P9-CQK-286

Law School Bound®

www.lawschoolbound.com

<u>The</u> Manual For:

Choosing A Law School

Applying To Law School

Mastering The LSAT

Surviving Law School

Being Admitted To The Bar In Canada And The U.S.

Choosing The Right Legal Career

And Much More...

Also includes Supplementary LSAT Preparation Appendix

Law School Bound®

www.lawschoolbound.com

<u>The</u> Manual For:

Choosing A Law School

Applying To Law School

Mastering The LSAT

Surviving Law School

Being Admitted To The Bar In Canada And The U.S.

Choosing The Right Legal Career

And Much More...

Also includes Supplementary LSAT Preparation Appendix

John Richardson, B.A., LL.B., J.D.

RICHARDSON PRESS

TORONTO, CANADA

ISBN 0-9696290-2-8

Copyright© 2006, John Richardson. All Rights Reserved.

Book design by Bryan Babcock Design

No part of this book may be reproduced or transmitted in any form or by any means, electronic or otherwise, including photocopying or recording, or by any information storage or retrieval system except with written permission.

Requests for permission may be directed to:

Richardson Press
Box 19602, Manulife P.O.
55 Bloor St. W.
Toronto, Canada
M4W 3T9

ISBN: 0-9696290-2-8

Printed and manufactured in Canada.

Table of Contents

Foreword

Although law, as a profession, has been around for centuries, everyone's journey to a "law" career is different. Some students are very directed and plan their university studies knowing they want to become lawyers. Others arrive at their choice of law after extensive career exploration and research, matching skills, values and interests to the field of law. Still others drift more slowly toward law after trying out other fields of interest. John Richardson's latest book *Law School Bound* takes all of these students through the whole process – from confirming the choice of law as a career to law school research, the application process and the practice of law, as a professional. With extensive experience as both a lawyer and an educator who has advised thousands of students, John Richardson shares his knowledge in this very timely new reference. The accompanying website www.lawschoolbound.com will ensure that potential applicants have up-to-date factual information on preparing for the law school application process.

Law school takes a lot of time, money, and effort. *Law School Bound*, comprising of eight books within its pages, begins with Book I asking why you want to study law – what is the appeal for you? Is it a good match for your interests and skills? Are you passionate about the study of law? If your answer is yes, how can you ensure that you have your best chance at getting in to law school? Book II offers advice on finding and researching law schools. Not all law schools are the same. Their admission requirements, as well as their academic cultures, and even the degrees they award after completion of their law studies may differ widely. Which schools are most appropriate for you and your goals? Book III deals with "getting in" to law school, taking you through the application process. It offers examples of successful personal statements and autobiographical sketches, gives advice on obtaining effective letters of recommendation and includes tips on mastering the law school interviews. This book, along with the appendix on preparing for the LSAT, and the website www.lawschoolbound.com are invaluable for the application process.

Even once accepted into a school of your choice, *Law School Bound* continues to serve as a reference and guide. Book IV shares information on navigating law school itself, offering hands-on accounts from successful students, along with advice on summer jobs and the non-academic aspects of the law school experience. Book V discusses articling and licensing requirements for becoming a barrister and solicitor, internationally as well as in Canada, while Book VI provides information on working as a lawyer in a global world. Additional information on the legal profession, as well as historical barriers to access are contained in Books VII and VIII.

Law School Bound is a complete resource for anyone contemplating a career in law. It is replete with advice, examples and information for all students and will serve as a needed reference for potential law school applicants.

Beverly Gilbert
Pre-Law Advisor
University of Guelph
Guelph, Ontario
Canada

Introduction

A New Book For A New World ...

In 1992 I wrote the first edition of Law School Bound. This book is not a revision. Much has happened since 1992. We have gone from a recession to an economic boom. The internet and other forms of digital communication are transforming the way that we live. There are areas of legal practice that didn't even exist in 1992. All of this has necessitated a completely new book.

What The Book Is ...

Law School Bound is a complete career counselor and performance coach for anybody wishing to attend law school and become a lawyer. It is composed of eight books and one appendix about the LSAT (Law School Admission Test). Each of the eight books and LSAT appendix is really a book on its own and is focussed on one stage on the road to becoming a lawyer. I considered breaking this complete "Law School Bound" book into eight smaller books. But, at the end of the day, I knew that serious pre-law students would want all eight books.

The Eight Books Need Not Be Read In Order ...

There is no reason why the eight books and appendix need to be read in order. I expect that you will want to refer to different parts of the book during different stages of your pre-law career. Think of it as a "Bible Of Law Admissions." You will probably find yourself rereading parts of it again and again. Don't forget to read the book in conjunction with the www.lawschoolbound.com site.

My Approach - We Are On A Tour And I Am The Guide ...

To use this "Law School Bound" book is to embark on a tour through every stage of the process from "thinking about law school" to actually "becoming a lawyer." Think of me as the "tour guide" - the "bus driver", if you will. I will take you from one stop to the next. Each stop will be an important one in terms of your decision of whether to become a lawyer and/or the mechanics of getting there.

VIPs Will Visit Us During The Tour ...

I recognize that when making career decisions you will want the input of many people. Therefore, almost every

Chapter includes "VIP" presentations. "VIP" stands for "Very Interesting Perspective." They are "guest speakers." I wish to thank the large numbers of people who have allowed their written work to appear as a "VIP". In addition, some VIP articles will be marked with different signposts, Stop and Yield, to indicate pieces that reviewers of this book found especially interesting.

My purpose in writing this book is to help you make career decisions and to then help you implement those decisions. To remember a famous football coach: process isn't everything, it's the only thing. The facts about certain law schools are interesting, but are less relevant than process.

The Challenge ...

To produce a book of this size and scope is very time consuming. The challenge is to produce a book that won't be outdated by the time it has been printed and THAT WILL STAND THE TEST OF TIME. Issues of process will stand the test of time. But facts change quickly. So, how have I ensured that the book won't become dated?

The Solution - www.lawschoolbound.com ...

The Chapters deal with issues and topics that are generic. They have enduring value. But of course, facts matter. So, I have ensured that facts will not become dated by: creating the website www.lawschoolbound.com which contains all the factual issues (for example what joint degree programs does a school have) that may bear on your decision. In the industry this is called using a "project specific domain name." The lawschoolbound.com site may be accessed for INSTANT UPDATES TO:

- rapidly changing facts;

- rapidly changing web addresses; and

- any major chapter updates.

The www.lawschoolbound.com site is a companion to the book and should be used with it.

Audience Specific Introductions ...

A great challenge in producing this book has been to make it relevant and interesting to a wide range of pre-law students. For this reason, I have included "Audience Specific Introductions" for different kinds of readers. They will appear in just a moment before the main book begins. I encourage you to read the one that you think applies to your situation.

Some Positive Thoughts ...

You are considering law school at an extremely exciting time. Applications are at a reasonable but not excessive level. Although it will always be difficult to earn acceptance at top law schools, acceptance is possible and achievable. There continues to be tremendous career opportunities for lawyers.

Some Well Deserved Gratitude ...

I would like to thank Pam Waechter of Career Services at the University of Waterloo and Betty Wong of Winpro Consulting for proofreading and editing parts of this book.

I am grateful to all of you who have allowed your work to appear as part of this book. Your generosity will be appreciated by future pre-law students. In the 1992 edition of this book I recognized the support and assistance of Ron Gurfinkel of Monarch Books. I continue to thank Ron for his advice and expertise. Twelve years later I acknowledge - and offer very special thanks - to his daughter Casey Gurfinkel for the final production of this huge manuscript. I doubt that the book would ever have been finished without her!

Finally, thanks to Bryan Babcock for the finishing touches and 26 years of putting up with me. Thanks Bryan.

A Dedication ...

This book is dedicated to the new generation of (possibly) "Law School Bound" people. Especially, "The Subject" and "The First Lady". Love and great lives to you all - whether or not you decide to become lawyers.

John Richardson

Audience Specific Introduction 1

Second Career or "Mature Applicants"

Please accept my congratulations on your interest in law. Most "mature" applicants either started their post-secondary education late or are thinking of a change in career. Either way, there are tremendous opportunities for you in law.

Many law schools have specific application categories for "mature" applicants. The problem is that although the categories may be called "mature student categories" they may be defined in very different ways. It is important that you focus on how "mature student categories" are defined and not how they are labeled.

The first piece of advice I would give you is to call the schools and talk to them directly about your situation. Try to determine the types of applicants they like to admit in the "mature student category." Remember that different schools will operate in different ways.

Note also the difference between the minimum requirements to be allowed to apply as a "mature student" and the probability of success in that category. Just because you are eligible to apply as a mature student doesn't necessarily mean that you should. You might in fact be a strong mainstream applicant. In any case, let the individual law schools guide you on this point. There is a perception on the part of some law school applicants that it is easier to be admitted as a "mature applicant." This is not so!

The application process for "mature applicants" may be different from the application process for regular applicants. For example, there is at least one Canadian law school that requires that "mature applicants" submit an earlier LSAT score. This school also admits "mature applicants" on the basis of an interview. In any case, you must learn the admissions process for every school you are considering.

The admissions process for "mature applicants" is often more stressful than for regular applicants. I think that this is (in part) the result of a greater feeling of isolation and the necessity of possibly making bigger life changes in order to accommodate the possibility of law school. Just stick with it! The extra "life experiences" that "mature applicants" bring to the law school benefit both the applicant and the school.

When reading this book pay particular attention to the Chapters on application categories and the interview. These are Chapters 12 and 17. You may find Chapter 6 (Non-Traditional Attendance) Ways Of Obtaining A Legal Education to be of great interest.

Audience Specific Introduction 2

Foreign Lawyers And Other Non-North American Applicants

There are many law schools in the United States and Canada. Almost all of them are based on the "common law" tradition. You will find that I devoted a complete chapter in the book to your situation. You may want to start there.

Foreign Lawyers

Chances are that you may be a lawyer already licensed to practise outside of North America. Your problem is to get licensed to practise in North America.

I urge you to read Chapter 30 - the "Foreign Trained Law Graduate". You need to begin by securing very accurate information on how "foreign lawyers" are treated in North America. This must be done on a state by state or province by province basis. Obviously some jurisdictions are more friendly to foreign lawyers than others.

In addition it is essential that you pay particular attention to Chapter 12 on marketing and application categories. One issue is (assuming you must go back to law school) how much law school you must do. Chapters 12 and 30 will be critical for you.

Other Non-North American Applicants

Chapter 9 has been created specifically for you.

Audience Specific Introduction 3

U.S. Applicants Applying To U.S. Schools

All of this book (in a general way) will apply to you. Because, I live and work in Toronto, Canada most of the VIP articles are taken from a Canadian context. But, the process of law admissions and the dreaded LSAT is the same in both Canada and the U.S. Obviously this would include the book on the law school application process.

I would also like to remind you that the United States, Canada and Mexico signed NAFTA (North American Free Trade Agreement). This has opened the door to a good deal of cross-border mobility for lawyers. Make sure that you read the Chapter on "Mobility." (Chapter 29)

As this book is being completed, the law school of MSU (Michigan State University) has introduced a program with the University of Ottawa in Canada to allow students to earn both American and Canadian law degrees. The University of Detroit has a program with the University of Windsor that allows students to earn both U.S. and Canadian law degrees in three years.

Obviously you should ignore Chapters 24, 25, 26 and 28 which deal with bar admission in Canada and the U.K. Book VII ("Learning About Lawyers And The Legal Profession") is relevant although most of the articles and discussion use examples from the Canadian legal profession. Canada through the use of provincial law societies, regulates the legal profession in a somewhat different manner than do its U.S. counterparts. Hence, you will find Chapter 37 ("Law, Society And The Law Society") irrelevant to the U.S. situation.

By the way, I have been through this process from both the American and Canadian perspective. I have both American and Canadian law degrees and am a member of the bar in Massachusetts, New York and the province of Ontario.

Chapter 27 will be of special interest to you.

Audience Specific Introduction 4

Quebec Residents Applying To Quebec Schools

As you know Quebec is based on the Civil law system and is not a "common law province." In general the law admissions process works in the same way. I encourage you to pay particular attention to opportunities that would allow you to earn both civil and common law degrees. This can be done in two ways:

First, pay particular attention to schools that offer combined civil and common law programs (examples include the University of Ottawa and McGill).

Second, many Quebec law schools have arrangements with other Canadian law schools that allow civil law graduates to earn a common law degree (LL.B.) in one year.

Chapter 26 will be of special interest to you.

Audience Specific Introduction 5

Canadian Applicants Applying To A Law School Outside of Quebec

You are the biggest winners. This book developed out of my 20+ years of teaching LSAT courses in Toronto and counseling Canadian law school applicants. There is NO part of this book that is not relevant to your situation.

The personal statements included in the book are those of Canadian applicants. My LSAT courses and pre-law seminars are offered in Toronto and other Canadian cities.

Further Resources ...

This book actually was developed from my monthly email newsletter, my LSAT courses and my pre-law seminars.

In order to subscribe to my FREE email newsletter send a request to: subscribe@lawschoolbound.com

There is a lot of pre-law information on our web sites at: www.richardson-prep.com and www.lawschoolbound.com

I teach LSAT courses all year around in Toronto - see www.richardson-prep.com and www.lawschoolbound.com

I am the author of Mastering The LSAT - How To Prepare Effectively And Successfully - ISBN: 0969629036

It is available through most university bookstores, general bookstores, Amazon.com and yes, even through us - info@lawschoolbound.com

Stop!! Before You Begin - How To Use The Book

This book along with the www.lawschoolbound.com site will be your companions from the time that you consider "Getting Into Law School", through the application process and can be used to prepare you for law school itself. Furthermore, during law school (as you look down the road to bar admission) you may want to reconsider Book V - "From Law School to Bar Admission - Your License To Practice".

I urge you to begin with the chapter table of contents to see how I have divided the main book into eight smaller books. You should understand the role that each book plays in the process of applying to law school, getting through law school and finally becoming a lawyer.

At the beginning of each of the eight books I have written a "Book Report" to describe the book and describe the contents of each Chapter. I advise you to begin by studying the outline of each of the eight books. After that, you can begin with the book that is of most interest and relevance to you at your present stage.

In order to encourage your beginning with the summaries, you will find the eight "Book Reports" both in the pages immediately following AND at the beginning of each individual book.

My live seminars and courses are posted at both www.lawschoolbound.com and www.richardson-prep.com. If you wish to subscribe to my email newsletter please email: subscribe@lawschoolbound.com

Acknowledgements

This book contains a large amount of third party material. Much of it has appeared in my newsletters over the years. I would like to begin with a general acknowledgement and thanks to all of those many people who have graciously allowed their work to appear in this book. Many of you will remain anonymous. Specific acknowledgements are in order for each chapter and as follows.

Chapter 2:

"How to get to the top - study philosophy" - Thomas Hurka

Chapter 3:

"Arguments for Toronto's two law schools" - Monique Conrod

Chapter 4:

"U. of T. to get J.D. Degree" - Joseph Berkovits

Chapter 7:

"Law faces a Boldt challenge and its perfectly paralegal" - Bill Schiller - Reprinted courtesy Torstar syndication services

Chapter 8:

"Some good advice .... So, you're thinking about getting an LL.M." - Michael Valihora

"From U. of T. to the Harvard LL.M." - James Hopkins

"Law School's part-time LL.M. course flourishes" - Monique Conrod - The Lawyers Weekly

Chapter 10:

"A Cross-Border Law School Actually on the Border" - Bruce P. Elman

Chapter 11:

"Getting Accepted: One Student's Story" - James Szyptman

"Old age and experience goes farther than youth and enthusiasm" - Victoria Cross

Chapter 14:

I thank those students who allowed their personal statements to appear in this chapter.

Chapter 18:

"Law school grads frustrated unprepared" - Michael Crawford

Chapter 20:

"Law 'n' ardour: How Bay St Courts Students" - Anne Perry - Reprinted courtesy Torstar syndication services

"Students must make case for themselves" - Terrence Belford

Chapter 21:

I thank the anonymous student for three years of contribution to my newsletter

Chapter 22:

"Atonement" - James Cowan

Chapter 23:

"Understanding Law School" - Professor Kenneth W. Graham, Jr. -

Reproduced with permission of Casenotes Publishing Inc.

Chapter 24:

"Law school not gatekeeper of profession: dean" - Miriam Ehrensaft - Courtesy the Queen's Journal

"B.C. lawyers' citizenship requirement falls in 'historical'

S.C.C. equality rights decision - Cristin Schmitz - The Lawyers Weekly

Chapter 25:

"Lawyers need to revisit articling process" - donalee Moulton

"Is articling obsolete?" - Janice M. Zima

"Clerking" - James Hopkins

"Bar Admission Across Canada" - John Jaffey - The Lawyers Weekly

"BAC Revamped" - John Jaffey - The Lawyers Weekly

Law School Bound® Book Summary

A Collection of Eight Books and One Appendix

Book I - Deciding On Law School - The Pre-Law Career Counselor

Book II - Understanding And Identifying Opportunities To Study Law

Book III - The Law School Application Manual - Executing A Plan

Book IV - Law School: Understanding, Surviving, Flourishing!

Book V - From Law School To Bar Admission - Your License To Practise

Book VI - The World Is Your Oyster - Lawyers' Mobility In A Global World

Book VII - Learning About Lawyers And The Legal Profession

Book VIII - Recognizing Historical Barriers To Access

Appendix - Introductory LSAT PREP - Get Off On The Right Foot!

> **Part A** - Introducing The LSAT - A PREP Primer

> **Part B** - Studying The LSAT - Past, Present And Future

Book I - A Report

Deciding On Law School
- The Pre-Law Career Counselor

Summary And Introduction

My Advice To You Is ....

Treat your undergraduate years as an opportunity to explore new things. Take the courses you like. Don't consider law school as a move into a new area. See law school as an extension of something you already like. Every academic background is relevant in law school and as a lawyer! By the way, the only good reason to go to law school is, that you want to study law!

We live in an age of unprecedented choice in career options. In fact, the options are so plentiful that many of you will have difficulty deciding which road to take. Some of you are sure you want to become lawyers. Some are considering law as one of a number of options. In the words of one commentator:

"A ranking of 'career desirability' shows that 36 percent of surveyed students are interested in law or another profession; 3 percent would consider teaching; 23 percent might become technology workers; and 22 percent would like to be filmmakers, musicians, artists or writers."

> *Virginia Galt - Globe Workplace Reporter - The Globe And Mail -*
> *December 9, 2000*

Some of you may be considering law school but have no intention of ever becoming licensed as a lawyer.

Book I has been designed to explore these issues.

Specifically:

- how to decide whether law school is for you; and

- what to do prior to the application process to assist yourself.

In Book I, I will play the role of a "Pre-Law Career Counselor."

Let's begin!

Book I - Chapter Summaries

1. So, You Want To Be A Lawyer - Is It REASONable For You?

Focus: The identification of a reason for attending law school

2. The Pre-Law State Of Mind - What Should It Be Filled With?

Focus: Pre-Law Years - 10 Specific Issues Of Concern To Pre-Law Students: how to select courses, summer jobs, extra-curricular activities, when to begin, etc.

Chapter 1

So, You Want To Be A Lawyer - Is It REASONable For You?

"Come, it's pleased so far," thought Alice, and she went on.

"Would you tell me, please, which way I ought to go from here?"

"That depends a good deal on where you want to get to," said the Cat.

"I don't much care where ..." said Alice.

"Then it doesn't matter which way you go," said the Cat.

"...so long as I get somewhere," Alice added as an explanation.

"Oh, you're sure to do that," said the Cat, "if only you walk long enough."

-From Alice's Adventures In Wonderland,
written by Lewis Carroll
as quoted in 'The Law School Game"
by Christopher Nuebert and Jack Withiam, Jr. (1976)

Planning, Goals And The Law School Decision

In all likelihood if you are reading this book you are in an undergraduate program and deciding on what to do after you graduate. As the Cat made clear to Alice, you will always end up somewhere. Your job is to take the steps to end up where you want to be. This book is about planning, goal setting and goal implementation. Specifically, it will help you decide whether:

1. Attending law school should be your goal and if so how to create and implement the plan; and

2. Whether practicing law should be your goal and if so how to create and implement the plan.

On the issue of planning - please remember that:

"Most people don't plan to fail, they just fail to plan!"

On the issue of goal setting - please remember:

"Don't wait for your ship to come in - go on out and meet it!"

Do You Really Want To Go To Law School? - An Overview

Not every applicant who applies to law school has a clear reason for wanting to go. Law school is a three year academic exercise. Following law school is a procedure for admission to the bar in the province or state in which you wish to practice. The complete process, from the beginning of law school to receiving a license to practice law, can take as long as five years in Canada and three and one half years in the U.S. That is a huge component of your life. Hence, you should **examine your reasons for wanting to go to law school**.

Is Law For You? What Kind Of People Go To Law School?

Obviously there is no one answer to this question. I offer five perspectives on this issue.

Perspective 1 - In general - My Personal Perspective:

Both law as a subject and law as a profession are so diverse that many kinds of people are attracted to them. I well remember conducting a "Pre-Law Seminar" for the counseling centre at a certain university. At the end, a young woman came and told me that she considered herself to be quiet, non-aggressive, shy and a very nice person. She asked me if there was a place for such a person in the legal profession. Well, obviously there is a place for a person like that in any profession. Lawyers are getting a "bad rap." The vast majority of lawyers are honest, decent, hard-working professionals with very high ethical standards. There is a place for almost anyone in the legal profession. So, if you want to be in the profession, the profession has a place for you. I share the view found in one pre-law handbook that says:

"Bound by few traditional stereotypes, the prospective lawyer should basically view his future career not as one which will mold him, but as one which he himself can mold, in accordance with his own interests, abilities and desires."

Perspective 2 - On the specific personality traits - From "Going To Law School" by Castleman and Niewoehner (1997) - pages 5 and 6:

"Along with analyzing why you may want to go to law school, you also need to consider the qualities, both personal and professional, that most lawyers possess. In this way, you can better determine whether you belong among them.

Not everyone has the personality to become a lawyer, that is good, because otherwise everyone would want to go to law school and our society would be even more litigious than it is. The traits that make a good lawyer do not necessarily make a good friend or companion. That is one of the reasons why it is so easy to poke fun at lawyers. In popular jokes, lawyers tend to be:

- picky

- two-faced

- argumentative

- evasive

- anxious to exploit an opponent's weakness

- always searching for a loophole

Well, a good lawyer often needs to be all of that, and more. That just comes with the territory."

Perspective 3 - On both the intellectual skills and personality traits - From "So You Want To Be A Lawyer" from Law Services (1994), pages 6 and 7.

"The kind of intelligence required for success in law school, and in law as a discipline, has to do with your analytical powers, your ability to reason and approach problems logically, your verbal and communication skills and your good judgment. You must be able to read and write well before you enter law school and you must be able to analyze diverse bodies of information to reach logical, viable solutions. Learning how to advocate a particular point of view within the context of the legal system can be both stimulating and frustrating. Being an effective lawyer calls for a fair amount of intellectual dexterity - the ability to juggle three or four ideas simultaneously. Skills in interacting with all kinds of people are also important. Depending on the kind of law you practise, you will deal with people from a variety of cultural backgrounds, professions, income levels, needs, and interests. Some of your relationships will be very rewarding both professionally and personally. Others may seem difficult if not distasteful. In any case, you must be willing and able to offer intelligent competent counsel to all of your clients: the practice of law is a service profession."

Perspective 4 - On the profile of law school applicants - From "The Lure Of The Law" by Richard W. Moll (1990) - pages 25 and 26

"What is the profile of the person attracted early to the law?

Alexander Austin heads the Higher Education Research Institute at UCLA. He publishes annually, in cooperation with the American Council of Education, an attitudinal study of America's entering college freshman. In a recent analysis of the freshmen who cited law as a career goal, he found the pre-law students to ... differ substantially from students in general. They come often from highly educated and affluent families, are better prepared academically than most of their college freshmen peers, and are more self-confident. A high percentage enroll in select private colleges and major in one of the social sciences. Prelaw students tend to have a strong political orientation, with the women more likely to identify themselves as liberal and men more likely to identify themselves as conservative. In addition, they give high priority to goals such as keeping up-to-date with political affairs and influencing the political structure. Like students in general, prelaw students have become more conservative over the past decade or so. Indeed this trend to the right is more pronounced among prelaw students, especially the men, than among all freshmen. Their attitudes manifest an interesting mix: Though they tend to be conservative on such questions as government intervention, academic standards, and legal issues, they are fairly liberal in such issues as equality of the sexes and student rights. They are strongly oriented toward material and power goals; making money, becoming an authority, winning recognition, succeeding in business ... and less inclined to be concerned about social issues and problems."

Perspective 5 - On People's Motives For Becoming Lawyers: From: Dancing With Lawyers by Nicholas Carroll (1992) - Introduction:

"People enter law school for a variety of reasons: The pursuit of justice - or power; to change the world - or feed off it; to get the respect they deserve - or lord it over secretaries; to make their parents happy; to (mistakenly) get a general education; to prolong school and delay work; to make big money; and on occasion, because law interests them. Many of them do not intend to practice law. Most do.

Though they start for different reasons, life beyond the entry exams is much the same from school to school. So is the entry-level work afterwards. The training involves a way of thought more than the study of facts. The hours are long, and ambition is high. They have limited time or inclination for outside interests; law becomes reality. They are taught to argue - endlessly. Their sense of humor erodes; original goals are forgotten. The strange and meaningless rules they obey gradually close the doors of imagination. It remains true that "The law sharpens the mind by narrowing it.

A product of legal education is likely to be the most troublesome temporary employee you will ever hire. ..."

Becoming A Lawyer - The Process In A Nutshell

Law school and the process of becoming formally licensed to practice law are distinct. The general process (I will discuss the case of "special applicants" later) of becoming a lawyer consists of three components from the time that you start university. They are:

1. *Pre-Law*

Canada - In general Canadian law schools require at least two (and commonly three) years of full-time university work as a prerequisite for admission to law school.

U.S. - In general, U.S. law schools require a bachelors degree.

2. *Law School*

In both Canada and the U.S. a law degree will require the equivalent of three years of full-time study. Many law schools have part-time programs. The first year at all the Canadian and U.S. law schools is basically the same. Most Canadian law schools (common law) award an LL.B. degree. The University of Toronto awards a J.D. (Juris Doctor) degree. U.S. law schools award a J.D. degree. Quebec law schools award a "civil law" degree.

3. *Bar Admission Process*

Canada - In Canada, admission to the bar results from successful completion of the bar admission course in the province in which you wish to practice. The course typically consists of a combination of articling and lectures. In order to enter the Bar Admission Course you will be required to have a law degree from a Canadian law school or (for those who have degrees from foreign law schools) a Certificate of Equivalency from the National Committee on Accreditation (more on this later). Hence, for the purposes of becoming a lawyer, the practical benefit of obtaining a law degree is that it allows you to enter the bar admission course.

U.S. - In order to be admitted to U.S. state bars you are required to pass the bar exam of that state. In order to be allowed to take the bar exam you must either:

1. Graduate from a law school approved by the American Bar Association (ABA); or

2. If you have not graduated from a law school approved by the ABA, receive permission to take the bar exam. A number of U.S. states will allow Canadian law graduates to take their bar exam.

In the U.S. neither articling nor a formal bar admission course is required for admission to the bar.

Please note that each of these stages is distinct and should be thought of as an end in itself. It is entirely possible to attend law school and never take the further step of becoming a lawyer! There is nothing wrong with that. In fact you shouldn't go to law school **unless you think that studying law would be a sufficiently worthy goal in and of itself - even if you never actually became a lawyer!** A legal education is valuable by itself. To quote Chief Justice Brian Dickson:

"A legal education is a superb education for non-lawyers. Accordingly, persons who intend to be business persons, journalists, secondary school teachers, public administrators and human rights activists, to name a few, may well want to receive a legal education before embarking upon those careers. The legal profession and the law schools should be proud of the fact that many such people value highly a legal education. They should encourage such people and make an effort to allow them to receive the benefits of a legal education."

Reasons Versus Excuses - You Need A Reason

Let's explore some reasons for wanting to go to law school or become a lawyer. You should have a **reason**! Considerable time and work are required to complete all the stages of the process.

First, let me suggest that nobody should go to the trouble of applying to law school **without actually going and sitting in on one or more law school classes!** Remember, different law teachers have different teaching styles. Try to visit more than one law school class.

Let's distinguish between an **excuse** and a **reason**. A **reason** for wanting to go to law school is some justification that is related to the academic content of law school. A reason for wanting to be a lawyer should be related to what a lawyer actually does! An excuse is something else. Let me suggest that the following answers to the question "Why do you want to go to law school?" qualify as **excuses and not as reasons**.

- I like school. I don't like the prospect of entering the work force. Three years of law school will help me avoid the work force for another three years.

- A law degree is a guarantee that I will have money, power, and prestige.

- My father is a lawyer. He's putting pressure on me to become a lawyer to take over his firm.

- A law degree or license to practise law is something that I can always fall back on. (Most insurance policies are too expensive!)

- All my friends are going to law school. Therefore, I should too.

None of the above justifications for wanting to go to law school is related to the content of law school or the work of a lawyer. Hence, none of them justifies the decision to become a lawyer.

Many of you have no way of learning what goes on in law school or what it is like to be a lawyer. Here are some suggestions for learning about each.

What Goes On In Law School?

You can:

- sit in on a law school class.

- join the Pre-Law Society at your university.

- read *One L* by Scott Turow. This is an account of his first year at Harvard Law School. (It is a very extreme account of law school.)

- view the original movie *The Paper Chase*. This is a movie made about the experience of a group of first year students at Harvard Law School. (The movie is an exaggeration, but does give an example of the Socratic method of teaching which is used by some professors.)

- talk to as many law students as you can.

- read the numerous books about law school. (For an excellent reading list, check the bibliography in the LSAT Registration Book.)

- subscribe to my free monthly email newsletter at: lawnews@prep.com.

What Is It Like To Be A Lawyer?

You can:

- try to obtain summer employment at a law firm.

- court hearings are open to the public. Why not check some out!

- read books about lawyers. (Jack Batten has an excellent series of books about Canadian lawyers. There are hundreds of books about U.S. lawyers.)

Please remember that the practice of law is diverse. Any reading you do or summer employment you may experience will give you a very small snapshot of what it is like to be a lawyer. Furthermore, the practice of law is becoming increasingly specialized. It is possible to change careers a number of times and still be a lawyer.

If, after having done your homework, you have decided that there is something about law school or the practice of law that provides you with a **reason** for wanting to go to law school or becoming a lawyer, then make the decision that admission to law school is your **goal!**

So What's In A Goal?

"Goals are nothing but dreams with a deadline!"

A goal is a serious commitment made to yourself to achieve a specific result. **A goal is not a wish.** A goal, honestly set, implies a commitment to do what is necessary to achieve the result!

Breaking The Goal Into Manageable Components

The most important considerations are:

1. When Should You Go To Law School?; and

2. When Should You Begin Organizing Yourself?

3. When Should You Take The LSAT?

4. When Should You Complete Your Application File?

Re 1: When Should You Go To Law School?

Although some Canadian law schools require only that you complete two years of university, it is more difficult to gain admission after two years. Hence, as a practical matter most applicants find that they must complete a degree before being accepted.

Those considering applying after only two years of university, should consider the following point. I graduated from law school in 1980 and have many friends who are lawyers. Most are happy with their careers, but some are not. A change into a new career may require that you have a degree in addition to your law degree. It would be a shame to go to law school after only two years of university and discontinue work on a degree in an area that interests you. This is particularly true if the effect is to close future options. If you like your current program, you should complete that degree. The most you gain by starting law school after two years of university is that you finish law school a year earlier. The long run cost may be too high!

Re 2: When Should You Begin Organizing Yourself?

As you read this book you will begin to realize the time and expense that are involved in applying to law school. **The process will take time! Ensure that you have enough time to complete the process**. Ideally you should begin to acquire information about the LSAT and research law schools no later than the year before the year in which you plan to apply! For example, if it is your intention to apply while you are in your third year, you should begin to acquire information no later than your second year. Those who are particularly keen may wish to begin the acquisition of information in your first year. You should obtain all the application material for all law schools to which you wish to apply. Study the application forms. This will help you organize yourself mentally.

Re 3: When Should You Take The LSAT?

The answer is: the earlier the better. There is no reason to delay the test. The LSAT is not a test of general knowledge.

It is important that you:

1. Not do the LSAT at a time when it conflicts with your academic commitments; and

2. Ensure that you leave yourself a second chance to take the LSAT **should this become necessary!**

At present, the LSAT can be taken in June, October, December and February. Statistics from Law Services reveal that those who take the LSAT in June and October have the highest average scores. This may be true for the following two reasons.

First, those who take the test in June or October are taking the test early, which means they take the test with the full knowledge that they can repeat it if necessary.

Second, there is less conflict with academic commitments than there is in December.

My advice is to take the LSAT the first June that is convenient for you. Don't presume to delay the LSAT until the June or October before your applications are due. Get it out of the way. Further academic experiences will do nothing to improve your LSAT taking ability!

Re 4: When Should You Complete Your Application File?

To put it simply, **the earlier the better**.. Many law schools use a "rolling admissions" process. This means that the school may consider your application file at the moment that it is complete and not wait until the deadline for applications to be received.

Early completion of your file can only be an advantage! It can never be a disadvantage. Make every effort to ensure that your application is complete at the earliest possible date.

Conclusion

What follows is a "Planning For Law School Calendar." It has been designed to help you achieve your goal. Remember, admission to law school is your **goal**. All of your work must be focussed toward achieving that goal! As I said in my **Mastering The LSAT** book:

"Your acceptance to law school is not a matter of luck. The road to law school is paved with the bricks of hard work and discipline. Stay on the road and an acceptance to law school will be yours!"

APPENDIX A

Your Planning for Law School Calendar

(To be used in conjunction with the guidelines in this book)

First Year

1. Meet with an academic counselor to devise an academic strategy for your undergraduate career.

2. Choose your courses with care. If at all possible, enroll in classes that will help to develop your reading and writing skills. Work hard to earn good grades. Your grades will be the most important factor in determining whether you will go to law school.

3. Consider attending a "writing workshop" to improve your writing skills.

4. Involve yourself in extra-curricular activities. This could include volunteer work. Do your best to become a well rounded person. Make sure that your academic work does not suffer as a result of your participation in extra curricular activities.

5. Get to know some of your professors. Keep in mind that you will need academic references for law school.

6. Obtain the current LSAT Registration Book. This will acquaint you with the law admissions process and give you up-to-date LSAT information.

7. Begin obtaining application materials from schools that interest you. Begin to learn how the admissions process works.

Second Year

1. Maintain a rigorous course load. Balance your extra-curricular involvement with your studying. Take an active role in school clubs and/or sports. Stress activities that show leadership and organizational skills.

2. Research specific law schools. Learn how they are different and what to emphasize when you apply to them. Think about how to market yourself differently to different schools.

3. Talk to lawyers and law students. They will be able to provide you with a personal glimpse into law and law schools. Read books about law school and the legal profession. Make sure that law is really for you.

4. Obtain a copy of the current LSAT Registration Book. The Canadian edition contains information about both Canadian law schools and the LSAT. The U.S. edition contains only information about the LSAT. Try to take the LSAT at a time when it will conflict least with other academic commitments. You should take the LSAT as early as possible. Plan for the first June that is convenient for you. Decide how to prepare (i.e. a course or self-study or both).

5. Obtain copies of law school calendars and applications for all schools that are of interest to you. This should be done in the early part of the school year. Peruse them to learn what is needed for each form. Practice completing the application form(s). Begin to identify things that you may want to include in your "personal statement."

6. Decide whether to apply after two, three or four years.

Spring Semester - Academic Year Prior To The Academic Year When Your Applications Are Due

1. Determine which schools require letters of recommendation. Learn what kinds of letters are required and for what purpose. Determine what you hope to accomplish by submitting the letters. Next decide who are the best people to write those letters on your behalf. In selecting your referees, you must accomplish two tasks. First you must ensure that the person will write a good letter. Second you must teach the person enough about the law

admissions process (and about you) so that an effective letter can be written.

Example - Hi Professor X. I am applying to law school. An academic letter of reference is required. In particular, the schools are interested in _____. Do you feel that you could, and would you be willing to write me a good letter of reference?

(For more information, see the chapter on letters of recommendation).

2. At the earliest opportunity sign up for the June LSAT. This may be done online at www.LSAC.org. Register early to ensure that you get your choice of test center.

3. Decide how you plan to prepare for the LSAT. If you plan to take an LSAT course, remember that many of them start in early May.

Summer Prior To The Deadline For Your Law School Applications

Many law school applications are due in the fall prior to the year you wish to start law school. The proper completion of the application file will consume lots of time. Hence, it is to your advantage to complete your applications during the summer.

Final Year

Let's assume your applications are complete or will be complete in the early fall. During your final year you should:

1. Complete your course of study. Continue to maintain a good grade point average, and your involvement in non-academic activities. Think about both law school and any other possible alternatives.

2. Reconsider your file. If there is new information that will make a difference to the acceptance or the rejection of your application, ensure that it is added to your application file. If retaking the LSAT may improve your chances for admission, then consider doing so. Ensure that the law school receives your final grades.

3. If you receive an offer of admission, notify the school of your acceptance immediately. Do not be discouraged if you are rejected. Be mindful of any rules that prohibit you from holding more than one seat in a law school at a time.

Let's hope that you are successful, but if you are not YOU SHOULD APPLY AGAIN! Should you apply again, remember that many schools still have access to your first application file. Therefore, you should retain a copy of every document that is included in every application file to every law school!

Consider retaking the LSAT, upgrading your average or anything else that may strengthen your application in the following year. Many students who eventually are accepted to law school are not accepted the first year that they apply.

APPENDIX B

In Closing....

Are you still struggling with the "pre-law decision?" Read (for a bit of humor) the following perspective of one of my students on why he selected law:

The following is an excerpt from 'My Road to the Bench" by Hon. F. Fitzgerald de Freitas —

When I was about 23, I began considering possible career options. I decided that the best possible approach to determining my future would be to draw up a list of 4 things I like to do and then, attempt to match careers to the list.

So, I sat down at my desk and the first criterion hit me, "I like to sit!". In fact, I love sitting. If it were at all possible, I would sit all day. After that, I began to think about what else should be on this list. Think, think, think. There it was...thinking! "I like to think!" I thought. I'm obsessed with it. I do it non stop; it's like a curse. This was fantastic. Only two minutes of effort, and my list was half done.

The next point came to me as I looked down at the pen in my hand. "I like to write!" and almost instantaneously I announced, " and I like to read too!". It was so simple it almost felt wrong. But it wasn't and that was the key.

Now I figured that if I could just find a job that would meet all four criteria and pay me well to do them, I was done. So I talked to some of my friends who were already out working to find out what their jobs entailed. Unfortunately, the vast majority of them involved a tremendous amount of standing and walking. One of my friends mentioned that his dad was a lawyer. So I asked, "does he spend a lot of time sitting?" and he replied, "almost all day." A good start. Then I asked, "what about thinking? Would you say his job requires him to think a lot?" And he said, "well, I guess." That was good enough for me. Finally the reading and writing issue. When I asked him about these two items his reply was, "well, he has a library in his office and he's always writing notes for his secretary." Could it be that the law profession was for me? It met all of the necessary conditions and I knew it paid well. Without wasting another moment my mind was made up. "I want to be a lawyer" I said to him, "it's the perfect job for me!"

Obviously shaken, my friend replied, "are you sure, dude. I mean, nobody likes lawyers." And the rest as they say, is history."

Chapter 2

The Pre-Law State Of Mind - What Should It Be Filled With?

The "Top 10" List Of Commonly Asked Questions

I publish an email newsletter for pre-law students. The newsletter includes a "question of the month." There are really ten questions that pre-law students ask over and over. What follows are the questions and the best answers I can give.

Warning!! The answers to these questions are my opinions. I urge you to pay close attention to my reasoning. You should consult your academic advisor or career counselor to see if my suggestions make sense for you!

Question 1:

Does it matter whether you have a bachelors degree?

U.S. law schools require a Bachelors Degree. Some Canadian law schools will admit applicants with only two years of University. Other Canadian law schools require a Bachelors Degree. Outside of North America law school is usually an undergraduate program. Hence, one attends law school after the equivalent of high school.

The number of Canadian law schools that will accept applicants after two years is diminishing. It is very difficult to be admitted to law school after only two years. To put it simply, superior grades and a superior LSAT are required. One school commented that:

"An applicant applying in the second year of undergraduate studies must meet higher standards for admission and may not be considered competitive when compared to applicants with lengthy records of academic achievement."

Hence, as a practical matter most applicants who are accepted have either a three or four year degree. Are you better off with either a three or a four year degree? In general Canadian law schools do not distinguish between three and four year degrees. There may, however, be strategic reasons for obtaining one or the other. (See the discussion on trends in grades below.)

The two most important criteria for admission to law school, for mainstream applicants continue to be grades and LSAT scores. Law schools are interested in your grades because law school is an academic exercise and your grades provide the law schools with direct evidence of your capacity to do academic work. (On this point please remember that all communication with the law schools should be premised on the assumption that law school is an academic experience.) Upon completion of law school you will be awarded the degree of Bachelor of Laws (LL.B.) in Canada or the Juris Doctor (J.D.). in the U.S. (The law degree offered by the University Of Toronto is a J.D.) A law degree is an academic degree and not a professional certification. In fact, it would be a mistake to think of law school as the equivalent of professional school. In the words of one law dean:

"Legal education is, first and foremost, education - an opportunity to gain understanding of the social practices that comprise our system of justice, an opportunity to reflect on why those practices are the way they are and what that means for the lives of the people of our country and, finally, an opportunity to criticize those practices and to suggest reforms."

There is one other strategic consideration governing your decision to apply after three or four years. This consideration takes into account how the LSAT score is weighed. For some schools - the larger the number of undergraduate years, the less important is the LSAT. The smaller the number of undergraduate years, the more important is the LSAT. If you are applying to a school that weighs the LSAT in this way, a fourth year of study will diminish the importance of the LSAT. This will be a consideration for only those of you with low LSAT scores. Conversely, if you have marginal grades and a high LSAT score, applying after three years would have the effect of maximizing the value of your LSAT score!

Question 2: Will a graduate degree help?

Yes, a graduate degree is helpful. But, high graduate grades will not compensate for low undergraduate grades. (Of course, you probably couldn't get into graduate school without high undergraduate grades anyway!) The only legitimate reason for going to graduate school is because you are interested in studying that subject. If you have a graduate degree you should contact the law schools individually to determine what role (if any) your graduate degree may play in your application to law school.

Bottom line: Graduate education is a good thing in your application file. But, it is hard to say exactly how it will be weighed. Consider the following comment from a law school:

"Grades obtained for work done in graduate schools are not used as part of the GPA but are considered when assessing the qualifications of applicants."

Question 3: Does it matter what "pre-law" university you attend?

In general, the law schools are not concerned with your undergraduate institution. Your grades are far more important than the school you attend.

Question 4: Does it matter whether you carry a full-load of courses?

It may. Your file will be compared to the files of many other applicants. It is not fair to compare an applicant who has consistently taken a full-load of courses with an applicant who has taken a half-load. Consider the following comment from a law school:

"More weight is given to academic work done on a full-load basis in consecutive years."

Question 5: What about trends in grades?

Common sense dictates that if your grades are not perfect an upward trend in your grades will be helpful. This principle has been acknowledged by many schools.

It is important that if your poor grades are the result of external circumstances or dislike of the program you started in, that these facts be called to the attention of the committee. If you don't explain the circumstances in your application, the circumstances won't be considered.

(See the later discussion on how to deal with "false starts.")

One law school commented that:

"Applicants may request the Admissions Committee to disregard part of their pre-law academic performance in the following circumstances:

(a) where that part of their pre-law academic performance has been seriously and detrimentally affected by factors beyond their control, particularly where their academic difficulties are as a result of medical or compassionate grounds, or

(b) where they have experienced a false start in their university studies, particularly where that false start occurred during their first year of study."

A second school stated that:

"Admission decisions rest primarily upon the relative strength of an applicant's academic record. Academic averages are calculated on a yearly basis and note is taken of individual grades and trends. Note is also taken of LSAT trends. The Admissions Committee looks for consistent academic achievement and increasing intellectual demand in courses taken."

It is important for all applicants whose grades have been affected adversely by external circumstances that these circumstances be brought to the attention of the admissions committee. If possible the circumstances should be documented by a letter from a third party!

(Downward trends in grades should be avoided!)

Question 6: Should I know what kind of lawyer I want to be when I start law school?

This is a matter of opinion. I would advise you to start law school with no preconceived idea of what kind of law you wish to specialize in or what kind of lawyer you may want to be!

My reasons are as follows.

There will always be many opportunities for lawyers. But, the opportunities in specific areas of law will be increased or decreased by changes in society. Every important change in society or new social issue will bring about a corresponding change in opportunities in the legal profession. This means that by the time that you become a lawyer there will be opportunities that don't exist today. There will also be opportunities that exist today that will either cease to exist or become less attractive over time.

Consider the following example. The back page of the technology section of a recent issue of the Globe was devoted to "careers in technology." There was an article that focused on a lawyer (not an engineer or programmer) whose law practice was in large part based on advising clients on Y2K compliance issues. Recently the Toronto Star ran a long article in the technology section titled "Y2K could be a bonanza for legal profession." This is a great example of the principle that where there is an important societal issue, there is sure to be an important legal issue. It is also a good example of an area of law where the opportunities have decreased rather quickly. Law and the opportunities in the legal profession follow trends and issues in society as a whole.

Remember - **the trend is your friend!**

It is probably not even a good idea to have a rigid idea of what kind of lawyer you want to be when you have finished law school. What follows is an excerpt from the remarks of Chief Justice McLachlin at the Ottawa call to the bar in February of 2000:

"There is no set path to finding one's place in the law and thus oneself. But I offer this piece of advice: Avoid getting prematurely boxed in to an aspect of the law that you do not truly enjoy.

Keep your options open. Keep trying until you find something that suits you and gives you deep and lasting satisfaction. Do not be put off by a bad day, three bad days, or even five.

But if all the days - or even most of them - are bad, perhaps the reason is that you have wandered into an aspect of the legal profession that does not suit you, that does not maximize your potential, that does not, to return to Kipling's phrase, allow you to be true to yourself."

Approach law school with a flexible attitude. Never assume that you are NOT interested in a specific area of law. Follow your heart. Be receptive to emerging trends and opportunities. Don't miss out. I once saw a bumper sticker that read:

"When my ship came in, I was at the airport!"

Question 7: Should I take law or law related courses in my undergraduate years? What kind of "pre-law" courses should I take?

It is NOT important that you take law or law related courses. Law schools do not prefer any particular pre-law program. In general, you should take the courses that you find to be of most interest. This will ensure that:

A. You are happy; and

B. You will get higher grades because of your interest in the courses.

There is no such thing as a "pre-law program." Hence, provided you take courses of substance, you may take any program you want. Consider the following excerpt from a law school calendar:

"The Faculty does not prescribe a program of pre-legal studies for those intending to enter law school, nor does it recommend specific undergraduate courses for those intending to enter law school. Indeed, the Faculty suggests that applicants treat their previous study as an end in itself in the event that they should not be admitted to the study of law. A solid academic background is an advantage in the practice and study of law. Applicants should select a challenging program of studies that will assist them in developing good study habits; courses designed to develop reading and writing skills are strongly recommended. Such skills should be acquired before entry into law school."

A second school commented that:

"The committee looks for outstanding academic ability, a competitive LSAT score, subjects of a rigorous nature which provide the opportunity to develop powers of analysis, and skill in written and oral communication."

Note the emphasis on reading, writing and powers of analysis! Hence, any program that develops "problem solving" skills will be of value.

Your university years before law school should be thought of as an end in themself. Treat them as years of personal development that are unrelated to law school or becoming a lawyer!

Question 8: Will my undergraduate program be useful to law school and a career as a lawyer?

There is no academic background that cannot be directly related to some aspect of the practice of law. Let me give you some examples of legal issues that have been topical:

- a relationship between understanding psychology and the discussion of "recovered memories" through therapy;

- a relationship between actuarial science and the litigation of "vanishing premium" life insurance cases;

- a relationship between engineering and patent law;

- a relationship between political science and the constitutional issue over whether Quebec can separate;

- a relationship between sociology and the constitutional issue of "same sex benefits";

- a relationship between computer science and the Microsoft antitrust issue;

- a relationship between economics and the Microsoft antitrust issue;

I am not saying that a specific academic background is a requirement for working in any particular area of law. I am simply saying that certain academic backgrounds will make certain areas of law more interesting to you, thereby giving you an initial advantage in them.

Question 9. Am I required to attend law school in the province/state in which I wish to practice?

No. Graduates of any Canadian common-law school are free to enter the Bar Admission Course in any province. Graduates of any U.S. ABA approved law school are free to take the bar exam in any state. Graduates of Canadian law schools may be allowed to take the bar exam of certain U.S. states. Graduates of U.S. law schools may (after becoming involved with the National Committee On Accreditation) be able to enter the Bar Admission Course in a Canadian province. (See the later book on Mobility.)

The purpose of a legal education is NOT to teach you the law - rather the purpose is to TEACH YOU HOW TO LEARN AND APPLY THE LAW! Law school is not for the purpose of preparing you for the bar exam (or exams in the case of Canadian provinces).

There is little difference between U.S. and Canadian law schools. Both countries are based on a system of common law (except Quebec and Louisiana which are based on the civil law system) and are constitutional democracies.

In Summary:

A. In terms of learning the law - you could attend law school in either Canada or the U.S. (or probably England, Australia, South Africa, New Zealand, etc.) and learn basically the same things.

B. But, where you attend law school may affect whether you can be admitted to the bar! Graduation from any Canadian law school will allow you to enter the bar admission course in any Canadian province. But - on the issue of "cross border mobility" - only graduates of Canadian common law schools have the automatic right to enter the bar admission course in a Canadian province. Graduates of foreign law schools must obtain a certificate that their education is equivalent to a Canadian law degree. In a later chapter, I will explain the process of obtaining this certificate from the National Committee of Accreditation.

Question 10: Will a "law related" part-time or summer job help me get into law school? Will it help me in any other way? How would I find such a job?"

A "law related" job will not make you a more attractive candidate to a law school admissions committee. But, a "law related" job may give you better insight into what lawyers do. This insight may help you with the "law school decision."

Getting The "Law Related" Job

Jobs do exist in various levels of government and in private firms. Some jobs will give you a "ring side" view of what kinds of work lawyers do. Contact firms and ask if they hire summer or part-time university students who are not law students. Also, contact the various levels of government. Let them know that you are willing to do anything. I would think that networking would be important here. Cultivate contacts you have. Your goal is to get close enough to the inner workings of a law firm so that you can see what some aspects of the practice of law are about. Getting that job may require persistence. But, the results can be worth it. What follows is part of an email that I recently received:

"Just a short response in regard to your article on legal related summer jobs.

My daughter will be attending Osgoode Hall year one in September. Last summer she wrote a letter asking for employment in a legal environment-she made 250 copies and I delivered them to every lawyer in the Niagara Region. She found a job in a law firm last summer. That experience was mentioned in her personal statement and she submitted it to 3 law schools along with her marks, LSAT scores etc. I don't know how much it helped but she was selected to attend the Law School of her choice, as early as January of this year. This summer she is working part-time for two Criminal Law firms in the same region. Networking from last summer's jobs led to this summer's employment. Her work this summer included (to date), attending court sessions, using the City Hall court library, speaking with clients, typing letters to clients and to other lawyers, making suggestions to her bosses on possible defenses especially in those cases where she had to transcribe police tapes of discussions with the clients of her bosses, lunching with the bosses at the Lawyers "hang out", knowing how to run a small law firm including billing procedures and a number of other experiences that will be of help to her while attending Law School and afterwards. One of her bosses has already indicated that she could article with him upon graduation. I would say that this 3-4 days per week of "legal work" that she has is more valuable than the additional money that she would have made by working for McDonalds.

By the way, she did attend one of your LSAT preparation courses."

Will A "Law Related" Job Help With Your Career Plans?

It depends. But, most of you have to work somewhere. So, why not go for the "law related" job. The primary benefit of working in an environment where you are close to lawyers is that when you go to law school you will see how the law fits in with the real world practice of law. In terms of creating opportunities down the road - a "law related" job may provide you with contacts that could be helpful.

Pre-Law Students Talk About Their Summer Jobs

What follows are three perspectives of three pre-law students. As you read them, please remember that different people can experience the same events differently. There is no guarantee that you would experience these opportunities in the same way that these students did.

Perspective 1 - A Private Law Firm

"I am currently a fourth year undergraduate student majoring in Finance. I've been thinking about law school for a long time now but was never really sure what the profession entails. So last year, I wanted to look for a summer experience at a law firm to learn more about it. I wanted to know what being a lawyer involves before I seriously consider this option. During a sleepless night, I surfed on several Canadian law firms' websites. Being a business major with a particular interest in international transactions, I was specifically interested towards law firms with an international presence. I first came across the website of _____. I was very impressed with the variety of services they offer as well as their specialization in corporate and security laws.

I sent them my resume and a month later I was called for an interview for a legal assistant position. I started working right after I finished my final exams.

I worked for a lawyer who specializes in corporate and security laws with an emphasis in the high-tech industry. My major task involved revising and formatting legal documents. Some of the documents consist of shareholders' agreements, escrow agreements, stock option plans, information circulars, prospectuses, and so on. I particularly liked this part of the job because it was an opportunity to see how some of the business concepts I learned at school being applied in the real world. I was also responsible for file requisitions, issuing statements of accounts, minor accounting and maintaining timely records of lawyer's time billings and expenses.

Overall, I had a valuable work experience this summer. Although the hours were long (especially during closing times) and the workload seems endless, I am still very much interested in law. I was particularly lucky to work with a lawyer who was involved in some interesting cases and who also took the time to explain some of the legal theory with me.

I would definitely recommend this to anyone who wants to learn more about the legal profession and in general, how a law firm works. Perhaps the most appealing aspect of the legal profession to me is that it is always intellectually challenging and I am definitely up for that."

Perspective 2 - **Another Private Law Firm**

"Summering in a Bay Street Law Firm

Being a summer student is not an easy task, and can take a lot of time and energy out of a person. I have been a summer student for the past 2 summers in a big law firm on Bay Street in Toronto and when asked to write this column I decided that I would divide it up into the 3 major sections: Who, What and How Much to allow me to cover any questions individuals may have. Hopefully this will help any of those who are looking to summer in a law firm, both University students and law students.

Who:

Unfortunately in this world, intellect and personality alone does not get most individuals where they want to be. The legal practice is no exception. Commonly individuals ask me how I acquired a summer student position in a large Bay Street law firm. Basically to sum it up, I had connections through connections. I knew an individual who worked for an accounting firm affiliated with a law firm and therefore my resume was sent internally, unlike the 1000 other applicants for my position that were not. Therefore I was the only one they interviewed and moreover the only one they hired. Don't get me wrong, the application and interview process was still long (I went through 3 or 4 different interviews and took computer tests and other tests) however eventually after a lot of persistence on my part I was offered the position and was rushed out to the firm to start working right away. Although this may come across very negatively, it is meant to do the opposite. I was extremely surprised when my personal connection told me that she had connections. She is an investment banker and an accountant, and I never thought that she would be able to get me a job in a law firm. I truly recommend that you talk to different individuals, even your relatives and close friends. When I told her that I was thinking about going to law school, she recommended that I forward her my resume and cover letter to her, and the rest is history.

What:

To sum up my job in one word is very easy; everything. As a summer student, I do everything from administration work to research and big projects. Last summer I worked on a few very large projects in which I headed, prepared and coordinated. Some days I may be revising agreements in our Corporate/Commercial department, and the next day I might be helping to allocate domain names in our Intellectual Property and Information Technology department.

It is a day-to-day job and whatever department is busy that day, is where I can be found. Our firm is a large practice, with over 120 lawyers in many different countries (mostly in Toronto) with many different specialties. This is an excellent opportunity for those students who do not know exactly what kind of law they want to pursue, and this is definitely the category I was in. Being in a full practice firm allows me to receive an in-depth experience in different areas of law, which one wouldn't receive in a Boutique firm (a much smaller firm in which specializes in one very specific area of law). For a student pursuing a general degree in law, and not knowing what kind of law they want to pursue or specialize in, I recommend trying to get a placement in a full practice firm.

How Much:

These are the questions I receive the most: How much time do you put in a week; How much do you really get out of it; and the most famous, How much do you get paid.

Some may think this is a dream job and that it would be extremely educational as well as interesting, and most of the time I would agree with you. I was ecstatic when I was hired last summer. However, it is a very demanding job and extremely tiring. Basically if you truly analyze my job I basically go where it is busy for 4 months. I have worked some nights until 2 or 3 a.m. and this is a long night when you start at 8 or 9 a.m. Weekends? What's a weekend? For those who like to take some time off, travel and relax in the summer this is definitely not the job for you. When I came back this summer in May they were waiting. The first week I was back I put in about 17 hours of overtime. Which is a lot considering I started back May 1st and finished my exams the last Wednesday in April. I didn't take a day off last summer, and my contract expired at the end of August, but I ended up working until the Friday before school started both last year and this year.

Bay Street is extremely fast-paced, everything is a rush and there is never enough time in a day to get everything that you need to get done. If you are the kind of person that likes checking things off your "To Do" list, think twice about being a lawyer!

It's funny because no matter how early I came in, or how late I left there was always lawyers getting in before me and leaving after me. I have also learned that it is extremely hard to be a corporate Bay Street lawyer and expect to be much more. Very few are married, and even fewer are happily married. Don't get me wrong, I'm not saying that it cannot be done, but it is rare and extremely hard. I do not have a lot of free time, and when I do I'm often really tired and run down anyway to do much. It is hard, but I do it, because for me it's worth it. It is worth the learning experience, it is worth the money, and when it comes down to it, you know that you are not the only one going through it. The students here often go out together, and we have a baseball team in the law firm league which is an excellent break. There was many extremely late nights last summer where I would go out with the articling students for a very late dinner to get away from work for a couple of minutes. We would just complain and say how we didn't want to still be at work and how we needed a vacation, vent all of our frustrations and then feel better going back to work. Everyone is an amazing support system and my experience here has been incredible.

In summation, my tip for anyone wanting to get into a big firm is; never cut off ties and keep getting to know people. I would have never thought that the individual that I knew could help me get into a law firm, but she did, and I am extremely grateful. Law firms like mine look for the outstanding resumes and the extremely well-rounded individuals, and to be quite honest their standards are extremely high. Therefore the more people you know and the more people you impress the more influence and pull you have on getting in. However, don't be surprised to be worked to death, whether summering or articling, or even being an associate. Someone told me a quote a couple of years ago, and it is very true "If it doesn't kill you, it will make you stronger". In this case, I truly believe it."

Perspective 3 - Working With The Government

"The Summer I Spent Exploring Law

In 1997, the provincial government initiated a formal and comprehensive strategy of eliminating illegal gambling.

This constituted the creation of the Ontario Illegal Gaming Enforcement Unit. In early 1999, the government began a cost efficiency initiative that required an analysis of the activity of this unit. That's where I came in. Through a provincial youth employment program, I was selected to work as a summer student at the Ministry of the Attorney General. As part of the Ministry that oversees prosecutions across Ontario, I worked with senior prosecutors responsible for overseeing gambling prosecutions around the province. I prepared a report surveying the use of prosecution resources in such cases. In collecting this data, I became familiar with the relevant Criminal Code sections and the various processes of the justice system. Beyond writing the report, I was lucky enough to be taken along on some of the 'field trips' that the articling students went upon. I toured the Centre for Forensic Science, Provincial Court, Court of Appeal, and all the law libraries in Toronto. For a law school hopeful, this job provided me with invaluable insight into the daily practices of crown work and the overall working of the provincial justice system. Working at the Ministry put me in contact with numerous crowns, lawyers and articling students. The legal expertise and passion for the law I was exposed to daily was simultaneously motivating and overwhelming. I learned that crowns spend a great deal of time researching cases and writing factums. Dramatic courtroom speeches, as depicted in "Law and Order" or "The Practice" are few and far between. Articling students warned me repeatedly that if I don't love to read, that I should not go to law school. As I have always wanted to practice criminal law, one of the most important insights I gained was the necessity of an iron stomach. Part of a crown's work is ploughing through unpleasant pieces of evidence, such as videotapes, photographs and graphic testimonies. The ability to distance oneself from one's job is thus essential to work in criminal law. Overall, I gained first hand knowledge (or as close as possible) of what my prospective career would be like. This was much more than a summer job, it was an immeasurable opportunity to make an informed career choice."

Advice From The ABA - Preparation for Legal Education

The American Bar Association (ABA) has a statement giving its position on preparation for law school. In substance, the document affirms the need for a broad background and the development of verbal and analytical skills. It also affirms that there is no specific pre-law curriculum and that one can be an effective law student coming from virtually any kind of academic background.

The ABA identified the core skills and values that are essential for competent lawyering to include the following:

- Analytic and Problem Solving Skills

- Critical Reading Abilities

- Writing Skills

- Oral Communication and Listening Abilities

- General Research Skills

- Task Organization and Management Skills

- The Value of Serving Others And Promoting Justice

The ABA identified the following areas of knowledge that are important for a sophisticated legal education and to the development of a competent lawyer:

- a broad understanding of history

- a fundamental understanding of political thought and theory

- a basic understanding of ethical theory and theories of justice

- a grounding in economics

- some basic mathematical and financial skills

- a basic understanding of human behavior and social interaction

- an understanding of diverse cultures.

So, you must be a "jack of all trades" and a "master of none!"

Conclusion

You should treat your undergraduate career as an end in itself. Treat law school as an extension of an interest you already have. Use joint degree opportunities to squeeze maximum benefits from the law school experience. Do not arrive at law school with too many preconceived ideas about what you like or don't like.

APPENDIX

How to get to the top — study philosophy*

How should Canada educate students to compete successfully in the business world? Some provincial governments think it is by teaching them business.

The Alberta government has announced plans for an "unprecedented" expansion of business education at its three universities. Already, 120 extra students are studying management at the University of Calgary.

Recent evidence suggests this approach is mistaken. We will produce better managers if we educate them first in traditional subjects in the arts and sciences. We may do best of all if we educate them in philosophy.

Each year, thousands of undergraduates write admissions tests for the prestigious graduate programs. There's the Law School Admissions Test (LSAT), the Graduate Management Admission Test (GMAT) for business study, and the Graduate Record Examination (GRE) for other fields. A 1985 study for the U.S. Department of Education compared tests of students from different disciplines, with surprising results.

Consider the GMAT, used for admission to MBA programs and, ultimately, to the highest levels of management. Undergraduate business students, whom you would think would be especially well prepared for this test, do badly on it, scoring below average for all test takers. The best results are by math students, followed by philosophy students and engineers.

This is typical. Business students score below average on almost all the tests, as do, excepting engineers, all other students in applied or occupational fields. The best results come from students in the natural sciences and humanities. The study concludes that, on tests measuring aptitude for advanced professional study, "undergraduates who major in professional and occupational fields consistently underperform those who major in traditional arts and science fields."

The most consistent performers are philosophy students. They are first out of 28 disciplines on one test, second on another, and third on a third. On their weakest test they are still 4.6 per cent above the average, the best performance on a weakest test of any group.

Although data here are less consistent, the superior performance of arts and science students continues after university. According to a book by sociologist Michael Useem, they have more difficulty finding beginning managerial jobs than those with business or professional degrees because they lack specific skills in finance or engineering. When they are hired, it is usually lower in the company hierarchy. Once hired, however, they advance more rapidly than their colleagues.

On average, arts and science graduates end their careers level with business and engineering graduates, having closed the gap. In some companies with less of an engineering or MBA "culture," they pass them. An AT&T study showed that, after 20 years with the company, 43 per cent of liberal-arts graduates had reached upper-middle management, compared with 32 per cent of business majors and 23 per cent of engineers. The Chase Manhattan Bank found that 60 per cent of its worst managers had MBAs while 60 per cent of its best managers had BAs. At IBM, nine of the company's top 13 executives had liberal-art degrees.

What explains the success of arts and science students? Many arguments for liberal education cite a contemporary cliche — that we live in a time of unprecedented change. If the world is in flux, an applied education will soon be out of date. Better the breadth and flexibility given by general studies.

A better explanation points to what cannot change: the basic elements of reasoning and problem-solving. The study of admissions test found that students do best "who major in a field characterized by formal thought, structural relationships, abstract models, symbolic languages, and deductive reasoning." The more abstract a subject, the more it develops pure reasoning skills; and the stronger a person's reasoning skills, the better he or she will do in any applied field.

This fits the data from business. Corporations report that, though technical skills are most important in low-level managerial jobs, they become less so in middle and top jobs, where the key traits include communications skills, the ability to formulate problems, and reasoning. Liberal-arts education may be weak in the prerequisites for beginning managerial jobs, but provides just what's needed for success at the top.

This doesn't mean there's no place for business education. Canadian industry needs specialized business skills, and our universities should supply them. But in the increasingly competitive world economy there will be a premium on vision, creativity and analytical power, traits better fostered by liberal education.

This points to the recommendation now heard most from chief executive officers: first an arts and science degree in a field like English, physics, or philosophy, then an MBA. First some general intellectual skills, then the specific knowledge needed to apply them in business.

So to train successful business leaders, Canada should strengthen education in the arts and sciences. And this will have another effect. Students educated in the liberal arts will be better rounded individuals, knowing more of the natural world or the history of their culture, and better at reasoning about morality and politics. At the very least, a nice side-effect.

Thomas Hurka, January 2, 1990.
Reprinted with permission of the author.

Book II - A Report

Summary And Introduction

My Advice To You Is ....

Some of you may know what kind of law school you wish to attend. Even if this is so, I suggest you spend some time on Book II. It will identify opportunities that you may or may not have known exist. Book II will teach you what different law programs are about. This will allow you to read effectively and critically promotional literature from various law schools - allowing for an intelligent comparative evaluation.

In Book II, I will play the role of the law program educator.

Book II - Chapter Summaries

3. How To Find And Research Law Schools - Because Not All Law Schools Are The Same

Focus: How to find appropriate schools in Canada, the U.S. and the U.K. and ...

4. Your Law Degree - LL.B. or J.D.

Focus: J.D. vs. LL.B.

5. Accredited Law Schools - Part-Time, Evening And Weekend Opportunities

Focus: Opportunities that are "accredited" and personal experiences of these kinds of programs

6. Non-Traditional Ways Of Obtaining A Legal Education That MAY Lead To Bar Admission

Focus: Correspondence law schools, external study, U.S. states that allow bar admission based on law office study ...

7. Ways Of Learning About Law That Will NOT Lead To Bar Admission

Focus: Undergraduate degrees in law, paralegal programs, etc.

8. Graduate Education In Law - An Investment Worth Making

Focus: Why take an LL.M.? What is it? Personal Experiences

9. For Those Outside North America - Coming To North America

Focus: What you need to know about North American law schools and bar admission

10. The Law Schools Have Chosen You! - How To Choose A Law School

Focus: How to interpret rankings, what is an "appropriate school", availability of joint programs ...

Chapter 3

How To Find And Research Law Schools - Because Not All Schools Are The Same

North American Law Schools

This chapter assumes a North American perspective. Furthermore, it is best understood within the framework of wishing to attend a three year "full time" program. Subsequent chapters will discuss other kinds of opportunities to study law in North America. (For law Schools in the U.K., Australia, New Zealand see the chapter appendix.)

I will discuss 6 areas of concern for pre law students. These are:

Concern 1 - Locating Law Schools In The U.S. And Canada

Concern 2 - Finding Specific Data About Specific Schools

Concern 3 - Finding Law Schools That Specialize In Certain Areas

Concern 4 - Employment Prospects - Does Your Law School Matter?

Concern 5 - Determining The Reputation/Quality Of Law Schools

Concern 6 - Determining Suitability For You

We will address these concerns in order.

Concern 1 - Locating Law Schools In The U.S. And Canada

One of the best sources of information is the Law Services web site at: www.LSAC.org. It has links to all the ABA approved law schools in the U.S. and Canada's common law schools. In addition check your Pre-Law Advisors and Pre-Law Societies. Furthermore, there are many books written by third parties which describe the law schools in the U.S. and Canada.

It is critical that you read the calendars of information for each school. Pay particular attention to the courses offered and the Dean's message.

Concern 2 - Finding Specific Data About Specific Schools

This topic is important. But, the information about law schools changes rapidly. It is necessary to ensure that the information does not become dated. Hence, school specific information will be provided online at: http://www.lawschoolbound.com. On this site you will find links (either directly or indirectly) to many of the law schools in North America and the rest of the world.

It is well worth spending time researching the schools. At a minimum you will spend three years of your life there.

Concern 3 - Finding Law Schools That Specialize In Certain Areas

In general, law schools do not specialize in specific areas of law. Hence, this should not be a concern. At most, a school may offer an extra course or two in a certain area. (This hardly qualifies as a specialization.) Many schools either offer (or require) independent research projects. You might consider using any independent study opportunities as a way to create your own "specialization."

You should also understand that certain areas of law - for example - entertainment or sports law - are not unique areas of law. They are just basic courses like contracts and trademarks applied to fact situations involving sports or entertainment. So, you should be a bit careful about choosing a school just because it claims to have a specialty in a certain area.

Concern 4 - Employment Prospects - Does Your Law School Matter?

The U.S.

It will matter where you attend law school in the U.S. The reason has to do with the method of bar admission. In the U.S. there is no articling or bar admission course. Hence, hiring decisions are based at least in part on where you attend law school.

Canada

It matters less where you attend law school in Canada. The reason is that many hiring decisions are based on your performance during the required articling period. Nevertheless, different schools do have different personalities and you should try to attend the school appropriate to you.

Concern 5 - Determining The Reputation/Quality Of Law Schools

DON'T Pay Attention To Law School Rankings!

Not all law schools are the same. Schools are more or less suitable for different kinds of people. Nevertheless, law schools are not susceptible to numerical rankings. In fact, to try to rank schools in this way is stupid. The Law Services web site at www.LSAC.org has a statement from U.S. law school deans explaining why numerical rankings are suspect. This statement from the law deans includes the following excerpt (with which I agree):

"The idea that all law schools can be measured by the same yardstick ignores the qualities that make you and law schools unique, and is unworthy of being an important influence on the choice you are about to make. As the deans of schools that range across the spectrum of several rating systems, we strongly urge you to minimize the influence of rankings on your own judgment. In choosing the best school for you, we urge you to get information about all the schools in which you might have some interest. An abundance of information, far more information than is used in any ranking system, is available from the sources noted in the box below. The next step is to seek information directly from the law schools, including catalogs or bulletins and other materials that will answer the specific questions relating to your special needs and interests. Finally, there is no substitute for on-site visits to the law schools that most interest you as you reach the end of the admission process. Law schools may all have met the same standards of quality to become accredited, but they are quite different from each other. The unique characteristics of each law school will inform you why one school may be best for you and another school best for someone else. We want you to make the best choice for you."

Nevertheless, rankings are interesting and impossible to avoid. Therefore, when you read rankings you should

pay attention to the facts that gave rise to the ranking and not to the ranking itself!

DO Pay Attention To Books And Articles About Law Schools

But, recognize that the information in them reflects only the author's point of view. There are many sources of third party information. Examples include: Peterson's, Barrons, Arco, Princeton Review, Kaplan, etc. Also, U.S. News and World Report publishes an annual ranking (pay attention only to the facts on which the ranking is based) of U.S. law schools.

Again I must caution you - these books and articles are to be used by reading the facts on which the rankings and/or discussion is based.

Concern 6 - Determining Suitability For You

So, How Do You Determine Suitability?

The issue of "suitability" involves much more than reputation and quality. Different people may be better suited to different schools.

Suitability cannot be determined with precision. A "suitable school" would include the following characteristics:

1. The quality of teaching is good.

Research by talking to current students.

2. The school offers a sufficient variety of courses.

Research by investigating current course offerings.

3. Joint programs are abundant.

Research by checking the calendar of information.

4. If in Canada, graduates have easy access to articling positions.

Research by talking with the career development officer. (In this regard, I am not aware of any problems with any Canadian law schools.)

5. If in the U.S., graduates find employment easily.

Research by talking with the career development officer.

6. If in the U.S., graduates pass the bar exam.

Research by asking the school.

7. Current students are happy.

Research by talking to them.

8. If in the U.S., it is ABA Approved.

Research by checking the list of ABA Approved law schools.

9. Last and most important - you must be happy in the school environment.

Do visit the campus! The campus visit is invaluable!

It is common for applicants to have narrowed the choice to two or three schools. They appear to be the same on paper. I suggest that you visit the campus, the school and the city of location. After all, you have to spend three years there. It is amazing how often a "feel for the place" will clarify the decision. I once had a student who had based his whole undergraduate career on wanting to attend a certain school. He was accepted, but after having visited the school, he went to a different school.

What follows is an account of a U.S. law school tour made by two Canadian students.

"As a 4th year undergrad at U of T, I have very limited time to visit the law schools I've applied to. In light of this, I decided to invite a friend on a four-day, four-school US road trip just before Christmas. After approximately 4000km of driving and very limited sleep over the course of a week, I strongly suggest to anyone applying to law schools to visit all schools you are considering, regardless of the inconveniences. When visiting a law school you get a real sense of the atmosphere surrounding the place you may have to spend the next three years of your life. Admissions officers and students will provide surprisingly honest critiques of what it is like to live in the area.

Here are some examples of important information I received on my tour.

Duke: the city of Durham is a former tobacco-manufacturing center. Most students prefer to live in Chapel Hill, seven miles away, making a car almost a necessity.

Harvard: A law student criticized the fact that Boston is falsely advertised as student friendly due to the numerous post-secondary institutions in the area.

Georgetown: the Law Center is not located on the Georgetown's main campus but instead consists of three buildings located in an unspectacular part of Washington.

Cornell: the law school is located in the very corner of campus, less than half a kilometre from the part of Ithaca called Collegetown.

Additionally, visits provide the most up-to-date information on the law school. For example, Harvard changed the size of its sections from 140 to 80 students this year. In choosing law schools you should collect as much information as possible on each in order to ensure you make the best decision for yourself. If you like to study late at night, you would avoid Harvard, regardless of its reputation, because their library closes at midnight.

Valuable info awaits you if you visit potential law schools. You must go out of your way to collect as much relevant info as you can. However, this does not mean a law school tour must be all business. Over the course of my trip I took some time to have a drink at Cheers in Boston, visit a sister living in the US, and saw MJ play basketball. To everyone awaiting admission decisions good luck and I feel your anxiety. Happy New Year!"

It sounds as though there was nothing to lose and a good deal of fun to be gained!

Conclusion

This chapter has been designed to help you locate law schools and determine if they are suitable. In the U.S. there are over 180 ABA approved law schools. Hence, there are wide ranges in quality. In Canada, there are few schools, they are small and do not vary significantly. In the UK, there are many schools and law school is something that is commenced after the equivalent of our high school.

APPENDIX A

Those of you thinking of attending law school in Toronto may find the following article interesting on this point.

March 28, 2002

Arguments for Toronto's two law schools

Monique Conrod

The classroom at Osgoode Hall Law School is beginning to fill up. Sixty students are plugging in laptops, getting out books and talking with friends about their weekends. Then conversation fades as Professor Patrick Monahan begins his first-year constitutional law class the same way he does every Monday morning: "OK, what happened last night on The Practice?"

What seems like small talk quickly turns into a discussion of what the TV show's defence attorneys did wrong, and a lesson in the fundamentals of cross-examination. It's all part of the process of learning about law.

Osgoode is the original training ground for lawyers although it's sometimes seen as the left-wing upstart while its downtown rival, the University of Toronto Faculty of Law, is seen as the school for the establishment. During the loud debate recently over U of T law tuition hikes, it was easy to forget about the city's other school also churning out new lawyers.

"University of Toronto is generally perceived as being focused more on corporate law - business law in its broadest context," says Christopher Sweeney, president of the ZSA Legal Recruitment agency in Toronto. "Osgoode is seen as being more focused on social issues."

Sweeney said U of T's law school is considered academically superior because Osgoode accepts more students and has less demanding admission prerequisites. In 2001, Osgoode admitted 287 students out of 2,000 applicants while University of Toronto accepted 170 of about 1,700 applicants.

A key factor in both cases is an applicant's score on the Law School Admission Test, or LSAT. Among students accepted on the basis of their academic records at Osgoode last year, the median LSAT score was in the 81st percentile. At University of Toronto last year, the comparable score was in the 94th percentile, with few of those accepted scoring below the 85th percentile.

Sweeney said this "best and brightest" reputation translates into articling positions with Toronto's big downtown firms. "Virtually all graduates of the University of Toronto school find openings on Bay Street. That cannot be said for Osgoode graduates," he said.

Articling salaries in the Toronto bar are the highest in the country, ranging from about $35,000 to $70,000 per year, with the big houses of law paying absolute top dollar. "And if you start off by articling at a large Bay Street firm, your future has more options to it than if you do not," says Sweeney. "So it impacts on the rest of your career."

But it also comes at a price. University of Toronto law school made headlines recently when it announced plans to raise its tuition fees to an unprecedented $22,000 over the next five years. The school was already commanding a premium tuition. Basic tuition for first year students last fall was $12,000, compared to Osgoode Hall's $8,000.

Osgoode is considering bumping its tuition to $12,000 as of September, 2003. A decision by York's board of governors is expected by May. Law dean Peter Hogg said this is not an attempt to match U of T's fees. "This is not a way station to a much higher figure," he said. "The proposal is that we would move to, and stay at, $12,000."

A sampling of some top Toronto firms reveals their articling students are currently drawn from both schools in roughly equal numbers, based on their Web sites. So while the percentage of U of T alumni on Bay Street may be higher, top students from Osgoode can land there, too, if that's what they want. But not everyone dreams of a career piling up billable hours for A-list corporate clients.

"We're very proud of the fact we prepare our students not just for a Bay Street practice," said Hogg. "We encourage students to think about alternative careers. We promote the idea that the law is a force for social good, and there are many careers which are very satisfying and important."

A sampling of Osgoode Hall graduates who have taken other paths include Ontario Tory leadership rivals Ernie Eves and Jim Flaherty, Ontario chief justice Roy McMurtry, cable czar Ted Rogers, Studio Two co-host Paula Todd and Toronto harbourmaster Lisa MacCormack Raitt.

Nevertheless "a very large number of our students do end up practising on Bay Street, and we have very strong business law programs," says Hogg. "There's a demand for that, and in the city of Toronto that's a very important thing for a law school to be strong at."

Osgoode is meeting that need, in part, through an innovative new program which allows upper year students to specialize in a particular area of law. The students take a series of courses that become progressively more difficult in terms of the ideas and skills mastered. Typically, these studies culminate in the school's intensive program, where practising lawyers serve as instructors and students spend a semester working or observing in a clinical setting.

The concept of hands-on experience began in 1971 when Osgoode established Parkdale Community Legal Services in west end Toronto. At any time about 20 students are working at the clinic under the supervision of staff lawyers, delivering legal services to low-income clients.

Clinical experience is now offered in a range of areas, including business, immigration, criminal and aboriginal law. In the criminal law intensive program, students are placed in the offices of a defence lawyer, prosecutor or judge for a semester. In the business law program, they will work at one of three large Toronto firms participating in the program.

"We get a really high degree of co-operation from the profession, and I think the profession appreciates the added value which these kinds of clinical programs add beyond the normal classroom setting," said Hogg.

While U of T does not offer specialized courses of study to its upper-year law students, it does provide other opportunities for hands-on experience, some of which defy the school's "big business" image. The International Human Rights Program places 30 students in programs throughout the world, while the June Callwood program in Aboriginal Law offers internships which places students with aboriginal community organizations.

Students can also get involved in Pro Bono Students Canada, a network of 16 law schools that places students with public interest and non-governmental organizations, and through

U of T's Public Interest Clinical Intensive Program, which combines seminars with clinical work at the school's Downtown Legal Services clinic.

Ron Daniels, dean of the University of Toronto law faculty, said one of his school's greatest strengths is the calibre of its students and faculty. He said the student body ranks in "the top 10" among law schools internationally, based on entrance scores and prior achievements. Not only do most students have an undergraduate degree before entering the law faculty, about 25 per cent also have a graduate degree in another discipline.

To reflect these high attainments, the school recently replaced the standard Bachelor of Laws (LL.B.) degree with a Juris Doctor (J.D.) program. "The law school has adopted the JD designation as the appropriate way of signalling our degree's 'second degree' status," said Daniels.

Daniels spoke with pride about his faculty's international reputations and said the professors are engaged in most of the important scholarly debates in Canada and internationally. Faculty members recently produced a book on the federal government's anti-terrorism legislation. Many have been cited in Supreme Court of Canada decisions, or acted for interveners in cases reaching the high court. "They are not merely contributing to those debates, but often helping to define them," Daniels said.

Daniels said his school plans to increase the number of faculty members from 50 to 57, making the ratio of students to teachers 9 to 1. Retaining current faculty, as well as attracting new ones, is cited as a key reason for U of T's dramatic tuition hike. Salaries need to be elevated, the argument goes, if the school is to compete with U.S. law schools for top academics.

Legal recruiter Sweeney, the owner of a law degree from Osgoode, expects the tuition hike to broaden the gap between the two schools in coming years. Raising salaries means the downtown school will attract a superior calibre of professors, he said.

"And if Osgoode does not respond, they will basically be left in University of Toronto's dust."

Monique Conrod is a Toronto legal affairs writer.

Sidebar

Admission to Ontario law schools is based primarily on Law School Admission Test (LSAT) scores and your cumulative academic record.

Writing the LSATs is a make-or-break event for virtually anyone determined to become a lawyer. The tests are held across North America to one standard - four times a year at both Toronto law schools.

The testing is multiple choice and aims to measure an individual's cognitive, reasoning and writing skills compared to his or her peers - the scoring is by percentiles.

One cannot "study" for LSATs in terms of content. Even so, the stakes are high and a thriving cottage industry exists to tutor students on how to ace the Big Test. A local firm called Richardson LSAT typically offers 60 hours of instructional classes for $300.

All applicants are urged to do sample tests under timed conditions. "Very few people achieve their full [LSAT] potential without preparing at all," the U of T law school warns on its Website.

In special cases - for example, mature or disadvantaged applicants - law schools give more weight to other factors such as non-academic achievements and personal interviews in the application process.

Most students accepted into a Toronto law school will have a bachelor's degree in another discipline. Both schools stress that the area of undergraduate study is not important. "A lot of students think they really should do something law related in order to go to law school," said Osgoode Hall Law School Dean Peter Hogg. "We don't find that that makes any significant difference. A person who's done well in biology or French, we find, will do just as well in law school as somebody who majored in political science."

Bonnie Goldberg, assistant dean of career services at the University of Toronto law faculty, said students come to the school from diverse backgrounds. "So you might hire a U of T graduate knowing that you could get someone with an engineering background, someone who's an Olympic athlete, someone who has four languages.""

Monique Conrod, March 28, 2002. Reprinted with permission of the author.
(Note although we were happy to receive a mention in this article, the pricing for our LSAT courses as described is obviously not accurate.)

APPENDIX B

Law Schools Outside Of North America

A. Law School In The U.K.

I am indebted to a University Of Victoria law student for the following contribution.

(Please remember that law school in the U.K. is not a "graduate degree." People commence law school after completing the equivalent of North American high school. If you attend law school in the UK, your classmates will be younger.)

"Applying to Law School in the U.K.

So, you want to go to Law School in the U.K. There are a few good reasons to do this. First of all, you can apply to most schools straight out of high school. This is because the UK university system considers an LL.B. to be yet another undergraduate degree, like a B.A. or B.SC., not like a graduate degree as we do here in North America. Going abroad to study is a positive and broadening experience for most people, it will bring you an international perspective and increase the uniqueness of your professional qualifications.

The first thing to do when you decide to apply to university overseas is send away for information. You will need the Universities and Colleges Admission Service Handbook. This is a thousand-page heavy book detailing the application procedure, providing information about each school, entrance requirements and other key information like deadlines. Going through the UCAS is the only way to apply to law school or post-secondary education in the UK. You cannot apply directly to the school, they will refer you back to UCAS. But, that being said, you should still write to the individual schools for information and pamphlets about programs since all UCAS provides you with is general listings of programs and contact information. The UCAS is dedicated to "promoting a partnership between applicants on one hand and universities and colleges on the other". Basically they serve as a gatekeeper, and as opposed to Law Services or the OLSAS in Ontario, actually provide a straightforward and accessible service. Most of the information in the Handbook is available there, as well as a convenient online application form. Contact them at the following address and make sure to check out the website.

Universities and Colleges Application Service, Rosehill, New Barn Lane, Cheltenham, Gloustershire, GL52 3LZ. Applicant enquiries by phone: 01-242-227788. Website: http://www.ucas.ac.uk

To apply to an LL.B. program in the UK you need to be ready early. Applications for the following September must be submitted early.

Applicants applying from outside the UK, be they British citizens or not, must go through the overseas applicant process. Forms can be obtained through either a British Council Office or directly from the UCAS. Addresses for the British Council Office in your area can be obtained from your local phone book, at http://www.britcoun-canada.org or in Ottawa or Montreal at The British Council - Canada, 80 Elgin Street, Ottawa, Ontario K1P 5K7. Tel: (613) 237-1530 Fax: (613) 569-1478. The British Council - Montreal 1000 ouest rue de La Gauchetire Bureau 4200 Montreal, Quebec H3B 4W5. Tel: (514) 866-5863 Ext. 222 Fax: (514) 866-5322 E-mail: britcnl@alcor.concordia.ca.

There are several hundred law and law-related programs available in the UK listed in the UCAS Handbook. They range from Environmental Law, to European Union Law, to Patent Law, and even the ever popular Conveyancing and Executry Law. An interesting and unique opportunity exists for "dual-system" law degrees in the UK. These degrees are generally called something like LL.B. Law with French, as offered at the University of Newcastle Upon Tyne in Northumbria http://www.ncl.ac.uk, or LL.B. Law with Korean, as offered at the University of Leeds http://www.leeds.ac.uk/law/law.html. They involve taking a year of study abroad in a law school in the country of your specialization. This is generally done during the second year of a three year program.

Funding your legal education in the UK can be an inexpensive venture for foreign students who have a parent or a grandparent who is a British citizen or a citizen of any European Union country. This may qualify you to be charged (or not charged, as the case may be) tuition fees on the basis of this parentage. To do this you should contact your local British Council office or the Consular office of the country your parents are citizens of and see if you qualify to obtain your own citizenship.

For everyone else, however, it can be a more expensive prospect. Some UK schools are entirely independent of public funding and charge tuition based on the full cost of your education. Other schools are fully subsidized and charge a nominal fee based on ability to pay. You should contact the schools you are applying to directly about tuition fees.

Finally, before going abroad for a legal education you are advised to contact the Law Society in the province where you intend to practise upon returning to Canada. It is important to note that there is a more lengthy Bar Admissions process for those holding foreign degrees, and the UK is no exception to this rule. (See the "Mobility Chapter" in this book.)

B. Law School in New Zealand And Australia

I am indebted to the same University Of Victoria law student for this contribution.

"Applying to Law School in New Zealand and Australia

The process of applying to law school in New Zealand and Australia is similar to the process in Canada. You must apply to each school individually, and each school organizes itself differently.

Tuition costs in New Zealand for foreign students range between $12,000-17,000 NZD (New Zealand dollars). At the time of writing that was equivalent to $9,000-13,000 CAD (Canadian dollars). This range changes depending on the school and the program. For the most part Honours Law degrees (LL.B. equivalent) are at the lower end of that range while Master of Laws degrees are at the higher end of that scale.

You can enter law school at most Australian and New Zealand universities straight out of secondary school. This is a positive head start that is not available from any Canadian law program. The degree granted at most New Zealand/Australia law schools is an LL.B. but occasionally there is also a B.A. in legal studies also offered. Keep in mind that there are several entrance exams that you may be required to write if you are a secondary school applicant. This exam is called the NZUEB or New Zealand University Entrance Bursary and Scholarship Examination.

There are several reasons for seeking out a legal education in New Zealand and Australia. Family reasons may make this an attractive option, or the desire to travel abroad and experience a different culture. New Zealand and Australian Law Schools offer an exotic experience of overseas education, while remaining in the British Common Law legal tradition, and comfortably translated into Canadian legal practice. (Please contact the Law Society in your province, to ascertain the bar admission process, for people holding foreign degrees, if you are interested in practising law in Canada after your law degree.)

Chapter 4

Your Law Degree - LL.B. or J.D.

So, What's In The Name?

Let's begin at the end. What is the law degree that you will earn? You have survived three years of a "common law" law school in North America. You have earned a "law degree." There are two questions that might be of some interest:

1. What is the degree called that you have earned?; and

2. What role does that degree play for you in terms of becoming a licensed lawyer?

To cut to the chase, in the U.S. you will graduate with a J.D. In the common law provinces of Canada you will graduate with either a J.D. or an LL.B. In Quebec or the Civil law program at the University of Ottawa you will earn a Civil law degree. What is the difference and why does the difference matter?

First, A Bit Of Background ...

In North America (but not in other parts of the world) a law degree is undertaken after a period of undergraduate, post-secondary, academic work. There are certain applicant categories (example the "mature student" category) where prior post-secondary work may not be required.

How Much Post-Secondary Work Is Required?

Law Degrees In The Common Law Provinces

In Canada, some law schools will admit applicants who (at the time of starting law school) have completed two years of a university degree. Other law schools require three years of university (which in most cases means that the applicant will have a degree). The fact that it is possible to earn a law degree, without having a prior degree, means that for some, a law degree is a first degree. As a result, a law degree in Canada has (until the decision of the University of Toronto to offer the J.D.) been a Bachelor of Laws degree, commonly known as the LL.B. Please note that almost all law students in Canada enter law school after having earned an undergraduate degree. Hence, for all practical purposes the LL.B. is a second university degree or a graduate degree.

(The LL.B .is a degree that may also be earned in many other common law countries. Examples include the U.K., Australia, South Africa, etc. Note that in these countries the LL.B. program may be undertaken after graduation from high school. But only a Canadian LL.B. is approved for entry into the Bar Admission Course in Canadian provinces.)

The LL.B. and Becoming A Licensed Lawyer in Canada

Although you can earn an LL.B. from law schools all over the world, only an LL.B. from a Canadian law school will guarantee entry into the Bar Admission Course.

Law Degrees In The U.S. States

In the U.S., law school (in almost all cases) is undertaken after the applicant has completed at least one post-secondary degree. Hence, (in almost all cases) a U.S. law degree is a graduate degree. A U.S. law degree is called a J.D. (Juris Doctor). This designation reflects the fact that the degree is a graduate degree. (Law degrees in the U.S. used to be called LL.B. degrees.)

In the U.S. there are two kinds of J.D. degrees. The first (and the only one you should consider) is the J.D. that is "ABA (American Bar Association) approved." A J.D. from an "ABA approved" law school will give you the right to take the bar exam in any state that you want. A non-ABA approved J.D. will give you the right to take the bar exam in only certain states.

The J.D. and Becoming A Licensed Lawyer in the U.S.

Not every J.D. will allow you to take the bar exam in the state of your choice. Only a J.D. that is "ABA approved" will give you that flexibility. Some states allow holders of non-approved J.D. degrees to take the bar exam. Examples in the past have included Massachusetts, New York and California.

What Of The University Of Toronto J.D. Degree?

The University of Toronto now awards its graduates the J.D. This is a fascinating decision. What is the reason for this? What is its practical application?

First, what it is not. This University Of Toronto initiative is not the equivalent of the program that the University of Windsor has with the University of Detroit that allows students to graduate with both a Canadian LL.B. and an "ABA approved" J.D. from the University of Detroit. It is important to note that, without approval from the ABA, the University Of Toronto J.D., is not an "ABA approved" degree for the purposes of HAVING THE RIGHT to take the bar exam in any U.S. state you wish. (Obviously this does not make it a "better" or "worse" degree.)

(At the risk of confusing the situation, please remember that many U.S. states, as a matter of discretion and courtesy, will allow Canadian law graduates to take their state bar exams. The University Of Toronto J.D. designation will not change that courtesy and University Of Toronto "J.D. graduates" will continue to take U.S. bar exams.)

Second, what it is. The University Of Toronto J.D. is the same as the U. of T. LL.B., with a name change. Why the name change? A recent article in the University Of Toronto "Ultra Vires" (law students newspaper) suggested that the change was motivated by two factors. These factors are:

(1) the importance of recognizing that a University Of Toronto law degree is actually a graduate degree; and

(2) marketing University Of Toronto graduates to foreign (meaning primarily U.S.) law firms, in an increasingly global world.

Third, the J.D. and Admission To The Bar Admission Course.

The Univeristy Of Toronto J.D. is the same as any other Canadian law degree for the purpose of entry into the Bar Admission Course.

Long Run Implications Of The University Of Toronto Decision

University Of Toronto graduates now graduate with a degree that is different from the degrees of other Canadian law schools. This may give the University Of Toronto law degree a certain "cachet" that other schools do not have. Will other law schools follow the University Of Toronto example? Maybe. But, if I were the dean of a Canadian law school, what I would do is:

Get my law school approved by the ABA, thus giving my graduates a truly North American law degree! Such a degree would meet the academic requirements for both the U.S. state bars and the Canadian law societies. This is an idea whose time has come!!

Some Additional Law Degrees

The focus of this chapter has been on the common law jurisdictions. In addition to the LL.B. and J.D., you may see reference to the following other law degrees:

LL.L. = A civil law degree offered by certain Quebec law schools

BCL = A civil law degree offered by McGill as part of its national law program

LL.M. = A Masters degree in law (see the chapter on graduate degrees in law).

Conclusion

This chapter has been provided to help you understand the kinds of degree programs that law schools offer. Always be clear on what kind of degree you wish to earn.

APPENDIX

Read the following interesting perspective from a University of Toronto law student.

October 17, 2000

U of T to Get J.D. Degree

Opinions divided over whether new degree is forward thinking or a sign of Americanization

Joseph A.G. Berkovits

The class of 2001 will be the first set of Canadian law students who will have the option of graduating with a Juris Doctor (J.D.), the degree earned by American law students, rather than a Bachelor of Laws (LL.B.) The key difference between these two degrees is that the J.D. is a second degree - meaning that students must have an undergraduate degree before entering law school, while the LL.B. is recognized internationally as a first degree. In Europe and Quebec, students earn an LL.B. straight out of high school. In the rest of Canada, most students have one, if not two, degrees behind them when they enter law school; yet the designation has always been Bachelor of Laws.

Assistant Dean Lois Chiang recently wrote a memo in Headnotes outlining the benefits of the impending replacement of the LL.B. with a new J.D. designation. "Explaining away the confusion," caused by the LL.B. in an era of "increased mobility," she promised, would soon be a thing of the past. But there are those among the students and faculty who worry that the prestigious-sounding Juris Doctor degree will raise its own set of questions.

Professor Denise Raume is among several faculty members who are skeptical of the move. She predicts that the "confusion" that Faculty Council had sought to avoid will be far from over once the change is complete. The LL.B. degree may be a second degree for most students, but the fact remains that it is a first law degree.

Students in the LL.M. program, for instance, may end up being perceived as getting more junior degrees than the Juris Doctors. And as for the American market mistaking our LL.B.'s for first degrees, Professor Raume finds "it hard to believe that employers aren't sophisticated enough to realize that. Canadians will have to explain themselves no matter what the initials are. No matter what, Canadians will have to prove they're as good as Americans and a change of degrees won't make that any easier."

She does not deem it "terribly important for our mission to protect" U.S.-bound careerseekers. Ultimately, "just because the Americans are doing it doesn't mean we should do it. At a conference I attended recently someone described 20 Canadian law schools plus one off-shore American Institution [U of T]. This is not terribly healthy for the reputation we are garnering for ourselves in the Canadian context." "To my mind," Professor Raume concludes, "the arguments put to Faculty Council were weak at best."

From his perspective as a member of the faculty at Osgoode Hall Law School, Professor Lorne Sossin sees the new designation as part of an inevitable Americanization of legal education. "Faculty and students at Osgoode are viewing this development at U of T with great interest. Some quarters see this as a longer term response to an Americanization trend and a globalizing market. Others view it as a shorter term and opportunistic response to Wall Street recruiters. Most are waiting to see the reactions of students and faculty at U of T and the larger legal community in general before they pass judgment."

Dean Ron Daniels is enthusiastic about the J.D. designation. As far as he is concerned, there is no downside to the change. "The student body is quite excited" about the new degree and it is "a wonderful way of signaling that law is a second degree. It is simply designed to enhance the status of the U of T degree and make it absolutely clear that it is a second degree."

He rejects any claims that the J.D. would be an Americanization but rather insists that it is a function of "the law school recognizing the international standard." He also strives to make clear that the school has not sought nor received accreditation from the American Bar Association and that the J.D. is neither a change in admission policy nor curriculum. The school is simply trying to be responsive to student concerns, especially graduates of the faculty.

"Students will be better off by the choice," he predicts. "The J.D. will be well received and well regarded by the public and the profession." As a graduate of the law school himself, Dean Daniels indicates that he will convert his old LL.B. degree to a J.D.

Students are generally positive about the changeover to the J.D. designation. Edan Howell, a third-year student representative on Faculty Council, feels that it in a globalizing market, "the J.D. opens up doors and maximizes options for students. The J.D. degree will boost the international stature of the degree, especially in the United States. The overwhelming motivation for the new designation," he feels, "is simply to remove the impression that for most of us the law degree is our first degree." For his part, Edan will be choosing the J.D. degree when he graduates.

First-year student Jeremy Streeter wonders if students who chose an LL.B. might appear to be "dated" in the future. He is also concerned that Canadian clients who are used to dealing with lawyers with an LL.B. might not understand what the J.D. means. He would prefer it if all law schools in Canada got together and made a joint decision.

First-year student Michael Hong thinks the J.D. is "a nice option to have because I do believe that because my friends have the J.D. designation it puts them at a perceptual advantage or even a perceptual par if you are interested in doing something outside of Canada."

Joseph A.G. Berkovits, October 17, 2000. Reprinted with permission of the author.

Chapter 5

Accredited Law Schools -
Part-time, Evening And Weekend Opportunities

This chapter is for those of you who wish to attend an accredited law school but cannot do so on a Monday to Friday 9:00 a.m. - 5:00 p.m. basis. By "accredited law school" I mean either:

1. A Canadian LL.B. program; or

2. A U.S. law school approved by the ABA.

A school that is "accredited" means that graduation from the school will allow you to become a lawyer.

The opportunities are more extensive in the U.S. than in Canada.

Part-Time: Your Law Degree Will Take Longer Than 3 Years

Many Canadian law schools allow students to attend on a "part-time" basis. The principle is that by attending "part-time" you will take longer to complete the LL.B. For example, attending "half-time" will mean finishing in six years instead of three years. Consider the following perspective from a student doing a "part-time" LL.B. at a Canadian law school.

"Half-Time Law School

As Dickens wrote, "It was the best of times, it was the worst of times...", half-time law school boasts both advantages and disadvantages to the student. The main advantage is that it exists. Prior to just over a decade ago, a law degree could only be had by people who could commit all their time to the program.

Other advantages to the half-time program include a lengthened exposure to legal academia, professors and research technique. This may translate into opportunities for enhanced understanding of more areas of law as well as potential for more meaningful mentorship. The program also softens the blow of the effects of the first year learning curve especially for the student who is returning from a long period away from university studies. A key advantage to protracted legal studies is the opportunity to meet several years of colleagues. Not only is this a socially enriching experience, but it also means that as the student progresses through school contacts for advice, summaries, interview connections [sometimes it may actually be a colleague from the first half of your first year interviewing you!], and wonderful supportive friendships that foreshadow the necessary network in our profession, enhance his or her legal education. Finally, but not exhaustively, the student of the half-time program can rightfully attend a five year reunion every year of his or her life!

As promised however, the program suffers a dark side too. Exactly how dark it gets can depend on many factors, both internal and external to the law school machine. Firstly, it has been my experience that 'half-time' is probably a very misleading name. Because classes, assignments, exams and those 'extras', of which there are many, are attached to the full-time program, they often bear the markers of a full-time commitment. For example, professors often switch class times based on majoritarian criteria, forcing the half-time student to contort their lives into the full time configuration, at least for that particular week or time impacted by the change. There is absolutely no slack in the schedule. School, if poised against a genuine reason supporting the half-time status of the student, is not the flexible part of the equation. Deadlines, exams, moots et cetera wait for no half-timer! Flexibility must be crafted into the non-school part of the student's life. Secondly, half-time students may suffer disadvantages in courses where group work, legitimate or not [i.e, take home exams], is involved. Often students avoid these types of courses because of the profound impact on grades this disadvantage can have. The reason for the difficulty is grounded in the half-time student's impeded ability to remain and converse and study into the night with other students. Thirdly, half timers are often very limited in course selection and therefore exam scheduling, depending on their outside commitments.

Finally certain strategies can be offered to offset some of the shortcomings of the program while still capitalizing on the opportunity to obtain the degree. Building up a good library at home is a tremendous help. Library time is often difficult to find on top of class time. Having a decent home library alleviates some of this struggle; the benefits often outweigh the increased costs of the resources. The always improving computer technology is extremely welcomed here too. Attending all the courses offered on perfecting computer research is time well spent. In addition, the half-time student cannot be a shy student for at least two reasons. First, he or she must be aggressive about initiating and remaining in contact with study groups. Secondly, the half-time student must be their own advocate, yanking the chain of the administration when their position is unduly threatened with unfair schedules, deadlines, exam structures pursuant to their status as half-time.

It is hoped that this is not too negative a review of the half-time study of law. It is true to say that it is a challenging, at times exhausting undertaking when balanced with serious outside commitments. Often the balance will feel skewed because it is. The student, when granted half-time status, enjoys a great opportunity hitherto not possible, but must at the same time remain clear on the reality of the nature of the pursuit of such a profession. Law is indeed a jealous mistress. Half-time law school is not an easy path, but if it is approached with some understanding and acceptance of both its limits and its priceless, life-altering benefits, tremendous satisfaction and learning is possible.

Good luck!"

By the way, part-time articling is also possible!

Evenings Or Weekends - It may be possible to complete your degree in three years

As far as I am aware, these opportunities currently exist only in the U.S. There are many U.S. law schools that have an "evening division." Obviously this allows students to maintain a job during the day.

Another opportunity that has arisen is attending law school on the weekends for three years. Read the following perspective of a student who attended law school on the weekends and earned her J.D. degree in three years.

"Law School on the Weekend

The buzz of the alarm went off and I rolled over to hit the snooze button - again. It was 7:30 Saturday morning. "Mmmmm, I can sleep in," I thought to myself. "Wait, oh, no, I can't! I have to go to class!" That's right, class. I'm a law student at the Thomas M. Cooley Law School in Lansing, Michigan, and some of my classes are held on Saturdays and Sundays.

I remember early on in my law school career talking to my Dad on the phone one Saturday afternoon. "Where were you this morning when I called at 9:30?" he asked.

"I had class, Dad."

"Class? On a Saturday morning? I didn't just fall off a turnip truck, you know," he replied.

When I started at Cooley, there were many scheduling options from which to choose. My goal was to get in and out of law school as soon as possible. Coming from Canada, I would be a long way from home, away from my friends and family. I chose to do the accelerated schedule which meant completing three years of law school in just two years. I knew that it would be a challenge, but I felt confident that I could do it.

The next obstacle to overcome was just how to fit everything in under this compacted schedule. As a Canadian student, I was not eligible for any of the U.S. student loans, and with the exchange rate being so low, money was going to be tight. My immigration status allowed me to work for the school, so I began working at the law library. Working during the week meant that selecting some weekend classes would be the perfect solution for me. In fact, a fellow Canadian student managed to work full time during the week in Canada and commute on weekends to Cooley. He earned his entire degree on Saturdays and Sundays. The same professors that teach the weekday classes teach the weekend classes, so I knew that I didn't need to worry about the quality of what I would be learning. But classes on the weekend?

At first, it was strange sitting in a class on a Sunday morning. I would think of all the other things I could possibly be doing at that precise moment, like still sleeping! Then I reminded myself that these weekend classes were allowing me to fulfill my goal: two years from now I would have my J.D. degree. Besides, there seemed to be a closer bond between the students in the weekend section. Classes tended to be smaller and as a result people got to know each other and their professors better.

I'm happy to report that my plan was successful. I will be graduating in May 1999 and taking the Illinois bar exam in July. I'm still taking weekend classes, but one day in the not too distant future I hope to be able to sleep in again on Saturday mornings."

Conclusion

It is possible to become a lawyer by attending law on a part-time basis, on evenings or on weekends. Obviously this is a harder route, but for those of you who are self-motivated it is possible!

"You can learn the law in Canada, or you can experience it at Cooley Law School."

Nico Santi
*Thomas M. Cooley
Law School student
Canadian citizen*

"I decided to get my law degree in the U.S. because of its 200 year history. I chose Cooley Law School because it provides students with sound legal knowledge and training. At Cooley, I went from student to lawyer in just over two years. I gained valuable legal experience through class lectures and a judicial clerkship provided by Cooley."

For more information about Cooley Law School, with its flexible scheduling options and straightforward admissions policy, contact the school at (517) 371-5140 ext. 5461. We will be glad to talk with you, and send you any additional school materials. E-mail: cooleyadm@aol.com

THE THOMAS M.
COOLEY
LAW SCHOOL
*In corde hominum
est anima legis.
1972*

The Thomas M. Cooley Law School, P.O. Box 13038, Lansing, Michigan 48901
Thomas M. Cooley Law School does not discriminate against qualified applicants or students on the basis of race, color, religion, age, national origin, disability, or gender. *Website: www.cooley.edu*

Chapter 6

Non-Traditional Ways Of Obtaining A Legal Education That MAY Lead To Bar Admission

Introduction

This chapter has been prepared for those of you who REALLY WANT TO STUDY LAW, but are in one of the following categories:

- you don't have the time to attend a traditional three year full-time law program at a Canadian law school or U.S. ABA approved law school;

- you fall short of the entrance requirements for acceptance to a traditional three year full-time law program at a Canadian law school or U.S. ABA approved law school;

- you can't attend a Canadian or ABA approved law school, part-time, evenings or on weekends;

- you want to study law but may not want to become a licensed lawyer

Please note that this chapter does not include a discussion of opportunities at U.S. ABA approved or Canadian LL.B. programs that may allow for study on weekends, evenings or on a part-time basis during the day. These programs do exist and you are encouraged to research their availability! (See the chapter devoted to this topic.)

Opportunities That "May" Lead To A License To Practise Law

Before proceeding please note the following warning!! The opportunities discussed in the following pages will not (without a certificate of equivalency from the National Committee On Accreditation) allow you to become admitted to the bar of any Canadian province. In addition, (unless a school is ABA approved) the opportunities to be admitted to U.S. state bars are somewhat limited! Hence, this discussion is intended for those who understand these limitations!

1. A law degree - but can't attend a traditional law school.

In North America we are accustomed to the idea that one attends law school at a fixed location. We are not accustomed to the idea of a correspondence law school or the concept of "external study."

Opportunities Outside Of North America - Correspondence

Both the University of London (England) and the University of South Africa offer LL.B. degrees through correspondence. I emphasize that these are highly respected degrees. You may contact the University of London at:

University Of London
Senate House
Malet Street
London, England WC1E 7HU
Telephone: 171 667 104
Fax: 171 436 0938

Opportunities Outside Of North America - External Study

This is a situation where classes are organized locally in preparation for the exams offered at another University.

Consider the following perspective on the U.K. bar exams written by a law student in Singapore. This person earned an "external degree." This means that she actually studied law for three years in Singapore, but received her law degree from a law school in the U.K. Specifically, the external course was at the Singapore Institute of Commerce. She took the exams of the University of London and received its degree.

The courses she took during the three years were:

Year 1

Contract law, Criminal law, Constitutional law, English Legal System

Year 2

Land Law, Evidence, Law of Torts, Equity & Trusts

Year 3

Jurisprudence, Family Law, Probate & Succession, Company Law

Her goal was to be admitted to the bar in both Singapore and the U.K. What follows is an account of her experience preping for the U.K. bar exams in London.

"Undertaking The English Bar Final Examinations In The U.K.

The Beginning:

As I had read my undergraduate law degree *externally* with the University of London (i.e. I studied under Singaporean lecturers, but sat for the University of London's examinations and obtained my degree from the University), my first taste of studying in the UK came when I undertook the postgraduate English Bar Finals Course in London. This was a ten-month course culminating in the dreaded English Bar Finals Examinations (which is set by the Council of Legal Education). On hindsight, it wasn't so much the course or the examinations that was so difficult. What made the course and examinations difficult were the reputation and the horrible legends that shroud the examinations. Even as undergraduates, we had all heard the rumours about how grueling the course is; how stringent the examining standards are; how even top degree students are felled at this final hurdle.

Still, nothing prepared us for Day One, when the dread and terror of the examinations were indelibly ingrained for a whole year. Approximately a thousand of us were herded into an auditorium for the orientation-lecture given by a member of the Council of Legal Education. He looked out at the sea of eager young faces and said, "Look at the person to your left, and to your right .... Only one of the three of you will make it."

Not at all an auspicious or encouraging start for a twenty-year-old whose family has just invested $40,000 into the crucial ten-month course and examination that separates her from legal practice. The queasy feeling in the pit of the stomach takes hold and stays there for the next twelve months, until one receives the result-slip.

The Stumbling Blocks:

(a) Radically Different Emphasis:

The contents of the course represent a quantum shift for the student.

While for the past three years, the undergraduate has been training with the academic side of the law, the Bar Finals Course teaches him to apply the law: how to get his case to court, how to respond to an opponent, how to use the law in court, and to advise clients using a realistic, pragmatic approach.

It requires the student to transcend the purely academic when answering and to take into account "real-life" issues when giving advice. So while an undergraduate essay may have been concerned with "Yes, you can sue because the other party has breached the contract and/or misrepresented the facts to you", the English Bar Finals answer would require "Yes, you can sue, but the amount is too small to be worth suing for, as the legal fees will subsume most of what you recover; so you should opt for the Small Claims Tribunal" or "Yes, you can sue, but you cannot afford the publicity of an open-court trial, so push for an (albeit smaller) out-of-court settlement instead".

(b) The External System:

I believe it was my experience with an "external" course that ultimately helped me do well for the Examinations.

While many of my course-mates (even those from the top universities) struggled to accustom themselves to the external system on which the English Bar Finals are based, it was the only system that I had ever known. (An "external course" is in essence a course in which your teachers (or members of your faculty) are not your examiners. This means that you take the examinations "blind", without having been taught by your examiner, and therefore not getting any indication of the areas on which he places emphasis.)

On such a course, the crucial study-tool is past-examination papers. Only then can you sift out the issues upon which the examiner places importance.

All in, it is a challenging examination, with room for creativity. It is an examination where theory is generally put aside and where practical, "real-life" solutions are rewarded. And while it is a truism, it helps to have established a strong foundation at the undergraduate level, though it is not too late to brush up during the course.

Living in the U.K.:

What's wonderful: The architecture, the plays/ballets, the antiques and flea markets, London in springtime, people from all over the world, the restaurants, the quirky independent boutiques. Although living in London is costly (mainly due to the unfavourable exchange rate), it was wonderful to be steeped in the ambience of the city.

An additional attraction for a student of law is being able to attend and become a part of the Inns of Court. It was sobering and awe-inspiring to be amongst judges and Queen's Counsel when one has become familiar with their names and their work in the course of one's studies.

All in all, London is a vibrant, inspiring city and one can gain a lot (both at school and outside) from a stint there.

Epilogue:

The Bar Exams were recently split into two categories — one for persons intending to practise within the U.K.; and the other for persons intending to practise overseas. The former placed more emphasis on procedure (advocacy skills, etc) and I believe is one-year longer. The latter (which I undertook) assumed that you would learn these when qualifying to practise at the other overseas Bar. And in the case of a person holding a UK Law degree intending to practise in Singapore, in order to qualify for the Singapore Bar, one would, after passing the English Bar Finals Exams, be required to undertake a 6 month Postgraduate Practical Law course (at which we are taught the local court procedures, local rules of evidence, advocacy skills). This system is possible because Singapore's legal system and laws are based largely on the British legal system and laws."

Opportunities Inside Of North America

1. Non-ABA Approved Law Schools

There are more than 180 ABA (American Bar Association) approved law schools in the U.S. Graduation from an ABA approved school will allow you to take the bar exam in any U.S. state. In addition, there are a number of law schools that are not ABA approved. In general these schools will allow you to take the bar exam only in the state where the school is located. This restriction will put severe constraints on your professional mobility. When it comes to non-ABA approved schools California leads the way. There are approximately twenty non-ABA approved schools in California. California also has a unique way of tracking the progress of those attending non-ABA approved schools.

The California "Baby Bar"

The "Baby Bar" is an eight hour exam which tests contracts, torts and criminal law. Students at non-ABA California schools are required to pass it in order to receive credit for their legal studies. It is also a prelude to the three day multiple choice and essay examinations given at the end of law school.

Medium Of Instruction For Non-ABA Approved Law Schools

Many of these schools run their program in the traditional way. i.e. live classes, etc. But, this is the age of information technology and some law schools are starting to take advantage of it. Examples include:

- at least one California school offers its law school program on video;

- at least one California school is offering its program on-line; and

- at least one California school is offering its program through traditional methods of correspondence.

Since legal research is now done "on-line", there is less need to have a traditional law school library. This removes the primary barrier facing an entrepreneur wishing to create a law school.

2. An Apprenticeship - Or How To Become A Lawyer Without Attending Law School!

Legal apprenticeships have a long history. They began with the beginning of legal education at Oxford University more than 800 years ago. From that point it evolved into the traditional way of becoming a lawyer. Apprenticeship has been the Canadian custom until quite recently. It was not until 1960 that a law degree became mandatory for admission to the bar in every province. Prior to that time legal education took the form of a vocational school run by the Law Society - consisting in large part of an apprenticeship called articling. Articling has been retained and is the still the major component of the Bar Admission Course in Canadian provinces.

(The significance of the apprenticeship has been recognized by the National Committee On Accreditation which will soon be recognizing the value of experience working as clerks under the supervision of a practicing lawyer. The experience will be recognized to the extent that it has contributed to the clerk's state of preparedness to practise law in Canada.)

States That Allow Bar Admission Through An Apprenticeship

In nine U.S. states it is still possible to qualify to take the bar exam by serving an apprenticeship. The idea of serving an apprenticeship in order to become a lawyer is deeply rooted in history. (Beginning with legal education at Oxford University more than 800 years ago.) In fact, the legal apprenticeship is the most traditional (why call it non-traditional?) way of becoming a lawyer. In fact, prior to 1950 in the U.S., there were more lawyers who had served apprenticeships than lawyers who had attended law schools.

The advantage of serving an apprenticeship is that it provides an opportunity for people with family and career commitments to stay employed while they work their way through law studies.

The following nine U.S. states (at the time of writing) allow people to qualify to take the bar exam by serving an apprenticeship (private study with a practicing lawyer): Alaska, California, Maine, New York, Vermont, Virginia, Washington, West Virginia and Wyoming. The rules vary from state to state. In some cases a minimal amount of law school is required in addition to study in a law office. For example, New York will allow law office study only after successful completion of one year at an ABA approved law school. No law school experience is required for law office study in the state of Washington. Further information may be obtained by contacting the regulatory (bar admission) authority in the state you wish to practice.

Conclusion

Obviously the easiest way to become a lawyer is to attend a three year law school program and become admitted to the Bar. Although this route is (provided you pass) sufficient, it is not necessary. As the article in the following Appendix demonstrates - it is possible to take an alternative route to becoming a lawyer.

APPENDIX

Read the following fascinating perspective written by somebody who became a U.S. lawyer in record time without attending an A.B.A. approved law school.

"I always wanted to be a lawyer, but my dream had to be put on hold because I married at the tender age of 19 and, over the next 20 years, found myself raising my three wonderful boys. I don't regret for a moment that I had family obligations, that was a choice I made, a wonderful choice. During those years I held several positions with the New York City municipal government, including that of police lieutenant. It was during my tenure in law enforcement that my dream of becoming a lawyer was revived, but I had a major barrier standing in my way, I did not have any college credits.

I knew I would have to get a college degree first before even thinking about law school, but I did not want to wait four years for a Bachelor's degree. (I later learned that there were methods available that didn't require an undergraduate degree). I was fortunate to learn about a system called testing out. Testing out is basically studying college courses at home and then taking examinations for accredited college credit. It isn't as easy as it sounds, but it does work very well if you cannot commit to a regular class schedule. And the education you'll receive can be remarkably good. Working with the police, my shift was subject to frequent changes, so there was just no way I could attend regular classes at the local college. After about two years of testing out I earned enough credits for a B.A. degree and applied my credits for graduation at Regents college, a fully accredited university in New York State (now called Excelsior College). It is also a great way to save thousands of dollars over the cost of a traditional college degree.

Even though I worked extremely hard at my studies and scored well in my examinations, for some strange reason I had a sense that my education was somehow tainted or lacking. I wanted to know that I was at least equal to those who earned their degree through traditional education, so what I did was to enroll in a traditional Master's degree program just to see if I was really good enough. Well, with a 3.9 GPA, I guess I felt that my nontraditional education was good enough and I was now validated OK, I supposed, I might now humbly try to get into law school, any law school.

When I first began to research law schools, I was shocked by the cost and the incredibly complex admissions process with the Law School Admissions Test, GPAs, and most frightening of all, those huge student loans that I would need to pay off. I mean, it would be like taking on another mortgage, wouldn't it? I began to think about my undergraduate education and thought, wouldn't it be great if I could obtain a law degree by distance learning. It would, and I soon learned about California's distance-learning law schools and I enrolled in one, Saratoga University School of Law. Now mind you, Saratoga is not approved by the American Bar Association (ABA) or accredited in the traditional sense, but it is registered with the State Bar of California and it is authorized to confer the Juris Doctor degree. More importantly, its graduates may sit for the general bar examination.

While I was studying for my Juris Doctor degree, I learned about the University of London External Programme, a fully accredited law school offering law degrees by distance learning. I thought it might be nice, though not necessary, to work toward an accredited law degree, so I cross-registered there to supplement my studies at Saratoga. The combined cost of enrollment in both universities was less than $4,000.00 per year.

After I graduated from Saratoga in May of 2000 I enrolled in an LL.M. program in International Taxation at St Thomas University School of Law, an ABA approved law school. I did this for two reasons, 1) my own self-validation concerns about my unaccredited law degree and, 2) I confess to being one of those geeks who loves crunching numbers, but that's another story.

What did all of this do for me? Quite simply it fulfilled my lifelong dream of being a lawyer. I passed the Bar examination, started a law practice and have published legal articles on international taxation that were well received in the professional community. But all of this pales in comparison to the enjoyment and fulfillment I receive working as a legal-education consultant helping others like you to fulfill their dreams of becoming a lawyer. Not too bad considering this was all just a dream six years ago.

That's enough about me. I must tell you that while I love and believe in alternative legal education, I admit that I am biased, and quite frankly you might even question my using myself as an example of what can be achieved through the strategies discussed in this book. After all, maybe I was just lucky, right? Well, I do consider myself lucky, but just so you will know that I am not alone, I have peppered this book with case studies of other lucky people so that you will know that you too can be lucky if you're willing to work hard.

Can you really become a lawyer without going to an ABA law school? Absolutely!"

This author may be found at www.lawschoolbible.com
Reprinted with permission of the author.

Interested in more?

Make sure you check our site at www.lawschoolbound.com for more information about non-traditional ways of becoming a lawyer. This is an evolving and growing area!

Chapter 7

Ways Of Learning About Law
That Will NOT Lead To Bar Admission

Introduction

This chapter has been prepared for those of you who REALLY WANT TO STUDY LAW, but are in one of the following categories:

- you want to study law but are VERY SURE that you have no desire to become a licensed lawyer;

- you want to work as a non-lawyer in the "field of law" (doing some of the things that lawyers do).

Opportunities That Will NOT Lead To A License To Practise Law

1. A North American Undergraduate Degree In Law

In England and many other places in the world, law is typically a subject studied at the undergraduate level. In many cases, these NON-NORTH AMERICAN opportunities can lead to a license to practise law.

There are undergraduate programs in law in North America. But these will NOT lead to Bar Admission. For example, Carleton University in Ottawa, offers both a B.A. in law and a Masters In Legal Studies. The content of these programs overlaps with what is taught in the LL.B. programs of many Canadian law schools. Nevertheless, these degrees will NOT lead to your becoming a licensed lawyer. But, if your objective is simply to study law, they are great opportunities.

2. Paralegals - Technical Training In Specific Aspects Of The Law

It is possible to obtain training in and work in a number of areas where lawyers also work. These areas may include: small claims court, mediation, conveyancing, litigation file management, court administration, simple wills, motor vehicle offenses, trade mark applications, etc.

There are many areas where parties can be represented in court by either a lawyer or an "agent." These "agents" are generally referred to as "paralegals." They compete with lawyers and are therefore a "thorn in the side of the legal profession." It is possible to generate a very decent income working as a "paralegal."

Paralegals are non-lawyers who work independently performing legal services before boards, tribunals or some courts for a fee.

As paralegals became widely recognized as a source of legal services, public pressure to regulate them increased. In June of 2000, Mr. Justice Cory (formerly of the Supreme Court Of Canada), delivered his report "A Framework For Regulating Paralegal Practice In Ontario."

In recognizing the importance of paralegals Justice Cory noted that:

"The importance of legal services to society is self-evident. The public needs access to adequate, effective, affordable legal services. To increase access to justice in a manner that protects the public must be the aim of the legal profession and goal of society.

The presence of paralegals in Ontario has steadily increased. They are now playing an important role in the delivery of legal services particularly in their work before boards and tribunals and in court on provincial offenses. Paralegals have a significant role to play in increasing the public's access to legal services."

In suggesting the areas of law where paralegals should be allowed to assist the public, Justice Cory stated:

"These areas of practice will include:

Appearances before specialized boards and tribunals after passing examinations such as the Ontario Rental Housing Tribunal; the Ontario Labour Relations Board; the Financial Services Commission of Ontario (Dispute Resolution Group); the Ontario Workplace Safety and Insurance Appeals Tribunal; and the Ontario Municipal Board; appearances in Small Claims Court and in court on provincial offenses; and appearances on appeals from the decision of some tribunals and from the decision of the Small Claims Court and the Ontario Court of Justice on provincial offenses.

A suggestion but not a recommendation has been made that qualified licensed paralegals may appear before the Immigration and Refugee Board of Canada.

Paralegals should be able to draw simple wills in the following restricted circumstances: where the assets are limited to a matrimonial home, bank accounts, RRSPs, insurance policies and savings bonds and where the distribution under the will is limited to situations where the sole beneficiary is to be the spouse, and if the spouse predeceases the testator or there is no spouse, and the assets are to be divided equally among the children per stirpe. They should also be able to draw and have executed powers of attorney and living wills.

In the family law area paralegals should be restricted to undertaking uncontested divorce proceedings in any one of the following three circumstances: first, where the parties have no children and no significant assets or the assets are jointly held, and if there is no need for, or no issue outstanding, as to spousal support; second, where the proceedings are commenced within one year of the execution of the separation agreement which resolves all collateral concerns; third, where there was a court order resolving all of the ancillary issues granted within one year of the commencement of the divorce action. Licensed paralegals should also be made available by Legal Aid Ontario in a role similar to that of duty counsel for proceedings in family court.

Licensed paralegals should be authorized to practise in the real estate law area where he or she is acting for the vendor in the sale of a residence that is either clear of any mortgage encumbrance or subject only to one mortgage.

The practice of paralegals in the criminal law area will be strictly limited to appearances in court on a small number of true summary conviction offenses such as vagrancy.

Paralegals should have the authority to swear affidavits. This is an essential requirement that is integral to their work. Confidential information imparted to paralegals must not be divulged unless a judge deems it necessary for the administration of justice and orders it to be disclosed."

These suggestions are quite sweeping. The implementation of these suggestions will ensure that much of the legal work done for the general public will be done by paralegals. Lawyers have simply priced themselves out of the market.

So, how would one become a paralegal? Justice Cory suggests attendance for two years at a community college offering a paralegal program followed by a period of mentoring (similar to articling).

Warning!! Justice Cory's recommendations are just that - recommendations. Even if they are not adopted "as is", his report has clearly demonstrated that paralegals play an important role in the delivery of legal services and that they are here to stay! Since paralegals are "here to stay" it is possible to have a career in the law as a paralegal! I predict that it will be a high growth area.

Justice Cory's report, if acted upon, will make Ontario one of the few North American jurisdictions to regulate paralegals.

Conclusion

Remember the following two points:

1. It is possible to study law outside the traditional three year Canadian LL.B. or U.S. J.D. program

2. It is possible to work in the "legal field" (as a paralegal) and not be a licensed lawyer.

APPENDIX

The Law Society And The Public Interest

Those of you who are interested in exploring the role of the Law Society in relation to the public interest may find the following article to be of interest. As you read this, ask yourself whose interest is really being served by the persecution of this paralegal?

March 12, 2000

Law faces a Boldt challenge and it's perfectly paralegal

Bill Schiller

Toronto Star Feature Writer

NORTH BAY - Among Ontario's 1,000 or so paralegals - people without law degrees who promise simple, uncomplicated legal services, sometimes for a fraction of the cost of a lawyer - only Maureen Boldt can lay claim to being the "Paralegal from Hell."

One recent morning in room 306 of the courthouse here, a defendant in a nasty landlord-tenant dispute chose to verbally spar with Boldt, rather than answer her questions.

But Deputy Judge Victor Vere would have none of it.

"Look," Judge Vere told the man sternly, "I don't want you

arguing with counsel."

Judge Vere then paused for a moment, looked out at Boldt and offered, respectfully, "I apologize for referring to you as counsel, Ms Boldt."

Boldt, a blonde, broad-shouldered woman with a purposeful stride, nodded her acceptance and smiled.

She doesn't want to be mistaken for a lawyer.

Indeed, she has even erected a billboard in town proclaiming as much: "I'm not a lawyer and I'm proud of it!" the board on North Bay's Cassells Rd. announces, encouraging passersby:

"Mediate Don't Litigate."

That billboard, and Boldt's day-to-day work as a paralegal, have got up the nose of local lawyers here.

Small wonder. Since at least 1994, she has openly and brazenly challenged what lawyers say is their exclusive right to dispense specific legal services throughout Ontario.

That challenge has brought her into direct and sometimes brutal conflict with the Law Society of Upper Canada, the Toronto-based body mandated to govern the practice of law in the province.

The six-year square-off with the society has cost her her home, her health and just about everything, she says, "except my sense of humour."

That's not to say the conflict has been any laughing matter for Boldt, a popular North Bay city councillor. But neither has it been for the law society and its 31,000 lawyer-members.

Since 1994, the society has reportedly spent upwards of $250,000 investigating and prosecuting Boldt through the courts, trying to restrict the scope of what she calls her "business."

They say Boldt, a qualified teacher with mediation but no legal training, is guilty of "practising law."

She disagrees.

"I do not practise law. I do not give legal opinions. I do not offer legal advice. I operate a business."

Specifically, the law society wants Boldt, and other independent paralegals in the province, to quit working on uncontested divorces, simple incorporations and wills - areas it insists are the exclusive domain of lawyers.

The society's efforts, however, have had little practical effect.

Over the course of the dispute, 35 of 36 charges against Boldt have been withdrawn or tossed out of court; a court injunction seeking to stop her from "practising law" has been denied; and Boldt has entered a single guilty plea and paid a fine of $100. She gave her commitment, as well, not to "practise law."

Although she does continue to work.

The law society, meanwhile, continues its pursuit. But starting tomorrow, in Toronto, retired Supreme Court of Canada Justice Peter Cory will begin mediation hearings aimed at resolving the larger dispute between the province's lawyers and its paralegals. The process was initiated by Ontario Attorney-General Jim Flaherty, who wants an end to the long-standing conflict.

The hearings won't stop the society from pursuing Boldt through the courts, insists law society staff lawyer Ajit John. Another trial is tentatively scheduled for April, he says.

But the six days of hearings might finally define what paralegals may and may not do in Ontario - and help resolve a conflict that has simmered since the mid-1980s.

There is, however, one agreement between lawyers and paralegals: both want to see clear lines of demarcation established.

"I wholeheartedly support the meetings before Mr. Justice Cory," Boldt says. "I have been asking the province to recognize us and to regulate our sub-profession for the past six years."

Her files are filled with correspondence with politicians and bureaucrats, including her own MPP and now Premier Mike Harris, calling for clarity on the issue.

Law society Treasurer Robert Armstrong also wants clarity. He emphasizes "the public must be protected." Although he will not comment directly on the Boldt case, currently before the courts, he does say that unresolved issues surrounding paralegals constitute "a serious problem" that has to be addressed.

"There are law clerks operating in this province without any particular (legal) training or any particular (legal) education. And that's where the concern lies. There needs to be regulation of paralegals operating in unsupervised settings in order to protect the consumer," he says.

Almost 10 years ago, the late dean of the University of Windsor Law School, Ron Ianni, tabled a detailed report with recommendations that sought to resolve the conflict. But it has never been acted upon.

Still, the need to act is obvious, says Armstrong. He cites a judgment from the Ontario Court of Appeal last year, Regina versus Romanowicz, which put the issue of unlicensed paralegals into sharp focus.

"The court noted that someone standing out in front of a courthouse selling T-shirts must have a licence," Armstrong says. "But that same person can walk into that courthouse and defend people charged with criminal offences that can carry sentences of as much as 18 months imprisonment. That makes no sense."

Under current law, paralegals may act as agents in small claims court, some immigration matters and traffic offences. Yet there are no specific legal requirements for paralegals. A Toronto-area college offers a two-year training program, but it's not compulsory.

But while the law society insists it is motivated by consumer protection, some paralegals say there is another factor at play - money. "The issue turns on remuneration," says David Goddard, of Toronto's CORE Paralegal Services and a former head of the Paralegal Society of Ontario. "It's the taking of money. That's the difference that makes the difference. The minute you accept it, it's seen to be the practice of law."

In the mid-1990s, before the law society supported the prosecution against Maureen Boldt, she grossed more than $90,000 annually, a sum that a few North Bay lawyers might envy. But with mounting legal bills to defend herself and with failing health, she was forced into bankruptcy in 1998.

Undaunted, she has resumed her work.

Goddard, a former police officer who has been a paralegal since 1987, argues there are two good reasons to license paralegals. They can specialize in lesser areas of law for which lawyers have little enthusiasm, and they charge less money.

"People are intimidated by lawyers," he says. "There is a perception among the public that once they engage a lawyer, the meter is running. Paralegals, on the other hand, offer a flat rate."

But the law society's Armstrong says the protection of the public is primary. "What is important is that standards be established and regulations be set so that the public knows that these folks are accountable."

He says lawyers have seen problems land on their desks originating from work done by untrained paralegals. Boldt doesn't deny there are paralegals who have made errors - a fact that lends even greater urgency to establishing regulations.

"We need to be regulated, and the sooner the better.'

Reprinted courtesy Torstar Syndication Services.

Chapter 8

Graduate Education In Law - An Investment Worth Making

Some of you may be considering a graduate degree in law. The LL.M. (masters degree in law) is the most common graduate law degree. It is normally earned in one year of study after the LL.B. or J.D.

The usefulness of an LL.M. is two-fold:

1. Many professors in Canadian law schools hold an LL.M. (this is not as true of professors in U.S. law schools).

2. It can provide a year of focussed study in a specific area of law.

The LL.M. And Bar Admission

Does an LL.M. qualify one for entry into the Bar Admission Course in Canada or allow one to take the bar exam in the U.S.?

Canada - An LL.M. is not equivalent to the LL.B. for the purposes of entry into the Bar Admission Course.

U.S. - In most states the LL.M. is not equivalent to the J.D. for the purposes of being permitted to take state bar exams. There is a small number of states that will allow holders of U.S. LL.M.s to take the bar exam.

Canadian Accounts Of U.S. LL.M. Programs

Account 1:

Some Good Advice......

WELL, I DID IT and it was an incredibly rewarding experience worth every minute and penny. But don't take my word for it. Read on and I will try to point out some of the things you should consider if you want to do an LL.M.

For those of you who are only reading this because you have read everything else in the magazine but are not yet ready to leave the loo, an LL.M. is a post graduate law degree. It takes about a year or two to complete and usually focuses on one or two specific areas of law.

One of the reasons why more people are contemplating the LL.M. route is that there are so many areas of study now offered. Not long ago, LL.M. programs were offered only in tax and a few other technical areas. However, as law has become more specialized and law schools look for more sources of income, the variety of programs has increased dramatically.

WHY GET AN LL.M.?

There are many different reasons for pursuing an LL.M. It is often a requirement if you plan on being an academic. It is allegedly a way to gain knowledge and understanding in a particular area. The degree can demonstrate your interest in and commitment to a certain area and make you more marketable. However, this can also work against you in that it could have a pigeonholing effect. It can help you transfer into a different field but it could also keep you stuck in one.

You could do it for the same reason you went to law school: you couldn't think of anything else to do. It could be done for the sheer joy of the experience and for some intangible benefits that may not be evident or come to fruition for years. Finally, friends and colleagues will be expected to address you as "Oh, wise one."

In my case, I had finished articling and was looking for work. In between sending out resumes and watching The Young and the Restless, I started looking into LL.M. programs. I was drawn to it for many of the same reasons I wanted to go to law school: an interest in the subject, the value of the experience, and the illusion of increased job potential. I also suffer from the "climb-a-mountain-because-it's-there" syndrome.

WHERE TO GO?

It can cost over $50.00 for each program you apply to so you need to limit the number of applications you make. Try to apply several months in advance. Not only does this improve your chances of acceptance in some cases, it also gives you time to apply for loans and grants. Canada student loans are available for those who study abroad. If you plan on starting studies in August or September, many scholarships and grants must be applied for by the previous December.

A threshold decision that will help you narrow the field is if you want to do a lot of course work or write a thesis. The program I was in was primarily course work with a paper requirement. The course work approach is a lot like law school but your studies are more focused and more advanced. Many schools have courses specifically designed for LL.M. students. Some course programs allow you to design your own program and get a "general" LL.M.

The thesis approach is even more focused. You will spend your year writing a behemoth paper, doing loads of research in one subject area, and not getting to know your fellow LL.M. candidates. I decided against this approach because I did not want to be so specific in my studies. I also feared getting halfway done a thesis and then deciding that I loathed the subject.

Obviously, you want to go to the "best" school you can. That will be different for each person depending on what your area of interest is and what you want to do after your degree.

I did my degree in the States. One of the drawbacks to being out of the country is the expense of foreign schools. This decision will also be driven by what you want to study. If your interest is in Canadian Aboriginal Law, there is not much point going to Oxford. I looked at other countries because my areas of interest are international trade and cross-border transactions.

I also recommend looking at the make up of the student body. You may have done this before you went to law school with respect to gender and race. You might also want to consider other elements such as nationality. Since I focused on international law, I saw no use in studying with a bunch of people who had never been outside the confines of the Mega City.

Try to speak with as many people as possible when you research the different programs. Speak with potential employers. They will be able to tell you what they think of particular schools and it is a good way to meet people practicing in your area. Speak with current and former students. Most schools keep track of their alumni and there may be some in a cubicle near you. The Placement offices of the schools may be able to provide you with information about how successful their graduates are at finding employment and what type of jobs they tend to find. There are also published guides to programs and the occasional survey conducted. For example, U.S. News and World Report publishes a yearly ranking of graduate programs in the States.

In addition to the expense of applying, there is also the burden of the application process. Every school has different forms and requirements. They all require transcripts, references and money. Some also require essays of varying length. Do all this as early as possible as it takes a lot of time, and more money. Remember that the people writing your references have lives of their own and may not act as quickly as you like.

MY YEAR

I spent a year in Washington, D.C. getting my degree. Living in a different city can be a valuable and worthwhile experience. No matter what you think about those damn Yankees, they are an interesting lot. The disadvantage to moving is that it obviously adds to the expense and effort required to get your degree.

One of the benefits of the program I was in was the large number of foreign students there. Every day was like being on vacation. I met people from different countries and were all as eager to talk about their own countries as they were to learn about others. Unfortunately, all of the Americans saw me as a foreign student, but the other foreign students did not. In addition to the cultural exchange benefit, this also provided great global networking opportunities. If nothing else, I can at least now go skiing in Chile in July.

WHEN IT'S ALL OVER

There are no guarantees about getting a job. The people from my program who found employment in Washington or New York, were not necessarily the people who had the best marks. Many firms hired people who happened to be from countries that were hot for foreign investors. A class mate of mine was told that he was given an interview because his last name was the same as the Venezuelan Minister of Finance.

You may not get a job as a direct result of your LL.M. However, if you have a strong interest in an area, and can afford the time and money, I would highly recommend the experience. Eventually, your training and knowledge will be useful in some way. For me, I know that it was an invaluable experience that I will always treasure."

Michael Valihora graduated from Windsor in 1993 with an LL.B. He obtained his LL.M. from Georgetown University in 1996. He is presently general counsel for Fund Monitor.Com.

Reprinted with permission of the author.

Account 2:

From U. of T. To The Harvard LL.M.

The decision to do an LL.M. at a U.S. law school is not to be done lightly. The first thing you will notice is that the cost is very high and you will require to show proof of funding before you enter the U.S. The total cost to attend Harvard's LL.M. program is about $45,000 U.S. If you ultimately want to work in New York City, it is no longer necessary that Canadian law degree holders require the cache of an ivy league LL.M. However, the experience in and of itself is often enough to justify the taking of a second mortgaging your parent's home. The thesis requirement at Harvard is minimal and can amount to a 25 page paper. You have the option of taking on a great workload, but the majority of students opt for the minimal requirements. In contrast, Canadian LL.M. programs usually require a rigorous thesis paper that is akin to publication material.

Harvard's LL.M. students themselves are international. Canadians make up about 10% and Americans comprise roughly 5% of LL.M. enrollment. The pursuit of a general LL.M. by Americans is not a common practice. The exception tends to be specialized LL.M.'s such as taxation offered at NYU. A general LL.M. can sometimes be viewed in the U.S. as a means to boost a lack lustre J.D. experience. This is not always the case for Ivy League LL.M.

candidates, but you may hear of this perception just the same. Consider for example that in Canada the LL.M. is an industry standard for academia whereas in the U.S. the ranking of your law school, law review involvement, and publication record are by far the most important factors.

If you decide to stay in the U.S., perhaps the most important thing to concern yourself with are the vast number deadlines for recruitment and job fares. This includes academia and law firms. You will find the Career Services at Harvard to be adequate, but they are not proactive. You should inquire with law firms and prospective employers directly because job fairs attract a tremendous variety of employers who have varying degrees of interest in a particular event."

James Hopkins earned his LL.M. from Harvard in 2000.
Reprinted with permission of the author.

Account 3:

A Canadian Part-Time LL.M. Program

The following program is of great interest to practising lawyers.

December 19, 1997

Law school's part-time LL.M. course flourishes

400 students enrolled in Osgoode Hall's downtown Toronto classes

By Monique Conrod

TORONTO—They call the part-time master of laws program at Osgoode Hall Marilyn Pilkington's baby, and she has every right to be a proud parent.

"What we've done in this program is really right at the cutting edge of a new way of conceiving legal education," said Ms. Pilkington, dean of the law school since 1993.

"And it's been an amazing success."

Although Osgoode's part-time LL.M. program has been around for 25 years, it underwent a complete transformation in 1995, expanding from one course in a single area of specialization to a choice of ten different specialties, and from 25 students to about 400.

Subject areas now include banking and financial services, alternative dispute resolution, international trade and competition law, securities, intellectual property, taxation and constitutional law, with new programs currently being developed in criminal and family law.

Classes are generally held one night a week in downtown Toronto, or in intensive three-to-six-day sessions. A degree can usually be completed within two years.

Instructors are drawn from Osgoode faculty, and supplemented by members of the Bar and visiting professors from schools such as UCLA and Cambridge.

Students come from a variety of backgrounds, ranging from recent graduates to experienced lawyers in private practice, legal clinics and government.

Most are from the Toronto area, but a significant number commute from southwestern Ontario, Ottawa, Thunder Bay, and even Manitoba and New Brunswick. Inquiries have come from as far away as Singapore.

Plans are currently in the works to extend the reach of the program through distance learning, including short intensive courses, live videoconferencing and use of Internet bulletin boards and discussion groups.

The new and improved part-time program was born out of Dean Pilkington's experience on the Law Society of Upper Canada's certification of specialists board.

"That board really certifies de facto specialists, people who have turned themselves into specialists over the years," she said.

"It seemed to me that what we needed was a program that developed specialists."

Osgoode's part-time program fills that need on many levels. Dean Pilkington attributes its success in part to the fact that it replaces the traditional mentoring model that formerly made up a significant portion of a new lawyer's education, but now is no longer feasible for many firms or individuals.

Specialization

The program allows new lawyers to specialize in the area of their choice, even if they were unable to find articles in that area.

It also helps lawyers who have been practising in one area for a while to make the move to another speciality—whether from personal preference or due to economic considerations.

"There are quite a few students who take one of these programs because they're interested in switching practice areas, say from real estate to securities, and this is a very good way of doing it," said John Claydon, director of the professional development program at Osgoode Hall Law School.

"It brings them up to date in a relatively short period of time, through a really comprehensive approach to a particular area."

For others, it's a matter of maintaining a thorough and profound knowledge of their own field as the profession becomes increasingly sophisticated, specialized and global.

"For many people, what they learned in law school even a few years ago is no longer all that relevant," Mr. Claydon told The Lawyers Weekly." The whole practice of law is now becoming internationalized...and we find we're building that quite extensively into all of our programs."

And then there are those for whom acquiring professional expertise is secondary to the opportunity to reflect on the law and legal institutions in an academic setting.

"In practice, people are dealing with close-up problems," noted Dean Pilkington.

"They appreciate the opportunity to stand back and see what all of those close-up problems add up to, in terms of the way the law is serving a particular area of interest."

INTELLECTUAL CHALLENGE

Mr. Claydon agrees. "They miss the intellectual challenge that perhaps they didn't appreciate in law school.

They come back to think about things and discuss things with their peers."

Brooke McNabb is a case in point. A sole practitioner in the Ottawa area, he found his interest shifting from traditional litigation to options such as mediation.

When his wife was transferred to Winnipeg, he sold his practice and went back to school—first for an undergraduate degree in conflict resolution studies at the University of Winnipeg, and then in Osgoode's part-time LL.M. program.

"I felt that this was the direction that law was going to move in, and society was moving in," said Mr. McNabb.

Now, in addition to doing part-time legal work, he commutes one night a week to Toronto for classes.

His fellow students come from all across Ontario, and include new graduates, some QCs and a judge.

REAL MIX

"Everybody's there because they want to be there," he said. "There's a real mix of people who are all quite interested in this subject and really articulate, so there's lots of great group dynamics."

When he moves back to Ontario in another year or two, he plans to set up an ADR practice, either on his own or within a firm.

"[The master's program] is a chance to take the experiences that you've had, and take a look at some of the theoretical and academic perspectives and combine them," he said. "I find it really very rejuvenating."

Monique Conrod - The Lawyers Weekly

Conclusion

There are many reasons that law graduates undertake a graduate degree in law. Is it worth it? Well, it depends on the person, but never forget that:

"If you think education is expensive, try ignorance!"

Chapter 9

For Those Outside Of North America -
Coming To North America

Author's note: This chapter reproduces an article that I wrote in 2000 for a newspaper in Trinidad. It is reproduced here because of its obvious relevance.

The article follows:

"Getting Into Law School - North America"

I recently created some material for a web site dedicated to helping "Non-North Americans" access law school opportunities in North America. What follows is a slightly edited version of that contribution. As a person who has both American and Canadian law degrees and is a member of the bars in the U.S. (Massachusetts and New York) and Canada (Ontario) I am uniquely qualified to write about both countries. Additional information may be found on my two websites: www.richardson-prep.com, www.lawschoolbound.com and in my monthly "Law School Bound" email newsletter.

In order to assist you, I have divided this article into the following 6 parts.

Part 1 - North America - A Common Law Tradition (Mostly)

Part 2 - Law School In Canada

Part 3 - Law School In the U.S.

Part 4 - Applying To Law School In Canada And The U.S.

Part 5 - Bar Admission In Canada

Part 6 - Bar Admission In The U.S.

Part 1 - North America - A Common Law Tradition

As you are probably aware the United States is composed of fifty states. Canada is composed of ten provinces and three territories. With the exception of the province of Quebec in Canada and the state of Louisiana in the U.S., the North American legal system is historically based on the system of common law that originated in England. This means that in many respects, law school curriculum in Canada and the U.S. is similar to law school curriculum in the U.K., Australia and New Zealand. In Canada and the U.S., students normally enter law school after earning a bachelors degree. This is not so in the U.K.

Part 2 - Law School In Canada - The Common Law Provinces

Links to all of Canada's law schools may be found at my www.lawschoolbound.com site or the Law Services site at www.lsac.org.

Law school in Canada normally takes three years of full-time study. I say normally, because, it is possible to attend law school on a part-time basis. Part-time students would earn their law degree in five to six years.

During the first year of law school students take a prescribed set of courses. There are slight variations among the individual law schools, but in most cases the courses include most of the following: contracts, property, torts, criminal, public/administrative/constitutional law and civil procedure. In second and third year students have tremendous flexibility in choosing courses. Virtually all schools have a requirement of a "moot court" and a "research paper."

Upon completion of the three year law school program (at the common law schools), students are awarded the degree of LL.B. (Bachelor Of Laws)

(The University of Toronto has recently begun to offer its graduating students the option of receiving a J.D. (Juris Doctor) degree instead of the traditional LL.B. degree. But, as of this date, it is NOT a J.D. that is approved by the ABA (American Bar Association). For the significance of this see "Part 3" as follows.)

Part 3 - Law School In The U.S.

Links to all U.S. ABA (American Bar Association) approved law schools may be found on my www.lawschoolbound.com site or the Law Services site at www.lsac.org.

Pay Close Attention!! It is important that you graduate from an "ABA approved" school. Only graduates of ABA approved law schools have the right to sit the bar exam in ANY U.S. state!

As is the case in Canada, law school in the U.S. is a three year academic program which is undertaken after the completion of a bachelors degree. There are many law schools in the U.S. and it is possible to attend law school part-time and in the evenings.

As is the case in Canada some courses are required and some are optional. The curriculum in first year law school is almost identical to the first year curriculum in Canadian law schools. The law degree you will earn from a U.S. law school is called a J.D. degree (which stands for Juris Doctor).

Part 4 - Applying To Law School In The U.S. And Canada

In general you must apply individually to North American law schools. The exception is the Canadian province of Ontario which uses a common application form for all six of its schools. (You may contact them at 519-823-1940 Ext. 558 or at www.ouac.on.ca). Sources of information about law schools - www.lawschoolbound.com

Some Frequently Asked Questions:

Q. What law schools exist in North America?

A. All law schools have web sites. A great collection of links to all the North American law schools may be found at the Law Services site at www.LSAC.org (or of course www.lawschoolbound.com).

Q. How much does law school cost?

A. It varies tremendously. Furthermore, some schools have different tuition fees for out of state/province students.

Q. What are the deadlines for applying?

A. Different schools have different deadlines. But, I advise you to try to have your "application file" complete no later than the November 1 prior to the September you wish to begin law school.

Q. You mention an "application file." What is it and what does it consist of?

A. The application file consists of the:

- application form

- transcript of grades

- LSAT score

- LSAT writing sample

- Letters of reference

- Personal statement

Q. That sounds like a lot of information. How much work is required to complete the file?

A. Lots of work. I recommend that you start as early as possible. You will want to construct different personal statements for different schools in order to tailor your application to the requirements of different schools.

Q. What is this "LSAT" thing?

A. "LSAT" stands for Law School Admission Test. It is required by almost all North American law schools. It is a standardized test - meaning that all applicants answer the same questions. There is no passing or failing score. Each school is free to decide what score will satisfy its admission requirements.

Q. How can I sign up for the LSAT?

A. The easiest way is to visit the Law Services site at www.LSAC.org. The site also provides lots of good information and has a free sample LSAT for you to download. I suggest you visit it.

Q. When should I take the LSAT?

A. My recommendation is that you take the LSAT the first June that you are free. In any case, you should take the LSAT no later than the June prior to your application deadline. Taking the LSAT in June will ensure that you:

- take the LSAT at a time that you are free from other academic commitments; and

- have the opportunity to retake the LSAT (should that be necessary). FYI: Many law schools will average multiple test scores.

Q. How should I prepare?

A. That is one of the things that we do. For information about our books and courses, visit www.prep.com

Q. I can't take a course. What books should I use?

A. In addition to our "Mastering The LSAT" book, it is essential that you have access to as many actual LSAT exams as possible. Actual LSAT exams may be ordered from the Law Services site at www.LSAC.org

Q. How do I get guidance on reference letters and personal statements?

A. Our "Mastering The Personal Statement" book (see above) is a complete guide to constructing all components of the application file.

Part 5 - Bar Admission In Canadian Provinces

So, you want to be a lawyer! Unfortunately, graduating from law school is only the first step. After graduating from a Canadian law school (be careful it is hard to become a lawyer in Canada without graduating from a Canadian school) you must complete the Bar Admission Course in the province you wish to practice. You may graduate from any Canadian law school and become a lawyer in any Canadian province. You need not graduate from law school in the province you wish to practise.

The Bar Admission Course consists of a combination of "articling" and a "classroom component." It takes from twelve to eighteen months to complete (depending on the province).

Further information on the requirements for each province may be found at: www.flsc.ca

Part 6 - Bar Admission In U.S. States

After you finish law school you must pass the bar exam in the state you wish to practice. There is no articling or bar admission course. Hence, it takes less time to become a lawyer in the U.S. than it does in Canada. The bar exam is a two or three day exam (depending on the state) and is administered twice a year - in February and in July.

Further information about the requirements for each state may be found at: www.ncbex.org

I also recommend the site of the American Bar Association at: www.abanet.org.

Conclusion

North America in general and the United States in particular has many quality law schools. Those who avail themselves of the opportunity will receive a legal education second to none.

Summary Of Useful Links

Note: In addition to these links I highly recommend that you subscribe to my monthly Law School Bound email newsletter. Subscribe by sending an email to: lawnews@prep.com (it is free) www.prep.com - Richardson Prep Centre - Preparation For LSAT and a wealth of information about the test.

www.lawschoolbound.com - Richardson Law School Bound - A web site designed to help you through every stage of the law admissions process and links to all North American law schools.

www.lsac.org - Law Services web site - LSAT test dates, how to register for the LSAT, order actual past exams etc.

www.flsc.ca - Federation Of Law Societies in Canada - Good information on how to be admitted to the bar in every Canadian province.

www.abanet.org - American Bar Association Site - Great information on the legal profession and U.S. law schools

www.ncbex.org - Will help you determine the requirements to be admitted to the bar in any U.S. state.

Chapter 10

The Law Schools Have Chosen You! - How To Choose A Law School

"... I want to mention the importance of an interdisciplinary focus in legal education. I know that there is already something of this focus in most Canadian law schools. There are, for example, combined degree programs which permit many students to take courses and receive degrees in law and such other disciplines as business and public administration. These programs are, without question, highly desirable. But I have something additional in mind. We all know that most law school curricula deal with roughly the same substantive subjects - contracts, property, torts, criminal law and the like. Furthermore, at least traditionally, these courses have been taught very much from the legal perspective. None of this should be criticized. But, it seems to me something needs to be added to this traditional mix. I believe that law students, while in law school, need to be made more sensitive to the valuable contributions of philosophers, economists, historians, scientists and social scientists."

-Chief Justice Brian Dickson

My monthly newsletter includes a question of the month. What follows is a question I received and my answer.

"Hi Mr. Richardson,

I know you're busy, but I'm just hoping you might have a quick piece of advice for me. Toronto was my first choice for law school and I did not get in, but I have been accepted to all of the other schools in Ontario. I'm really not sure how to decide between them. Does it much matter where I go in Canada (Ontario)? I don't know what type of law I'm going to want to practise, and most schools seem to sell themselves on the basis of their "specialties".

I know you have your disclaimer, etc., and I wouldn't put the pressure on you of making my decision strictly on the basis of what you say; I'm just looking for as many informed opinions as I can find. Anything you might have to say would be greatly appreciated.

Thanks for your help (getting into law school as well as any advice)."

My answer is: First the usual disclaimer - it is imperative that you discuss this with any school to which you are thinking of applying. In addition, consult your academic advisor.

So, the question is - how do you select law schools? You mention that you don't know what type of law that you want to practise and that you have lots of choices.

First, I suggest that you should approach the law school decision assuming you might not want to practise law at all. Law school is an excellent general education. You can do lots of things with it. One example that comes to mind out of yesterday's paper is the fact the new president of American Express is a Harvard Law School graduate who went into business. And yes, there are countless other examples. Law school and becoming a licensed lawyer are two distinct steps and two distinct decisions.

Second, I would not approach the law school (assuming that you do want to practise law) decision based on any assumption that you want to practise a specific kind of law. How can you possibly know what you might want to do after law school without ever having been to law school? You should attend law school with the attitude that you don't know what kind of law you wish to practise. Keep yourself open to experiencing many new and interesting things. If you go to law school with the attitude that you already know what you want to do you may avoid subjects that ultimately are interesting and enriching. Also, law courses are not compartmentalized. The analysis of most legal issues requires knowledge of a number of subject areas.

Third, how do the law schools differ? You mention that you perceive law schools as promoting themselves based on a specialty. Well, it is really not possible to specialize in anything in law school. The most you can do is take an extra course or two in a particular area. This hardly qualifies as a specialty. Besides, most schools require some kind of research project as part of the requirements to graduate. You can probably do this in any area of interest to you - thus in a sense creating the opportunity to specialize where none is promoted. Proceed on the basis that all the law schools will afford you the opportunity to study what you want. All the Canadian law schools are good. They are all small. They use many of the same books, etc. They all are approved law schools for the purposes of entering the bar admission course.

Fourth, what about the relationship between a given law school and articling opportunities? You can talk to ten different people and get ten different answers to this question. If you do well in law school and you do a proper job of marketing yourself to the law firms (and make no mistake about it - some people do a very poor job in this regard) you will do fine. What if you are a mediocre student? Well you are going to have more trouble regardless of where you attend law school. But, if you plan on being a mediocre student, and you plan on articling in Ontario, then my instinct is that you should go to an Ontario law school. The reason is that articling decisions in Ontario tend to be made by Ontario law graduates. REMEMBER THAT ALL OF CANADA'S LAW SCHOOLS ARE APPROVED FOR ENTRY INTO THE ONTARIO BAR ADMISSION COURSE. People making articling decisions include graduates of all law schools.

Fifth, let's deal with the issue of the prestige of the school. Prestige - by definition - is distinct from the reality of the quality of the school. Many of you are aware of Canadian Lawyer's annual law school rankings. In addition, MacLean's recently published an issue that appeared to rank the Canadian law schools. Although these articles make for fun reading, they should not influence your decision in any way. Law schools are simply not susceptible to numerical rankings. The issue of rankings is also perceived to be a problem in the U.S. A number of deans of U.S. law schools have issued a joint statement ("Law school rankings may be hazardous to your health") urging prospective law students to ignore them. (This may be found on the Law Service's web site at www.LSAC.org.) Obviously the law schools are not identical in content and approach. But, schools do not differ in ways that lead to one school being better than another for all purposes. Differences among law schools, may however, make certain schools more appropriate than others for the needs of specific individuals.

In the U.S., (unlike in Canada) there are variations in the reputations of the law schools. There are more than 180 ABA approved law schools. Although the law schools cannot be ranked with numeric precision, the law school you attend will impact on how your legal career begins. There are a number of books on U.S. law schools. In addition, U.S. News And World Report attempts an annual evaluation of the schools.

Sixth, okay so how should you make the decision? I would consider two things.

1. If I were going to law school again I would choose the school that gave me the best opportunities for joint programs. My personal view (and I emphasize that this is my personal view) is that there is no reason to go to law school and get just one degree. The fact is that you have to be there for three years (in most cases) anyway.

Use the time to get two degrees. Look through the law school calendars. Examples include: the McGill National Law Program, Law and Environmental Studies, LL.B./M.B.A. The list goes on and on. I repeat: there is no reason to attend law school and earn just one degree!

2. Consider lifestyle - you will be there for three years. Leaving aside the content of law school - will you be happy? I have had students who have avoided schools because they didn't like the atmosphere, the town, the lack of parking, the distance from family, too far from family, not far enough from family, etc. These are all valid considerations.

But, the main consideration in my opinion should be the availability of joint programs!

Remember also that your law school grades will ultimately be much more important than the name of the school awarding you the LL.B. degree!

> *Congratulations on your success!*
> *John Richardson"*

Joint Programs Leading To Joint Law Degrees

Canada has two legal systems. The first is the common law system that is in effect in every province except Quebec. An LL.B. is the degree obtained when one graduates from one of Canada's common-law schools. Quebec is based on the civil law system. In order to be admitted to the Quebec bar candidates must have a civil law degree. Law schools in Quebec offer a civil law degree.

National Law Programs

McGill National Law Program May Be Completed In 3 Years

"... students will obtain both a civil (BCL) and common law (LL.B.) degree after completing 105 credits taken over three or four years. Concepts from the two legal systems are presented through an innovative, integrated methodology that fosters critical analysis. Joint degrees in management or social work are also possible, and students have opportunities to take part of their legal education abroad."

- the McGill information book

Those who attend McGill will have a tremendous opportunity. As you know Canada has two legal traditions - the common law system used in all provinces except Quebec and the civil law system which is used in Quebec. In order to become a lawyer in Quebec, one must have a civil law degree. By itself, this would take three years to complete.

McGill students complete a National Law Program, leading to both civil and common law degrees in three years! WHAT A FANTASTIC OPPORTUNITY! (Note also, the possibility of combining degrees in management, social work and the possibility of study abroad. How could it get any better?) As you know, some of your course work at McGill is in the French language. "Knowledge" of French is required to participate in the program. So, brush up on your French and consider McGill!

You should also be familiar with the programs at other Canadian law schools that allow students to obtain both the LL.B. and a degree in civil law by spending an additional year studying civil law. The program at the University Of Ottawa is very well known (it has both civil and common law faculties housed in the same building). Other Ontario law schools have partnered with Quebec law schools to offer both degrees in four years.

(You should also be aware that it is possible to do the LL.B. degree at the University of Ottawa in French.)

Programs Leading To Both Canadian and U.S. Law Degrees

The Windsor/Detroit J.D./LL.B. Program

In most cases law school takes three years to complete. Why not earn both a Canadian law degree (LL.B.) and a U.S. law degree (J.D.) in those three years?

The University of Windsor has a program with the University of Detroit that makes this possible. It is an incredible deal and well worth considering.

There may even be a possibility of going one step further and spending a fourth year of law school at one of Quebec's civil law schools and add a Civil law degree in a total of four years! Or spend 5 years at the University Of Ottawa (see below) and earn three law degrees - Canadian Common Law, Canadian Civil Law and U.S. Law.

The Ottawa/MSU J.D./LL.B. Program

This is a very exciting opportunity for law students. What follows is the "news release" issued by the University of Ottawa. The University of Ottawa will soon have a similar arrangement with American University of Washington D.C.

"University of Ottawa introduces unique joint law program with U.S. university

OTTAWA, Wednesday, November 20, 2002 - The University of Ottawa has been a leader in training lawyers to work in Canada's bijural legal system for decades. Now, students can prepare to practice in any of three legal systems - Qubec's droit civil system, the common-law tradition in other provinces, and the United States.

A new joint program between the University of Ottawa and Michigan State University will allow students to obtain a dual LLB/JD degree in four years, spending two years at each institution. Students can then spend a third year at the University of Ottawa to obtain a LLL through the existing "National Program." The program is unique in North America.

"This program will graduate students who are uniquely prepared to work in today's legal profession, where business, government, and law regularly cross borders," says Prof. Constance Backhouse, who is in charge of the program.

Three students have already begun taking classes at the Detroit College of Law at Michigan State, and enjoying life at a Big Ten university. Nadia Campion, originally of Toronto, says "this degree allows you to gain an upper hand when applying for summer and articling positions. It makes you stand out as a candidate for employment because it's new and innovative." The joint program is also excellent value for University of Ottawa students, who will pay tuition to the University of Ottawa for the program's four to five years, including the years spent in the United States, where tuition is significantly higher.

While at first blush the program might seem to respond to the need for commercial and trade lawyers with expertise in both Canadian and American legal systems, Backhouse says the program will also be attractive to law students with interests in human rights law, as well as legal issues related to immigration or the political structures of both countries.

"We anticipate sending between five and seven students from here to Michigan each year," says Backhouse, "but if the program develops well, we may send as many as 15. We anticipate similar numbers coming here from the American schools."

Facts And Figures

The University of Ottawa is ranked second in Ontario for its graduate programs and co-operative education.

The University's Faculty of Law offers students the widest selection of technology-law courses in the country, as well as top-notch courses in all other aspects of law.

Graduates of the Faculty include five current federal cabinet ministers, the mayors of Ottawa, Montreal, Gatineau and Qubec, and many prominent lawyers and judges.

Faculty members include technology law experts Michael Geist and Daniel Gervais, Secretary of the Law Society of Upper Canada Vern Krishna, and many other well-known legal scholars.

Michigan State University's Detroit College of Law is the partner institution in the joint program."

Joint law programs in law are highly desirable. The world is getting smaller every day. Successful completion of these joint programs will enhance your professional mobility. In the long run these joint degrees can only benefit you! I recommend that you take advantage of them!"

A Joint Degree That Includes Articling

One very interesting example is a program at Queen's which is a joint law degree and Masters in Industrial Relations. The program is unique in that work done in the program will also satisfy part of the articling requirement in Ontario. How about that? Two degrees and the articling requirement solved!

What follows is information from the Queen's site:

"The MIR/LL.B. Co-operative Program is a four year, full-time joint degree program offered by the School of Industrial Relations and the Faculty of Law. Graduate training in industrial relations is combined with a degree in law in order to meet the increasing demand for industrial relations specialists with legal backgrounds. The two co-operative work placements provide students with valuable practical experience in the areas of labour and employment law, and have been approved by the Law Society of Upper Canada to count as the equivalent of articles."

Joint Degree Programs In General

Don't be satisfied with the idea of attending law school and just getting the LL.B. degree. All law schools offer joint programs. You have to be in law school for three years anyway. Why not get an extra degree out of the experience?

Why Not Design Your Own Joint Program?

You may not be restricted to existing joint programs. All joint programs operate on the basis of work toward one degree also counting as work towards a second degree. (An advanced standing principle).

Therefore, you may be able to construct your own joint program in your own area of interest. This question can and should be raised with the administration of the law school you wish to attend!

The moral of the story - why get just a law degree when there are so many joint degree possibilities available!

Conclusion

It is impossible to determine the reputation of schools. Go with the one that you think will suit your long term interests. The opportunity to earn joint degrees makes some programs far more attractive than others.

APPENDIX

Two First Hand Accounts Of Joint Programs

The following accounts are included to show how enriching joint programs can be. As you read these accounts remember:

1. The nature and even existence of these programs can change; and

2. Consider how much they add to the law school experience.

Account 1 - The Joint LL.B./MBA Program - York University

(This article originally appeared in the Osgoode Hall student paper. It is reproduced with the permission of the author.)

"For twenty-six years Osgoode Hall and the Schulich School of Business have offered a joint MBA/LL.B. program. The Osgoode/Schulich program was the first of its kind in Canada, and it allows students to complete an MBA and an LL.B. in four years. Students spend their first year in Law or in the MBA, the second year in the MBA or Law, and the final two years doing a combination of both programs.

One of the first graduates of the program was John Bankes. Bankes decided to do a joint degree because he was torn between law and business; the joint program offered a way to avoid committing to one field. Bankes is now an instructor of the joint program seminar. He describes the joint program as an "intellectual biathlon" in which students pursue two distinct but complementary fields of study. The program creates many career opportunities. Popular occupations include corporate law, investment banking, management consulting and entrepreneurial endeavours.

Prof. Ian McDougall, one of the Directors of the joint program, suggested that joint degree students are in demand among law firms that practise corporate and commercial law. Firms are interested in these students because they know the students have an understanding of basic business concepts, they relate more readily to business clients, and they have greater interest in business transactions. For many firms, corporate and commercial law is a mainstay. The joint program gives students a comprehensive business background and his credential that distinguishes them from other law graduates.

Folklore of the joint program has it that joint degree students do well in their articles. But many students seriously consider non-practice options. It is common for students to do their articles, complete the Bar Admission course, and receive their call to the Bar. But then they reevaluate their career direction and transfer into the commercial sector, often into investment banking. Students are drawn to the commercial sector by starting salaries and salary growth that is much higher than they could hope for at law firms. Several students also end up in the U.S. Students are told when they enter the program that at least 1 person in their class will never practise law; many more than this moves out of law after a few years.

The Osgoode/Schulich MBA/LL.B. is the only program in North America to offer an integrated course between the two faculties. In the final term of the fourth year of the program students take the MBA/LL.B. Seminar, which is an advanced corporate finance course. This class gives students an opportunity to ask career-related questions of their instructors, who are practitioners and business people. Prof. McDougall said that these sessions convince many students that they don't want to practice law.

Admission to the joint program is competitive. Students who apply must satisfy the entrance criteria of both Osgoode and the Schulich School (yes, you do have to write both the LSAT and the GMAT). After clearing both of these hurdles, applications are reviewed by the Joint Committee. For admission in September 1997 36 applications were received. Twenty-nine offers of admission were sent out and 17 students enrolled.

Students and directors are frank about the weaknesses of the program. Doing the MBA/LL.B. means dealing with 2 faculties, neither of which has any knowledge of what the other is doing. Students are left to their own devices to resolve administrative issues. There is no single person employed full-time to handle the administration of the program, so students must endure these inconveniences. Surprisingly, this problem is not unique to York. Students at other Canadian MBA/LL.B. programs experience similar frustrations. The Osgoode/Schulich program is attempting to unify its administration, but more work needs to be done.

The program Directors are hoping to develop more integrated courses to take advantage of the common skills and complements of the two schools. Very little time is spent integrating the two sides of the program. C.J. Scott, a second year joint program student, commented that "sometimes you wonder why they call it a joint program at all". The programs are not integrated to maximize the benefit of both schools. Only one integrated seminar is currently offered, but there is potential for more in the areas of tax, business and corporate finance. The fourth year seminar course attempts to identify subjects that lend themselves to both legal and business study, and to draw on the expertise acquired in both schools. For example, finance and accounting are natural tie-ins to corporate law. One future possibility is accepting the Business Administration law course as students' elective option for the winter term of their MBA year. Offering more integrated courses would be a significant change that would make the Osgoode/Schulich program more specialized and unique among joint MBA/LL.B.s in North America. Students give a variety of reasons when asked why they chose to enroll in the program. Cameron Goodnough, a 3rd year student said that his rationale was to delay the making of a decision between two careers. He expressed an interest in both areas. He said that the advantages of the program are that it provides students with an advanced understanding of business, which is invaluable to corporate lawyers. For students who intend to go into business the program is valuable because there are legal implications to everything in business: contracts, employment, and environmental regulation. Business students are on a curve, but there is greater flexibility among faculty when determining grade profiles. The workflow in the business school is different than in law school. Assignments are smaller and are due throughout the term. This affords the opportunity to receive feedback and adjust study and work habits where needed. Goodnough suggested that the downside is that students need a split personality; the fields are two different ways of thinking. The politics of the two schools are entirely different, which is a function of the questions that are raised (or not raised) by each. Also, students who begin the program in their first year of law will not graduate with their law class or with their MBA class. Another drawback is the extra year of study. It makes for a long program, with 4 years of MBA/LL.B. study, 1 year of articles, and the Bar Admission Course. Scott suggested that one drawback of the joint program is that it significantly narrows students' academic options in the law school. Students enter a highly specialized stream of study that is incompatible with some of the other opportunities Osgoode offers, such as the Intensive programs. Joint program students have few law electives, which is particularly problematic given Osgoode's extensive menu of courses to choose from. It is possible to do a specialization in the business school, but students have no room to maneuver and must ensure that every elective counts toward a specialization. One possibility might be to allow joint program students (and others) to take intensive programs during the summer.

Overall the joint MBA/LL.B. is an exciting program that offers students the opportunity to acquire a deeper understanding of two complementary fields. Legal study develops an ability to rigorously analyze a situation; business study focuses on resolving problems. The synthesis of the two methods in the MBA/LL.B. creates an exciting academic opportunity. Students and directors admit that the program needs some fine-tuning, but are satisfied with the possibilities it offers."

Account 2 - Windsor - Detroit LL.B./J.D. - A Cross-Border Law School Actually on the Border

I was pleased to see a recent article in the Sept. 15, 2003 *Law Times* by Julius Melnitzer which addressed the subject of "Cross-Border Law Schools". However, I was somewhat disappointed not to see the University of Windsor Law School mentioned in the article. We have a long history as "a cross-border law school" in partnership with the University of Detroit Mercy School of Law.

In his article, Melnitzer stated "... it was an American school, Michigan State University, which recognized the need and started the trend towards a dual degree." In fact, this is not correct. The University of Windsor Law School initially instituted its J.D./LL.B. Program with the University of Detroit (now called Detroit Mercy) in the summer of 1981, with the first students entering in the fall of that year. This program continued from 1981 to 1998. The program started out small, with 6 students in its initial year of operation and, by 1998, there were 42 students registered in the Program.

Thus, for more than two decades, the law faculties of the University of Windsor and the University of Detroit Mercy have cooperated in offering an academically successful and pedagogically integrated J.D./LL.B. Program. This successful cooperation is only possible because of the extremely close geographical proximity of the participating schools.

A student at either law school can physically access the other school by car within 20 minutes using the Detroit/Windsor Tunnel or the Ambassador Bridge. The object of the J.D./LL.B. Program has been to provide students with the opportunity to experience the unique legal and social cultures of each country while acquiring an ABA approved J.D. and a recognized LL.B. within three calendar years.

In 2000, the J.D./LL.B. Program was restructured and our first class under the new format entered in August 2001. This restructuring created a unique joint and integrated American/Canadian law degree program with a Corporate/Commercial focus.

Two of the unique features of the Program are the Applied Legal Theory and Analysis

(ALTA) course and the modules that have been added to many of the fundamental courses. First, the ALTA course, in the first year of the Program, is specifically designed for students to learn the legal research methods and legal processes involved in both the United States and Canada. Students prepare a number of written assignments and participate in Moot Court experiences specifically designed for each jurisdiction.

Second, the modules provide students with a truly comparative study of both legal regimes. Courses on Canadian law which include modules on U.S. law are Property, Contracts, Criminal Law, Law of the North American Free Trade Agreement, and Secured Transactions. Courses on American law which include modules on Canadian law are Evidence, Torts, Commercial Law of Sales, Payment Systems, Business Organizations, and Canada-U.S. Business Transactions.

In June 2004, we will graduate a class of 21 students from the J.D./LL.B. Program. Today, we have 75 students registered in the Program, including 20 second year students, and 34 first year students. J.D./LL.B. students are involved in many of the activities, committees and clubs at both the University of Windsor and the University of Detroit Mercy. Indeed, a third year J.D./LL.B. student is currently President of the Student Bar Association at Detroit Mercy.

Today, the U.S. and Canada represent the most important trading relationship in the world with more than $1.5 billion a day traveling between these two nations. The long term impact of the J.D./LL.B. Program has yet to be fully realized, but in a world where business and commercial practice is heavily influenced by NAFTA, the development of a corps of attorneys on both sides of the border with sympathetic understanding of the similarities, as well as the differences, between the legal systems of the two countries is a significant development.

Many of the graduates of the original program have become influential members of the Canadian legal society and leaders in their communities. From 1981 until today, the J.D./LL.B. Program of the University of Windsor and the University of Detroit Mercy has provided significant opportunities to develop cross-border professional and personal friendships, which have significantly enhanced the lives of both groups of students and members of the legal profession.

I hope that this additional information will serve to provide *Law Times* readers with a more complete picture of cross-border law schools in Canada and the United States.

Bruce P. Elman is the dean and a professor of law at the University of Windsor.
Reprinted with permission from the author.

Gain Command Of Two Legal Systems!

For further information about the Windsor Detroit LL.B./J.D. Program:

Director of J.D./LL.B. Program - jd-llb@udmercy.edu

University Of Detroit Mercy www.law.udmercy.edu

University Of Windsor www.uwindsor.ca/law

Earn a Canadian & U.S.
Law Degree
in Just Four Years!

Michigan State University College of Law's joint degree program with University of Ottawa Faculty of Law will give you the edge in international law, trade and business. You can earn a U.S. juris doctor (J.D.) law degree and the Canadian bachelor of law degree (LL.B.) in just four years! If accepted into the program, you will spend two years at each law school, giving you the most comprehensive dual U.S./Canadian legal education available in either country. Both U.S. and Canadian students may apply to MSU College of Law.

For more information about the Joint J.D./LL.B. Program, please visit www.law.msu.edu, call MSU Law Admissions toll-free at 800/844-9352, or e-mail us at law.msu.edu.

MICHIGAN STATE
UNIVERSITY
COLLEGE OF LAW

You will receive the Canadian Law Student Handbook, a must for any Canadian wishing to attend law school in the U.S., as well as a viewbook detailing the legal education program at MSU College of Law, when you contact the MSU Law Admissions office.

Canadian student, Kate McNeill, began the Joint J.D./LL.B. Program at MSU Law and served as 2003-04 Student Bar Association President. She is now at Ottawa completing the program.

Book III - A Report

The Law School Application Manual
- Executing A Plan

Summary And Introduction

My Advice To You Is ....

Treat applying to law school as though you would treat the process of applying for jobs. Your applications must be targeted to the requirements of different law schools. Applying to law school is "academic marketing."

Okay, law school is for you and you are going to apply. Book III has been designed to take you through every single step of every component of your law school application file. Let me warn you!! Applying to law school is a lot of work. Get started early. I recommend that you start looking at application material in the year before you wish to apply. Most law school applicants underestimate the amount of work required to do a proper job in the application process. Read Book III well in advance. It will be your Bible as you go through the process. It includes actual samples of letters of reference and personal statements (of successful applicants).

In Book III I will play the role of the "Law Admissions Coach."

Book III - Chapter Summaries

11. Getting Accepted - "Chicken Soup For The Pre-Law Soul"

Focus: Personal Success Stories - How success relates to planning

12. How To Apply - Different Marketing For Different Schools

Focus: Preliminary Considerations - What is the most appropriate application category? How to identify the "mission statements" of different schools.

13. How To Develop Effective Personal Statements And An Autobiographical Sketch That Works

Focus: How to develop personal statements. What works. What doesn't.

14. Twenty-Six Actual Personal Statements Of Successful Applicants

Focus: Samples of real personal statements

15. The Personal Statement Workbook - Tools To Develop Your Personal Statement

Focus: A plan for developing your personal statement

16. How To Obtain Effective Letters Of Recommendation

Focus: How to obtain effective letters. What makes an effective letter, effective?

17. Excelling At Law School Interviews - Seven Real Accounts

Focus: If you are invited to an interview, this chapter is for you. "Mature Applicants" take note!

Chapter 11

Getting Accepted -
"Chicken Soup For The Pre-Law Soul"

Getting Accepted - Oh What A Feeling!

"When I first found out that Ontario law schools would be sending out admissions on a rolling basis this year - that is responding to applicants as soon as their file was complete - I breathed a little easier. I was sure that it would be a lot easier on the nerves knowing that I could get a letter before reading week, maybe even before the winter break, instead of having to wait until some distant point in the spring or early summer. I became all the more enthusiastic when at one law school's information session the speaker - the Dean of Admissions - said that she may start sending out responses as early as November. But as is often the case, the exact opposite of what I expected happened. I began checking my mailbox for something (anything!) with a law school letterhead as early as mid-November, two weeks after I sent in my application. By early December I actually found myself getting nervous as I looked for my mailbox key every day, even though every logical instinct was telling me that I shouldn't expect any kind of response till the new year. So, all in all, I was anything but relaxed thanks to the rolling admission system until about two weeks ago when I discovered a large and well filled envelope with Osgoode Hall's letter head peering out of my box.

It's hard to describe the feeling that came with reading a letter of acceptance. A lot of excitement along with a bit of relief probably sums it up best. Relief that all those weeks of preparing for the LSAT were not in vain - come to think of it, I really should have been able to bring myself to throw out that pile of old practice tests by now. Relief that my personal statement seemed better to the admissions committee then it did to me when the time came to put it into the envelope.

The excitement is a bit more difficult to put into words, possibly, because I am not a hundred percent sure of what kind of career I want to pursue within law. Still, I've known that I want to study law since high school and there are a number of fields within it that interest me. The knowledge that I'll now be able to study law in what I consider to be a very good law school is very satisfying. I feel like a lot of doors have suddenly been opened and one important one - that of admission has served its purpose and been closed behind me. Although, a friend of mine did recently ask me if I knew when this summer's LSAT was being held."

-An Osgoode Hall Law Student

"Most people don't plan to fail, they just fail to plan."

This section of the book deals with application issues. Specifically, we will focus on how to plan the components of your application and execute that plan. Your acceptance to law school will be an achievement. It will require hard work. The purpose of this chapter is give you a glimpse of how much work can be involved and the satisfaction you will feel when you succeed. For this purpose we will use real success stories. As you read these accounts of the law school application process, be conscious of how hard these applicants worked to devise a plan and then to execute that plan. Getting into law school is not luck - but hard work!

"I remember last summer. Dragging an LSAT book with me everywhere I went, the heat in the classroom where we spent hours going over questions and reading comprehension passages. There were days when I wondered if I'd ever get into law school, or if the LSAT was just going to swallow me whole.

I'm 33 years old, a single mother of three. I married at 17 and I spent 13 years being a housewife and mom before I returned to school at 30 to earn a Bachelor of Arts degree in Psychology. What on earth would law school see in me? Will I be the oldest person there? I must be crazy to put myself through this; the application process, the LAST courses, the never ending practice tests, laying awake at night wondering if I'll fit in, will I feel out of place?

Was it worth it? Yes, very much so. I am part of the class of 2005 at Osgoode Hall Law School. I applied under both the mature student category and regular access. I wrote my LSAT in October 2001 and I won't lie to you, it was intense. My score was not stellar, but it wasn't horrific. Heed what they tell you during your prep course, the LSAT is not the be all and end all, just simply a part of your application package.

For a mature student application they conduct interviews; they want to know about your life thus far and why you chose to apply to law school. I had little time to worry about my interview; they called me and asked me to come in the very next day. It was obvious throughout the interview process that the school is concerned about your life as a mature student, many of us have children and other responsibilities. At Osgoode they value the mature student, we have life experience, often the mature students excel while in school and come out at the top of their classes. There is a mature students' association, there are many functions to meet other mature students, and a large number of students accepted are from the mature student category. You will certainly not be alone. There are support systems, programs and the like set up to help you, particularly if you are a single mom, as some of us are. I can tell you from personal experience, trying to run a household, balance responsibilities, and raise children that it will not be easy but it is possible. Being organized is the key!

I attended the open house at Osgoode Hall on August the 11th 2002. What I found were a sea of friendly faces, not all of them were early 20-somethings. The vast majority of students I saw were like me, with kids and families, smiling faces. I am not alone, and neither will you be. I'm looking forward to the next chapter in my life; the next 4 years will be interesting with classes, bar courses, and articling.

I suppose the point to this letter is that if you want something badly enough and are willing to work for it then you can achieve it. Have faith in yourself; believe in your goals. We are all unique and have a variety of personal experiences, that's one thing law schools look for, particularly in a mature student. The ride may be bumpy and often takes the odd turn but when the phone call came that day in April, I can honestly say I'd do it all over again."

-An Osgoode Mature Student Applicant

Two Accounts Of Accepted Applicants - Two Stages Of Life

We will hear from two students. The first was planning to make law his first career. The second was planning to make law a second career.

Account 1 - Regular Applicant - Law As A First Career

Getting Accepted: One Student's Story

Getting into law school was as exciting as I imagined it would be. I still remember the moment when I anxiously ripped open my courier-delivered letter to find the words "you have been accepted." Those four words marked the culmination of my efforts over the last few years of my life. It also meant a new beginning for me. Suddenly my days as a pre-law hopeful were over. Moreover, I no longer had to wonder what it was like to be on the other side - I was there!

For those of you still eagerly awaiting that day, let me offer you some solace. I know what you're going through and can relate to the precariousness of your pre-law position. I am also aware that there is something profoundly disconcerting about not knowing whether your dreams will be realized. But relax, you've taken a step in the right direction by purchasing the book of etiquette on the law school admissions process (John Richardson's Law School Bound). I know I referred to the manual time and time again during the course of my endeavour, and it clearly offered much sound, tenable advice.

Like everyone else, I had my own reasons for seeking admission to law school. Some were enticed by the prospect of money, prestige and power, Hollywood style. Then there were those whose interests transcended the often pretentious glamorization of the law. Whatever your reason may be, I am here to offer my experiences as a seasoned veteran of the law school admissions process.

I applied twice to the University of Windsor's Faculty of Law, once in the third year and again in the final year of my four-year honours program. Although I was not accepted in my initial attempt, going through the application process proved to be an invaluable experience. After the dust settled and I had my rejection letter in hand, I was able to identify the many mistakes I had been guilty of. This knowledge was a stepping stone to my success a year later.

One of my deadly sins involved reference letters. So obvious and careless was this error that I could have kicked myself for it. Rather than asking a tenured professor for a letter of reference, I requested one from a sessional (a temporary instructor contracted by the university to teach on a semester by semester basis). This was a mistake of considerable proportion, as I was later told by a professor on the admissions committee. Quite simply, the council would rather refer to someone who is a permanent and respected part of the university. Different sessionals may come and go every semester, and the committee may be apprehensive about trusting the credibility of someone they do not know or have known for only a short period of time.

To further exacerbate the situation, I found myself in large, informal classes and did not make the proper effort to meet the instructor and let him learn something about my ambitions and attitude. As a result, my letter of reference did not say much about me as a person, and the referees' confidence did not shine through.

I took a number of positive steps in order to circumvent the previous year's reference letter debacle. In my fourth year, I set my sights on tenured professors right from the start. I sat at the front of the room and participated zealously. I often stayed after class to discuss the topic of the day, or just to simply chat. When the time came to request a letter of reference, I approached them with a mature attitude, and they agreed to it.

It is at this point where many students make a mistake by assuming that their job is done. Be prepared for the next step. Now you must canalize their letters in the desired direction so that it can be demonstrated to the law faculty that you possess the qualifications that they consider important. If the school you are applying to values extracurricular activities, think about outlining your relevant experiences to the professor in addition to your academic achievements. Perhaps he/she can comment on how well you balanced your academic and extracurricular activities. I handed in a detailed letter to my references explaining what the law faculty considered desirable in a candidate and how I matched those particular qualifications.

Another blunder I stood guilty of in my initial attempt was handing in my application at the last minute. I procrastinated and procrastinated until the deadline arrived and I ended up submitting something that was hastily thrown together. If that wasn't bad enough, I later learned from my colleagues that Windsor utilized a "rolling admissions process," which meant that they evaluated applications in the order they received them. In other words, if your application is processed later they will inform you of their decision later. As a general rule, I feel that the earlier you know whether or not you have been accepted, the better. I handed in my application right before the deadline the first time I applied. Not surprisingly, I did not receive my rejection letter until late June. The only problem was that I had planned to re-write the LSAT if I was not accepted. However, at this point it was too late to write it in June, the statistically and logically best time to write the test. Some rejected applicants who applied weeks ahead of the deadline received their rejection letters as early as April, giving them ample time to register and prepare for the June LSAT if they wanted to. Needless to say, I applied well before the deadline the following year. Perhaps it was no coincidence that I was among the first to be notified.

There is no doubt in my mind that applying early is for the better, rolling admissions process or not. Think about it. You can take your time and fill in the information neatly and carefully. Perhaps you can have a friend or a professor look over your vital personal statements. Moreover, you can afford the luxury of putting it away for a few days and reviewing it later with a fresh mind. The chapter on personal statements in this manual relates how important and controllable they are. Do not compromise their quality by giving yourself insufficient time!

There is another point I should mention with respect to law school in general. It is never wise to put all your eggs in one basket, as the saying goes. In other words, do not make law school your one and only option after graduation. I can relate numerous anecdotes of students who staked all of their hopes on getting accepted. When their dreams were shattered by a rejection letter they were clueless as to what their future held. They are now meandering around, pondering their next step. Why? They did not have an alternate plan of action. Don't let it happen to you! Examine other options such as teacher's college, a masters program, an entry-level position, etc.

If law school is the brass ring you are striving for, then it is necessary to continually remind yourself of the countless students who are reaching for that same ring. It is very competitive out there and you must set yourself apart, or risk being lost in a myriad of applications. Be creative. Be different. But don't forget that style over substance will not get you anywhere. Being familiar with the admissions process is vitally important but it cannot stand alone. Your hopes and dreams hinge on a multitude of factors - hard work, good grades, a good LSAT score, a proper marketing strategy, etc. Law school is a dream worth chasing, so don't give up. Hopefully one day you too will experience the fulfillment of realizing your dream. Good Luck!

James Szpytman
Reprinted with permission of the author.

Account 2 - Law As A Second Career

Old Age and Experience Goes Farther Than Youth and Enthusiasm

There is a mathematical equation that proves the best way to get between two points is to follow a straight line. That may be true of a triangle, but when it comes to people, individual circumstances have a way of shattering theories. I'm a case proving that for some of us, the best way to get to law school is to take a crooked path.

Here are some bare facts. I'm as old as Jack Benny. Like Jack did, I plan on staying 39 forever. I didn't complete a traditional high school education and I never finished University. I am an immigrant to this country without any evident old-school ties to Canada's academic elite or legal community. I'm the mother of a grown daughter, married to a folk singer, and for the last year and a half, I've been working as a freelance writer. Nine months before I filed my application, thoughts of Law School hadn't entered my mind. Not exactly your blue-suited profile of a keener young law student, eh?

Yet, one rainy April morning, Gerry the letter-carrier knocked on my door. "Haveta sign for this," he said waving a thin envelope bearing the blue and white logo of the University of Windsor. Water dripped from his uniform hat visor onto his clipboard. "Looks important," he said, hoping I'd share my news.

I tried to deflect his curiosity by commiserating about our damp spring. When I initialed the form and said goodbye, I blamed the chill for my shaking hands.

I ripped open the envelope to learn I had been accepted to the University of Windsor School of Law.

This is how I earned an acceptance letter. Some of my plan might work for others.

First, I clarified my goal. I decided that law school was an avenue that was right for me, and chose an area of interest that matched my skills and personal history. Second, I learned the "right" way to apply to law school — and then, I carefully chose which rules to break. Third, I overcame the Law School Admission Test and the application blues.

That's one of the benefits of being Jack Benny's age. Usually, if you're old enough to remember when "I Want To Hold Your Hand" hit number one, you know enough about yourself to make decisions, challenge the conventional wisdom, and face up to doing what it takes to get a job done.

Gotta Work

Yes, there's more to me than meets the eye. That's also what happens when you've lived a long time.

I've had a wide range of experiences and developed a moderate level of street smarts. Also, I've seldom been more than a few days without paid work when I wanted it.

As did many people who suffered through the last recession, I lost a great full-time job. My situation was dramatic, but not as heart-rending as most plant shutdowns or office closures. I lost my paid work when the Member of Parliament I worked for as constituency representative for 7 1/2 years lost in the 1993 wipe-out of Ontario New Democrat seats.

I had spent up to sixteen hours a day on the telephone or at the computer dealing with an endless round of constituency concerns. I argued Canada Pension, Unemployment Insurance, and Worker's Compensation cases. I handled news releases and constitutional debates, had first hand experience in how laws were made and changed. I reveled in the immediate, dual satisfaction of both challenging the system and making it work for people.

Suddenly, the path I had been on for 15 years — advocacy journalist, union staffer, leftie organizer, pamphleteer, back room political maneuverer — ended in a black hole. Setting aside the politics of my work, and the fact that I actually did help people, most potential employers thought I was no different than any jobless mid-level office worker. I was a generalist without specific skills, looking for a niche.

There's nothing like a mortgage to get you on your feet with a new plan.

I started writing again, landing decent pieces in good outlets. But the loner life of a writer is a far cry from the crisis filled office of an activist political team. And I missed my cases.

One by one, I started polling my friends for ideas. A pal gave me a copy of *What Color is Your Parachute?* I figured it was a subtle way of saying, "I'm tired of your kvetching, get a life."

Finally, a lawyer buddy who knows intimately the ins and outs of life after politics took me out for coffee and suggested I think about the law. "You miss advocacy work. You know how the legal system does and doesn't work. You speak well on behalf of others. You write. You love long hours. Why not be a lawyer?"

I pointed to my sketchy formal education. My friend waved away my concerns. "Many schools accept mature students. It's just a matter of finding the right one."

I thought about it for two months. I concentrated on weighing options regarding the actual work lawyers do. I tossed aside fanciful images of Rumpole's bewigged jests and Cynthia Dale's Street Legal wardrobe. Finally, I decided law school might be a useful path for me. Given my background, I decided to focus on labour and international contract law.

I read the mission statements and rules for admission for every school in Canada. Luckily, the one right for me was in front of my nose. I live only blocks from the University of Windsor.

To see if we could get around my electric pint politics and my education gap, my lawyer friend arranged a meeting with a kind U of W Law professor. In a brief interview, to which I wore my best suit and tried hard to show I wouldn't spill the sherry at student-faculty events, the professor sized me up. "It might work," he said.

Tenting his hands the way professors do, he rocked back in his chair and gave me three pieces of advice.

1.   I should avoid the conventional view of applying to more than one school. I should apply only to U of W, because we know it is the right (and only) school for me. I should subtly make that clear in my application.

2.   Since I entered the process with a "gap" in my education, but high credits on the "life experience" side, I should concentrate my energies on recommendations and my essay answers.

3.   I shouldn't worry too much about the Law School Aptitude Test. I took most of his advice.

The LSAT

It had been over fifteen years since I had taken an exam. No matter what my friendly professor said, the mere thought of the LSAT sent me into a theatrical flop sweat. Luckily, I didn't have time to think about it too much. I had a book to finish writing, get on press, and distribute. I had a very ill parent in intensive care to visit. Life experience was again outstripping school.

Oh, I took some practice tests. During lulls in round-the-clock editing sessions, I struggled with timers and exam booklets. I feared I'd disgrace myself by "failing" the exam. Most of all, I struggled with the annoying "analytical reasoning" questions. Who cares how you order the people with blue hats and green jackets among those with yellow shirts?

Thanks to inevitable printing delays, the test was exactly two days after my book came off press. My co-editor and I had no time to celebrate. I turned down radio interviews. My husband and I didn't take a weekend away. My sick dad went un-visited. Instead, I fumbled through more analytical reasoning problems and tried breathing exercises to keep my stress levels down. It didn't work. The night before the exam, I dreamed an audience booed me off stage.

The next morning, there was a queue waiting for the test-room doors to open. Not a man in the crowd wore 501 jeans. No other women had dark circles under her eyes. If any dyed their hair, it was for effect — not to cover the grey. These folks were young! Luckily, they make you pay to take the LSAT. The thought of wasting the fee without taking the test kept me in line.

And then I started listening to the conversations around me. There was discussion of last night's dorm keggers. Chat about some bands. A bit of computer lingo floating about. No art, politics or literature. In ten minutes I realized — no sweat. In the fifteen years since finances forced me to drop out of University, I had read more books, government documents, and filled out more forms than these folks had seen in a lifetime. And fully 75% of the LSAT is based on exercises testing reading comprehension and logic. I deduced the group huddled in the doorway was a representative sample of those taking the test that day throughout North America. Therefore, I would not disgrace myself. "Old age and experience," I thought, "will get me farther than youth and enthusiasm."

Thanks to years of cramming for parliamentary question period and a lifetime voracious love of books, I knew I would do well on the reading comprehension and logic portions. At the last minute, I remembered a tidbit from *Mastering The LSAT*, and chose to guess on the analytical reasoning portion of the test. I figured it would keep my head clear for the sections where I would be strong. I arbitrarily ticked the letter "B".

When the marks came, it turned out my score was acceptable for most Canadian schools. Too bad I hadn't picked the letter "C" on the analytical reasoning portion. If I had, I would have bumped my score into the 90s. But I survived the LSAT. So can anyone.

It was time to talk to my lawyer friend and the professor again.

The Application Case File: Turning Onions to Roses

Once the LSAT was mastered, we treated my application as if it were a legal case. We defined objectives, marshalled arguments, and ensured witnesses were lined up. In an effort to do what I called "turning onions to roses" in my organizer days, I made a list of negative issues requiring resolution in my application, and possible positive approaches.

Onions

1. Some people believe constituency work is really a glorified secretarial job

2. Perhaps too heavy on partisan politics

3. The annoying gap in my education; so many different interests

4. U.S. origins

5. Would I have the drive, and focus to complete the program and carry out my expressed interest in labour law, since I have such an interest in journalism and politics?

Roses

1. Stress advocacy work, hands-on contact with law at all levels of government, range of demanding duties (Letter: former boss)

2. Delineate work with Women's Incentive Centre, Essex County Citizens Against Fermi II, Clean Water Alliance, Committee to Preserve Public Broadcasting, Windsor Folk Music and Arts Society; attach examples of "academic" briefs and backgrounders (Letters: community group activists; find a Tory to send a letter, too!)

3. I'm a late vocation student with varied life experience. (Attach writing samples for proof of literacy, use "lawyer words" properly to show some knowledge of field and issues. Letters to reflect also.)

4. Ability to work in two countries, understand two court systems (Letters: U.S. referee, labour leaders)

5. Address directly, admit interest in ensuring democratic, popular understanding of law and systems, and potential continued work "community work" — leave open the issue of electoral politics. Stress writing skills. (Letters: Labour leaders again. Attach writing samples.)

I ignored the application instructions to provide two letters, because two letters weren't sufficient to deal with all the onions. It's true my recommendation letters were signed by some great "names". But the names weren't as important as what the letters said. Each was from someone who knew me well, and highlighted a different aspect of my life, work, and community involvement, which I in turn reiterated in my personal profile answers.

After I phoned in to each letter writer, I encouraged content control with a thought-out thank you letter also outlining which issues I would stress in my parts of the application.

I made it as easy and fun as possible. For some writers, I attached a list of "words law school admission committees love to see". I suggested to a local Tory that if he wrote a good enough letter, his work might ensure that I would be locked in the law library for four years, thereby removing a thorn from his political side.

I asked the letters be hand delivered to the school and requested a copy "for my records". When I received them, I naturally sent a thank you note to the writer. I also learned my approach to content-control plan worked. Reading the responses, I felt as if I were Sally Field receiving her Oscar for Norma Rae. "You like me! You really like me!" I said to myself, utterly overwhelmed with the kindness of my friends.

During the 10 days before the close of the application process the school received a package each day regarding my application.

I sent copies of recent published articles with a cover letter requesting they would be "added to my file". Same for my book. And the community organization briefs. Each time, I hand-delivered the properly-addressed manila envelope, and thanked the school office staff for their hard work.

I worked for three weeks on the short essay questions on the application form. I had three readers for each of five drafts. In the likely case admissions committee members wouldn't read every word of my file, I honed the answers so they flowed from start to finish, but each answer stood on its own, too.

Meanwhile, I told everyone I knew in Windsor that I was applying to the University's Law School. Never can tell who will put in a good word, eh?

Finally, the day before the close of applications, I put on my best suit, and walked it over to the office. By then, the staff knew my name. I thanked them again, and they wished me good luck. I stopped by my friendly professor's office to thank him, and let him know all the pieces were in. I assured him that I had given it my best shot.

And then I went home, returned to real life, and forgot about law school until Gerry the letter carrier rang my doorbell."

Victoria Cross will continue to provide The Windsor Star with a weekly column while she attends the University of Windsor School of Law. Her work has appeared in a variety of publications, including the Globe and Mail, Toronto Star, Our Times, and Canadian Dimension. She is co-editor, with Steven Langdon, of As We Come Marching: People, Power, and Progressive Politics.

Reprinted with permission of the author.

Conclusion

These applicants were extremely methodical and focused in their approach to their law school applications. They are very different people. But, what they had in common was a clear plan which was executed to perfection. The next chapters have been designed to help you create and execute your plan!

Chapter 12

How To Apply -
Different Marketing For Different Schools

" ... I want to say a few words about the gatekeepers to legal education, namely those involved in the admissions process. Those who fulfill this role are, in a real sense, the gatekeepers of the legal profession. Ultimately, the ethos of the profession is determined by the selection process at the law schools. In order to ensure that our legal system continues to fulfill its important role in Canadian society, it is necessary that the best candidates be chosen for admission to law schools. By "best" I mean more than just the most academically qualified. I also mean young people who exhibit other qualities such as compassion, unselfish service to their community and idealism."

-Chief Justice Brian Dickson

Developing School Specific Application Strategies

Introduction - What Research Is Required?

Applying to law school is a huge, time consuming job. It should be thought of as a process of marketing yourself specifically to specific schools. Start early and leave yourself sufficient time to complete each step of the process. Effective marketing requires the acquisition of strategic information for each school.

But First, Avoid These Two Mistakes!

Law school applicants frequently make two mistakes.

Mistake 1 - Assuming Schools Use Identical Information

The first mistake is to assume that all admissions committees work in the same way. In fact admissions committees are working with different priorities, categories of applicants, different rules for interpreting trends in grades, different rules for weighing the LSAT and different objectives in filling their first year classes. Some schools require personal statements and/or letters of recommendation and some don't. In short each school will be different in some material respect from the others.

Mistake 2 - Assuming Law Admissions Is Hierarchical

The second mistake that applicants make follows from the belief that admissions committees work in the same way. This mistake is to assume that law admissions are hierarchical. Applicants often assume that if one can't get into school "A" that one can't get into school "B", etc. Since, admissions committees operate differently they certainly don't operate in a hierarchical manner.

Your Complete Task - Two Jobs

Job 1 - Locating The Relevant School Specific Information

Strategic information is information about what individual law schools are looking for. By understanding what individual schools are looking for, we can better understand how to construct our application file in a school specific way. Strategic information falls into the following four categories.

1. The Determination Of The School's Objectives

2. Determining The School's Application Categories

3. The Identification Of Objective Criteria Used By The Committee

4. The School's Interpretation Of Grades And LSAT Scores

Each of these categories will be discussed individually.

Category 1 - The Determination Of The School's Objectives

Because, Not All Law Schools Are The Same!

Understanding The Ad - What Are The Schools Looking For?

Even nice people market! The fact that each law school is different implies that each school has a different objective in admitting its class. If you were applying to different jobs you would market yourself differently to each prospective employer. You would submit different resumes and you would research the companies to determine what each one hoped to accomplish by filling the job. You must do the same thing when applying to different law schools. How do you determine what each law school hopes to achieve by admitting its first year class? Answer: we try to find the school's "mission statement."

What Do The Law Schools Hope To Achieve?

Law schools have clear objectives in selecting their first year class. These objectives can be gleaned from reading the school's statement of its generalized policy on admissions. Think of a statement of a generalized policy on admissions as being analogous to a job ad. Since the schools have differing objectives, they will have different admissions criteria. These differences will be reflected in different advertisements that the schools use to attract their first year classes.

For each school, the admissions criteria are a function of the school's objective in filling its first year class.

Sources Of Mission Statements - Hypothetical Examples

The primary sources of "mission statements" are:

1. A school's calendar of information - pay particular attention to the dean's message (or visit the school's web site)

2. The current edition of the LSAT registration book (available from any law school or from Law Services at www.LSAC.org or by calling 215-968-1001)

3. Information sessions organized by the individual law schools

4. Law forums where a number of law schools attend

5. The question(s) that is/are the basis of the personal statement that you may be required to submit

6. Information on the application form

So, What Do Mission Statements Look Like?

This section is designed to give you practice in reading "mission statements." For each of the following sample schools let's look first at the statement of the school's objective (the advertisement) in filling its first year class. Next we will look at how the objective shapes the admissions criteria (who gets the job).

Sample 1

Objective - Advertisement

"The Faculty of Law is interested in creating a vital and diverse academic environment and in graduating competent and compassionate professionals. ..."

Admissions Criteria - Who Will Help Us Meet Our Objective

"To ensure that the student body represents the fullest possible range of social, economic, ethnic and cultural perspectives in our society, we consider many factors. Among these are the candidates' significant achievements in extracurricular activities at their University or in their community, adverse economic circumstances which may have required more than casual employment during the undergraduate school year, outstanding qualities or achievements in previous careers, unique linguistic or cultural factors in the applicant's background that add to the candidate's overall academic background, or physical or learning disabilities."

Sample 2

Objective - Advertisement

"The Faculty of Law seeks to identify and select a student body of diverse interests and backgrounds joined by a commitment to academic excellence and intellectual rigor and demonstrating unusual promise for distinguished performance at the law school and, subsequently in the legal profession and community."

Admissions Criteria - Who Will Help Us Meet Our Objective

"The admissions committee ... chooses those applicants whom it judges are likely to complete the program with the greatest intellectual return. The Faculty believes that the qualities of mind and personality necessary to satisfy its requirements are:

(a) high intelligence,

(b) sound judgment,

(c) the capacity and motivation for demanding intellectual effort,

(d) the capacity and motivation to engage in sophisticated legal reasoning, and

(e) an understanding of and sensitivity to human interaction."

Sample 3

Objective - The Advertisement

"The Committee's goal is to identify those applicants whose records indicate the greatest likelihood of success in law school."

Admissions Criteria - Who Will Help Us Meet Our Objective

"The Committee relies primarily upon the average grades obtained during the applicant's undergraduate studies and the applicant's LSAT score(s). This objective data will enable the Committee to identify those applicants who are clearly eligible for admission, and those candidate's who are clearly not competitive with the other applicants. ... In addition to the categories of clearly acceptable and clearly unacceptable applicants, the Admissions Committee will have to consider a large number of relatively undifferentiated applications from competitive applicants. Along with the objective data, the Committee will also consider any other factors which it considers relevant to the applicant's probable success in law school. The applicant should, therefore, ensure that his/her application is accompanied by any validated evidence which indicates that his/her undergraduate averages or LSAT score, or both, are not truly indicative of his/her academic potential. For example, the Admissions Committee will consider documented medical evidence that a serious illness had adversely affected the candidate's academic performance. There are, of course, many other relevant factors, often depending upon the particular circumstances of the individual applicant, which will be taken into account. Make it clear on the form that you wish us to consider any special circumstances."

Sample 4

Objective - The Advertisement

"It is our policy that no applicant be denied admission to any program on the basis of race, creed, colour, age, sex, marital status, ancestry, or place of origin. Further, the Faculty of Law has adopted a commitment of principle relating to equality in legal education for women and members of minority groups."

Admissions Criteria - Who Will Help Us Meet Our Objective

"Any qualified person can apply for admission to the Faculty of Law. No regional or other quotas are imposed on the Admissions Committee. Admissions decisions are discretionary and are based upon comparisons of academic records, LSAT scores, and other relevant factors. ... The competition for admission leads to a fluctuating class composition. However, the Admissions Committee strives for equal gender representation and a significant number of special and minority students."

Sample 5

Objective - The Advertisement

"The objective of the admissions policy is not only to select from among the many applicants those students who will excel in the study of law but also to select those students who, while doing well in the study of law, have the potential to contribute creatively and meaningfully to the Law School and the community."

Admissions Criteria - Who Will Help Us Meet Our Objective

"The majority of applicants are considered by the Admissions Committee in the framework of the following criteria:

1. University Program:

This category includes averages and performance trends in light of relevant considerations; awards and prizes; the nature and content of the program taken (if particularly relevant to the study of law); the level of any degree(s) obtained.

2. Work Experience:

Part-time, summer, and/or full-time work experience will be analyzed for its indication of organizational and administrative skills and initiative. Vocational, professional or other special qualifications will also be considered.

3. Community involvement:

Contribution to the community (city/town; university; religious; etc.) will be assessed for indications of talent demonstrated by the applicant, and commitment to the community. Factors examined include the nature of the applicant's participation in service clubs, community service organizations, religious, athletic and social organizations.

4. Personal Accomplishments:

Factors considered in this category include extracurricular activities; hobbies and special accomplishments (including activities outside regular academic programs in high school and university); artistic and athletic accomplishments; communication skills and languages spoken.

5. Career objectives:

The applicant's career objectives, including how and where the legal education will be employed, are considered.

6. Personal Considerations:

Personal factors affecting the applicants are recognized in this section. Any personal factors such as illness, bereavement, unusual family responsibilities or other such circumstances which may have some bearing on the applicant's qualifications will be noted.

7. LSAT Scores

The Admissions Committee has decided the LSAT scores written more than six years prior to the academic year of application will not be considered.

It must be emphasized that no one factor is solely determinative of admission to the law school. The Admissions Committee assesses applications in light of all the above criteria. It should also be noted that the chief source of the Admissions Committee's information is provided by the applicants themselves in their personal files. Therefore, it is very important that an applicant take care to present a full and rounded view of himself or herself to the Admissions Committee."

Sample 6

Objective - The Advertisement

"The objective of the Faculty's admissions policy is to select those students who can best study law in our school's unique comparative and bilingual legal environment. The Faculty's students are drawn from all parts of the country and have varied backgrounds. They will in various ways have demonstrated sound judgment, a capacity for intellectually demanding study and motivation, in addition to academic ability and substantial fluency in English and French."

Admissions Criteria - Who Will Help Us Meet Our Objective

"The Faculty looks to select students who have followed a challenging course of pre-law study that has given them a sound command of language and the ability to reason. A wide range of disciplines can produce such a command and such an ability. The Faculty has in the past welcomed excellent students with diverse intellectual backgrounds. Its admissions policy thus has no particular profile of pre-law courses, but rather a focus on the intellectual demands applicants have experienced."

Conclusion - The School's Objectives

In the same way that companies have different objectives in hiring employees, law schools have differing objectives in filling their first year classes. The school's ad (generalized admissions policy) and statement of who is most likely to be admitted (admissions criteria) provide the guidelines for targeted marketing. Your application must demonstrate that you are one of the applicants who will best serve the schools objective in filling its first year class!

Category 2 - Determining A School's Application Categories

Application Categories And Personal Positioning

Once you have determined the school's "mission statement" you must decide in which category to apply. There are many categories of law school applicants. Different applicant categories give you the opportunity to market yourself in different ways to a given school. Be careful, categories are not always designated by the same descriptive labels at each law school. In addition, not every school has every category. Your job is to research the law schools individually and determine:

1. The application categories available to you;

2. How a particular application category furthers the schools admission objectives; and

3. Whether you have met the jurisdictional requirements to apply in that category; and

4. Whether if it makes sense for you to apply in that category - your probability of success.

Important! When considering an applicant category ask: how does the existence of this applicant category further the school's admissions objective?

Examples Of Common Application Categories

(Most schools will have these application categories.)

Regular: This is the main category into which most applicants are streamed. The main criteria for admission are high grades and a high LSAT score. In order to apply in this category applicants must have completed at least two years of university. It is much more difficult to be accepted after two years. Some schools require three years of pre-law study and/or a degree.

Native: Almost all the Canadian law schools have special access programs for native Canadians. In general, native Canadians who wish to take advantage of this program must complete an eight week summer program offered by the Native Law Centre at the University of Saskatchewan. The University of Alberta has a program for Native Canadians in the law program itself.

Part-Time Applicants: A number of schools have part-time study programs. Part-time programs are common. Full details may be obtained by communicating directly with the school.

Letter of Permission: This is a "visiting student" who wishes to spend a semester or a year at another law school. The applicant will not receive an LL.B. degree from that law school. The applicant will receive his or her law degree from the school of his or her origin.

Transfer: A transfer applicant must have completed his or her first year of law school at another law school. A transfer applicant is applying to a law school for the purpose of doing his or her final two years of law school at that law school to receive an LL.B. degree from that law school. It is not easy to transfer from one law school to another. Some schools will consider transfer applications only from other Canadian schools. Other schools will consider transfer applications from foreign schools as well.

Advanced Standing: An advanced standing applicant is an applicant who has completed some previous legal studies somewhere in the world. The purpose of the application is to be accepted to a Canadian law school and to obtain credit for all or some of those previous legal studies. An advanced standing applicant, if accepted, will receive the LL.B. degree from that law school.

National Committee Applicant: Law school graduates or lawyers from outside Canada need to obtain a "Certificate of Equivalency" for the purpose of being able to enter the Bar Admission Course. The National Committee On Accreditation will assess the applicant's foreign legal studies and experience and determine what Canadian law courses are required to ensure that the person's legal education is the equivalent of a Canadian LL.B. When the Committee requires that a person complete Canadian law courses at a Canadian law school, the person must apply to a Canadian law school. The person will apply for the purposes of taking specific courses and will not receive an LL.B. degree from the law school!

Examples Of Special Or Residual Categories

(Most schools will have some variation of one or more of these application categories.)

By providing examples of "special or residual categories" I hope to open your mind to different ways of applying to law school.

Residual Category - Special and/or Mature Student: A large number of schools (but not all) have an additional category to accommodate applicants who do not fit into any of the preceding categories. Each school defines these categories differently! For some schools the defining characteristic is age coupled with distinction and for others it is socioeconomic background. The following discussion is intended to be of a general nature and is to give you ideas for how to interpret information in law school calendars and application forms. Some schools may incorporate the "Native Category" into this residual category.

Age Coupled With Distinction - What follows are hypothetical examples of applicant categories that condition eligibility on age. These examples are offered to alert you to how these categories may be defined.

School A - Persons who are at least 28 and do not have two years of university may apply on the basis of experience, maturity and an outstanding previous career.

School B - Persons who are at least 26 and have been out of school for at least five years who can, through the length and quality of their non-academic experience, demonstrate the rough equivalent of formal university training are eligible to apply.

School C - Persons without the usual pre-law background but who have five or more years of non-academic experience will be considered on the basis of experience, maturity, and outstanding qualities as demonstrated by their previous careers, are eligible to apply.

School D - Mature applicants are those with five or more years of non-academic experience. Applicants in this category may or may not have completed two years of university.

School E - Mature applicants are required to have the normal academic prerequisites but they qualify as "mature" because they have been away from academic work for "some years." The admissions committee exercises discretion in considering these applications.

School F - Applicants must be at least thirty years of age and have completed at least two years of undergraduate work and exhibited evidence of past achievement in non-academic areas indicative of comparable ability to compete in the areas of study in law school.

School G - Persons who are least 26 years old are eligible to apply as mature students. Normally the admissions committee will not extend an offer of admission to an applicant who has not completed at least one year of university.

Socioeconomic Background - The following are hypothetical examples of schools that condition eligibility on socioeconomic background. These examples are offered to alert you to how these categories may be defined.

School H - Special applicants must fall into one of the following categories.

1. The applicant has demonstrated sustained or distinctive achievement.

2. The applicant has suffered from a seriously disadvantaged social or economic background.

3. The applicant has substantial record of activity on behalf of persons in disadvantaged circumstances and intends to continue such activity after obtaining a legal education.

4. The applicant is physically handicapped.

School I - Special consideration will be given to applicants whose educational opportunities have been hindered by circumstances such as cultural or economic disadvantage, physical impairment or learning disability, or significant interruption of the pursuits of post secondary education.

School J - The category includes persons whose academic achievements have been significantly delayed, interrupted or adversely affected by physical, cultural or economic disadvantage, family or similar responsibilities and the consequent need to attend to these responsibilities or to maintain employment.

School K - Applicants presenting special circumstances are those persons who are asking the committee to consider unique aspects of their background. These, might include linguistic or cultural factors, physical disabilities, learning disabilities, and adverse economic circumstances which require more than casual employment. Once again the onus is on the applicant to explain how or why these factors have affected the applicant's grades, LSAT score and/or abilities. Supporting documentation is required.

School L - In recognition of the concern that the sole use of grades and LSAT scores can have a discriminatory effect, our school has devised an access Admissions Programme. The purpose of this programme is to recruit individuals with good academic potential who are from groups that have experienced social, economic, or educational barriers to education. For applicants in this category the Admissions Committee will consider a number of factors including language barriers, family background, work responsibilities while attending school, physical handicaps, etc. It is important that your personal statement be supported by statements from individuals who can comment on the relevant factors. A primary consideration of the Admissions Committee for applicants in this category is the "perceived likelihood of passing." Hence, a good academic reference will be a major positive factor in your file! Applicants in this category are required to have completed two years of university education as is the case for regular applicants.

School M - Pursuant to the terms of this programme, applicants are asked to indicate any significant matters which they believe should be considered in addition to grades and LSAT scores. The admissions has the authority to relax the criteria of grades and LSAT scores when it concludes that pre-law performance has been seriously affected by either factors beyond the control of the applicant or by extraordinary involvement in worthwhile activities of a non-academic nature. Every effort should be made to corroborate the relevant facts with letters from third parties who have knowledge of the facts.

Applicants should note that there are few spaces available in the "residual categories." Admission is at least as competitive as it is in the "regular category." It is critical that applicants clearly understand how the category is defined and market themselves specifically to that category." One school commented that:

"Applicants requesting special applicant status should be aware that the number of persons who request such status greatly exceeds the number of offers that can be made to special applicants."

Applicant Categories And Marketing Opportunities

Different applicant categories give you the opportunity to market yourself in different ways to different schools. An applicant category may give you the opportunity to make certain aspects of your life relevant to the admissions decision. By way of example, imagine that you are a thirty year old university dropout who started the world's largest software company. A "mature student" category gives you the opportunity to make your age and success relevant to the admissions process. Your ethnic background might be irrelevant in the regular and mature student categories, but might be relevant in some kind of "residual" category.

Jurisdictional Requirements Versus Probability Of Success

The "jurisdictional requirements" of a category are the requirements that you must meet in order to be considered in the category at all. For example, a "mature student" category may be defined so that applicants must be at least 26 years old. But, meeting a jurisdictional requirement is no guarantee of acceptance in that category.

The "probability of success" depends on whether you are the type of person that the applicant category was created to accommodate. You may be 26, but have you accomplished extraordinary things? Are your extraordinary accomplishments of such a kind that the law school will want you?

Conclusion - Applicant Categories

The law admissions process is a marketing process. Part of effective marketing is deciding which category to apply in at each law school. Applicants may find that they are able to increase their chances of acceptance by applying in a category in addition to or other than the "Regular" applicant category. Ask:

1. How does the applicant category further the school's admission objective;

2. Do you meet the jurisdictional requirements of the category; and

3. Are you the kind of person that the category was designed to accommodate?

Category 3 - The Identification Of Objective Criteria Used By The Committee

You will need to know:

- the specific components of the complete application file (reference letters, personal statements, etc.);

- the date the complete application file must be complete;

- the deadline for taking the LSAT; and

- the kind of supporting documentation that is required.

All schools use grades and LSAT scores. Most schools require letters of recommendation and personal statements. Letters of recommendation and personal statements should be thought of as your opportunity to "link yourself" (sell yourself) to a specific application category and the school's admission objectives.

In subsequent chapters we will work on how to develop the components of your file and how to link those components to the school's objectives.

Category 4 - The School's Interpretation Of Grades And LSAT Scores

Different schools have different rules for interpreting trends in grades and multiple LSAT scores. These considerations may influence your decision of when to apply to law school and whether to retake the LSAT.

A Timely Reminder - Where Should You Apply To Law School?

The answer is EVERYWHERE! The most that you have to lose is a small application fee. In the long run this loss is not important. Costs associated with the law admissions process are an investment in your future! The long run cost of applying to few schools (if you are not accepted) is far greater than the cost of applying to many schools (if you are accepted).

If you think the cost of applying to lots of schools is high, consider the "long run" cost of applying to too few!

Job 2 - Analyzing And Using The Relevant School Specific Information

This is what the next chapter is about, but in general:

Your task is to:

First, determine the school's admission objective ("mission statement");

Second, determine how various application categories are linked to and further the school's objective;

Third, determine what application categories you can and should use;

Fourth, develop every component of your application file in a focused and purposeful way.

Conclusion

Now that you have done your research you are ready to prepare your application file. The next chapter will be devoted to helping you complete this exercise.

Warning!!! Many of you will be applying to law schools in more than one year. Some schools keep files from previous years and will use the files from both years when evaluating an applicant. The information which you give to the law schools in different years must be consistent and truthful! It is imperative that you copy every document which you send to the law schools.

APPENDIX A

Application Information

When applying to law school you must be aware of which schools are part of a centralized application process and which are independent. This information may change from year to year. But, in a general way you should know that:

1. Ontario law schools use a centralized application process. http://www.ouac.on.ca

2. Canadian common law schools outside of Ontario use a process where you apply to the school individually.

3. Quebec law schools use a process where you apply to the school individually.

4. U.S. law schools may participate in the LSDAS (Law School Data Assembly Service). For further information visit the Law Service's site at: http://www.lsac.org

APPENDIX B

Transfers, Advanced Standing and National Committee Applicants

Applicants Who Are Applying Into The Upper Years

The distinguishing feature of each of these categories is that applicants are applying to law school on the basis of having previously completed legal studies.

The rules for "transfer" and "advanced standing" applicants differ from school to school. In general you will find that transfers, in particular, are extremely difficult. There are few spaces available for transfer students. The law schools have indicated that they consider the following (depending on the individual law school) when they consider transfer or advanced standing applications:

- the applicant's performance in first year of law school. Some schools have indicated that they will not admit a transfer student unless he or she would have been admitted if the person had applied to that school for first year.

- compatibility of the courses taken with the school's curriculum

- the applicant's reasons for wanting to transfer

A specific reason or compelling reason for the transfer will enhance the application.

From what parts of the world can one transfer? Some Canadian law schools will entertain transfer applications from only Canadian law schools. Others will entertain applications from the United States and other common law countries.

It is also difficult to obtain "advanced standing." In general the same considerations will apply to an application for "advanced standing" as to "transfers." There are few places and it is difficult. Most "advanced standing" applicants will have done their legal studies in a foreign country. Hence, the National Committee On Accreditation may become involved in assessing the quality and content of the foreign legal studies. What is the National Committee On Accreditation and what does it do?

Introducing The National Committee On Accreditation

The National Committee On Foreign Accreditation is appointed by the Federation of Law Societies of Canada and the Committee of Canadian Law Deans. Its purpose is to assess the quality and content of foreign legal studies with a view to determining what Canadian legal studies are necessary in order that the applicant has the equivalent of a Canadian law degree.

A "certificate of equivalency" issued by the National Committee is considered to be equivalent to an academic qualification for admission to the Bar Admission Course in Ontario. Other law societies and law schools use the Committee's recommendation on a more informal basis.

After having completed a review of an applicant's file the committee will make one of the following three recommendations.

1. That the applicant be denied further standing. (This means the applicant must earn a complete Canadian law degree.)

2. That the applicant take further education at a Canadian law school. (This will generally be one or two years. The applicant is responsible for applying to law school as a "national committee applicant." This will not guarantee that the applicant will be admitted. If admitted, the applicant will not receive an LL.B. degree. This category of applicant is called a "national committee applicant.")

3. That the applicant pass examinations in specified areas of Canadian law. Examples may include: constitutional law, civil procedure, etc.

The Committee issues a "certificate of equivalency" upon successful completion of the requirements set out in its recommendation.

For current information visit: http://www.flsc.ca (I have included a more comprehensive discussion of the National Committee On Accreditation in the "Mobility" chapter later in this book.)

Chapter 13

How To Develop Effective Personal Statements And An Autobiographical Sketch That Works

"GPA/LSAT figures may provide law schools with quick and handy ways to sort applicants into categories but it is often the personal statement that makes the difference in an admissions decision."

-Pre-Law Advisors National Council

"The personal statement is especially important when you consider that most law schools do not include formal interviews as part of the admissions process. Therefore, think of the personal statement as an interview - a chance to tell admission personnel who you are and what you have done that makes you uniquely qualified to study and practise law."

-So, You Want to Be A Lawyer

"As the Admissions Committee does not grant interviews, the Personal Statement is an applicant's opportunity to inform the Committee about interests, accomplishments and goals."

-Commentary From A Law School

---

1. Introduction - Marketing Is Job 1!

Although the above quotations all concern the personal statement, they are applicable to the complete application file. The application file in its entirety is your interview for a seat in a law school class. Effective applicants treat the application file as a "marketing tool" which is targeted to the specific requirements and personalities of different law schools. For a good example of targeted marketing, consider the following excerpt from a recent biography of Bill Gates by Stephen Manes and Paul Andrews:

"Toward the end of the year, Lakeside senior classman Bill Gates took on a different marketing project: the selling of William Henry Gates. Potential customers? College admissions officers. Bill had scored 800 on his math SAT and five achievement tests (although only in the low 700s on the verbal SAT), and he put it, "I wanted to know which personality of mine would appeal to the world at large."

Witness the transformation! To Harvard, he was Bill Gates, son of a prominent lawyer, someone with connections, "the guy who was into politics ... so my whole page experience was the central part of that application." For Princeton, "I positioned myself as a computer nerd," the programming magician who could hypnotize a minicomputer or mainframe into doing anything he commanded. For Yale, he was a consummate do-gooder and sensitive artist with thespian aspirations, "the guy who did drama, the guy who was Boy Scout." It was one of the earliest displays of his chameleonlike, Thomas Crown-like ability to change his skin, to transform his persona-and eventually, his company's-in order to "do business."

The personal statement and autobiographical sketch are controllable and afford the most opportunity for "direct applicant input." They should be targeted to meet the requirements of specific schools.

2. The Marketing Tool - Your Complete Law School Application File

The application file is your interview for one of the few seats in a law school class. This interview consists of some or all of the following separate components:

The Covering Letter - Name, Rank and Serial Number

1. **Application form** - make copies and practice completing a copy before completing the original.

Third Party Statements - What Others Say

2. **A transcript of your grades** - You will not be able to change the numbers, but you may be able to influence the interpretation of the numbers. For example, if a grade of B is the top grade in the class, ensure that the committee is aware of this.

3. **Your LSAT score** - Many schools average scores. But, if your second score is higher than your first score, you may have grounds for requesting that the school use only the higher score.

4. **LSAT Writing Sample** - Can be compared to the personal statement to determine if the applicant authored his/her personal statement.

5. **Letters of recommendation** - Can be enormously helpful. Don't ask somebody to write a letter for you. Ask a potential recommender if he could and would be willing to write a positive letter of recommendation. In this way you can exercise some control over the content of the letter.

Direct Applicant Input - What The Applicant Says

6. **Personal Statement** - Written by the applicant and the most controllable part of the application file. This will either be in the form of one long question or a number of very specific short questions.

7. **Autobiographical Sketch** - Many schools (including the Ontario Law School Application Service application) ask for a list of jobs, awards, extracurricular activities, community service, etc.

3. Direct Applicant Input - Three Types

Grades, test scores, and letters of recommendation are all instances where a third party makes a statement about an applicant. The personal statement and autobiographical sketch afford the applicant the opportunity to make his best case in his own words!

Not all schools require a personal statement. However, most schools require some kind of "autobiographical sketch" in which candidates are required to list activities and achievements. Completing an "autobiographical sketch" in an effective manner requires more than "substance." "Form" matters as well. It must be well written. There can be neither typos nor grammatical errors. It must be visually pleasing. The way you describe your activities matters as much as what the activities are.

Three Forms Of Direct Applicant Input And Examples

Direct applicant input will take one of the three following forms:

1. Autobiographical Sketch - The applicant is asked to list his activities, jobs, awards, education, etc. The answers are generally to be completed on a prescribed form. Here are some examples:

"List in chronological order, beginning with the most recent year. It is important that you complete this section carefully providing details of extracurricular activities, non-academic achievements and community involvement. Indicate the nature and duration of your involvement beginning with the most current activities."

"List in chronological order, beginning with the most recent year, all post-secondary schools attended. Include all courses completed through professional associations."

2. Multiple Questions Personal Statement - Short answers to a number of specific questions. This form of personal statement has the effect of forcing the applicant to think about himself in terms of very specific issues. Some examples of these kinds of questions are:

A. How has your university program aided in your personal development and prepared you for the study of law?

B. Do you think that your employment, business or professional experience will aid you in the study of law?

C. Which of your extracurricular activities have been important to you?

D. Why do you want to study law? What is your career objective?

E. Do you have any special skills or interests that will assist you in law school or in your future career?

F. Are there personal facts or issues relating to your application that you would like the admissions committee to know about?

(Notice that all these question focus on the applicant.)

Short answer questions are often required to be answered on a prescribed form. Practise completing copies before completing the original!

3. One Question Personal Statement - The applicant is required to write an essay in response to one specific question (or in some cases to no specific question). This form of personal statement gives more room for the applicant to determine what is important. Some examples of these kinds of questions are:

A. With specific reference to your experiences, concerns and values, what is your objective in seeking a legal education?

B. Each applicant is required to submit a brief but reasonably detailed personal statement. This is your opportunity to inform the committee about your interests, accomplishments, and goals. It should include any special facts which should be brought to the attention of the committee.

---

4. What Are The Schools Looking For? - Know Your Market

Before attempting to formulate answers you must understand the purpose(s) of the question(s) asked. If you knew how the answer to the question influenced the admissions process, you would know how to better answer the question. How do you learn what the school is looking for?

The Basics - What All Schools Look For

All schools seek applicants who have the tools required to complete the program. The two primary tools are:

1. Ability - intellectual and academic

2. Motivation - because intelligence without focus is wasted

Applicants must have the academic and intellectual ability to complete the program. For many applicants their grades and LSAT scores provide adequate evidence of that ability. Intellectual ability is not sufficient. The world is full of intelligent people who have never achieved anything. A high achiever is motivated to direct his ability in a focused way to achieve results. Hence, schools look for evidence that the applicant is motivated to complete the program.

Beyond The Basics - How They Are Different!

Beyond attracting students with ability and motivation, different schools have different objectives in admitting students. Hence, you may wish to emphasize different things about yourself at different schools.

Targeted Marketing - The Importance Of Researching The Schools!

Consider the application process as being analogous to a job search. Imagine that you are applying to ten different jobs. Effective applicants would not send exactly the same resume and cover letter to each potential employer. Effective applicants would research two major issues.

First, what is the business of the employer?

Second, what role does the specific job play in the business of the employer?

The applicant would then design the job application to target the specific requirements of the employer. In the same way that prospective employees must research potential employers, applicants must research the law schools. On the basis of this research, all forms of direct applicant input should be targeted to specific law schools. This may mean writing different personal statements for different schools!

Great! But, How Do I Do This Research?

Research each school by asking the following two general questions:

1. What Is The School's Generalized Policy On Admission?

Different schools have different agendas. Ask, what is the school trying to achieve by admitting applicants to its program? Look for statements about generalized policies on admission. Sources of information include:

For Law Schools In General

-   the calendar of information (pay particular attention to the dean's message);
-   the application form itself (there is now one common application form for Ontario law schools - U.S. and other Canadian law schools have their own forms);
-   the school's web site

For U.S. Law Schools

-   The Official Guide To U.S. Law Schools published by Law Services;

For Canadian Law Schools

-   the section of the LSAT Registration Book which has information about all Canadian law schools;
-   the information about Ontario law schools in the Ontario Law School Application Service (OLSAS) package

What follows is an example of a generalized policy on admission:

"The purpose of the admissions policy is to admit students from among the many applicants, who will excel at the study of law and, at the same time, contribute creatively and meaningfully to the law school and the community."

2. What Application Categories (Marketing Avenues) Are Available?

All schools have a "regular applicant" category. In addition, some schools may have categories for "mature students", students in an "access" or in a "special circumstances" category. In determining whether an application category is suitable for you, carefully review the requirements of the category and determine how the category furthers the school's generalized policies on admission. Different schools use different applicant categories. Even if two schools use the same name to describe a category, that category may be defined differently at each school.

Different schools use personal statements in different ways. Try to determine how the school uses the personal statement or other form of direct applicant input. For example, is it appropriate to use direct applicant input to talk about grades and LSAT scores? Take care to respond to the specific question asked.

The most effective direct applicant input is tailored directly to the requirements of a specific school. All other things being equal, any admissions officer would rather admit somebody with a specific interest in that specific school.

---

5. Your Image Isn't Everything. It's The Only Thing!

Direct Applicant Input As Image Control And Development

Your application file is your interview for law school. Your objective in an interview is to create positive images about yourself. Therefore, all forms of direct applicant input should be aimed at image control.

Inside Perspective - The content and development of many personal statements suggests that the applicant doesn't realize that they serve as a replacement for an interview.

Think Of The Personal Statement As A Job Interview.

Imagine that you were at a job interview. You want to project a positive image of being: competent to do the job, organized, prepared for the interview, capable of following directions, well dressed, interested in that job and company, and having the potential of "fitting in" with the company. This can be achieved only if you present yourself in a way that the interviewer gets to know you. You would want the interviewer to think that working with you would be a pleasure. Finally, all information that you convey during the interview must be consistent with any other information that the interviewer has about you! All components of your application file must be consistent and work together to create a positive image where the whole is greater than the sum of the individual parts.

Inside Perspective - You must use your personal statement to sell yourself to the school. Thorough preparation and thought are essential for a well written personal statement.

Competent To Do The Job

Law schools are academic institutions. Schools seek applicants with the ability to do their academic work. For most applicants this will be established by grades and LSAT scores. Do not use the personal statement to simply repeat your transcript of grades and LSAT scores.

Inside Perspective - If your numbers place you on the borderline between acceptance and rejection at a school that uses subjective factors in its admissions decisions, then your personal statement will be scrutinized with care for evidence that you can do law school work.

Organized

We will spend more time later on how to organize personal statements. A well organized file, autobiographical sketch, and personal statement will depict a sensible and clear minded person.

Inside Perspective - If your essay is carefully organized and unified, it will be natural for the readers to assume you are a neat and careful person.

Your direct applicant input should show evidence that it has been written to satisfy the specific requirements of that school. If you are applying in something other than the regular category (for example the mature student category), make it clear why you satisfy the requirements of that category!

Inside Perspective - A big mistake made by applicants is not explaining why they are applying in the special category.

Capable Of Following Directions

Answer the precise question asked. For example there is a difference between a question that asks you to explain why you want to attend law school and a question that asks you why you would make a good lawyer.

Inside Perspective - Our personal statement requires applicants to tell us why they want a law degree. Too many applicants simply review what they think are their positive qualities for admission without explaining what they think society will get back if a scarce resource is allocated to them.

Inside Perspective - A big mistake is failing to read and follow simple directions in organizing the application.

Pay special attention to any requirements respecting length. George Bernard Shaw once apologized to a friend for having written such a long letter. He commented that he hadn't had time to write a short one. There is no virtue in length.

Inside Perspective - By far the biggest mistake is that applicants provide statements that are too long. It is a mistake to think that sheer length is an asset; the readers of these statements are more interested in concise presentations.

Well Dressed

Your personal statement or autobiographical sketch must be beautiful! There is no room for a single typo or grammatical error. Use a font that is visually pleasing. The key is readability. A font size of 11 or 12 pitch is best. Allow yourself plenty of time. The best personal statements are developed slowly and deliberately over a reasonable period of time. They are subjected to numerous revisions and refined to perfection. Have your work reviewed by a friend or associate. Ask, what image(s) does it convey?

Inside Perspective - "… spelling mistakes and grammatical errors are a personal pet peeve of mine which I find particularly annoying, especially when I read approximately 1200 applications a year."

Showing An Interest In That School

Inside Perspective - One law school admissions director at "school X" revealed that they receive many personal statements in which the applicant says he is looking forward to attending "school Y " the following year. This is a very careless error. Avoid it!

If a school has a particular program that attracts you to that school make it clear that you are interested in that program!

Will You Fit In With The Student Body?

In the back of the mind of any admissions director is the question: can I see this person at our school?

Is The Reader Getting To Know You?

Direct applicant input is about you. It must be a reflection of your personality. It must make you come to life as a person. Without direct applicant input the admissions director will not have you in sharp focus. A well written personal statement will bring you into focus - bring you to life. An application file without an autobiographical sketch and/or personal statement is like seeing the applicant on black and white television. The personal statement should move the applicant to living color!

Inside Perspective - A big mistake is that many statements are vague and provide no real information about specific characteristics of the applicant.

Pleasure To Have Around

How do you know if you have written a good personal statement? If after reading your personal statement the reader thinks: I would like to meet this person, then you have done a good job!

Inside Perspective - A director of a law school admissions committee that interviews applicants once suggested to me that some applicants are given interviews because the personal statement has made the applicant an interesting and likable person.

The Consistency Requirement

The admissions director will look at the complete file for the purpose of trying to get an impression of you. All parts of the file must fit together properly. While writing your personal statement and/or autobiographical sketch ask if it fits well with the other components of your complete file.

---

6. The Facts Don't Always Speak For Themselves! - Making Sure They Do!

Learn to describe facts so that they create maximum impact!

A. The Autobiographical Sketch - Describing Activities, Jobs, And Awards In A Positive Way

It is your responsibility to tell the committee anything that you want it to know!

Inside Perspective - Please remember that the Admissions Committee cannot know what the applicant wishes to have considered unless it is included in the admissions materials submitted.

At a minimum, when describing things, you must be concerned with both length of time and content.

Length Of Time

The length of time that you have been involved in an activity is strong evidence of your commitment to that activity.

Inside Perspective - A big mistake made by applicants is the failure to give meaningful time frames to community service and other activities.

Inside Perspective - If an applicant has worked 40 hours a week but only states that she has worked "long hours" and there is no letter from an employer, the Committee can only guess how long and guess to the applicant's detriment.

Content Of Activity

Avoid listing only the title of the job, activity or award. In many cases the title will not be sufficient for the reader to understand what you mean. After having listed the title you must describe the responsibilities, qualifications for award, etc. A well written entry can document a history of advancement, achievement and the assumption of greater and greater responsibility. Here are some hypothetical examples that might be found in an autobiographical sketch.

Western Pre-Law Society, 92-94; organized trips to Law Fair; President 1993-94.

Researcher - Department of Justice, Summer 95; was only non-law student hired to do legal research in the criminal division.

State University Dean's List; (A- average or higher), 5 consecutive semesters.

Debating Club, 1991-94; Attended weekly meetings, placed second in North American competition 1993, Vice-President 1994.

Big Brothers Organization, 1993; Averaged 8 hours per week providing tutoring and mentoring to two boys aged 8 and 12.

Cambridge Scholarship, 1996; Awarded each year to Cambridge student who makes the greatest all around contribution to the university in the areas of athletics, academics, and university community involvement.

Head Of Orientation Committee, 1996; From an applicant pool in excess of 100 applicants I was selected to plan and organize the orientation activities for 5,000 first year students.

The Applicant Is More Than The Activity!

In each of the above examples the explanation clarifies the activity and is evidence of a quality that is desirable in a law student. The reader will use the descriptive material to infer additional things about the applicant. For example the winner of the Cambridge Scholarship (because of interest in athletics and the university community) is much more than an academic. Attending weekly meetings of a debating club is evidence of both commitment and discipline. Spending eight hours each week as a Big Brother is evidence of ability to manage time and a commitment to public service. Three years of involvement in the Pre-Law Society is evidence of an interest in law and an interest in working along with people. Being elected president is evidence that he is held in high regard by his peers. Notice how much better the summer job with the Department of Justice sounds once you know that the applicant was the only non-law student selected for the position. The fact that the person was the head of the orientation committee is evidence that the applicant is responsible.

The descriptive material will allow the committee to make inferences about the applicant that extend beyond the activity itself. In this way the descriptive material will assist in the creation of positive images.

Creating Images Through Facts - The Personal Statement

The single biggest mistake applicants make in developing personal statements is that they write a statement rather than a personal statement. A personal statement will help the reader get to know you better. This means that a personal statement must be about you as an individual and NOT about your view of the world in general or law in particular. A statement (in contrast to a personal statement) is not about you but is either about how you see the world or about some other topic.

In order for someone to get to know you, you must reveal something about yourself. It's time to get personal. Don't be abstract. An effective personal statement must talk about you in a very personal way. Focus on the facts. For example you could: write about the best thing that ever happened to you, the worst or the most unusual. You could write about your greatest achievement - making it clear why that is important to you. You could write about your greatest failure or disappointment - saying what you learned from the experience. Go into detail! Be specific! Use concrete examples to make your statement distinctive. Avoid the generalities and platitudes that apply to every law school applicant and will make it impossible for your statement to be distinctive. For example, it does little good to say that you want to make the world a better place. Be specific. What motivates you specifically? Why?

You cannot tell the school directly that you have the qualities it seeks. Rather, you must describe yourself in such a way that the school will infer that you have those qualities. For example, imagine that a law school is seeking applicants with the following characteristics:

Maturity

Disciplined

Hard Working

Honest

Generous

Motivated

Intelligent

Responsible

Well Rounded (diverse interests)

Community Oriented

Sound Judgment

The school requires a personal statement. You cannot write a personal statement that says:

"Hello, my name is Stanley Student. I want you to know that I am mature, disciplined, hard working, honest, generous, motivated, intelligent, well-rounded, community oriented and have sound judgment. Please send my offer of admission to:

> Stanley Student
> 123 Main St.
> Anytown, Canada
> A1A 2B2"

Describe specific aspects of yourself that will allow the reader to infer that you have the above qualities. Describe something you have done that will show that you are honest or responsible or motivated, etc. Don't write that you have sound judgment. Describe some event or incident in which you exercised sound judgment.

Your job is to describe specific things about yourself that will convey the kinds of images that are consistent with what the law school is looking for!

---

7. A Special Situation - Coming To Terms With Negatives

Every component of your application file should convey the image of a positive person. Avoid emphasizing negatives. If you must mention negatives try to show what you learned from the experience. There may be situations where you wish to place low grades and/or LSAT scores in perspective. The law schools are interested in your ability to do academic work. Your job is to convince the school that such grades or LSAT scores are not indicative of your academic ability.

Low Grades

You may be able to minimize the effects of a semester of low grades if you can show that they were an aberration. If you have grades that are high there may be room to argue that the law school should consider only the high grades. This may be possible if you can demonstrate that the low grade(s) were the result of a temporary external problem and that the problem has gone away. Perhaps you started in the wrong academic program. For example, many students change programs (Arts to Sciences) because they didn't like the first program. Poor grades are often the result of a program that is not liked. If the student switches to a new program and the grades improve:

1. The student has a proven ability to get good grades; and

2. The problem that caused the poor grades has gone away.

What follows is a good example of a student dealing with a "false start."

"I am asking the Admissions Committee to overlook the false start I experienced during my initial university studies.

I think of my academic career as being divided into two distinct chapters, the first chapter being when I enrolled at University X in 1986. In my first year of studies I obtained a C+ average in the four credits I completed. The following September I transferred to University Y as a visiting student on a letter of permission for one year. Late planning prevented me from registering in courses that matched my academic interests and my grades suffered. As a result, I decided to leave university life all together. The next September I enrolled in the two year Financial Management Program at Community College Z. At its conclusion, I was a half credit short of a diploma and had some major decisions to make regarding my future.

During my time at University Y and Community College Z, I was an immature young man who lacked career goals and objectives. While these traits were exhibited by many in my age group I must admit that if this young man were applying to law school today, I would advise the admissions committee to reject his application without delay. Fortunately however, a dramatic transformation occurred in the second chapter of my academic career and I believe that my academic accomplishments during the last three years prove that I have the academic ability to be an excellent law student.

The second chapter of my academic career began with my decision to return to University X in the fall of 1990. I was determined to succeed in my second attempt at university and entered fall classes with a good attitude and the motivation to succeed.

I am now twenty-six years old and will earn my Honours B.A. in the spring of 1993. Maturity and self-direction have vastly increased my academic success and the marks I have achieved during the last three years attest to this change. I know that I will be a first rate law student and would ask with respect that the Admissions Committee disregard or assign less importance to the academic results I experienced during my initial university studies. I know that my enthusiasm, motivation, interest and goals will ensure that I will make a positive influence on the law school and the community."

LSAT Scores

If your grades are competitive argue that in spite of your LSAT score you have strong academic ability. This ability is proven by your good grades. Under no circumstances should you attack the validity of the LSAT in general.

8. Okay, I'm Ready To Write. How To Write, "Right."

Inside Perspective - A good piece of writing is a good piece of writing; it has unity, force, and coherence. It communicates clearly and persuasively.

Good writing takes time. Personal statements should be developed over time with great care. What follows are some suggestions for both process and content.

Some Suggestions For Content And Organization

There are no right and wrong ways to write a personal statement. The following are some suggested things to do:

- Begin with a strong first sentence. You can make an instant good impression. You have a greater chance of catching the attention of a bored reader.

"A wise man (my grade 8 teacher) once gave me the following advice: "try as many different jobs as possible while you are young because it will be of great help in determining what you want to do in life."

"A #2 pencil and a dream can take you anywhere."

- Tell who you are by telling your story. This will focus the personal statement on you. Write about the best thing that ever happened to you, the worst or the most unusual. Write about your greatest failure or accomplishment. It will make you come alive as a person and make the personal statement more interesting.

"Although my grades were satisfactory, they did not reflect my abilities. As a result, I decided to work for the summer and travel Japan, Korea and Thailand from September 1994 to December 1994 in the hopes of "finding myself." To my dismay, I found myself out of money with mononucleosis in early November."

- Use simple language and short concise sentences. Avoid legalese or abstract language. Here is an example of what to AVOID:

"My rigorous domicile in Russia was the result of a hard fight to obtain a highly coveted work visa which entitled me to enter Russia as one of the few official working residents sanctioned each year by the Russian government."

- Ensure that there are no typos or grammatical errors.

- When listing accomplishments or achievements explain why they are important to you. What role did they play in the development of your personality or your interest in law school?

"I got involved in rowing in high school. Rowing is an extremely tough sport requiring intense dedication. This sport taught me how to organize my day and use each hour efficiently."

- Work with a plan or outline. Ensure that there is a main idea or theme that you wish to communicate. Pretend the personal statement is a thirty minute interview.

- If you have been out of school for some time, explain how your interest in law developed through jobs or other activities. For example:

- A police officer could justify an interest in criminal law because of interaction with the legal system.

- If your interest in law developed as a result of a significant life experience, then describe how that experience contributed to your interest in law. For example:

- An accident victim could justify an interest in law through interaction with the legal system.

The following are some suggested don'ts:

- Don't write about the law. The audience knows about the law.

- Don't write a resume in prose.

- Don't dwell on negatives.

- Don't draw conclusions. Simply provide facts that will support the conclusions that you want the reader to draw.

The Reader Is A Human Being - Avoid Upsetting The Reader!

- Admissions directors are overworked and read many more personal statements than they would like. It is human nature to experience positive or negative feelings about personal statements and to experience these feelings quickly!

Inside Perspective - The first 40 personal statements that are read are tolerable. But after the first couple of hundred I start to lose interest and read them very quickly. They had better have something interesting to say!

And Finally -

The personal statement is about you. Make sure that everything in the personal statement is for the purpose of making you come to life as a real, breathing, feeling, interesting person who the reader would like to meet! Use concrete examples and facts. In order to accomplish this you must do some thinking about yourself. The Personal Statement Workbook (following chapter) has been designed to help you focus your thinking about yourself!

Conclusion

A personal statement should:

1. be about you

2. ensure that general statements are backed up by specific facts and experiences

3. show that you are competent, well-rounded, positive and motivated person

4. explain how significant events contributed to the development of your personality

5. be interesting and tell a story

6. explain why you are interested in that specific school

7. be responsive to the precise question asked and the personality of the school

8. have some kind of theme or organizing principle

9. explain jobs, activities and awards

10. describe facts from which the reader will infer that you have cetain qualities or attributes

11. have a strong opening

12. be well-written

13. use simple language

14. have no typos or grammatical errors

15. not be too long and respect the directions concerning length

Chapter 14

Twenty-Six Actual Personal Statements of Successful Applicants

Personal statements come in the following two formats:

1. **Multiple Questions Personal Statement**

2. **One Question Personal Statement**

Each of these examples was written by a real, living, breathing, pre-law student. Most importantly each of these students was accepted! The examples included here cover a wide range of styles. Each example is quite good but far from perfect. Each is an example of what is achievable by a "mere mortal." I have not included any of the "rare dazzling" personal statements that are crafted by professional writers. You should view them as examples. As you read each one ask how it could be improved. How well do you feel that you are getting to know the applicant? After having read the personal statement, would you be able to describe the personality of the applicant?

You will note that these samples have been written by different kinds of applicants, with different motivations, and at different stages of life. This is for the purpose of completeness. A personal statement will be read in the context of what kinds of life experiences the applicant has had. Therefore, don't be upset if you feel that you have not had experiences as varied as some of these applicants.

The publication of this book will guarantee that admissions officers will be familiar with each example. It would therefore be a mistake to copy them.

As you read these samples, ask yourself:

- is there a strong opening?

- does the writer use the facts so that we get to him/her?

- does the personal statement make the writer come to life as a living, breathing, interesting person?

- is this the kind of person you would like to have in your class?

- is there evidence of the person's motivation for wanting to attend law school?

- what is your overall impression of the applicant?

Format 1 - Multiple Questions Personal Statement

(1) How do you think your academic, business, employment and/or professional experience have contributed to your development as an individual and prepared you for the study of law?

As a graduate student in Jurisprudential Philosophy, I have thought in-depth about the purpose of law from a philosophical perspective. My education in Philosophy of Law has lent itself to a consideration of justice and to moral reflection about the law. Philosophy of Law has prepared me in particular to examine the concept of a just legal system, and to consider the appropriate range of judicial discretion. I have spent a great deal of time considering grounds for obligation to obey the law, and what sorts of justifications hold in particular legal systems. For example, do considerations of fairness ground a general obligation to obey the law? What should citizens do in legal systems which fail to meet minimum requirements of justice?

My record as a graduate research assistant and as a tutorial assistant has prepared me to conduct research and to teach. I have always believed that tutorials should be more than a meeting place to negotiate grades, and that graduate students have a special obligation to guide their own students as much as possible. I have worked as hard as I can to foster co-operation, non competitiveness, among my students. I am proud that in a course with an attrition rate of one-third, I have maintained fifty-five of my original sixty students.

On a personal note, being born in South Africa and spending my adolescent years in a legal system which is anathema to the majority of the people has provided me with an acute sensitivity to fighting for justice. I was raised in a family that despised the system, tried to oppose it, and opted to leave rather than devoting the lives of their sons to its defense. That, more than anything, has left a profound impact on me. This upbringing, and my record in academia, researching and teaching, have prepared me for the study of law.

(2) If you have been involved in extra-curricular activities (such as community service, political, religious, social or athletic, etc.), which of these experiences has been most important to you? why?

By far the most important experience has been as a member of the Executive Committee of the graduate program in Philosophy at _____ University. To begin with, it was an honor to be elected to this position as I was the sole student representative. This position was important to me because student representation on committees had been something I was working toward since transferring to School A from School B. I felt that students were not represented in issues that concerned them the most. For example, while I favor preferential hiring policies and believe that concerns of equity should govern hirings, I felt that it was wrong that the formula adopted by the Philosophy Department was instituted largely by tenured faculty members without any input from graduate students. Since the policy would undoubtedly have an impact on our job prospects in the future, I was convinced that it was unjust that we were not consulted. Graduate students at other universities in Ontario shared this opinion and I supported them in bringing forward our concerns to the Canadian Philosophical Association, and in convening meetings at School A to discuss these issues. With student representation in mind, I was instrumental in arguing that graduate students should have a vote on the Search Committee for the Director of the Graduate Program. As a result of my work on the Executive Committee, I was asked to serve as a member of the Search Committee for the Director of the Graduate Program. I worked as one of four people on this committee with the Chairpersons of the Philosophy Department of School A, and I brought forward twelve issues that concerned graduate students. It is no coincidence that this year, graduate students were "invited" to participate on the Admissions Committee, and on the Committee for Scholarship Ranking Procedures, and that I was personally asked by the Graduate Program Director to continue representing the Philosophy Graduate Students' Association in order to maintain continuity. I am the current representative on the Faculty of Graduate Studies, and I am especially proud of my commitment to ensure graduate students' representation, and of my university service that has been helpful in achieving this goal. I have learned just how much one can do with solid, unwavering commitment, and I shall bring that dedication to law school if given the opportunity.

(3) Do you feel that you have developed any special skill interests other than your university program work experience outlined above? How may these skills assist you in the pursuit of your legal studies and future careers?

As an individual, a young chess player learns that dedication for long periods and concentration for hours on end are rewarded. I learned through playing chess competitively that to perform well requires a tremendous amount of work. The most important lesson came later, however, when I realized that winning as an individual "wasn't everything," and that working with a team or helping young chess players to fulfill their dreams are just as rewarding. Teaching and working co-operatively with groups are special skills which I have cultivated for my own happiness. I did not work for years with Aphasic Stroke survivors twice a week for solely altruistic reasons. To say I did so would be a lie. I volunteered to assist these people because it made me feel good about myself. I saw how people, when severely challenged, can rise beyond circumstances if they have support. I learned how good it feels to provide that support as a friend, and while I cannot classify those lessons as a skill, I believe they are more important than my academic learning. I will continue in my own studies and future career to focus not only on myself, but on others as well.

(4) Why do you want to study law? Do you have a career objective other than the traditional practice of law? Please describe.

I want to study law because I believe in pursuit of justice. I am currently engaged in a doctoral dissertation on equitable health care rationing. Because the dissertation parallels my interest in law, I shall outline its ambitions. My aim is to balance concerns of maximizing human well-being while allowing individual autonomy to pursue health care options which may lie outside the scope of a national health care plan. Jumping ahead on waiting lists and "quality health care" should not be synonymous with going abroad. I am convinced that national health care plans become minimal plans when people who can afford it have an incentive to go abroad. The result of this incentive means that we have a two-tiered system: Those who need treatment quickly, and can afford it, can get it immediately. I believe that equal access should be a guarantee of primary care, and instead of a constraint at the low end, people should be able to get the care they need based on: need, benefit, and an upper level constraint. Provisions must always be maintained for primary care.

This dissertation parallels my interest in law at the University of _____, in particular, through access to justice. My interest in an equitable health care system is in keeping with studying law at the University of _____. I feel well prepared to write on the normative and philosophical issue of equitable health care, but I am not yet well prepared to deal with the legal issue. The Faculty of Law of the University of _____, with its emphasis on access to justice, will provide the legal background and the requisite legal reasoning necessary to complete the dissertation, and enable me to work beyond it to completion. I want to work in public policy and legislation, and it will be essential to have a background in law. I have chosen the University of _____ Law School also because I can obtain a grounding in European Constitutional Law by availing myself of the one year study abroad program. Even more so, though I recognize how competitive selection to the program is, I shall work as hard as I can to have the opportunity to Clerk to the Supreme Court. Access to justice, be it in health care, be it in working in under serviced areas, or be it in fighting against unjust regimes such as South Africa's, is a theme I will commit myself to in law school and out.

I can summarize my reasons for wishing to study law at University of _____ Law School in one word: "Flexibility." I even want the opportunity to gain practical experience. The Law School provides this through the community legal aid plan. The blend of practical and theoretical study promises an enriching education at the University of _____ Law School. I could go on. Having completed a large part of my education in Toronto, I look forward to being at a largely non-commuter school with many students in my own age group. The University of _____ Law School is the one I want to attend most for all of these reasons, but mainly, for the single word which summarizes what it offers. I hope I am given the opportunity.

Format 2 - One Question Personal Statements

Sample 1

Education and work experience (particularly in the legal profession) have been the two factors which have most influenced my decision to apply to law school at _____.

My education has allowed me to develop expertise in a wide variety of fields. I completed a Bachelor of Arts (Honors) in Political Studies. I am currently completing a Bachelor of Education at the Intermediate/Senior level. My studies have included a year abroad, at _____. Studying international relations interested me in the relationships between existing laws and the resolution of politically contentious issues, for example through new or amended legislation. My work as an educator has expanded my understanding of interpersonal relations, social and political systems. Both subject areas have dealt with social and political philosophy, which is relevant to the study of law. Thus, the pursuit of legal studies would allow me to expand upon knowledge and skills I have developed in previous areas of study.

At the same time, my work in the legal profession has given me insight into the nature of the practice of law and the many possibilities open to those who hold law degrees. Having been employed as an assistant in a large corporate law firm, I have found the work is challenging, requires creative problem solving and necessitates dealing with clients and colleagues on a regular basis. Labor law and criminal law hold particular interest for me, and arbitration is an area I would like to explore further. Nevertheless, I am also open to other options, such as teaching at the university level, and other areas of business.

These experiences have taught me that I enjoy dealing with a variety of people; that I enjoy challenging, stimulating work; and that I feel it is rewarding and useful to broaden one's perspectives by considering the social, political and economic structures. Given these interests, I have chosen to apply to the _____ Faculty of Law because it offers strong programs in public law and legal theory.

In conclusion, I feel that law at _____ would be the ideal program to suit my interests, and would enable me to be effective and successful in fulfilling my career goals. My work, and educational experiences have allowed me to develop skills and knowledge which could be best explored by a career in law. If given the opportunity, I will use these skills to make productive and thoughtful contributions to _____'s Faculty of Law, and eventually to the legal community.

Sample 2

I will be completing my undergraduate honors degree in Family and Social Relations in April of 1995. A Bachelor of Law Degree at University of _____ interests me very much because of the learning opportunities provided by the proximity of the Supreme Court of Canada, the Federal Court and federal government institutions. I feel that my academic background, interests, community service, and goals make me an excellent candidate for the study of law at the University of _____.

With regard to my Academic background, the programs of Akademia, and Family and Social Relations have taught me to approach problems from a multidisciplinary perspective. Akademia is a one-year program at the University of Guelph in which students take courses in both the Arts and the Sciences as well as Integrated Courses that examine certain problems using a variety of disciplines. Following the first year, students transfer into another program. I chose Family and Social Relations because it is a program in which students study human interaction from an interdisciplinary approach and I wanted to gain some background for family law. Society in general and legal problems specifically are becoming more complex. Therefore, looking at problems from a multidisciplinary perspective is an asset in the study of law.

Being a well-rounded person, I have many interests outside of academics. I have continued to provide leadership for the Akademia program throughout my four years at Guelph. In my second year, I was treasurer on the Akademia planning council which promotes Akademia and arranges interdisciplinary events for first-year students. In the past two years I have continued to provide leadership for the Akademia program by attending events and program planning meetings.

Religion and athletics are also of interest o me. I have been a member of the University of Guelph Navigators for the past three years. The Navigators is an interdenominational club committed to helping others and examining how religion relates to modern day life. With the Navigators I have also done some community service work. Athletics have been particularly useful to me for two reasons. First, they mentally restore me and allow me to approach my academics with vigor. Second, they give me important social contacts, some of which may be helpful in the future.

Community service also plays an important part in my life. Particularly valuable to me has been my experience with the Big Brothers Association. Through Big Brothers I have been entrusted with a "Little Brother". I have done many activities with him like reading, building models, camping, operating computers, and watching movies. When I am in the Sault I devote an average of six hours a week to my Little Brother. Both his mother and his teachers feel that our relationship has assisted his development. I have also helped Big Brothers run community events such as barbecues, bingos, and bowlathons.

Considerable thought has gone into my career goals. One area of law that particularly interests me is the area of family mediation. Ideally, I would like a married couple who is contemplating a divorce to come and discuss their problems with me. I would try to use the experience that I have gained to help the couple to determine if their problems were irreconcilable. If they were irreconcilable and divorce was inevitable, I would try to work with them to draw up a mutually agreed upon, equitable separation agreement. There is evidence to indicate that couples are happier with this type of arrangement and are more likely to comply with its terms.

On the other hand, my career as a student has not been free of difficulties. During the Winter Semester of my first year I suffered from depression and needed to drop one course to lighten my academic load. Additionally, I am not pleased with my June 1994 LSAT score. Because of the significance of the LSAT and my desire to gain admittance to law school, I put a great deal of pressure on myself and under performed as a result. I would ask you, the admissions committee, to wait to see my February 1995 LSAT score, as I am hopeful that it will be more reflective of my true abilities.

In conclusion, I think that I am an excellent candidate for the University of _____ Law School. I am intelligent and have a strong work ethic. I have developed good research, critical-thinking, and essay-writing skills. I feel that I would be an worthwhile addition to the incoming class of 1995!

Sample 3

My name is_____and I am twenty-five years old. I am originally from Calcutta, India and my mother tongue is Bengali. I graduated from the University of Toronto with a B.Sc.(hons) in Toxicology and Human Biology, and a M.Sc. in Pharmacy. I am presently working on a part-time basis for the Canadian Armed Forces in the Royal Canadian Naval Reserves. I am training as a Maritime Subsurface and Surface (MARS) officer and working toward a Bridge Watch Keeping (BWK) ticket for vessels of the minesweeper class. This ticket would give me responsibility for the conduct and operations occurring aboard Maritime Coastal Defence Vessels (MCDVs), both under routine operation and in times of maritime or national threat. I am interested in studying law because the study of law would not only enhance my educational and career background, but also my considered career options for the future.

I am interested in pursuing the study of law at the University of _____ because I can offer a significant contribution to the school and in return, the school can provide me with distinct educational opportunities.

My background education has been sound, liberal and intensive. To broaden the scope of my science-based education, I have pursued study in the arts. I studied classical piano at the Royal Conservatory of Music for ten years; participated in cultural functions in the Bengali Cultural Association; studied martial arts and obtained a black belt in five years; worked as a volunteer instructor for two years, with women and children affected by domestic or street violence; and presently I study drums and percussion music in private lessons. I have participated in student government bodies in university, which have included being the vice-president of the Pharmacology Course League in 1991-1992, an active member of the Indian Student Association from 1988-1992, and a member of the Caput Committee in residence in South House at Victoria College from 1991-1992. I also have four years of experience working with computers and interfacing with internet and "information super-highway" technology.

My ethnic and racial background, diverse educational background, and my military career has given me a strong commitment to social equity and human rights. In seeking social equity and safeguarding of human rights, there are a number of aspects of our legal system which I would be able to contribute to.

My ethnic and racial background has given me insight into many problems in the Indian community, the foremost of these being problems with immigration and the protection of prospective immigrants' rights. Many people that come to Canada from India are coming from a system where justice is available only to the rich or the powerful. As a result, they are afraid to seek retribution for wrongs committed against them and are not trusting of the legal system. Being new to the country, they are afraid of lawyers that are from outside of their own community, as they feel vulnerable due to language and cultural differences. There is a large population of East Indians in Canada, with few Indian lawyers available to represent their interests. By studying law, I would be able to effectively represent interests of members of the Indian community, so that they are not excluded from the process of social justice.

My science and biotechnology background gives me a unique insight into a problem which exists for many Canadians. That is, many Canadians are hurt or damaged by medical products or procedures which are available to them. In order to seek compensation, or to re-enforce their rights which have been violated, they require not only representation by someone who has an understanding of the underlying legal principles, but someone who also has an understanding of the scientific processes and issues involved. This broader understanding would make it possible for victims to become more informed and as a result, be better represented in their quest to resolve their situation. The study of law would allow me the possibility of making a significant contribution in this area.

As a potential UN peacekeeper, I am sworn to uphold the human rights of individuals, by mental, physical and possibly, lethal means if necessary. It is a difficult job which requires not only understanding of the human and ethical issues involved, but the legal issues as well. Canada has a proud history in peacekeeping of understanding well, the human and ethical issues involved, in spite of recent difficulties. However, Canada's ability to assert its legal rights of its peacekeepers has historically been clouded, obscured and essentially impotent. Canada maintains an international voice in humanitarian efforts, but lacks a strong Canadian legal precedent which would allow it to enforce the mandate of the United Nations. As a result, in the attempt to restore human rights and social equity in troubled places, Canadian soldiers, sailors and airmen/airwomen are placed in unnecessary and grave risk. As an officer in the Canadian Armed Forces, legal training would provide me with a dual understanding of the issues involved. It would allow me to pursue the investigation and enforcement of social equity and human rights not only throughout Canada, but on an international scale as well.

The three reasons I have outlined above demonstrate most accurately why I am interested in law studies. I am interested in law studies because I have a number of unique perspectives which I can offer to this field. Accordingly, the University of _____, faculty of law, is well suited to my choice of studies. The school is expanding and is developing its commitment to human rights and equity issues. My diverse and flexible background would allow me to introduce to the school, a number of different perspectives which may not have been previously considered. In return, the schools strong commitment to human rights research and education would not only allow me to broaden and strengthen my educational background, but provide me with the basic tools necessary to make a significant contribution to these areas.

Sample 4

While attending the Law Fair in Toronto, a good friend asked me "Why are you here?". This person was not an existentialist but, rather, concerned about my decision to leave a promising career in order to pursue the study of law. I was taken aback not only by the question, but by the strength of my conviction. A legal education has always been one of my aspirations and I feel that it is a privilege to be earned. As a person raised in the welfare system, I have learned many valuable lessons about privileges and can appreciate them. In addition to being prepared to undertake the task, I believe that my life experiences would greatly benefit the University of _____ as well as the community.

It has taken me a long time to realize that I should be proud of myself for surpassing the limits that the majority of people unknowingly set for children in poverty. For much of my life I was ashamed of where I lived and what it stood for, namely failure. My mother and I lived in a subsidized housing project, and my father left soon after I was born. Thus it was that my mother, with her limited knowledge of English, began receiving social assistance.

Life in Moss Park was eventful, to say the least. A large housing area in downtown Toronto, it was plagued by poverty, crime and, most of all, despair. The passivity of the adults was so overwhelming that children were afflicted by it as well. It was solely because of my mother's devotion to my studies that I was saved from the fate of my classmates.

Her determination that I receive the best possible education is what prompted her to transfer me, to a predominantly upper class junior high school. There I was able to see the disparity of wealth in our society, and it was also where I first experienced discrimination. I suddenly had to work twice as hard to meet the higher standards, both academically and socially. Thankfully, I was able to stay on the honor roll and was accepted to an advanced level high school rather than the local general level one. There I was involved with both the yearbook committee and the student body. As a class representative I was able to hone my public speaking abilities and have become a confident and effective speaker.

Attending university was a natural step for the students at my high school. I, however, had to motivate myself to continue on, because I could not see past my situation to the benefits that would eventually come. I was the only one of the children in my community who continued on past Grade Twelve. Unfortunately, due to financial constraints, I had to work not only during the last two years of high school but through the four years at York University as well. The time that I had to devote to my studies often conflicted with my obligations at work. This prevented a sincere commitment and as I grew older I realized that I had cheated myself out of what I wanted the most; a legal education.

In an attempt to pacify myself, I completed the Law Clerks of Ontario program. I did this in one year by enrolling in both first and second year courses concurrently. The classes were an intense study of the practical aspects of Real Estate, Litigation and Corporate Law. However, instead of satisfying me, they only served to heighten my desire.

Currently, in addition to working over forty hours a week and volunteering at the Daily Bread Food Bank, I am attending a third year social science class involving an in-depth analysis of how the law functions.

My interest in law stems from exposure to both the impoverished and the affluent cultures of society. This unique experience has given me the ability to look analytically at both sides and has become an important aspect of my character. Furthermore, having studied French, Greek, and Spanish extensively, I have gained skills that will aid me in breaking down the barriers that hinder many in our communities, and I believe this will enable me to become an effective link between the legal system and the community.

It is for this reason that I would like to attend the University of _____. I am particularly interested in the Legal Aid Clinic and I strongly believe that I would make a significant contribution if accepted into your faculty of law. I believe I now possess the maturity to handle the responsibility that accompanies the privilege of law school. I would like to thank you for your time in considering my application.

Sample 5

Born in Jamaica and the son of Jamaican immigrants, I was celebrated within my family as the first to attend university. After first year, it became my goal to earn a degree in international Economics and join the department of External Affairs as a Foreign Service Representative. During my first academic year I held two part-time jobs, one bartending at a campus pub and another with the Council of the Student Federation event coordination staff. This involved organizing speeches, dances and other events held in the student commons. I also made the time to play for the varsity rugby team, volunteer as an event planner for the my College Student Council, and participate in the Caribbean Students Association (CSA).

In my second year I decided to take initiative - and control my finances-by creating my own business. I started a boat care company providing and subcontracting cleaning/servicing at three marinas. By working up to 30 hours per week throughout subsequent school years, I graduated without indebtedness. The financial burden eventually demanded that I lighten my course load and even miss a semester in 1989. This venture took quite a toll on my academic performance but it was also a source of tremendous satisfaction and helped to develop my organizational and communication skills. Regrettably, I was forced to cut back on other activities as well and gave up my jobs on campus, the CSA, and of course, the rugby team. In the summer of 1989, I earned two A's in third year courses when the availability of high school workers allowed me to apply a reasonable amount of time to my studies. I chose X as my educational referee primarily because he was aware of my work schedule and the effort that I was making under the circumstances.

My current career began with a customer relations position at Z Life Insurance Company. I was assured that if I worked hard, showed a unique commitment to achievement, and earned my F.L.M.I., I would advance within the company. The Fellow of the Life management Institute program consists of ten courses that touch on all aspects of life insurance administration. These courses include: maths of finance, Canadian life insurance law, marketing, and information systems.

Over the past five and a half years my career has seen three phases. In the first phase, I represented the company in the customer service department. This responsibility provided the occasion to polish my interpersonal skills. I learned to quell situations by listening intently and analyzing issues in a logical order. Besides plenty of patience, success as a service representative requires strong research and writing skills and the ability to deal with the often complex issues of the Insurance Act. After eight months, a second phase began when I was chosen among fourteen staff members to represent customer service in an information systems project. Representatives from each division of the company spent a year designing and testing the data processing software. My responsibility was to ensure the accuracy of all calculations and documents made by a new computer system. The project stressed the importance of cooperation and demanded very strict attention to detail. By this time, I had earned my F.L.M.I. diploma in an uncommonly short nineteen months.

The third and final phase began when I was promoted to Coordinator of Marketing. In this capacity I am responsible for writing brochures, manuals, and descriptive elements of our computer software. A large amount of my time is spent analyzing the products of other companies and comparing them to ours. I make presentations in our brokerage offices throughout Ontario and in Montreal, in French and English, and represent the company at industry discussion groups. These responsibilities have been mine for the past four years and I welcome the daily challenges to my writing and public speaking skills.

From the age of sixteen I have participated in rugby at the high school, varsity and provincial levels. Having found the rugby club atmosphere extremely supportive, in 1991 I decided to see what I could do to help some boys in trouble and promote the rugby club. I wrote to a probation office and was successful in an application to have work with the club to serve as community service for young offenders. My proposal centered on the importance of community as well as guidance and showed how they can be provided by a team setting. Through my experiences with these young people and subsequent discussions with crown and defense lawyers, I have developed a very deep desire to study law and contribute to a fair and representative system. As a criminal lawyer, I will be in a better position to help assess and influence the ways in which we punish and rehabilitate Canadians.

For me, the University of _____ Faculty of Law is ideal for several reasons. The Community Legal Services program and Clinic courses represent an excellent opportunity to prepare for my career in advocacy. I am drawn to the opportunity to study under a faculty so accomplished in my area of interest such as professors _____, _____, _____ and _____. Also, I will be sure to apply to the _____/_____ Joint Program to earn my LL.B. Civil Law as I may eventually seek employment in the federal Ministry of Justice.

While other universities may boast an emphasis on criminal law, I appreciate that the University of _____ shares my belief in the importance of a strong sense of community —an aspect of university that I will not go without again.

I believe that qualified people of all races should be represented in the legal profession and that given my aptitude, experience, and desire to make a positive difference in society, I will make a unique contribution to The University of _____. By sitting in on law classes and taking the time to discuss the merits of a legal education with lawyers and law professors, I have gained full confidence in the fact that I have not only the motivation but also the ability to succeed in law school.

I have clearly demonstrated my ability to do academic work with first year grades and my studies with the Life Management Institute. I am hard working, motivated, and I have excellent analytical, logical and communication skills as confirmed by my success in the workplace. Active community involvement has been a part of most of my adult life. At the age of twenty-eight, my maturity level has allowed me to carefully consider and pursue this career change with confidence. Finally, I have established the study of law as the right step toward meeting my personal goal of participating in a criminal justice system that serves us all equally. I hope that in the future, exercises such as the Provincial Committee on Systemic Racism in the Criminal Justice System will not be necessary.

Sample 6

First as an undergraduate at Trinity College, then later as a graduate student in the Near Eastern Studies department and as a theological student at the Toronto School of Theology, I pursued my deep interest in the foundations of Judaism and Christianity. In addition to mastering the languages of Syria-Palestine (Hebrew, Greek and Aramaic), which was my main area of interest, I explored the literature, history and archaeology of the whole Ancient Near East. One of the highlights of my studies was a summer spent working on an archaeological expedition in Israel sponsored by Harvard University. I also valued the many hours I spent studying ancient Greek manuscripts as part of my research assistantship. The rigorous discipline required in the analysis of detailed textual material and the necessity of understanding the import of precedents and underlying principles for purposes of arriving at the meaning of a text have provided me with an excellent background for the study of law. Throughout this period, I expressed my equally deep commitment to the community by doing volunteer work during the school year and by choosing summer jobs in the social services area.

In 1980 I married an Anglican clergyman and moved to the Niagara peninsula, where I continued to be involved in various social service and community organizations (Crescent Park Nursing Home, Niagara Women in Crisis, Nova House (a shelter for abused women), Family and Children's Services of the Niagara Region, Fort Erie Palliative Care Association). I was also a leader in an on-going Youth Leadership Training Program sponsored by the Diocese of Niagara.

However, by far the most important preoccupation in my life during the past five years or so has been meeting the special needs of my son,_____, who was born with a profound hearing loss. After considering the various approaches to educating hearing impaired children, my husband and I decided that the oral method would provide

_____ with the greatest opportunity of becoming a fully participating member of society. Our commitment to the oral approach led first to daily trips to Children's Hospital in Buffalo, and eventually to a move to Toronto in order to take advantage of the special programs offered by the Toronto Board of Education and the Auditory-Verbal Therapy Program sponsored by VOICE (a parent self-help organization) at North York General Hospital. I consider it a major achievement that my son is a happy, well-adjusted little boy in a regular Grade 1 class, at home with both his hearing and his hearing-impaired peers.

When we moved to Toronto in the fall of 1986, my husband went back to university and I looked for a job with flexible enough hours to enable me to meet _____'s needs. In September I obtained a position as a Library Assistant in the Learning Resources Centre at _____ Institute. A few months later I became the supervisor of the Reserve Department, a position which I hold up to the present. My responsibilities include overseeing the maintenance of a collection of some 12,000 items, participating in the implementation of an on-line system in the Reserve area, and training and supervising the Library Assistants. I am actively involved in our union (O.P.S.E.U.), and am a member of the Human Rights Committee of our Local. I am also taking advantage of the facilities at _____ by taking courses in photography.

Now, as a single parent of a school-age child, I intend to develop my own potential by pursuing a career in law, building on the foundation of my previous academic accomplishments and my various experiences over the past several years. I believe that the study and practice of law play a central role in ensuring that the rights of all citizens in a society are advanced and safeguarded and that their obligations to society are guided with fairness, reasonableness and humanity. In my law studies and practice, I would like to focus on the field of regulatory law as applied to either the disadvantaged (particularly the disabled) or labor and labor-related problems. In this way I hope that my career as a practising lawyer will both benefit society and allow me to meet my responsibilities and desire for personal growth.

If I am accepted into the program, I am fully confident I will do well in my studies and complete successfully all the degree requirements. I hope also to contribute in a positive way to the life of the Faculty during my years of study there. I am fortunate to have a supportive family who have always encouraged me in both emotional and practical ways, and I have their assurance of continued support as I embark on this new and challenging enterprise.

Sample 7

A passionate interest in politics, the principles of government, and the values that Canadians seek to live by, motivates my desire to study law at _____. I was 13 years old and growing up on a farm in rural Ontario when I first attended a constituency meeting for the nomination of our local candidate. The power and influence of the ideas I heard were exhilarating. That experience excited my curiosity about the processes and structures that organize ideas into a framework for the structure of society. I quickly discovered that law is the medium through which human values are articulated. Thenceforth I have been certain about my decision to study law and make a contribution to Canadian public life.

My interest in politics and political theory led to an undergraduate education in Political Studies at Queen's University. The program is intellectually demanding and has helped me to acquire the knowledge, skills, and habits required for further scholarship. The program requires that students complete 19 credits for a B.A.(H), and I will graduate with 19.5 credits in May 1996. My studies have sharpened my capacity for critical thinking, strengthened the quality of my judgment, and heightened my understanding of interaction between humans and political structures that shape human demands. One of the greatest pleasure of my undergraduate experience has been the opportunity I have had to enjoy learning for its own sake. The challenging academic standards of the program enabled me to prove my intellectual abilities by maintaining a consistent record of academic achievement. I believe that my undergraduate program, with its emphasis on rigorous reading, writing, and thinking, has not only been an excellent preparation for the demands of law school, but also has provided an intellectual foundation that has developed the attributes of effective communication, cultural sensitivity, and an ability to reason critically. My studies have focused on Canadian politics. During 1995-96 I served as a research assistant to Professor _____. In that capacity I have worked on a B.A. honors thesis.

Another important factor in my personal and intellectual growth has been the activities and distinctions I have achieved outside the classroom. Extra-curricular involvement has broadened my experiences and developed my leadership skills. I have devoted a substantial amount of time, energy and creativity to student government and academic issues during my four years at Queen's. My participation in student government has reinforced my interest in law and community service. As my involvement and experience have progressed, I have embraced opportunities to assume more responsibility and face greater challenges. These experiences, particularly my appointment to an office in student government, have strengthened my organizational abilities, enhanced my interpersonal skills, and proven my managerial capabilities. In this position I have demonstrated originality in problem solving, intensified my sense of personal and professional integrity, and emphasized my conviction about the importance of education. One of my goals has been to facilitate the publication of course evaluations in an effort to educate students about the academic opportunities available. I have worked with members of the Faculty and Administration addressing concerns about the availability and accuracy of this information. As a recipient of the Arts & Science Undergraduate Society Achievement Award, my dedication and commitment to student government received public recognition. These academic and extra-curricular achievements have stimulated my passion for life and my appetite for knowledge. I am also proud of the extent and quantity of my employment experiences, which entail a great deal of responsibility and demonstrate the tenacity which has enabled me to finance a major part of my education.

I believe that acquiring an education entails a responsibility to contribute to society. I have realized the need for sensitivity to the social and political environment in which the government operates, and developed an understanding and respect for the history of the Canadian political system. I have faith in the ability of the Canadian government and Canadian citizens to make the changes and decisions that will allow Canada to prosper in the twenty-first century. I intend to apply the knowledge I have gained in my undergraduate experiences to the study of law, to formulate and implement public policy, and to make a contribution to public life. A legal education will develop the analytical abilities and problem solving skills I will need to tackle the challenges and complexities of the modern world in a career in the federal public service. The contributions I have made to community service during my four years at Queen's signify a lifelong commitment to public service. I sincerely believe that my choice of a rigorous undergraduate program, my quest for academic excellence, my achievement in extra-curricular activities, and my success in positions of responsibility in employment exemplify the capabilities and characteristics that will enable me to succeed at law school and in my career as a legal professional.

Sample 8

Any summer evening I would walk onto the grounds of Maranatha Gardens and spend time with its tenants, many of them, friends. The four floor apartment building stands at the end of a gauntlet of thirty well designed townhouses. A few years ago, this patch of land was merely three acres of weeds and garbage in the hear of Simcoe, Ontario. Now it is home to seventy families, many of whom could not previously afford decent housing.

It is difficult to resist a sense of pride. Although the conception and building of Maranatha Gardens was not part of my job description as a Pastor, it became an extension of it. It was one of the accomplishments that made the ministry worthwhile.

Becoming a minister was an unusual move for someone from our home. While we were raised Lutheran (my grandparents immigrated from Iceland to Gimli in 1926), we rarely attended church.

I was born in Winnipeg in 1956, the third of eight children. At the age of thirteen, our family moved to The Pas, Manitoba. Two years later, my parents separated, leaving my father to support and raise all of the children. Perhaps that is why he did not protest too loudly when, at seventeen, I left home and moved to Ontario to become involved in the rock music industry in Toronto as a bass guitarist.

While in Ontario I met and became impressed with a number of evangelical Christians. In the fall of 1974, after committing my life to Christ, I entered a Bible College in Lindsay, Ontario. I attended the three year full time course, graduating in 1977 with a B+ average.

That same year I married my wife, Lynn, and moved back to The Pas, where we lived until 1981. It was then that I was asked to take over a struggling congregation in Simcoe, Ontario. I accepted the invitation and moved to Simcoe in September 1981. I received my ordination in 1984 from the Apostolic Church of Pentecost of Canada, headquartered in Calgary, Alberta.

I was the Senior Pastor of the Full Gospel Fellowship in Simcoe from 1981 to 1996. During that time,the church grew from seven families to over one hundred. It also progressed through two building programs, added additional staff and started other congregations.

Early in my career as a clergyman, I decided that my ministry would be governed by three principles. First, growth (we would resist the trend of declining church interest and would become a noticeable force in our community). Second optimism (we would resist the image of negative legalism and offer people a positive message of hope). Third, relevance (we would resist the tendency of answering unasked questions and, instead, relate to the nitty-gritty of people's lives). Everything we accomplished was guided by these convictions. I believe that we were successful in changing lives because of these principles.

It wasn't always easy. Being the Pastor of a growing congregation, coordinating over seventy staff and volunteers, demanded the continual learning, development and deployment of different skills, many of which will be helpful in the pursuit of law. Some of these skills are as follows.

The skill of administration. I enjoyed the art of forming and chairing boards, committees and organizations. Along with numerous groups within the church itself, I led one Ministerial association, founded another, created a "church planning" organization, was Vice-President of a Missionary Corporation and served in different capacities within my denomination. These endeavors were fulfilling, so long as we accomplished clear goals and objectives.

The skill of research. The constant necessity of writing seminars, messages and manuals sharpened my research and creative abilities. Staying fresh, original, motivational and instructional was a satisfying challenge.

The skill of counseling. A steady caseload of crisis, marriage and behavioral counseling enhanced my interpersonal skills as well as cultivated the areas of problem identification and solving. Although I found counseling to be intense and demanding, it was a high value activity. Many people, from children to professional adults found direction and encouragement in our offices. It was always gratifying to see the lives of others rebuilt and redirected.

The skill of leadership training. One top priority was the development of leadership abilities in others. Some people took senior positions within the church. Many of our young people went on to full time ministry. We are particularly proud of that. Also, I have had the privilege of teaching the dynamics of leadership internationally to hundreds of people in colleges and churches. Motivating and instructing others to take ownership of their lives is a rewarding task.

The skill of writing. Writing has also become a very useful talent. Between 1981 and 1996 over five hundred of my articles have been published in newspapers and magazines. Targeting the unchurched, the columns, addressed lifestyle issues in terms that anyone could understand and enjoy. The blend of directness, relevance and humor built a weekly and monthly readership of well over five thousand people. I will endeavor to bring the same mixture of textual integrity and enjoyable style into the practice of law.

Community involvement has been important to me both as a clergyman and as a private citizen. Simcoe is a town of fifteen thousand people with a strong economic base. However, in 1988, the need for affordable housing was brought to my attention. It was then that the dream of Maranatha Gardens was born. I founded Kent Park Community Homes of Simcoe, a nonprofit corporation dedicated to providing housing with dignity to the underprivileged. After forming the corporation, we hired consultants and acquired the appropriate land. Next we attained a government allocation and built a positive relationship with the Ontario Ministry of Housing. Then it was a matter of patiently working with architects, contractors and local groups. Finally, in 1992, Kent Park Community Homes opened the seven million dollar "geared to income" housing facility. Since then, the project, christened Maranatha Gardens, has given young adults a "head start", seniors a decent residence and families an attractive home. As mentioned previously, this accomplishment has been source of pride for myself and my wife Lynn, who also served on the board.

My community involvement also involved chairing committees for the Chamber of Commerce, radio broadcasting and teaching music in local schools.

During my tenure in religious leadership. Lynn and I not only raised up healthy congregations, but, more importantly, two sons, Dallas, 17 and Brady, 15. They have different opinions, different goals, different shoe sizes (13 and 14), but both have exceptional personalities and active social lives.

Music is a large part of church life and became an enjoyable part of our home. I have taught myself piano, keyboards, guitar and bass guitar. I am delighted to see these interests beginning to blossom in our children.

Now, after fifteen years in the ministry, it is time to shift direction. I originally entered the ministry in order to help others and lead our church to success. I feel that I have come as far as I can in my ministry. On Sunday, October 13 (my fortieth birthday) I stood before my congregation and announced that a time of transition had come for myself and for them. It was to become, for all of us, a season of change.

It is my hope that the field of law will allow me to increase my ability to serve others in practical ways. I believe that the skills that I have acquired as a minister will enhance my ability to excel in the legal profession. It is also my intent to expand my leadership into the political arena. I do not feel that I can adequately do this without first being educated in the discipline of law.

Thank you for considering this application. I look forward to the opportunity to study law at the University of _____ and contribute to the class with any sensitivities and perspectives into religious, social and organizational issues that my experience has afforded me.

Sample 9

In the wee hours of the morning last week, as I was stealing a bit of time to try a few LSAT questions while working overtime at my law firm, a young associate noticed the LSAT book and asked incredulously, "Are you crazy? Why would you want to give up a promising new career as a trademark agent for three years of intense study, followed by one year of very long hours as an articling student, only to be followed by even longer hours as an associate?" I could not answer the question in a few words, so I merely assured her that I considered myself to be in full possession of my faculties. In the following paragraphs, I intend to explain to the Members of the Admissions Committee why I am so determined to continue with my studies.

I was in third year of Nursing Science program at the University of Ottawa when my son John was born in 1980. At that time, I made the decision to leave my studies to devote all my energies to raising a family. Between 1980 and 1987, I gave birth to five children. By economic necessity, I was forced to start work in 1986, first part-time and then later full-time. I thoroughly enjoyed the assignment, and have held a contract position there through my company, Cortage Corporation, continuously since then.

After working as a float secretary, having the opportunity to be exposed to and learn about many areas of law practice, I "fell into" the intellectual property department. Due to the nature of this area of practice, secretaries are traditionally given more responsibility than in other area. Some secretaries advance to become Canadian trade-mark agents. I successfully wrote the October, 1996 examinations, and am now a qualified Canadian trade-mark agent.

My five children are now adolescents, or nearly so. Although each is very much an individual (which makes for some very interesting moments for my husband and me as parents!), we are both very proud of how they are developing as young individuals. We are also pleased with their academic achievements. All three boys have been honours students at high school. The oldest is studying first-year math and science at the University of British Columbia. The two girls are home-schooled, working above their grade level.

As my children have become older, more independent, and more grounded, I have been able to devote additional thought and energy to my career. During the past year, I have been working on a procedures manual for my department. This project had its inception when I was asked to train a new person with no knowledge of intellectual property, to enter due dates into our trade-mark tracking database. I hope to have it completed by the time I am at law school in 1998!

Last year, when my firm developed an association with a patent agency, I was asked to set up a patent due date tracking system. This involved learning the patent process, worldwide, from filing to expiry, and then programming a set of codes into our existing database to track the flow. The agents have been pleased with the results, given the limitations of the software package. Over the next six to eight months, I have been asked to work with them and our Systems Department to create a new trade-mark and patent database that will satisfy all of us. I am very excited about being able to apply my knowledge and experience to work with this team to create the "ideal" database.

One of our clients, needed to track infringers of "knock off" items or grey market goods, and I created a database. Although we have not yet discovered any common infringers, the client is happy to know that a system exists to "flag" them.

It did not take long for the chair of the IP Department to discover that she could use my French-language skills to translate French-language correspondence and documents, thereby saving our clients time and money.

I was grateful to be given the opportunity to participate in all of these projects and have enjoyed each for its new challenges. However, I still felt that my direction was limited. For this reason (among others), I made the decision to become a trade-mark agent. Studying for the exams, I was exposed for the first time, to analysis of case law and applying it to new situations. This greatly aroused my interest in law. It was while preparing for the exams that I made the decision to continue my studies and to become a lawyer.

The University of _____ is an ideal school for pursuing studies in intellectual property. Gordon Henderson's spirit and influence remain there.

Being bilingual, the University is also an ideal program for me. Even though my application is for the English language common law program, I look forward to having the opportunity to take some courses in French. Being a citizen of a province and country with two official languages, I believe there should be more Anglophones capable of expressing themselves in French. The University of _____ will prepare me for a career in both official languages.

Members of the Admissions Committee, I trust that I have been able to present sufficient evidence as to why I will be an ideal candidate for the University of _____'s common law program.

Sample 10

An ancient Chinese proverb tells us that if one makes a mistake and does nothing to correct it, then one is making another mistake. I learned that this is the case concerning how one approaches a university career. My first year was relatively unfocused. I did not yet know what I wanted to study, and spent most of my available time with readings in a number of different topics and adjusting to university life. My grades, being somewhat lower than those of the succeeding years, reflect this uncertainty. Having decided to major in Philosophy in my second year of undergraduate studies, I have felt a drastic increase in my ability to speak and write since my first year, which I regard as a testing ground and not an accurate measure of my academic potential. I believe my transcripts reflect this hypothesis. I learned the same lesson through the experience of the Law School Admission Test. The first time I took the LSAT, I underestimated it, and received a score that I did not consider satisfactory. But I have always believed that immediate failure does not entail ultimate failure, and after preparing to a greater extent for my second writing, experienced a fifteen-point increase from my first score (145 to 160, or, 29th to 83rd percentile). That this happened to only a small percentage of test-takers only reinforced my belief in the idea that no challenge is so great that it cannot be overcome with persistent effort. It would appear that the LSAT itself contributes to one's preparation for law school! Having eventually double-majored in Philosophy and York University's unique Social and Political Thought Program, I have been exposed to a number of theoretical and practical issues, including topics in ethics, logic, and political theory. I went on to take two courses as part of my undergraduate career which were conducted at the graduate level. My particular interest in political thought and ethics in general lead to my acquisition of a Certificate in Practical Ethics, the requirements of which included two 2000-level ethics courses taken in my fourth year of undergraduate study. This interest continued with a Major Research Paper completed as part of my M.A. dealing with ethical issues and the nature of ethics itself.

My academic success can be at least partially attributed to my employment history. Throughout all of my undergraduate life, I have held full-time summer positions, most of which entailed industrial and laboratory positions. I worked 40 to 50 hours per week, and 8 to 12 hours per day. Notwithstanding the short-term economic benefits of my employment, the industrial setting gave me the long-term benefit of discipline. Industrial labour is challenging and physically difficult, as one must be able to clearly think, communicate, and work rapidly under conditions that impede such activities. But more than this, it taught me that one's economic circumstances are often closely connected with one's world view and opportunities. The focus of laboratory work is precision. Working under conditions where the elements of procedure must be exact, one learns to pay conscientious attention to every detail. Experiencing all of this alongside my academic life made me a stronger student, and I experienced a heightened appreciation for university courses, viewing education not as a chore but instead as a relatively rare opportunity.

Despite this personal development, I always wanted more out of labour; more thinking, more autonomy, and more personal development. I wanted, and still want, the feeling at work that I still get at school, to be thinking and judging for a living and to see this manifest itself as a direct and visible contribution.

The transformation that I desired first occurred when I was given the opportunity to work as a supervisor. The level of responsibility entailed by this position was surprising. I was responsible for allocating employees to various jobs, updating production records, and participated in quality control. This trend continued in the latter portion of my undergraduate career, when I began essay tutoring. I had always wanted to teach at the university level, and I thought that tutoring others in the art of essay writing would be a good preparatory activity. I found that tutoring helped me to work and communicate with others towards the achievement of a common goal. In addition to improving one's ordinary editing skills, tutoring also helps one to interpret what a student wishes to say and to help the student articulate it.

During my M.A. in Philosophy I was offered a Graduate Assistantship. I had the opportunity to work in close proximity with one faculty member, assisting her with departmental and personal academic projects, often under pressing temporal constraints. At first, I suspected that such a position might be tedious, but as it played itself out, I found myself conducting more efficient research, and interpreting specific instructions with greater ease than ever before.

When I began my PhD, I was offered a Teaching Assistantship. This entails seminar instruction and discussion with two groups of undergraduate students on the issues, concepts, and readings of an undergraduate course in philosophy. But more than this, it involves a great deal of verbal explication and interpretation, both of course texts and students' concerns. In some cases, a Teaching Assistant may even offer assistance in regards to students' personal problems. This personal interaction has generated a unique bond between me and my students such that they now feel as though they can approach me with almost any concern. Currently, I am a teaching assistant for a course focusing on law. Leading tutorial groups in this course has refreshed my interest in legal questions, and has turned my studies once again towards the concrete questions of justice, fairness, civil disobedience, and the various theories, nature, and functions of law. I find that each tutorial involves approaching at least one critical legal, philosophical question and then coming to some type of resolution through discussion.

I see a future legal education as an enrichening of what I have studied thus far. I feel that I have the interest, discipline, employment history, and academic background to succeed in law school and make valuable contributions to the academic life thereof. I hope that you have enjoyed reading my personal statement, and I look forward to the Fall 2000 semester at your Faculty of Law.

Sample 11

"A #2 pencil and a dream can take you anywhere."

Joyce A. Myers

I have entertained the same dream for the last five years. Even before applying to university, I knew I wanted law school to be a part of my future. At the beginning of first year I made a sign that read: "LAW SCHOOL". Through the last four years I have developed and struggled, to try and make my dream become a reality. The sign still hangs over my desk today and represents a dream that has never been anything but my top priority. I am hungry for the day that the sign over my desk reads: "GRADUATE FROM LAW SCHOOL".

I started my undergraduate program with this goal in mind. I felt an English degree would develop my writing also improve my vocabulary, my reading, and my analytical skills. I believe I'm a much stronger writer and thinker than I was going into university. I did not, however, reach this point overnight. I found the first year very difficult mainly due to the separation from home and my family. The adjustment of living on my own was very upsetting, and it took me awhile to adapt. I was also not prepared for university; I did not yet know how to study and do well in exams and essays. I eventually learned that going to class and taking proper notes was essential to being a good student and I have now developed a pattern of studying and an approach to preparing for exams that I find very effective. I have improved in each year of university, and I feel my third and fourth year results reflect my ability and the seriousness with which I regard my studies. Last year, for example, I stood first in two of my classes with an A+ in both.

I consider myself a very active person, and I get involved in many different types of activities. For the past three years, I have been a member of Alpha Omicron Pi (AOTT), an international Woman's Fraternity. The sorority offers me many opportunities, and each year I participate in and help run our annual philanthropic events. My sorority won an award for the most successful philanthropic program in the school's (UWO) panhellanic society. One example of the activities we do is Derby Daze, a week long contest between the six sororities with the proceeds going to charity. AOTT has been the winner every year I've been a member. During this week I participate in all the activities: the cheer off, air bands and bottle drive. In addition, I participate in other AOTT charitable events including: going at least once a year to the London Food Bank and lifting and sorting food, serving pancakes at our annual pancake dinner for charity, and working at our annual Halloween pumpkin carving contest.

For the past two years, I've been elected to the Officer's Council, which runs our chapter of the sorority. This year, I hold the position of Centennial Liaison and am working on getting my chapter involved in celebrating AOTT's 100th birthday. I am in charge of fund-raising, getting my chapter to brainstorm and then decide on what our chapter's gift/project to the community will be, and raising money for the centennial scholarships fund. Last year, I was elected to the officer's council as reporter to "To Dragma" (AOTT's international magazine). I wrote reports on individual member's achievements and our chapter accomplishments including activities the chapter participated in. I enjoyed this position and it sparked my interest in journalism. I am hoping to be active in a law school journal.

I have always been very athletic and enjoy both competitive and recreational sports. The first sport I showed interest in was figure skating. Until age 15, I skated singles competitively, and also on a precision team. Next, I got involved in field hockey and rowing in high school. Rowing is an extremely tough sport requiring intense dedication. This sport taught me how to organize my day and use each hour efficiently. It is the ultimate team sport, and the crew only performs as well as its perfectly coordinated effort.

Because of the unpredictability of my work load at university I have chosen not to play on a university team, however I have found a sport that lets me release my energy and frustrations. I work out every day, including weight lifting or training for an hour each day in addition to an aerobics or step class. My work outs are very important to me because they structure my day, regulate my sleeping and diet and I really enjoy them. I feel that working out is my sport and my dedication is equal to that of any serious athlete. In the summer I continue with weight lifting and aerobics but I also play some of my favorite sports including racing canoes and sailboats. Athletics are not my sole interest. I have also been a member of two choirs, one vocal and also the St. Johns Handbell Choir which performed in church services across North America, including various locations in Ontario and also in Wyoming and Texas.

My work experience has been steady and I have tried to work with children at every opportunity as I enjoy being with kids. For two summers I worked at Havergal Day Camp and was responsible for twenty campers. I had to plan their activities, ensure their safety, and take them on field trips. Prior to 1991, I spent summers up north with my family and worked as a mothers helper for a family with four boys. I feel I have a lot of interest, experience and natural ability with dealing with children and perhaps may have a future in a child and law related profession. Currently, I work part-time with the Toronto Dominion Bank as a teller. I also worked full time during summer and over Christmas break.

My experiences and interest are widely varied and I am very dedicated to everything I do. The things I choose to do I put one hundred percent into. I am interested in perhaps incorporating my legal degree with writing, children and women's issues. For now, I am mainly interested in studying law, and seeing where the future takes me. "From everyone to whom much has been given, much will be required; and from the one to whom much has been entrusted, even more will be demanded." (Luke 12, v. 48) I feel that an education is a privilege and to go to law school would be a wonderful opportunity. If given this privilege I would use it to its fullest, and give back to the community in equal measure what I have been fortunate to receive.

Sample 12

During my school years in the Soviet Union every year around November 7, the anniversary of the Socialist Revolution, my friends and I heard the same speech on how this day marked a new beginning for the Soviet people. As young children we could not fully comprehend the meaning of those words and the only significance it held for us was that we did not have to go to school that day. As we grew older and started to better understand the life around us, our indifference turned into skepticism. However, November 7 did, indeed, mark a new beginning for me in a way that my teachers could not have imagined. On November 7, 1989, my mother and I came to Canada. I was twenty years old.

This was a very sad and emotional time for me. I was leaving behind my father and grandmother and saying goodbye to life-long friends. I was also giving up my sociology studies at the University of Leningrad. At the same time I knew that I had a unique opportunity that only a few people in the Soviet Union had - a chance to get out and have a better and more productive life. By the late 80's there were fewer and fewer opportunities for young university graduates, especially for young women. Most of the available jobs were low-paying with no possibility of growth.

My dream was to continue my education in Canada. One of my aspirations was to receive a law education. I became interested in studying law back in Leningrad when I had taken a course in Soviet law and wanted to turn my interest into comprehensive studies. I believe that a democratic system of justice is a framework upon which society should be based. In the Soviet Union even minimum requirements for justice were not met and people in positions of power were above the law. For me, a chance to study law in Canada would not only be a right step in the way of personal growth but also an opportunity to participate in a system of justice that serves all equally.

I had, however, one major obstacle to overcome. Although I was fluent in Russian and Italian, and had some knowledge of French, I spoke no English. While working to support myself I devoted all available time to learning a new language. In April 1990 I spoke English well enough to be eligible for a government sponsored work-study program. I worked full-time as a receptionist at a Canada Employment Centre and took a course in typing twice a week in the evenings. I also kept studying at home to further improve my English. My years of training in classical piano helped me cope with my busy schedule. From the age of eight to fourteen I spent, in addition to my time in regular school, fifteen hours a week in music school. My musical studies not only taught me discipline and patience but also helped me learn to organize my time and use each hour effectively.

In 1991 my dream moved closer to becoming a reality when I was accepted at the University of Toronto. During my first year, however, I was able to take only two courses, since I had not received a permanent resident status yet and therefore was not eligible for OSAP. To support myself I had to work over 20 hours a week. Throughout my university years I was able to combine my studies with work and other activities. During my second year I found an exciting opportunity to volunteer for the department of education of the Consulate General of Italy. This not only helped me to improve my Italian, but also allowed me to learn about the life of another community.

I did my undergraduate studies in the History of Fine Art. As a child, growing up in a city like Leningrad, surrounded by beautiful art and architecture, I would spend hours in the halls of the Hermitage and the Russian Museum. My studies in Art history gave me a deeper understanding and appreciation of Art. I also believe that they were a good preparation for the demands of law school. My program was not just an art program, but an economics, politics, history and humanities program combined. It required extensive reading, writing and critical analysis. It allowed me to deal with complex political and social issues, to think critically and to analyze relationships between things.

In 1995 I obtained a 3-year BA in Fine Art History but unfortunately could not continue my education. My family in Russia unexpectedly became my priority. My father, a retired navy officer, and my grandmother were struggling to survive and needed my help. Even that limited amount of money that I was able to send made a big difference for them. Although I don't work in the field of my studies I continue to maintain a great interest in Art. I spend an average of four hours a week doing volunteer work at the Lismer Library of the Art Gallery of Ontario. I don't regret the fact I had to postpone my education. The years of work gave me important life experience and confidence. These years didn't weaken my interest in law and my desire to pursue a legal education.

It would be an honor to be accepted at the Osgoode Hall Law School. Having come from a country where civil rights were not protected and justice was available to very few, I would be greatly privileged to become a part of a school known for its strong commitment to social justice and equality. The area of Immigration and Refugee Law holds a particular interest for me, especially Osgoode Hall's strong clinical program in this subject. I am also looking forward to taking advantage of the school's diverse curriculum and exploring other areas of law. I believe that I have a number of unique perspectives I can offer to the school and, in turn, benefit from its long-standing tradition of academic excellence and its diverse student body.

Thank you for considering my application.

Sample 13

An elderly woman asked a younger man from her neighborhood to assist her with her banking. Although she had lived in England for quite some time, she had remained within the confines of London's Indian community; consequently, she had never mastered English. The young man, whose English skills were good, agreed to help her with the paperwork involved in conducting her transaction. All she had to do was sign the applicable forms. Several days later, the woman discovered the 30,000 was missing from her account. Anxious relatives contacted the bank, only to find that she had unwittingly authorized her young "assistant" to withdraw all her money.

The woman described is my grandmother. I was only nine when she was defrauded out of her entire life savings, but I seethed at the injustice that was done to her. A man whom she had thought she could trust had taken advantage of her old age and inability to communicate in English. Several years would pass before that man was apprehended, charged, and convicted of fraud. However, my grandmother never recovered a penny of her money. Although this incident did not immediately trigger my desire to pursue a career in the legal profession, it awoke within me a child's sense of justice which, with experience and observation, I came to understand the importance of protecting individual and social rights and freedoms against abuse.

I am currently interested in studying law because there is a great need for lawyers who have a first-hand knowledge of Sikh Indian culture to represent the growing number of Sikh Canadians and inform them of their rights and responsibilities under the law. My own first-hand experience is more than a birthright; for the past four years, I have volunteered for approximately ten hours per week at the Sikh Temple at 7080 Dixie Road in Mississauga. I have devoted part of this time to helping members of our community with their tax returns, which have been known to confuse even the most fluent Anglophones. My fluency in Hindi, Urdu, and Punjabi has been particularly beneficial to new Canadians among us who have yet to master English, as well as our elders-many of whom have never been comfortable enough to venture outside our community to learn and practice English. I also participate in the organization and administration of our temple's summer camp, which draws over 2,000 Sikh children from all over Ontario to share in the celebration of our languages, prayer, and songs.

Living in Toronto, the most multicultural city in the world, I am also well aware of the need for persons to act as liaisons between cultures outside their own. As an Air Canada Sales and Service Agent at Pearson International Airport, I am reminded of this need on a daily basis. Although my knowledge of both English and Indian languages enabled me to help numerous Indian and Pakistani clients, I took the initiative to learn Japanese at the Berlitz Language School in order to provide better service to our airline's Japanese customers. In addition, I learned sign language, and worked for one year on a Special Assistance assignment, which gave me the opportunity to serve travelers with disabilities. In international travel cross-cultural communications are crucial, especially when crisis-such as medical emergencies, disputes, or lost children-arise. Likewise, one of the most important roles a lawyer can play is to act as her client's interpreter, for in essence, the law itself comprises a sort of culture, with its own dialect, practices, and rituals; some or all of which may be foreign to clients' understandings.

I expect that the study of law will require tremendous self-discipline, effective time management skills, the ability to juggle tasks, and a commitment to excellence-qualities which I have been developing since childhood. Since childhood, I have been accustomed to leading a busy life. Between the ages of six and thirteen, I participated in gymnastics teams. At eight, I began training in Kathak-classical Indian dance. I also learned to play two instruments, the tabla and the sitar. To juggle all of these arts with my schooling, I had to develop good time management skills. I continue to use my time in a disciplined manner to this day, balancing my career at Air Canada with my volunteer work, parenting my ten year old son, Jesse, and working a part time consulting job.

At the age of fifteen, I began to apply the basic organizational skills I had learned from my busy childhood at Crown Travel, my first place of employment. I provided general help around the office by filing documents, book-keeping, and using my fluency in the three Indian languages to assist with customer queries. As I become more familiar with the travel industry, I realized that Crown Travel had not managed to reach a significant, largely untapped market of Indian businesspeople. This was a major oversight; the travel industry is highly competitive and profit margins are very low. After I was made manager, I developed different advertising strategies and we brought the agency out of the red to become a highly successful business.

After many years of work in the travel industry, I would now like to apply myself to the study of law. Reviewing Osgoode's literature, I was particularly impressed with the school's focus on law as a means of providing public service and achieving social justice. I am also certain that, with its wide array of programs, centers of research, societies, volunteer opportunities and clubs, Osgoode would be a most exciting school in which to embark on the engaging, interdisciplinary path of legal study I intend to pursue. I thank you for your time in considering my application.

Sample 14

I am Metis, a direct descendant of Gabriel Dumont, who with Louis Riel was one of the leaders of the Red River Valley rebellions. My grandmother, Rosanna Goulet, was functionally illiterate, married at 15 and moved to Athabasca. My father was the youngest of 11 children to survive past childhood, and he has the characteristically bowed chest from whooping cough in infancy. Conditions were difficult. Sometimes there wasn't enough food to go around. My father was called 'half breed'. Later as a career professional with the Department of Indian Affairs and in government, he presented his background as 'Spanish'. When I took my baby brother out in the stroller, people commented on the cute Eskimo baby and asked where we had adopted him.

When I tried to talk to Grandma about my background, she got very angry with me and refused to talk about it. In my 20's I investigated attaining status and was told that as a Metis, I "didn't count". This hurt, and I dropped the issue, but never stopped thinking about it.

Two things occurred that rekindled my Metis identity. First, I have two sons, and it is important that they know about- and feel proud of- their heritage. Secondly, I was forcibly reminded of my Metis status when we nearly lost my second son after birth due to a blood incompatibility between my husband and myself. Simply put, the haematologist advised that I had the blood type of 95% of all Native Americans; (AB positive, with no 'C' antigen.) I haven't been involved with the Metis community because I didn't know until now that I would be accepted. I welcome the opportunity to reclaim my heritage and contribute to the Metis and First Nations community- I am looking to get involved.

My family moved around a great deal- I had been through 10 moves and three provinces before I was 10 years of age. I learned to be outgoing and make friends quickly. I became self-reliant and an independent thinker at an early age. My mother still tells the story of how the local priest asked my class of 7-year-olds whether the Devil sent us to hell. All hands went up- except mine. I stood firm, to announce that our choices, not the Devil, sent us to hell. Years later, I discovered that St Augustine had said it far better in his doctrine of Free Will!

I won public speaking awards in Grade 7 and the Sir Robert Borden trophy (for best all round student) in Grade 12. I was involved in Band, Volleyball, Theatre Arts, and a Leader of Student Council. My family supported me through my Grade 12 Summer Scholarship and 1st year at Brock University. When they 'suggested' I move again and I refused, I was left solely to my own resources. It was difficult. I worked my way as a waitress through an Honours B.A., completing a 4-year program in 3 years and graduating 1st in Programme. I learned to be extremely disciplined with my time, to focus completely on the task at hand and complete it efficiently and thoroughly. I became very resourceful and tolerant of other's opinions and behaviors. I also experienced the rougher side of the employment sector. As one example, once when I was working as a cocktail waitress the owner asked the staff to attend a 'private party' after work. I begged off, citing schoolwork commitments.

When I came into work the next day, I discovered I'd been fired. This experience taught me that there is a price to ethical conduct but that the reward- self respect- is worth it. I also started thinking about disequities in the employer/employee relationship, and how jurisprudence and legislation could address these issues. While at McMaster University I won three consecutive Ontario Graduate Scholarships and I became the first Graduate student to be recognised for the Student Union Award in Teaching, for the 1997-8 year.

When I completed my Master's in Philosophy at Brock University I applied to Law School at the University of Alberta, and to the Ph.D. program in Philosophy at McMaster University. I was accepted to both, and decided to follow the Ph.D. for the wrong reasons. I have always regretted not pursuing the study of the Law.

I have continued to teach, both at the adult level at Ryerson and McMaster and St Clair College, and at the children's level, at church Sunday schools for 6 years, and at my local Christian School's literacy program for 1998-1999. Teaching is very personally rewarding to me. I have also taught Aikido (a martial art) for the last two years to children aged 6- 16. Aikido requires that you 'blend' with your opponent, redirecting his energy without injuring him. I apply this paradigm shift in other aspects of my life as a conflict management approach, and am very interested in how the Law views Arbitration and Mediation. Aikido is very difficult to do well, and requires complete focus. I return from a class feeling virtuous, refreshed and ready to tackle my readings with new vigor.

My community work has been a natural outgrowth of my interests in addressing disequities and affecting positive change. I am a past President, Toronto Business and Professional's Women's Association. In that capacity, I worked with Mary Cornish as a founding member of the Pay Equity Coalition, and coordinated activities with L.E.A.F. (the Legal Education and Action Fund) and Nellie's., a home for battered wives and their children. When the local hospital (Toronto East General) intended to close down its paediatric ward, 3 other individuals and myself organised public meetings and other events positioning this as a bad choice. This process took the better part of a year, but in the end they did not close the paediatric ward and despite continued cutbacks it is thriving today. This is something I am very proud of. I discovered that a few committed individuals CAN make a difference. I see the study of Law as offering many different career streams, which position someone like myself to be more effective in making such a difference.

Over the past 18 years, I have had a varied career in the Financial Services Industry, as a Manager and administrator, as a Risk Manager for the LCBO and as a Broker. My career has developed strong organisational skills and a critical and disciplined approach to information. In projects such as the $2 million insurance placement for the Credit Unions of Ontario, I have learned to lead teams and to focus on the positives in moving objectives to completion by due date. My maturity and work experience afford a unique perspective in my coursework, such as Employment Law, (which I am doing as part of a Human Resource Management Certificate). The Professor is Matthew Certosimo, an Employment Law specialist with Borden and Elliot. The text is Labour and Employment Law, by the Labour Law Casebook Study Group. While most of the students find the course abstract, dry and difficult, the cases come alive for me. It is exciting and challenging. I find I have an almost pictographic recall of the events, and an analytical ability to grasp the issues and principles at law. This has restored my confidence in my abilities to succeed at law and rekindled my desire to practice , originally awakened when Pierre Elliot Trudeau came to my high school to discuss policy and its impact on my generation. I still remember my 10-second clip on national TV, when I inquired that I would be 18 in a few months, would I be able to vote in an upcoming election? (the date was not yet set). I realised then that new ideas and social change come to life through jurisprudence and legislation. The study of Law offers many career paths in addressing the difficult issues of equity and equality, especially in view of First Nations peoples.

Society and the Courts are grappling with how best to include First Nations peoples in social justice, without disenfranchising others. I would like to be part of making that process work.

My educational background in Philosophy has taught me how to read critically and my work has ingrained in me how rewarding it is to work with others to accomplish a goal.

A career in Law would provide a venue for me to apply my gifts and be one of those who as Roberta Jamieson said in the 23rd Annual F.B. Watts Memorial Lecture recently, "...put forward solutions that will improve the system in order to prevent problems in the future." I want to look back on a career and a life where I made a difference, and I believe that the study of Law presents the most appropriate opportunity to do so.

Sample 15

My name is _____ and I am thirty-one years old. I was born in Mersin, Turkey in 1968. I have six siblings. My father died when I was two years old and my mother raised seven children by herself. From my mother, I learned that being a responsible person is the most important thing in one's life, and also that following one's own path was paramount. When I was asked in fourth grade what I wanted to be when I grew up, I stated emphatically, "a lawyer".

I graduated from a high school in Mersin with a grade point average of 8.5 (out of 10) in 1985. When I was seventeen years old, I passed the entrance exam allowing me into a law school in Turkey. I was third out of 850 students accepted into the Law Faculty of Ankara University. While I was attending university, I was employed as a legal secretary for five years. I worked from 3:30 p.m. to 7:30 p.m. on weekdays and 8:30 a.m. to 5:30 p.m. on Saturdays. Needless to say, I had to work to earn my way through school.

However, by the same token, it was extremely important for me to gain as much experience as I possibly could in order to prepare for the time when I would graduate. Immediately upon graduating from university, I was trained for six months in a lawyer's office and for six months in the courts in Mersin. During this period, I obtained extensive training in the various areas of law.

Upon passing the bar exam, I opened my own law practice. Initially, there were only myself and my secretary. During the first two years in practice, I worked very hard preparing my cases. It was important for me to excel, to do the best job for my clients, and to obtain a reputation for my skills and ability. After two years, my case load increased to such an extent that I had to hire another lawyer. Prior to immigrating to Canada, my firm consisted of myself, two lawyers, one paralegal and my secretary. During my law practice for five years, I also worked as a volunteer for the Legal Aid Center of the Mersin Bar Association. There were only eight lawyers involved, including myself, out of 600 lawyers in Mersin. The center offered free legal services to people in need, especially young offenders charged with offences against private property due to extreme child poverty in the city.

My daughter was born in May of 1996 and we immigrated to Canada in October of that year. I completed the English as Second Language courses first and then the English for Academic Purposes course offered at Centennial College in Toronto. Subsequently, I completed various Grade 10, 11 and 12 courses at the Adult High School in Richmond Hill, Ontario. While I was studying English, I have worked as a volunteer for the Turkish Community Culture and Folklore Association and for the Turkish Community Television in Toronto.

Upon passing the York University English Language Test, I was accepted in the Refugee and Migration Studies Certificate Program. I decided to study part time at the time because my daughter was still young. My daughter is now more independent and is attending a Montessori School full time. I am now prepared to commit myself full time to my academic career.

I have chosen to apply to the University of Ottawa Law School because it offers a strong general legal education. As I stated above, I obtained my degree from the Turkish Civil Law System which is drawn by the French Civil Law System taught in your school. I am very impressed with the fact that the two main legal traditions of civil and common law are taught in the same faculty and the same building. In addition to its strong general legal education, The University of Ottawa Law School's commitment to human rights and equity issues greatly attracts me. I also know that there are a number of courses offered in criminal law, which I want to specialize in.

In conclusion, I am interested in pursuing the study of law because I have a number of unique perspectives which I can offer to your school, as follows:

1. My academic knowledge on the Civil Law system in Turkey,

2. My work experience as a lawyer,

3. My work experience in public relations in the Turkish

Community Culture and Folklore Association, which has given me

insight into Turkish society's needs and problems in Canada.

Because there is only one Turkish lawyer in Ontario, the need for my legal services is evident.

I believe that I would be a worthwhile addition to the incoming class of 2000. I would like to thank you for your time in considering my application.

Sample 16

When I first entered university in 1996, I did not know what to expect: I struggled to decide what courses to take, I thought about what it would be like to live in a new city with new people, and I wondered how my academic abilities would stand up at the university level. Looking back, I consider my undergraduate years to be the most defining period of my life to date, and also the most enjoyable.

I chose to attend Trent University for many different reasons. For example, I wanted to go to a school that would offer close personal attention, that had a strong reputation in the area of liberal arts, and that emphasized discussion and debate. I also wanted to see what it would be like to live in a smaller city after having grown up in Toronto (I am now ready to return to Toronto).

I chose to take a joint-major because I had too many interests to narrow myself down to just one major. As a result of my many interests, I also found it difficult to determine my specific majors. However, I eventually decided that I was more interested in history and politics than I was in any other subjects.

One of the main reasons that I am interested in history and politics is because they both involve a great deal of writing and debating. While I have always had a passion for both of these activities, my university experience expanded this passion tremendously. I enjoy all forms of writing (argumentative, fiction, nonfiction, etc.) and I have developed a great deal of confidence in my ability to write in a way that is creative, powerful, logical and grammatically correct. As well, I feel that I am a good debater, and someone who can hold an educated conversation on many topics.

Throughout my university career, I made a point of enrolling in courses from many very different disciplines. From physics to philosophy, I made every attempt to expand my interests. Along the way, I feel that I have developed a tremendous drive. I work extremely hard and have a high ambition.

During my time at university, I have constantly searched for opportunities to take part in extracurricular activities. Many of the activities that I have been drawn to have allowed me to indulge in my desire to write and debate. Among other things, I have been an elected member of student council, I have sat on several decision-making committees, I have been a student don, and I have done some work for Trent University's student newspaper.

My experiences in the working world have been as enjoyable and educational as have my experiences at university. For the past two summers, I have been employed as a politician's assistant. In the first of these two summers, I was employed by a City of Toronto Councillor. In the second summer, I worked for a Member of Parliament. As a politician's assistant, I performed a wide variety of tasks such as writing correspondence, assisting constituents, and following relevant news items. In my position as an assistant to the MP, I also attended meetings as the MP's representative, and I assisted in preparing speeches and conducting research. My experience as a politician's assistant helped me to gain a greater appreciation of the legal profession. I was regularly confronted with legal documents and with people who required legal advice (of course, I was in no position to give legal advice since I have no legal training). I also came to realize just how many people there are who desperately need legal assistance, but who cannot afford to pay for it. Some day, I hope to do my part to help such people.

Debating, writing, politics and history are only a few of my interests. I am also very interested in baseball (both watching and playing), photography, philosophy, astronomy, swimming, reading, sailing, electronics and music.

I believe that I would benefit from studying law in many ways. It would help me to build on my writing and debating abilities. It would improve my ability to help others. It would give me the option of establishing my own law firm. And, it would also be a major asset in the world of politics and business. This flexibility is extremely important to me, as I have always been someone who desires to keep my options open.

Sample 17

"Why do you want to practice law?" This question is by far the most common aspect among all law school applicants. I have always been prepared with an all-encompassing, very general, very safe answer that would possess the right degree of discretion and personal insight. However, when the senior partner of the law firm that I currently work for challenged me with the question, I found that my answer had changed. I realized that my response was passionate and that the values, ideas and commitments that I have come to develop throughout the course of my life motivated it. While I am aware that law school admissions is objectively centered around one's G.P.A. and LSAT, I am confident that the admissions committee will be in an optimal position to judge me as an individual if they are to understand the evolution of my character.

Life can be evaluated through a series of events that warrant critical decision-making. From this, one may triumph in the opportunity or suffer the reality of defeat and thus, estimate the total number of right over wrong. However, I believe that embracing all these events as essential elements towards forming my character have enriched my personal development.

While my formal education has led me to a Bachelor's degree in Law with a Minor in Political Science, my desire to study and practice law stretches far beyond the scope of Carleton University. As an individual whose charismatic demeanor would often lend people to establish the label of lawyer or politician, I am quite capable of tracing the catalyst of my interest in social justice. In my final years at St. Peter's High School, I can recall a time where I had successfully convinced several of my peers to skip our French Immersion class.

In light of my interest in articulating the goals of others, my teacher and fellow members of the administration decided that a suitable punishment would be to host or MC the talent show, realizing my sincere lack of interest in performing such a task. Nevertheless, this event prompted Ms. _____ , a teacher who would later be instrumental in my personal journey, to forward unbenounced to me, my application to a Student Council Leadership camp. In the least, my final two years of high school were completed with having served as Head Boy of the Student Population and by far my most memorable achievement of having the honor of delivering the valedictorian address at our graduation ceremony.

Attending university was a natural step for the students of my high school. I, however, met my first year of studies with a great deal of hardship, both personally and financially. I began to realize the harsh reality of how one's access to available resources often equals one's access to achievement. This became apparent to me through, not only my own situation, but also that of others in society. I can recall thinking about individuals within society that were facing the truly difficult events that I could not possibly fathom. The homeless, the mentally ill, the drug addiction. I believe that I have a character that has an inherent need to impart efforts that could enhance or improve another's life. I had always taken great pride in my commitment towards enhancing positive changes. While working approximately 45 hours a week at bars and restaurants, I realized that I sacrificed the community and extra-curricular involvement that I had enjoyed so much just several months before. Consequently, my first year of studies at Carleton University suffered and I found myself on academic probation.

I believe that the events that occurred during my first two years at Carleton solidified my intention of studying law. I also realized that while one may have the idealistic testimony, admission to law school is highly competitive.

I adopted a notion that is reflected in most of my work in the last two years of Undergraduate studies. I realized that my access to education was in essence, like access to justice. Throughout the course of my time at Carleton, I have been capable of holding up to three jobs at a time while maintaining a high academic standing in my studies. I made the necessary changes in my life that would enrich every possibility of gaining access to my goal of law school admission. Virtually every event that has occurred in the past two years has contributed to both my political and social insight. It was within these times that I have come to understand the importance of opportunity. At one time, I believed that working the number of hours I had would have been counter-productive if I didn't fair well in school, however, it proved rewarding in emerging from adversity and added to the development of inner strength and resiliency-testing limits and pushing further still. It is within these aspects that I found outside the scope of academic literature that I take great pride in possessing as true elements of my character.

I have placed considerable thought in the goals I wish to achieve in the coming years. I believe that my original sentiment towards a system that is primarily catered to the affluent has changed to a hidden ambition of social justice, not only within the sphere of access to education but all services in general. In realizing that, at times, opportunities must be created, I explored the many avenues open to myself at the time. Since, I have enjoyed with great pleasure the past three and a half years that I've worked as a student law clerk with the law firm _____. I decided to venture this route, not because the employment was financially rewarding, but challenging in every aspect. My experience with this office has lent me valuable insight into the nature of the practice of law and the many possibilities open to those who hold law degrees. The senior partners of the firm, understanding both my ability to converse intellectually and my enthusiasm for law school admission, were eager to lend compounding responsibilities each year. My work ethic and my ability to react and think critically have been instrumental in dealing with clients, other lawyers, and fellow staff members. I have found the work challenging and intense since creative problem solving requires an educated degree of charisma and the desire to learn in a fast-paced environment.

The rejuvenated spirit that I had found following the disappointment of my first year of studies has been the fundamental building block in the evolution of my character. During my final year of studies at Carleton, I once again felt the emptiness of not being involved or challenged outside of a classroom. Prior to September, a friend who was acting as President of an organizing committee called the Undergraduate Business Games approached me for some aid and advice with the project. By mid-July, I was appointed the Vice-President of all Logistics' of an event that is recognized as Canada's foremost network-building intercollegiate business school activity.

This event presented me the opportunity to use all political and social tact that I had acquired in my studies within a very aggressive and demanding setting.

The event, responsible for bringing together over one thousand students from 21 universities across Canada for three days of interactive network development demanded a great deal of commitment and creative thought.

The non-profit event requires sponsorship generated from the corporate community. As VP of Logistics, my responsibilities included, but were not limited to, overseeing team arrival's, inter-city mobility, hotel liaison and general itinerary planner. The obvious humor is my distinct lack of experience or course related credentials in the area. This was later confirmed by other members of the executive and participants that it was my sincere passion for the task and organization that inevitably placed me in this leadership role. This was the same feeling I had felt in high school.

Opportunity.

I firmly believe that law school is the next logical step. While my results on the LSAT clearly do not reflect my ability to succeed in law school, I am confident that the admissions committee may look towards my dynamic character and individual strengths. This year away from studies has also given me the opportunity to reflect on my future goals and truly develop my character through other opportunities. While completing my application, I have been traveling through Western Europe, which I'm sure upon my return should have been included in this explanation of my character as truly the most inspirational. In January, I have been enrolled in taking both a Level 1 and 2 courses in mediation with the Center for Dispute Resolution in Ottawa-Carleton. Alternate Dispute Resolution is an area that I became very intrigued by in my undergraduate studies and will be an avenue I wish to pursue, considering it's positive effects in the areas of access to justice.

I urge you, the Admissions Committee, to take into consideration the contribution that I may bring to the Faculty and the profession through my passion for the discipline and my ability to articulate fundamental values and ideas necessary to foster insightful thought and discourse. Thank you for your consideration of my application to the Faculty of Law. I look forward to the opportunity to study law at your institution and would welcome the opportunity to discuss with the Admissions Committee, in person, regardless of time or expense, the merit of my application and the contribution that I could be to the Faculty.

Sample 18

According to Psychologist Abraham Maslow "What a man can be, he must be." The implication of his theory played a big part in my life. I am and am thirty-two years old. I am originally from Sri Lanka and my mother tongue is Tamil. I came to Canada six years ago in January 1995 with my husband and two small children. We came as political refugees and became citizens of Canada in 1999. I am presently working towards a Bachelor's Degree, majoring in psychology at York University. I am very interested in studying Law and am thus submitting my personal statement for your kind consideration.

I was born in Mannar in 1968, a small town in Sri Lanka, the third of three children. I was interested in studying Law from a very young age. My Aunt and Uncle who were both Lawyers gave me an initial interest in Law. They helped many people in the community and were well liked and respected. They became my role models. I developed a passion for their profession and promised myself to become a part of it. Attending university was not a natural step for all the students in my high school. Only five percent were admitted to the university and less than 1% of these were admitted to the law faculty. To enter the Law school you must have high grades in English (which was my second language) and be willing to move to the country's capital, Colombo, since it has the only Law School in Sri Lanka. I knew of all these hurdles but I was determined and committed to becoming a lawyer. My passion, motivation, hard work and commitment ultimately paid off when I was finally admitted for undergraduate study at the University of Colombo, Faculty of Law, in 1985.

I was a few steps away from fulfilling my dream. The situation in Sri Lanka became worse because of the war between the majority and minority communities. There were communal riots and insurgency to overthrow the government. I belonged to the minority community and became a target. The University was closed for most days, lectures were cancelled, and exams were postponed a number of times. I stayed at the Law school for two and a half years (1985 - 1988) and managed to finish the first year of the programme.

Frustrated with the situation, most of the students left the university and started working. In Sri Lanka you cannot do part time work and part time studies. You must either study or work full time. I decided to work since we did not have any lectures or exams. I worked for three years, first as an account executive for the Motorola pager company, and next as a ground handling agent for my country's national carrier, Air Lanka.

Even after three years things did not change or improve. I could see my dream fading away. It was frustrating to think that I had no control over my situation. In 1991, I married and decided to start a family. I had to put my dreams on hold. From 1991 to 1995 I was a homemaker and raised two children. In 1995, my husband and I decided to leave Sri Lanka when trouble came to our doorstep. We arrived in Canada in January 1995.

When we arrived in Canada my second daughter was only six months old. My husband and I decided that I should stay at home till she became two years old. In 1996 I started work at a bulk food store. I then moved to Japan

Camera and worked as a head printer. Although I was working and having a peaceful life in Canada, I still felt a void inside since I could not attain my dream of becoming a lawyer. One of my friends suggested that I do a legal secretary's course since I was interested in law. This made me think hard and I refused to accept that proposition. I started asking myself why I should become a legal secretary when my dream was to become a lawyer. I decided that I would not settle for second best. "What a man can be, he must be". So I decided to try for law school admission.

To pursue this goal I joined York University in 1998 so that I could try to get admission at Osgoode Hall Law School. I had mentioned this to the admission office in 1998 during my admission process (Copy attached). I knew the tough requirements for Law school and thus started working hard from the very first day itself at York University. It wasn't always easy being the mother of two active young children and trying to be a full time student. During my first year at York (after an 11 - year gap) I had to re-teach myself how to study, to learn, and to achieve my dreams again. My schedule was overwhelming at times. Most of the days I had to get up by 3 AM to finish my schoolwork before my children woke up. I have always been a self-motivated person, someone who enjoyed working hard to produce results. Thus, I took this as a challenge and did it. I received an above average GPA for my first two years, and I am really proud of my achievement.

My undergraduate studies have sharpened my capacity for critical thinking and strengthened the quality of my judgment. The courses, which ranged from philosophy to the economics of law, involved extensive reading and placed emphasis on developing verbal and written communication skills. Our professors challenged us to conduct research, write analytical essays, engage in class debates and make presentations. This experience has prepared me well for the real world where the ability to write well, analyze precisely, facilitate discussions and speak persuasively are essential skills.

I believe that acquiring an education entails a responsibility to contribute to society. My ethnic and racial background has given me insight into many problems in the Sri Lankan community. One of these is the problem faced by new immigrants. Being new to the country, the immigrants are afraid of Lawyers who are outside of their community. They are afraid and feel vulnerable due to their language and cultural differences. There is a large population of Sri Lankans in Canada, with few Sri Lankan Lawyers available to represent their interests. By studying Law, I will be able to effectively represent their interests and serve my community. My Christian faith also requires me to serve my community to the best of my ability.

I trust that I have been able to present sufficient evidence why I am so determined to continue my studies. I have worked as hard as I can to fulfill my dream. I believe that qualified people of all races should be represented in the legal profession, and given my aptitude, experience and desire to make a positive difference in my community, I will make a unique contribution to the Osgoode Hall Law School.

In summary, I will bring maturity, determination and seriousness of purpose to my legal studies. I have learned just how much one can do with solid, unwavering commitment, and I shall bring that dedication to Osgoode Hall if given the opportunity.

Thank you for considering my application. To be accepted by an institution such as Osgoode Hall would be an honor.

Sample 19

"The people who get on in this world are the people who get up and look for the circumstances they want and, if they can't find them, make them"

George Bernard Shaw

I left home at a very young age - 16 to be exact. My family was in turmoil. My father was drinking heavily and at times abusive. My mother was simply out of control and my sisters, well they were just too young to understand.

On the surface this was hard to believe, given it could be said that I came from the right side of the tracks. I had money, clothes, a roof over my head, what more could a teenager ask for?

In many ways, the life I stepped into was far worse than where I came from but I am proud to say that it was the most profound and influencing experience of my entire life. It literally shaped the person I have become and hopefully will shape the lives of my children.

I continued with my high school education and held part time jobs to support myself. Thing s changed quickly when I entered into a relationship that would last for the next 5 years. It was a time that was filled with physical and mental abuse, domination and control, manipulation and sadness. The environment I lived in exposed me to poverty, alcohol and drug abuse, and violence.

Through it all, I kept my focus on a promise to myself that I would not fail. My father's last words to me were that I would become "a resident" on the corner of Jarvis & Wellesley and I took that to be a challenge to succeed. I continued to go to high school and work as I learned very quickly the responsibilities of being on my own. To survive, I developed an ability to withdraw into myself and I become very immune to the pressures and influences that were a large part of my environment.

I had tried to leave many times but the emotional turmoil that I lived with had taken away my self-confidence and self-esteem. Everything changed when I learned I was pregnant. At 21, I was a single mother and now had someone else's life to fight for as well as my own. At the end, the violence got worse and we literally escaped into the night with the help of a very dear friend. I have taken what could have been an experience that ruined my life, and turned it into a driving force. That time taught me that a person's life and who they are is not shaped by their experiences, but how they choose to make use of what can be learned from them instead.

I refused to become part of the welfare system and planned a future for my son with the same focus and commitment that had gotten me through the past 5 years. I had to find a decent place for us to live. I became a member of the Board of Directors of the Duffin's Creek Co-Operative Housing Development. As this concept was in its initial phase it faced great opposition from the community. I attended Board meetings, Town Council meetings, lobbied the provincial government for approval and participated in the resident interviews. We resided in this complex and I stayed on the Board during it's 1st year of operation.

As for my professional life, I worked as a customer service representative and in public relations for the next 2 years and attended night school. These roles taught me how to communicate with others and the insight into effectively deal with opposing views and perceptions.

I had always had a fascination with the law and decided that was where I wanted my career to go. I entered the legal profession as a receptionist with a local law firm. I enrolled with the Institute of Law Clerks of Ontario as I saw this program as a challenging opportunity that would give me the knowledge and ultimately, the experience which would bring me closer to the practice of law. I spent the next 2 years going to night school and graduated with honours in 1991.

My first job as a law clerk was with the Metro Toronto Housing Authority, legal branch. My training and skills acquired in public relations became invaluable tools that I was able to use to enhance my abilities as a law clerk. I left public service to work with private firms in 1992.

My work history has provided me with practical legal experience and an opportunity to observe first hand the demands of being a lawyer. It has taught me how to deal with clients and their perceptions of lawyers and the law. I have worked with many different lawyers over the years and seen many different styles of practice. This has allowed me to assess both the good and the bad aspects. I have taken what I perceive as right and used this in my own professional development.

By far, the most important aspect of my career occurred when I decided to become self-employed. I successfully competed for acceptance into a self-employment program so I could learn the fundamentals of running a business.

For the past 3 years I have been working as an independent law clerk but I remain under the direct supervision of a lawyer. My services are designed to meet the individual needs and demands of each lawyer or firm that I work for. My objective is to be able to provide my clients with the opportunity to offer a more streamlined and cost-effective service to their clients. I am very aware of the issues surrounding the practice of a paralegal. I have taken great care in planning my business and in marketing my services to ensure that it is clear that I do not operate as a paralegal. My respect for the profession of law and what it stands for has guided me in this endeavor. I hold myself out to have the same principals and ethics that would be expected from a lawyer as it is very important to me to be able to provide my clients with a service that mirrors their profession.

My personal life also flourished as I continued to be faced with further personal and financial struggles. I am married and now have two boys ages 8 and 14. Although, my life has been filled with the responsibilities of working and being a parent, I have become involved with my community through volunteering with the various sporting associations that my sons participate in. I have also spent time volunteering at the schools my children have attended and am currently a member of the Student Activity Council (SAC) at our local catholic school.

I am confident that my personal experiences have provided me with the skills and training equivalent to the fundamentals of a university education. I have lived my life with resolve and determination to learn what I need in order to face every challenge, and to organize my thoughts and plan my actions so I may achieve the goals I have set. That is not to say that I have been successful each time, but I truly believe some of the best learning experiences come from failures. Discipline, hard work and commitment have been key to my personal and professional development.

It is difficult to put into to words the reasons why I want to a lawyer. My years of hardship and struggle have shown me what it was like to be disadvantaged and to be wronged by another. I know what it feels like to believe you are helpless and have no choices. As a result, I am driven to helping others and fighting for justice. Today, I stand with strength and conviction in my beliefs of what is right not only for myself but for others around me. As a reflection of this, I have recently volunteered my services to the Association in Defence of the Wrongfully Convicted. Should I be accepted at Osgoode Hall Law School I am looking forward to taking an active role in C.L.A.S.P.

I believe that the role of the law in society is to provide the rules for the playing field that we are on. As a part of society, I feel that everyone has a duty to be responsible and to live in a way that betters our communities and ourselves. I feel that the law provides an avenue whereby we can be held accountable for the choices we make and more importantly, the choices that are made by others. Everyone has the right to make their own decisions but with this right comes a responsibility for the outcome. The law attempts to be the guidelines in considering what is just together with a moral reflection. The lawyer's role is not to control and manipulate the rules for the benefit of another. It is to be the mediator; the person who can interpret and apply the law with the end result being the fulfillment of our own responsibilities to each other and to continue to develop a balanced society.

I have placed a great deal of thought into my decision to apply to Osgoode Hall Law School at this time. I fully realize and am able to accept the sacrifices that will be required of not only myself but also my family. I understand that I will be away from my family for periods of time and that there will be a substantial personal and financial commitment required from me if I am accepted at Osgoode Hall Law School. More importantly, I also know the personal rewards that can come from sacrifice.

I have looked upon my experiences with optimism and have transcended above my circumstances. The paths I have taken in my life have prepared me for where I am right now. Should I be given the privilege of studying law at Osgoode Hall Law School, I will continue with that same strength, conviction and focus.

Thank-you.

Sample 20

My name is _____ and I am twenty-three years old. My family and I are originally from Trinidad, West Indies, and since coming to Canada, I have been very involved in my school and cultural communities. This past June, I obtained my Honours B.A. from the University of Toronto with a Specialist in Management and a Minor in Women's Studies. I am interested in the study of law because my experiences as an immigrant, my community involvement and my undergraduate program have motivated me to want to make a difference in the lives of those people who are disadvantaged as a result of race, gender and/or socio-economic situation. A legal education from the University of Ottawa's Faculty of Law would provide me with the necessary tools to accomplish this goal.

I have always taken my academic career seriously, but unfortunately, there was a period in which I encountered difficulties as a result of external circumstances. Throughout high school, I was a member of the Honour Roll and graduated as an Ontario Scholar. These achievements earned me an Entrance Scholarship from the University of Toronto. However, my first two years at university proved to be extremely challenging. In my first year, due to financial necessity, my father moved to the Caribbean in order to work. We had always been a really close-knit family of four, and my dad's departure was a major disruption to our family, and to me personally. The true effects of this were felt during my second year, which was emotionally difficult. Even though I was beginning to cope with the added workload at university, I still felt lost and confused, and at times, the situation seemed hopeless. However, I called on my inner resolve and persevered, knowing that this was only a temporary situation. Unfortunately, my grades had already suffered.

In addition to my family situation, the area in which I lived was also causing me stress. Although I had lived in this housing complex for nine years, it had gotten progressively worse during my first two years at university. There was an influx of drug traffickers, which led to loud music being played day and night, open drug dealing, and eventually, gun shots.

In the summer before I began my third year, we moved to Ajax and my whole outlook on life improved. I returned to school determined to get the most out of my university education. It was during this time that I became interested in Women's Studies, and decided to pursue a minor in this program. Through Women's Studies, I learned about the plight of women from diverse cultures. However, my moment of awakening occurred when I took Gender Issues in the Law and was immediately intrigued by the various ways in which the law affects women's lives. I knew that this was something that I would like to investigate further.

Community involvement is a very important aspect of my life. From 1998 to 1999, I was the Membership Commissioner for the Kinara Society - a black students' association at the University of Toronto at Scarborough. This position required a commitment of at least ten hours each week from May to April in order to attend Sunday meetings, plan and organize social events, contact club members, and liaise with similar clubs at other universities. This experience allowed me to interact with other black university students, but I also came to the realization that the number of blacks in university is not representative of the number in the general population. I decided that I would work with disadvantaged black children, so that they would realize the importance of a university education and have the self-confidence to eventually break the cycle of poverty.

In 1999, I began to volunteer with Tropicana Community Services Organization's tutorial programme. From October to June each year, I tutor a grade school class in order to bring their performance up to grade level in Math and English. This requires a commitment of an average of seven hours per week because not only do I tutor each Saturday, I must also plan and prepare the curriculum for the upcoming week. My students are the children of immigrants, and many are underprivileged. Unfortunately, these children do not have many positive role models, and once I saw the impact that I was having on them as a mentor, I decided to continue to tutor the same group of children each year, so that they will have some consistency in their lives.

For many immigrants, the transition from their native country to Canada may prove to be difficult. In the case of refugees, they may require legal services in order to settle their immigration matters. My Women's Studies background has also made me aware of some women who flee their lands for fear of persecution, such as in the case of female genital mutilation. My role will be to provide legal services to those immigrants who may need it, and also to defend the rights of people who are discriminated against on the basis of race or gender. I believe that as a black woman and an immigrant, I will be able to tend to these people's needs in a sensitive manner.

I am interested in attending the University of Ottawa's Faculty of Law because I can use my experiences to contribute a lot to the school community, and in return, the school can provide me with a legal education that is comparative to no other. Since I am interested in human rights law, the University of Ottawa is my choice because of its commitment to human rights research - as evidenced by the Human Rights Centre - and its encouragement of diversity. I have demonstrated that I am capable of overcoming adversity and succeeding. I am a woman who knows the importance of community involvement as a way to make a positive contribution and to better the lives of the disadvantaged. I will extend this conviction to my legal career, and armed with an LL.B. from the University of Ottawa in conjunction with my life experiences, I will have what it takes to make a difference!

Sample 21

I am _____, a twenty-two year old currently enrolled in my fourth year of study at the _____. I will be graduating in April of _____ with an Honours Bachelor of Arts Degree, majoring in Economics with a minor in Political Science. I believe that my education and personal experiences have prepared me for the study of law at _____ Faculty of Law.

The pursuit of higher education has always been a high priority in my family. Growing up in rural _____, my parents never had the opportunity to pursue higher education. My father did not thrive in a formal education setting, leaving school before graduating. Despite my father's lack of a formal education, he has gone on to enjoy a fulfilling life. He has successfully created his own home renovations business in _____. My parents have recognized that I have an ability to excel at school. They continue to give me the tremendous amount of support and encouragement necessary to recognize the value of an education. I am inspired to continue with my education at _____ Faculty of Law by the examples set by my parents every day.

As a result of studying economics and political science at the _____, I have been able continue to develop my critical analysis and research skills through examinations of such issues as banking policies in Canada and unemployment strategies in Ontario. Similar to the law, economic and political concerns permeate through many aspects of our society. Studying these complex issues has helped to develop my critical thinking skills and research techniques. By analysing the multi-faceted demands of economics and politics, I have developed a better understanding of the decision-making processes that governments and businesses must engage in if they are to achieve their goals.

My undergraduate work has helped me prepare for the intensified study of law at _____. I have learned to manage my life between my full-time academic schedule, community service commitments, and my personal relationships. I am confident in my abilities to manage the psychological pressures associated with the study of law.

Community involvement continues to be an important component of my character. I would like to apply my values, coupled with knowledge of the law and legal system, in order to improve my community. My involvement with the YMCA-YWCA of _____ over the past 3 years, has provided me with the greatest sense of giving back to my community. I have been elected twice to the post as a member of the Board of Directors for the _____ largest YMCA-YWCA in the country. In the history of the organization, I am the only person below the age of twenty-seven to hold this position. Of the current Board, I am the only person below the age of forty. The Y has provided me with the means to help give back to the community which has been generous to my family. My _____ required the help of the Y through their _____ Program. I have twice chaired a committee that implemented a new style of annual fundraising that is designed to provide support for programs such as _____. Through my participation on the Board of Directors of the YMCA-YWCA, I feel that I am able to make a measurable difference in many peoples' lives.

I believe that communication is a key component to the study of law. Throughout my university career I have written many papers on complicated issues. These experiences have allowed me to improve my written argumentative techniques. While I enjoy written communication, I am passionate about public speaking. This passion started when I was a member of my high school Debating team and flourished when I was appointed to the _____District School Board as a Student Trustee in my final year of high school. My final duty as a Trustee was to address a dinner commemorating the teaching accomplishment of all retiring staff in the district. I poured my heart and soul into writing a speech that would be memorable. Returning to my seat after the speech, I was met with handshakes of congratulations from Trustees and Superintendents, of whom remarked that they had never seen the Director of Education upstaged before, let alone by a student. On my way out of the event, dozens of teachers stopped me to thank me for my remarks. Even weeks later I received phone calls of appreciation from teachers I had never met, from schools of which I had never heard. I will never forget that feeling of accomplishment, which made me truly understand the power of language. I hope to use my communication skills to concisely convey complex legal issues and arguments, indispensable skills in any aspect of the legal profession.

My Law School Admission Test experience was a tumultuous one. I wrote the LSAT exam for the first time on _____. Unfortunately on the day of the exam, I failed to perform to the best of my abilities. This placed me in the very uncompetitive 47th percentile. Resolved that I was going to fulfill my dream of attending law school, I immediately registered to take the LSAT again at the next available sitting. On my second attempt at the LSAT, I improved my score to 154, which places me in the 63rd percentile. I have mixed feelings towards this LSAT score. One the one hand, I improved my score by an amount outside the normal 3-point range and improved my percentile ranking significantly. On the other hand, this score is not as competitive as I would have desired. In the dozen or more practice test I wrote under strict time constraints, I never scored below 158. I am disappointed that I did not perform as well as I had anticipated. Regrettably, I will not be able to rewrite the LSAT exam during this admission period as the December test date conflicts with my examination schedule and the February test date is unfortunately timed with my academic programme. My purpose in writing this section is not to challenge the validity of the LSAT, but rather to illustrate that my LSAT scores do not entirely portray my abilities. The consistency of my academic performance at a high level, while simultaneously being active in my community, illustrates that I have the intellectual ability to succeed at the study of law.

My ultimate career goals are not limited to the field of law. Rather, I plan to apply my personal values, life experiences, and education to the practice of politics. Politics seems to be a natural progression for my commitment to society. I want to be a part of the process that makes public policies that positively affect peoples' lives.

I have been politically active in the _____ Party for the past six years as a volunteer, both at the Federal and Provincial level. As a volunteer, I worked with the local party leadership to help recruit members and raise awareness of our party's philosophy. During election campaigns, I perform many different functions to assist in the campaign including door-to-door campaigning, office work, setting up signs across the city, and many other duties. The political arena is one in which leadership, personal values, and vision can be applied to a nation. I hope for the chance to express my ideas and values in an electoral forum. I know it sounds naive, but I want my chance to help create a more just society, applying the fundamental principles I will gain by participating in the community at _____ Faculty of Law.

For as long as I can remember, I have wanted to be a lawyer. I am drawn to the study of law for a romantic reason: using the power of language to argue a point in the pursuit of justice. Throughout my life, I have experienced the power of language. The study of law and politics would be a way for me to use language and the application of values as a means to help establish a sense of justice. I know it is idealistic and a romanticized version of reality, but we all have to start somewhere. At a major milestone along my chosen path, I anxiously await the Faculty of Law's decision on my application.

Sample 22

"What this power is I cannot say; all I know is that it exists and it becomes available only when a man is in that state of mind in which he knows exactly what he wants and is fully determined not to quit until he finds it."

Alexander Graham Bell.

The pursuit of the study and practice of law has been a genuine, life-long goal for me. My academic background as well as my distinct life experiences have led me to an interest in the University of ————— to successfully complete its full-time program in the study of law. (*I inserted a personal message to each specific university here.*) My strong academic foundation would be an asset to the University of —————. I have maintained excellent grades while working part-time and volunteering throughout the academic year. Scholarships and a placement on the Dean's Academic Achievement List each year have recognized my major accomplishments. I attribute this success to an intense interest in and commitment to my academic endeavors.

My expansive educational background has equipped me with the necessary tools for success in law school. First, my undergraduate program in Psychology has allowed me to develop critical judgment, strengthen my debating skills, fortify my leadership qualities and attain teamwork expertise. I have learned that people are diverse and complicated entities and working successfully with them requires understanding, not only of others but also of one's self. Second, my special interest courses in History have provided me with a unique context for the study of law in Canada. Finally, my educational interests also extend to an appreciation for the fine arts. Studying the piano at the Royal Conservatory of Music as well as the violin through private lessons has provided me with a form of self-expression as well as an unreserved educational experience.

I am an extremely focused and dedicated person as a result of several distinct life experiences. I was challenged at a young age by a serious medical condition that required both the commitment and support of my entire family as well as the determination and inner strength to undergo several years of intense treatment and therapy. By overcoming such diversity I have been able to experience a resolve of self-worth and conviction, thus learning the true meaning of success.

One of my most exciting experiences was the pursuit of international culture and travel. Without previous training, I entered a modeling contest and won a contract with a leading international modeling agency. Throughout this venturesome commitment I have lived and worked independently in countries such as Japan and the United States as well as Canada, developing such personal attributes as diplomacy and the appreciation of cultural diversity. I have learned a great deal about myself and of my true potential.

I am also committed to influencing positive changes within my community. I have volunteered in several community-oriented programs. While assisting in a number of elementary school classrooms, I realized a need for volunteers in a "Before-and-After" School Program in my community. I was motivated to initiate volunteer involvement in the program because of its importance to the many families it served. The experiences I have had in working with young children have given me the opportunity to apply my leadership abilities as well as an expression of compassion, creativity, and imagination.

I am very proud to admit that my commitment to community outreach programs continues to this day. Specifically, I volunteer at York University by taking notes for several classmates who suffer from disabilities. These students rely on me to help provide them with equal access to educational opportunity in a society where, despite our best efforts, inequalities often persist.

My professional experiences have also helped develop my aspirations to follow a career in law. Specifically, one of my greatest career experiences has been working as the only non-postgraduate law student at a prestigious labour relations law firm. I was extremely motivated and inspired this past summer and therefore decided to continue my work part-time throughout the academic year. The practical knowledge I have gained there has provided me with a new perspective of the legal profession and has confirmed this as my career goal.

My academic background and distinct experiences have taken me to a point in my life where I am motivated and determined to meet the demands of the study of law. I cannot imagine a more noble profession than one that is determined to uphold the basic rights and freedoms of every person. Alexander Graham Bell once said that one could only attain the power to achieve one's goals if "he knows exactly what he wants and is fully determined not to quit until he finds it." I have found it.

Sample 23

"The best way to find yourself is to lose yourself in the service of others."

> - 'Mahatma''Mohandas Karamchand Gandhi.

This quote is one of the most influential and stirring that I have ever come across. It reminds me of the road I have travelled to get to where I am today, it inspires me to travel down new paths in life to get to where I am going, and it humbles me. I have made mistakes in my life; I have experienced the sorrow and pain life offers, and the joy and excitements that each day brings. I believe that it is only when you learn from your mistakes that you can truly begin living.

There are many ways to define who I am. My name is _____ _____; I am thirty-two years of age. I am a single parent, the survivor of a violently abusive marriage; I am a student, a friend, and a daughter.

Describing the essence of who I am in a letter is a difficult task. My academic background is a colourful one, influenced by a teenage marriage and a return to academia more than thirteen years later. The failure of the marriage is not a surprising one, what is surprising is the journey of finding myself and what it has taught me. I have been raising three children for the last fifteen years; I have little professional or volunteer experience, but I believe my life experiences have given me insight of incredible magnitude and that they will continue to do so in coming years.

The decision to return to school was not a difficult one; although the process was arduous then resulting experiences have been valuable. I am a high school dropout, however, this has not deterred me from reaching my goals. I attended an upgrading program through Durham College and subsequently enrolled in a college level program. Only after achieving excellent grades did I realize I wanted to go farther than this program I had chosen would enable me. I enrolled at Trent University as a Psychology major and I have had continued success in my academic endeavours.

It is this background in psychology; along with my life experiences, that have lead me to apply to law school. I have an intense interest in purusing an education that specializes in criminal law. My goal is to some day attain a position with the Attorney General's Office as a Crown Prosecutor, specializing in domestic violence and abuse cases. I feel strongly that my undergraduate degree in psychology, combined with my life experience, has prepared me well for a life of working to ensure that justice is served so that barriers to a safe and happy life such as domestic abuse are eliminated. If I can help just one person realize that they can achieve their dreams and live without fear then I believe that I will have accomplished something meaningful.

Osgoode Hall Law School is the only law school to which I have applied. The level of success that Osgoode graduates have achieved, combined with a curriculum that is, in my opinion, unequalled by that of any other law school is what has made Osgoode Hall Law School my one and only choice for an education in law. That Osgoode offers considerable flexibility and innovation, while providing a solid foundation for a legal education, is a main attraction. The intensive program in criminal law, as well as the Community and Legal Aid Services Program are of particular interest to me. I look forward with anticipation to dedicating time and effort to CLASP, principally in the women's division, should I be fortunate enough to attend Osgoode Hall Law School in the future.

My Access supplementary form explains in greater detail many of the points I have mentioned in this letter. I believe my grades speak for themselves. I have written the October 2001 Law School Admission Test and, although I scored in the range required for consideration in both the Mature Student and Access categories, I will be rewriting the LSAT again in December 2001. I do not feel my mark is an accurate reflection of my abilities and I wish to improve my score for personal reasons.

I believe that, in the future, I could make a significant contribution to the legal profession as a whole. I feel that my experiences, my drive and determination, combined with an immense desire to help those around me, make me a strong candidate for admission to Osgoode Hall Law School. I have confidence that not only do I possess the motivation and academic ability to succeed in law school, but that by practising a career in the legal profession I will help benefit society by continuing my responsibilities to my community.

I would like to thank you for your time in considering my application.

Sample 24

I made the decision to apply to _____ after many years of interest in how our political and legal institutions resolve fundamental issues in our society. The 1993 federal election sparked what would become both a personal and academic interest in the questions that surround contemporary Canadian democracy. Though I have always enjoyed school, it was not until I began the pursuit of an undergraduate political science degree that I found the field of study that I truly and enthusiastically enjoyed, that is, the area wherein politics and law overlap. Constitutions, human rights, criminology and the influence of lawyers and the law upon society are of particular interest to me. I look forward to studying these subjects in much greater detail as a law student, particularly how court decisions shape the society we inhabit and how systemic inequities are addressed by cogent thought and practice.

I am confident that both my work and school experiences have prepared me for success in the study of law. At the end of the current winter semester, I will have completed all of the course requirements for a degree in political science. If it is necessary for my acceptance into law school, I will enroll in summer courses to take the remaining 1.5 electives to finish the degree. The program places a strong emphasis on developing the ability to both critically analyze and persuasively articulate ideas and arguments. My grades reflect the development of these skills, which I expect will be a valuable asset to me as a law student.

Since the age of 16, I have worked in industries as diverse as hospitality and real estate. While working for a real estate corporation over the past three years, I assisted in the sale of upscale Toronto condominiums and in the administration of a busy sales office. In addition, my ongoing experience working with lawyers to develop pension law software is giving me valuable experience interpreting Ontario statutes and should be excellent preparation for a more detailed study of law.

My extracurricular experiences in campus, provincial, and federal politics over the years have been very rewarding. As a member of several campus political associations, I have developed leadership and teamwork skills that I hope to bring to the University community at _____. I also pride myself on my skills as a public speaker, as I have addressed audiences as large as two thousand people at the invitation of my local M.P.P.

I believe that my academic, work and extracurricular experience make me an excellent candidate for the privilege and responsibility of acceptance into Law School. Thank you for considering my application.

Sample 25

Just recently when my mother was going through her filing cabinets she came across my grade 1 report card. In reviewing it, the teacher commented that I had a tendency to talk more than was necessary. This trait, one which all my teachers throughout both elementary and secondary school thought would lead that an incident occurred which I think has had a fairly large influence on me. As a member of a soccer team that had worked extremely hard all season, we lost the most important soccer game I had ever played up to that point in the championships by an unfair decision made by an obviously partial official.

I think it is funny how events which seem so minor can have such a major impact on one's life. My parents always taught me that you can either be part of the problem or part of the solution and so I decided to become a soccer referee myself the next year at the young age of twelve. By 2000, I was recognized as a senior soccer official within the York Region Soccer Referees Association, and was scheduled routinely to officiate games involving men, women, as well as older teenagers. To say that there was immense pressure on me as an official in some of the games I had to officiate is an understatement. I took great pride in being a soccer official and took my responsibilities very seriously, and this could be part of the reason why I was given the privilege of refereeing some of the most competitive games in the province at several Ontario Cup championship tournaments.

Extracurricular involvement has broadened my experiences and strengthened my leadership skills. Aside from refereeing soccer for eight years and playing competitively for the majority of my life and every year while at secondary school, I was a retreat leader for several years and participated in over 40 hours of community service in conjunction with the Religion department. I was also captain of our Law team, which was victorious in both the regional and provincial championships in 1998. I was chosen to prepare the opening and closing statements for the final mock trial, and the exhilaration I felt when our team won is indescribable and only served to strengthen my resolve to pursue a career in law.

In my last year of high school, I was asked by one of my teachers to participate in an accredited physical education class that allowed us to work with those who were physically and/or mentally delayed. I saw how people, when severely challenged, rise above circumstance with support and encouragement. The gratification I felt at the end of the year when I saw the progress that was made by the students was incredible, and becoming friends with students I probably would not have been in much contact with otherwise taught me a valuable lesson: it is only when we allow ourselves to experience new things do we grow as people and become more aware individuals. Wanting to experience something different and exciting was part of the reason why I chose to study at Bishop's University for my undergraduate degree. I entered the school knowing nobody, and will leave knowing that if I decide to travel anywhere across Canada or around the world, I will have a place to stay with a fellow Bishop's student that I met and became friends with over the course of my time there. Another aspect of Bishop's that appealed to me was the close-knit atmosphere in which students and professors would be able to get to know one another. This small atmosphere has enabled me to get involved in things that I have a passion for, from hockey coach, a member of numerous intramural sports teams, resident assistant, school newspaper columnist to vice-president of the student council. In these capacities at Bishop's, I have been able to grow socially, personally, and academically.

Being a resident assistant in my second year at Bishop's allowed me the opportunity to draw on my leadership skills. This experience taught me a great deal about myself, as well as how to handle the most delicate and personal situations one could deal with. These situations involved students of different backgrounds and academic and social strengths, which made it more challenging. The main responsibilities of the job were to always be available whether to offer peer counseling on academic or personal matters; to act as an information source; to assist with emergencies, and to provide leadership in areas such as human relations, conflict management and mutual respect. In this role, I was able to work with the heads of security, housing and food administrators, as well as health services to ensure that my residents had a safe and fun time at Bishop's while in residence.

This year I am serving as Vice-President on Bishop's University's Student Representative Council. This elected position not only entails organizing events, but also heading several student safety committees, and being an ex-officio member of the Committee on the Life of the University. I am the chair of the Department of Internal Affairs and as one of only five student executive members at the school, this experience will continue to strengthen my organizational abilities, enhance my interpersonal skills, and my managerial capabilities. Along with being a member of the executive council, I will be writing for the school newspaper, The Campus, as a freelance sports writer while taking a full course load in this, my final year.

My interest in politics has led me to pursue a minor in political science and criminology to go along with my major in sociology. My program, while intellectually demanding, is both rewarding and invigorating. The small class sizes allow students to have open debates and discussions about the material being covered, and often time they are continued with after class. My studies at Bishop's have sharpened my capacity for critical thinking, strengthened the quality of my judgment and heightened my understanding of society and the way it functions. These are just some of the skills that I believe have prepared me well for the upcoming challenges I will face if given the opportunity to pursue law at _____.

My strong self-discipline has served me well allowing me not only to maintain my scholarship throughout my years at Bishop's, but to also be able to pursue outside interests as well. I am confident that my undergraduate program with its emphasis on rigorous reading, writing and analyzing has provided me with an excellent preparation for the demands of law school. Having been involved in extra-curricular activities and successful in positions of responsibility, I intend to continue to be an active member in campus life while pursuing the study of law at _____. I am confident that I have the abilities that will enable me to succeed at law school and in my career as a legal professional.

Thank you for considering this application. I look forward to the opportunity to study law at _____ and to contributing to the school and class in a most positive manner.

Sample 26

Learning Italian has always been an extraordinary passion for me. During the summer of 2000, I was given the opportunity to study Italian at Middlebury College, an institution renowned for providing the most demanding and effective language immersion program in the world. My Middlebury experience not only dramatically improved my language skills in Italian, but it strengthened my confidence and learning strategies. It was at Middlebury that I developed my true inner will to study, and my abilities to think, decide and express myself independently, tools for success that I would be able to apply in any other facet of life. As a personal intellectual challenge which I saw through to fruition, I came to realise the extent of my academic potential as a student and was awarded with the Director Prize for Academic Excellence(22). I realised that the intense and competitive atmosphere of Middlebury is what motivated me to excel. With this wider vision of knowledge and learning, I returned to the University of Toronto, eager to continue my Italian and European Studies. My study of Italian was a continuous process of development and refinement and my commitment and perseverance were critical in achieving the highest level of proficiency. My language education has instilled in me an ability to critique and has sharpened my understanding of the analytical process. These skills will prove to be invaluable in the study of law, an academic discipline rooted in the fluidity and precision of language. Also, as I commence my fourth year of university, I now have a greater awareness of the linguistic reality of our society and to this end the potential value of my competence in the Italian language. My ability to communicate in Italian has helped me become a well-rounded individual and an effective communicator in the Italian-Canadian community. Particularly valuable to me was my experience this past summer with World Youth Day(12). I was engaged in this international event as a language service volunteer. My mastery of the Italian language allowed me to help bridge the communications gap for the visiting Italian pilgrims.

I have always possessed a profound respect for human dignity. This respect stemmed from my own participation, on a personal level, with my elderly grandmother. Having had my grandmother reside with my family, I was confronted with the inevitable reality of aging and its inherent patterns and problems. My grandmother's life was slowly taken over by human frailty and dependence, and as a result my life became a test of mental and physical resistance. At a young age, I came to a deeper, personal understanding of the human condition and of life itself. My family and I felt it particularly important to ensure my grandmother with conditions that would allow for her to grow old with dignity. When her health dramatically deteriorated, we were forced to place her in a home where she spent the final stages of her life. It was in this social context that I gained a deeper awareness of the position of the elderly in our society. I personally witnessed socially isolated elderly people in need of good medical care and other supportive services and felt compelled to contribute actively. I began to volunteer at the Trillium Health Care Centre(11) on a weekly basis and continued my services for two years. Visiting with the patients, I directly contributed to their well-being and helped in preserving their quality of life. In turn, I recognized the complex interplay between good systems of health and social support, and basic human rights. It became clear to me that I would be fulfilled as an individual defending the rights of others.

I now recognize the complex interplay between good systems of health and social support, and basic human rights. By making this conscious effort to acknowledge and appreciate these people, it was my intent to directly contribute to their social well-being and preserve their quality of life. These experiences played a role in my personal growth and the forging of my character. I began to perceive the strength and determination I possessed, and how fulfilled I felt as an individual when I defended the rights of others.

Today, my desire to help others is not static, but an active force. Motivated by a sense of communal duty, I took the initiative, and now devote time and energy to organizations in my local parish that are actively engaged in just this task. I began my involvement as a Lector(13). As such, it is my objective to deliver effectively the word of God to all types of people, because true human dignity can only be achieved in community. In addition to promoting the common good, as a lector I continue to strengthen my skills as a confident communicator. Also, I have just recently been commissioned as a Eucharistic Minister for my local parish(13). Through my ministry I have renewed my interior commitment to serve. I am now a conscious and active participant extending community care and concern to the poor, the disabled, the elderly, the sick, and the homebound members of society. I have come to fully respect others in all their diversity, and through my societal involvement, it is my aim to challenge the structures of injustice by affirming a sense of peace and equality. Guided by a strong moral compass, I believe that I have grown to be a confident and resourceful leader in my community, and as a result this ministry has become a natural extension of me.

My commitment to educational development has also been extended outside of the formal school setting, and it is these self-directed ventures in the professional field which have enriched the texture of my life and have cultivated my capacity as a critical thinker and leader. What began as summer employment at the Islingtion Kumon Centre(1), developed into a long-term opportunity which I maintained with interest and focus for nine years. Kumon, being the world's largest supplementary education provider for students, allowed me to actively guide the overall achievement of young children enrolled in our centre. Exposed to this complex interrelation of individuals, it was my duty, as Assistant Supervisor, to listen actively and think creatively in order to solve problems in a constructive way. Not only did I act as an instructor and observer of the students, but also as a medium of communication between the students and their parents. With a position of such responsibility, I was faced with multiple demands which needed to be met with composure and a professional attitude. Kumon provided me with a solid base of skills which I would soon employ as a legal assistant at the law firm of _____.

Immersed in the intense law environment, I am constantly faced with new stimulating challenges and an exciting opportunity to gain hands-on application in this field. Presented with a wide-ranging set of duties which involves drafting letters, pleadings and other legal documents, my effective research capabilities and skill in writing prove to be vital. In my legal interactions with clients it is crucial that I think objectively and analytically, and in turn, I have developed superior communication skills and effective thinking strategies. I am one who takes great pride in what I do, and the demanding atmosphere of the firm motivates me further to take initiative and perform with diligence, resulting in a higher quality of work. Interacting closely with a team of Personal Injury lawyers and their diverse cliental, I now recognize the wider benefits of a law degree with its intrinsic social and ethical dimensions. By impacting all corners of society, law can provide innovative responses to the world's ever-changing needs. It is clear to me that a degree in law involves direct interaction with real people and real problems. In turn, it is only through the successful completion of legal undertakings that society is ensured deserved access to justice.

My personal endeavours have not only broadened my individual scope, but more importantly, developed in me a moral strength and an enthusiasm to be a life-long learner. A degree in law would nourish my understanding of human institutions and values and supply me with the essential skills to make a profound impact on society.

Since you are "Law School Bound™" you will be interested to know about John Richardson's live seminars:

▶ *LSAT Prep Courses*
▶ *Law School Bound Seminars*
▶ *Personal Statement Workshops*

Can't make a live seminar? Continue your journey to law school with John Richardson's LSAT text:

▶ *Mastering The LSAT: How To Prepare Effectively And Successfully*
ISBN: 0969629036

(Available at your local university bookstore, Indigo, Chapters, Amazon.com and Indigo.ca)

Have a friend or family member interested in MBA, Medical School or Graduate School? The Richardson Prep Centre also offers live:

▶ *GMAT Prep Courses*
▶ *GRE Prep Courses*
▶ *MCAT Prep Courses*

For Complete Information visit:
www.lawschoolbound.com
www.richardson-prep.com

▶ *416-410-7737*

Chapter 15

The Personal Statement Workbook - Tools To Develop Your Personal Statement

Developing The Personal Statement - The Workbook

An earlier chapter of this book was designed to teach you what a personal statement and autobiographical sketch are about. The purpose of this chapter is to help you develop your own personal statement. This will be done in two stages. Stage 1 provides you with a "Personal Statement Gameplan." Stage 2 provides you with the "Personal Statement Workbook" which has been designed to help you research the most difficult and interesting topic of all - yourself.

Stage 1. The Personal Statement Gameplan - The Process

Personal Statement Development - The Nine Essential Steps

(This "Gameplan" will refer to various tools. These tools are part of the Personal Statement Toolbox and will be introduced below.)

1. Begin early. The complete application process can be as much work as an extra half course in university.

2. Research the school. Try to determine what the school is trying to achieve by admitting its first year class. What kinds of students is the school looking for? This information may be found in the school's calendar of information (pay attention to the dean's message), the LSAT Registration Book and the school's website. (Use Tool 1 in the Personal Statement Toolbox.)

3. Research the application categories available to you. All schools have a "regular category." Many schools have "residual categories." These are called "mature student" or "access", etc. If you are applying in something other than the regular category, think about how to justify your application in that category. How do the various application categories further the school's admissions policies? (Use Tool 2 in the Personal Statement Toolbox.)

4. Research yourself using this Personal Statement Workbook. There are three steps.

   (i) Complete the Comprehensive Applicant Questionnaire (Tool 3 in the Personal Statement Toolbox) provided.

   (ii) Arrange for others to complete Third Party Questionnaire (Tool 4 in the Personal Statement Toolbox) provided.

   (iii) Complete the Applicant Inferential Imaging Exercise (Tool 5 in the Personal Statement Toolbox) provided.

5. Think about how to link yourself to the application category and the school's general admissions objectives.

6. Write a first draft. Put the first draft away for a few days. Look at it again and write another draft.

7. Circulate the draft of the personal statement along with the Third Party Personal Statement Questionnaire (Tool 6 in the Personal Statement Toolbox) provided.

8. Rewrite and continue to circulate the draft statement along with the Third Party Personal Statement Questionnaire (Tool 6 in the Personal Statement Toolbox) until you are satisfied.

9. Produce a final copy for each school that is suitable for framing. Not only should it be well written, but it should look beautiful.

Stage 2. The Personal Statement Workbook - Getting To Know You!

Applicants often have difficulty writing personal statements because they have not thought sufficiently about themselves, what is important to them, and their goals. It is difficult to think about yourself. In order to assist in this process I have created six tools to be used during various stages of the development process. Tools 1 and 2 focus on the school. Tools 3 to 6 focus on the applicant.

Introducing The Personal Statement Toolbox

The toolbox contains the following tools:

Tool 1. School Research Exercise -

Purpose: To determine what the schools are looking for in applicants.

Tool 2. Category Identification Exercise -

Purpose: To help you determine the appropriate application category for you.

Tool 3. Comprehensive Applicant Questionnaire -

Purpose: To help you focus on yourself.

Tool 4. Third Party Questionnaire -

Purpose: To seek the input of third parties and to learn how they see you.

Tool 5. Applicant Inferential Imaging Exercise -

Purpose: To help you identify facts that will result in the reader receiving positive and relevant images about you.

Tool 6. Third Party Personal Statement Questionnaire -

Purpose: To obtain ongoing "feedback" about your personal statement. This "feedback" is to be used to improve and rework successive drafts.

Each of these six tools will be used at various stages in the Personal Statement Gameplan.

Introducing The Tools Individually

These tools are to be used as directed in the process described above. Each tool is to be used as an aid for a specific step in the personal statement development process. Tools 1, 2, 3 and 5 are to be completed by the applicant. Tools 4 and 6 are to be given to third parties to complete. They are then to be returned to assist the applicant.

Tool 1: School Research Exercise - Getting To Know The Schools

Take a separate piece of paper for each school. By using the calendar of information, the dean's message, the LSAT Registration Book, the application form and any other material you have, identify any:

- statement(s) about how the school sees itself;

- statement(s) about the objective of the admissions policy;

- statement(s) about any special programs that the school offers;

- statement(s) about anything that suggests the school is unique

in any particular way.

Tool 2: Application Category Identification Exercise - Discovering Additional Marketing Opportunities

Different schools have different applicant categories. For example, the "mature student" category is common. Each different category provides a new and different opportunity for direct marketing.

Take a separate piece of paper for each school. For each specific school list:

- the category by label

- determine exactly what makes one eligible to apply in that category at that particular school

- determine how the category further the school's admissions objectives as a whole

- assess whether you are eligible to apply in that category

- consider whether it makes good sense for you to consider applying in that category (would you be more or less competitive?)

Tool 3: Comprehensive Applicant Questionnaire - Getting To Know You

These questions are to be completed by the applicant. It is impossible that the answer to every question would be directly relevant to every personal statement. Nevertheless, the questions will help you explore the various dimensions of your life. Do not attempt to incorporate the answers to every question into your personal statement.

Geographic Origins

1. Were you born outside North America? If so, under what circumstances did you arrive in North America?

2. Is your mother tongue a language other than English? If so, at what age and under what circumstances did you learn English? Do you speak a language other than English at home?

3. Do you consider yourself to be a member of an ethnic or religious minority. If so, in what way(s) are you active in that community? How has your minority status made it easier or harder for you to achieve your goals?

Economic Circumstances

4. What were the economic circumstances of you and your family? Have you had the financial support of your family during your university years? Were you required to work while attending university? If so, how much? Can you think of any way(s) in which your family's economic circumstances created or restricted opportunities for you?

General Considerations - The Holistic Approach

5. How many languages do you speak? What are they? Where were they learned?

6. Do you participate in sports? If so, in what way and how much? Have you been on a university sports team?

How much of your time have you devoted to this? Why is participation in sports important to you and how has it contributed to your life? Have you received any recognition in the form of awards?

7. Do you play any musical instruments? What? For how long? Have you received any certificates that recognize your proficiency? In what way does playing a musical instrument enhance your life?

8. Are you a member of or an active participant in any religious organizations? In what capacity? Why is this participation important to you and how has it contributed to your life?

9. Are reading and learning important to you? If so, what is your favorite book? Describe a course that made a major contribution to your life. Why was this book or course important to you?

10. Have you made any contribution to the university community and/or your community at large? In what capacity? List three things that you have done for the sole benefit of somebody else.

11. Have you had the opportunity to travel? Where and for how long? How did your travel experience help to shape your understanding of the world and your understanding of others? Is there any way in which your travel experience(s) have contributed to your interest in law?

12. Reflect on your history of employment and/or self-employment. List every job and determine what that job taught you beyond the requirements of the job. (For example, being a sales clerk will teach you things about human nature that extend beyond sales.) What was your worst job? What was your best job? Why? Are there any special skills that you learned which may help you in other jobs or in law school? In what way(s) has your employment history contributed to your interest in law school?

13. Each of us has our share of successes and failures. Describe two failures and describe what you learned from each of those failures. Describe two successes and describe what you learned from each of those successes.

14. Have there been any unusually difficult periods in your life? (For example: illness, family problems, divorce, etc.) If so, did the difficulties adversely affect your academic or work performance? Have the difficulties been resolved? In what way did the manner in which you coped with the difficulties teach you something about yourself and contribute to your personal growth?

15. Do you consider yourself to have any skills or abilities that are not common to your peers or beyond those commonly attained by university graduates? What? Where did you acquire them?

16. What about non-degree academic experiences? Have you taken any extra-curricular courses? Have you attained any certificates of achievement? Why did you undertake these courses? Was it for general interest? Was it for self improvement? Was it for advancement in your employment? How did these experiences contribute to your life and your interest in law?

Academic And Professional Plans - Why Law School

17. In addition to law school, list three opportunities (educational or professional) that you would be interested in pursuing. (Examples: teaching, medical school, graduate work in your current area of study, jobs, etc.)

18. What is your current area of study? Are you happy in it? If you attend law school will you abandon your current area of study? Will you be able to combine law with your current area of study? Are you interested in pursuing any joint degree programs?

19. If you are happy in your current area of study and you think that by attending law school you will abandon that area of study, why do you want to attend law school?

20. At what stage in your life did you decide that you wanted to attend law school? Is attending law school your primary objective or one of several suitable objectives?

21. What is it about the study of law that appeals to you?

22. Has your interest in law school resulted from experiences you have had in the work force? If you become a

lawyer, will that be a second career for you?

23. Are you able to point to any significant life event that stimulated your interest in attending law school or becoming a lawyer? If so, what?

24. A law degree will not by itself entitle you to practise law. After law school you must become licensed as a lawyer. Are you sufficiently interested in law as an academic discipline that you would attend law school even if you were unable to be licensed as a lawyer?

Emotional Dimensions And Your Mind

25. What do you consider to be your greatest strength? How has this strength assisted you in life?

26. What do you consider to be your greatest weakness? How has this either strengthened or weakened you in life?

27. Where would you like to be professionally and socially:

- in five years

- in ten years

- in fifteen years

28. Identify and describe a person who you greatly admire. What do you admire most in that person? Why?

29. What is the one characteristic you have that you value most? (Integrity, athletic ability, etc.) Why?

30. If you could improve one thing about yourself, what would that one thing be? Why?

31. If you were dead and buried, what would you like to have written on your tombstone?

Tool 4: Third Party Questionnaire

People often see you very differently from how you see yourself. What follows is a questionnaire that you can ask third parties to complete. The results may give you food for thought.

I am applying to_____. As part of the application process I am required to submit a personal statement. I have included a copy of the specific question that I am required to answer. The statement is to be about me. I am aware that often other people see me in a different light from how I see myself. I value your judgment and ask that you answer the following questions about me from your perspective. Thank you!

1. Please pick three words that you feel best describe me.

2. If you were writing my personal statement, what would be the most important fact about me that you think the admissions committee should know?

3   In your opinion, do I have any special qualities that make me uniquely suited for the study of law or being a lawyer?

4. Is there anything in general about my background that you think it would be helpful for the admissions committee to know?

5. Describe one actual experience that you have had with me that (in your opinion) summarizes my basic character.

Tool 5: Applicant Inferential Imaging Exercise

EXERCISE: Describe something about yourself or an event in your life that would allow the reader to infer that you have the following characteristics.

Maturity

Disciplined

Hard Working

Honest

Generous

Motivated

Intelligent

Responsible

Well Rounded (diverse interests)

Community Oriented

Sound Judgment

Example: Being selected to be the "don" in a University residence might be evidence of being responsible.

Tool 6: Third Party Personal Statement Questionnaire

After having completed one or two drafts of your personal statement you should circulate it for evaluation. What follows are a list of questions that you may want to ask your outside readers.

Attached is a personal statement that I have written for the purposes of applying to_____. I have also included a copy of the specific question that I am answering. I would appreciate it if you would take some time to read what I have written and answer the following questions. I am particularly concerned with the overall image(s) of me that are suggested by this personal statement. If you find any grammatical errors or typos would you please circle them. Please include any additional comments you have that are not covered by the questions asked.

1. Was my opening paragraph (and particularly the first sentence) engaging and attention grabbing?

2. Did you find any grammatical errors or typos?

3. Did I seem to be a positive person?

4. Was the personal statement responsive to the precise question asked?

5. Was it well written and well organized?

6. Are there any specific words that should be omitted?

7. Do I sound like a likable, honest, sincere, interesting person?

8. Can you think of anything that you know about me that I should have included?

9. Was there anything included which you don't think should have been included?

10. Did you learn anything new about me from reading this personal statement?

11. Do you see me in a different way after having read this personal statement?

12. If you didn't already know me, after having read this personal statement, would you want to meet me?

13. Please try to paraphrase the main point of the personal statement as a whole.

Conclusion

Although it may seem like a daunting task, writing your personal statement is more easily approached with this step-by-step process to help you research the most difficult and interesting topic of all - yourself. When given a reasonable amount of time and effort, this very important step in the law admissions process can provide a valuable and necessary addition to your application package.

3 Years	
2 Countries	United States & Canada
2 Cities	Windsor, Ontario & Detroit, Michigan
2 Universities	University of Detroit Mercy & University of Windsor
2 Law Degrees	J.D. & LL.B.
1 Program	Joint J.D./LL.B. Program

Study two legal cultures simultaneously at two law schools in two cities located in two countries, with a travel time of 20 minutes or less between the two campuses. Gain an understanding of the role of law in domestic and international commerce in an economically vital and culturally diverse environment.

The J.D. is approved by the American Bar Association and the LL.B. is recognized by the Federation of Law Societies of Canada.

Contact us now for enrolment
Application Deadline: 1 March of each year

Director of J.D./LL.B. Program	jd-llb@udmercy.edu
University of Detroit Mercy	www.law.udmercy.edu
University of Windsor	www.uwindsor.ca/law

Chapter 16

How To Obtain Effective Letters Of Recommendation

Learn From Real Samples

A Guide For The Applicant

Some schools use letters. Some don't. Some of those who don't use them will read them if sent. Others won't. But, each of you will be applying to at least one school that requires at least one letter of recommendation.

Although letters of recommendation are third party statements they are very controllable. Actually the phrase "recommendation" may be a misnomer. Few "recommendation" writers will compromise their personal integrity. As a result, I have seen many letters that are either neutral to the point of being useless or go so far as to suggest that the applicant be rejected. At the other extreme I have seen many letters that are certain to enhance the applicant's chances of receiving an offer of admission. This part of the book has been designed to help get the most out of the "marketing opportunity" that letters of "recommendation" afford.

From Whom Should You Seek Letters?

You should seek letters from someone who is in a position to comment on something that the school considers relevant. In most cases the prestige of the writer is irrelevant. Applicants often seek letters from famous graduates of the school, lawyers, politicians, judges, etc. Unless the person can comment on factors that the school considers relevant you will have wasted a marketing opportunity.

Who Is In A Position To Comment?

In a perfect world one could say that the best recommenders are people who:

1. Are Objective - Avoid getting a letter from someone too close to you.

2. Know You Well - Seek a recommender who can comment on the most important activities in your life.

3. Have special skills or experiences that make them good judges of applicants. Examples may include employers who have been able to observe your job performance and can comment on your motivation, ability to work, and level of responsibility. Coaches and trainers who know you well from frequent contact can often comment on your drive, dedication and persistence. Some professors and teaching assistants will also qualify. But remember every recommender must comment on matters that the school considers relevant.

So, What Does The School Consider Relevant?

"Remember that law schools are academic institutions interested in your academic potential. University and college faculty are the people whose judgments tend to carry the most weight with admissions personnel. Therefore, try to have at least one letter from a professor in your major field of study (even if you have been out of school for a while)."

-The Right Law School For You

Academic ability is not the only consideration. Schools also want to know that you will bring your academic ability to bear on law school work. Hence, letters that comment on drive, dedication, and other similar qualities will also be helpful.

Academic References

All schools are interested in your ability to do their academic work. Therefore, many schools require that at least one of the letters be an academic reference. A professor is a logical choice. Those of you who do not know professors may want to consider teaching assistants. (Often the teaching assistant knows you in a way that the professor does not.)

Remember that the academic reference is for the purpose of hearing what a professor says about your ability to do university work. Therefore, you should do your best to ensure that the letter comes from a university professor.

Those applying in the residual categories (mature student, etc.) may have more difficulty getting a current academic reference. The schools understand this. If you cannot get a current academic reference ask yourself what qualities are consistent with and lead to superior academic performance. (Examples may include: discipline, strong writing and organizational skills, motivation, etc.) Consider getting a reference from someone who can comment on these qualities. (See particularly Sample 4 at the end. It is a good example of how to get an academic reference from a non-academic source.)

Every applicant should do his best to ensure that there is at least one strong academic reference in the file. Non-academic references should be used as a supplement to and not a substitute for academic references!

Non-academic References

In selecting non-academic references ask: can this writer comment on something in which this particular school has an interest? Remember, beyond academic ability, different schools may be looking for different things. For example:

- If community service is relevant then you may want to get a letter from someone who has worked with you in that capacity.

- If employment history is relevant then you may want to get a letter from an employer.

- If your medical history is somehow relevant then you may want to get a letter from a doctor.

How Unorthodox Can A Non-Academic Reference Be?

There is no right or wrong answer to this question. Ask: what are you trying to contribute to your application file by using a certain letter? Remember that the application file is greater than the sum of its parts. Will the inclusion of the letter (in conjunction with other parts of the file) improve or diminish the overall effect?

An Exercise In Determining Suitability

Consider the following example.

Imagine that you are opposed to the death penalty and that your reason for attending law school is that you want to do "death-penalty work". Imagine also that you have spent a great deal of time working with an inmate who has received the death penalty and is waiting for his execution. You consider this particular inmate to be articulate and intelligent. Should you get a letter of recommendation from him?

This question was posed to a number of experienced pre-law advisers in the U.S. Here are samples of the answers received.

"Our committee would be happy to receive such a letter on your behalf."

"If I were you I would try to demonstrate your qualities in more traditional ways. This would ensure that the letter will not be ignored."

"The letter would be attention getting and would distinguish you from other applicants."

"I would use this as an additional letter and not as a substitute for the required ones. Some admissions officers will find it helpful but others will ignore it."

"The schools want academic references that compare you to other applicants. This person could not write such a letter."

Author's opinion: I have the following thoughts.

1. If used, it should be used as a supplement to the academic reference(s).

2. If used, it should be used only if your interest in working with death row inmates is relevant to your application to a particular law school. It could be relevant in two ways. First, it is arguably evidence of community service for a lengthy period of time. Second, it could improve the effectiveness of your personal statement by lending additional credibility to the claims made in it.

3. Use of this letter does have a degree of risk. Experienced pre-law advisers have given different advice about the suitability of this letter.

How Many Letters Should You Send?

In general you should not exceed the required number of letters. Consider this question from the perspective of the admissions committee. First, you are burdening the committee with extra work. Second, you are not following directions. Finally, you will find it difficult to obtain two good letters. The more letters you have, the greater the chances of the positive impact of the good letters being diminished by weaker letters.

Select Your Referees To Avoid Repetitive Information

Every letter should be thought of as an additional marketing opportunity. Therefore, you should try to obtain letters that complement each other rather than repeat each other. I have already alluded to the possibility of using letters to enhance certain parts of your personal statement.

Avoid a referee who will simply repeat what is already on your transcript. Example:

To The Committee:

"Stanley Student was in my political science course. He got an A."

Yours Truly,

Professor X."

This letter simply repeats something from another part of the file. It is repetitive and is therefore a wasted marketing opportunity.

How To Qualify People To Write Letters For You

You are now at the point where you have decided who you are going to ask. You have no right to see the letter and the letter should be sent directly by the writer. Obviously you must be careful. Never ask somebody if he/she would be willing to write a letter on your behalf. Remember, they might write an unhelpful letter. In most cases you will not have the opportunity to see the letter before it is sent. So, you must protect yourself by asking the right qualifying question. The right question is:

"Do you feel that you could and would you be willing to write me a positive letter of recommendation?"

If the person answers "yes", then the person has agreed not only to write the letter but to write a positive letter. The person is now qualified.

Qualification Isn't Enough - The Person Must Now Be Educated!

You now have a willing partner in the letter writing process. Your next job is to help the writer do the best that he/she can. Schedule an appointment with the writer. Show the writer your personal statement and all other parts of your application file. Specifically you should bring:

- your transcripts

- personal statement

- resume and/or autobiographical sketch

- photocopies of anything you want the writer to specifically refer to

Suggest the importance of all parts of the file working together. Alert the writer to any special programs to which you are applying. Tell the writer who else is writing on your behalf. In short - give the writer as much information as you can. All of these things should be done well before the deadline date. It takes the better part of a full day to write an effective letter of recommendation. Be respectful of this. Make sure that you thank the writer for his/her hard work. You should offer to pick up any out of pocket costs. Don't forget to notify the writer where you were accepted.

How To Deal With Standard Form Letters

Many schools or application forms include "standard forms" for recommenders to use. Frequently these "forms" are not a required form of letter, but rather a convenience for the writer. In most cases your recommender will be able to do a better job for you by writing his/her own letter and not using the form. First, ensure that a "non-standard form" letter is allowed. Then encourage the recommender to NOT use that "standard form." If the "standard form" is required, your recommender may be able to write a supplementary letter as well.

The Necessity To Follow Up

Ultimately it is your responsibility to ensure that your file is complete. It is important that the letter be sent directly from the writer. (Some writers will allow you to see the letter and others will not.) Take steps to ensure that the letter(s) has actually been sent and received. Make sure that you thank the writer and notify the writer where you have been accepted.

A Guide For The Recommender

Those in the academic community generally know how to write letters of recommendation. These comments are not directed toward them. But, potential recommenders in the non-academic community may have never written a letter of this type. For example an employer or clergyman may be very anxious to help, but simply not know how. These suggestions are primarily for them. In addition, these suggestions are just that - suggestions. There is no one way to write an effective letter of reference.

If you have read this far I assume that you have been asked to write a letter and are seeking some guidance. Begin by reading the sample letters included in this book. Look at both the academic references and the non-academic references and see how they supply facts, convey enthusiasm and help the applicant come to life.

I would like to offer two sets of guidelines for the letter writing process. First, guidelines for an initial meeting with the applicant. Second, guidelines for the actual writing.

Guidelines For The Initial Meeting

The applicant should supply you with all the other components of the application file. Ask the applicant to bring a current resume. Review these documents with the applicant. Try to determine how your letter is to fit in with the marketing of the applicant as a whole. Ask if there are any special considerations that should be discussed at any specific law school. Agree on whether the applicant will have an opportunity to see the letter. Ask who else may be writing a letter in support of the applicant. Clarify deadline dates, number of letters, addresses, etc. Remember that the complete application file is the "marketing tool." Your job is add a specific component to the file so that the whole file has an effect that is greater than the sum of the individual parts.

Guidelines For Actually Writing

Your meeting with the applicant is complete. You are ready to collect your thoughts and write. Here are some suggestions.

1. Introduce yourself and qualify yourself.

2. Explain how you know the applicant, for how long and under what circumstances.

3. Supply specific factual evidence that will support the conclusions that you want the reader to infer.

4. Compare the applicant to other people you have observed.

5. Try to make the applicant come alive as a person by:

   A. Writing in such a way that it is clear that you know the applicant; and

   B. Writing so that you convey your enthusiasm about the applicant.

6. At all times imagine that you are a witness in a trial. You must show that you are qualified to make judgments about the applicant, have had the opportunity to observe the applicant, have actually observed the applicant and support the applicant both as an individual and in comparison to others that you have observed.

Good Writing Is Like Good Cooking - It Takes Time

Ensure that you leave yourself enough time to write, put it aside, reflect on what you have written and rewrite. An effective letter has the potential to make a difference in the applicant's life. The applicant will appreciate your efforts.

Some Sample Letters

Samples - Academic References

Sample 1:

Dear Dean Admissions Committee

RE: Stanley Student

<u>John Franklin University</u>

For a number of years I taught a part-time course at John Franklin University entitled Introduction to the International Law Of Human Rights - Political Science 410. This was a challenging course intended for second and upper year students during the course of which students were required to read, analyze and digest a large number of judicial decisions as well as participate in the classes/seminars. Evaluation was on the basis of a term test, a major paper and final examination.

I recall Stanley Student from the 1993 fall session as having been in regular attendance, always obviously prepared and an active and able participant in the class. He wrote an excellent paper for the course dealing with the complexities of the law of citizenship as it is influenced by the International Covenant On Civil And Political Rights.

Based on my experience of him in my course, I am of the opinion that he clearly has the ability and diligence to successfully complete a course of studies in law and would advocate his admission to the school.

Yours very truly,

Stephen H. Adjunct, LL.B.

Author's Comments: This is not a particularly helpful letter. I am left with the impression that the writer has neither the knowledge of nor interest in the applicant to do a good job. There is no enthusiasm in this letter. Compare this letter to the next two.

Sample 2:

Members of the Admissions Committee:

<u>Re: Stanley Student</u>

Stanley Student has asked me to supply you with a letter of reference in support of his application for admission to your program. Stanley has been a student of mine in Labor Economics (fall 1993) and advanced econometrics (fall 1994). I have been teaching at John Franklin University since 1971 and before that as a doctoral student, I taught at the University of California for 4 years. I am one of 9 full professors in our department of 39.

Stanley Student would fit into the top 100 students I have taught, measured against approximately 12,000 students. He may not have all the theoretical courses as background that some of the other top 100 would have but he has the logic, the maturity, the clarity, and the communication skills, all of which I view as extremely important in his planned career.

In my labor economics class, students participated in debate and in the advanced econometrics class, there were presentations. Stanley excelled in both. Without being loud or interruptive, Stanley was a ready and regular participant in class discussion and always added value to such discussions, a rare occurrence indeed. His writing skills are similarly strong.

Stanley Student participated as a representative of the class and the University at the Foundation For Economic Education and was selected there to attend a session on investment and free market economics. He readily shared what he had learned when he returned to campus. Despite the age difference (6 to 8 years), I found Stanley to be held in high regard by his peers and indeed there was close cooperation instead of a coldness often accorded excellent students.

Economics is extremely demanding and I am not noted as an easy grader. Stanley topped both classes that I taught. Economics also has a reputation for forcing students to use logic, the same logic which is a necessary characteristic of "excellent" lawyers.

I am aware of and share Stanley Student's ethical concerns. I believe he would be a highly professional individual, both as a student and as a member of the bar.

It has been a pleasure to write for Stanley Student. I hope you take account of the demands of the earliest period of his enrollment (carrying a full-term job and many related activities) and look at his full-time marks as being more representative of his ability. I cannot think of another reference to law school that I have written where I felt as strongly about the student's ability to complete law school. That may be seen by the A+ and A which I assigned him as first in both my classes.

Sincerely yours,

John M. Keynes, Ph.D.

Professor of Economics

Author's Comments: This is a superb letter. The author demonstrates that he is well qualified, writes with enthusiasm and compares the applicant to other students. The author uses lots of very specific examples to provide independent evidence in support of his claims. In summary, this letter provides lots of detailed evidence that the law school can use.

Sample 3:

The Registrar, Faculty of Law

Justice Law School

Dear Sir:

I am writing a letter of reference for Sarah Student who is a student in my Russian literature course.

Ms. Student is an outstanding student. In the first term Ms. Student has received "A" grades in all four written essays (two research essays and two test essays) and "A" grades in both oral reports. In these essays as well as in her oral reports, she has demonstrated superior analytical and communicative skills. I am impressed with her exceptional ability to identify the central thesis and to develop her argument with clarity and with well-chosen and well-documented examples.

The literature course which I am teaching is an intensive seminar with a heavy reading list of nineteenth century Russian literary texts in English translation. The texts in the course present complex moral, philosophical and social issues. This course is also very demanding and students must participate actively. Sarah Student is always well prepared for class and participates enthusiastically in class discussions. In class discussions as in her written work, she identifies major issues and presents her arguments persuasively and lucidly.

Sarah Student also has excellent skills in interacting with other students in the seminar. Clearly her extensive experience in community work and human rights issues as well as her work in administration, management and education have been an asset and have provided her with valuable insight and skills in interacting with other people.

Ms. Student is one of the best students that I have ever taught. My qualifications include a Ph.D. in Comparative and Slavic Literature and twenty years of teaching experience.

Yours sincerely,

Dr. Shelia Wisdom
Associate Professor

Author's Comments: This is a superb letter. The author demonstrates that she is well qualified, writes with enthusiasm and compares the applicant to other students. The author uses lots of very specific examples to provide independent evidence in support of her claims. In summary, this letter provides lots of detailed evidence that the law school can use.

Samples - Non-Academic References

Sample 4:

To The Admissions Officer

Any Law School

Anytown, Canada

To The Admissions Committee:

Re: Stanley Student

Stanley Student has asked me to write as a referee as part of his application for law school. In my judgment, Stanley is educationally, intellectually and emotionally well suited for the study of law. I am very pleased to write in his support. Frankly, I know of nobody whom I could more enthusiastically recommend for the study of law. Allow me to elaborate.

My background is in law. I hold both U.S. and Canadian law degrees and am a member of bar in the Province Of Ontario and the states of Massachusetts and New York. In addition, I teach and work with a number of pre-law students. As a result, I have extensive and regular contact with "would be" law students. I first met Stanley in 1987 when he was a student in one of my courses. I have kept up with him since that time. For the last year Stanley has assisted me in instructing a course that I teach to prepare students for the Law School Admission Test. You can see from his transcripts and academic achievements that Stanley is a gifted scholar. In addition to his being a first rate scholar he is a first rate teacher!

When Stanley approached me to write on his behalf, I asked him why he wanted to study law. As you can see from his academic records Stanley is completing his Masters Degree in the philosophy of law. His dissertation will discuss the rationing of health care from a sociological, ethical and philosophical point of view. My many conversations with him reveal that Stanley realizes that social, ethical and philosophical problems are intimately connected to legal problems. In addition to an independent interest in the study and practice of law, Stanley sees a law degree as a way of improving his work in the area of philosophy of law in general and his dissertation topic in particular, in that a law degree will equip him to consider constitutional and other legal issues relating to the right to health care.

I recognize that there are a finite number of spaces in your program. Hence, it is in your interest to ensure that students you accept will benefit from your program and that participants in the program will also benefit from other students. As well as being intelligent and an accomplished student, Stanley is intellectually suited to the study and practice of law. From my many conversations with him I have learned that he has a fine mind for discerning and developing general principles and determining to what extent these principles apply to specific factual situations. Stanley is a "natural" at legal reasoning and has an agile and inquiring mind. I expect that he will be a first rate legal scholar.

Stanley has the maturity and discipline that is required to excel at law school. During his work with me as a teaching assistant I have observed that he understands the value and necessity of hard, consistent and disciplined work. Furthermore, he puts his understanding into practice. To put it simply, Stanley has the values and work ethic that are needed to excel at law school.

Finally, Stanley is generous with his time and talents. On numerous occasions I have seen him assist both his peers and students. (In many cases going far beyond what one would reasonably expect.) Should Stanley attend your school, I have every reason to believe that he will enhance the lives of his colleagues. Certainly, he has been a positive influence in my life.

In closing, I repeat that I enthusiastically support Stanley's application to law school in general and the University of _____ in particular. His academic qualifications are evident from his transcripts. His values, ethics, character, effectiveness and belief in hard work make all those around him perform better!

Sincerely yours,

John Robertson, LL.B., J.D.

Author's Comments: This is a cross between an academic and non-academic reference. It is in part an academic reference from a non-academic person. Applicant's having difficulty getting a real academic reference should take note!

Sample 5:

To The Admissions Officer, Any Law School

Anytown, Canada

To The Admissions Committee:

Re: Stanley Student

Please accept this as a letter in enthusiastic support of the application of Stanley Student to the faculty of law.

I have known Stanley's family for approximately 20 years. Stanley's older brother and I were roommates at University. At that time Stanley was approximately 3 years old. I am currently a Chartered Financial Analyst and have developed a financial planning company. Beginning in 1990 I began the process of franchising the Financial Planning Offices.

Although I have been a friend of Stanley's brother since 1974 I did not meet Stanley until 1983. In 1989 he immigrated to Canada from Germany. Since that time he has been employed in my business (full time in 1994 and part time during other years). He is a likable young man who I also consider to be a personal friend.

The process of franchising my financial planning business has required the planning and marketing of seminars aimed at potential franchisees. Over the years Stanley has been involved in every aspect of this. He has designed promotional material, arranged for its printing, handled its distribution, been the contact person for those attending the seminars, and handled every other aspect of this business. This has always been a big job. But, what is most significant is that he accomplished these tasks with a minimum of direction. He always took the initiative to ensure that what needed to be done was done. During my 20 years in business I have worked with a number of students and young adults. To put it simply, Stanley has been the best, most responsible, effective and trustworthy employee with whom I have had the pleasure of working. Although he is in his early 20s, he has the maturity and common sense of a person much older.

During 1994 Stanley worked with me on a full time basis. It was also the best growth year that I have had. The spectacular growth during 1994 was largely attributable to Stanley's work. During this time period Stanley reorganized our whole marketing program. He recreated both our promotional material and its method of distribution. Stanley has a unique ability to put a "new spin" on old ideas and the ingenuity and ability to see a project through to completion. Many of his ideas are still being used by my company.

Stanley has demonstrated that he is a highly intelligent, competent, effective person. But he is also a pleasure to be around. His interests range from soccer to piano to history to simply being around people. His experience growing up in Germany has given him a cross-cultural perspective that should serve him well in later years. In addition, to his accomplishments, integrity and strengths of character, Stanley is a "nice guy."

I enthusiastically support his application to the faculty of law.

Yours truly,

James R. Wealth III, CFA

Author's Comments: As you can see this is a letter from an employer. The employer comments about the applicant - in a way that makes it clear that he is much more than an employee.

Conclusion

If managed properly reference letters can enhance your application. To follow the guidelines in this chapter will improve the quality of your application.

Chapter 17

Excelling At Law School Interviews - Seven Real Accounts

How Prevalent Are Interviews?

Interviews will play no role in the application process for the majority of applicants. Almost all applicants who are interviewed are applicants in a "residual category." Nevertheless, this chapter has been designed to assist those of you who have been invited to an interview.

This chapter has been divided into:

Part A - Understanding Law School Interviews; and

Part B - Seven First Hand Accounts Of Law School Interviews.

Part A - Understanding Law School Interviews

Informal Contact - The Process Of Creating An Impression

Any contact with the school will leave an impression. This includes any telephone call, letter, email (I could tell you stories about email that I receive - tone matters!) or entry into the admissions office. Every time a school has contact with you, it should be left with a positive image. Treat everybody in the admissions office with respect.

I know of one law student who had been placed on the waiting list. During the summer she telephoned to ask about the status of her application. During this conversation she had a lengthy conversation with an admissions officer. That conversation left the admissions officer with a definite impression of what kind of person she was. The next day she received an offer of acceptance. She feels that her informal conversation was part of the reason that she was accepted.

Bottom line: Treat any interaction with the school as being part of an ongoing interview!

Official Interviews - You Know You Are Being Interviewed

There are few law schools (in contrast to medical schools) that use interviews as part of the admissions process. In most cases, if an interview is used at all, it will be for those who apply in a category other than the "regular applicant category." The opportunity to be interviewed is something that you achieve. If interviews play a role in the process, only a select number of applicants are interviewed. Hence, as a general rule, being invited to an interview is an accomplishment.

There are many different kinds of interviews conducted by many different interviewers. Hence, no two interviews will be the same. It is therefore difficult to give specific advice for specific schools. Nevertheless, what follows is an excerpt from my Mastering The Personal Statement book.

The Steps To A Successful Interview

"Imagine yourself to be a lawyer who is required to argue a case before a court made up of judges. The court requires that you first submit your arguments in writing. You then have the opportunity to make an oral presentation which is to be largely based on your written material. The judges will have read your written material in advance. They will certainly begin by asking you questions about it. Although these questions will control the direction that the hearing will take, through your answers you are anxious to control the content. Although you are anxious to answer any questions that you are asked, there are some specific facts that you want to ensure the court hears about. You are given one hour to make your oral arguments on a fixed day at an appointed time. On that day your job is to deliver the most effective presentation possible and to answer the judges questions in an effective way. You cannot anticipate all the questions. Therefore, it is important that you are sufficiently flexible to respond to anything that might be asked. Furthermore, you know that your presentation will be most effective if you engage the judges in a dialogue. This will keep the presentation more interesting. Not only must you be an effective lawyer., you must look like an effective lawyer. Therefore, you understand that you must be well groomed and well dressed. As the date for your court presentation draws near, you find out the identity of the judges who will actually hear your case. You should learn everything that you can about the court.

The lawyer's written arguments are analogous to the application file without the interview. The oral arguments are analogous to the interview."

An Interview Is A Sales Call

Organizing Yourself For The Interview

Step 1: Know Yourself - The Seller

General

You must know yourself in a general way. Rethink your values, interests and goals.

Career/Academic

Be prepared to answer: Why law school? Why at this school? Why at this stage of your life?

Step 2: Know The School - The Buyer

If you are being interviewed it is likely that you have applied in a specific application category. Make sure that you understand the requirements of the category and the kind of people the school looks for in that category. For example, from the perspective of the school - what kinds of applicants do they like to admit in the "mature student" category?

School Specific Opportunities

If the school has a specific niche or area of specialization or joint program you should know about it and be interested in it.

Important!! You must make it clear that you are interested in attending the specific school that is interviewing you!

Step 3: Prepare For The Interview

<u>Research</u>

Anticipate possible questions.

Read the papers. Be familiar with current events as they bear on your chosen profession. For example, should the government cut funding to legal aid?

<u>Practice</u>

If possible do some practice interviewing. Ideally this should be done with somebody who is experienced in admissions or has been through the process.

<u>Prepare Questions You Would Like To Ask</u>

Think of questions you would like to ask if given the opportunity.

Step 4: Logistical And Tactical Considerations

If you are given a choice, schedule the earliest possible interview.

Know where the building is. Know where the room is.

Arrange to arrive three or four minutes early.

Prepare to dress appropriately. Remember the interview is a "sales call." Be well groomed. Have your clothes laid out the night before.

Bring a copy of every document in your application file.

Step 5: Conducting The Interview

The interviewer will control the direction through the questions. You will control the content of the interview through your answers.

Respond to the questions asked. Don't react. Think about your answer.

Don't sit on the fence. Answer questions decisively. In life it is more important to be decisive than it is to be right.

Be positive. Maintain eye contact. Smile and be animated. Make sure that you display a firm handshake.

Don't disparage anybody or any school under any circumstances!

If you don't know an answer, simply say so.

Appear interested in the interview.

Don't exhibit relief when the interview is over.

And finally,

Don't Interrupt The Interviewer!

Step 6: It's Over - What Now?

Send a thank you note. In most cases the interview is a privilege which you have earned.

Some Practice Hypothetical Interview Questions

1. What characteristics do you have that would make you an outstanding lawyer, law student, leader, etc?

2. Tell me about your greatest strength or greatest weakness.

3. Where do you see yourself 10 years from now?

4. How do feel about increasing government involvement in the legal profession?

5. What appeals to you about our school?

6. What is your favorite book?

7. What have you read lately?

8. What if you find that your friend had cheated on the LSAT? Would you report him/her?

9. How did you choose your undergraduate institution and area of academic concentration?

10. How has your undergraduate major prepared you for Law?

11. Why should we choose you over all the other applicants we have?

12. What do you know about our school?

13. You have had an interesting career. Why do you want to go to Law school anyway?

14. Who is your favorite historical figure? Why?

15. What do you think is the strongest part of your application file? What do you think is the weakest?

And Finally - A Picture Is Worth 1000 Words

Interviews, when used, are the final step of the marketing process. If the school goes to the trouble to interview you, the interview will be a major factor in determining your fate!

Part B - Seven First Hand Accounts Of Law School Interviews

I have included student impressions of interviews they attended at five different schools. What follows is an accurate account of their perceptions. It doesn't mean that another person interviewed would share the same perception.

Again, please remember that these accounts are included only to provide some perceptions of how different people have experienced interviews as part of the law admissions process. ALTHOUGH THE ACCOUNTS ARE INTERESTING, THEY SHOULD NOT BE CONSIDERED TO BE A BLUEPRINT FOR WHAT YOU MAY OR MAY NOT EXPECT!!

Account 1 - Manitoba - "Individual Consideration Category"

"The Interview - Individual Consideration At The University Of Manitoba"

The interview takes place at the Law Society of Manitoba which is located in the heart of downtown Winnipeg. The interviews are held over a weekend, usually around the first weekend of June. The panel interviews thirty people out of which fifteen are chosen for the "Individual Consideration Category." The Law Society is easy to find and within walking distance of the major hotels. The entire interview takes between fifteen and twenty minutes. When I arrived at the interview, I waited in a small reception area. The Chair of Admissions came down the stairs from the second floor and greeted me. On the way upstairs to the interview room, he made "small talk" and assured me the interview would be very relaxed and informal and not to be nervous. He further stated that they already knew a lot about me and simply wanted to fill in the "bits and pieces."

Once I entered the interview room, I noted a panel consisting of four people: the Chair of Admissions, a Law Professor, a second year law student and the Director of Legal Aid. (two men and two women) I was introduced to each and there was some "chit chat" before the "real" interview commenced. The "chit chat" consisted of questions like: "Have you ever been to Winnipeg?" "How long are you staying here?" "What have you been doing since you arrived?"

The "real" interview then commenced. Starting with the Chair, each member of the committee asked me questions that targeted a specific area of my application.

The student asked: "How will your experiences help you in law and what are the disadvantages of being a lawyer?"

The Director of Legal Aid asked: "Tell me more about your community activities."

The Law Professor asked: "I notice that you have taken two criminal law courses. Have they peaked your interest? Also, what kind of law do you want to practice?"

Finally the Chair asked: "Can you comment on your poor performance on the LSAT? Why are you working two jobs and only taking two university courses per semester? Did I have any financial dependents?"

While I was giving my responses to the various questions, the entire panel was taking notes. Hence, it was difficult to maintain eye contact. Different committee members interjected with comments and/or additional questions for clarification about my responses. The committee then invited me to ask any questions that I had.

The interview was concluded by the Chair, who advised me that they would be making their decision within eight days and that I would be informed of the decision in approximately two weeks.

Although the atmosphere is friendly and informal the committee is looking for well-prepared (or thought out) answers. It would be a mistake to enter the interview without being well versed in potential answers about your work experience, your community activities, and your scholastic activities. In addition, you should be informed about the university in general and the law program in particular. The reasons as to why or why not you are accepted into the program are an unknown quantity. More specifically, the Chair of Admissions stated in a follow-up letter that: "Decisions in this category being of necessity, both subjective and relative, the Interviewing Committee does not and indeed cannot provide reasons for its decision."

Dalhousie - Regular Category and Indigenous Blacks and Mi'kmaq

Note that Dalhousie does interview students who have applied in the regular applicant category.

Account 2 - An Applicant In The "Regular Category"

"As far as the interview with Dalhousie, it took place at a law firm in the TD tower in downtown Toronto. Someone from Dalhousie called about a month earlier and gave me a choice of three days to choose from. Afterwards, I was told that I would have to remit a $50 fee for the interview. At first, this request seemed fine, but I must admit that I later felt gauged.

The interview took place in an office with a professor from Dalhousie, a former student who was articling at the law firm, and another student who was part of the admissions committee. The majority of the questions were posed by the professor and the articling student.

I don't remember the exact order of the questions, but here is what I do remember:

The professor introduced himself and the two other interviewers. He then proceeded to explain the purpose of the interview which was to narrow down the list of candidates.

He then began to ask questions:

Why do I want to go to Dalhousie?

Why do I want to practise law?

How would I explain my LSAT score?

How would I explain my graduate and undergraduate marks?

What are my feelings about the situation in the former Yugoslavia?

What makes me mad?

Why have I done so many extra-curricular activities?

How have they benefited me?

What books am I currently reading?

At this point, the professor asked me if I had any questions for them about Dalhousie. After I posed a couple of questions about university life at Dalhousie the professor reiterated much of the same from the beginning of the interview. He did mention this time that there were about 150 students being interviewed across the country and that I would receive a response in 2 to 3 weeks.

In retrospect, I must admit that I found some of the questions odd and I left the interview ambivalent. I couldn't figure out where they were going with some of the questions that they posed to me. Nonetheless, the interview somehow lasted somewhere around 45 minutes."

Account 3 - Category For Indigenous Blacks and Mi'kmaqs

(See the chapter on minorities for information and disscussion about this category.)

"Here are the details of my interview at Dalhousie Law School.

I applied to Dalhousie under the 'regular' category. They had a special category for Indigenous Blacks and Mi'kmaqs, but I did not meet the requirements of this category because I am not a resident of Nova Scotia. However, I did indicate on my application and in my personal statement that I am black.

In mid-April I received a telephone call from the person in charge of the Indigenous Blacks and Mi'kmaq Programme. She informed me that even though I was not a resident of Nova Scotia they wished to consider me under this category. Consideration in the Indigenous Blacks and Mi'kmaq category required an interview. As you know, I was given a choice of attending an interview in person or having the interview conducted over the telephone. I chose to fly to Halifax to be interviewed in person.

As I mentioned to you, I had problems getting to the interview. My interview was to be at 3:00 pm (all times referred to will be Toronto time) on April 11. I took a Royal Airlines flight that was to leave Toronto at 9:00 am that day and arrive in Halifax at 11:00 am. This would give me plenty of time to check into my hotel and change my clothes before my interview.

The flight left the terminal shortly after 9:00 and was taxied out to the runway. Upon reaching the runway the Captain informed us that there was a problem with the plane and we returned to the terminal. After about 45 minutes the plane was fixed and we were instructed by the Captain that he was waiting for an alternative flight plan. Once an alternative flight plan was received we were again taxied out to the runway. This time the plane actually took off. However, about 15 minutes into the flight the Captain indicated that there was another problem with the plane and we returned to Toronto.

By the time the plane was finally repaired it was 1:00 pm! Since the flight time to Halifax is about 2 hours, there was no way I could get there for 3:00. I telephoned the Indigenous Blacks and Mi'kmaq Programme Coordinator and requested a change of time. She rescheduled my interview for the next morning.

I was interviewed by three professors for a period of about 40 minutes. There were three types of questions posed to me:

1) Questions involving my race and the Indigenous Blacks and Mi'kmaq Programme

Why do you think Dalhousie Law School has an Indigenous Blacks and Mi'kmaq Programme?

Do you see the world in black and white?

Why do you want to represent blacks through the legal profession, rather than through, for example, a career in medicine or engineering?

2) Questions about myself

What books have you read lately?

Why have you worked throughout your university career?

Do you feel that your LSAT mark reflects your abilities?

3) Questions about current events, hypothetical situations, etc.

What international issues interest you?

Do you see a problem with colonialism?

Do you think that Harvard University was right to withdraw its offer of admission from a young woman who, as a teenager, had killed her mother? (This referred to a case that occurred a few years ago.)

You are Dean of the law school. A student of the school accuses a fellow student of rape. What would you do in this situation?

At the interview I gave each professor a presentation folder which contained my personal statement, my resume, and a copy of a recent essay for which I received a grade of A (a Sociology essay in which I compared the Juvenile Delinquents Act to the Young Offenders Act). The interviewers seemed to be impressed by this and they commented that I was definitely prepared! If you would like to see a copy of this presentation folder, just let me know."

Osgoode Hall - The Mature Student Applicant - Two Accounts

Account 4 - Osgoode Mature Student Applicant

"The Mature Student Interview

I've been to the personal interview and survived! It was at the beginning of March that I received a phone call from the admissions office at Osgoode Hall Law School informing me that I had been selected for a personal interview - the next day! As a mature student, with no university background whatsoever, I had no idea what to expect from this process and I was caught between absolute joy and terror.

Preparation was key. I made sure that I read everything I had about Osgoode. The book a Guide to Law Schools in Canada by Catherine Purcell was a very valuable resource. I wanted to make sure that my characteristics and strengths matched those of Osgoode. The interview itself was surprisingly pleasant and informal. I was interviewed by 2 professors. They asked the standard questions - why I wanted to be a lawyer; why Osgoode; did I do my best on the LSAT? I had the standard answers ready - I had prepared! But then, as I began to answer, the words came from the heart instead. From there, the interview turned into the 3 of us simply sitting around having a chat - each question turned into a discussion. This is where the preparation really paid off. I was able to incorporate the strengths and weaknesses of the school, the clubs and extra curricular activities, into my comments and opinions. There were personal questions as well - what did my family think about me going to school, would I have to work during the school year?

I left feeling totally elated and by the time I got home I was crushed. I relived the entire interview and began second guessing my answers. Eventually I realized that they, must have been pretty impressed from what they saw on paper to want to meet me and I knew that I did not say or do anything to lessen that opinion so I was certainly no farther behind.

The best advice I can give anyone who faces the interview is prepare but be yourself. Make sure that your answers are what you really believe and simply not what you think they want to hear, be honest and don't be afraid to say I don't know. Remember, they are not looking to see if you will be a good lawyer - they are looking to see if you will be a successful law student."

Account 5 - Osgoode Mature Student Applicant

What follows are my notes based on an interview that I conducted with a female mature student applicant who achieved an interview at Osgoode.

Warning! What follows is based on one student's experience. Although it is interesting, different people can and will have different experiences.

Applicant's Personal Profile

This applicant is married, in her early 30s and has school aged children. She does not have a university degree, but runs a small business and is also employed. She speaks three languages in addition to English.

Length

The interview itself lasted approximately 30 minutes. She was asked to bring a photograph of herself to the interview. She was told that the purpose of the photograph was to assist the interviewers in remembering her when they made their final decision. (Apparently 70 of the most "competitive" applicants in the mature student category were granted an interview.)

Interviewers And Physical Layout

The applicant was interviewed by two people. The interview took place in a very small room. The applicant sat on a couch and the each of the two interviewers sat in a chair. It was a triangle setup.

Style Of Interview

It was very informal. Although questions were asked, the purpose of the questions was NOT to acquire information (remember that they already have the complete file). Rather the purpose was to engage the applicant in a dialogue. The dialogue was to facilitate communication.

Comment: On this point it is important to remember that communication includes:

- language

- intonation

- tone

(One can learn more about a person by their intonation and tone than from the language that they use.)

The interviewers were friendly and there was a great deal of laughter. In fact, this particular applicant felt uncomfortable with the degree of informality. She mentioned that it was:

"Far too casual for my liking - too much laughing."

Although the interview was informal, the interviewers took copious notes!

Use Of The Personal Statement In The Interview

Remember that most "mature student" applicants are NOT granted an interview. The interview is an achievement and is granted largely on the basis of the personal statement. Hence, it should come as no surprise that the interviewers made use of the applicant's personal statement during the interview - basing many questions on it. In fact, the applicant thought that about three quarters of the interview was based on the personal statement.

Comment: Make sure that you bring a copy of everything in your application file to the interview!

The applicant had the strong impression that - at least to some extent - that the interviewers were testing the veracity and substance of the information in the personal statement. To put it simply: some of the questions were for the purpose of probing information in the personal statement.

Questions Asked During The Interview

The questions seemed to fall into two categories.

Category 1 - Questions to get to know the applicant better

Q. Why do you want to go to law school at this stage in your life?

Q. Tell me more about your work in (such and such) area of community service.

Q. What was it like to learn (such and such) a language?

Q. What are you currently reading?

Q. What do you like about that book?

Q. What type of books do you like?

Q. How do you select the books that you read?

Q. If you could travel anywhere in the world, where would it be?

Category 2 - Questions to see if the applicant could manage the logistics of attending law school and doing well

Examples include:

Q. The first year of law school is quite intense. Your son is relatively young. What does your husband think of your going to law school?

Q. Are you aware that the tuition fees are increasing from $5000 to $8000 next year?

Q. Where do you live? How many minutes are you away? We are trying to work out how long it takes people to get to school.

Comment: The clear purpose of these questions is to ensure that the applicant could pay for law school, get to law school and while in law school be free of distractions.

Ending Impressions

The applicant left the interview feeling neither good nor bad, but very confused. Her confusion was primarily a function of the informality of the interview - that is, the attempt to engage her in a dialogue.

Account 6 - A Mature Student Applicant At McGill

"After getting sick and canceling my mature student interview with the Admissions Committee of the Faculty of Law at McGill once, I was finally aboard a train from Toronto to Montreal to attend the interview scheduled for me for the second time. I had been through so many interviews in my life that this one should not have made me nervous at all, yet, sitting on the train, I was feverishly rummaging through my mind trying to anticipate questions of the Committee and my possible answers.

After all, the interview experience proved the old theory that during an interview we must be our own selves and be ready for any possible twists of fortune. That means any thorough preparation may box up our thinking and work against us. Leafing through the law school booklet to make up a couple of questions about the school may be quite enough.

In the beginning, having a French-speaking Montreal girl beside me on the train seemed a God send - why not prepare better for the interview in a relaxed atmosphere? However, after chatting in French for two hours, I found myself mentally and linguistically drained: my only desire was to return to English, and I admitted that if the interview was to be in French, I would probably have to pack my bag and go home.

When finally, after the train was more than an hour late and I was late for the interview, I got terribly nervous about everything, the interview happened to be completely in English. No one checked my ability to speak in French. The assumption of the Admissions Committee is that since there are certain materials not available in English, applicants must realize what they are getting into themselves.

The interview with representatives of the Admission Committee (there were two professors interviewing me) was a lively chat about a variety of things - with impressive topical swings. This clearly told me that the members of the Committee had no desire to hear anything prepared and gift-wrapped. Since - by their call of duty - they are supposed to ask why applicants wish to go into law (Montreal, McGill University, and the variations of this), the question was asked, but I told the Committee point-blank that I was not going to bother them with stories about love for social justice. They appreciated it very much and lost their interest to the question before I embarked on the real "why".

When the Committee asked me about my opinion on whether the LSAT is able to measure analytic abilities, I told them that I did think so. With my LSAT score being relatively low, I figured I'd be better off admitting that I was just not sufficiently prepared, rather than mud-gushing LSAT developers and claiming that all those 90th percentile winners are a bunch of lucky idiots. The Committee seemed to be quite pleased with my answer.

The fun part commenced when the Professors inquired whether I had any questions about the University or its new weird programme. I happened to have a lot of questions, and, had I not felt that the time had come for me to shut up, the Committee might have probably sent me to hell. In any case, being prepared to ask detailed questions about the curriculum or the faculty will never hurt.

Thus, going through an interview at McGill University Faculty of Law was a memorable and pleasurable experience, which another time proved that people are always people, and they - irrespective of how high they fly - prefer a lively spontaneous conversation to a castrated, prepackaged, and learnt-by-heart speech of an intimidated applicant, fumbling with his fingers. Just a touch of preparation will do enough good to the forthcoming interview."

Account 7 - Interview At Cornell

"Hi prospective law students,

If applying to law school is a stressful endeavor, the admissions interview could be considered the pinnacle of pressure. Imagine your life plan resting on your performance on a half-hour question and answer. I myself had to recently clear this admissions hurdle. At first I was rather intimidated by the request to show up for an interview. However, my initial apprehension proved unwarranted.

The interview was more of an informal chat than an intimidating interview. I was interviewed by a gentleman who recognized my face from the tour of the law school he gave me 2 months earlier. At the time I asked about athletics at the school and he remembered this and put me at ease by opening the interview with an update as to how the hockey team was doing and a story of an undergrad who had just returned from Salt Lake City with a bronze medal (for those of you trying to guess the athlete or school, my interview was at Cornell and the athlete was an American snowboarder if I am not mistaken).

This is another example of how it can be helpful to visit law schools to which you are applying.

The interview consisted of two broad questions:

1. Why law?

2. Why school X?

For those of you that took care in writing your personal statements the answers to these questions should be a repetition of what you have already thoughtfully documented. The answers should easily flow off your tongue.

What I believe to be important is to be sincere and to know what school X has that appeals to you specifically. If you show that you have a sincere interest in the school and that you will benefit from and contribute to the characteristics that make school X unique, then the admissions committee will happily admit you to the study of law. Also, this is another opportunity to collect information about the character of the school. Just the fact that someone wants to meet you should be taken as a sign that the administration might actually care about what you are like as a person rather than just a number.

Conclusion

For most law school applicants the interview plays no role in the admissions process. However, for those applicants who are interviewed, the interview is important. If you are invited to an interview, I suggest you do some practice interviewing in advance. Although the preceding accounts of law school interviews are interesting, they should not be construed to be a "blueprint" for what your interview might be.

Book IV - A Report

Law School: Understanding, Surviving, Flourishing!

Summary And Introduction

My Advice To You Is ....

Law school is an academic experience unlike any other. In fact law school really is a "way of life." Those who enjoy it most, benefit the most and achieve the most are those who have the most balanced view on it. Law school will be your full-time job for three years. But, there is a difference between having a job and having a life. Do make sure that you have a life!

Book IV will explore every aspect of law school that I think could possibly be of interest to you. Read it. Enjoy it. And finally, try to sit in on at least one law school class before starting!

In Book IV, I will be your guide through law school.

Book IV - Chapter Summaries

18. The Academic Side Of Law School - Courses, Workload, Cases, Exams

Focus: What courses will you take? What is the workload? Read your first legal case and participate in some analysis. What are law exams like?

19. Keeping It Interesting - Enhancing The Academic Side Of The Law School Experience

Focus: Your life is more than school. Can you incorporate other activities? What about exchange programs?

20. Summer Jobs And Non-Academic Aspects Of The Law Student Experience

Focus: How does one find a summer job? Why is it important? How competitive is it?

21. "Law School Cafe" - A Law Student's Diary

Focus: The Canadian "One L" - a law student's diary from the first month to graduation.

22. Ethical Aspects Of The Law School Environment

Focus: Ethics matter. Consider the recent cheating scandal at one Canadian law school. How might it change the law school environment?

23. Excelling In Law School - What I Wish I Had Known Before Starting

Focus: To Excel you need to know much more than the law. How to get the grades you deserve.

Chapter 18

The Academic Side Of Law School - Courses, Workload, Cases, Exams

"The primary goal of legal education should be to train for the legal profession people who are, first, honest; second, compassionate; third, knowledgeable about the law; and fourth, committed to the role of law and justice in our democratic society."

-Chief Justice Brian Dickson

So, What's It All About?

Law school is a highly personal experience. North American law schools are very good. In particular, one will receive a quality legal education from any Canadian or U.S. ABA approved law school. Your return from the law school experience will be directly proportional to your investment. Although different people experience law school differently, almost everyone regards law school as a valuable experience. I have met few people who regretted going to law school!

A Truly Mind Altering Experience

A legal education will enhance the way you see the world. I remember so vividly, how studying corporate law and constitutional law changed the way that I processed information that I read in the morning paper! It's a great experience. Go for it!

Here is the account of a recent law school graduate of her legal education:

"One law student's comment about her legal education

Looking back, I have benefited a great deal from my legal education.

For instance, I now better understand the "constitutional issue" when I hear it mentioned on the CBC, although I will still be flipping a coin to decide who to vote for come this federal election; I now know that a corporate entity is a natural person and that like us, a corporation is entitled to talk freely as accorded by our Charter of Rights; just as corporations are humans, I also found out that dogs could be cats and cats could be dogs if they confine themselves to the four corners of a statute; I realize that as a land owner, I would have rights over not only the portion of land that is registered under my name at the Land Title Office, but also have rights over the air space above the land, all the way up to heaven, as well as the soil beneath the land, all the way down to hell, ... the list goes on.

Aside from these tidbits of information, however, my legal education has also given me an insight into how society officially organizes itself and how it regulates the relationships amongst the individual members.

In summary, my legal education has rewarded me in many different ways: my new membership status at the law society, a sense of awareness of the legal dimension of our social existence, and ... my new corporate law firm, navy-blue suits which I live in 15 hours a day.

To those of you who have decided to go to law school, best of luck!"

What Is The Purpose Of Law School? Theory, Practice Or Both?

Law school is an academic exercise and NOT a professional school. Many students forget this and measure the quality of their legal education by the number of "practical skills" that they learn. Practical skills can be learned quickly and easily in the Bar Admission Course and during your early years of practise. Law school is your only opportunity to learn legal theory and your only opportunity to learn how to continue learning about law. Much of the "black letter law" that is learned in law school is obsolete by graduation. The law is in a constant state of change. The purpose of law school is to teach students how to research, understand and apply current law.

There has always been, and will always be a disagreement about the purpose of a legal education. Some believe that law school should be used to learn practical lawyering skills. Although the following article was written in 1991, it could have been written in the 70s, 80s, 90s or 21st century.

WARNING!! This article should be used only to illustrate the debate over what law school should be about. Given the age of the article (1991) it should not be used to evaluate any of the schools named in it. (The article could not even have been used to evaluate the law schools mentioned in 1991.)

February 21, 1991

Law school grads frustrated, unprepared

Michael Crawford

It might surprise, even anger, many people to learn that a fresh-faced law school graduate these days likely has little or no idea how to draft a contract, a will or real estate agreement.

It certainly frustrated many budding lawyers and their employers, according to a Canadian Lawyer magazine poll of recent law school graduates published this month.

The survey went out to 2,500 lawyers who graduated between 1986 and 1990 and more than 700 responses were returned. The graduates not only commented on their preparedness for the practice of law, but also rated their alma maters on everything from quality of curriculum and faculty to library and classroom facilities.

More than half, 54%, said their law school did not prepare them sufficiently. Graduates of the universities of Victoria, Toronto and Windsor were most pleased with their legal education, giving the schools an average grade of A for offering relevant and practical law courses, as well as for cultivating a personal and open atmosphere between students and teachers.

Schools faltering

Schools rated as faltering in certain respects included some top names — York University's Osgoode Hall, the universities of Montreal, Western Ontario, Queen's and Laval.

Many graduates claimed these schools focused too much on theory and failed to offer enough courses in practical legal skills. They noted that some professors often had no law practice experience.

There were other complaints. At York, some students cited overcrowding and poor or inadequate testing standards. "Osgoode Hall is over-rated as a law school" was one 1989 graduate's comment.

Queen's got bad reviews for a perceived lack of business and advocacy courses, and some complained about the well-publicized political in-fighting between feminist and "mainstream" teachers.

The reactions from poorly rated schools are defensive.

The deans of Osgoode, Western and Queen's all say their schools will unlikely veer from their emphasis on theory, and feel it is not unusual for graduates to be critical of their education.

"If they're just starting their jobs, for example, they may feel it's very important to know how to search a title or draft a will, or any of the technical things that, frankly, could be taught in a community college," says Western's dean, Peter Mercer. But he adds that later in their careers the graduates will value the broader, theoretical education.

While most of the survey respondents said they recognized the need for a theoretical grounding, many felt there should be only one year of theory and two years of "practical nuts-and-bolts courses."

One said, "We do not need to concentrate on turning out legal technicians, but I doubt anyone's education would suffer from at least being shown legal documents that they will have to deal with in the future."

That opinion is echoed by senior lawyers who deal with each year's crop of fresh graduates. "I think it's burying your head in the sand not to realize that 90% of the people you're educating are there because they want to practise law," says Eric Gertner, director of research at McCarthy Tetrault in Toronto.

The debate is not new, but some schools appear to have found a happy medium.

Top-rated University of Victoria law school, started in 1974, features small classes, a first-name basis, open-door policy and a curriculum with a high practice-oriented content. But, says dean Maureen Maloney, theory is also important, so teachers are encouraged to find new ways to teach, such as problem-solving assignments.

'Law in context'

"Here we have what I like to call 'law in context,' so we look at the economic, political and social ramifications of law, and the way it works in society," she says.

For example, a teacher may focus on how the Income Tax Act affects certain groups. "In fact, women come out quite badly in the Income Tax Act, so it's very easy to put into that a feminist critique," says Maloney.

"At the same time, you have to go through in quite rigorous detail how the registered retirement savings plan rules actually work, and what people have to include for employment income and what they don't."

Victoria is also the first Canadian law school to try out a concept that many say is the wave of the future — co-op education. Students earn their degree over four years with a staggered agenda of teaching terms and work experience in law firms, government and courts.

The program is in its second year and limited to 30 students because of funding, but Maloney says each year the pilot project has been oversubscribed by applicants who see it as a better alternative to traditional legal education.

Reprinted with permission of the author.

Law School Content - What Courses Will You Take?

You may have heard the old adage about law school:

In first year they scare you to death.

In second year they work you to death.

In third year they bore you to death.

First Year Law Course Content

The first year of law school is basically the same at every Canadian and U.S. law school. The courses typically taught include:

Constitutional law: An introduction to the Canadian or U.S. constitution from a legal perspective. This course deals with the structure and the history of the constitution, the powers of all levels of government, civil liberties and the constitutional rights of individuals, including The Canadian Charter of Rights and Freedoms and the Bill of Rights in the U.S.

Contracts: An introduction to such general concepts as the formation and enforcement of contracts, remedies for breach of contract and the rights of contracting parties.

Criminal law: An introduction to basic concepts and principles in criminal law. Procedural aspects, the rights of criminals, the types of defenses and criminal liability are discussed.

Torts: An introduction to the concept of liability within private wrongs. Injuries to persons, damage to property and reputation are some of the areas that are studied.

Property: An introduction that examines the nature of property, its concepts and uses. Ownership and possession, covenants, easements, adverse possession, and future interests are covered during the course.

Legal Writing: This is a course which deals with legal research skills and legal writing. Students are typically given practice in the research and drafting of memoranda in various aspects of the law.

What Courses Will You Take? - Second and Third Year Course Content

After first year, students have more freedom to choose their courses. Many schools have a requirement of a "major research project." In addition, virtually all schools require students to participate in a moot court.

How Law Is Learned - The Case Study Method

Law schools use the "case study method." This method involves the detailed examination of a number of related judicial opinions that describe an area of law. Professors don't tell you what principles of law the cases are designed to illuminate. Instead, they expect the student to discover this by reading the case. It is the job of the student to discover the relevant legal principle. Since law is generally not "black and white", learning law by reading cases can be difficult. Consider the following comment, which although a bit extreme, can be true some of the time.

"You work out of a "casebook." As the name implies, this book contains reprints of bits and pieces from important cases that judges have decided down through the years. The cases are often difficult to understand, not only because the law is complex, but also because the judges who wrote them talk in circles.

Half the time, when you've finished reading a case, you say to yourself, "Now what the hell was that all about?" You look at the notes after the case, hoping for answers, but all you see are a bunch of questions or, at best, some comments that seem to be moving forward, as though you were itching for more. You turn the page, and they're starting a new case. You're baffled. You turn some more pages, and you discover that this goes on, case and notes, case and notes, for 50 or 100 pages. And then it's a new chapter, and you're still utterly confused."

A U.S. Law School Graduate

So, What's A Case? - An Example ...

Here is an example of case that is included in many first year courses on criminal law. Cases are based on real facts and include the decision of the court.

Exercise: Read the following case and see if you can answer the questions that follow.

"FAGAN V. METROPOLITAN POLICE COMMISSIONER
[1969] 1 Q.B. 439; [1968] 3 All E.R. 442 J.P. 16; 112 Sol. Jo. 800; 52 Cr. App. R. 700. Queen's Bench.

James J.: The appellant, Vincent Martel Fagan, was convicted by the Willesden magistrates of assaulting David Morris, a police constable, in the execution of his duty on August 31, 1967.

The sole question is whether the prosecution proved facts which in law amounted to an assault.

On August 31, 1967, the appellant was reversing a motor car in Fortunegate Road, London, N.W.1, when Police Constable Morris directed him to drive the car forwards to the curbside and standing in front of the car pointed out a suitable place in which to park. At first the appellant stopped the car too far from the curb for the officer's liking. Morris asked him to park closer and indicated a precise spot. The appellant drove forward towards him and stopped it with the offside wheel on Morris's left foot. "Get off you are on my foot," said the officer. "Fuck you, you can wait," said the appellant. The engine of the car stopped running. Morris repeated several times "Get off my foot." The appellant said reluctantly "Okay man, okay," and then slowly turned on the ignition of the vehicle and reversed it off the officer's foot. The appellant had either turned the ignition off to stop the engine or turned it off after the engine had stopped running.

The justices at quarter sessions on those facts were left in doubt as to whether the mounting of the wheel onto the officer's foot was deliberate or accidental. They were satisfied, however, beyond all reasonable doubt that the appellant "knowingly, provocatively and unnecessarily allowed the wheel to remain on the foot after the officer said 'Get off, you are on my foot'". They found that on those facts an assault was proved.

Mr. Abbas for the appellant relied upon the passage in Stone's Justices' Manual (1968), Vol. 1, p. 651, where assault is defined. He contends that on the finding of the judges the initial mounting of the wheel could not be an assault and that the act of the wheel mounting the foot came to an end without there being any mens rea. It is argued that thereafter there was no act on the part of the appellant which could constitute an actus reus but only the omission of failure to remove the wheel as soon as he was asked. That failure it is said, could not in law be an assault, nor could it in law provide the necessary mens rea to convert the original act of mounting the foot into an assault.

Mr. Rant for the respondent argues that the first mounting of the foot was an actus reus which continued until the moment of the time at which the wheel was removed. During that continuing act, it is said, the appellant formed the necessary intention to constitute the element of mens rea and once that element was added to the continuing act, an assault took place. In the alternative, Mr. Rant argues that there can be situations in which there is a duty to act and that in such situations an omission to act in breach of duty would in law amount to an assault. It is unnecessary to formulate any concluded views on this alternative.

In our judgment the question arising, which has been argued on general principles, falls to be decided on the facts of the particular case. An assault is any act which intentionally-or possibly recklessly-causes another person to apprehend immediate and unlawful personal violence. Although "assault" is an independent crime and is to be treated as such, for practical purposes today "assault" is generally synonymous with the term "battery" and is a term used to mean the actual intended use of unlawful force to another person without his consent. On the facts of the present case the "assault" alleged involved a "battery". Where an assault involves a battery, it matters not, in our judgment, whether the battery is inflicted directly by the body of the offender or through the medium of some weapon or instrument controlled by the action of the offender. An assault may be committed by the laying of a hand upon another, and the action does not cease to be an assault if it is a stick held in the hand and not the hand itself which is laid on the person of the victim. So for our part we see no difference in principle between the action of stepping on to a person's toe and maintaining that position and the action of driving a car on to a person's foot and sitting in the car whilst its position on the foot is maintained.

To constitute the offence of assault some intentional act must have been performed: a mere omission to act cannot amount to an assault. Without going into the question whether words alone can constitute an assault, it is clear that the words spoken by the appellant could not alone amount to an assault: they can only shed a light on the appellant's action. For our part we think the crucial question is whether in this case the act of the appellant can be said to be complete and spent at the moment of time when the car wheel came to rest on the foot or whether his act is to be regarded as a continuing act operating until the wheel was removed. In our judgment a distinction is to be drawn between acts which are complete-though results may continue to flow-and those acts which are continuing. Once the act is complete it cannot thereafter be said to be a threat to inflict unlawful force upon the victim. If the act, as distinct from the results thereof, is a continuing act there is a continuing threat to inflict unlawful force. If the assault involves a battery and that battery continues there is a continuing act of assault.

For an assault to be committed both the elements of actus reus and mens rea must be present at the same time. The "actus reus" is the action causing the effect on the victim's mind (see the observations of Park B. in Regina v. St. George [1840], 9 C. & P. 483, 490, 493). The "mens rea" is the intention to cause that effect. It is not necessary that the mens rea should be present at the inception of the actus reus; it can be superimposed upon an existing act. On the other hand the subsequent inception of mens rea cannot convert an act which has been completed without mens rea into an assault.

In our judgment the Willesden magistrates and quarter sessions were right in law. On the facts found the action of the appellant may have been initially unintentional, but the time came when knowing that the wheel was on the officer's foot the appellant (1) remained seated in the car so that his body through the medium of the car was in contact with the officer, (2) switched off the ignition of the car, (3) maintained the wheel of the car on the foot and (4) used words indicating the intention of keeping the wheel in that position. For our part we cannot regard such conduct as mere omission or inactivity.

There was an act constituting a battery which at its inception was not criminal because there was no element of intention but which became criminal from the moment the intention was formed to produce the apprehension which was flowing from the continuing act. The fallacy of the appellant's argument is that it seeks to equate the facts of this case with such a case as where a motorist has accidentally run over a person and, that action having been completed, fails to assist the victim with the intent that the victim should suffer.

We would dismiss this appeal."

EXERCISE: Your first case related assignment. Based on the case, try to answer the following questions.

1. What is necessary to constitute an assault?

2. What is meant by "mens rea?"

3. What is meant by "actus reus?"

4. What is the temporal relationship between the "mens rea" and the "actus reus?"

5. Can the "actus reus" requirement be satisfied by an omission to do something?

6. What is the legal argument made by Mr. Fagan's lawyer?

7. What was the court's decision?

Some suggested answers may be found in the Appendix at the end of this chapter.

How Are The Cases Used To Teach? - The Socratic Method

"Judging by the results, "though this be madness, yet there is method in't."

- Dr. Bernard Diamond discussing the Socratic method - 'Psychological Problems Of Law Students"

How are legal cases used in class? In many cases the professor will call upon students to answer questions designed to explore the facts of the case and determine the legal principles involved in reaching the result. This method of instruction is called the "Socratic method" and is designed to teach the student to think like a lawyer.

The "Socratic method" places the onus of learning on the student. Those of you who have read *One L* or seen the movie *The Paper Chase* will know how it works. The classroom discussions can be exciting, illuminating, frightening (if you are not prepared for class) and emotionally draining.

The Socratic method of teaching is widely, but not exclusively used. It can be used effectively only by professors with very effective teaching skills.

What follows is one description of the Socratic method.

"The method is named for Socrates, who supposedly never made statements, but just kept on asking questions. So in law school, your professors ask, and you answer, until they stump you. At that point, you may finally be ready to listen and learn.

I grant that, as compared to a lecture, it's more entertaining to watch some poor jerk squirm under the professor's relentless badgering. But when you move beyond sadism and start to ask how much you're learning, you have to wonder. It always seemed moronic, to me, to use a question-and-answer format in a class of 150 students. You can't hear what the students are saying, you can't believe they're saying something that stupid (or that complicated), you can't stand a particular student who likes to dominate the debate, etc.

In most of those large classes, no one is assigned to the row of seats in back of the big classrooms, near the exits. As the semester grinds on, you see a growing fringe of students sitting back there, where the lights don't shine too well. These are obviously not their assigned seats, and you realize that this is a form of truce. They'll attend classes, even though they don't understand what's going on, as long as the professor pretends they're not there and doesn't call on them.

By semester's end, many students have lost track of what's happening in the intimate little chat that goes on between the professor and the few students who are still on his/her wavelength. Does a student's love of the Socratic method have anything to do with his/her ability to practice law? No. Is it a better way of teaching than the one they use in, say, engineering school? No. But the Socratic method will arbitrarily help to determine whether the student understands the professor, earns a higher grade, and gets a better job. When I ran head-on into this teaching method, I had no patience for it. And, of course, it had no patience for me either."

A U.S. Law School Graduate

Law School Exams - What Do They Test And What Do They Look Like?

What Law Exams Test - Law school exams are not for the purpose of testing whether you know the law. They assume that you know the law. Rather law school exams test your ability to apply the law to a given set of facts for the purpose of reaching a resolution.

What law exams look like - What follows is a sample of what one law school exam question looked like. Remember, exams are set by individual professors. Therefore, they will differ. But, they all assume that you know the law and test your ability to apply the law to the facts.

"NOTE: This problem is set in Dullsville, an imaginary common law province of Canada. Decisions of the Supreme Court of Canada are therefore binding on the Dullsville courts.

The accused, Jim McCormack, was charged with impaired driving causing death, and elected to be tried by judge alone in Dullsville Provincial Court. The trial judge, Maude Prov. Ct. J., made the following findings of fact:

For some years, Jim McCormack had been in the habit of taking a few Valiums in the evening. These Valiums had been prescribed for his brother, not for him, but there is no indication in the evidence that his driving, his performance at work, or any other aspect of his conduct, had ever been adversely affected by this habit. On 31 January 1998, McCormack was feeling somewhat depressed, and decided to take some Valiums just after lunch. He rummaged around in his brother's bedside table, found a pill bottle, and took four tablets. He then settled down to listen to the the hockey game on the radio. According to McCormack's evidence, which I accept on this point, the next thing he remembers is being taken out of his car by ambulance attendants following a crash on Massachusetts Avenue. The tragic events that preceded this crash founded the charge against him.

The pills that McCormack took were not Valium at all but halcion a commonly prescribed remedy for insomnia. The Valiums that McCormack usually took are largish oval blue pills, while the Halcions he actually took are smallish round blue pills. McCormack testified that he noticed this difference, but assumed that the shape of the pill had changed; he did not know that his brother had begun taking sleeping pills, nor did he bother to read the label on the bottle because, as he testified, "I can't tell the name of one drug from another." McCormack reads and writes at about a Grade 4 level, and I accept his evidence that he was unable to read the label and unaware of the effects that Halcion might have on him. The medical evidence at trial clearly establishes that four tablets amounted to a massive dose of Halcion that could well have placed McCormack into a state where he could conduct, albeit unreliably, routine tasks, and not remember later that he had done so. It appears from the evidence that after taking the Halcion McCormack got into his car and began to drive erratically along Massachusetts Avenue. The street was covered with a thin layer of snow at this time. McCormack's driving was sufficiently poor to attract the attention of two Dullsville police officers, Constables Smith and Souter, who were patrolling Massachusetts Avenue in their cruiser. When they turned on their light and siren to pull McCormack over, McCormack increased his speed, driving ahead, in Souter's words, "like a bat out of hell." Smith and Souter gave chase, and also called on their radio for other police vehicles to intercept McCormack. In response to this call, Constables Heart and Heath quickly set up a road block about three miles farther along Massachusetts Avenue, while Detectives Doody and Yang tracked McCormack's path from a police helicopter. McCormack crashed into Heart and Heath's roadblock. Meanwhile, Smith and Souter lost control of their cruiser and mounted the sidewalk on Massachusetts Avenue, killing a pedestrian named Donnelly.

I am satisfied beyond a reasonable doubt that McCormack was impaired by a drug when he drove his car on 31 January, and that Donnelly's death was a direct result of the impairment. The accused is therefore guilty as charged.

McCormack is appealing the verdict to the Dullsville Court of Appeal, and has retained Frank Bailey to represent him. You are an articling student in Bailey's office. Write a memorandum outlining the possible grounds of appeal and assessing their probable success. Your memorandum should be carefully reasoned and should make appropriate reference to relevant constitutional and statutory provisions and case law. If you think the facts as stated by the trial judge are insufficient to resolve any issue, do not speculate about what the facts might be, but please indicate how your answer would be affected by additional facts. (Bailey will assign another articling student to search the trial transcript for more evidence.)"

Answering Law Exams - The Importance Of Technique

Many law students underperform on their exams because they simply don't have the proper technique of answering law exam questions. Learn the basic principles of answering law exam questions!

Conclusion

Although all law schools will get you to the same destination, they do it in somewhat different ways. Although all roads may lead to Rome, it doesn't mean that each road has the same scenery. What you get out of law school will depend on what you put in. No two people experience law school in exactly the same way. It is suggested that you learn enough about law school in advance so that you can get the most that you can out of your experience.

APPENDIX

Possible Answers To Fagan Questions

1. What is necessary to constitute an assault?

An assault is defined as any act which intentionally causes another to apprehend immediate and unlawful personal violence.

2. What is meant by "mens rea?"

"Mens rea" is the intention to cause the unlawful act. In this case "mens rea" would be the intention to perform an act which caused another to apprehend immediate personal violence.

3. What is meant by "actus reus?"

The "actus reus" is the act causing the apprehension of immediate personal violence.

4. What is the temporal relationship between the "mens rea" and the "actus reus?"

The intention to perform the act and the act causing the apprehension of violence must be present at the same time.

5. Can the "actus reus" requirement be satisfied by an omission to do something?

No, an omission to do something cannot constitute an "actus reus."

6. What is the legal argument made by Mr. Fagan's lawyer?

Fagan's lawyer argued that the car had rested on Morris's foot long before Fagan was aware of it. At the time Fagan formulated his "mens rea" the car was already stopped on Morris's foot. Hence, at that time there was no "actus reus." Remember that an omission cannot constitute an "actus reus." Therefore, no "mens rea" and "actus reus" existed at the same time. Hence, Fagan should be acquitted.

7. What was the court's decision?

The court agreed that the "mens rea" and "actus reus" must exist at the same time. The court also agreed that omissions do not satisfy the "actus reus" requirement. But, the court simply decided that, as a matter of fact, there was an ongoing "actus reus" and at a certain point the "mens rea" sprung into existence to co-exist with the "actus reus." Result - Conviction. Poor Fagan.

Discussion And Debate

Do you think Fagan should have been convicted? Do you think the court is bending over backwards to convict Fagan? In this regard consider the following debate between a future prosecutor and future defense lawyer. It is typical of what you will hear in a law school class.

Defense: I feel so sorry for Fagan. Such a misunderstood man. The problem is that, at the point that anyone could possibly infer "mens rea" there was no "actus reus."

Prosecution: Ah, but did that happen? Were they separate events or did they overlap? All moot points because there was no doubt the courts were going to convict any schmuck who, when "accidentally" treading on a policeman's toes with his car, refused to remove the car and uttered a profanity at the officer.

Defense: He simply didn't do anything. Poor guy - convicted for what he should have done.

Prosecution: No, convicted for leaving his car on the officer's foot, turning off the ignition and making the officer wait before he moved his car because he was pissed off. Don't forget that courts tend to characterize the offence with respect to the accused's actions. I understand your stance on this. He was convicted for "not" moving his car but I think the judgment was further characterized by the actions surrounding that negative act.

Defense: At the point that one could argue there was an "actus reus", there was no "mens rea." They just don't go together. (kind of like my shirts and ties) The whole episode was nothing more than a tragic accident. The police officer accidentally let his foot get under Fagan's car.

Prosecution: Agreed, but when you accidentally do something that causes physical pain to another person, are you not quick to act to redress the situation? Or do you normally tell someone, "Fuck off, you can wait" before you give your humblest apologies and remove the harm inflicted?

Defense: The result is determined by how you feel about Fagan.

Prosecution: I have no feelings for Fagan one way or another. But if he did that to me, I'd feel some redress would be prudent.

Defense: Then the courts will try to invent the "actus reus" to convict.

Prosecution: I don't think the courts did this but it's all in how you interpret it.

Defense: A bit like the Greek myth of Procrustus (cut off the legs to fit the size of the bed).

Prosecution: Agreed. I think we can put Fagan to bed now.

Chapter 19

Keeping It Interesting - Enhancing The Academic Side Of The Law School Experience

To paraphrase a recent advertisement:

"Some people live and some people live well!"

Most law schools have programs that allow you to enhance the academic side of law school. You should explore your opportunities.

Joint Programs - Everything To Gain And Nothing To Lose!

All law schools offer joint programs. You have to be in law school for three years anyway. Why not get an extra degree out of the experience? (To read some experiences on joint programs, review the chapter on how to choose law schools.)

Exchange Programs Which Don't Lead to Joint Degrees

Although these programs don't lead to joint degrees, they are academically enriching. As a bonus, they may also offer the opportunity to travel the world!

Taking Advantage Of Clinical Or Co-Op Programs

Some schools have programs that offer academic credit for work down in some sort of practical setting outside the law school classroom. Here are some first hand accounts.

Account 1 - A Legal Clinic

"Reflections On Law School

Many people that hear that I am on my way to becoming a lawyer (a student at law) often seem to paint all lawyers with the same brush, characterizing them as money hungry corporate sharks. As a second year student currently at Osgoode Hall, I am telling you that is simply not the case. I am sure, given the fact that you are subscribed to this newsletter you have already realized this is a myth. However, I would like to shed some light on the more altruistic side of law.

Thus far, law school has consisted of reading case after case after case after case and then culminating all this case reading in a 100% three hour final. Don't get me wrong - law school has been great, and I have learned a great deal of how to think like a lawyer. However, I was really lacking in terms of practical knowledge. That is, I had no idea what lawyers really did, day in, day out. I was fortunate enough to be chosen to participate in an intensive program in poverty law at a poverty clinic in Ontario. I figured this would give me some practical knowledge as to how the law works, and give me humble beginnings by serving low income residents in Toronto. My experiences in the past month have been incredible. Not only has it humbled me and made me more thankful for living a comfortable, financially secure life, but it has allowed me to create legal solutions to various problems the Parkdale community is currently faced with.

What I have learned is that law has no one easy legal solution, and it really does involve using one's imagination and innovation to craft the most effective legal solution for one's client. This could mean anything from arguing in a provincial or federal court, mediating, negotiating, lobbying, or simply writing letters to the opposing party. Parkdale is certainly not the only place that a blossoming law student such as myself can make a difference - there is your school legal aid clinic, pro bono work, and various legal aid clinics that are in dire need of help.

I can sit back and reflect tonight and realize that I chose the right career for myself - I am challenging my mind and helping others in need - what could possibly be better??"

Account 2 - A One Of A Kind Adventure

"My job is with the legal aid office for Nunavut - Maliiganik Tukisiiniakvik. It services all of the Eastern Arctic including Cape Dorset and the Arctic Circle communities but the head office is in Iqaluit, the capital of the new territory. Most of the work I do will be in Iqaluit, but I'm going to get sent on at least one circuit, probably the Arctic circle circuit (they usually run that one in the summer months).

Since there aren't many lawyers up there (the Premier of Nunavut, Paul Ogalik, is the only Inuk lawyer in the North) law students do lots of heavy work. I will be in court most days doing bail & sentencing hearings, have my own files, and possibly be the "lead" counsel for a summary trial (if one comes up). It is a different world up there though. The guy who is there now doing this job from the UVic Co-op program has had some amazing experiences. For example: he was the 2nd lawyer-type person to interview Salamonie Jaw, the guy who shot the RCMP officer a few weeks ago. Imagine, in Toronto, it would be a battle amongst high rolling partners to be the one to interview someone who shot a cop - in Nunavut they send the student in. The experience should be intense.

My job isn't related directly to the law school, but since there are only a couple of UVic people who are going to be up there over the summer I'm sure they will rope me into something. I am the co-op rep. at UVic, so there might be some work for me up there in that capacity with the new students. For the most part this first year is going to be a "pre-law" basics type year. There is a lot of catchup to be done before the substantive law stuff can be started for most of the people in the new program.

There are two other students from UVic co-op going to Iqaluit this summer, they are both working for the Court of Justice and will have much more to do with the development of the new school and the local bar. My job is more people-focused than administrative or research-based."

Account 3 - A One Of A Kind Adventure Continued

What follows is an email I recently received from a student.

"Hi John,

Hope you're doing well and enjoying teaching these days. I thought I'd just send you a quick update as to what I'm up to - I always appreciate how much your help contributed to getting me to this spot I'm at now.

Right now I'm in Ottawa working at the Department of Foreign Affairs and International Trade in the Oceans, Environmental and Economic Law Division as a legal researcher co-op student. It's interesting work spanning everything from extraterritoriality issues in future cyber-crime laws to arctic sovereignty and oceans law to multinational environmental treaties. I get to do work for a variety of lawyers here in the Department, all of whom are also foreign service officers with lots of interesting stories to tell.

The big news is that I finally heard back from the UN International Criminal Tribunal for Rwanda and ...

I've been accepted to do my third and final co-op placement with the Office of the Prosecutor! I'll be at the Tribunal's main office in Arusha, Tanzania. It's going to be a long summer of fundraising and grant-seeking to afford this unpaid internship but I'm still awfully excited. What a wonderful chance to contribute something positive - this is why I came to law school. Two other students from UVic are going to work for the Yugoslav Tribunal in The Hague in September as well - co-op is really a great program.

Anyway, thanks again for helping me get this all started.

J"

Conclusion

Remember that law school is an opportunity for exposure to many different things. Take full advantage of the available opportunities!

THE LAWYERS WEEKLY
NEWS FOR THE CANADIAN LEGAL PROFESSION

STUDENT DISCOUNT ▶ GET 75%
OFF THE REGULAR PRICE

In interviews, on the job and in the classroom, a strong store of practical knowledge, a familiarity with what concerns practitioners in the real world, will make you stand out from the pack.

● **BLACK-LETTER LAW KNOWLEDGE ISN'T ENOUGH**. THE BEST WAY TO PREPARE YOURSELF FOR ARTICLING INTERVIEWS AND A LEGAL CAREER IS TO BE CONVERSANT IN CURRENT LEGAL AFFAIRS, PRACTICAL TRENDS AND THE LATEST CASES.

● AS YOU READ THIS, SIGNIFICANT RULINGS ARE BEING HANDED DOWN, IMPORTANT LEGISLATION PASSED, AND PRACTICE DIRECTIONS RELEASED BY THE COURTS.

● THERE'S ANOTHER HALF TO YOUR LEGAL EDUCATION—THE DEVELOPMENT OF **PRACTICAL KNOWLEDGE** AND SKILLS. IN THE YEAR 2000 AND BEYOND, A PRACTICAL EDUCATION WILL GIVE YOU UNTOLD BENEFITS AND A DISTINCT COMPETITIVE ADVANTAGE.

● USE THE LAWYERS WEEKLY, CANADA'S PREMIER LEGAL NEWSPAPER — IT'S ALL THE PRACTICAL EDUCATION YOU'LL NEED.

Subscribe to The Lawyers Weekly newspaper for only $49*

TO ORDER, COMPLETE A PHOTOCOPY OF THE SUBSCRIPTION FORM BELOW AND MAIL TO:
THE LAWYERS WEEKLY, 75 CLEGG ROAD, MARKHAM, ONTARIO L6G 1A1
OR CALL TOLL-FREE 1-800-668-6481 OR FAX YOUR ORDER TO 1-800-461-3275
MAKE CHEQUES PAYABLE TO: BUTTERWORTHS CANADA LTD.

☐ **YES!** SEND ME A STUDENT SUBSCRIPTION TO THE LAWYERS WEEKLY
IMMEDIATELY FOR $49 + GST = $52.43 (TERM: 48 WEEKLY ISSUES)

TLW STUDENT RATE

NAME

ADDRESS

CITY   PROVINCE   POSTAL CODE

METHOD OF PAYMENT:
☐ CHEQUE ENCLOSED   CREDIT CARD: ☐ VISA ☐ MASTERCARD ☐ AMEX

CREDIT CARD NUMBER   EXPIRY DATE

PHONE NUMBER   SIGNATURE

SCHOOL NAME   STUDENT #

* Offer valid in Canada, to law school students only. GST not included. Price subject to change without notice. Regular one-year price $205+GST. Allow 2-3 weeks after receipt of payment before delivery of first issue. Not to be combined with another TLW offer.

Room No. 2328

Chapter 20

Summer Jobs And Non-Academic Aspects Of The Law Student Experience

Law School And Your Life - Stress, Activities and Lifestyle

For many the thought of law school is a frightening experience. Law school is not hard, it is just different. Law students are required to think, study and organize time in a way that is different from their previous studies.

It is possible to be a law student and have:

- a balanced family and/or social life;

- a part-time job; and

- a healthy collection of extra-curricular activities. You don't have to spend all your time on your law studies. In fact, participation in other activities will make the time that you devote to your studies, more effective.

Is Stress Real Or Just Part Of The Culture?

How stressful is law school? It depends on who you ask. What follows are the perspectives of two people with conflicting points of view.

Perspective 1 - The Words Of A U.S. Law School Graduate

1) "What the Pressure Does to You

Perhaps you've had the experience of dealing with people who've been working 80 or 100 hours a week for months on end. At times, they're irrational. Their moods swing with the wind. They have no patience. This experience is not limited to law students.

But there's something special about law school. It goes beyond the quantity of work and the pressure to get it done. Law school is the door into a hard new world. It brings you face-to-face with a different, less friendly kind of person, and eventually that's what you become too.

I sometimes wonder whether it's anything like what people feel in the moments before their first act of cannibalism. In law school, people seem to hope that you'll fail, and you find yourself thinking the same way in return. Some classmates may share your unhappiness with this, but others seem eager to say, "Hey, if you don't like it, go somewhere else. It'll be one less body for me to climb over."

Sometimes, the tension was impressive. One law student punched out a clerk at a copy center when the clerk told him that his photocopies would be delayed. During an otherwise relaxed pick-up game of volleyball, one of my fiercely competitive classmates, a top-flight athlete, could not resist spiking hammer-blow shots at the two out-of-shape women on the opposing team. I cut my roommate's telephone cord, in the middle of a phone conversation, when he wouldn't stop talking right outside my door and disturbing my study. And I remember, one night in the Third Phase bar, being reduced to tears, when I didn't even think that was possible anymore, by a vicious verbal attack from a classmate whom I had considered one of my better buddies.

Scott Turow, describing his experience as a Harvard 1L (i.e., first-year student), put it this way:

'I know of at least one suicide attempt in my class, and there were more people than I can count who confided that they'd been driven through the door of the psychiatrist's office for the first time in their lives by the experience of being a Harvard 1L. ...'

[He quotes one of his professors as saying that] men who fought in World War II or Korea or Vietnam ... never felt as scared or oppressed as they did when they were law students at Harvard....

Supporting that, studies comparing law students to medical students and other graduate students have found far more depression, anger, stress, and hostility, and much less contentment and feeling of friendliness, in the law students."

Persective 2 - An Osgoode Hall Student

"First Year at Osgoode

One of the (many) stereotypes that surround lawyers is that they tend to make things much more complicated than they need to be. Maybe it was a sub-conscious attempt to fit in with the members of my future profession or the result of having a lot of free time over the summer, but I found myself doing that very thing following my acceptance to law school. The closer I got to September the more times I asked myself just what law school in general and Osgoode in particular would be like. As everyone else, I too had heard my share of opinions. It seemed almost everyone I talked to had an idea of what life in law school was and many of those opinions were fresh in my mind as I made my way to orientation just over two months ago.

The first year class at Osgoode is made up of 280 students divided into four sections of seventy. The people in your section are the ones you have almost all your classes with throughout first year. Having done my undergraduate at a school where classes of several hundred people is the rule rather than the exception those numbers didn't strike me as particularly daunting, but several people I knew were somewhat worried about being "lost in the crowd". Following the first days of orientation it quickly became apparent that those worries could easily be dealt with. I got to know the vast majority of my section very quickly. For the most part it is made up of friendly, outgoing people with incredibly diverse backgrounds.

Previous university degrees ranged from engineering to philosophy to physics to archeology with some people having received graduate degrees. Others had taken a couple of years off school to work. Still others were mature students with families and previous careers. All this made for some interesting and easy conversation in the first weeks.

As a result of a great orientation I was far more familiar with the school in mid-September than I thought I would be. The large number of extra-curricular activities Osgoode offers were all put on display for our benefit from the Legal Aid Clinic to the Law Journal to Pro Bono (through which students can do legal work for various causes) to the seemingly endless number of clubs and societies in various areas of the law.

In class, the professors were friendly and accessible. At Osgoode first year is designed so that all faculty members have to teach first year at some point. In the words of the Dean "no-one is too good to teach first year". The result is that first years are taught by some of the most accomplished experts in their respective fields. Classes are a combination of full section lectures and small groups. First year professors are also each assigned an advisee group of about twenty students which meets informally several times a term giving first years the chance to discuss questions and concerns with a professor and upper year students.

All law schools have a unique personality and in making a choice you should definitely investigate as many as you can. Osgoode is a school with tremendous depth and variety in all it offers. At the same time it preserves a sense of community which one would associate with a smaller faculty. To me it represents an ideal balance, an environment I'm glad I became part of."

Law Students And Summer Law Jobs

This is a major concern of many law students. There are two reasons:

1. Most students need summer employment to finance their lives.

2. Summer jobs at law firms are perceived to be valuable in terms of future employment. In fact this concern was the reason for the 2001 cheating scandal at the University of Toronto law school.

What follows are three perspectives on this issue. First, from a University of Toronto law student. Second, from a writer for the Toronto Star. Third, a writer for The Globe and Mail.

Account 1 - A University of Toronto Law Student - Fall 2000

"To paraphrase a famous Lord Denning judgment, it was summer jobs interview time in Toronto. For the second year law students it meant even more stress and anxiety as usual. As if that were even possible. Many consider the summer job interviews one of the most crucial stages in law school. It is a well-known fact that most of the big firms now have a guaranteed hire back. It is equally well known that a tremendous pressure put on law students to excel stems from the fact that the better your grades the easier it is to get a job. This means that those fortunate who at the end of November are notified of being hired by a firm, can pretty much sit back and enjoy the rest of the law school relatively stress-free.

The process of summer jobs interviews is as fascinating as it is nerve racking. While some people manage to keep their cool and remain true to themselves, others completely fall apart and do things that, in any other circumstances, would be absolutely out of character. The usual law school schmoozing reaches its peak in pre-interview time. The recruiting directors are being called, e-mailed and written to excessively. I was amazed to find out that some of my friends were on a first-name basis with the recruiting directors of some of the major firms. Mind you, in many cases it did no good.

There really is no recipe for surviving this time of the year. Having good marks certainly helps. Undoubtedly, people with a better GPA have a much higher chance of being called for an interview. At the same time, it is not just the marks that count. I know a number of people with marks considerably worse than mine who got more interviews that I did. It remains a mystery to me on what criteria the recruiting directors base their decisions. I can fashion a guess and say that it is the overall picture. It may be your undergraduate degree that they are interested in or your volunteer activities. There is no right answer. It should also be kept in mind that the high marks, although necessary, are not sufficient. They are very important in getting your foot in the door but come the actual interview it is your personality that plays a crucial part. Considering that the first round interviews are only 20 minutes, it is safe to assume that the interviewers are looking at whether you, as an individual and not as an academic transcript, will fit with the people in that particular firm. I heard from a friend of mine that last year, apparently, someone who had 16 interviews (a very high number) did not get any job offers. I don't know whether it is just a law school myth designed by those who don't have any interviews to make themselves feel better or, in the alternative, to make people with a lot of interviews feel worse, or a true fact. Be that as it may, the proposition that it is not just your marks that count certainly has a lot of validity behind it. Despite all the anxiety that precedes the interview process, the OCIs (the on-campus interviews) proved to be a great experience. With the exception of one firm, whose recruiting director was considered a jerk by everyone, people who conduct the interviews are great, very friendly and accommodating. None of us got the dreaded questions on the substantive issues of law, which we know nothing about. For the most part we were asked about out hobbies, our summer jobs and our life experiences. So relax, look forward to the interviewing experience. Even if you don't get a job after the second year of law school it is not the end of the world. Enjoy the summer, after all it is the last one before you sign your life away to the law society."

Account 2 - A Writer For The Toronto Star

November 14, 1999

Law 'n' ardour: How Bay St. courts students

The Toronto Star

Competition fierce among top law firms for tomorrow's best

Ann Perry

It's what they don't teach you at law school that really counts. Like how to balance a glass of white wine, a delicate canap and a cocktail napkin in your left hand while leaving the right free to shake the hand of someone who, just maybe, will offer you a summer job on Bay Street.

Welcome to recruiting season, a week-long frenzy of interviews, parties and expensive dinners where the country's most prestigious corporate law firms and most academically accomplished second-year law students engage in an elaborate mating dance for money, prestige and power.

During the first week of November, law students from across Canada converged on Toronto's downtown office towers to test their cocktail mettle against one another in an intense competition for the ultimate prize: a summer job at a top corporate law firm complete with a $1,000-a-week salary, a tuition bonus of $4,000, a health club membership and all-expense-paid nights on the town at Toronto's toniest eateries.

'It's really a personality contest, a beauty contest. I like to call it the Miss America Contest in a gray flannel suit' - A Bay Street insider

Although the Bay Street firms are ostensibly interviewing students for summer positions, the partners are really looking to the future. Who among these earnest 25-year-olds nervously sipping cocktails in plush law firm boardrooms will work the hardest, attract the biggest clients and bring in the most money? But it's a crapshoot on both sides. Law students passing through the reception areas of the major firms arm themselves with sheaves of research and attend pre-recruiting sessions held by law schools, but in the end must base important career decisions on a few hours spent at a firm that is intently showing itself off. Students "see a very controlled, marketed view of the firm," says one Bay Street insider who has worked at four Toronto corporate law firms - and doesn't want to take a chance on never working at another by letting her name be used. "They're putting their best foot forward." But firms also may not have a good idea of who they are admitting into their elite club, because who and how they interview is tightly governed by regulations set by the Law Society of Upper Canada. This year, firms were allowed to collect applications until Oct. 8th. Then came a nervous two weeks for students, who rushed home between classes to check for all-important letters that law firms send out by courier. The lucky ones get notice that a firm intends to make an appointment for an interview. More often, it's a politely worded rejection letter - what the students call the "PFO," or "Please F— Off" letter.

The next critical step in the process, known as Call Day, occurred on Oct. 20th this year, when firms were permitted to set up formal interview times with the lucky, shortlisted few. In keeping with the tenor of the legal profession, even this turns into competitive sport. Dozens of partners and associates at each firm station themselves at telephones with lists of students they want to meet, index fingers poised in anticipation. At exactly 8 o'clock in the morning, the Olympic speed-dialling event begins. The ensuing 10 minutes are sheer mayhem for students and firms alike. Students leave strict orders with family and friends not to call that morning. The telephone must stay free, because a call from a legal firm might come through even if it didn't announce its intentions by mail. Particularly accomplished candidates may have 15 firms simultaneously trying to get through, all jousting for favourable interview slots on Monday morning, when students are fresh and enthusiastic. And for students whose phones don't ring, these are the longest few minutes of their lives. By 8:10, the race is over. Students and firms now have two weeks to regroup and prepare for the onslaught. Peter is one of the lucky ones. His phone rang off the hook on Call Day, and he had a busy schedule between Monday, Nov. 1, and Wednesday, Nov. 3, the three days set aside by the Law Society for recruiting. When Peter phones after a marathon first day - four interviews, two meals and two cocktail parties - his voice is flat. "I've been all over God's green acres today," he says wearily. "The firms are all blending into each other." He describes a methodical interview process that appears to be almost uniform across the firms. Lawyer A greets Peter in the reception area, ushers him into the office and starts a conversation about points of interest in his application. The questions are never substantive and generally have nothing at all to do with law. One student was quizzed about her jive lessons. Another, with a musical background, was asked if he would like to play in the firm's rock band. Although student directors at some of the firms say the informality of these quizzings allows the interviewers to decide who, among the hundreds of academically qualified candidates, will be a "good fit," the Bay Street insider has a more cynical take on it, in view of the legendary long hours most Bay Street lawyers put in together. "They want to know if they will be able to spend a weekend in a boardroom with you," she says. About 20 minutes into the interview, Lawyer B appears, joins the conversation for a few minutes and then takes Peter to meet Lawyer C or an articling student, who either shows the candidate around the firm, introduces him to more lawyers and gives him the full court press, or sees him out quickly. Peter realizes that it's no coincidence that every lawyer with whom he has interviewed works in a practice area in which he has expressed interest, attended his law school or comes from his home town." I do have this feeling that it's carefully scripted to get students to work for them." Carefully scripted may be a polite way of putting it." The firms are putting their most personable people out there," says the Bay Street insider. "There are certain lawyers whom the firm will never allow the students to meet." Even students who thrive on the endless self-promotion the week requires admit that after a few interviews it becomes tiresome. "This must be how models feel," says Susan. "You're judged on what you wear, your hair, your pantyhose, whether your shoes are polished - you're judged on everything." "It's really a personality contest, a beauty contest," agrees the Bay Street insider. "I like to call it the Miss America Contest in a gray flannel suit." Minus the swimsuit competition, of course.

And recruitment for the show is early and intense, driven by prestigious New York and Boston firms that scoop up top students at the University of Toronto, Osgoode Hall and McGill University with summer salaries of $2,000 (U.S.) per week before the Toronto firms are even allowed out of the gates. The moment first-year students walk through the front door of the Faculty of Law at the University of Toronto, the Bay Street marketing machine begins an elaborate process of wining. Frosh T-shirts are always given to first-year students, but where the arts undergraduates get campy logos from beer and pizza sponsors, law students get the staid, conservative crests of Toronto's top corporate law firms. Orientation packages overflow with firm-branded goodies, from highlighters to stress balls and engraved pens. And many firms thoughtfully include brochures describing their articling programs so particularly keen first-year students can make career choices while the dean delivers his opening address. Aggressive marketing by the firms continues throughout the first year, even though the number of Bay Street summer jobs for first-year students is extremely small. Distinguished alumni preach to the novices about how to succeed on Bay Street, and firms invite students to attend seminars with innocuous names like "The Practice of Law," which are always followed by meet and greet events complete with the ubiquitous open bar. Indeed, the acquisition of cocktail skills may be more important to a law student's success than mastering the intricacies of contract law. For that reason, some students who have always succeeded on the strength of their excellent academic records find the recruiting process to be a perplexing experience that induces fear and, sometimes, paranoia. Like fortune tellers looking for patterns in a tea cup, students dissect their interview schedules for clues as to how things will go. Most have heard from upper classmates that the earlier in the week an interview is scheduled, the more interested the firm is. Likewise, students believe that the number of meals offered and the swankiness of the restaurants signal a firm's intentions. "They don't want to see me until Wednesday," Susan laments shortly after Call Day about one of her appointments. "It's a mercy interview!" She later recants after the interview goes particularly well. But in the end, it seems futile to speculate on how firms choose their summer students. By Wednesday at 4 p.m., the earliest that firms can extend job offers, Peter has three and, although the Law Society regulations allow him 24 hours to think about it, he accepts one on the spot. Susan has also learned the recruiting dance steps well. She has received one offer and an encouraging phone call from another firm after getting only three interviews in total. "I'm very much aware of the fact that I want them, but they also want me," Susan says pragmatically. "I look for honesty and you don't see a lot of that during Interview Week. I don't want to be spoon-fed the firm line. We're all grown-ups here." But the Bay Street insider doubts that law students really know what they're signing up for. "Everybody talks about the firm, the firm culture and the deals," she says. "But nobody ever talks about the work the students will be doing." Because underneath the sexy deals and glittery parties of corporate law, somebody has to do the grunt work. Before these law students are invited into the partnership, each faces years of grinding hours as an articling student and associate, catering to the needs of corporate clients, bowing to the demands of senior partners and postponing personal plans, eyes constantly on a carrot that may always dangle elusively just beyond reach. "This is what's so sad," says the Bay Street insider. "You have all of these very bright students who have been seduced by money. "But it really is a seduction on both parts."

Reprinted courtesy Torstar syndication services.

Account 3 - A Legal Commentator

"Students must make case for themselves

Terrence Belford

For McGill law student Jeff Feiner the pressure is over. Last January, he beat the 40 to one odds and won a summer job with Canada's largest law firm, McCarthy Tetrault LLP. Not only does McCarthy pay among the highest rates for summer students — $1,300 a week — but winning a spot in its summer program almost certainly means an invitation to article with the firm followed by a full-time job. His career is off to a running start.

This month, marks crunch time for law students entering their second year. The process of finding a job for next summer has begun. In Ontario, applications to law firms must be in by September 9. In other provinces, the deadline is October. Getting summer work with the right firm can mean a fast-track to professional success.

"Today getting a summer job with the right firm is looked on as a great career move," says Curtis Stewart, chair of the student recruiting committee at the Calgary office of Bennett Jones LLP. "Here, for example, close to 100% of the summer students we hire are asked back to article with us and close to 100% of articling students are asked to join us as associates."

For the law firms, the student recruitment process is an intensive and expensive one. They regularly update web sites to present the best possible face to students. Partners and associates maintain year-round involvement with law school activities. In September, Ontario firms will invite applications; in October, those in the rest of Canada will do the same. Starting the third week in September, teams of recruiters from 35 law firms across Canada will make cross-country visits to university career fairs, talent spotting and interviewing potential candidates.

In Ontario, the week starting November 3 becomes crunch time. All Bay Street firms hiring summer students invite the finalists to Toronto for interviews. In the rest of Canada, January is the final cut month. The competition is fierce. McCarthy Tetrault, for example, will receive more than 1,000 applications this year and hire just 56 to work in its seven offices across Canada. Of them, about 30 will work in the firm's Toronto office and 25 of them will be second-year students, says Sheena MacAskill, director of professional resources.

"What we are after is the best and the brightest," she says. "For law firms like ours, student recruitment is crucial. It is a tough, competitive process but the students we choose will almost always be asked back to article and then to join the firm as associates. From there on, some will become partners eventually. They are our future."

The effort and expense are well worth it, says Nancy Stitt, director of student programs at Osler, Hoskin & Harcourt. Osler hires only second year students and this year plans to take on 20 of them in Toronto and another eight spread among offices in Ottawa, Calgary and Montreal. "The idea is to do it once and do it right," she says. "These young people are going to stay with us and be the people who create the future of this firm."

The idea of recruiting summer students for life is a relatively recent phenomenon, says Bennett Jones Mr. Stewart. When he was a law student in the mid-1980s, many law students found summer jobs outside the profession, mainly because they could make more money.

"I worked the oil fields; the money was a lot better," he says. Today however, law firms pay increasingly high salaries to summer students, especially in Toronto. There, $1,300 a week is standard among big firms. Pay depends on local conditions, however. In Calgary second year students can count on between $2,800 a month and $3,500 a month. In Halifax, $2,500 a month is the norm.

"It is a different market out here and a different billing structure,"says Mark Bursey, chair of the recruiting committee in the Halifax office of Stewart, McKelvey, Sterling Scales.

His firm has 200 lawyers in six offices throughout the Maritimes. This year it will hire six students in the Halifax office and another six spread among its other five offices.

Like law firms in the west, Maritime lawyers start their big recruitment push after their Ontario counterparts are well underway. The time lag does not seem to alter the

chances of finding top-notch legal talent in the bud, however. Stewart McKelvey's Halifax office alone regularly gets 260 or more applications for its six summer student positions.

"Sometimes it is young men and women who could not find a spot with a Bay Street firm but more often it is a student who wants to work both with this firm and in Atlantic Canada,"he says. To ensure a pick of the legal litter, the firm maintains close year-round ties with law schools at Dalhousie University and the University of New Brunswick. "Every law student at Dal knows us," he adds.

While Bennett Jones' Mr. Stewart says he personally would prefer to start recruiting earlier in the year, his firm has no trouble attracting between 400 and 500 applications for the 11 to 13 summer jobs it offers students each year. He does see one advantage once a student is hired.

"If we get a summer student out here, they generally love it so much they want to stay out here," he says."They come back to article and they stay to practise."

That is Mr. Feiner's plan. He heads back to McGill this fall to complete his BCL and LLB degrees, then returns to McCarthy to article.

"This is exactly what I wanted," he says. "I actually did get offers from

other firms but my interest is litigation. If litigation is going to be your field where better to start than at Canada's biggest firm."

Reprinted with permission of the author.

Conclusion

For most law students, law school is the main part of the journey towards becoming a lawyer. As a law student, it is both possible and quite necessary to lead a balanced life. Although summer jobs and grades are important they must be kept in perspective. If they are not, problems will arise. In this regard pay special attention to the chapter dealing with "Ethical Aspects Of The Law School Environment."

Chapter 21

"Law School Cafe" - A Law Student's Diary

"The profession is reaching a point of crisis. Students graduate without learning the technical skills required, because professors aren't technicians. Instead of training students to respond to people as real people, and to care about these people and their problems, we are training students to see the larger political implications behind these people's problems. The students generally don't give a shit about this. Students want to enter the world of the professional knowledge elite. They want to be part of a world in which membership in the elite permits the member to harbour "contempt for the mulititude." We should be doing something to counter these pretentious aspirations; instead, the law schools keep breeding politically correct little bastards."

- Law Professor Alan Young - Justice Defiled

"Law School Cafe" - A First Hand Account Of Law School

Beginning To End

Law School Cafe appeared over a three year period in my newsletter. It was written by a student at a Canadian law school. To his credit - he wrote a column each month. It seems appropriate to include his column from the beginning of law school until the end.

As you read this be conscious of what concerns him at each stage of his law school career.

Keep in mind the old adage about law school.

"In first year, they scare you to death.

In second year, they work you to death.

In third year, they bore you to death."

Enjoy!

First Year - Scaring You To Death!

Month 1 - September 2000

"The first week of law school was surprising—the opposite of what people expect. People think that law school is fiercely competitive, torturous, and without remorse. But these myths could not be further from the truth. On the contrary, the kind of solidarity that has developed among all of us first-years is staggering. The attitude is not "sink or swim", but more, "we're all in this together". The work load is demanding, but manageable. I find that two or three hours per day, in addition to lectures, is sufficient to stay where I should be for readings.

Really, law seems like any other undergraduate program. Nobody has to read a thousand pages per week! Also, the professors are understanding and patient in that they understand that we have come in with mythological preconceptions. The film, *The Paper Chase* really is not a good source for insight into what law school is like! The point is, we are never asked to do things that we can't do. I find that anyone that wants an LL.B. will get one. Hopefully, it will all stay as manageable as it has been throughout the exam periods."

Month 2

"Things are heating up as time goes on, with some readings being quite complex, and assignments coming up that test our knowledge of entirely new things. The thing to master right now is the so-called "case note", which is basically an analysis of a case that one would find in a journal containing law reports. It's a student's chance to read a case and attempt to spell out the important issues in the case, with reference to the facts that relate to these issues. Reading cases has become such a normal thing that we all have learned to just keep on reading. Each course demands anywhere from 2 to 6 cases per week, with each case ranging from 5 to 50 pages. It sounds intimidating, but the number of pages per week is fairly consistent. A large case, for example, would not usually accompany additional work. It's all mostly a matter of learning principles and applying them to facts. Now it's just a question of beginning to gather together our Fall term knowledge in time for the December exams..."

Month 3

"The big issue now is course summaries—study guides that students put together containing summarized lecture notes, case notes, and summaries of the readings. What a lot of people don't realize about law school is that memorization really isn't the focus most of the time. A lot of exams across many law schools are open-book. We're all finding that the skill that counts is being able to extract legal principles from cases and apply them to new fact situations, or to other cases. The cases one reads in law school are the relatively hard cases; the controversial cases that produce a lot of discussion among judges, scholars, and the like. The one big question to keep in mind when reading a case is:

Why am I reading this case? Why is it important? And the same goes for legal writing. It has to be to the point— no more, no less. So my piece of advice for now is: for all those who think that you have to have written a dissertation to survive law school, it just isn't true.

When summarizing ideas for any purpose, be it course summaries or case reports, you're bound to have picked up the necessary skills through a variety of courses in university."

Month 4

"Well, exams are fast approaching, and the big concerns are course summaries and how exactly to compose an exam answer. Rumour has it that law school exams ask more of students than we've been given. They present new fact situations, demanding creativity in the application of the legal principles that we've absorbed in the past three months.

It's been the fastest semester we've all had in school. Three years may sound like a long time, but it races by when you're doing this much.

The name of the game for exams is clarity: less is more. The best answer can be the shortest. Once again, if people think that composing lab reports as an undergraduate can't be of any use in law school, think again! Similarly, it's not how much we've read that will make the crucial difference, it's what we've been able to pick up that will.

The importance of one case can be summarized in three lines; that's all it really takes to apply it. I find that everything in law is pragmatic. If you're writing something, the first question should be, "Why am I writing this?" The next big thing on the agenda will be the moot court exercises, but that will be for a future meditation..."

Month 5

"Well, exams are over with, and everyone is relieved. The Christmas exams are more of a practice run than anything, given that they are usually worth less than a quarter of our final grades. Really, they are essentially the same as regular undergraduate exams, but in every one of them, time is of the essence. Much like the LSAT, time must be commodified, preserved, and spent wisely. That's part of one's legal education—learning how to do an hour's worth of work in half an hour.

To provide a bit of a preview, exams are usually hypothetical fact situations that demand of the student an original application of legal principles learned throughout the semester. It's about seeing issues in the facts that have legal significance, applying the appropriate principles, and deriving a conclusion. Really, it's a small memorandum that can only take about 90 minutes to plan and write."

Month 6

"All of us first-year students just got through our moot court assignments. This entailed putting together a factum (a document that is submitted to the judges that summarizes the case and the lawyers' arguments) and then presenting in a simulated court situation. Some of us had to defend the accused, while others were prosecutors. When it all begins, everyone is nervous. But when it all happens, there is a certain competitive rush that makes it exciting. Every detail must be accounted for—how one addresses judges, one's moot partner (co-counsel), etc. For anyone that gets stage-fright, I can't think of anything better to overcome it. For most people, the only things left are the April exams. Many of them are worth up to 75% of one's course grade. It's all a little daunting, I must admit, but the key is to have fun with it. And believe me—when moot court is over, most people look back and laugh."

Month 7

"With only a few more weeks of lectures to go before the April exams, the only things on everyone's minds are final grades and summer employment. While almost everyone applies to law firms in their first year of law school, only a handful of positions are granted. The truth is, most people don't obtain legal employment until at least two years of law school have been completed. With most of this first year now gone, I have found that the first year serves as an adjustment period; not only to the demanding schedule, but also to the language and norms of legal discourse. From the case reports to the moot court assignments, and writing of factums and memorandums; all of it is the gradual transformation into a person that thinks, speaks, writes, and even looks like a lawyer. And perhaps not surprisingly, it has been the fastest academic year ever. It may be a three-year degree, but to all those who find this an intimidating length of time, it feels like a mere few months."

Month 8

"Even amidst the increasing anxiety brought on by the fast-approaching exams in law school, there is a multitude of activity. What never ceases to amaze me are the opportunities here to get insights into the real legal world. With summer job start-up dates approaching too, there is a definite career-oriented feeling circulating around the law school. A definite must for any law student is taking as much advantage as possible of the opportunities to visit law firms, court houses, and any other aspect of the legal practice. The insights one gains puts law school in perspective and opens up a light at the end of what is often perceived as a very long and intimidating tunnel. It shows you what you can expect and what options are available. For those of you still doubting the LL.B., I can say with sincerity that it really is a versatile degree. You say you don't want to be a traditional lawyer? No problem—there are a growing number of lucrative fields in which one can apply an LL.B. yet never be a traditional lawyer. There are as many things one can do with a law degree as there are law students."

Month 9

"With the exams finally over, there is an astounding sense of relief inside the law school. The issue of summer employment is the going concern.

With only a small number of us working for law firms over the summer, most of us have to look for regular jobs. There is, though, a growing number of research positions open to law students within the law school. This gives a law student the chance to work for a law professor, assisting that professor with whatever research he or she is presently involved in. Not only does this provide insight into what's going on in the law right now, but it also provides valuable previews on things to come in 2nd and 3rd year courses. Also, and perhaps most importantly, it is practical experience that lets the law firms know that a student knows how to do legal research. Ultimately though, when it comes to part-time experience, anything can be of interest to the law firms when they review their applicants. The truth is, with the incredible variety of backgrounds here, and the number of things that one can do with an LL.B., any of a number of work experiences can be impressive. The fact is, no firm on Earth is expecting legal experience! In closing, for all those writing the June LSAT, good luck, and see you in law school."

A student was recently charged with defrauding the government out of about $19,000 in OSAP. Income on the student's application was misrepresented, as welfare income was omitted. The student also had more than one name circulating, which played a part in the fraudulent activity. The student appealed the charge, but lost the appeal. The punchline—the student was a law student. Who says law is not a creative discipline?

In retrospect, I still feel like it is still September. I am convinced that the LL.B. is one of the fastest degrees around. Like I've often said, it may be advertised as three years, but it feels like a few months. Law teaches us how to think, how to write, and even how to read all over again. It teaches us how to navigate through a society that is a sea of rules and competing interests. You enter a person with a regular degree—you come out a lawyer."

Month 10

"Last month I mentioned research positions in the law school, and the benefits of doing legal research both for the benefit of acquiring a preview of courses to come, and of learning how to do legal research for one's career. Most of us summer researchers are working directly with law professors, and all of us are finding that it's not only a good source of legal information, but also a great way to get to know the professors. Working closely like this also discloses the leading edge of Canadian legal thinking, and reveals the possibilities of legal developments to come. Many people do not realize that professional research often serves as direct support for the decisions that judges make in actual cases. The further we all proceed in law school, the more we all feel like we are a part of the greater legal world.

While there is a great deal of emphasis placed on working in a law firm for the summer, the vast majority of students cannot do this. And while the remuneration for the summer at some firms is impressive, (approaching $1500/week at some firms) most firms outside of Toronto do not pay summer students that much. Academic research, then, can be the ideal alternative in an otherwise chaotic summer job race. As I've already tried to emphasize, the experience can be just as high-profile as law firm experience, and the money is competitive. Summer research can pay up to about $500/week, which is what many law firms outside Toronto will pay summer students. And once again, good luck to everyone on the June LSAT."

Second Year - Working You To Death!

Month 11

"As yet another September approaches, the things on everyone's mind entering second year are course selection and job applications.

At most law schools, second year is the first time that one has any choice in what one will take. Selecting courses is a combination of interests and an acquisition of the kind of legal knowledge that one wishes to apply to a future career. While some rush to specialize in one type of law, others sign on for a wide variety of topics. While some believe that specialization is the key to success, it's a good idea to keep in mind that firms offer extensive training to all of their new lawyers.

Speaking of firms, for all prospective law students reading, everyone soon discovers that firms often expect applications, even for summer positions, months before one actually begins a potential job. In the summer, we have to spend quite a bit of time putting applications together. Again, while some concentrate heavily on only a few firms, other apply everywhere, hoping to secure a point of entry into what seems like an intimidating world. No matter what, though, it's a good idea to research the firms, and know who you are applying to. How old is the firm? What kind of law do they practice? What is the work environment like? A good application process provides answers to these questions.

In either case, whether it be courses or job selection, there will always be those who have a clear idea concerning what they wish to do in mind, and others that are still deciding. There really is no rush to decide on the type of law one wishes to engage in, and almost everyone changes their mind at least once throughout the LL.B.

Have a great summer, and good luck to everyone in September."

Month 12

"Now that my class, the class of 2003, is in our second year, summer jobs have become more of an issue. This is not merely because we are closer to graduating and articling, but also because we now have a much higher chance of obtaining a summer position at a law firm. The deadline for applications into Toronto firms is always in early September. This is accordance with the rules of the Law Society of Upper Canada, an institution that sets out rules regarding the manner in which lawyers practice.

Coming out of first year, the chances of such a job are slim. Out of second year, there is a sudden flood of opportunity. About a fifth of last year's second year class acquired summer jobs in Toronto, and all of them (yes, ALL!) have received placements to article. Speaking of articling, given the way things are today, a person can often secure an articling position through impressive work at a summer position. As such, summer work is often a right of passage into full-time status.

A growing number of the Toronto firms conduct what are known as "on-campus interviews". That is, representatives of the firms travel to the various campuses across Ontario in order to interview students in their own locales. This is a lot easier than driving to Toronto every time one has an interview.

Now, it's just a matter of waiting. Everyone is nervous and excited, awaiting what could be the beginning of a long and lucrative career at a firm. As for what the firms are looking for, anything could be of value. In recent years, I have noticed that the firms want a diverse group of eclectic, interesting people in their offices. As such, there really is no way to tell who will obtain a job and who will not. Sometimes the interview is the deciding factor. Resumes and cover letters can only indicate so much, and interviews give firms the opportunity to get to know their candidates as real live people. It can be stressful, but it is always rewarding.

Once again, for those of you writing the LSAT and applying to law school this year, I wish you all the best of luck."

Month 13

"For many second-year law students, this month is interview month. Accordingly, it is for some (a fewer number than those who have interviews, unfortunately!) the first major transition from the academic side of law into the mainstream legal world. For most who obtain positions, this occurs at a law firm with several lawyers.

When one begins at a firm, whether as a summer student or as an articling student (though more the latter), most firms have programs designed to gradually introduce students into the legal practice. Often, this involves a placement in close connection with a lawyer who has been at the firm for some time, and who can supervise the student's work, and provide advice. Over the years, this has come to be known as "mentoring". At some firms, especially the larger ones, mentoring has become extremely sophisticated, sometimes taking the form of a formal program, almost as though one's first few months at a firm is itself a program of study. Rotation is extremely common, this being a process whereby articling students move throughout the firm's various departments and try a bit of everything. This can even include the opportunity to temporarily transfer to another of the firm's offices, say from Toronto to New York. The novelty of being able to sample the legal and social world of another city is hard to beat.

The other summer or articling option is the clerkship option. Some students obtain positions as clerks, working in close connection with judges. This can occur locally, or even at the federal level. At the Supreme Court, for instance, each of Canada's nine Supreme Court judges is allowed three clerks. Clerks do all manner of things, from clerical assistance to thoughtful discussion concerning the outcomes of cases. This experience is invaluable because with it, one can learn how judges arrive at their decisions, and develop a familiarity with court procedure. This, in turn, is invaluable for those who wish to pursue a career in litigation. It makes communication with judges that much better, and when it comes to this, there is no such thing as too good!

For those of you who have just sent in your materials for the November application deadline, I wish you the best of luck. See you "out there..."

Month 14

"With exams fast approaching, we are once again facing the prospect of constructing summaries for open-book exams. As I've mentioned before, most law school exams are open-book. Any student can have any material that he or she wants in front of them, subject to minor exceptions. Accordingly, the issue is not memorization, but is instead legal analysis. Most exams are hypothetical fact scenarios that have legal implications. The student's job is to provide an assessment of the facts' legal meaning.

Summaries are, as the name implies, summaries of a law course's key cases and concepts, and are meant as a convenient reference for time-sensitive exam conditions. There are two primary sources of summaries: you, and others. One can write one's own summaries, or try to acquire summaries from previous years through other students or various websites. There are advantages and disadvantages to either approach. Writing one's own summaries is time-consuming, occupying several evenings per summary, but the act of writing it is the best way to become familiar with everything in the course. Getting external summaries saves vast amounts of time, but there is no direct interaction with the material. Also, the accuracy of other students' summaries is always an issue. Every course is taught differently, and your summary must reflect the particularities of the course it is based on."

MYTH OF THE MONTH

I've added a new section to the Law School Cafe. I call it "Myth of the Month". As many of you know, there are always several myths circulating concerning law school, lawyers, and the practice of law in general. Every month I want to post a myth and put it in perspective.

THIS MONTH'S MYTH: "There are too many lawyers"

This one really gets under my skin, and it is a common excuse put forth by those who decide that "law is not for them". The truth is, there is a greater magnitude and variety of legal work now than ever before. Issues that were a few short years ago nonexistent (i.e., bioethics, the Internet) are coming to the fore as the next generation of hot legal issues. The law is more prolific than ever. Law school populations are at record numbers, and from what I have seen, there is enough work to go around to keep every lawyer busy for the next several decades of our working lives. In my humble opinion, there are not yet enough lawyers.

Month 15

"For this month, I thought I would talk about a place for which January is a special month—the Faculty of Law at the University of Western Ontario. At Western Law, students have the opportunity of participating in what is known as the "January Term". Throughout January, every law student takes only one course. It is an opportunity to specialize in a topic of interest and concentrate one's efforts on that topic alone. Historically, students at Western have found the January Term to be tremendously rewarding.

For those of you who are not yet in law school, 1st-year law students complete what is known as their "1st-year moot" in January. Their entire January Term is devoted to the preparation of an assignment in which 1st-year students must, at the end of January, argue a hypothetical case in front of their professors and, usually, some senior law students, all of whom play judges. This involves writing what is known in the law as a "factum"; a summary of the lawyer's arguments that he or she will present in court. Students are graded on proper attire, the ease with which they respond to questions from the judges, proper speech, clarity, and the overall soundness of their arguments. While this all tends to be an anxiety-provoking experience, everyone ultimately has fun with it. Also, it is a great way to get into the litigation spirit and get used to the courtroom setting and civil procedure."

THIS MONTH'S MYTH: "You know, lawyers don't really make that much money"

This is something you hear from a lot of people who really haven't bothered investigating the average lawyer's standard of living. The truth is, everyone that comes out of law school is guaranteed a good living, if they so choose. Many law firms will pay an articling student well over $1200/wk, with the maximum in Toronto now approaching $2000/wk; and this is in addition to what is now an impressive compensation package at most firms, including the payment of one's third year of law school tuition. Accordingly, many (if not most) lawyers earn well over $100,000/yr, which is almost twice the average family income in Canada. If this isn't "that much money", I don't know what is!

Month 16

"In law school, February is a time of anticipation. Now that we are in our second year, quite a few of us have secured employment of a legal nature for the approaching summer. Actually, the job hunt continues right into the spring and summer for those of us who have not.

Some firms' summer hiring is regulated by the Law Society of Upper Canada, an organization that you will learn more about in law school, and a lot of whose activities deal with the professional conduct of lawyers. There is, for this group of firms, an application deadline imposed (usually early September).

However, the vast majority of firms announce job opportunities much later in the academic year. These other firms, which are usually smaller, are not so strictly regulated in their hiring deadlines. Accordingly, you will find when entering law school that there are several firms who immediately announce themselves in a variety of ways. However, other firms will be discovered, further down the road.

The purpose of keeping these two "layers" in mind is to maintain a healthy level of morale. It is surprising how soon in our legal careers (i.e., the first month of law school) that the stress of market competition sets in. The truth is, most people do not secure legal employment until they are articling. This is not something to be depressed over—it is merely the nature of the legal field. A student is infinitely more useful to a law firm with a legal education than without one. The point is, NEVER GET DISCOURAGED."

THIS MONTH'S MYTH: "Lawyers are immoral"

Well, it's no secret that there are a million stories concerning the supposedly nefarious deeds of many a lawyer, and about twice as many jokes reflecting this general reputation. However, it is this writer's opinion that lawyers are no more immoral than those individuals that comprise most other groups that we can delineate in the labour market. In fact, lawyers are often directly instrumental in bringing about justice. Evidence must be collected and submitted, such that a court can get a correct view of the facts, and lawyers are responsible for this. Even if defending a client who has committed a crime, a lawyer must make sure that his or her client's interests are properly and fairly represented, and that the court determines guilt in the ways set out in our legal tradition, such that the punishment suits the crime. Also, as I've said before, there are several things that can be done with an LL.B. If you have ideas concerning good things you would like to do in the world, an LL.B. will facilitate those things.

Month 17

"This week, many lawyers and law students met for Articling Day, an annual exhibition of law firms held at the London Convention Centre. Every firm that attends creates a display, has lawyers on hand to answer questions, and gives away items such as T-shirts, stationary, and various other novelties. The event is an opportunity to determine which firms do what and what they offer, especially in terms of work experience, locale, and salary. I've spoken about articling before, but perhaps not in this context. Articling is an interesting phenomenon because it can have a variety of purposes. For some, it is an inception into a firm for which they will work for several years and, accordingly, marks the beginning of a series of possible promotions. For others, it is merely a temporary sojourn, seen as an opportunity to gain experience and knowledge that will be applied somewhere else. I try to caution a lot of people that are not yet in law school not to adhere to a rigid pre-conception concerning articling."

THIS MONTH'S MYTH: "Articling is an essential part of what determines the rest of one's career"

This proposition can be true, but is not necessarily true. Wherever articling takes place is not, for most lawyers, the place where any given lawyer will spend most of his or her career. Nor must articling be spent within a law firm; clerkships at courts working with judges are becoming more popular. It would also be a mistake to think that just because one does not do a certain type of work or work at a specific place that that type of work or even that place cannot be explored in the future. Perhaps the biggest misconception that one can unfortunately hold is the belief that if one does not earn relatively good money during their articling phase then one is committed to eternal poverty. This could not be further from the truth. I think that articling must be viewed as a part of one's overall repertoire of experiences. Accordingly, it opens doors, and does not close them.

Month 18

"With exams less than a month away, it is once again "that time". For many readers, the approaching exam period precedes the writing of the June LSAT, and possibly a course to prepare for it. It is also a time in which grades really count, since many readers will be either applying to or soon attending law school. Since the overall principle which binds these things is stress and anxiety, I thought I'd offer a few relaxing words for all of you pre-law readers.

First, everyone gets into law school that wants to. Many people write the LSAT a few times, or stay in university longer than they thought they would. Often, all of this occurs for the sole purpose of getting into law school. I have spoken to countless people who want to get in, and I have never met someone that could not who really wanted to. The point is, all it really takes is sufficient desire. One must never believe that one element of their application file will prevent admission. The admission decision emerges out of a holistic process in which every element of an applicant's materials are considered.

Second, many people believe that there are certain deficiencies on their resumes or transcripts that will prevent them from getting into law school. The truth is, everyone who gets into law school has these little scars on their materials. The law school student population is one of the most diverse groups of people you will ever encounter, with a variety of backgrounds, work experience, grades, and LSAT scores. If there are things about your academic career that concern you, I guarantee that everyone who is presently in law school has had these sorts of concern at one time or another.

Third, many people that have invested a lot of time and energy into getting into law school begin having second thoughts about whether law is the right career for them. As many readers will remember, I often say that a law degree in North America is one of the most opportune pieces of paper that any institution can issue. Many people that obtain LL.B.'s never enter courtrooms, read case reports, or do anything commonly associated with what it means to practice law. Whatever assumptions you have, get rid of them. Whatever stereotypes you encounter, ignore them. Although I, and those around me, are almost finished law school, I can honestly say that none of us knows what practice will be like, or what we will do for a living.

Some readers undoubtedly think that this sort of "advice" is patronizing. If that's the case, then I have to congratulate those people for their ability to relax. However, everyone that applies to something like law school has these sorts of concerns at one time or another. The bottom line is that if you want it enough, it will all happen."

Month 19

"The academic year is over for most of us, and the primary thing on most people's minds is summer earnings and OSAP, all orbiting around the question, "Can I afford another year of school?" In recent years, though, I have heard a lot of talk concerning "pre-law experience", where people either 1) search for temporary work that will (supposedly) give them an "edge" in law school or the legal world which follows it, and/or 2) try to determine which undergraduate courses constitute "better" preparation for law school or the legal world which follows it. As we all know, many universities even offer courses and programs relating to law.

Though you may not know it yet, all of that summer experience in industrial furnaces, fast food kitchens, lawn-mowing, coaching, camp supervising, etc. will be invaluable. You say that you wish that you could enter law school with law firm experience on your resume? The truth is, everyone wishes that, and it's a wish that rarely comes true. There will be a small minority of people in law school with this sort of experience, but no one really expects it on your resume until you are well into a legal education. Furthermore, a dynamic resume containing a mish-mash of work experience is not only expected, but desirable. It signifies ambition, persistence, and a maximization of a person's first few years in the employment world.

The second issue, that concerning university courses, is usually met with much more resistance. A lot of people simply refuse to believe that molecular biology could be as useful to them in law school as a course dealing with law. It may be one of those things that must be seen to be believed, but the unique worldview, thought processes, and style of learning offered by every single course is a contribution to the student. Idealistic? Maybe, but I know people whose first exposure to law was law school, and who nevertheless obtained impressive grades. In summation, it's more about how you think than what you already know.

So how does all of this cash out in regards to summer work and course selection for next year? First, however you employ yourself, do it well. Letters of recommendation from any boss in regards to any type of work can be impressive. Second, whatever you take in school, do it well. And how do you maximize academic performance (other than through hard work)? Take what you like. If you like molecular biology, then study it. If you like certain professors because of, say, the way that they teach, communicate, write, etc., then take courses offered by them. If you like a certain university because of something as simple as the design of the campus, attend that university. In short, be the happy student who wants to go to class. This may make some of you laugh. If that's the case, glad I could be of service."

Month 20

"There is often a distinction made between theory and practice between general principles and the difficulties faced in applying them. Sometimes, as we've all experienced, a given practice seems to entirely contradict the theory we're told supports it. I think it's fair to say the same of the legal world. Law school is about grasping fundamental principles and learning rules which reflect those principles; the meaning, for instance, of terms such as "contract", "property", and "tort". This summer, I am finally working for a law firm. The theoretical background that I have is useful, but the real frontier is the practice of applying it.

The surprising thing is the extent to which the practice goes "back to basics", so to speak to those fundamental terms I mentioned. Through all of the phone calls, faxes, conversations, clients, arguments, and transactions, it is often a simple legal principle at play. But the simplicity of the law is clouded by these distracting things. The difficulty is not in learning the law, but in convincing others of it not in doing one's job, but in relying on others for it to reach its completion. The practice is a vortex of noise a machine whose parts (people, that is) often do not work well together. The law is like the eye of the storm the stillness which remains quietly at the center while we all stumble around it.

Despite its essential importance, I think that one has to think of law school as something that gets added to the world experience that is already there. Accordingly, there are things about the practice of law that are learned in other places, other jobs, other people, and even other ages. I find that the lawyers that have the easiest time of it out there are those who have done a lot of things in life, thus giving them the ability to adapt to new situations through a greater openness to other points of view. These are the people who can flow through a situation like water because they are able to negotiate conflicting elements. Given this, I think it's fair to say that law is surrounded by phenomena which are sometimes best analyzed through other disciplines economics, politics, ethics, technology, and (frighteningly) psychology.

Oh yes, and for those of you beginning law school in September, please relax and keep a clear head. Few things will feel as tough as getting accepted."

Month 21

"The summer months preceding the third year are all about securing an articling position. This is, as most of you know, the largest portion of the Bar Admission Course in Ontario.

There are a lot of mythical nightmares circulating concerning this process. Perhaps some of you have heard that some people must article for free or that they look for years for an articling position after the end of their LL.B. While I must admit that I am not certain that all of these stories are false, what I can say is that it is hard to believe that all of them are true given that it is often all of the students of a given graduating year that already have articling positions. Most of these people have a guaranteed position by the time they begin their third year in September. This is because most people will have already applied for articling positions in the Spring of their second year, and gone through interviews in July or August. While they are not all high-paying or prestigious, they all provide valuable experience and the potential for one to shape one's future career.

The interview process is really not essentially different from any other. It's about who you are, and what you can contribute to the firm to which you are applying. I have found that there is no special magic or elite code required, other than clear speech, confidence, and enthusiasm for what you are asking for, namely a chance to produce and be compensated for it. Much of the time, one who spends a summer at a law firm will be offered an articling position, and the same principles apply. Just as it is often perplexing deciding on things like what firm or type of firm in which one wishes to practice, or, for that matter, even the type of law, it is equally perplexing for the firms to make selections out of the hundreds of candidates that approach them. I have found that the better the indication you can provide as to your attitude and ability, the better they can assess you.

In closing, I know that by now the June LSAT has been written. For those of you who scored high, congratulations. For those of you who did not, congratulations on your continuous reading of this newsletter, despite your disappointment, and your commitment to writing the LSAT again, no matter who tells you that you cannot improve your score. Personally, I jumped 54 percentile points from the first to the second writing. Most people thought that I was not going to be able to do that. I was happy to prove them wrong, and wish you the same satisfaction."

Third Year - Boring You To Death!

Month 22

"As first year students, we always knew this year would come; our last year of law school and, for most of us, our last year of formal education. The priorities are different now. It used to be about getting a grasp of the fundamentals, the firms, and the practice areas. But most of us already have articling positions to look forward to. A certain plateau has been reached for us third-years, and we're all getting the definite feeling of rolling downhill. Don't get me wrong-we're still immersed in course work and working hard, though to a large extent, the waiting is over.

The main project right now is the upcoming registration for the Bar Admission Course. As I've said in the past, most of this year-long course is comprised of the so-called Articling Phase, in which we will do real legal work. The other part is comprised of topical modules in which the so-called "lawyering skills" are discussed and applied. Most of us will dive right into this in the Spring of 2003, right after we graduate. There are options concerning when the various phases of the Bar Admission Course can be completed, and where the so called "Bar Ads" (exams marking the end of the modules) can be written. I want to say more about this as information concerning it becomes available to us.

For the time being, then, we are in a kind of in-between state-between theory and practice, between student life and full-time work, and even, in a sense, between childhood and adulthood. For the first time in life, for many of us, the way is fully paved and in clear view-it is just a matter of playing out what has already been achieved. And once again, for those of you working to have your applications in by the November deadline, good luck as always-and apply to as many schools as possible."

Month 23

"In the context of articling, many of you have probably heard of something called the "match". This is a term referring to a process by which prospective law students are matched with a firm with which to article. It is a process approved and regulated by the Law Society of Upper Canada. A few words about the process:

When students enter the match, they are asked to list the firms of their choice, from favourite to least favourite. This increases the efficiency of the interview process since more of any participating firm's interviewee population will be comprised of people that actually want that firm. This is also more efficient for students because it is a process that gets them inside the doors of the firms that they want, and less interview time is spent trying to secure whatever one can get.

The firms that participate in the match are the relatively large Toronto firms. Their interest in the match seems to be, other than being able to isolate those that are interested in their particular firm per se, that it is a way to more quickly evaluate all of the thousands of potential candidates that constantly knock on their doors. It may be a harsh fact of life, but if there's a really big, impressive downtown firm that you would give your life to work for, then guess what-there are droves of other people that share your sentiments. The match helps to organize this competition in a way which better fulfills everyone's interests.

Initially, the match may end up placing about half of its participants. This may sound bleak, but this has the effect of reducing competition for those that don't yet have articling positions, resulting in almost 100% placement for any given 3rd year class by the end of the school year. I hope that I have revealed the truth concerning yet another law-related myth-no, it is not impossible to find an articling position. In fact, it is hard to keep away from one."

Month 24

"With law school drawing to a close fairly soon, I'm thinking a lot lately about development; specifically, the development that one goes through in a program like this. People enter law school with certain popular conceptions, but then overcome them through an exposure to "the real thing". However, there are certain persistent myths that continually recur. Those of you who have been reading for awhile know that I sometimes focus on one myth, and try to expose it for what it really is.

One such myth is something that a lot of you pre-law school readers will encounter, this being the seemingly ambitious acquaintance who proudly states that he or she wants to do "corporate law". The myth of corporate law is a serious one that a lot of people buy into. It seems to be an empty, unexplained term that just about anyone can drop into a conversation, with little investment and a lot of return. Next time this happens to you (as it invariably will), ask the person to define the term. Ask the speaker to define exactly where his or her interests are. Chances are, you'll discover no conception of what this term means.

What you'll likely find is a person that is in love with the term "corporate" and who derives a lot of inspiration from their favourite cutthroat, climbing-the-corporate-ladder films.

The truth is, most of the kind of law that is relevant to corporations is the same kind of law that could be relevant to anyone. When one corporation sues another, say for a breach of a contract, the principles that come alive in their proceedings are the same principles that you would need to sue a service company for not installing your furnace properly. Accordingly, the term "corporate" is so general a label, it is almost as broad as stating that you want to specialize in human clients. Admittedly, I can't tarnish the shine of this term in its entirety, there are rules that are particular to this entity that we've invented called the corporation (i.e., shares, limited liability, etc.), but most of the trouble that corporations get into can be analyzed through generally applicable principles.

Here's another common myth that goes something like this: "I could never defend someone that has killed someone!" I'll talk about that one next month."

Month 25

"Last month I mentioned that I wanted to talk about criminal law. One of the most common and enduring myths in law school and popular culture at large is the belief in the supposed "evil function" of criminal lawyers. How many times have you heard someone say, "I could never defend a criminal" or that criminal lawyers "just keep criminals on the streets". Consider for a moment, though, the way that criminal law works.

For those of you who aren't yet in law school, criminal law works by way of the government (or "Crown", as they are always referred to in this context) charging an "accused" with a crime listed in the Criminal Code of Canada. In order to convict the accused, the Crown must prove "beyond a reasonable doubt" (this is called the "standard of proof") that the accused did what the Crown claims he or she did.

The function of one's criminal defence counsel is not to lie, withhold the truth, or otherwise obstruct justice. The function of one's criminal defence counsel is to ensure that the accused is treated fairly during the procedural process of questioning, the gathering, presentation, and interpretation of evidence, and sentencing. It must also be ensured that the accused is being convicted of the correct offence, if at all. For instance, an accused may tell a criminal lawyer that he or she has killed someone. In such a situation, the Crown may have charged this person with first-degree murder. The question is not whether the accused has killed someone, and it is not for the criminal lawyer to deny this fact. The question is the legal meaning of this fact, as there are a number of charges that could arise out of the death of a human being. The defence of the accused must ensure that this determination is conducted fairly and accurately.

Unfortunately, the general public knows very little of this, and seems to think that criminal lawyers have the freedom to do whatever it takes to allow his or her client to be released from custody. Of course, criminal lawyers are people, and are free to do their jobs however they want. But, to conclude my rant atop the soapbox, dishonest behaviour is far from what is proper to criminal law. If there's one thing that a legal education might do for quite a few people, its overturn the preconceptions that a lot of them enter law school with."

Month 26

"As this degree draws to a close, one of the persistent themes on my mind lately is the extent to which I overestimated a lot of things. When I think of the hours of work, the pages of notes, and the immeasurable stress that surrounded a lot of it, I really just wish that I had taken more time to explore where it is I have been living (or maybe not really living) for three years now, or more time for plain old relaxation. I have found no correlation between stress and grades-some of the most relaxed people I know are very high performers.

Everyone that wants to go to law school asks me different questions, but all of their questions seem to gravitate to one common intention-they seem to want a unified theory that explains law school's nature, that reveals how it works. I now believe that there is no such answer. There is no real way to enter into something here with a method in mind and guarantee oneself a definitive result.

I should qualify this doom-and-gloom approach by saying that my answer that is no answer is not attributable to institutional disorganization. Rather, I have come to believe that the seeming randomness that exists here is due to the fact that everyone experiences it differently. The institutions that make law school possible struggle with a student body that have a multitude of competing interests and agendas. The utilitarian result is program content that is meant to maximize satisfaction, yet which is destined not to please everyone. That being said, there is an additional point that must be raised.

I am noticing lately that some of you pre-law rumour-theory-junkies have prematurely decided that law is not "for you" on the basis of some of the things that I have mentioned. The problem is, no career or institution ever proceeds on this basis. If you are looking for a perfect world, look somewhere other than this one. But then again, why see it as a problem? I have come to believe that when a program is this fluidic, that is, when experiences within are so variable, all that this really means is that it is a place in which anyone can find opportunity. Law is the kind of thing that can channel you into anything because it touches everything. It is never in one place, yet exists everywhere. I have found that whatever special interest you might have, law can accommodate it-in fact, it has to. Nothing that anyone does today is "lawless"-all issues are legal issues.

Having said all of this, I have no regrets. Some of this was painful, joyful, cheap, expensive, anxious, relaxed, traumatic, uplifting, spirit-crushing, and spirit-saving. So there's the future, as undetermined as ever-the usual dark place that we are all committed to. On a closing note, "undetermined", for me, means "free"."

Month 27

"We will be finished law school in a matter of days. With so much else going on, things like moving, the pending BAR Admission Course, correspondences with employers, and the like, (not to mention good weather), concentrating on course work has become exponentially more difficult. We all feel as though we've learned enough, that there's nothing more that our respective institutions can teach us, that it's time to move on. This is one of those major turning points in life, where even many relationships with relatives and significant others are being compromised in the name of a life-altering career. It seems that the pull of the great legal machine is becoming stronger by the day. By now, we are all definitely a part of it. We are no longer asking the early, anxious questions of the LL.B things like, will I like this?, should I do something else?, etc. Personally, I think that questions like that are, at this point, irrelevant and weakening moves in the face of futility. Having come this far, we have no choice but to want a taste of it, to dig in with all of the fierceness that we can muster. It is a rapid, aggressive, forward-looking time during which we are no longer looking back. The choices have been made, and these are our careers. Oddly, despite this feeling of destiny, a lot of us have never felt more free - finally some money, some freedom, some autonomy, some real stuff (the really big toys that you have to finance!). I guess that after several years, some of us might return to those early questions; in a future dark age that we of the golden age have yet to comprehend. But in the meantime, why dwell on such possibilities?"

Month 28

"It is now all over. The feeling that I had leaving the law school, never to return for another lecture, exam, or even study session, was surreal. Those of you who have been reading for awhile have often heard a lot of people say what I am about to say: this LL.B is one of the fastest ways to accelerate that I know of. Admittedly, at the beginning, I was apprehensive about the length of time that I would be here. The phrase "three years" has a certain ring to it, much the same way as a three-year sentence, or so part of me thought at the time. And yet, as I recall the first day of law school, the morning of which I found myself walking up the same road that I stared at when I left the building for the last time, it's really all quite clear, as if I am still there. Some of you may think this sounds quite cliche, but I can assure you that after something like this, a sense of nostalgia will set in. And no sooner am I ending one thing than I'm beginning another in a few short days, the Bar Admission Course begins.

The Law Society of Upper Canada, the organization that you pre-law people keep hearing about, now requires that we do the seminar work for the course in the four-month period from May to September, absent some special circumstances. Accordingly, articling typically begins in September. The course is divided into a series of sections, i.e., Real Estate, Criminal Procedure, etc., and each section has exams. Seminars occur everyday for about three hours. However, there is now a new option whereby students can complete the course strictly with software, and without seminars. Actually, those that opt for seminars have access to this very same software.

So that's all - some of it was horrific, fantastic, boring, and exciting. To those of you beginning law school in September, I'm not just going to wish you luck; you'll learn that it is definitely not about luck."

Conclusion

You were just exposed to the experience of one law student at one school. There are as many different law school experiences as there are people.

Congratulations...

To the author of "Law School Cafe" on his 2004 call to the bar.

Chapter 22

Ethical Aspects
Of The Law School Environment

"The person who undertakes to become an attorney must approach the law disposed to becoming a good lawyer sensible to the daily process of practical deliberation required to live a life in the law of integrity."

-S. Steir - 'Legal Ethics - The Integrity Thesis" as quoted in
'Integrity Testing For Lawyers - Is It Time?" by Marvin Huberman

What follows is so shocking that it is deserving of a separate chapter.

The Facts - Those Stubborn Things!

In the Winter and Spring of 2001, almost 20 percent of first year students at the University of Toronto were involved in a cheating scandal. The effects of this scandal should force the school to examine the conduct of the faculty, students and the administration. In the case of the students, I suspect the school will be forced to reconsider its admissions policies. "Good character" is a requirement for admission to the bar. Should the school attempt to evaluate character as part of the admissions process? Were the penalties in this case appropriate?

The facts and progression are well canvassed in the following article by James Cowan.

Atonement

James Cowan

When 24 students at U of T's faculty of law lied about their grades to land summer jobs, they tarnished the school's reputation and risked their futures. Punished and penitent, they've paid for their folly. Why won't the school shoulder its portion of the blame?

His summer job application is almost finished. The cover letter is composed, edited, proofread and laser-printed on buck-a-page high-bond paper. The resume lists education (a bachelors from a good school, a masters from an excellent one), awards and scholarships (there are a few - enough to merit a special section), professional history (from camp counsellor to teaching assistant in five short years) and interests (public speaking, photography, golf). Now it's 3:30 in the morning, and there's only one thing left to do: key in his December exam results.

Torts: B

Contracts: C

Constitutional: C

Property: B

Criminal: C+

Civil procedure: B

As the page prints, he stares at those Cs. The Bay Street firms don't interview people who get Cs. If the Cs weren't there, he might have a chance. Rumour has it that students have inflated their grades before. Hell, rumour has it that students are doing it this year. And an acquaintance told him a professor had actually encouraged students to alter their grades. If only his marks were a bit better, he'd have a shot at the $4,000-a-month gig, the nearly guaranteed hire back for the following summer, the subsequent articling position-maybe even a chance to join a Wall Street firm. People lie on their resums all the time, right? And it's not like the firms are playing fair. These marks weren't meant for them. That's why the school doesn't verify the grades or issue official transcripts. So no one will ever know. He tosses the page in the garbage and starts again.

Last year, when the dailies discovered that a couple of dozen first-year students at the University of Toronto's law school had inflated their grades in job applications, the story got full play, often on the front page. By this one act, these students not only jeopardized their own careers; they tarnished the school's carefully cultivated, increasingly strong international reputation. Soon the scandal migrated to the opinion pages,where letter writers, columnists and editorial boards provided their own answers to the question everyone was asking: Why would anyone, particularly a student at the country's most exclusive law school, take this risk? Greed, some said. Ambition, others argued. This, as it turns out, is the easy question. Yes, money played a part, as did ambition, but the harder question here is not why a single student would lie about his grades, but why 24 did.

The law school's campus is singularly unprepossessing. It sits at the northwestern edge of Queen's Park in a tiny enclave between the legislature, the university proper and the Children's Own Museum. Founded a little over 50 years ago, the faculty originally occupied Falconer Hall, a house, and Flavelle House, a hall. When its population grew too large, the very modern Bora Laskin Law Library was added to the back of Flavelle House, transforming the faculty's main building into a strange hybrid of Casa Loma and the Starship Enterprise.

The school's founders, John Willis, Bora Laskin and Caesar Wright, were dissatisfied by what they saw as Osgoode Hall's focus on the nuts and bolts of legal practice. Determined to establish a school where serious intellectual engagement with the law could take place, they resigned their teaching positions at Osgoode and marched up University Avenue to what one historian called the "promised land of U of T." Since then, the faculty they founded has produced more than its fair share of Supreme Court justices (including former deans Laskin and Frank Iacobucci and former students Ian Binnie and John Sopinka), as well as politicians (Bob Rae), writers (Andrew Pyper and Jack Batten) and several thousand straight-up legalists.

 Walk past the school at night, after the library has closed and the last students have fled, and you stand a good chance of seeing an office lamp burning on the second storey of Falconer. It belongs to Dean Ron Daniels. A graduate of the school and a professor who specializes in law and economics, Daniels has spent the past 14 years at the school, six as dean. He's 42, but his youngish looks, slight frame and polished speech give the impression of a high school debater who's borrowed his dad's sports coat for the big tournament.

A fervent booster of his school, Daniels is reluctant to revisit last year's events. His reticence is understandable, perhaps doubly so with me: my ex-girlfriend is a student at his school and works part time for Clayton Ruby, the lawyer who defended the majority of the accused students. (She was not involved in this case.)

When Daniels became dean in 1995, he launched a campaign to make it one of the top five in the world. The same year, the provincial government cut U of T's operating grant by 15 per cent. The school faced shrinking revenues, while Daniels wanted to increase funding for student aid and expand the size of his faculty. Despite the loss of funding, the school's faculty swelled from 33 full-time professors to 50. Meanwhile, the school substantially increased its undergraduate student aid offerings from about $100,000 in 1995 to almost $700,000 in 1999. Professor Michael Trebilcock, a revered 30-year veteran, notes that the school can now compete with its American cousins. "For as long as I can remember, we simply have not recruited professors from the U.S. market," he says, "because we couldn't make competitive salary offers. This year, for the very first time, we sent a recruitment team down to the U.S."

Add to all this an ambitious proposal for physical expansion. Plans are under way to spend at least $20 million to enlarge the existing complex. Appointed to a second term as dean in 2001, Ron Daniels should have been focusing his attention on some serious fundraising. Instead, he had to consider whether and if so, how to punish some of the students he'd welcomed aboard the previous fall.

When the notorious class of '03 arrived, on September 5, 2000, they began an indoctrination process that would transform them from unwashed peons into members of a scholarly and dignified profession. In those first few months, there were Latin phrases to be learned and basic but slippery legal concepts to master. More important, the incoming class had to begin the long-term undertaking of learning to think like a lawyer. Along with the academic training, incoming students are also inundated, almost from day one, with lore about "the firms." "The day I walked into orientation, I didn't even know what a Bay Street firm was," said one of the students who falsified his grades. "And all of a sudden, orientation was full of T-shirts and paraphernalia from the firms. People were saying,'You've got to get in with Torys or McCarthys!' It was a whirlwind."

The firms' ubiquity has, over time, caused most students to obsess over landing a first-year summer job. "The students create the buzz," says Denise Raume, a professor who found herself in the middle of the controversy, "about which firms to pick, what makes you a schnook and what makes you a high flyer." Students size each other up based on their success in the pursuit of these jobs. "Half of law school is about impressing people," one student said. "It's about impressing your peers so they think you're smart. And people thought it was prestigious to work at the firms."

The central irony in this case is that the grades that caused the school and the students so much pain weren't supposed to matter at all. The first-year class writes a set of practice exams each December, which aren't generally counted toward final marks, allowing students to work out the kinks before their first real exams in the spring.

Faculty and students agree this long-standing system has educational value, but not everyone cares that the exams are meant only for the students to measure their own progress. The downtown firms, which are hiring more first-years than ever (11 firms recruited first-year summer students in 2001, compared with only five the previous year) do so based largely on the students' first-term, first-year, first ever law school exams. Increasingly concerned about Wall Street's poaching, Bay Street firms see early recruitment as the only way to guarantee them a shot at Canada's top prospects.

Landing a summer job after first year raises the chosen few in the estimation of their fellow students; more to the point, you may never have to hunt for a job again. If you're hired as a first-year summer student, there's an excellent chance you'll be hired back the next year. Most firms also guarantee second-year students return to article and then be hired as associates.

In January 2001, the school's career development office hosted an information session that the students dubbed "Bay Street Day." Superficially, the event was a return to high school guidance class, with recruiters delivering lectures on such topics as "Effective and Ineffective Cover Letters and Resumes" and "Distinguishing Yourself in an Interview."

But while the school's job information package told students "The submission of first-year marks will continue to be at the discretion of the student," during these speeches the recruiters made it clear that an application that did not include marks from the practice tests would be considered incomplete. "We had five lawyers telling us that if we wanted to be considered, we'd better have good grades on our December tests, because they're the only means of assessment they have," explained a student who bumped up her grades. "That left a lot of us confused."

It was a confusion the school's administration failed to dispel. While the dean has often warned firms that first-term marks are a poor indication of a student's legal aptitude, he didn't directly confront the firms about their hiring practices. To reinforce the marks' informal nature, the administration refused to issue official transcripts, advising students to "simply append a piece of paper to your application listing your results." But that didn't solve the problem.

The school's policy, meant to protect students, had the opposite effect. "I got a C plus in one course, and I told the law firms I got a B," an accused student said. "My thinking was the school wasn't doing anything to prevent anyone else lying, so I could very well be the only one submitting a C plus. I'd be putting myself in a seriously disadvantaged position in vying for these jobs."

This student wasn't alone. While early media reports suggested that students had replaced Cs and Bs with straight As, people close to the case claim the actual adjustments were much smaller in scope. "I was told the vast majority effectively took the Cs off their transcripts," says Jim Phillips, a professor whose forte is legal history. "The word among the students was that if you got Cs, you hadn't a chance of getting an interview. They didn't fabricate their grades in order to get a job; they fabricated their grades in order to not be immediately rejected without even an interview. They did it to get into the game, not win the game."

At 520 students, U of T's law school is small compared with many other Canadian schools, and gossip is relentless; gospel truth can be turned into rank falsehood within a half-hour. One common tale about this scandal suggested that an administrator had advised students to bump up low marks, since the school would never verify the marks submitted to the firms. Another said students in past years had inflated their grades, that the practice was commonplace and tacitly accepted. A final bit of gossip had it that a professor was encouraging students to alter their marks.

The first rumour was duly investigated and deemed to be false, but at least a grain of truth lay at the core of the other two. According to Dean Daniels, the faculty had never received a complaint about marks misrepresentations before last year, but others say the absence of formal complaints means little. "A lot of us were under the perception that it was convention and practice," one of the accused students said. "I've spoken with people who worked for the firms, and a lot of people have said this has been going on for years." Word of a long-standing practice of grade fudging also reached Peter Russell, an emeritus political science professor who for a time headed an investigation into the affair. Rumours that some students would be submitting false grades to the firms first came to the attention of associate dean Mayo Moran and assistant dean Bonnie Goldberg on January 19. The students' applications were due on January 26, which should have allowed the administration a full week to dissuade the students. However, the administration moved cautiously during the first month of its investigation - so cautiously, in fact, that the dean himself didn't become aware of any problem at all until January 31, five days after the offending applications had been signed, sealed and delivered.

On February 8, persistent reports of marks misrepresentation led Moran to circulate an e-mail, crafted with the dean's assistance, that advised first-year students of the administration's dim view of grade inflation. The next day, an envoy sent by the offending students approached Moran. The students' representative (who had not lied herself) told Moran that the e-mail had made students realize the seriousness of what they had done and suggested that more than 10 students were involved.

On February 15, Daniels followed up on Moran's message with an e-mail of his own, recommending that students who had lied should withdraw their applications. A single student may have heeded the warning. When school officials obtained copies of the applications from the firms, they found 34 students' applications contained higher grades than those actually awarded. Five days later, after a report in The Toronto Star, the marks affair became a national scandal.

If Daniels has used his tenure as dean to attempt to move the school into the big leagues, long time professor Denise Reaume has fought to preserve the faculty as a refuge for serious academic thought. Save for some grey hair, Raume could easily be mistaken for a graduate student, but she has taught feminist legal analysis and other, more mainstream "black-letter law" courses here since 1982. Her acerbic wit, commitment to teaching and occasionally brutal candour have made her a respected, and some times loved, professor. Last winter, Reaume's unwavering commitment to academia put her at the centre of an affair within the affair.

During an informal how-are-you-all-adjusting conversation in a torts law seminar led by Reaume in early January 2001, the topic of first-year job applications came up. As an offhand remark by one of the students flowered into a heated discussion, Reaume suggested that all the first-year students enter a pact and submit straight A's to the firms. It would be an act of civil disobedience, she said, and send a message that asking for the grades was inappropriate.

By February 9, the day after Moran's e-mail alerting students to the school's concerns, five students had contacted the administration to report rumours that a professor had counselled students to alter their grades, though only one of them had been present when the remarks were made. That student said she believed Reaume's comments were made as a joke, "to get students to relax," but she still felt "the students had not thought of being dishonest until being made aware of the loophole arising from the non-verification policy."

Daniels e-mailed Reaume on February 12, asking for an explanation. Reaume promptly responded: "It should be clear that this was suggested as a political protest strategy and not as an individual strategy to gain over one's classmates." With that, Reaume thought the matter resolved and left a week later to attend a conference at Oxford.

But the matter was far from resolved. On Valentine's Day, a student from Raume's seminar approached Daniels. The first marks inflator to approach the dean directly, she didn't believe Reaume's comments were a joke or part of a political agenda. Based on her accusation, the dean asked the university to appoint an external examiner to investigate.

An investigating committee was promptly set up, with Russell, the emeritus political science professor, as chair. While he was successful in his bid to expand the mandate of the committee to include any issues that led the students to misrepresent their grades, no one disputes that the committee was primarily established to investigate Denise Reaume. Indeed, the press release posted on the university Web site announcing the formation of the Russell committee was entitled "Law Investigation Extends to Include Professor."

The decision provoked howls of protest from the international academic community. An open letter from a group of professors from Oxford, Yale, Columbia and the London School of Economics expressed concerns about U ofT's commitment to academic freedom, as did a petition from U of T law students. Although there was some muted disgruntlement among the law school's professors, less than half the faculty signed circulating letters of support for their embattled colleague. "There is a general atmosphere in the school that the leader knows best," tenured professor Hudson Janisch asserts. "There is no doubt in my mind that junior faculty members are very conscious of the goodies that the dean can give you. He can give you sabbaticals, and he can determine salaries."

Upon her return from England, Reaume wasted no time in launching a pair of legal actions against the university. Reaume and the U of T faculty association sought an interim order to stop the Russell committee investigation in its tracks. At the same time, she served notice that she was prepared to sue Ron Daniels and vice-provost Paul Gooch for libel. Both legal actions argued that by announcing that the Russell committee's job was to look into Reaume's behaviour, the university denied her certain protections, such as anonymity, provided to faculty members under investigation. Furthermore, they suggested that Daniels and Gooch, by giving interviews in the press about the investigation, had injured Reaume's good name.

In response, the university contended that Daniels and Gooch had only confirmed what reporters already knew (perhaps by reading the university's Web site). At a preliminary hearing in the interim order application, a grievance committee concluded that, yes, there was a chance the investigation would tarnish Reaume's reputation, and so it ordered the committee to halt its work until the grievance could be heard.

The anticipated hearing never occurred. When the university settled Reaume's libel case on June 18, it apologized to her (while noting it still believed what she had done was "inappropriate") and asserted its commitment to academic freedom. It then disbanded the Russell committee. All in all, it seemed a clean victory for Reaume.

But it wasn't over for her just yet. In an interview given with the law school's student paper, Ultra Vires, this fall, Daniels made further comments. "I regret the university had publicly revealed her name," he told the paper. "We should have been more attentive to her interests, and the university apologized, and I endorse that. As to the investigation...I don't regret that for a moment."

 In response to the dean's comments and similar remarks by the university's president, Denise Reaume, who retreated to McGill to teach this past year, wrote her own letter to the paper. "Having been threatened with dismissal, subjected to an ad hoc investigation not contemplated by the university's agreement with faculty, pilloried in the press and consequently hounded by the media for months," she wrote, "I get the message: you didn't like what I said."

While Reaume and the dean fought their public battles, a more private, internal investigation of the students was moving forward. Bruce Chapman, a lanky, soft-spoken professor, met with each student individually to determine whether there were honest mistakes that could account for the discrepancies between the university's records and the student's application. These meetings identified a number of students who had not out-and-out falsified their marks. Some had been given split grades like C to C plus and had only indicated the higher mark to the firms. These students were weeded out of the investigation, as were those who had sought a professor's permission to substitute a mark from a first-term paper for the mark from their practice exam.

On March 23, Chapman informed the students that nine would be excused on these grounds and the rest would have to attend another meeting with the dean. This reduced the total accused from 34 to 25. Of those 25 students, Clayton Ruby represented 18. (The remainder had other lawyers or represented themselves.)

A distinguished alumnus of the school, Ruby, the silver-haired defence lawyer and regular antagonist of the powers that be, had for a number of years addressed the first-year class during orientation. Each year, he would argue that the school's increasing tuition and its cozy relations with Bay Street were leading more and more students astray - toward highly remunerative corporate law and away from worthy government or criminal defence work. Ruby's reputation and his intense disapproval of the school's direction made him the natural choice to represent the students. Although he and the dean disagree on a number of matters, they essentially agree on one key issue. They both believe many of the students here were motivated by their own financial bottom lines. Daniels has contended that some of the students involved in the case had dollar signs in their eyes. Some, he says, went so far as to tell him, "I simply wanted the money." For his part, Ruby suggests the dean is ignoring the factors that may have fuelled the students' pecuniary desire. "For many kids, particularly the ones who are poor, these are plum jobs," Ruby said. "They have huge debt, and then someone offer's them a summer job that pays a thousand bucks a week. That's a huge amount of money for someone with no real skills."

The money is even more of an incentive for students who've borne some of the cost of Dean Daniels' great leap forward. In the past five years, tuition has gone up by 380 per cent, from $3,400 to $12,800, and the school plans to increase it to $22,000 by 2006.

In his defence of the students, Ruby argued that the increased fees prompted the students to lie. "If you see that 30-odd people misrepresented their grades on job applications, then the first question has to be 'What's going on?'" he says. "If it were one or two students, then you would say they're a couple of bad apples. But when you consider only 55 or 60 people applied for these jobs, you realize 50 per cent of the applicants misrepresented their grades. Why? The answer has to be that the school places such pressure on these people that they do what they have never done before. They become people who lie."

In a building elsewhere on the U of T campus (its location a closely guarded secret), a comfortably appointed anteroom was briefly transformed into hell. In the waiting room, students sat together and waited for their hearings. Many sobbed; some called their parents or spouses for support; one made frequent trips to the bathroom to vomit. "Sitting in that room was the worst experience of my life," one student said.

Daniels' meetings with the students began on Monday, April 2, and should have ended on Wednesday, April 4. That timetable quickly fell apart. "I was scheduled to go into my meeting at 9:30 in the morning, and I actually got in at 9:45 that night," one student said, "and that was because one of the students' interrogations went about six hours. They interrogated her, sent her away for a little while and then brought her back in." Another student had a similar experience. "We walked in there willing to confess what we did, but I felt I was under inquisition."

David Scott, an Ottawa-based lawyer who specializes in administrative law, advised the dean throughout the proceedings. His recollection differs markedly from those of the students. "It was a completely open, frank exchange. There was a penetrating process of questioning by the dean but I saw absolutely no evidence of overbearing questioning or inquisitorial behavior of any kind," he said. "What I saw was an environment that was driven by care and compassion, but in the face of an enormously serious set of allegations against these people."

It is very possible the dean believed himself to be acting with compassion toward the accused students while remaining blind to the pain this "compassion" was causing. For example, Daniels had originally planned to inform the students of their punishments on April 6. That day, due to the dragging meetings, he e-mailed the students to tell them he was going to reserve his decision until the following week. On April 11, he e-mailed them again and informed them he was not going to release his decision until May 1. "The dean spent hours ruminating over this," Scott explains. "He took the time and made the effort to think about the punishments in a responsible way." The unfortunate side effect of the dean's careful ruminations was that the students had to write their spring exams at the end of April, uncertain whether they would be asked to return in the fall.

On May 1, Daniels finally brought the students' wait to an end. Seventeen of them would receive one-year suspensions and notations on their academic records - black marks that would remain there until three months after graduation. Another five would receive lesser sanctions, ranging from simple reprimands to a notation on their records (without suspension of their studies). Finally, three students would be referred to the provost to decide if they should be formally charged. If so, they would face a full hearing and possibly stiffer penalties.

The bulk of the suspended students were shocked by the gravity of their punishments and aired their complaints in the media. "You've essentially been identified for life," one student said, "because there'll be gaps in your transcript."

Scott contends that none of the students would have blamed institutional pressures or criticized the dean in the media if the penalties had been lighter. "I didn't hear a single complaint about how these things were managed until the punishments were announced," he says, "and then suddenly the whole thing wasn't working any more."

After the dean delivered his decision, almost all the students took their punishments and began serving them in anonymity. The one who didn't, the only one to go public, was Roxanne Shank.

A 48-year-old mother of two, Shank has a brown belt in aikido and a master's degree in philosophy. Until her meeting with Ron Daniels to discuss her punishment, her story was much the same as the other accused students'. There is, however, one salient difference: Shank says she never intended to lie about her grades.

Shank has consistently refused to speak with the press, but the court documents outline her story. At 4:30 a.m. on January 26 (the day the applications were due), after a day of school and caring for her children, Shank settled down to complete her summer job packages. She typed a column of plus signs beside her grades, intending to go back and edit out the inaccurate pluses. She removed the one from beside the B she had received in property law, but she forgot to remove the pluses beside the Cs she had received in contract law and torts. In short, she claims that it was poor proofreading and not poor judgment that led to her submission of two C pluses rather than two Cs.

Her explanation raised eyebrows among fellow students. "How do you accidentally change your mark from a C to a C plus?" one asked me. Others accepted the explanation, suggesting that a change from a C to C plus would do little to improve Shank's chances. That said, the veracity of Shank'saccount mattered little to her court case. You don't have to buy her contention to argue that the dean had no right to punish her.

On August 23, the day of Shank's review, the courtroom was nearly full, packed with at least 40 students. In the day long proceeding, Ruby spoke on behalf of Shank, and other lawyers represented the dean (who was out of town), the university and the school's students' administrative council.

On Shank's behalf, Ruby contended that because she had never admitted an academic offence, the dean lacked the jurisdiction to punish her. (Under the academic code, the dean isn't allowed to make findings of fact - he can only impose a sanction if the student admits to the offence.) According to both sides, Shank had been extremely contrite during the meetings, breaking down and crying. She apologized for her mistakes and the trouble they were causing; she did not "intend to cheat," but she had been "very careless, "she had "screwed up," there was "no excuse" for her carelessness. In the administration's view, these statements constituted an admission of the offence.

Until she met the dean to discuss her punishment, Shank apparently never realized that he was approaching her case in the same manner as he did those of other students who had admitted intentionally changing their marks. Detailed meeting notes seem to pinpoint the exact moment Shank discovered she and the dean weren't on the same page. He tells her she will be suspended for one year, and Shank responds:

Shank: Is this the punishment for the lion's share of the students?

Daniels: Any student I determined intentionally misrepresented their grades will be suspended.

S: You believe I intentionally put two pluses on two Cs?

D: Yes, I'm sorry I wasn't persuaded by it. I was not prepared to see it as a mere transcription error. Bruce Chapman felt the same way. There are other students in similar circumstances.

S: What do you think - what possible advantage is there in putting two pluses on two Cs?

D: It's a stronger record [The two discuss why the dean didn't consult Shank's character references.]

D: I think this is appropriate.

S: Why?

D: In the end, I do not believe your account. I don't believe they ended up there by accident.

Professor Hudson Janisch explains Shank's case: "Daniels said, 'I don't believe you. The moment you say, 'I don't believe you, you are acknowledging that the person hasn't admitted the offence, and you are in effect judging them and determining that an offence has taken place.'"

On this issue, the court eventually sided with Shank. "The applicant recognized her responsibility but at all times denied the essential ingredient to an offence that involved a 'knowing' or intention to deceive - the very thing the dean found against her," the court wrote. "It is patently unreasonable to conclude that a denial is an admission. Shank's supporters were thrilled by the ruling, but she could still be referred to the university's disciplinary tribunal for a full hearing.

A week later, Daniels circulated an e-mail to the student body announcing that the charges against Shank would be dropped. "As I have told Ms. Shank," he wrote, "I am sensitive to the protracted and public nature of these proceedings and the toll that the process has undoubtedly taken on her. It is now time to put the matter behind us and move forward." The university also reversed its decision to refer two others to its disciplinary tribunal, giving them one-year suspensions instead. A third did have to appear before the tribunal. This final student not only lied about his exam marks; he tried to change them on the exam papers themselves to match the grades submitted to the law firms. He received a five-year suspension.

In the aftermath of the controversy, the school has addressed some of the systemic problems that led to the widespread lying - even as the administration steadfastly denies that such factors contributed. There's been a drastic reduction in the Bay Street firms orientation-week profile, and the school has begun issuing official transcripts for practice tests. Ron Daniels doesn't believe the firms' high profile contributed to the cheating, but even he doesn't contest that their early involvement may not be productive. The dean has convened a committee, co-chaired by assistant dean Bonnie Goldberg and Professor Michael Trebilcock, to study the relationship between the faculty and the profession. The dean denies the committee was conceived as a response to the events of the past year, but Trebilcock isn't so sure. "Recruitment pressures on first-year students have intensified," he indicated. "We hadn't really, until the marks scandal broke, wrapped our minds around it."

In a report delivered in early March, the committee suggested U of T band together with other Canadian schools to forbid any recruitment activity during the first half of first year, and to restrict such activities at other times. Students can't afford recruitment restrictions that would hurt their chances of landing a job, but many faculty members worry that the intrusion of the profession into the school may hamper their ability to teach. "Fifteen years ago, we had to write off our students in the second half of third year," Denise Raume said, "because they were all off planning their futures. Then we had to write off the whole third year, because by the end of second year they'd gotten their articling jobs. To the extent that a first-year summer job is conceived of as putting you on track for an articling job, the long-term threat is that within months of coming to law school, students will know what the future holds, and they'll have less incentive to engage in the intellectual enterprise."

The dean's plan to raise tuition to $22,000 over the next few years has angered many students, and the often bitter interfactional debate has again caught the attention of the national media. But as a fresh skirmish begins, the casualties of the last one are still recovering. Seventeen suspended students are waiting out their punishment with varying degrees of patience and grace. Some are making the best of their time in purgatory, working at legal clinics or travelling. Others are in therapy. Not one of the students I spoke with wants to be excused for submitting false grades to the firms.

"Obviously, lying to potential employers is wrong," one said. "I can offer some explanation as to the kinds of things that may have led to that, but certainly there's nothing that could justify it. I brutally, extremely regret having done it."

The students know they were responsible. They only wish the school would acknowledge its mistakes as well. "I think at the end of the day, it's been horribly myopic to focus on us," one said. "But now that we've fessed up, can we start looking elsewhere? Can we start looking for room for improvement?"

It's unlikely that the faculty will ever admit culpability in the scandal. Seated in the dean's spacious office last December, I asked Ron Daniels a simple question, the simple question.

"Why did this happen?"

He didn't answer then, but later he e-mailed me a response.

"We may never know," it read.

I was disappointed. I had spent a couple of months interviewing students and faculty, and a consensus had emerged, a list of contributing factors on which even the dean's supporters could agree. The students made their decisions based on money and ambition. Those decisions were made within a context of rising tuitions, unchecked gossip and innuendo, peer pressure and undue influence on the school by the big firms. All these factors played a part, but the school will never admit it. Why? Perhaps they don't believe you can be one of the top five law schools in the world and admit a mistake. Perhaps they fear alienating their Bay Street supporters. Perhaps they just want to pretend the whole thing never happened. We may never know.

Reprinted with permission of the author.

Conclusion

The account of this event reinforces how disconnected the university has become from society as a whole. All of the participants behaved poorly. The law school should never have made public allegations against the professor without first discussing those allegations with her. In the case of the professor, it is hard to understand how her comments are somehow protected by the notion of "academic freedom." "Academic freedom" does NOT mean that a professor is entitled to say anything in a classroom. And finally, (although it seems to have become the least significant issue) the students should never have cheated! Facts are stubborn things!!

Chapter 23

Excelling In Law School -
What I Wish I Had Known Before Starting

Advice From An Armchair Quarterback

Like most law students, I started law school with little idea of what to expect or of what was expected from me. In retrospect I realize two things:

First, I didn't know that I could benefit from some advice; and

Second, there was no place to get advice anyway.

The advice I would give any student in or starting first year law school is:

1. Law school is not to learn the law - it is for learning how to learn and how to apply the law.

2. Law exams don't test your knowledge of law - they presume you know the law and test your ability to apply the law to the facts.

3. You will learn the course by preparing the summary of the course.

4. Answering law school exam questions is a very specialized skill. I recommend you get some instruction in that area - earlier rather than later.

Work Habits and Study Skills

In spite of the fact that, the evaluation in many law school courses is based on 100% final exams, law school is not difficult to pass. You will, however, have to work both consistently and effectively to do well! At many schools, grading is quite competitive.

Begin working at the beginning of the year and work consistently and effectively. You know what it means to work consistently. To work effectively will require the acquisition of certain specific skills.

Consistent Work - You Must Spend The Time

Working consistently does not mean working all the time. It means working a certain amount every day. It is also essential that law students receive regular exercise and entertainment! Extra curricular activities are essential.

Effective Work - The Time Spent Must Be Productive

Effectiveness requires that:

1. You be mentally and emotionally focused.

Regular exercise and extra-curricular activities will allow you to focus better on your work. To focus on your law school work - you need activities and a life outside of the study of law!

2. You are skilled in processing the cases that you read.

A systematic way of organizing the information from the cases is essential. The traditional way that law students organize information from cases is through a "case brief." A "case brief" is an organized summary that consists of the following parts:

1. Case name and citation and court deciding the case - the citation is a statement of where the case may be found in the official law reports.

2. Facts - a brief summary of the relevant facts

3. Issue - the point of law in question

4. Holding - the decision of the court

5. Principle - the legal rule that the court uses to justify its result

When you review for your final exam you will not have the time to reread every case! You will have time to review only your case briefs and lecture notes. You should use your case briefs and class notes to develop an outline of the course. Through the construction of the outline you will learn the course and prepare for the exam. Learning the law is a gradual exercise.

Advice From A Professional On These Issues And More ...

The following article, written by a California law professor will give you a "head start." Read it, and think about it before you arrive the first day.

The following article has been reproduced with the kind of permission of Casenotes Publishing.

Understanding Law School

By Professor Kenneth W. Graham, Jr.

Introduction

There are many good books that tell you exactly how you should brief cases, take notes in class, make an outline of your courses, or write answers on law school examinations. What they don't tell you is why you should do these things. Programming is fine for computers, but we humans get tired, bored, and suffer pain when we have to perform tasks we do not understand. This essay tries to ease the pain by giving you an understanding of law school and letting you program yourself.

Law students are surprised when they discover, sometimes too late, that the study skills that got them into law school are not enough to keep them there. It should be obvious that law school is different. The casebooks don't seem to explain, and the professors don't seem to lecture. Why law school is different is frequently explained but seldom understood. The explanation goes like this: law professors are not trying to teach you a bunch of rules you will forget when the exam is over; they are trying to teach you professional skills that will last a lifetime.

The distinction between learning rules and acquiring skills is clearer in this sentence than it will ever be in the classroom. Perhaps this is because one of the skills you have to learn is how to find the rules and another is how to apply the rule after you have found it. Since you have to learn some rules in order to practice these skills, it is easy to think that it is the rules and not the skills that you ought to be studying. But professors don't make understanding the distinction any easier when they describe the skills they are trying to teach you by some vague description such as "learning to think like a lawyer." Let me try to be a bit clearer.

Thinking Like a Lawyer

During my last year in law school, I once tried to study while I was baby-sitting our two children. Distracted from my work by the sounds of forbidden activities, I dashed to the bedroom, threw open the door, and bellowed: "How many times have we told you kids not to jump on the bed?" My three-year-old daughter replied (innocently?): "But, Daddy - we weren't jumping on the bed. We were jumping off the bed!" This was a precocious example of "Thinking like a lawyer."

If we were to analyze this as legal rhetoric, we would say that I made "an argument from authority"; that is, I cited a rule ("No jumping on the bed") from an authoritative source (me). My daughter, unable to challenge the authority of the rule (for example, by arguing that it was unconstitutional), responded with a "conceptual argument"; that is, she defined a key concept ("Jumping on the bed") in a way that made the rule inapplicable to her conduct ("Jumping off the bed"). If you focus on the type of argument made, rather than the specifics of the argument, this interchange between my daughter and me is the same sort of argument that lawyers make every day.

Lawyers make many other kinds of arguments. Historical arguments: "This is a good rule because it has survived for hundreds of years" or "this is a bad rule because society has changed too much since it was first adopted." Process arguments: "This is a bad rule because it will be hard to enforce" or "this is a good rule because it was drafted by legislative experts who know more about the subject than anyone else." Instrumental (or "policy") arguments: "This is a good rule because it will produce some result that is good for society (such as encouraging investment or deterring negligent behavior)." Legal rhetoric — thinking like a lawyer — requires that you understand the various types of legal arguments so that you can tailor them to fit any specific case.

Legal arguments resemble plays in football or openings in chess because if you understand their basic structure, you will be able to see some common ways to defend against them. For example, an instrumental argument involves both a prediction about the effect of a rule and an evaluation of that rule as either good or bad; e.g., "The 'no-jumping-on-the-bed rule' is good because it allows Daddy to study." Therefore, you can respond to an instrumental argument in three ways: by disputing the prediction ("jumping on the bed is not noisy"); by contesting the value placed on the result ("who says studying is good?"); or by pointing to some bad consequence of the rule that outweighs the good effect it is supposed to produce ("if we can't jump on the bed, we'll grow up to be juvenile delinquents").

Understanding the structure of a particular argument does not tell you whether it is good or bad. Learning to make a good legal argument is a skill that takes lots of practice. As I will explain, much of your time in law school will be spent practicing this skill - and others as well. Let us see how understanding that legal education is primarily skills training can affect how you study in law school.

Preparing For Class

You will probably arrive for your first year in law school eager to get a start on your studies. But you may find that the law school is not as ready for you as you are for the law school; class assignments are not posted, books are not yet in the bookstore, and the professor is not due back in town until the first day of classes. Don't panic or waste your time and energy frivolously. Instead think about what you need to do to be a successful law student.

Studies of successful students show that one trait they all share is the capacity for self-reflection and analysis; that is, they constantly ask not just "what should I do to prepare for class?" but also "why am I doing it this way?". Emphasize the personal pronoun in that last question. The most important person in determining your success or failure in law school is you; you cannot be a successful law student if you do not constantly look at your study habits from that perspective.

In thinking about your success in law school, the first question you must ask is "how should I define, 'success'?" Some students unthinkingly adopt the popular definition: "success in law school means finishing in the top 10% of the class." But by that definition, 90% of the class is doomed to fail. At the other extreme, after a few weeks of law school, many students begin defining "success" as "not flunking out." But defining "success" so that it is easy to achieve is not very rational either.

To get your own definition of "success," define it in terms of things that you can control rather than those that are in the laps of the gods; for example, define "success" in terms of the effort you put in rather than the effect it has on your professor's evaluation of your exam. Or try to make success an immediate and concrete possibility rather than a remote and grandiose goal; for example, "success" means "studying 10 hours on Saturday" rather than "being editor-in-chief of the law review in my third year." Always keep in mind your own strengths and weaknesses. If calling yourself a "success" is not sufficient to motivate you to brief all the cases before you go home today, then promise yourself a triple-dip ice cream cone if you get the job done.

Time and the Law Student

Despite your uniqueness, there is one way that you are like all other law students: none of you has more than 168 hours per week to study. Despite the stories you may have heard about "straight A" students who never crack a book after sundown, all the evidence shows that the more time you spend studying, the better your grades are likely to be. So, some students spend 100 hours per week studying, which still leaves them nearly 10 hours a day to eat, sleep, exercise, and perform other bodily functions. But if you have to work 40 hours per week to support your family (as I did), you can't be that profligate with your study time. You have to budget it carefully.

The best way to budget your time is the way lawyers do it: by keeping time sheets. Time sheets break down the day into increments of 10 to 15 minutes. Carry them with you and get in the habit of recording exactly how you spend your time as you are doing it; e.g., "10:57 am. - 11:50 a.m. - attended contracts class" or "briefed pages 30-41 in property" or "stood in line at the registrar's office and thought of several crimes." Go through your daily time sheets at the end of each week and "bill" each professor for the time you spent studying for each class and "bill" yourself for the rest.

Keeping time sheets is not only a good way to acquire a professional skill; it will also help you to avoid some common mistakes. One of these is spending more time on classes that you understand and enjoy than you do on those you hate because they are difficult. Another error is to suppose that you spent an hour studying between torts and contracts by ignoring the 10 minutes you spent going to and from those classes, the 10 minutes you spent in conversation by your locker, and the 10 minutes you spent in the john. Time sheets can help you distinguish between "quality hours" and the kind where you spend 60 minutes staring at the page, understanding nothing, and slapping your face to keep awake. "Billing" your hours will help you to schedule them more productively and show you where you can squeeze in the time you need for a major research paper or a visit from your lover.

Know Your Enemy

If you focus on skills rather than rules, you can see why people have been as important as principles in shaping our law. This is why we have battles over Supreme Court appointments. It is also why lawyers try to learn as much as they can about the judge who will hear their case. Whether an argument is "good" or "bad'" either in the courtroom or the classroom, depends upon the person to whom it is addressed. For example, an instrumental argument showing that capital punishment is "efficient" is not going to be very effective with a judge or law professor who thinks "fairness" is a more appropriate criterion. This is why you need to know as much as you can about the person who will be evaluating your arguments in class and on the final examination.

Some professors are political mavericks who make their views well-known in the classroom (and give students their first taste of making arguments that are acceptable to someone whose values they do not share). But other professors hide behind a Socratic mask so that determining their values requires a good bit of detective work. A good place to start is the professor's biographical entry in the Directory of Law Teachers, published annually by the Association of American Law Schools and available in most law libraries. You can also read or skim any books or articles the professor has written. In some schools, you can inspect evaluations of the professor by former students. Finally, looking over some of her old examinations can provide some useful clues about the professor's values.

When assignments are posted, your first task in preparing for class is to simply read the assigned cases or statutes. This will be difficult at first because legal writers use unfamiliar words or familiar words in unfamiliar ways. You will have to stop frequently to look up definitions in a legal dictionary. This is not always easy because the definitions themselves may use other words that you will also have to look up or the definitions may simply be unclear. But don't give up. If you stick with it, you will gradually begin to master the language of the law. But if you just plow ahead reading words you don't understand, the pain may persist for the rest of the year.

After you have read the case once, you are ready to analyze it. Lawyers analyze the case in three steps. First they examine the facts of the case to determine what legal issues were presented to the court; this requires separating the facts that are legally relevant from those that are not. Second, lawyers try to deduce what rule (or rules) the court applied in deciding the dispute; this is called "the holding" of the case, and determining it is not as easy as you might suppose. Finally, lawyers will examine the legal arguments the court used to justify applying this rule rather than some other rule; those arguments are called "the reasoning" of the opinion. This part of the opinion provides important clues as to what arguments the court might find persuasive when asked to apply the holding of this case to a case with slightly different facts.

Briefing Cases

Lawyers record their analysis of an opinion in a "case brief" (not to be confused with a "legal brief," which is a written summary of a lawyer's argument to a court). Casenotes offers a free publication you can print called "How to Brief a Case." However, some of these books obscure the fact that briefing cases is a lawyerly skill and convey the impression that it is some special drill for law students. It is true that your brief will be more elaborate than a lawyer's because you have to consider the case from all points of view where the lawyer is only concerned with how the case can hurt or help her client. But the purpose of the brief is the same in both cases; namely, to provide a written summary of your analysis of the case so that you do not have to re-read the case when preparing for classroom or courtroom arguments.

Learning to brief cases takes time, but with a little practice you will be able to read and brief a case in little more time than it takes you to analyze the case without briefing it. Real briefing does take more time than "book briefing" because preparing your own brief requires you to analyze the case, while merely underlining sentences in the opinion does not. If a month into law school, you find that it takes all your class preparation time just to read and brief the cases, you have a problem that will not be solved by abandoning briefing. It may be that your briefs are not "brief" because you have not mastered the abbreviations and other shortcuts that reduce the required verbiage. But you may also have some problems in your analytic technique. Ask for help from your professor or writing instructor.

After Briefing, Then What?

Sooner or later you will find that reading or briefing the cases takes only a small portion of the time you have allotted for studying. You can use part of this new-found time for reviewing and planning for the final exam, but I doubt that you can or should devote all of your extra time to exam preparation during the early part of the semester. I used much of this time to read and brief ahead in all my classes because I had been warned that some teachers will pile on work at the end of the semester when you need the time for exam preparation. For reasons you can probably deduce, most of my classmates thought this an insane way to spend valuable time.

On the other hand, not everything my classmates did seemed completely rational to me. Most law schools have an ample supply of well-meaning quacks or fast-buck artists who have just the thing to reduce your anxieties and make education effortless. Their nostrums range from flashcards to computer programs, from songs you can sing in the shower to weekend seminars in flea-bag hotels. I have not tried any of these, but I can tell you that each of them has proved helpful, or so they tell me, to at least some students. Be that as it may, I only have space here to cover some of the more conventional secondary sources.

Law Review Articles

I spent a lot of time in law school reading the law review articles that were cited or excerpted in my case books - too much time. Most law review articles are written to impress other law professors or to change the law, not to explain it to neophytes. You can learn from some of them about the "cutting-edge issues" that make good examination questions or about the outer limits of permissible legal arguments, but lucid explanations of the law are infrequent. I kept slogging away on many articles because I was too stubborn to admit that I was getting nothing out of them. Don't you make that mistake.

By all means, read anything your professor has written - even if it is so incomprehensible that you wouldn't dare try to parrot it back on the final examination. Read the "classic" articles, those that have changed the way lawyers and judges think about the subject; you can identify these from the way your professor talks about them in class or from the way they are cited in your casebook. Student writing is useful, especially casenotes that analyze the principal cases in your casebook; student writers may not be as knowledgeable as professors, but what they do know is closer to what you need to know than are most faculty articles. Finally, don't overlook articles in bar journals; they are often written by practicing lawyers so they are shorter, more practical, and can provide a refreshing change from the academic alfalfa you are fed by the faculty.

Hornbooks and Other Student Texts

My favorite form of secondary reading was student texts, often called "hornbooks" after the title of a series of such texts from the West Publishing Co. I used them in law school and continue to do so - even as a substitute for a casebook in one of the classes I teach. Some professors will advise you not to use hornbooks-and with good reason. A hornbook is essentially a written lecture; which is to say that it is good for conveying information about the rules but will not teach you much about the skills you use to apply them. But if you understand that limitation you can safely use them to quickly satisfy your need to know the rules and thus free up more of your time for practicing your lawyerly skills.

Student texts, unlike law review articles, are written for students and by professors who are in the mainstream of legal thinking. They can be a useful antidote to the weirdos whose ideas get more attention in law school classes then they ever will in the courts. Most hornbooks also do a good job of showing you the way the rules are related to each other. This is a big help when you are trying to organize the rules for your outline. Finally, a hornbook is a good source for a "second opinion" when your professor's explanation leaves the subject unclear.

Classroom Training

Class Attendance

Some people believe they can do well in law school without attending classes; we call such people "ex-students." If you have understood what I have been telling you about legal education you will see why. The classroom is to the law student what the practice field is to the athlete - a place to practice your skills with and against your peers under the guidance of a coach who can correct bad habits and suggest how to improve your technique. Moreover, the classroom gives you a chance to see what your professor thinks are "good" and "bad" legal arguments, so you know what kind to use on the final examination.

The accreditation standards of the American Bar Association require class attendance, and conscientious professors will take attendance even if the law school does not require this because missing classes is the first sign that a student is having educational or emotional problems that require help. If you think you are getting nothing out of classes except the next day's assignment, talk it over with a friendly faculty member. She can help you understand what your professor is trying to do and, perhaps, point out how you can better prepare to meet those goals. Sitting in on the class of some other professor who is teaching the same subject is rarely a good way to prepare for your professor's final examination. Use it only in the rare case of the truly incompetent teacher. ("Yes, Virginia, there are . . .")

Just Before Class

Make sure you bring all of the assigned texts, your case briefs, and everything you need to take notes with you to class. If you have a choice, select a seat someplace in the middle of the room where you can see everything written on the chalkboard and hear what is said even by your soft-spoken classmates. (Contrary to what cynics may tell you, the last row in the classroom is not the best place to avoid the professor's eye.) Use the minutes before class begins to review your notes from the previous day and your briefs of that day's cases. Two minutes of such review each day in a class that meets 60 times will save you two hours of study - almost enough time to take in a movie as a reward!

Notetaking

Most law students have plenty of notetaking experience so they are not likely to think of taking notes as a professional skill. But if you get to court and watch a real trial, you will see that good lawyers do not spend their time staring at the witness or opposing counsel like lawyers on TV shows do. Instead, they and the judge are busily taking notes of the testimony. This may seem strange when you see the court reporter making a verbatim stenographic record of everything that is said. But if you could see their notes you would understand the difference. The reporter records everything that is said - the relevant, the irrelevant, and the insignificant. The lawyer takes down only what is useful for cross-examination or final argument; the judge notes only what she needs to rule on motions and objections.

Notetaking is a tool for critical listening, not an inefficient substitute for tape-recording. The skill you should master in class is selectivity in notetaking. Make it a habit to think "why am I taking this down?" rather than just scribbling away whenever the professor's mouth moves. If he is just repeating something that is already in yesterday's notes (that's why you reviewed them before class), the only reason for writing it down again is to help fix it in your memory. This is not the best use of the limited strength in your writing hand.

Noting Class Discussion

Students who think that law is just rules will copy down every pseudo-lecture delivered by the professor but record very little of the most important part of the traditional class — the discussion or "Socratic dialogue." Even students who do take notes of the discussion will only record what they suppose to be the "right" answers and disregard everything else. Students who understand that the classroom is the place where they practice argumentative skills also know that they have to record specimens of both "good" and "bad" arguments if they are to learn the difference between them.

Taking good notes of class discussion is not as difficult as you might suppose. In learning to brief cases, you will develop a set of abbreviations for the major rules and concepts in each subject. If you devise a set of symbols for the various types of legal argument to help in recording the "reasoning" portion of your case briefs, you can use these symbols and abbreviations to capture both the form and content of an argument or response. For example, if the student makes the instrumental argument that the Mapp rule (requiring the suppression of illegally obtained evidence) is "good" because it will encourage the police to follow the law, you might record the argument this way: "Mapp cops cops law-abiding" (the arrow indicating the causative element of the argument). If the professor questions the causative part of the argument, you just add underneath: "P:?? ".

Noting the structure as well as the content of the argument will help you see that what other students think is the professor's disapproval of a student's argument is simply an attempt to demonstrate the standard responses to that type of argument. For example, when the student makes the instrumental argument for the Mapp rule just mentioned, the professor might respond, "How do you know the rule deters police misconduct?" (attacking the causative claim) or, "Who says illegal searches are 'bad'?" (attacking the evaluation of the result) or, "A lot of guilty people will escape punishment if we suppress illegally obtained evidence" (pointing to some supposedly "bad" effect of the rule). Students who ignore this entire interchange on the ground that what the student said was "wrong" will never learn that they could have attacked the professor's last argument the same way she attacked the student's; e.g., "How do you know we need illegally obtained evidence to convict the guilty?"

Demystifying the Socratic Dialogue

Socratic teachers usually begin the class discussion by asking a student to "state the case"; that is, to describe the salient facts and the court's decision of the disputed issue(s). My purpose in "stating the case" is to make sure students have the correct understanding of the legal dispute and its resolution. The professor may quiz the student to elicit any relevant facts omitted or to question the relevance of some of the facts stated or simply to test whether and when the rule it states will be available in future cases with different facts. The best way to record this part of the dialogue is by additions to, or deletions from, your brief of the case.

The professor will next ask about "the holding" of the case. Whatever the student says will be criticized or questioned by other students egged on by the professor. This can be confusing if you do not realize that there is no single, unequivocal holding for most cases. The case can, and in subsequent litigation frequently will be, cited for any number of possible "holdings." The purpose of this part of the discussion is to enable you to see how malleable the idea of a "holding" is and to open your eyes to all the possible "holdings," not to arrive at some determination of what is The One True Holding.

At some point, students will be invited to describe and criticize the court's "reasoning." This part of the discussion allows you to practice your skills in making and analyzing arguments. It will become more sophisticated as student understanding of argumentative techniques deepens. If one student seems to approve of the court's use of some concept, such as "consideration," "malice," or "minimum contacts," other students will respond with conceptual arguments suggesting other definitions that will change the result. If a student attacks the court's instrumental argument, the professor may respond with another argument the court did not make to see if the student can shoot the new argument down as well.

Good Socratic teachers make extensive use of hypothetical cases (or "hypos," for short). Hypos are designed so that students can see how the case under discussion (usually called "the principal case") might be used as a precedent in some subsequent case. For example, if the principal case holds that the landlord is not liable for injuries suffered by a fireman who comes into the building to fight a fire, the professor may pose a hypo where the fireman is there to sell tickets to the fireman's ball or where a policeman enters the house to catch a burglar. The student will be expected to see whether the principle case can be "distinguished" by revising the holding so that it does not apply to the hypo (the rule only applies to firemen who are on duty) or "extended" by expanding the holding to cover the hypo (the rule applies to "public safety officers, not just to "firemen"). It is a good idea to take note of the professor's hypos; they have a nasty habit of popping up again on final examinations.

To Participate or Not To Participate?

This question would seem to have an obvious answer if you view the classroom as a place to practice your new-found skills - or if you have seen movies about the "good days" before the "no-hassle pass" when students had their names stricken from the class for failure to answer. However, even when I was in school the stress of participating in a legal argument - even with someone of limited skill and venom of the typical law professor - seemed so forbidding to many students that they preferred to falsely claim they were "unprepared" and endure the abuse that followed rather than attempt to match wits with the professor. And today in many schools, there is a student "ethic" of non-participation that is enforced by "hissing" when some "handwaver" volunteers answer.

My advice is to ignore the hisses. How will you know if you are making any progress in learning legal rhetoric if you don't try your arguments in class to see how far they will fly? (Ironically, the same idiots who hiss at "handwavers" and bad-mouth rigorous Socratic teachers will often be heard to belly-ache about the lack of "feedback in legal education.") As you learn to distinguish between a response from your professor that says "that was a pretty weak argument" and one that says "not bad - now let's see if you can hit this curve ball," you will find that arguing with the teacher becomes less stressful - even fun! Besides, and I am ashamed to say that this is what motivated me to become a "handwaver," if you volunteer often when you are well-prepared and reasonably certain of your answer, this makes it less likely that the professor will call on you when you are unprepared or have not the slightest clue as to what he is after.

Why Don't We Do It In The Road?

Many professors hang around the hallway after class to answer questions or continue discussions that were cut off by the bell. If you are too scared to jump right into class discussions, you might get your feet wet by posing your questions or making your arguments in these post-class "seminars." Since many professors drop the Socratic mask when they step out from behind the podium, yours may seem less frightening out in the hall. But stick around even if you aren't terrified of the teacher. I find that some of my best explanations of complicated subjects come after the class is over, and I do not have to worry about covering the next case, students are more candid about what they don't understand, and I can tailor my explanation to the particular student's needs.

If the professor does not hang around after class, he or she may hold formal "office hours" to meet with students. If you fear that asking your question during office hours will lead to a "one-on-one" Socratic dialogue, you can invite a friend or your study group to come along and share the abuse. However, you will probably find the professor much less forbidding in her office than she appears in class. Besides, an office visit is a good way to learn a bit more about the person who will be grading your examination paper, you don't want to write a bluebook filled with cross-outs and interlineation if your professor is one of those anal compulsives with a neat desk. (Guess what mine looks like.) The pictures and diplomas on the wall and the books in the bookcase can provide useful clues into the Professor's values and socio-political philosophy.

Debriefing the Class

As soon as possible after each class, go over your notes, fill in any gaps and make necessary corrections while the discussion is still fresh in your memory. As you go over the notes, ask yourself "why did the professor ask this question?" and "are there any kinds of arguments that were not made?" If you focus on the type of argument being made, rather than just the specific content of the argument (that is, seeing that the argument "if we apply the fireman's rule to policemen, how can we not apply it to garbage collectors and meter readers?" is simply another variant of the infamous "slippery slope" argument), you will see the kinds of arguments your professor favors as well as the values she holds. You will see how similar arguments are being made in classes with quite different specific content. This makes your skills training more efficient. If you argue in torts that a common law liability rule is a good one because it has been refined by centuries of use (the historical "good because old" argument) and your teacher responds with "but we need a rule that is more attuned to socioeconomic conditions of the twenty-first century" (the historical "good because new" argument), this should teach you how you can respond in property when your professor tries to defend some medieval doctrine by arguing that it must be a good rule because it has survived for so many years.

Each week, or at the end of every casebook chapter, you should go through your notes and briefs and attempt to integrate and synthesize the cases into a coherent set of rules. This requires that you determine whether one case overrides another case or creates an exception to the rule in the other case or is a "minority rule" only in effect in a few states. If this is unclear from your notes, ask your teacher or check the hornbook. This integration of the cases is the first step in preparing the outline of the subject. You will need to be able to apply all these rules on the final examination.

Preparing For Law School Exams

A sage once observed that legal education resembles the method used to induce schizophrenia in laboratory mice; namely, you train them to run the maze in one way, then abruptly change the goal. All semester, law students are told that rules are not important and are rewarded for making oral arguments; then on final examinations, they are expected to memorize a bunch of rules and make good written arguments. Why we test you on what is testable on a written examination rather than on your mastery of all the skills you are taught in class is too complicated to be discussed here. But this practice creates a tension between learning what you need to be a good lawyer and learning skills that are only useful on examinations.

I have no desire to foster the all-too-prevalent notion that law school is an intellectual track meet, and I certainly do not want to make you think that your potentiality as a lawyer is captured by your grade-point average. But the fact is that if you want to be a lawyer, you have to pass law school exams (and in most states a bar exam as well). The trick is to learn the skills you need to pass these examinations without taking too much time away from learning the skills you will need after the bar exam is over. My suggestions aim to show how you might do that - not to make it appear that there is nothing in law school besides examinations. If you are lucky, you may have teachers who try to make the discontinuity between lawyerly skills and examination skills less sharp than is usually the case.

Looking at Old Examinations

From what I have said about the importance of knowing your audience in designing your arguments, you may already have deduced one of the most important maxims for exam preparation: never take a law school examination without looking at samples of the professor's past examinations. One of the first things you want to do when you begin law school is to find out where the law library keeps old examinations. Some students delay looking at old examinations until late in the semester on the theory that until you know most of the rules, you will not be able to understand the examination. Poppycock. The real reason they postpone this vital task is that they are afraid of what they will find. This is irrational. The best way to reduce fear of exams is to know exactly what to expect when you walk into the examination room.

In going over our corporations teacher's old exams, my study group discovered that the old gentleman had been using the same dozen questions for more than 40 years, but this recycling had gone unnoticed because most students only looked at exams for one or two years. You can imagine how confident we felt walking into that examination, knowing that we had already worked out answers to all the questions we were going to be asked. In fact, I felt so good that I got my lowest grade in law school. This may prove that there is a fine line between complacency and confidence — or that grading is inherently arbitrary (the rest of my study group did fine) — but it does not disprove the wisdom of looking at old exams.

What to Look For

Look first at the instructions. They will tell you if the exam was "open-book" or "closed-book" or what materials students were allowed to use if the exam was "semi-open-book." Make note of these materials and make sure you bring them to the exam; feeling like a fool because you forgot to bring your statutory supplement to the exam is not the best state of mind with which to begin the exam. Watch out for idiosyncratic instructions: e.g., "don't write in red ink" or "don't use small bluebooks." You may say it is safe to ignore these petty preferences, but I have a colleague who enforces his request that students "write on only one side of the page" by refusing to read what appears on the other side when grading exams.

Check whether the past exams were in the traditional essay form or whether they also used multiple-choice, true-false, short-answer, or other so-called "objective questions." The form of examinations can influence your method of preparation for them. An essay examination tests such skills as making legal arguments and the ability to write English prose under severe time constraints. An objective exam is more likely to test your ability to recall or recognize rules and your skill in applying them to varying facts. Moreover, if the exam is "open-book," you are more likely to be tested on esoteric rules than you would be on a "closed-book" exam; it would be an outrage to expect you to memorize some obscure provision of the Internal Revenue Code, but it is not outrageous to expect you to find and apply it if it appears in a book beside you.

Be wary of examinations if the past instructions suggest your teacher likes to give "take-home" exams. A take-home exam is "good" if you prefer to have your anxieties stretched out over 24 hours rather than compressed into three. It also frees you from the distractions of being cooped up with 100 sweating paranoiacs. But a take-home exam requires a bit of advance preparation if you are to get all of its presumed benefits. For example, the law school administration is not going to summon you from the examination room to answer a telephonic inquiry from a parent or lover into your pretended celibacy; in a take-home exam, you have to make your own arrangements for screening out such distractions. Moreover, you may feel pressured to buy books that all of your classmates will have beside them when preparing their answer on a take-home examination when you might well forego this expense on an in-class exam where you wouldn't have much time to consult the book even if you had it.

Study Groups

For learning legal skills, having a high L.S.A.T. score is less valuable than being in a good study group. However, since many students have a mistaken idea of the purpose of a study group, they have a hard time finding a good one. The purpose of a study group is two-fold. First it gives you a chance to practice the skills you are learning in class with a group of your peers. Second, it gives you a chance to develop an important lawyerly skill not taught in class - how to work in a group. Many students in law school like to think of themselves as intellectual "Lone Rangers," but it is unlikely that many of them are going to practice law that way. Besides, if you are in one of those law schools with a highly competitive student culture, you can find your study group to be a comforting enclave of cooperation.

A study group is not a "briefing pool" or an "outline combine," though some good ones may share such tasks, nor is it a "legal bull session" or "support group for the alienated," though some poor ones do little more than that. The ideal study group is more like a debate team where you practice making arguments and criticize arguments made by others. When you are just getting started, the subject of these debates can be whose brief has the best statement of the facts or holding; later you can choose up sides and argue some classroom hypothetical case or some issue raised by the notes in your casebook. When you get closer to exam time, you can practice making up hypotheticals for the rest of the group to argue. This gives you a chance to look at the rules from the perspective of a teacher trying to devise an exam or a lawyer trying to work her way around them; that is, you search for gaps and ambiguities in the rules and try to imagine factual situations that exploit these weaknesses.

My law school study group met only one evening a week (we were married with children so this became our spouses'"night out"). In advance of the meeting we would assign topics, rotating weekly, so that one week I might take criminal law and torts, the next week civil procedure, and so on. I would dig out several old exam questions on my assigned topic and try to work out answers to them by using class notes, hornbooks, outlines, etc. At our weekly sessions, we would take turns presenting the questions we had prepared to the other members of the group and criticizing or supplementing their attempts to give oral answers to the questions. I don't claim this is the "ideal method", but it will illustrate how one good study group functioned.

Forming a Study Group

A good size for a study group is three to five students. With only two people, there is no one to criticize (or referee) debates; with more than five students, you decrease the participation of each and increase the likelihood of including someone whose personality or purpose does not mesh with others in the group. Keeping the group going requires effort under the best of circumstances; you don't want to end up spending more time debating what you ought to be doing instead of doing it.

Some students think the primary criterion for membership should be intellectual that is, that an ideal study group is "me and two other people with high L.S.A.T. scores or who seem to know more than I do about what is going on in class." Avoid students who express such sentiments. It is hard to build a cohesive group with people whose primary motivation is what they can get out of the rest of the group rather than what they can contribute to the group. Compatibility of purpose should be the primary criterion for a study group. If you want a skills-practice group of the type I have described, you will not be happy in a study group with people who really want a "briefing pool" or an "outline exchange." Similarly, if you are a working parent who has to carefully budget your time, you don't belong in a study group with "100-hours-a-week" overachievers who will kill themselves (or you) in order "to make law review."

Outlining

Why does everyone who offers advice on law study tell you that you "gotta outline?" The best answer is that an outline helps to overcome one of the major disadvantages of the case method of law study; namely, the way that it tends to fragment the law. Studying the law by close examination of individual cases can be like learning about forest ecology by examining the individual trees; the things you learn this way are true and useful, but terribly incomplete. In some caselaw courses, the only synthesis you get is the analysis of a group of cases to develop "the rule" and its myriad exceptions and qualifications. But this leaves you with some serious questions about the relationship of this rule to other rules - to say nothing of the relationship between this subject and other branches of the law. This is an important problem in the practice of law because clients do not come through the office door with the announcement: "I have this novation problem." Indeed, the client usually does not know whether the problem is one of torts, contract, or property.

I can make the same point in more concrete terms with a more immediate pay-off. All semester long, you will be honing your rhetorical skills on hypos that the professor presents in class. You may get pretty good at this and feel confident going into the final examination. Yet when you read the first question, you can be dumbfounded if you are not prepared for it. Why is that? One reason is that each time you looked at a question in class, you knew from the day's chapter headings that the applicable rules were those dealing with "novation" or "burglary" or "indispensable parties." Now on the examination you are faced, often for the first time, with a set of facts that are not only more complex than the classroom hypos but that lack the clues you have been getting in class about the relevant rules. Like the lawyer, you have to decide whether the appropriate rules to invoke are those dealing with "novation" or those that govern offer and acceptance, though unlike the lawyer you can be pretty sure that the appropriate rules will be found in contract law rather than property or torts. Not only are you faced with an unfamiliar task, but you are asked to perform it on a set of facts more complex than anything you will have faced in class - more characters than a Russian novel and moving faster than a Max Sennet comedy. Facts that are relevant to contract formation may be intermixed with those that concern issues of breach or performance. Worse yet, some facts may be relevant to more than one issue and some may be totally irrelevant. It is little wonder that many students who were doing well in class can flounder on a law school examination.

This is where outlining comes into play. You make one monster outline of the entire course - what one of my classmates used to refer to as "the Poppa Bear." The purpose of this outline is to figure out how the rules fit together, which rules are separate requirements, which are subsidiary rules or exceptions to major rules, which are competing rules that are inconsistent and in effect in different states (the so-called "majority rule-minority rule" classification). Making this big outline can serve other functions as well - review, testing to see which rules you don't understand yet, and helping to implant the rule in your memory - but its major function is to organize the course so that it can be compressed into an exam outline.

The purpose of the exam outline - the "Momma Bear" in my friend's terminology - is two-fold. The second, and less important, function is to condense the course to a length that you can realistically expect to memorize for a closed-book exam. The first, and most important, purpose is to give you a program for processing exam questions through your own "thinking-like-a-lawyer" hand-operated computer. It should be obvious that you cannot discuss all the facts in an examination question at the same time and that the legal rules cannot be applied simultaneously. You have to deal with some issues first and others second and third. Does it make any difference which issue you discuss first and which you discuss second? Or is the law like long addition where you get the same answer regardless of the order in which the numbers are taken? If you cannot answer these questions, then I have just successfully illustrated the problem that an outline is designed to deal with.

The last step in outlining is the preparation of a one-page document that is less an outline than a check-list or index of the exam outline; this is the "Baby Bear." When I say "one-page," I mean that literally. The Baby Bear is a mental check-list that you will use as you go through a complicated exam question, searching for issues that the professor has buried and planning how you will organize your answer. I will explain the use of the mental check-list in the portion of this essay suggesting how to go about writing an answer to a law school examination. For now, you will simply have to take it from me that the Baby Bear has to be so short that you can visualize it in one corner of your mind's eye as you read the question — something like that little picture that appears in the corner of the screen on television sets that allow you to monitor one channel as you are watching another.

Commercial Outlines

As the author of a commercial outline, anything I say on this subject is suspect - and rightly so. But if that were grounds for silence, no one could say anything on the subject. My views on the subject were biased before I wrote an outline, albeit in a somewhat different fashion. As courts do with biased witnesses, don't treat me as a total incompetent but hear what I have to say and discount it for bias in making up your own mind.

From what I have said above about the function of outlining, you will have deduced that while a commercial outline can be an adequate substitute for some of the purposes of outlining, for others it is no substitute at all. A commercial outline can demonstrate how someone else organizes the rules, but it does not give you much practice in that skill. Moreover, by letting someone else do the outlining for you- whether it is me or a member of your study group - you lose the review, memorization, and learning that are the by-products of the outlining process as well as the psychological sense of progress that comes from producing your own. These are the reasons I did my own outlines and urge you to do the same.

But having said that, I must acknowledge that not every student has the time to do outlining. Despite the importance of outlining, only the most devout worshiper of the Great God G.P.A. would claim that it should rank above spending time with your children or engaging in political activity or reading poetry. Moreover, commercial outlines do offer something that your own cannot - namely, a second opinion on organization or another explanation of difficult rules and concepts. Indeed, some students buy an outline not as a substitute for their own outline, but as a substitute for a hardbound student text and a model for their own outline.

The issue with commercial outlines, as with any study aid, is not one of use, but abuse. If buying an outline increases your passivity, makes you a spectator rather than a participant in the educational process, and prevents you from developing your own critical skills, then buying it is a bad idea regardless of how good the outline may be in other respects. On the other hand, if you use the outline as a tool to encourage your own critical aid to free up more time for the practice of your rhetorical skills, it is probably worth the price in dollars and foregone opportunities.

Mid-semester Melt and The Marathon Metaphor

If you plotted study effort over time, for most law students the graph would look like a cross-section of the San Joaquin Valley; two towering peaks at either end with a flat, foggy miasma between them. We all find it easy to study at the beginning of the term, when our enthusiasm is high, or at the end, when fear of failure towers over us. The trick is to maintain study in the middle weeks when the subject matter is no longer fresh, the faculty's foibles become annoying rather than amusing, and when job interviews, research memos, or co-curricular activities (such as law review, moot court or other student organizations) provide a handy excuse for decreased study time. If weekly review of your time sheets shows a decline in your efforts, it is time to think about a strategy for the long haul.

One model for such a strategy is a marathoner's training schedule in preparation for a 26-mile run. Viewed over the entire period, a typical plan would show a slow but steady increase in mileage each week with a tapering off just before the race. A look at the daily or weekly schedule would show a more varied pattern. One day might have a long, slow run that is interspersed with short, sudden bursts of speed. Some days the runs are up a hill to strengthen leg muscles, while on others the runs are supplemented by lifting weights to build up unused muscles. There are even days of total rest. Your mind is also a muscle, perhaps not the same as the gluteus maximum, but with a similar need to recover, recharge, and rebuild after stress and with the same need for variety. If you spend all your time exercising your logical and analytic capacities, your imaginative and empathetic faculties may atrophy like non-stressed pectorals.

Don't make your "training plan" a prison; as the runners say, learn to "go with the flow." If you are "on a roll" when briefing cases for property, you don't have to come to a screeching halt just because the plan calls for you to switch to some other task. On the other hand, if you are having trouble just staying awake when you are scheduled to read the hornbook, don't push the "no-pain, no-gain" philosophy to the point where you stick pins through your nostrils to keep from drowsing off. Switch to lighter reading, like a legal novel or a lawyer's biography; that will clear your mind of academic torpor. If you keep track of your time, you will find that your efforts will balance out over the long run.

Did I just tell you to read a novel? Yes, I did - and do some legal history or jurisprudence or legal jokebooks while you are at it. I am a believer in the "serendipity theory" of education, which holds that learning is a process of making connections between what is already known and what you would like to know so that the more you know, the easier it is to make these connections. But you don't have to understand or believe in this theory to take my advice. Just understand that learning to "think like a lawyer" requires you to know our legal culture. That culture is deeply embedded in materials that seem rather far removed from the cases, statutes, and treatises that are your daily diet. You have to immerse yourself in other manifestations of the legal imagination if you expect to understand the thinking of lawyers and judges. This is why I never felt guilty about stopping by the rack in the library, when I had a few moments before class, and skimming the front page of a legal newspaper or giving a fast read to an article in the local bar journal. Let your reading roam beyond the syllabus and you will find many rewards.

Writing Law School Exams

The Prof's Eye View

When I entered law school, I had prior experience as a teacher. I found my experience in giving and grading examinations helped me when I returned to taking them. I urge you to try to think about law school examinations from the professor's point of view. If you do, you will realize that your professor could devise an exam that everyone could pass (well, almost everyone) or an exam that everyone would fail (contrary to what students may think, this last is not the strategy professors follow). From the professor's point of view, the reason for giving you an exam is so that she can give you a grade. All schools require grades and most of them expect or require that grades be distributed in a manner resembling the infamous "bell-shaped curve." Thus, the professor's strategy in constructing an exam is to ask some questions everybody can answer, some questions almost nobody can answer, and a range of questions between these two extremes.

Students need their own strategy for taking examinations. If your only plan is to walk into the exam room, read the question, and "wing it" in writing your answer, you are much more likely to panic when you see all those facts and issues crawling off the page toward you (or worse yet, when you see no issues at all). A sound strategy will help you to avoid common errors. For example, good students sometimes think that if a legal question is easy to answer, then it must not be an issue when they see it on the exam; so they lose points for not discussing an issue that the teacher thought everyone in the class would be able to answer. It may help you to devise your strategy if I describe the method I used to write law school examinations.

The "Three Times Through" Method

My method was to read an essay exam question three times before I began to write my answer. The first time through, I read quickly to get a general understanding of the facts and to make sure that I understood the task that I was expected to perform. The task instruction or "call" is usually at the end of essay questions, despite the fact that these instructions should make a difference in how you read the question. You will look at the facts one way if you are instructed to "discuss all possible claims and defenses" and another way if you are told to "write a legal argument in opposition to defendants motion to dismiss."

The second time through, I read the question much more carefully and with this thought in mind; "Why did the professor put this fact in?" I knew from my experience as a teacher and in devising hypos for my study group that you raise legal issues by first making up facts needed to raise these issues, then gluing them together into a plausible story with other non-essential facts. Hence, the second time through the question I was just reversing the process. I would ask "what legal issue(s) would this fact be relevant to?" and jot down the abbreviation for the issue in the margin of the exam next to that fact.

If you practice this technique on old exams, you will see some patterns that make it easier to spot issues. For example, the more specifically a fact is stated in the question, the more likely it is to be relevant to some issue; if the professor wants to raise an issue about the amount of damage recoverable for negligent destruction of a vehicle, he is going to describe it as a "1990 Mercedes" rather than as "plaintiff's automobile" because the latter gives you no idea what the car is worth. Similarly, if the professor goes to the trouble of making up specific dates for some events in the question, it's a pretty good bet he wants to raise an issue like the statue of limitations that turns on the dates of those events.

The third time through the exam was another quick trip. This time I flipped on the one-page mental checklist I had memorized just before the exam and kept it in my mind's eye as I looked over the facts and my notes in the margin regarding their potential significance. I used the checklist for two purposes. First, to organize my answer (I would suggest that you outline your answer on the first page of the bluebook if your professor is one of those who will give you credit for seeing issues you don't have time to discuss). Second, I used the checklist to make sure that I had not missed some issue that did not leap out at you from the facts but was easy to see if you were looking for it with the assistance of the checklist.

A strategy such as the "three times through" method takes time - but it is time well spent. If you make sure that you have found all of the issues and the facts necessary to resolve them before you start to write, you won't have to feel (and look) like a fool when you cross out pages you have already written because you remember a rule or stumble over a fact that demolishes your initial analysis of the question. Moreover, if you see all the issues and organize your answer, you can allot your time so you don't waste so much on the earlier issues that you can only skim the surface of the later ones. Finally, if you practice this system on old exams of a professor who uses the "Easter egg hunt" method of constructing exams, you may discover the tricks she uses to conceal issues so that only a few students can find them.

To Type or Not to Type?

There is only one good reason for typewriting your answers to an essay examination; namely, you can write a better answer with the machine than you could with a pen. Since most law students have poor handwriting, the professor is unlikely to be particularly biased against you when she has to pause now and then to decipher a word. I know of no evidence, including my own grading, that typewritten answers are scored higher than handwritten answers with the same content. Because typists are a small minority, law schools do not administer examinations with them in mind. For example, corrections to the questions that are chalked on the board where students are writing the exam are not always communicated to the typists. When you add in all the things that can go wrong with the machine, it is clear that while typing the exam may make it easier for the professor to read, it is not necessarily the best way for you to write your answers.

Common Errors - Some Rules of Thumb (Down)

(1) R.T.D.P. - Read The Damn Problem! Make sure you have the parties straight and the facts correct. Nothing exasperates a grader more than factual "mistakes"; somehow students always seem to "err" in the direction that makes the issue easier to answer (and the answer harder to grade).

(2)   Follow the "call" of the question, not the "call of the wild." If you are instructed to "write a legal memo supporting the plaintiff's claim", don't write your answer as if you had been told to "discuss." Put your answer in the form of a memo and only make arguments that favor the plaintiff.

(3)   Resist the temptation to show off how much law you know; discuss only those rules that are essential to resolving the issues posed. If the professor wants you to write a law review article, she will say so.

(4)   Don't write "formulaic" answers. "I.R.A.C." may be a way to remember the elements of a good answer, but it is not a recipe for wilting one. It is tedious for the grader to read and inefficient for you to write an answer that repeats over and over, "The issue is...The rule is ... The application of the rule is ... The conclusion is ....".

(5)   Don't "resolve issues in your head." If you think "this can't be a battery because the defendant never touched the victim," write that down in your bluebook. If you don't, you may miss cheap points that every idiot in the class is going to get; if you do, the act of writing it may remind you of some rule or reason that turns this "cheapie" into a more difficult issue.

(6)   Don't ignore the gorilla. If there is a major issue that you have no idea how to resolve, don't just pretend that it is not there. If you do, you look like a fool and miss points the grader may give you for seeing an issue that he really didn't think that anyone could answer.

(7)   Keep your eye on the doughnut, not the hole. If you have a gap in your recollection or knowledge, don't let that distract or discourage you. Start with what you do know and try to work your way toward the answer from there. If you can't think of a relevant statute or case, make an argument from policy. For all you know, there may be no policy!

(8)   Use legal terminology. I know you are not going to pass the exam when I read in your answer that "this case should be thrown out of court," instead of "The motion to quash service of summons should be granted." If you can't even talk like a lawyer, it is almost certain you can't think like one.

(9)   Don't whine or throw bouquets. If the exam is unclear or has an apparent error, don't annoy the grader by gloating or complaining about how his mistake has destroyed your concentration. Explain how you have resolved the ambiguity or corrected the error, then answer accordingly. And if you really think it was a "great class" don't write this at the end of your bluebook; send your professor flowers after the exam. Putting compliments in your bluebook makes you look like an insincere sycophant.

(10) Finish it off. Before turning in your bluebook, make sure it complies with all formal requirements (exam number attached, honor pledge signed, etc.) and all your answers are labeled so the professor can find the answer she wants to grade without guessing which bluebook has the answers to which questions.

"After The Ball Is Over ... "

Get away from the exam room immediately. If you stand around in the hall exchanging anxieties with your classmates, you will disturb other students still writing their exams. Even worse, you will hear about a whole bunch of issues that you never saw (and which may not have been there). You don't want to ruin your concentration for the next exam (or the first day of your vacation) by worrying about your performance on this exam. Besides, your subjective feelings are rarely a good indication of how you did. You may think you "creamed" the exam because you were not prepared enough to see all the issues you would now be moaning about missing if you were.

The time to "debrief" the exam is after it has been graded, but very few students do this, perhaps understandably so. It is embarrassing to admit to a professor you admired that you are the author of a bluebook he didn't admire. It may be painful to read what you wrote and to listen to a litany of your errors of analysis. However, if you wait until you have calmed down and go in with the attitude that you intend to learn from your mistakes, the confrontation may be less painful and more helpful than you might suppose.

If your grade on this exam was markedly worse than your others, tell the professor and ask (respectfully) if she will check or allow you to check the calculation of your grade. Over the past 25 years, such requests have turned up two cases in which stupid mistakes in addition by me have lowered the student's grade significantly. Two mistakes in over 4,000 bluebooks might seem like long odds, but keep in mind that there were probably less than 100 students who actually had the math checked.

Make careful notes as the professor explains the strengths and weaknesses of your answer; you probably won't be able to absorb the criticism adequately just by hearing it once. Ask the professor if you can make a photocopy of your answers so you can go over them more carefully later. (Most schools have rules that forbid the professor from giving you the original bluebook.) Don't be discouraged if you run across a professor who seems reluctant to take the time to debrief you. Insist. You paid your tuition like everybody else and are as much entitled to make demands on his time as his buddies on the law review.

When you have assembled comments on your exam performance from all your professors, you can go over them and the copies of your exam answers to see if any common threads emerge. Don't be surprised if the critiques of your work vary in both their direction and their quality. Professors vary widely in their notions of what makes a good answer and in the depth of their insight as to what is really going on when they give and grade examinations. This is why you have to put together the comments from all your teachers so that you can weed out the idiosyncratic and the idiotic before you make changes in your study habits and your exam strategies. The specific suggestions I have made here are less important than the premise on which they are based; that is, that you should see the examination as a part of the educational process, not as its end. If you have tried in your daily work to engage in self-conscious criticism of your learning practices, you will find it easier to respond intelligently to your exam grades, good or bad. It is foolish to look at a set of bad grades and decide to give up studying for partying; but it is also foolish to keep beating your brains out semester after semester using the same unsuccessful methods to try to improve your grades. The fact that your teachers have not taught you how to learn the law is a poor excuse for not learning to do it yourself.

This brings me to one final point. Maintain your dignity. If you thought the professor was a jerk for 15 weeks, don't suddenly discover his hidden virtues after your grade puts you in the top of the class. If you have studied hard and learned much during a semester, don't think you are a jerk if the grades don't seem to reflect your accomplishments.

Success or Failure?

One of the least pleasant side effects of legal education is the way in which students "internalize" their grades. It is most apparent in the case of the student who responds to a set of bad grades by thinking: "I am a 'C' student - a worthless person who will be lucky to get a job as a claims adjuster and who is doomed to a lifetime envying those with better grades." But it is equally invidious in the case of the "A" student who decides that his grades prove his self-worth and spends the rest of his life seeking a substitute for the G.P.A. in more money, faster cars, or better children than everybody else.

The fact that some employers seem to give grades a disproportionate significance should not fool you into supposing that all lawyers are unaware of the arbitrary nature of law school grading. Anyone who has ever graded law school exams can tell you that while there is a palpable difference between the best and worst papers in the class, other comparisons can be more problematic. A grade of 80 could go to either a student whose parents were both lawyers, who has learned nothing in law school, and who has gotten by on what was learned from listening to Mommy and Daddy talk at the dinner table or to someone who is the first person in the family to attend college and who has had to learn not only how to think like a lawyer, but how to understand people from a totally alien culture. In other words, the same grade can represent either an achievement or an accident.

Some law schools have done studies of their graduates that have produced one striking, and frequently suppressed, result. There seems to be an inverse relationship between grades and "success," regardless of whether success is defined in terms of financial rewards, professional stature, or personal satisfaction. Law professors, who are usually "A" students, have offered a number of explanations for these findings. Law professors are unrewarded in terms of pay and status. Other top students go to big firms where they exchange security for the opportunity to make the kind of money that personal injury lawyers make. Students with low grades are "too dumb to know they are unhappy."

But in their candid moments, even law professors will concede that law school grades measure (and often very poorly) only a few of the talents needed to be a "success" at the bar, irrespective of how that term is defined. Like many of my colleagues, I have no difficulty writing truthful letters of recommendation for students whose grades on examinations do not reveal the talents they have displayed in class. I could spend the next 20 pages just listing people I know who have had wholly admirable careers as lawyers despite "mediocre" grades. But I won't - because to do that would be to foster the very attitude that needs to be discouraged.

Sooner or later, we must all recognize our own strengths and weaknesses, whether these limitations are broader or narrower than those of others who we know. When we do that, we are ready to redefine "success" in our own terms rather than accept the definitions that seem to be thrust upon us. This requires us to give up the comparative ease of asking, "Am I better or worse than X," for more difficult questions such as, "Am I better or worse than I was yesterday?" "Am I really performing up to my capabilities or am I imagining limits as an excuse for my failure?," and "What difference will it all make when I'm dead?"

It is with these more difficult questions that education, even legal education, ought to be concerned. But because those questions are so personal, we have to learn to handle them with little help. I hope that the suggestions in this essay will seem to you not a "blueprint for success," but rather as encouragement to begin learning about yourself as you try to learn about adverse possession and the Commerce Clause.

Reproduced with permission of Casenotes Publishing Inc.

If you enjoyed *Understanding Law School*, check out:

Casenote Law Outline on Evidence

By Professor Kenneth W. Graham, Jr.

Casenote Publishing Co., Inc.

1640 5th Street, Suite 208

Santa Monica, CA 90401

(310) 395-6500

FAX: (310) 458-2020

Conclusion

I repeat - I wish I had known even some of this before arriving at law school. Your grades in law school are based on your exam performance. Your exam performance depends on:

1. How well you know the law;

2. How well you are able to apply the law you know; and

3. How well you are able to DEMONSTRATE your knowledge and abilities on exams.

Learn how to play the "law school game" at the beginning of law school and not at the end!

Book V - A Report

From Law School To Bar Admission - Your License To Practice

Summary And Introduction

My Advice To You Is ....

All jurisdictions have different requirements for becoming a lawyer. Learn those requirements at the earliest possible stage. Furthermore, you should become a member of the bar in both Canada and the U.S.

If your goal is to be a lawyer, more than a law degree is required. Book V will teach exactly what is involved in taking the further step of being admitted to the bar: becoming a lawyer in Canada, the United States or England. There are vast differences in what is required to become licensed in various countries. Those differences may even influence where you wish to receive your license.

Warning! This information is subject to change. Make sure that you always research the current requirements that may govern your situation.

In Book V I will role play the role of the "Bar Admission Consultant." You can tell from the Chapter Titles that lawyers are called different things in different jurisdictions.

Book V - Chapter Summaries

24. Becoming A Barrister And Solicitor - Bar Admission In Common Law Canada

Focus: Canadian lawyers are both Barristers and Solicitors - Educational and character requirements for both

25. Understanding Articling And The Rest Of The Bar Admission Course

Focus: The dirt on articling and the classroom component of the Bar Admission Course

26. Becoming A Notary Or An Advocate - Bar Admission In Quebec

Focus: Quebec lawyers are either Notaries or Advocates - Requirements to become either a Notary or Advocate

27. Becoming An Attorney At Law - Bar Admission In The U.S.

Focus: How to become an Attorney At Law - Opportunities for both U.S. and non U.S. law graduates

28. Becoming A Barrister Or Solicitor - Bar Admission In The U.K.

Focus: British Lawyers are either Barristers or Solicitors - How to become either a Barrister or Solicitor

Chapter 24

Becoming A Barrister And Solicitor
Bar Admission In Common Law Canada

Bar Admission In All Canadian Provinces Except Quebec

In the common law Canadian provinces lawyers are called "Barrister and Solicitors." Every person called to the bar in a common law province is both a barrister and a solicitor. Historically barristers would appear in court and solicitors would do other kinds of legal work. The U.K. retains the historical distinction between barristers and solicitors.

This chapter deals with the steps that must be taken and requirements that must be met in order to become a barrister and solicitor in a common law province. Ontario will be used as the model. The rules for Ontario are approximately the same as for the other provinces.

All persons practising law in the Province of Ontario must be members of the Law Society of Upper Canada. No person, other than a member of the Society in good standing, may act as a barrister or solicitor (lawyer) or hold himself or herself out as such.

The Requirements To Become A Barrister And Solicitor

The primary requirement is successful completion of the Bar Admission Course in the province in which you wish to practise. (The next chapter will focus on the contents of the Bar Admission Course.)

Admission to the bar is governed by a statute of the provincial legislature. In Ontario that statute is the Law Society Act. The Law Society Act provides for the structuring and governing of the legal profession in Ontario. (Every province has an equivalent.) The Act describes who is entitled to practice law and who is not.

The Law Society Act defines who is entitled to be a member of the bar. The actual text reads as follows:

the persons, being Canadian citizens or permanent residents of Canada,

(i) who are members on the 31st day of December 1990, or

(ii) who after that day successfully complete the Bar Admission Course and are called to the bar and admitted and enrolled as solicitors, or are members and entitled to practice law in Ontario as barristers and solicitors.

In addition, the Law Society Act requires that:

An applicant for admission to the Society shall be of good character.

The <u>Law Society Act</u> makes it clear that admission to the bar is not at the discretion of the Law Society by stating that:

"No applicant for admission to the Society who has met all admission requirements shall be refused admission."

These sections also make it clear that to become a member of the Law Society is to become both a barrister and a solicitor. In Ontario (and the rest of Canada) the historical distinction between a barrister and a solicitor has been abolished. No person may be called to the bar as a barrister only or admitted as a solicitor only; every applicant for admission to full membership in the Society must qualify both for call as a barrister and admission as a solicitor, and be called to the bar as a barrister and admitted as a solicitor on the same day.

In summary to become a member of the Law Society you are:

1. Required to be of good character; and

2. Assuming that the requirement is constitutional (and it may not be), be a **Canadian citizen or permanent resident** of Canada; and

3. **Complete the Bar Admission Course** administered by the Law Society.

What follows are some comments on each of these three requirements.

The Character Requirement - Not Good Enough Or Just Bad?

The crux of the matter is: Does any person who has completed the bar admission course and is of good character, at the time of his application for admission, have the right to be admitted to the bar? Or, are there instances of past misconduct, that are so severe, that an applicant should be permanently banned from the practice of law? This issue might be decided differently in different jurisdictions. I note that the Ontario Law Society Act says that:

"No applicant for admission to the Society who has met all admission requirements shall be refused admission."

After having been admitted to the bar lawyers are held to standards of ethics and behavior that exceed those applied to members of society as a whole. There have been cases of people completing law school and the Bar Admission Course (if applicable) and then having been denied admission to the bar. These cases are in an extreme minority. Although technically the burden is on the applicant to prove that he/she is of good character, in practice good character is presumed. What kinds of conduct will result in a failure to satisfy the character requirement?

Are Criminal Convictions Necessary?

The short answer is no. Conviction of a crime will operate as one piece of evidence used to determine whether one is of "good character." Here are some examples:

1991 - A former seminary student and teacher who was acquitted of sexual assault in 1984 was denied admission to the bar by the Law Society Of Upper Canada on the grounds of poor character. The applicant had graduated from law school and had completed the bar admission course. The hearing was called after the applicant disclosed that he had been charged with and acquitted of sexual assault and dismissed from his teaching position for gross misconduct. The committee believed that the applicant had sexual intercourse on more than one occasion with a 12 year old girl.

1995 - An applicant was refused admission to the Ontario bar even though he was acquitted of an assault against a woman who had received obscene phone calls which were traced to the applicant. He admitted making more than 100 obscene phone calls in the space of six weeks while he was a third year law student. The calls stopped when he was discovered by the police. Apparently he was not admitted to the bar because the Law Society was not satisfied that the applicant had rehabilitated himself. Obviously, this indicates that rehabilitation is an important issue. This case also makes it clear that one's conduct in his/her personal life can affect character for the purposes of admission to the bar. In a written decision the Law Society wrote that:

"... evidence as to why he did not tell his law firm of the charges against him was that he was innocent and that it was a personal issue which did not affect his articling services to the firm. This indicates a lack of understanding by .... of the importance of a lawyer's character as part of the profession and the fact that one's character and reputation have a very important impact on one's ability to provide services to clients and their desire to receive such services."

A case out of Illinois is a further example of how conduct in private life (outside the professional capacity of being a lawyer) can affect character for the purposes of bar admission. The Illinois Supreme Court ruled that an applicant did not meet the state bar's character and fitness requirements because of his rhetoric and racist views. (This case is particularly interesting because the applicant does have a constitutional right to freedom of speech. This right may have been violated by the ruling of the court.) Apparently the Supreme Court of the United States has agreed to hear an appeal of this case. This decision indicates that the court is of the view that the decision of the Illinois Supreme Court raises serious constitutional issues (of which I am sure "free speech" is one).

Are criminal convictions sufficient?

The short answer is no.

1999 - A University of Montreal graduate who had been convicted of murdering his mother (1990) by stabbing her at least four times applied to the Quebec bar course. The Quebec bar initially refused his application ignoring evidence of his possible rehabilitation. Through a series of appeals the applicant was able to adduce sufficient evidence of rehabilitation. A Quebec Superior Court judge ruled that he should be enrolled in the Quebec bar course. This decision underscores that rehabilitation is an issue that must be considered when considering what is important in an application to the bar.

You're Admitted To The Bar - Is Character Still An Issue?

The short answer is yes. Lawyers are disbarred every day of the week. Sometimes for violations of the rules of professional conduct in their capacity of being a lawyer. Sometimes lawyers are disbarred because of their behaviour outside their capacity as lawyers. Many of you will remember the case of Robert Alan Eagleson who was disbarred for various instances of "conduct unbecoming" (or as the title of Ross Conway's book suggests - "Game Misconduct").

1990 - a University Of Alberta law professor - Maurice Sychuk (known as "Screamin Mo" to his students) was convicted of the murder of his wife. He was disbarred because of it. His application for readmission raises a number of interesting questions.

Disbarred! - Is Rehabilitation Sufficient To Be Readmitted?

Rehabilitation is considered when assessing the character requirement. But, is a finding of rehabilitation sufficient? The Sychuk case is particularly interesting.

1999 - Maurice Sychuk served ten years of a life sentence prior to being paroled. He apparently had been a model prisoner. Mr. Sychuk then applied to the Alberta Law Society to be readmitted. The following summary of the facts comes from Robert Remington writing for the National Post.

"On New Year's Eve 1987, after an evening with three other couples that he described as "nothing short of a nightmare," the Sychuks returned home and began to fight. After Claudia (his wife) hit him in the mouth, "Screaming Mo" in an alcoholic haze, stabbed his wife 22 times."

Mr. Sychuk's lawyer presented evidence from experts in psychiatry, psychology, alcoholism and anger management that Mr. Sychuk was rehabilitated. Because of his rehabilitation, as goes the argument, Mr. Sychuk should have been readmitted to the Alberta bar. His application was opposed by many, including, eleven members of the University Of Alberta's law faculty (almost half the faculty).

On September 30, 1999 the Law Society of Alberta adopted the report of its own investigating committee (which heard all the evidence). Mr. Sychuk's application for readmission to the bar was denied.

Although the decision may have been "right", there is nothing in the Alberta rules which specifies what factors the law society was to consider in evaluating Mr. Sychuk's application. Furthermore, the rules did not specify what legal standard should have been used to decide the issue. Mr. Sychuk did not appear at the hearing where the Law Society voted to adopt the report of the investigating committee (which recommended that the application be refused). What follows are excerpts from the report.

"We agree with counsel for the Applicant that as a Committee of Inquiry, we must carry out our mandate and make our recommendation in accordance with the law. In our view, however, the lists of criteria contained in the textbooks and cases cited on behalf of the Applicant are not very helpful in this particular case.

In a case such as this, certain principles come to the forefront making other considerations pale in significance. We agree with counsel for the Law Society that rehabilitation cannot be the paramount factor at the expense of the standing of the legal profession.

In our view, an application for reinstatement is much different from an application for admission to the Bar. The Applicant in this case, in addition to committing the most serious of crimes, has broken faith with his oath, his role as an officer of the court, and as a member of our Law Society. As Deborah Rhode wrote in her article "Moral Character as a Professional Credential" in the Yale Law Journal Vol. 94 No. 3, January 1985 at p. 587:

"Clearly the rationale for monitoring practitioners' personal behavior is somewhat stronger than the justification for screening candidates'conduct. Attorney actions, unlike much applicant misconduct, cannot be discounted as remote in time or the product of youthful indiscretion. Moreover, violations of the law assume a different symbolic dimension when committed by those sworn to uphold it."

The life sentence imposed upon the Applicant reflected society's denunciation of the crime he committed. Moreover, at the time, he was an officer of the court sworn to uphold the law and this exacerbating factor calls for increased denunciation by the Law Society which governs the legal profession in the public interest. In our opinion, this denunciation by the public and the Law Society would be compromised or undermined if the Law Society were to reinstate him. One of the main reasons he seeks reinstatement is to improve his acceptability; in other words, his respectability in the community. Implicit in that is that membership in the Law Society and the Bar of Alberta carries with it a badge of respect, but that brings us full circle. In our view, the Applicant's admission to the Bar of Alberta would tarnish that badge, not because he is a bad person, but because of the enormity of the crime he committed while a member of the bar. In reaching this view, we are not rejecting the principle of rehabilitation or the qualities of forgiveness and mercy. Indeed, we recognize them as valid considerations. In the circumstances of this case, however, it is our view that these considerations cannot prevail where reinstatement may compromise the public's respect for the law and the legal profession.

Even if we are wrong, however, and rehabilitation is the controlling factor, we would not have recommended that the Applicant be admitted to the bar. We concede that the evidence of rehabilitation is substantial, and we concede that the Applicant has developed new ways to deal with his anger and his addiction. Nevertheless, he has only been out on full parole since January 1, 1998, and in our view, insufficient time has passed to provide us with sufficient comfort of complete rehabilitation."

By the way, Professor Sychuk is not the only professor at a Canadian law school to have been convicted of murder. For another interesting example, read the book "A Matrix Of Evidence" by Bruce Olson.

Character And Admission To Law School

Should individuals with character problems be admitted to law school in the first place? At what point should the inquiry into character begin. Read the following article which was written in response to an individual having been denied admission to the bar because of character.

October 17, 1989

The Queen's Journal

Law school not gatekeeper of profession: dean

Miriam Ehrensaft

A criminal record alone would not constitute reason to refuse admission to Queen's Faculty of Law, says John Whyte, dean of Law at Queen's in reference to a recent decision to disallow a convicted child molester to finish his education.

Whyte said that in a similar situation, the Queen's law "would not have taken any action to remove such a person from law school."

Whtye does not see the law school as having a responsibility to screen the character and moral values of their students.

"We don't have that duty because we're not in the business of gatekeeping the profession. We're an academic institution," Whyte said.

"I don't see a way at the admissions stage, of finding out if people suffer from social deviance to such an extent that he shouldn't be getting a legal education," he said.

The admissions procedure to Queen's law does not involve a criminal record check.

The candidate at U. of T. was refused admission to the Ontario bar when he failed a test of "good character." This incident had led to questions about the efficacy of admissions procedures within the Canadian law school system. Asked how the incident would affect prospective Queen's applicants, Whyte said, "externally the Queen's faculty of law could be pressured by the Law Society to be more forthcoming about character problems." Or, said Whyte, there may be need to "respond to the concern for professional integrity."

"If the applicant chooses not to divulge these details, then we won't know," said Virginia Bartley, the associate dean of law, director of admissions and registrar.

Bartley said admission to Queen's law is based on transcript marks and LSAT scores; letters of reference are optional and no interviews are given.

"There is no way that our admission procedures address moral character at all, because we don't ask questions about moral behavior," she said.

Whyte said an interview system would mean biased and subjective admissions procedures. "After all," he said, "interviews are measures of socialization, and we could not be sure that would get a good picture of the person."

Bartley explained that Queens' policy has traditionally been that either all or no applicants should be interviewed, rather than the select few.

"An interview is a way for an applicant to put forward positive information about themselves, so you wouldn't want to offer an interview to a select few," Bartley said.

There is, however, a category of "special admissions" reserved for 20 percent of all applicants. This discretionary list allows the faculty to examine the social context and situation from which the candidate comes as well as his/her maturity and background.

In the case of a past conviction, the admissions officers would attempt to "inquire whether the person has paid the penalty and understood his crime," said Whtye. "It is also a way to allow less socially-privileged people to obtain an education in law."

"It is a way of extending law school to people who have been disadvantaged in their lives."

Furthermore, Bartley pointed out that a law school with a wide range of classmates is a "positive environment. Queen's wants to encourage the broadening of thoughts and a variety of perspectives," said Bartley.

A national organization representing law school admissions officers, called Class I, has been established to address the issue of fair and appropriate inquiry in admission procedures, said Bartley, Queen's representative in Class I. She said the committee is "divided on the issue of fair admissions inquiries."

Whyte said that what can and should be done to counter poor moral character, is to develop students' sense of ethics within the classroom. "Any role in society has its ethical imperatives . We should be talking in the classroom about the ethical qualities of lawyering.

Courtesy The Queen's Journal.

Requirement Of Canadian Citizenship Or Permanent Resident Status

"A citizenship requirement for lawyers under British Columbia law violates equality rights guaranteed by the Canadian Charter of Rights and Freedoms, the Supreme Court of Canada said in a 4-2 ruling presented yesterday.

The court said a law that bars an entire class of people from employment solely on grounds of lack of citizenship is clearly an infringement of their rights.

The ruling came on an appeal by the Law Society of British Columbia against an attack on the citizenship requirement launched in the early 1980s by Mark David Andrews, a British subject, and continued by Gorel Elizabeth Kinersly when Mr. Andrews became a Canadian citizen."

The Globe And Mail - February 3, 1989

Canadian citizenship is defined in the Citizenship Act of Canada and permanent resident status is defined in the Immigration Act of Canada. As a result, both terms are defined by federal legislation. If you were born in Canada and have not renounced your citizenship you are a Canadian citizen. If you were born outside of Canada and came to Canada as a "landed immigrant" you are a permanent resident. At the present time neither of these requirements should present a barrier to many applicants. It is interesting to note that until 1989 permanent residents of Canada who were not Canadian citizens were not eligible for admission to the bar. This requirement was very unfair to people who had lived in Canada most of their lives but had not become Canadian citizens. In many cases people were unable to become citizens without automatically losing the citizenship of the country in which they were born. Until recently U.S. citizens automatically lost their U.S. citizenship if they became naturalized citizens of another country. Fortunately this is no longer the case.

Requirement Of Completion Of The Bar Admission Course

Why spend three years in law school if all that is required is that one complete the Law Society's Bar Admission Course? The answer is that a legal education is required to be admitted to the Bar Admission Course in the first place. What is required to be admitted into the Bar Admission Course and what does the Bar Admission Course consist of?

Prerequisites For The Bar Admission Course

The academic qualification for admission to the Bar Admission Course is:

(a) graduation from a law course, approved by Convocation, in a university in Canada; or

(b) a certificate of qualification issued by the National Committee on Accreditation.

All of the Canadian common law schools meet the above requirements and are approved for the purposes of entering the Bar Admission Course in every province. Hence, an LL.B. degree from any of these schools will allow you to enter the Bar Admission Course.

It is possible (but not easy) for one to attend law school outside of Canada and still be able to enter the Bar Admission Course. A certificate of qualification from the National Committee on Accreditation is required.

Components Of The Bar Admission Course

Every Canadian province has a Bar Admission Course. The courses vary in length from province to province. The approximate length of time ranges from twelve to eighteen months. For each province the Bar Admission Course consists of:

1. Articling; and

2. Written exams that may (depending on the province) include a classroom component.

The exact format of the course is in a continual state of flux. Hence, I advise you to contact the law society in the province where you wish to become a member of the bar.

Conclusion

To be admitted to the bar you are required to be of good character, have Canadian citizenship or the appropriate status under the Immigration Act, and successfully complete the Bar Admission Course.

APPENDIX A

The Law Society And The Law

In September of 1998 the Law Society Of Upper Canada allowed twenty-seven students, who had failed "to successfully complete the Bar Admission Course", to be called to the bar of Ontario. This decision:

- was picked up by the media (it was reported in the Globe and Mail, The Toronto Star, The Financial Post and campus newspapers;

- angered members of the public (On December 5 and 12 of 1998 the following ad ran in the Globe and Mail:

"APPALLED ONTARIANS sought to join a class action against the Law Society of Upper Canada for accrediting 28 flunkees to the Ontario Bar. (416)

> *- angered members of the legal profession*

In the spring of 1999, this became an election issue. A number of candidates for bencher expressed their discomfort with this decision. Sentiments expressed by candidates were articulated in the following ways:

"Why should students bother to study if students who fail are admitted to the bar anyway?"

"there was no public debate or prior authorization for admitting students who failed"

"the assertion that the competence of candidates could be assessed as a result of a 1/2 hour interview is an insult to the intelligence of lawyers and the public"

"I don't see how anybody can be judged competent to practice law based on a simple interview"

"the benchmarks for qualifying to practise law in Ontario should be uniform and consist of the successful completion of the skills-based component of the Bar Admission Course and the passing of those subjects"

motivated the Law Society to defend its decision to its members by responding in the following ways:

"As virtually everyone knows by now, the Law Society has come in for some heavy criticism since it decided on September 25 1998, to grant pass standing to 27 students who had not successfully completed all of the examinations of the Bar Admission Course. I say this because Convocation understands, even if others do not, that the test for a licensing body such as ours is not whether an individual can pass a prescribed set of examinations. Rather, the test is whether a candidate is competent to practise law."

The Facts As Stated In The Report Of The Admissions Committee

Fourty-nine students failed the Bar Admission Courses which ended in December of 96 and December of 97. Of the "group of fourty-nine" six were "transfer students." In August of 1998 the Law Society created an ad hoc committee to interview some of the "group of fourty-three" who were not transfer students. Thirty-six of the "group of fourty-three" were granted an interview that lasted for approximately thirty minutes. During the interview, the interviewer had access to the applicant's complete file. This file included information about the applicant's prior academic history and articling experience.

"In conducting its assessment, the ad hoc committee asked itself the following questions and considered the following factors:

1. Had the student attempted each examination? If not, he or she should be required to do so.

2. Had the student completed his or her articles? If not, he or she should be required to do so.

3. If the student had failed, was the failure(s) marginal or not?

4. Were there circumstances that convinced the committee that there were reasons for the failure(s) other than lack of competence?

5. Was the committee convinced that the student's competence had been otherwise demonstrated?" The Law Society reported that:

"In the interview process, what the committee learned from the students was at once significant and startling. Many of them proved to be extraordinary individuals, full of courage and tenacity and intelligence. In some cases, the students proved to be spectacular illustrations of how the BAC in its ordinary execution does not account for individual emotional, psychological, socio-economic, or cultural circumstances."

On the basis of the interviews, twenty-seven of the thirty-six were called to the bar. Members of this "group of twenty-seven" were deemed competent to practice law. The remaining nine were not deemed competent to practice law. Therefore, they were not called to the bar. (No explanation was given for the decision to deny admission to nine of the thirty-six.) Members of this group may not have been "extraordinary individuals, full of courage and tenacity and intelligence." Perhaps they were ordinary, run-of-the-mill cowards, who were discouraged by any obstacle and lacked intelligence.

The Law Society justified its decision on the basis that:

"The single criterion in every case was this: Is the student competent to practice law in the province of Ontario?"

Finally, it may be significant to note that the Law Society's decision took place after the discovery that many of the exams for 1996 and 1997 were leaked. Obviously, this provided an advantage to those students who had access to the leaked exams. There was a corresponding disadvantage to those who did not. In the words of the Law Society:

"For the two Bar Admission Courses in question, we relied for objectivity on the fact that we had a secure examination bank. We now know that this bank was not in fact secure. How much that impacted on the results is impossible to ascertain."

Analyzing The Law Society's Decision

Who are the parties with an interest in this issue and what are the interests that they have? The affected parties are:

- members of the public,

- members of the legal profession,

- the students involved,

- the Law Society as the administrator of the Law Society Act.

All affected parties have an interest in:

1. the jurisdictional aspect of the decision (is the Law Society legally allowed to admit students who fail the bar exams to the bar?);

2. the procedural aspect of the decision (if, in theory, the Law Society is allowed to admit them to the bar, what are the rules for deciding whether they should be admitted); and

3. the substantive aspect of the decision (if the Law Society is allowed to make the decision and if it follows a sound procedure, is the actual decision to admit the students to the bar a fair one?)

When called upon to justify its decision the Law Society does not comment on the jurisdictional and procedural aspects of the decision. It comments only on the substantive aspect - that is, the decision is correct because the students were deemed competent to practice law. The competency of the students to practice law is only one of the issues at stake. Jurisdictional and procedural issues are of equal importance.

Jurisdictional Issues

The Law Society is an administrative tribunal whose powers are defined by the Law Society Act. The Law Society Act requires successful completion of the bar admission course as a condition of bar admission. The Law Society is the entity that administers the Law Society Act. It has the power (and is in fact required) to admit those to the bar who successfully complete the Bar Admission Course and are of "good character." The law requires successful completion of the Bar Admission Course. The Law Society cannot change that law. (The Law Society does have the authority to decide what constitutes successful completion of the Bar Admission Course, but a successful completion is required. The interviews took place because the students did not successfully complete the course.) Once objective standards for successful of the course have been defined, the Law Society has no power to arbitrarily "grant pass status" to those who have not met that standard.

Conclusion: the Law Society doesn't have the power to admit "the group of twenty-seven" to bar even if it wants to.

The Law Society Act prohibits the practice of law without being a member of the Law Society. The Act further prohibits one from becoming a lawyer if one does not successfully complete the bar admission course.

Hence, assuming the Law Society does not have the jurisdiction to admit them to the bar, members of the "group of twenty-seven" are not lawyers within the meaning of the Law Society Act. In theory, they can be prosecuted for the unauthorized practice of law under the Law Society Act.

The Law Society's written report notes that one member of the admissions committee refused to participate in the decision because he or she objected to the process. In commenting on process, the Law Society stated:

" _ the process was credible, convincing and appropriate given the circumstances of the group of students under consideration. In short, as a one-time measure, it was the appropriate way to respond to the Law Society's mandate to ensure that the public is served by competent lawyers while at the same time preventing the erection of barriers that unfairly keep people who are competent from entering the profession after they have come so far.

There was a minority view on the Committee that while some process should be put in place for the group of the students under consideration, they could not approve the process that was used. In the minority's opinion, another process should be put in place with pre-approved and pre-articulated criteria. The majority agreed that it would have been preferable to have had the opportunity to pre-approve a process with criteria clearly set out in advance."

The above excerpt underscores that the interviews were conducted without any pre-approved or pre-articulated criteria. The thirty-six students were each given a thirty minute interview and at the end of the interview, the interviewer(s), without using pre-approved criteria, decided whether the applicant should be admitted to the bar.

Hence, it is unlikely that the process was procedurally fair. (Ask the nine interviewees who were still not admitted to the bar!)

It is also worth noting that only those who had failed in 1996 and 1997 were invited to the interviews. Why not those who graduated in 1995, 1994, 1993, etc? A fair process would have allowed all of those affected to have been interviewed.

Were only the 1996 and 1997 failures interviewed because these were the two years where it found that the exam base was not secure?

Conclusion: the process of reconsidering the thirty-six students lacked procedural integrity.

Substantive Issues

If we were to assume appropriate jurisdiction and process, can the decisions be justified? It is important to note that there were two decisions made in relation to thirty-six people interviewed.

1. Can the decision to deny admission to nine people on the basis of a thirty minute interview be justified?

2. Can the decision to admit twenty-seven people on the basis of a thirty minute interview be justified?

If the decision is to be made at all, then at least one appropriate criterion is whether the students are competent to practice law. Who can say whether the interviewers made the right or wrong decision? The Law Society is probably right when it states that:

"At the root of such criticism is the unexplained assumption that success or failure on written examinations is the only means available to an organization to judge the professional competency of its members. Let this be clear: any argument that the students in question are "failures" is false. So also is the notion that professional competence can only be determined by reference to written examinations. The single criterion in every case was this: Is the student competent to practice law in the province of Ontario?"

The Relationship Between Written Exams And Interviews - The Cart Before The Horse?

The Law Society is correct when it says that written exams are not the only way to judge professional competence. In fact, they may not even be a sufficient determiner of professional competence. New York, as a condition of bar admission, requires that all applicants who pass the bar exam submit to an interview (approximately thirty minutes). In other words, passing the bar exam is required to achieve the interview. An interview may be useful once there is an indication of basic competence. It is unreasonable that a 30 minute interview be used to determine basic competence!

In all probability, competence cannot be evaluated from a thirty minute interview. Hence, either all thirty-six should have been admitted to the bar or none of the thirty-six should have been admitted to the bar.

Conclusion: Without independent evidence of competence to practise law, a 30 minute interview is not sufficient to determine competence. Hence, each of the 36 should either have been admitted to the bar or refused admission to the bar.

Possible Noble Purpose But Definite Dangerous Effect

The Law Society refers to the decision as a "one-time" measure. If the Law Society really had confidence that it was doing the right thing, why make it a "one-time" measure? The Law Society is a "self governing" body. As such, it has a heightened obligation to consider the legality of its actions. In this case, the obligation was not met.

Summary

In my opinion, the Law Society has no jurisdiction to admit to the bar, those who do not successfully complete the Bar Admission Course. In addition, the decision was procedurally and substantively flawed. In short, it was an abuse of the Law Society's power and may well be subject to review by the courts.

Contact information for all Canadian law societies may be found at: www.flsc.ca

APPENDIX B

More On The Citizenship Issue. In the 1989 case of Andrews v. The Law Society of British Columbia the Supreme Court of Canada held that it was unconstitutional for a province to require Canadian citizenship to practice law. After the decision in Andrews, Ontario amended the requirement of Canadian citizenship to the present requirement of Canadian citizenship or permanent residence status. In the opinion of the author it is possible that the present requirement is still unconstitutional. If you are one of the very few applicants who is neither a Canadian citizen nor permanent resident and are unable to become one, it is suggested that you seek legal advice at the earliest possible moment! The Andrews case is discussed in the following article. As you read this article, consider what effect this decision may have on the rights of other minority groups in Canada.

Friday, February 17, 1989

The Lawyers Weekly

B.C. lawyers' citizenship requirement falls in 'historic' S.C.C. equality rights decision

Cristin Schmitz

OTTAWA-Lawyers representing disadvantaged groups were ecstatic following the release of the Supreme Court of Canada's first decision on the equality rights provisions of the Charter.

The 4-2 split decision handed down in February strikes down s. 42 of B.C.'s Barristers and Solicitors Act which said Canadian citizenship was a requirement for entry into the British Columbia Bar.

Similar provisions in many other provinces, including Ontario, are accordingly now also invalid: Law Society of B.C. v. Andrews.

But the real significance of Andrews extends far beyond the relatively narrow confines of its facts.

As the first time the top court has pronounced on the equality guarantees of the Charter since they same into effect April 17, 1985, Andrews sketches out the general analytical framework that the court will use in many upcoming equality rights test cases.

Subsection 15(1) says every individual is equal before and under the law, and has the right to the equal protection and equal benefit of the law, without discrimination, based on race, national or ethnic origin, colour, religion, sex, age or mental or physical disability.

Section 1 of the Charter guarantees these rights "subject only to such reasonable limits prescribed by law as can be demonstrably justified in a free and democratic society."

Lawyers and academics lavishly praised the court for its clear rejection of the "similarly situated" test, and for its clear affirmation that the purpose of s. 15 is primarily to promote equality for disadvantaged groups and individuals, rather than to protect the privileged who may occasionally be disadvantaged by the law.

Catharine A. MacKinnon, a visiting constitutional law professor at Yale University, called the Andrews decision "superb".

"It's not only positive," she told The Lawyers Weekly. "It's world-historic. There has never been one single equality ruling under any Constitution, in any country, that has repudiated the similarly situated test."

(The so-called "similarly situated" test is based on the principle that things that are alike should not be treated differently. This test has not been beneficial to disadvantaged groups, but it has been extremely popular with courts.)

Professor MacKinnon, who co-authored the factum of the intervener Women's Legal Education and Action Fund

(LEAF) with its counsel, Mary Eberts of Tory, Tory, DesLauriers & Binnington, explained that the court has adopted "the concrete conditions of disadvantaged people as the touchstone for understanding what equality means" under s. 15.

Helena Orron, LEAF's litigation director, agreed that the court's rejection of the similarly situated test will be crucial in helping women and other disadvantaged groups to progress towards equality.

"There are issues around pregnancy discrimination, reproductive choice, sexual assault where the similarly situated approach would not have allowed women to participate fully, and on the same basis, as men do in our society," she said.

Ms. Orron noted that the court accepted LEAF's argument that the purpose of s. 15 "is to alleviate the disadvantage of groups who have historically, or are presently, disadvantaged in our society in terms of social, legal, political and economic rights, and so a purposive approach to s. 15 would say that those are the people who should get the benefit of s. 15."

Thus with respect to sex discrimination, it is implicit in the judgment that s. 15 of the Charter is basically concerned, not with the "equality of men to women, but [with] the equality of women to men," Professor MacKinnon said.

Ms. Eberts described the court's decision as "outstanding." She pointed out that the court has tied s. 15 to the disadvantaged by focussing on the grounds of discrimination enumerated by s. 15, and on analogous grounds, and by accepting that principles developed under various human rights codes are applicable under the Charter.

"By tying [s. 15] into human rights legislation, I think it's implicit that they are really intending to benefit individual people [rather than corporations]," she noted.

"The court has very clearly served notice that s. 15 is for the use of the disadvantaged."

"...It is not for the makers of steel pop cans who complain that they're treated differently under the legislation from makers of aluminum pop cans, just to cite an infamous Ontario case."

Moreover, the court's view that the meaning of "discrimination" under the Charter corresponds to the concept of "discrimination" developed under Human Rights Codes further suggests that the grounds of discrimination prohibited under such codes-including marital status, and sexual orientation-may be accepted as grounds analogous to those enumerated in s. 15(1).

J. David Baker, counsel to the intervener Coalition of Provincial Organizations of the Handicapped, lauded Andrews as "an extremely positive indication that the courts are going to become the champions of disadvantaged groups in a way that they have not been up to this point in time."

The ruling is a quantum leap from the stance taken by the U.S. Supreme Court under its "equal protection" clause, he noted, and should be helpful to the disabled who are presently challenging various laws dealing with communication, education and transportation under s.15.

"We feel very, very encouraged," he said. "Overall, the decision is a very strong statement that systemic barriers are going to be removed."

Of particular importance is the court's position that the burden does not rest on an equality seeker to prove, under s. 15(1), that a distinction which harms him or her is unreasonable or unjustifiable. Instead, the onus remains on the state to prove that discrimination in violation of s. 15 is reasonable.

"Under the human rights principles adopted by the court as Charter principles, [the disabled] just have to prove that the inaccessible transit system which excludes them has the effect of denying them public transportation in order to get over the s. 15(1) hurdle," Mr. Baker explained. "And then the state has to justify it under s.1."

George Monticont, of the Advocacy Centre for the Elderly in Toronto, agreed that this aspect of the decision is especially welcome to equality seekers. "I think they have put the onus back where it belongs-on the government to try and justify the legislation in s. 1."

But despite their enthusiasm for the decision, some commentators were disturbed by the fact that at least two of the six judges were prepared to find that a "socially desirable" objective-rather than a "pressing and substantial" objective as cited in R. v. Oakes-may be enough to justify overriding a s. 15 right under s. 1.

"I think it's of concern that Justices McIntyre and Lamer chose a s. 15 case to initiate the discussion about diluting the Oakes standard," Mr. Baker observed.

"What is it about s. 15 that leads them to be more concerned than would apply to s. 7, or some of the other clauses? Is there a lesser commitment to s. 15?"

Ms. Eberts also noted that adopting a different standard under s. 1 for equality rights cases, at this early stage, could impoverish Charter jurisprudence generally, and could lead to s. 15 becoming a "second-class right with its own idiosyncratic level of tests."

Moreover, adopting a less stringent test for s. 15 would "would run the risk that you sanction government attempts to do social and economic engineering on the backs of the disadvantaged," she said.

An important issue which also needs to be developed in future cases is what "discrimination" means beyond a simple distinction. Professor Bill W. Black of the University of B.C. Law School, who is also research director at the University of Ottawa's Human Rights Centre, pointed out that "depending upon what you put into the word discriminatory, that will obviously have an effect on what goes into s. 15 and what we save for the s. 1 analysis."

However, "in terms of 'do we have all the answers to equality?' and 'do we just sit back and apply a rule?'...we can say that we are a long, long way from that.

"And since I would say much the same about U.S. jurisprudence 120 years after their section came into effect, I don't think that's a big surprise."

The decision also leaves plenty of scope for imagination in designing equality claims, although Professor Black applauded the fact "that it may crimp the creativity of those who are trying to turn s. 15 into a constitutional protection of occasional disadvantage for generally advantaged entities, which I just don't think was its intent."

Ms. Eberts noted that if s. 15 was relied on extensively by powerful interests, it could become a much less effective weapon in the hands of disadvantaged equality seekers.

"The fear of people in the equality seeking community was that if the courts continued to get a flood of these 'economic rights' cases, basically they would develop an approach to s. 15 that was designed to throw these cases out, because they would get impatient with them, and then when somebody who really needed the section came along and asked for help under s. 15, the test would be so rigorous that the truly disadvantaged couldn't use it."

Cristin Schmitz - The Lawyers Weekly

Chapter 25

Understanding Articling And The Rest Of The Bar Admission Course

"In his masterful 1991 diagnostic study on how we teach lawyers to be professionals, Professor Brent Cotter reactivated the haunting and persistent refrain sung by decades of young lawyers - why do we have articling and the bar admission course. Whose interests does this pedagogical gauntlet really serve? It has for too long survived the establishment of the university law schools whose absence was the original rationale for its existence. Is there really an evidentiary foundation for concluding that this is the most reasonable way for the Law Society to ensure that people entering the profession have the requisite educational arsenal of knowledge and skill? Has anyone taken a survey to gauge the utility of, or consumer satisfaction with the humiliating beauty pageant this is the gatekeeper to articling, or with the bar ad's income-delaying months which either repeat the job the law schools were doing, or teach the courses few graduates will ever need. How positively can a newly emerging lawyer be expected to feel about a Law Society which imposes either the frenzy of the match programme or the irrelevance of an accounting exam. Are the gains really worthy of the financial burdens these educational achievements impose on students?"

-Justice Rosalie Silberman Abella

Why A Bar Admission Course?

Law school graduates receive an LL.B. in Canada and a J.D. in the U.S. Neither degree, without bar admission, gives one the right to practise law. In Canada, successful completion of the Bar Admission Course is required. In the U.S. law school graduates must pass the bar exam.

General Components Of The Bar Admission Course In Canada

In general, the Bar Admission Course in Canada is composed of two components. The first is articling and the second is the classroom component. The classroom component consists of lectures, readings and exams. The course is somewhat different in each province. What follows is a general discussion of each. I will use Ontario as the model. But please remember that the form of the Classroom component will differ by province.

Articling

"... I know that historically the articling system that has existed in Canada has been one of the mainstays of legal education and the legal profession. This is still true today. The profession as a whole has always demonstrated, and still demonstrates, a collective responsibility and generosity towards those students who want to embark upon a legal career. Accordingly, in times of financial restraint, I think that it is laudable that most law firms in the country still regard it as a fundamental trust to accept and, in a very real sense, educate young members of the profession. But I know that there are problems with the present articling system, problems of inconsistency and uncertainties. My sincere wish is that the legal profession will address those problems with a view to making the articling experience rewarding to all young members of the profession."

-Chief Justice Brian Dickson

"Since signing on with the firm last June, Wentworth had been toiling something like one hundred hours a week. He was not getting overtime, unless one counted his share of the tab the firm picked up for the drunken debauches that Friday lunches at Au Saterne often evolved into. Au Sauterne being a restaurant across the square where individual entrees cost as much as the monthly payments on his new Outback 310 twenty-one-speed bike."

-Articling student Wentworth Chance described in William Deverell's 'Kill All The Lawyers."(pages 7-8 Ballantine Books 1995)"

Purpose And Role

In Canada, graduating law students must commence a period of articling, which is the practical component of the Bar Admission Course. (It should be noted that in the U.S., there is no such thing as an articling period.) This "internship" is a "hands on" experience lasting nine to twelve months (depending on the province) that allows the student to bridge the gap between the theory learned in law school and the practical aspects of the day-to-day practice of law. This is accomplished by the student working under the direct supervision of an Articling Principal, who is a lawyer or a judge. Traditionally, articling placements are within private law firms. However, it is often permissible to article within the public sector, corporate legal departments and non-traditional placements. The ethical application and practice of law are primary objectives of the articling experience.

What Does An Articling Student Do?

It is impossible for all law students to share the same experience during their articles. An ideal articling situation would expose the student to many common areas of private practice. These include: Business Law, Civil Litigation, Creditor's and Debtor's Rights, Criminal Procedure, Estate Planning and Administration, Family Law, Real Estate and Landlord and Tenant, and Commercial Law.

The articling experience is expected to be an educational opportunity for the student. It is the responsibility of the principal, a practitioner, to assume the role of teacher and provide the necessary instruction to the student.

The principal benefits when the student takes the maximum responsibility commensurate with the student's training, experience and abilities. Because articling students are not full-fledged lawyers there are both legal and practical limits to the kind of responsibilities they are able to assume.

The Mechanics of Finding An Articling Job

The student is responsible for finding an articling placement. It is not automatic. Where one articles, and the experience one receives can have a profound effect on one's career. The issues pertaining to the mechanics of securing an articling job may be divided into the categories of:

A. When

B. Where - Type of Law and Firm

C. How

Each of these will be discussed in turn.

A. When

In general students look for an articling job after their second year of law school. Those who are fortunate (or more likely approach the process in an intelligent way) obtain a position during the summer after second year. Others continue seeking a position during third year of law school and some others (see the comment below) continue during the summer after their law school graduation.

In some provinces there are no formal rules governing the search for articling positions. Students are free to arrange for interviews at any time. In other provinces (Ontario included) there are formal rules governing the timing and procedure for obtaining an articling job.

The Computer Match

In Toronto and Vancouver the determination of which student articles at which firm is generally determined through a computerized matching program. The matching process begins only after the students and firms have evaluated each other completely independently of the computer. Students apply directly to the firm and the firm decides whether or not to interview the student. Interviews take place without offers being made during the interview period. After interviews have been completed each firm ranks the students in order of priority. Similarly, each student ranks each firm in order of priority. The computer performs its magic and firms are matched to students. Students and firms are given only the final result and are not told specifically how firms and student were ranked by each other.

What follows is the perspective of a third year law student on the "match."

"In the context of articling, many of you have probably heard of something called the "match". This is a term referring to a process by which prospective law students are matched with a firm with which to article. It is a process approved and regulated by the Law Society of Upper Canada. A few words about the process:

When students enter the match, they are asked to list the firms of their choice, from favourite to least favourite. This increases the efficiency of the interview process since more of any participating firm's interviewee population will be comprised of people that actually want that firm. This is also more efficient for students because it is a process that gets them inside the doors of the firms that they want, and less interview time is spent trying to secure whatever one can get.

The firms that participate in the match are the relatively large Toronto firms. Their interest in the match seems to be, other than being able to isolate those that are interested in their particular firm per se, that it is a way to more quickly evaluate all of the thousands of potential candidates that constantly knock on their doors. It may be a harsh fact of life, but if there's a really big, impressive downtown firm that you would give your life to work for, then guess what - there are droves of other people that share your sentiments. The match helps to organize this competition in a way which better fulfills everyone's interests.

Initially, the match may end up placing about half of its participants. This may sound bleak, but this has the effect of reducing competition for those that don't yet have articling positions, resulting in almost 100% placement for any given 3rd year class by the end of the school year. I hope that I have revealed the truth concerning yet another law-related myth - no, it is not impossible to find an articling position. In fact, it is hard to keep away from one."

Articling positions outside the major cities are found without any computer intervention.

B. Where - Type Of Law And Firm

The majority of students article in the private sector. There are also a large number of articling positions available in government and corporate legal departments or non-traditional legal environments. In addition, some of the most exciting, rewarding and prestigious positions are clerks to judges in the courts. These positions are research oriented. Information about the availability of these positions may be obtained by contacting the court in question.

If you wish to article with a private law firm, you will have to decide whether to article with a large or small firm. There are both advantages and disadvantages to consider.

The Large Firm Articling Experience

Large firms provide a more structured experience. Large firms often have "rotations" which will rotate you through specific departments of the firm. For example, you might spend three months in litigation, three months in real estate, three months in corporate and three months in something else. In addition, large firms generally have more support staff which should minimize the "burdens of articling."

The Small Firm Articling Experience

In a small firm it is likely that you will have more responsibility. The reality is that small firms have fewer lawyers to do legal work. There is probably more opportunity for specialization than there would be in a big firm.

Where - Geographical Articling Location Preferences

When recently asked about their first choice of location for articles Ontario students answered as follows:

Location	First Choice Of
Toronto	67%
Central Ontario	8%
Eastern Ontario	21%
Southwestern Ontario	2%
North/Northwest Ont.	2%

Articling statistics - Geography and Type

Statistics from Ontario reveal that for the 2002-2003 there were 1063 positions.

They were broken down geographically as follows:

Number	Location
741 or 69.7%	Toronto
143 or 13.4%	Ottawa
35 or 3.3%	Greater Toronto
33 or 3.1%	London
22 or 2.1%	Hamilton
19 or 1.8%	Windsor
70 or 6.6%	Everywhere else

Statistics from Ontario reveal that for the 2001 year of 1124:

525 articled with firms of more than 25 lawyers

115 articled with government

27 articled with firms of 5-25 lawyers

127 articled with firms of 1-4 lawyers

C. How

Suffice it to say that researching opportunities for articling, preparing resumes, covering letters, and attending interviews is a time consuming and stressful process. A whole book can be written on that alone. In fact a superb book has been published by Edmond Montgomery on this subject. It is appropriately titled:

The Law Student's Guide To Articling And Summer Positions In Canada. ISBN: 0-920722-90-3

This book is a manual for how to secure an articling position in any province. In addition to strategy it provides information about which provinces will allow part time-articling. The book also includes a discussion of "International Articles." Yes, that is a way to have experiences outside of Canada count as part of the articling experience.

Towards the end of your second year of law school you should begin researching these issues. Your job is to market yourself to potential employers in the same way that your job at the present time is to market yourself to law schools.

The Uneven Articling Experience

Because students can article in a variety of contexts and it is virtually impossible for two students to obtain the same experience. Some firms have formal articling programs which involve systematic rotations through different departments within a law firm. Smaller firms often have no systematic rotations. There are advantages to both experiences. What follows are excerpts from the description of the articling program at a large Toronto law firm:

"... offers a focussed articling program, designed to provide the student with exposure to different types of practice in many different types of practice in many different areas of the law. It is intended to be a hands-on experience, to provide the student with some insight into what practicing law in those areas would be like and thereby to assist the student in making his or her career choices.

"... consists of rotations in the following areas of the firm's practice:

Corporate - Commercial and Tax

Litigation

Administrative

Commercial Transactions and Estates

The twelve month articling term is divided into five rotations of approximately ten weeks each. Four rotations will be spent in the areas above. The fifth rotation is an opportunity to spend additional time in one of these areas.

The firm relies on its articling program to identify future associates and partners."

Articling Moves Into The Future - "Part-Time" Articles

Traditionally articling has been in the form of a nine to twelve month (depending on the province) commitment. Part-time articles are now a possibility. In general, the process is that the student will article two, three or four days per week and complete the articling program in no less than three years. (For further information, contact the Law Society in the relevant province.)

Is It Hard To Obtain An Articling Job? - Facts vs. Fiction!

In all but the most unusual cases (for example significant lawyering experience in another common law jurisdiction) everyone must article. Therefore, everyone must obtain an articling position. At the end of the day, almost everybody does. The interview process can be stressful. Rejections are inevitable and painful. The following contribution from a second year law student underscores the stress and frustration (but reveals a healthy dose of humor) involved in searching for an articling position:

"For those of you in the legal field, I'm sure you are well aware that time of year is upon us. Yes, it's time to start thinking about which firms we would like to article with to become fully qualified lawyers. I think this year, I will send out something like this as a follow-up to my cover letter i.e. once I've received their rejection.

Dear _____

Thank-you for your letter of July 5th. After careful consideration, I regret to inform you that I am unable to accept your refusal to offer me employment with your firm. This year I have been particularly fortunate in receiving an unusually large number of rejection letters. With such a varied and promising field of candidates, it is impossible for me to accept all refusals.

Despite your corporation's outstanding qualifications and previous experience in rejecting applicants, I find that your rejection does not meet with my needs at this time. Therefore, I will initiate employment with your firm immediately following graduation. I look forward to seeing you then.

Best of luck rejecting future candidates.

Sincerely,"

Perspectives On The Value Of The Articling Experience

The articling experience is uneven. The sentiment towards it is both positive and negative. Articling could probably be described as one of the "Good", the "Bad" or the "Ugly" depending on the circumstances. What follows are a number of perspectives on the articling experience. The perspectives are those of both lawyers and articling students.

A Lawyer's Perspective On Articling

Lawyers need to revisit the articling process

donalee Moulton

The traditional role of articling clerks as learners who used to collect at the knees of lawyers, carry their books, and sit in on meetings with clients seems to have disappeared and with it so has much of the benefit the individual and the profession derived from the articling process, said the President of the Nova Scotia Barristers' Society (NSBS).

"The idea of serving an apprenticeship, once the foundation of he articling system, has been replaced by law office economics," Thomas Burchell, NSBS President, told The Lawyers' Weekly in an interview.

"We appear to have lost sight of the fact that we have a duty to ensure that our articling clerks are properly trained. We cannot assume that their law degrees and attendance at the Bar Admission Course absolves us from our obligation to provide hands-on training," he noted in an article written on this issue for the NSBS' newsletter, The Society Record.

Two critical factors have been at work to affect the articling process. And both are market driven.

The first is the competition among firms to hire the top students in a law class. The emphasis is often placed on whom it is that a firm hires and less on what the firm has to offer an articling clerk, Mr. Burchell said, who is a partner with the Halifax firm Burchell Hayman Barnes.

In that same vein, he added, articling clerks are generally more concerned with salary levels, employment benefits and hire backs and less on what they can learn from the lawyers in a particular firm.

This has had a significant effect on the role of both the principal and the clerk. The expense involved in employing an articling clerk has forced many firms to get their money's worth, as it were, out of the employee. Therefore, they relegate their articling clerks to researching material in the library or preparing memos behind the scenes.

"But research does not teach articled clerks about quoting fees, meeting with clients, negotiating settlements, framing pleadings, conducting discoveries, incorporating companies, drafting wills, collecting on overdue accounts (or) entering pleas," Mr. Burchell stated in his article.

Law firms, on the other hand, he added, "are concerned with snapping up hardworking, eager, bright students but not particularly focused on the duty they owe the clerks who article with them to train them to become lawyers."

One approach that could effect a balance between the needs of both students and the profession is to create a co-operative education program, similar to that run in business schools, or a clinical-based program similar to that used to help train medial students. In such programs, of course, government is a major financial contributor.

There are a number of benefits to a hands-on training program that runs while the student is still in school, said Mr. Burchell.

Students would, for example, be better immersed in the law and the practice of law, while law firms would not have to bear the full cost of training.

Regardless of what approach is ultimately adopted, said Mr. Burchell, change is necessary.

"The way we article has to change with the times and be responsible to the legal community out there," he stressed. "We have competing issues that need to be resolved."

Reprinted with permission of the author.

Some Perspectives Of Articling Students

The articling experience means so many different things to people.

Articling - The Good And The Bad - Five Perspectives

Perspective 1: A Downtown Toronto - Small Litigation Firm

"Articling

Thank God for articling. I can only imagine how much havoc must be wreaked in the U.S., where there is no articling when fresh law students are unleashed on the trusting and unsuspecting world.

I graduated from law school feeling like I knew a lot of law. I was nowhere near ready to represent clients, however, as I had only the vaguest notion of how, in practical terms, to implement that knowledge. Even at the University of Manitoba, which is reputed for having one of the most intensive civil advocacy and pre-trial process programs, no one taught us about the vast array of seemingly minor but crucial tasks which must be done along the way.

Phase I ended, and the general consensus among students from everywhere was that we were not even a little bit more competent than we had been a month before.

Articling started off slowly. After all, I am in a litigation firm, and the courts don't move into full swing until September. I was initially handed small tasks which were easily salvageable in the event that I erred. Then, after lawyers in the firm had ascertained that I was relatively conscientious and not a complete moron, they began to give me more meaningful and risk-bearing work. This was not an anomalous situation. Every other student to whom I have spoken initially felt insecure and incompetent. It is truly amazing how quickly that begins to change. The once seemingly large task of bringing a motion before the court has become straight-forward. There are now several files and minor areas of law in which I have done research and in which I am relied upon by the firm. It's quite an ego kick.

If I may forward a small tip to those of you who are presently in or about to enter law school: become a master at Quicklaw and any other form of computerized research which you can learn. Most of the lawyers presently practicing are helpless with computers. It has provided me with a few opportunities to make a great impression for doing virtually nothing. "Can you get this case for me? All I know is the name and that it has to do with amending pleadings." Then, you show up fifteen minutes later with the case and; "Wow, this guy's a real computer whiz!" Little does he know that I had little more to do than turn the computer on and type in pretty much exactly what he said. Still, what he doesn't know won't hurt him.

As the articling term proceeds, the level of responsibility increases, if you're lucky. This is a good thing for one's education and experience, but as for the condition of one's stomach lining, it sucks. I think I need a new watch on which every point on the dial is labeled as the "last minute". As the student, I am the lowest form of life on the "lawyer" totem. As the expression goes — or doesn't exactly go, but close enough — "crap flows downhill." Every emergency, ripe limitation date, and suicide mission falls into my lap. Technically, it's no excuse that it isn't your fault that your principal was the one who handed you the file the night before and sent you to trial without witnesses. Fortunately, most of the judges and opposing counsel are pretty good about not shooting the messenger. The Masters, however, are frequently less forgiving. Driven by fear of humiliation and a personal decision that I will not be trounced upon where avoidable, I have developed a much thicker skin and an ability to "peruse" very efficiently. I wonder whether there's a "make'em sweat" clause buried somewhere deep and the bowels of the standard form contract between the firm and the Law Society.

Notwithstanding these conditions, articling is extremely worthwhile, character-building and, yes, rewarding. We all just become well acquainted with the initials "CYA"... read, "cover you ass." You write letters and memos reflecting everything that you've said and done and everything that has been said and done to you. That way, if ever things go wrong as a result of circumstances in which others have placed you in, it will be clear that you are not responsible. All of this sounds very harsh and devious, but it truly is simply a practice which is done out in the open and without hard feelings as a matter of course.

Well, that's a taste of articling. Good luck!"

Perspective 2: A Downtown Toronto - Big Firm Perspective

"I clearly remember my first week at law school. My fellow students had already started talking about articling jobs in general and articling jobs in big firms in particular. Of course, some students had a "better" perspective than others. Why? Simply because they knew somebody who was a lawyer or an articling student. I did not want to be left behind on the articling bandwagon so I became a law student aspiring to definitely article but preferably in a big law firm. Three years later, I am happily articling in a "Big Law Firm."

Big firms have some unique advantages. And, I am told, some people might say some peculiar disadvantages. Being a curious articling student, I have asked many probing questions to ascertain what are those disadvantages. The answers I have received are many and remarkedly varied. However, based on my personal experience, the advantages definitely outweigh any disadvantages.

The principal advantage is that big firms really strive to make the transition from law school to the practice of law smooth. As a result, they arrange various seminars for their articling students. These seminars are focussed on a particular area of law and usually given by practising lawyers. To ensure that their articling students attend these seminars, big firms usually entice them by providing free lunch or breakfast. And, it is definitely time well spent, because these hours are docketed albeit to a non-billable firm account.

Big law firms are usually full service law firms. Therefore it is possible to work in an area of your interest. I have heard about articling students interested in business law primarily managing to do only commercial litigation and altogether skip intellectual property or estate or tax litigation. This essentially means that it is possible to become a well rounded professional who has had experience both in straight "chamber lawyer" type work and a "courtroom legal eagle" type work.

Big law firms make available extensive resources to their lawyers and students. The libraries are fairly big, computer systems and software are generally state of the art, telephone and fax systems are easily available. And let me not forget free coffee, tea, cookies, etc.

And after surviving a number of years on student loans and odd jobs, big law firms pay big bucks. It certainly helps to be paid handsomely because I can repay my student loans faster and ... later perhaps buy, do I hear ... a BMW?"

Perspective 3: Articling With The Government

"Appearing for the Crown: Some Thoughts on My Articles

Today is a happy day as today is my last day as an articling student. Soon to begin bar exams, I relish the thought of never again having to explain the meaning of "student-at-law". As I enter this new phase of my life, Phase III (of the Bar Admission Course) to be specific, the LSAT seems a million miles away, and vivid memories of law school are beginning to fade.

My articling experience was a good one. Big cases, small cases, motions, dispositions, discovery - I did it all. Small Claims Court, Provincial Court and in-house training have improved my litigation skills, while working as a junior on larger, more complex cases has given me the opportunity to think about some of the "big issues".

The experience is great, the money is not. Quality work is expected, long hours are not. More often than not, however, the former demands the latter. The atmosphere is warm, friendly, informal, and the people make the office a nice place to be. For every great legal mind, there is deadwood, and make no mistake about it, the Crown is replete with both species.

Broad exposure to vast legal subject matter has meant a lot of learning over the course of the past year, and for that I am most grateful. The old saying, "The more you learn, the more you realize how little you know" comes to mind as I reflect on my articling experience. Law school taught me how to learn, while articling has been more learning, as well as the practical application of all that learning to specific legal problems and issues. Oh yeah, I can also use "hitherto" in a sentence. Have I found my calling? For now."

Perspective 4: Smaller Specialty (IP) Law Firm Perspective

"Articling at an intellectual property law firm - all that glitters may not be gold

It may be, in the view of some law students, that the only thing more traumatic than attempting to secure an articling position, is articling itself. This I suppose, depends on where one chooses to article. My experience in obtaining an articling position, along with the articling experience itself, I dare say does not fit the mold of the majority. It does however, offer some hope to future students in the sense that anything is possible.

I offer some background to put my experience in context. Unlike the majority of my colleagues, I did not secure an articling position after the summer of my second year. Indeed, interviews were a rarity as compared with the wining and dining which many others experienced. The anxiety and fear, naturally, began to settle in by October of my third year. The thought that some nine years of post-secondary education was culminating in personal failure, was daunting. For others that may be in this position now, I offer one piece of comfort, and one piece of advice.

You may take comfort, however minimal, in the fact that you are not alone. Most students are unwilling to discuss the fact that they did not obtain an articling position. Instead, they silently blend in the background, in the hopes that no-one will expose their dark secret. However, the phenomenon of students returning to third year without an articling position is not as uncommon as one may think. Indeed, many students are in the same boat year after year. No student is alone in this.

The advice I offer is simply this - keep looking. There is a position for everyone. Look everywhere, and ask everyone. Your law school has resources for this matter - use them. Ask firms that have rejected you previously if a position has opened up. Most students think that this is an impossibility. Who would give up an articling position? Well, it happens for a variety of reasons. I know this because that is how I secured my articling position. Where am I articling you ask? Out of a van on some side street in an unpalatable part of town? No. I am articling at one of the top, if not the top intellectual property (IP) law firm in the country.

My good fortune stems from the fact that although my current articling principal did not offer me a position at the relevant time, he took a liking to me at our interview. When it came to his knowledge that I was without a position, he allowed me to tap all of his resources for articling prospects (i.e. he allowed me to use his name as a reference with his colleagues). After still many more applications and brutal rejections (I received over 100 rejections in this experience, not a word of a lie), I called him again to tell him of my situation. He informed me that an articling student the firm had previously hired decided to try her luck in the United States. That being so, a position was now available for me if I wanted it. I took it.

So, here I am, articling in Ottawa, thinking about my colleagues on Bay Street, in Toronto. How does my experience measure up to theirs? Well, it is like a bad broken record in some respects. I continually hear stories of my friends working weekends (yes full weekends, a good eight hours a day) and putting in late nights (which in some cases turn into late mornings). In contrast, I put in a steady ten hours a day on average, some times less, very rarely more. Although things have become a little hectic at points, I have not had the "privilege" of working weekends yet. I never bring a sleeping bag to work (yes I know of people that have done this). The educational experience however, is still intense and the learning curve is steep. My articling experience is turning out to be one of quality, not quantity. Working long hours is meaningless if the finished product is substandard. At this firm, the emphasis lies in quality of work, not quantity of hours worked.

But what is the actual meat and bones of my experience? I must confess that it is not as rounded as others working the larger firms. I don't attend court every day and I don't carry my own files yet. However, what I am getting in return is a very strong grounding in basics. Legal research is a large portion of the job here. Many lawyers will tell you that without strong legal research skills you cannot be a strong practitioner. I assure you this is true. The essence of a strong memo, statement of defense or factum is comprehensive legal research. As one senior partner of our firm has commented, the only way to build a pyramid is to start with a strong and wide base, proceeding brick by brick; only then will the structure be self-supporting.

The firm itself operates on a truly open-door policy. Even senior partners keep an open door. Most associates and partners insist that you call them by their first name, and treat you with dignity and respect (yes, this has been an issue for some friends of mine). Being a smaller firm, there is an emphasis on the learning experience of the articling student. Both associates and partners have called me into their office to offer constructive criticism about memos I've written, research I've been asked to conduct, or other matters. Although they have more pressing concerns, many partners and associates actively seek the time to provide useful and substantial comments to students in the hopes that students will learn as much as they can about the IP field.

As compared with my Toronto colleagues, I have not done as much drafting of legal documents. The opportunities for a student to practice these skills is less in IP than in more general areas of law. Matters of IP are heard at the

Federal Court and students are not permitted to appear as counsel. The consequences of this, I suppose, is that my colleagues are more portable in obtaining employment with other firms, and have a better chance of hanging up their own shingle (i.e. open their own practice). Their general knowledge of the law and legal procedure will be substantially broader than mine.

I, on the other hand, will be reliant on obtaining future employment with an IP firm, for quite some time. The skill set required of an IP lawyer is not completely imparted onto an articling student. The process of "apprenticeship" is substantially longer (at least two to three years as an associate). Even after working as an associate, an IP lawyer would still require more experienced resources in the field. As a newly trained IP lawyer, you will not be the master of your own domain for quite some time.

The flipside to this however, is that the IP community is closely knit. Although firms often become adversaries in matters of litigation, they form a unique community where members "look after their own" in a sense. They tend to respect each other and the reputation of one firm will generally carry well with another. In other words, employment prospects are usually quite good. In a society constantly bombarded by technological advances, employment prospects in IP tend to be stable. While larger Bay Street firms produce many qualified lawyers year after year, they call back only a small portion. IP firms prefer to train only a few students at a time, and offer more stability in the field. The competition pool among IP lawyers is much smaller than general practitioners.

In summary, my inability to initially get a Bay Street articling job, or indeed, an articling job at all, in retrospect, was not a failure. Looking around at my colleagues, I see that all that glitters is not gold. I may not be making a Bay Street salary and my skill base may not be as large at the end of the articling year, but I am at a firm where a personal touch exists. Associates and partners maintain a strong interest in my education and seek to provide me with as much constructive training as possible. The second pay-off is that while I am receiving an intense education, I am not forfeiting the rest of my life for it. The size and nature of the field afford me the opportunity to truly get to know my colleagues and build a strong working rapport with them. I have come to realize that in this sense, I am far better off here than I am on Bay Street. And so, as far as my legal career goes, this is my strongest success to date.

It is important that articling students receive an intense and well-grounded education. Bay Street firms definitely offer that. But in searching for an articling position, students should bear in mind that Bay Street firms are not the only place where one can obtain such an education. Larger firms have many features which are attractive to many individuals. In the end, it is a matter of personal taste. In determining one's personal taste, smaller firms shouldn't be ignored, and an open mind should be kept for the possibility of entering a somewhat more specialized field (e.g. IP, criminal, labour, etc.)."

Perspective 5 : Clerking For Judges

James Hopkins, LL.B., LL.M.

I clerked at the Ontario Court General Division. There are two differences that contrast this clerkship with appellate level clerking. First, you are not assigned to a specific judge. Instead, you are periodically assigned to a pool of judges defined either by an area of law (i.e. drug trafficking), or a region. Nonetheless, you are able to form good relationships with individual judges and you tend to get steady work from them regardless of your assignment. Second, you will gain superior insight into the trial process and I recommend this clerkship for those who have a serious interest in trial litigation. I was able to sit in on several high profile trials and see the entire trial process unfold. You will also see first hand some of the greatest litigators in the country on fascinating issues. As well, you will also see the daily issues that arise from motions and endless issues of law. The clerkship program at the trial level is very new. I believe it is now in its fifth year. The view that one gains from the clerkship is invaluable both from a practical level in becoming a good lawyer and from an academic and sociological commentary. As for salary, it is worth noting that outside of Toronto, it is generally the highest paying articling position and the hours are very reasonable in comparison to large firms.

Reprinted with permission of the author.

Articling - The Ugly

As part of the process of researching this book I talked to many articling students. Some of them reported enduring abuse in the extreme. None of them was willing to commit their experience to paper and have it included in this book. This is regrettable but not surprising. The articling student is completely powerless. He or she must complete the articling period with a satisfactory performance. For many, the articling year is a year long job interview. Quitting is possible only by going to a different firm. Outside the legal world there are employees who are subjected to many kinds of hostile environments. Sometimes, the hostility is based on race, sometimes religion, sometimes sex. As might be expected, the legal profession mirrors the employment market in general. Hence, I interviewed articling students who experienced abuse of all types. I am not suggesting that the abuse was rampant. However, given that the articling student can't leave, law firms should make a special effort to ensure the atmosphere is conducive to learning and growth.

Part II - The Non-Articling Component Of The Bar Admission Course

The General Classroom/Exam Component - Province By Province

The "Classroom/Exam Component" is the lecture and exam part of the Bar Admission course. It is a complement to Articling (or is it the other way around). As such it will vary from province to province. In conjunction with articling, students take courses in and sit exams in substantive law, ethics, practice management and in some cases accounting. The exact requirements vary in length and content depending on the province.

Bar Admission Across Canada - A 2004 Snapshot In Time

What follows is an interesting article comparing the Bar Admission Requirements for all provinces. The information in this article is true as of December 2003.

Toronto - With their new-found mobility, Canada's aspiring lawyers may be able to choose the fastest and cheapest Bar Admission Course (BAC). With that in mind, The Lawyers Weekly offers a list of comparative requirements for admission to the bars of common-law provinces, which shows the current cost ranges from $900 to $4,400 and the course length from seven weeks to 14 months, with Ontario's BAC the longest and costliest.

British Columbia - The one-year articling program includes a 10-week "Professional Legal Training Course," which emphasizes skills and problem-solving. Students are provided with materials and are examined on law and procedure in 10 areas, including law office management and professional responsibility. At the end of the course, they write two three-hour qualifying exams. The cost of the PLTC, including materials, is $2,500 plus G.S.T.

Alberta - The Bar Admission Course, run by the Legal Education Society of Alberta, is divided into two sessions: a three-week skills session and a five-week course in core practice areas. They take place during the articling year. Tuition for course andmaterials is $1,845 plus G.S.T.

Saskatchewan - The current Bar Admission Course consists of a four-week skills component and a four-week segment dealing with substantive and procedural law. The course is included in the 12-month articling period. Tuition is $1,335 including materials plus G.S.T.

Manitoba - Eight bar admission courses are currently interspersed throughout the 52-week articling period.

They consist of classroom lectures each followed by an exam. Fees are $1,100 plus G.S.T.

Prairies - Beginning next summer, Alberta, Saskatchewan and Manitoba will run a harmonized BAC, combining online instruction with some classroom sessions (held in each province using the same materials). The new course will focus on skills and professionalism. Throughout their articling year, over small blocks of time, students will read the materials, prepare assignments, write exams and prepare for face-to-face sessions. The new fee, including materials, will be $1,000 plus G.S.T.

Ontario - Ontario's Bar Admission Course lasts 14 months and costs $4,400 plus G.S.T. The present system consists of a 10-month articling component, a one-month course in professional responsibility and a three-month course dealing with substantive law and procedure. Ontario's new regime is to start in 2006.

New Brunswick - The Bar Admission Course consists of four two-week sessions in skills development (interviewing, drafting, negotiations and criminal), which occur during the 12-month articleship. Students, having been provided with a written Practice Manual, must write an exam on the first day of each BAC session to prepare them for that skills component. Tuition, including materials, is $900 plus G.S.T.

Nova Scotia - The BAC consists of a seven-week skills training course and one exam, which take place during the articling year. Tuition fee including materials is $3,250 plus H.S.T.

Prince Edward Island - Facing, perhaps, the most strenuous licensing requirement in the country, students must complete a 12-month articling term, a two-week bar admission course concentrating on aspects of substantive law and practice unique to P.E.I., as well as Nova Scotia's seven-week BAC. They must write seven exams in their own course and 12 in Nova Scotia, and pay a $500 tuition fee plus G.S.T. in addition to the N.S.tuition.

Newfoundland and Labrador - The law society's website describes the province's Bar Admission Course as "a 7-8 week intensive educational experience." It takes place in the middle of the articling year, and emphasizes lawyering and transaction skills. There are six 3.5-hour exams. Cost is $1,950 plus G.S.T.

In the U.S., graduates of law schools approved by the American Bar Association (which do not include Canadian law schools) need only pass a state bar exam to qualify to practise law.

John Jaffey - The Lawyers Weekly

As you can see, the requirements and style of course depend on the province.

What Goes On In The Classroom - A Student's Perspective

Please note that following perspective was written in the late 1990s when the classroom stage of the Ontario Bar Admission course ran from September until December. The format has changed (as stated above) slightly, but .....

"The classroom phase can be the most trying time for law students. This is because it comes at a time when students have most likely finished an extensive period of schooling, studying, and training. By this time, students are unsurprisingly tired and impatient with the process. It is the last four months of a four and one-half year marathon. For many, the prevailing sentiment is: I can't take it anymore!

The purpose of the classroom phase is to provide students with the basic elements necessary to successfully complete their Articles, and also to prepare students for the eventual practice of law. The classroom phase is completed by requiring students to pass comprehensive exams in different subject matters, in order to demonstrate their basic minimal competence.The exams are usually three and a half hours long and often become more stamina contests than tests of the students' knowledge. The areas of law tested include: Civil Procedure, Family Law, Criminal Procedure, Administrative Law, Business Law, Estates, Accounting and Professional Responsibility. (Most of these subjects are also taught in law school.)

Whether the classroom exams need "successful completion" is of course a debatable point. In 1998 LSUC reviewed the performance of a number of students who had failed Phase 3 of the Bar Admissions Course (BAC). After those reviews, they decided to admit 27 of those students to the Bar of Ontario, in spite of their inability to pass the bar exams. The Law Society has come under scrutiny for its decision in this regard.

The academic workload of the classroom phase is intense. It is common to read 50 - 80 pages per night. These required readings are unreasonably large and very often contain irrelevant sections. While many of the readings would be suitable for first year law school, they are not suitable for a course which is intended to train law students in the practical aspects of practising law. Nonetheless, all materials are examinable, including lectures.

Although the purpose is laudable, there are many flaws in the current classroom phase structure which make the classroom phase fall short of its goals. For example, there is a discrepancy among instructors. Although the Law Society has attempted to standardize the instruction among students, there still exists a marked difference in the quality of instruction from classroom to classroom. Further, the setting of the examinations by the Heads of Sections often results in material being examined which was not covered in class. Of course, the Law Society is continually modifying and restructuring the program in the hopes that it will serve its original purpose. The point however, is that as the structure exists, the classroom phase of the Bar Admissions Course is not well-suited to meeting the needs of today's students. The overly burdensome readings, the lack of standardization among the sections and instructors, and the ambiguities surrounding certain examinations leave the classroom phase well-meaning but not very useful.

Does the Bar Admission Course achieve it's purpose? Would somebody graduating from this long BAC both be and feel competent to "hang a shingle." No, they would not. The purpose and effect of the exercise are different. I can still see the purpose. It's just not happening. It could be accomplished in a shorter period of time provided they were willing to take the attitude of "let's cut the shit, here is bare bones of what you need to know. Do this as a minimum and you're okay."

Although this passage may leave some students with a negative impression, they ought to bear in mind that a student will get out of the legal education process, what they put into it.

Although the legal education process is flawed in some aspects, it doesn't mean that students cannot otherwise receive a good education and preparation for the practice of law. What it does mean, is that students must at all times keep their eyes open and avail themselves of all opportunities that best serve their own needs. To do any less on the student's behalf, is to deny one's own success.

In closing, the classroom component of the Bar Admission Course was long and tedious. On the last day I thought, I can't believe it's over. Four months of bullshit. Not long in the greater scheme of things but long enough."

As you can see, there have been problems with the classroom component of Bar Admission Courses. But, great news - read on!

Ontario Shortens And Revamps The Bar Admission Course

For those graduating from law school in 2006 or later:

- the length of the Ontario Bar Admission Course has been reduced to approximately 11 months;

- substantive law will be taught only in the law schools and not in the Bar Admission Course;

- the classroom component will be reduced to one month (prior to the commencement of articles);

- resulting in a savings of 11 weeks which according to the Law Society could be worth approximately $14,000 in additional salary.

This is fantastic news. Believe it or not, the Bar Admission Course has not been changed significantly since 1957 - the year that the law schools took over the teaching of law. In its current form the Bar Admission Course is seriously out of touch with reality and in some aspects (reteaching courses already taught in law school) a tremendous waste of time.

As you know, completion of the Bar Admission Course, along with "good character" are the requirements to become a lawyer in Ontario. A law degree provides the academic qualification for entry into the course.

So, What Will The Ontario Bar Admission Course Be Composed Of?

Beginning in 2006 the Bar Admission Course will be composed of:

1. A 4 week skills and professional responsibility course with (at least so far) a requirement of mandatory attendance. The purpose of this is to teach practice management - with a balance between litigation and non-litigation skills. This will start right after law school and is to be completed before articling starts.

2. A 10 month articling period. This is the same as the current 10 month articling period.

3. Two exams:

A. A barristers exam focusing on advocacy related areas; and

B. A solicitors exam focusing on solicitors related areas.

Each exam is available to be taken 3 times a year in - July, October and February. The exams may be taken together or separately. The Law Society will supply reference materials on which the exams will be based. The idea is that they will test a minimal amount of substantive law and continue the testing of professional ethics and responsibility. The exams will be done during (but not as part of) the articling year.

A Possible Time Line

In practical terms - if this were applied to the 2004 year, this would mean that the calendar for becoming a lawyer would be:

Law School Completed - April 30

Skills Program - May 19 - June 13

Available To Begin Articling - June 23

Exams - 3 times a year - July 7 - 11; Oct. 27 - 31; Feb. 23 - 27

47 Weeks Articling - ends May 15

Call To The Bar - June 1 - 10

This will reduce the time it takes to be admitted to the Ontario bar to a level that is closer to other provinces. Remember also the 2002 mobility agreement which will in effect mean that a license to practice in any province is a "national license."

The world is looking better and better for future lawyers!! The next step should be to abolish articling completely.

Conclusion

This has been an attempt to give you a taste of what the process of bar admission in the Canadian provinces involves. The bar admission course is constantly evolving. The combination of national mobility and Ontario's changes to take effect in 2006 are very positive!

APPENDIX A

This chapter began with a quotation from a distinguished judge urging that the role and value of the Bar Admission Course be considered. We will end with an interesting article questioning the value of the articling experience.

Warning! Warning! The following article by a Toronto lawyer was written while Canada (and the legal profession) was in the grip of a vicious recession. Any "doom and gloom" about the difficulty of obtaining an articling position is no longer applicable! Nevertheless, this article discusses a number of issues dealing with articling.

Is Articling Obsolete?

Janice M. Zima

It's getting tougher for law school graduates to get their articles. And what's more, not everyone's wild about the quality of law firm articling programs. Maybe, as in the U.S., it's time to do away with them.

A story is making the rounds of two articling students recently left alone to manage their principal's law office - not for a few hours, or a couple of days, but for two weeks. Their employer, it seems, needed a tropical vacation and didn't see anything wrong in leaving the fledgling lawyer to mind his clients' affairs.

Rare as incidents of student abandonment may be, this little yarn underscores the somewhat cavalier and haphazard attitude of some in the legal profession towards articling. This, though is one of many stories lawyers and students alike tell about the peculiar ritual of professional purgatory that lies between law school graduation and formal bar admission.

Babysitting, fetching coffee, endless photocopying, pointless memo writing, long hours in registry lineups and trips to the dry cleaners are part of the job for lawyers-in-waiting in many law firms. Although articling is supposed to be about learning the practical skills of being a lawyer, too often it becomes a beauty contest for prospective hires or a period of forced, albeit often well-paid labour with minimal legal apprenticeship.

Is articling worth keeping or is it an obsolete holdover from the days before law schools and bar admissions courses? Today, students in many provinces are caught in a classic catch-22 situation. They need a year or more of articles to get their ticket as a practising lawyer, yet the articling market has shrunk and practitioners are so far under no obligation to take on students - forcing some law grads to article for free, go into another career or return to school.

Meanwhile, those who do their articles report training experiences that are hugely uneven, ranging from organized, well-supervised programs to some that are nothing short of a waste of time. Professional educators are not surprised that the value of articling is being questioned "The theory behind articling is great, but the key, always, is what actually happens on the job," says Neil Gold, law dean at the University of Windsor and a legal education author. "I think law firms lack the `know how' to engage in supervision and in-house programs. "They're lawyers, not educators."

Right now is a bad time for articling in many centres across Canada. During the rich 80's annual salaries for students jumped to as high as $50,000 at the big firms, but the money is simply no longer there to take on students in the same numbers. Although employers in smaller firms don't pay much more than a living wage, articling is an expensive proposition for them too.

Aside from providing salary and benefits, employers have to devote office resources and billable time to supervising their young charges. In this tough economy, many practitioners are saying

"No thank you."

How bad is it out there? For the past few years in Ontario, the Law Society of Upper Canada has regularly dropped to its knees and publicly pleaded with law firms to take on students. A mid-summer notice to the profession this year indicates how far the law society is willing to go. Newly minted joint and part-time articling programs now offer employers the option of hiring someone for just a few days a week or a few months, permitting a student to stretch articling up to three years. In-house corporate and government law departments are being encouraged to take on grads and, departing from its own standards, the society now allows lawyers with less than three years' experience to train students. Other law societies are making similar concessions.

Though finding an articling job and a willing employer is far more difficult today than five years ago, most students eventually do get positions, according to Mimi Hart director of LSUC's placement service. By mid-July of this year, 114 students, or about 10 percent, were still looking for jobs for the 1995-96 term in Ontario. Hart says these figures are similar to July statistics for the preceding year, and by the close of 1994, 99 percent of students seeking articles had been placed. (Some would dispute this figure, noting that students who abandon their search are not included in the final tally. Clearly, though, a majority do find work.) The lean market for student jobs, however is not going to convince law societies that articles are unnecessary. "The current shortage of articling positions alone fails to justify the elimination of articling as a preparatory element for practice," says Marilyn Bode, LSUC's director of articling "Because economic factors are cyclical and ever-shifting, it would be tremendously short-sighted to eliminate articling on that basis. Decisions made regarding articling should be based on education, and not economic, considerations.

"What, then, are the educational merits of today's articling programs? When students spend three years in law school and as much as six months learning the practicalities of the local law in bar admissions courses, they can be forgiven for questioning the need for lengthy stints in a law office. "Do we really not trust our law schools?" asks Michael Fairney, a Toronto articling student. It's fair to at least question why law societies differ in length of required articles, with some needing almost two years, including bar ads.

Articling is by no means a universally accepted concept. Robert MacCrate, a prominent New York lawyer and U.S. legal education expert, says one of the reasons why law school eventually won out over clerkship as the leading vehicle for legal education in the U.S. was "the recognition that apprenticeship training was inconsistent, non-uniform and serendipitous." Today, in every state but Delaware, law graduates can write state bar exams and begin practising right after law school without doing any articles.

U.S. law schools, however, are more oriented towards teaching the practical skills than are their Canadian cousins. For now, the law societies argue that in-the-trenches articling is a valuable element in a new lawyer's training that simply can't be covered in classroom settings. British Columbia's students, for example, must enroll in the province's Professional Legal Training Course (PLTC), a 10-week program that teaches basic legal skills in a small-group setting. Bill Duncan, director of PLTC, believes this co-ordinated program of both articles and a professional skills training program is the best means of ensuring that students enter the bar competent to practise law.

Students themselves tell Don Thompson, director of competency at the Law Society of British Columbia, that there is no substitute for being in a well-supervised office-setting. "In a firm, students deal hands-on with clients, registry offices, support staff, all practical pieces of the pie," he says. "This just can't happen in the '10-week miracle"—as the PLTC is known.

This, of course, assumes articling principals are doing their job. In its pure form, articling should be an enriching and learning experience. The earliest-known reference in the English common law tradition, according to The Origins of the English Legal Profession, was in 1289 of one Nigel of Amcotts and an unnamed apprentice. The central feature of legal apprenticing between these two was regular court attendances, where officials would expand upon legal matters for the benefit of the young mind. Hundreds of years later, articling has become much more complex.

For one thing, most lawyers no longer have the time to devote to a proper training program. Indeed, Windsor's Dean Gold argues that many law firms can't train future lawyers while also serving clients. "What tends to happen," he says, "is that the student's interests get subordinated to the immediate practical aspects of operating a firm. The irony of this, however, is that unless an articling student is adequately trained, the client's position is ultimately undermined by the [lower] calibre of that lawyer later on.

"Moreover, very few law firms have formal training programs or the resources to stick with them. As a result, students tend to be assigned the infamous menial tasks that go to any employee who is standing around with little to do. At the other extreme are those firms that regard students as worker bees and demand "crazy hours," as one student puts it—up to 80 hours per week on a regular basis at some of the larger Toronto firms.

Adam Szweras articled at one such Toronto firm last year, but developed a somewhat philosophical attitude to it all. He believes that since long hours are inevitable at large firms, students who are unprepared for this one-year lifestyle sacrifice should just find another job or lower their expectations about making big money fresh out of school. Still, even Szweras sees a dark side to all this. He suggests that the forced level of competitiveness and long hours put in by articling students primes a workaholic mentality in the early years of practice that drives many lawyers to burn out later. "I start from the premise that the legal community has gone nuts—working long hours, yet complaining about them, while many other lawyers can't find work," he says. "It doesn't make sense. "Another student, who asked to remain anonymous, agrees. "The problem isn't articling; it's the legal profession. A firm's expectations of articling students reflect those of the profession. And some of those expectations are crazy."

"She tells the story of a fellow student recovering from an illness who was recently told to be at work 2:30 a.m. The student protested, noting he needed proper sleep to recover. But he was told to be at work by 5 a.m. at the latest. "However," she says, "what you may forget is that the lawyer was there, working at 2:00 a.m. and, if you want to get hired back, you have to keep the pace. "Student dissatisfaction with the articling process motivated about 30 Toronto students in a handful of firms to form a much-publicized union early this spring. While standardization of hours and working conditions was a part of their objective, the main aim was to give students a unified voice and wake employers up, says Shella Turkington, who articled with Cavalluzzo Hayes Shilton McIntyre & Cornish—appropriately, a labour law firm.

Most of the participating students saw the idea of student unionization "a principled, forward-looking endeavour, to establish formal expectations and grievance channels," she says. Though they all recognized that they are well-paid and better off than most workers, they believed there was a danger that some law firm employers could ride roughshod over students' basic rights.

While the fledgling union hasn't caught on in many other firms, it did send a shiver through some managing partners' offices. Not all students like the idea of unionization, though. Some wear their long hours and torturous schedules as a badge of honour, citing the medical interns whose work days are notoriously grueling and who are paid far less money. Long days are not bad as long as, in the words of one student, "the work involved is not menial or so routine that the learning value of the articles is diminished. "Roy Lizzi, who articled at another large Toronto firm last year, agrees. "You get dumped on at 5 p.m. Friday. So what? That's not a problem. You're there to learn." That's not to say, however, that articling always fulfills its promise of teaching practical skills. Lizzi observes that a critical element of learning—adequate supervision—is too often missing from the articling process. "If you are to be treated as a student, someone's got to be a teacher," he says. The quality of supervision is often what separates the good articling programs from the bad. Echoing Gold's view of lawyers as educators, Patricia Towler, author of Articling in Canada: A Survival Guide, says the failure of employers to supervise is not necessarily deliberate. "Lawyers don't always remember what they knew when they were articling students," she says. Ironically, the lack of supervision can cost the employer as much as the student. According to law firm consultant Antony Karabus of Toronto-based Karabus & Apple Consulting Group, "the single factor that will most affect the profitability of a particular student is how well he or she is supervised." In addition to minimizing the extent to which a firm must write off a student's research time, Karabus says, "proper supervision and mentorship minimizes losses down the road, by (instilling) good work habits right away.

"Towler suggests that the firm's size has a lot to do with the quality of its supervision. In smaller firms, she maintains, feedback and instruction are ad hoc at best, whereas larger firms tend to schedule regular reviews.

The program at Calgary's Bennett Jones Verchere is typical of what's done in many large firms. Douglas Foster says that students are assigned work on a rotation basis, using a supervising mentor system combined with work distributed through a single research co-ordinator. Though lawyers are expected to give feedback on an on-going basis, Foster notes that some are more diligent than others. Therefore, Bennett Jones, like many firms with structured programs, uses a formal evaluation system administered by a student liaison committee each May and December. In other firms, quarterly evaluations may be done, particularly where a rotation system is offered and no mentor program is in place. Small firm life is not bad for some, though, Andrea Saunders, who articled two years ago at a small firm in Kitchener, Ont., says supervision at smaller firms can be good since there's more opportunity to work with the same lawyers, and that can actually make feedback more frequent, even though it's often casually delivered rather than formally evaluated. Choosing the right size firm for the student's own needs is the "single biggest decision a student will make," says Towler. She suggests that in certain respects, articling students can only blame themselves if they pick the wrong firm. "Firms do have different cultures," she says, and she encourages students to "do their homework" before selecting a firm.

But in a tight market, many students have to take what they can get and may accept positions that don't fill their needs simply because they must meet the articling requirement to practise law.

"I am concerned that I may be channeling myself into an area of practice that might not be the best choice for me," remarks one student, who asked not to be named. "But after seven years at university, it's tremendously important for me to get my call to the bar. "One peculiarity of articling today that is distorting its original purpose is that it's not just about training lawyers anymore; it's about landing a job. Each year, students and law firms perform a ritual dance of interviews and matching services, with future earnings often the prime goal for both sides. Terence Dobbin, student committee chair at Osler Hoskin & Harcourt's Toronto office, says his firm takes its articling program very seriously for that reason. For example, Osler is one of the few megafirms with its own in-house director of professional education for all lawyers. Dobblin says Oslers sees articling, in addition to preparing a student for the rigours of practice, as an invaluable recruitment tool. The articling program allows the firm to mould a student into the type of lawyer best suited to the firm's culture and that of its clients. "If a firm recruits a good student and trains her [or him] well, it has improved its chances of hiring someone for the long term," he notes.

Fair enough. However, if law firms are using the articling process to screen new recruits, what happens when firms aren't hiring as many for entry-level positions? The articling market dries up, which is what's happening now. To some people, law firms are getting the best end of the deal. They can hire top recruits when times are good and cut back when they please. Is that within the spirit of articling's purpose? If law societies are to continue to make articling mandatory, this raises the question whether the profession should be forced to make positions available.

Michael Fairney's is an interesting case in point. He was one of five articling students who took unpaid positions with the federal Department of Justice in Toronto this past year after spending six months fruitlessly looking for a paying job. Ironically, Fairney had already proved his capability as a practising lawyer, having been called to the Manitoba bar in 1994. To qualify in Ontario, he simply had to do six months of articles.

His job hunt convinced him that one of the problems with articling is that it's market-driven. Although he didn't have bad marks and had already had articled with a top trial lawyer in Manitoba, no one was interested in him. "Law firms have these standards," he says. "You have to be a gold medalist." The fact that he had to sell himself to law firms in order to meet an educational requirement of the law society strikes Fairney as "ridiculous." In his view, the profession could better fulfil the practical skills requirement by building co-op work programs into the three years of law school. "It would take the market issue right out of it," he says. Interestingly, Fairney doesn't support the idea of eliminating articling itself; he sees more problems within the law schools themselves. "I found articling vastly superior to law school in turning me into a lawyer," he says.

In reality, though, it'll be a distant day when law societies dare to impose hiring quotas on law firms or force them into co-op programs. Instead, the societies are skirting the problem of inadequate articling courses. Several law societies are taking steps to ensure the hands-on experience of articling is complemented by critical skills training in the classroom. Though the societies have historically focused on matters such as insurance and professional discipline, in recent years their attention has shifted to legal education and skills training for all lawyers, says Darrel Pink, executive director of Barristers' Society of Nova Scotia. BSNS has also moved to make its articling requirements more flexible, as in Ontario. "Our response as a law society [to the difficulty of finding articling positions] has been to become more flexible with regard to the types of articles we will allow to be implemented to meet the needs of lawyers and students," says Pink. "To increase access, we have done a lot more one-on-one work with principals to make viable articles that in the old days would not have been acceptable. "He rejects the suggestion that this is a watered-down approach to articling. Pink insists the society's response simply accommodates the ever-changing needs of both the student and the profession. "There is now more recognition of the diversity of legal experience that's out there. We are recognizing that there are fewer generalists and more specialists practising law. Our obligation as a governing body is to give students as well-rounded an experience as possible," he says.

In Ontario, LSUC is constantly tinkering with the articling process to ensure that lawyers are prepared to practise. Students now complete their bar admission requirements in three phases over a 16-month period, alternating terms of law firm work with classes. More reforms are still to come to bolster the practical skills-development part of the bar ads, according to Alan Treleaven, director of education.

While law societies are making efforts to adapt their articling requirements to economic realities, what's still missing is uniformity in the articling terms across the country. Unevenness in this aspect of the articling experience is yet another rallying point for those advocating the abolition of articling. Pink, however, believes that even more important than uniform periods of articles are "nationally articulated standards and a clearer articulation of required skills."

Not everyone agrees. Treleaven says that modern law practice makes the unevenness in articling programs among law firms necessary, even desirable, where a student wants specialized experience. Unevenness in substantive law is acceptable as well, provided that a threshold of basic skills are met, he adds. "Bar admissions courses and the bar examination itself ensure that some degree of uniformity is achieved in spite of differences in students' articling experiences."

During the course of interviews for this article, with all the confidential asides about horrible principals and stupefying work assignments, not one student actually suggested that articles be completely abandoned. Most agreed that law schools and bar admissions courses didn't measure up in preparing graduates for actual practice, so articling is still a necessary evil.

What is evident among today's articling students, however, is a growing militancy towards law societies and articling employers, something that's not gone unnoticed. "Students are becoming increasingly more demanding," says Pink. "They know the threshold they have to get through in order to get admitted to the bar and for their eventual practices. They are demanding better quality articles." If law societies are to continue requiring articles, you can bet students won't be shy in the near future to press for better articling programs and some guarantee of articling positions. Whether law firms like it or not, articling students aren't willing to play the role of the good worker bees for much longer. As Fairney puts it, "If you don't like what you're doing, you should leave and assign your articles to someone else. You get the education you ask for."

Janice M. Zima is a writer and articling student.
Reprinted with permission of the author.

APPENDIX B

Watch Out For What The Firms Tell You!

Firms are anxious to impress potential articling students during interview week. Many students are wined and dined! But, do the firms accurately portray life at the firm?

"There once was an lawyer who lived her whole life without ever taking advantage of any of the people she worked for. In fact, she made sure that every job she did resulted in a win-win situation. One day while walking down the street she was tragically hit by a bus and she died.

Her soul arrived up in heaven where she was met at the Pearly Gates by St. Peter himself.

"Welcome to Heaven," said St. Peter. "Before you get settled in though it seems we have a problem. You see, strangely enough, we've never once had a lawyer make it this far and we're not really sure what to do with you."

"No problem, just let me in," said the lawyer.

"Well, I'd like to, but I have higher orders. What we're going to do is let you have a day in Hell and a day in Heaven and then you can choose whichever one you want to spend an eternity in."

"Actually, I think I've made up my mind...I prefer to stay in Heaven."

"Sorry, we have rules..."

And with that St. Peter put the lawyer in an elevator and it went down-down-down to hell. The doors opened and the lawyer found herself stepping out onto the putting green of a beautiful golf course. In the distance was a country club and standing in front of her were all her friends - fellow lawyers that she had worked with and they were all dressed in evening gowns and cheering for her. They ran up and kissed her on both cheeks and they talked about old times.

They played an excellent round of golf and at night went to the country club where she enjoyed an excellent steak and lobster dinner. She met the Devil who was actually a really nice guy (did you see the movie "The Devil's Advocate?") and she had a great time telling jokes and dancing. The lawyer was having such a good time that before she knew it, it was time to leave. Everybody shook her hand and waved goodbye as she got on the elevator.

The elevator went up-up-up and opened back up at the Pearly Gates and found St. Peter waiting for her. "Now it's time to spend a day in heaven."

So the lawyer spent the next 24 hours lounging around on clouds and playing the harp and singing. She had a great time and before she knew it her 24 hours were up and St. Peter came and got her. "So, you've spent a day in hell and you've spent a day in heaven. Now you must choose you're eternity." The lawyer paused for a second and then replied, "Well, I never thought I'd say this, I mean, Heaven has been really great and all, but I think I had a better time in Hell."

So St. Peter escorted her to the elevator and again the lawyer went down-down-down back to Hell. When the doors of the elevator opened she found herself standing in a desolate wasteland covered in garbage and filth. She saw her friends were dressed in rags and were picking up the garbage and putting it in sacks. The Devil came up to her and put his arm around her.

"I don't understand," stammered the lawyer, "Yesterday I was here and there was a golf course and a country club and we ate lobster and we danced and had a great time. Now all there is a wasteland of garbage and all my friends look miserable."

The Devil looked at her and smiled. "That's because yesterday you were a recruit, but today you're an associate.""

Moral: watch out for what the firms tell you in the articling interviews!!

APPENDIX C

December 2003

By John Jaffey

Toronto

In a special session of Convocation, the Law Society of Upper Canada voted 41-4 this month in favour of revamping and shortening its 45-year-old Bar Admission Course (BAC).

Starting in 2006, the existing program of substantive law lectures and exams will be eliminated. Instead, the law society will provide reference materials, learning tools and support services to enable candidates to self-study for two full-day licensing exams, which will test legal knowledge and analytical capabilities. Students-at-law will have a choice of three dates during their articles to write a barrister exam and a solicitor exam.

The only classroom instruction during the BAC will be a short course – four weeks was recommended - in legal skills, including professional responsibility and practice management.

Articling will continue to be part of the BAC; there is a consensus among the benchers that the mentoring aspect should be emphasized.

In addition, although the exact length has yet to be decided, the new BAC will be about 11 weeks shorter than the existing program. New lawyers can expect to benefit by about $15,800, through tuition savings of $1,800 and about $14,000 of additional earning power.

George Hunter, chair of the Task Force on the Continuum of Legal Education, said the new regime will make the BAC more relevant to the practice of law in the 21st century; remove unnecessary barriers to admission and respect principles of equity, and significantly reduce costs to students while continuing to serve the public interest.

He emphasized that the assessment of a new lawyer's competence at the time of being called to the bar is only a snapshot. The existing method of testing competence in substantive law was based on the outdated assumption that pre-call learning was thought to be the last opportunity for the lawyer to assimilate knowledge in a formal setting. The emphasis on continuing legal education belies that assumption.

"Realistically," Hunter said, "the BAC contribution can only set the foundation for all that follows." In making his pitch for adoption of the report, Hunter pointed out that thetypical BAC candidate is a 31-year-old with life experience. He also noted that attendance at the BAC lectures in substantive law is dismal. Some afternoon lectures are attended by only 20 percent of the class.

In addition, he said the recent passage of the National Mobility Agreement suggests that further steps will likely follow to remove all remaining unnecessary barriers to a lawyer's call to the bar and to harmonize admission processes across the country.

Hunter said three of the four western law societies are developing a new bar admission program that eliminates the teaching of substantive law in favour of the development of skills taught in large measure via the Internet.

Before the special convocation began, a seven-page letter from a former bencher, Professor Marilyn Pilkington of Osgoode Hall Law School, was circulated. The communication was highly critical of the Task Force's report, calling it"fundamentally flawed."

Pilkington concluded that the report "has the trappings of a major new policy initiative, but in fact it makes a rather narrow proposal to change the delivery method of the Bar Admission Course in order to generate efficiencies."

Other criticisms came during debate: bencher Gavin MacKenzie said, "I strongly feel that self-study is not a good substitute for ... a good teacher." Gary Gottlieb said he feared that American "cram schools" would open branch offices here in Ontario.

But most of the debate was positive. Derry Millar called the proposed changes a "leap of faith, though an informed leap of faith. Maintaining the status quo militates against improvement, and improvements are what we're trying to achieve."

Carole Curtis noted the current system spends $8 million a year to fail 30 students. The most graphic argument for change was made by a special visitor to convocation, Dean Alison Harvison Young of Queen's University Law School.

She told the benchers that when she was discussing the BAC with her daughter, who completed it two years ago, she was amazed to hear that it was still as full of "waste and duplication" as it was when she went through 20 years ago. The dean said the fact that they both had the same complaints was proof enough for her that the time has come for an overhaul.

John Jaffey - The Lawyers Weekly

Chapter 26

Becoming A Notary Or An Advocate - Bar Admission In Quebec

In the province of Quebec there are two kinds of lawyers. The Notary is analogous to the English Solicitor and the Advocate is analogous to the English Barrister. This chapter will explore how to become either a Notary or an Advocate.

One Canada - Two Legal Traditions

Canada has two different legal systems - the common-law system and the civil law system. All the provinces except Quebec are based on the common-law system: Quebec is based on the civil law system. In the common law provinces lawyers are called to the bar as both barristers and solicitors. In Quebec there are two kinds of lawyers - the advocate and the notary. How are they different?

Advocates and Notaries - The Distinction

A distinction must be made between Quebec's two types of lawyers:

(a) the advocate who is similar in function to the English barrister; and

(b) the notary, who is similar in function to the English solicitor. The notary does not have a related counterpart in the other provinces.

Whereas in the common-law provinces people are admitted to the law as both barristers and solicitors, in Quebec lawyers are either advocates or notaries.

Two Kinds Of Lawyers - Two Governing Bodies

In Quebec the legal profession has two governing bodies. The Chambre des notaires du Qubec governs the notarial profession within Quebec, while the Barreau du Qubec governs the lawyers (advocates). Each of theses governing bodies has its own licensing exams and requirements. In order to pass the course, one must be admitted to the course.

So, What Are The Requirements For Admission To The Course?

You must have a degree from a law school that has a civil law program. A brief overview of these opportunities is provided at the end of this chapter.

Admission to the Bar - Advocate

To be admitted to the Quebec Bar as an advocate, the applicant must have been granted a civil law degree from a recognized law school or a degree approved by the General Council of the Barreau du Quebec. (A degree from any of Canada's civil law programs will suffice.)

The Bar Admission Course is run by the Quebec "Bar School" and is comprised of the following three components:

1. A Practical Skills Component Which Includes Instruction In:

- doing research;

- establishing a consulting or counseling relationship;

- drafting legal documents and proceedings;

- negotiating;

- managing his or her own legal practice;

- mastering the art of representation;

- managing the rules of ethics in a law practice.

2. A Substantive Law Component Providing Instruction In The Following Areas:

- professional practice;

- civil law;

- evidence and procedure;

- public and administrative law;

- business law

3. A Training Period (The Equivalent To Articling)

Like articling, the "Training Period" is conducted under the supervision of a practicing lawyer. The "Training Period" lasts for six months and may not commence until the student has successfully completed the first two components of the course.

Admission to the Bar - Notary

The Quebec notary is of the Latin type with an LL.L., LL.B., or B.C.L. law degree. The curriculum and options for the first three years of law school are the same for both future notaries and future advocates. The latter leave university for bar school while notarial candidates continue at law school for an additional year of practical studies related to notarial areas of specialization, followed by one year of articling in a notarial law firm, and evaluation, after which the future notary is officially sworn in and admitted to the profession.

Law Programs Offering The Civil Law Degree - Where They Are

With the exception of McGill and the University of Ottawa, Canada's law schools teach either the common law system or the civil law system and not both. The University of Ottawa (civil law section) is the only school outside of Quebec that offers a civil law degree. The Quebec universities offering a civil law degree are:

- Laval University

- Sherbrooke University

- University of Montreal

- University of Quebec

- McGill

Instruction at these schools is in the French language. Therefore, to be considered for admission to one of the above faculties, the applicant must be fluent in both verbal and written French. (Incidentally, none of these programs requires the LSAT for admission.)

As An Aside - Common-Law (LL.B.) Degrees Offered in French

Recognizing the demand for instruction in the French language, law schools have introduced the option of earning the common law degree in French. The **University of Ottawa**, and the **University of Moncton** are examples. In fact, Moncton offers instruction only in French!

At the University of Ottawa, students in the common-law program have the option of taking some courses in French.

The University of New Brunswick permits its students to study upper year courses that are offered in the French language. To encourage bilingualism, the Faculty allows students to take non-law courses which are instructed in the French language.

It makes sense to consider schools offering civil law degree programs in the following three categories:

1. Schools Offering Only The Civil Law Degree

- University of Ottawa Civil law division (the only school opportunity outside of Quebec)

- Laval

- Sherbrooke

- Montreal

- Quebec

2. National Law Program - A Joint Civil And Common Law Degree

McGill is unique in that it allows students to achieve a joint civil and common law degree in approximately three years!

"McGill occupies a unique position among Canadian law faculties to pursue its dual mission of educating future professionals and promoting scholarship. The Faculty, quite naturally in the light of its location, has a long tradition of teaching and scholarship in both the English and French languages. The staff and students have always been drawn from these two linguistic groups. While English has been the primary language of the Faculty, the use of French in the classroom and as a language in daily life is firmly entrenched."

3. Achieving Both Civil And Common Law Degrees By Adding A Year

A number of Canadian law schools have arrangements with other schools that will allow holders of the Common law to degree earn a degree in Civil law by studying for one year at a school teaching civil law. The reverse is also true. Obviously this is a great opportunity. Current opportunities may be found by researching the individual schools.

By way of example, at The University of Ottawa, the **joint common-law and civil law degree** is also offered. After completion of third year, students from both streams may, through progressive studies, earn the other degree. Civil law students must apply to the Common-Law Faculty for permission to enter the program, while common-law students must apply to the Civil Law Faculty.

What follows are two perspectives written by those who have experienced both common and civil law degrees in this four year (two degree) format.

Perspective 1:

"No LSAT, two law degrees, two bar admissions and three years of practice by the age of 27! It is possible!

At 27 years old, I am a third year associate at a Toronto-Bay Street specialized law firm, and a member of both the Quebec and Ontario Bar. At such a young age, people often wonder how I got to where I am today.

I was raised in Quebec where the school system is different from the other provinces. Students graduate from high school after grade 11, and attend college (or CEGEP). CEGEP is designed to prepare students for university, and most CEGEP programs are for 2 years. I graduated from CEGEP in Health Sciences at the age of 19 and hoping never to study sciences again, I decided to go to law school. An undergraduate university degree and the LSAT are not required for enrollment under the Civil Law program in universities. However, some universities, such as the University of Montreal have an admission exam similar to the LSAT, and McGill offers a joint Civil Law/Common Law degree program of 4 years and therefore requires the LSAT and an undergraduate program. I attended the University of Ottawa after CEGEP, and obtained a Civil Law Degree (LL.L.) by the time I was 22. I then completed the Quebec Bar admission course, which is a full school year, and articling for six months after all exams have been successfully completed is required. I was called to the Quebec Bar at the age of 23. I was fortunate to have passed all of the Quebec Bar exams on my first try. It is no secret that they are very challenging and my theory is that, because the admission requirement to Civil Law programs are not very stringent, the Quebec Bar has to make becoming a lawyer in Quebec fairly difficult.

The University of Ottawa also offered a joint Civil Law/Common Law program where students who completed either the Civil Law program or the Common Law program can return to the University of Ottawa and obtain the second law degree in one year. I therefore returned to Ottawa and obtained a Common Law Degree (LL.B.) after I was called to the Quebec Bar, while in private practice in Montreal mainly in real estate and family law. Having practiced in Quebec for a little under a year, I was exempt from certain Ontario Bar requirements. I only had to write the Ontario bar exams (Phase III at the time) and I had to article for a period of 4 months. I was called to the Ontario Bar at the age of 25. I did not find the Ontario Bar exams extremely difficult compared to the Quebec Bar. My articling experience in Quebec was fairly similar to my experience in Ontario. I have no regrets, so far! My advice to anyone going to law school or who's just finishing up law school is to make sure to choose an area of law that you really enjoy. The hours are long and the stress level is high, so make sure you enjoy it!"

Perspective 2:

"Attending Sherbrooke Law has been a diametrically different experience from my 4 years at the U of T. Having studied in Ontario, I can objectively compare and evaluate the pros and cons of attending a French university in Quebec. Studying in my third language proved to be a true challenge, but thanks to close friends and a bilingual civil code, I was able to breeze through the curriculum. Sherbrooke's strength lies in the teaching methodology; the professors adopt an open-door policy which basically revolves around the students' schedules. In fact, recent bar results reveal that overall, Sherbrooke students scored higher than McGill's!! My first year courses consisted of the basics: Property, Civil Procedure, Obligations, Droit des Personnes, and Constitution Law. With only three hours of classes a day, I found time to improve my golf, and parallel skiing; Sherbrooke is located in the heart of the Eastern Townships. I am looking forward to my LL.B. Civil degree, followed by the ONE-YEAR COMMON LAW degree. In just 4 years, students can earn 2 (two) LL.B. degrees; the second being granted from Queens University, as an exchange option. Admittance into Queens is secured provided that your academic standards remain above average. Indeed, this scheme sounds too good to be true, but I must emphasize that admittance into Sherbrooke requires high academic excellence. While Sherbrooke does not require the LSAT, a strong score will only improve your chances with the exchange programme. If you have a basic command in French, and would like to explore the Quebecois culture to its fullest. I would highly recommend students to polish their French, and at the same time, acquire a joint degree!"

What Is The Value Of Having Both Civil And Common Law Degrees?

North American law graduates with a degree in civil law are in a minority. It is very easy for Canadian law students to earn both the civil and common law degrees. Consider the following comments:

"Quebec lawyers and notaries find their training in Civil Code matters is in great demand overseas.

Accustomed to both civil-law and common-law environments, Quebec lawyers and notaries have an undeniable edge in the international legal scene. They live in a bilingual universe and are familiar with North American business realities."

-From 'A Code For The Road'- Canadian Bar Association National -
June/July 2000

Conclusion

The process of law school and bar admission is similar to the common law provinces. Graduation from any of the common law schools will provide you with the academic qualification for entry into the bar admission course of any province except Quebec. Graduation from a civil law school in Quebec will provide you with the academic qualification to become a Notary of Advocate in Quebec only.

APPENDIX A

Addresses of the Civil Law Schools

Bureau de Registraire
Pavillian de la Bibliotheque
GÈnÈrale
UniversitÈ Laval
CitÈ Universitarie
Montreal, Quebec
(418) 656 3703

Bureau du Registraire
UniversitÈ de Montreal
C. P. 6205
Succursale A
Montreal, Quebec
H3C 3T5
(514) 343 6197

Service de l'admission
Bureau du Registraire
UniversitÈ de QuÈbec ‡ MontrÈal
C. P. 8888
Montreal, Quebec
H3C 3P8
(514) 282 6961

Admissions Officer
McGill University
3644 Peel Street
Montreal, Quebec
H3A 1W9
(514) 398 6666

Faculty of Law
Civil Law Section
Fauteux Hall
57 Copernicus Street
Ottawa, Ontario
K1N 6N5
(613) 564 2230

Bureau du Registraire
UniversitÈ de Sherbrooke
Sherbrooke, Quebec
J1K 2R1
(819) 565 2900

Contacts For Further Information

To become an Advocate:
Directeur de la formation permanente
Barreau du Quebec
445, boulevard Saint-Laurent
Montreal, Quebec
H2Y 2Y7
(514) 954 3460
htttp: //www.barreau.qc.ca/en/

To become a Notary:
Chambre des notaires du Quebec
http: //www.cdnq.org

APPENDIX B

This is a fasinating article about the legal profession in Quebec.

Notaries in Quebec

Jean Lambert, Notary at Montreal

According to official historic tradition, the Latin notary made his first appearance around the end of the first millennium. It is impossible to pinpoint the exact decade or century, since the origin of the notarial profession, as many other institutions, was not self-generated but rather the result of the gradual evolution of an ancient writing profession, the members of which were called the tabellio and the notarius, devoted exclusively to the mighty, the rich, and the merchant class.

Some believe that on returning from the Crusades, St-Louis, the Good King, found his court congested with unresolved cases, justice in those days being the sole prerogative of the monarch. He took up his sceptre and quickly began hearing cases in order to return his subjects to their work or regular business. It soon became clear to him that many of the parties appearing before him had already agreed to terms of settlement.

To increase efficiency, he determined to handle litigious cases himself and refer to the clerks of his court all those parties who had agreed to settle their disputes. Instruments evidencing the terms of their agreement were drafted and sealed, with the legal authority of the king attaching thereto.

It has been said that 60 of these clerks were appointed as the first royal notaries. They were not merely clerks but persons who truly knew the legal system and the law, and who had the capacity to give proper legal counsel and advice as they drafted. Those drafts are believed to have been presented to the King before they became official.

We know for certain that in thirteenth-century Europe, under the influence of northern Italy's Scuola di Notariato, created in Bologna in 1228, the notarial professional was well and truly acknowledged and the need to submit instruments to the court for legal effect disappeared.

The appointment of notaries was a prerogative of monarchs, sovereigns, and the Pope, and the model quickly spread throughout Europe.

Finally, with the Napoleonic Loi 25 Ventse anne XI of 1803, the rules of the modern notarial profession were established, and were either imposed upon, or willingly adopted by, all other European countries.

The notarial profession was exported by European imperial powers to their colonies, including the so-called "New World," with one notable exception: the British Empire. This exception is the result of two fundamentally different major legal systems of law in the world: the civil law and common law.

England And The Notary

Being an island, England (or the United Kingdom) developed its system of law independently from mainland Europe. The first notaries were introduced into England from continental Europe under papal authority, but in 1279, the Pope authorized the Archbishop of Canterbury to appoint notaries. Some two centuries later, relations soured between Henry IV and the Pope and one of the many consequences of religious reform was the transfer to the Crown, in 1533, by the British Parliament, of the power to appoint notaries. This power was later delegated to the Court of Faculties in 1801, which still appoints notaries today.

Notaries of the Latin type can be found today in England, though few in number (some forty) and all located in the "City." They act as a link between continental civil law institutions and the common law institutions of the United Kingdom. They are called "scriveners" and have legal training, and although they draft contracts (as do Latin-type notaries), they lack public-officer status and their writings do not have the probative value of Latin-type notarial instruments. Interestingly enough, their services are intended for foreign countries, where the instruments they prepare serve as attestations directed at judicial or other public authorities in the country where they are to be used.

As two different types of notary have developed since the end of the sixteenth century in European countries, England, and their respective empires, I will differentiate between them by designating the civil law notary of continental Europe as "Latin notary" and the common-law type as "notary public," even though many Latin notaries are designated as notario publico and notaio publico.

Quebec Notaries

The first notary to settle in French North America was appointed by Louis XIV and arrived in 1663, more than 130 years after Jacques Cartier first discovered what is now known as Canada.

The law of the land was, of course, the French Coutume de Paris, traditional law derived from Roman and Germanic laws. Under the French colonial administration, notaries rapidly and inevitably became legal professionals and business advisers. In those days, only a few inhabitants of New France had any education or writing ability, and advocates (lawyers of litigation) were expressly forbidden to settle in the colony by royal interdiction, the King having a very low opinion of their usefulness. It is interesting to note that advocates were prohibited and barred from the land even during the first fifteen years of British administration, i.e. until 1775.

1760-1867

To understand the survival of the Latin notarial profession in Quebec, and only in that province in Canada, we must again look to history.

Events following victory on the Plains of Abraham were the direct consequence of an astonishing fact: the British had no definite plan in mind when they attacked Nouvelle France. Their action was merely part of a greater plan to curtail French hegemony in Europe. It is therefore no surprise that the British conquerors were few in number and almost one hundred years passed before English settlers outnumbered (thanks to the American revolution) French inhabitants.

The smell of boiling tea having begun to waft over the New England colonies, London quickly convinced itself, in 1770, that gently keeping French Canadians quiet and turning them into loyal subjects of the Crown should be the primary objective.

British sovereignty over Canada was sealed in 1774 by the Treaty of Paris, but London had agreed to allow the inhabitants to keep their Roman Catholic faith and French civil law. However, the British military refused to be subject to French seigneurial tribunals and it succeeded in obtaining an English court system. The end result was a colony governed by French civil law applied under the authority of English common-law courts of justice.

After the turmoil of the conquest, life continued uneventfully in the colony. French Canadians resisted an American military incursion, confirming London's foresight.

One last historical point before proceeding to the essence of the notarial profession: in 1847, Canada was divided into two parts, namely, Lower Canada (Quebec) and Upper Canada (Ontario). This was done to curtail the power of the larger French population and grant parliamentary government to the English loyalists settlers who were then in the majority in Upper Canada.

In 1866, the Parliament of Lower Canada revoked the old Coutume de Paris by enacting the Civil Code of Lower Canada, a virtual replica of the French Napoleonic Civil Code, which is still considered today to be a legal masterpiece and Napoleon's greatest achievement.

Then in 1867, the British North America Act was adopted by the British Parliament as the constitution of Canada. It united the three maritime colonies of Nova Scotia, New Brunswick and Prince Edward Island with Lower and Upper Canada. Of interest here is the fact that the Constitution gave jurisdiction over the ius commune to the provinces, and all but Quebec then developed English-type common law legal systems.

II. ESSENCE OF NOTARIAL SERVICE

To understand the role of the Latin notary, we must consider a society with an integrated system of legal specialization. Whereas in the United States, there exists only one kind of lawyer for all aspects of law (though most law firms have their specializations), Quebec and European, Latin, and Asian civil-law countries have officially divided their legal professions between advocates, for advocacy or litigation, and notaries, for "non-advocacy," i.e. mainly contractual and non-litigious family matters. Five years ago, France had five divisions of its legal profession.

In Quebec, the notary acts in all areas of the law except litigation. The conveyancing of immovable property ("real estate" in common law) constitutes the major sector of activity at 55%. Like their European and Latin colleagues, Quebec notaries

1. are legal professionals acting in a liberal environment;

2. are vested with publica fides;

3. deal with non-litigious matters;

4. must be impartial in acting for all parties; and

5. are expected to

   a) give legal advice to all parties (all sides);

   b) draft legal documents on their behalf;

   c) authenticate those documents; and

   d) keep records of transactions.

Lawyer

The Quebec notary is of the Latin type with an LL.L., LL.B., or B.C.L. law degree. The curriculum and options for the first three years of law school are the same for both future notaries and future advocates. The latter leave university for bar school while notarial candidates continue at law school for an additional year of practical studies related to notarial areas of specialization, followed by one year of articling in a notarial law firm, and evaluation, after which the future notary is officially sworn in and admitted to the profession.

Liberal Environment

Although the Quebec government delegates publica fides to the notary, the notary is not a functionary or a public servant. He is not on the government payroll and does not operate out of some ministerial or government office.

The notary must set up practice privately, by buying or renting premises and equipment, hiring clerical staff, obtaining proper financing, and assuming both civil and professional liability. In fact, with over 95% of notaries in private practice, either for themselves or working in a notarial law firm, the Quebec notarial profession is probably the most liberal in the land.

Publica Fides

Publica fides is, in essence, the power of the state to authenticate or certify. Literally translated, it means "public trust" or "public faith"—"faith" in the sense of the trust people have (or must have) in official papers or acts of the state such as texts of law and court judgments.

In concrete terms, the Quebec notary has the authority to vest with an exceptionally high level of probative value the private documents he prepares, provided he complies with the formalism required by the law. A notarial deed is rarely invalidated by the courts, endowed as it is with the strongest possible presumption of truth. A party attempting to counter this presumption bears a heavy burden of rebuttal through a specific judicial procedure called "improbation." Probative value is justified by the duties (impartial counselling, expert drafting, etc.) notaries must fulfil at all times.

The evidential force of a notarial document is not limited to the identity of the parties and whether they have indeed signed the document, but extends to all the facts stated therein, including the date, whether asserted by the parties themselves or seen, heard, and verified by the notary himself.

For instance, back-dating a notarial deed en minute (the original of which is kept by the notary) is almost impossible, since each notarial instrument or deed must be recorded in an unalterable repertory, and is given a serial number that cannot be changed. If a notary attempts to alter a signed deed, including modifying the date and/or serial number, and is proved guilty, he will be suspended for some years at least and most probably disbarred for life.

Non-litigious Matters

The notary in Quebec, as with colleagues in all but a few of the seventy countries where the Latin notarial profession exists, does not represent clients in advocacy or litigious matters. The professional laws governing both notaries and advocates clearly distinguish between two approaches to the practice of law: notaries have the exclusive right to give authenticity to deeds and instruments, and the duty to inform all parties, while advocates take sides and represent one party with the aim of overcoming the adverse party. They have opposing functions because they are answerable to different legal philosophies. The notary, with a duty to inform and advise all parties, acts somewhat as a conciliator/mediator and, when sealing a document, even as a judge. He does not represent a party; he acts for them all, rising above partisan advocacy to ensure the legality of a transaction. The advocate, on the contrary, moves in adversarial surroundings and must make use of talent and professional skills (within the scope of the law) to promote the best interests of his client and obtain victory.

To conclude here, it should be noted that while Romano-Germanic systems of law have confined the adversarial approach to truly litigious cases, the Anglo-American approach has been to extend it to embrace all aspects of law. For example, in the purchase of a house, the vendor and purchaser are theoretically invited to seek independent advice even though an offer to purchase or sell in due form has already been signed; the same is true for financing, etc.

Impartiality

Notaries are prohibited by a code of ethics from being partial to any one party. Favouring one party would necessarily be detrimental to the other, and is contrary to the concept of the notarial institution, the notary being a multi-party counsellor.

It is probably not easy for a person raised and educated in an Anglo-Saxon society, and even harder for a North American lawyer, to believe that a legal professional such as the notary, an impartial private practitioner, does exist and, furthermore, really succeeds in being impartial in his day-to-day work. But the system works!

By impartiality, I do not mean that notaries are neutral, as we would expect mediators and arbitrators to be. The notary must be impartially active in the sense that he must ensure the equilibrium of the parties to a transaction. In other words, he must enquire as to the level of knowledge and understanding of each party and devote his counselling and advice not necessarily equally, but rather so as to place (in so far as possible) all parties on the same level of contractual ability.

Is this merely idealistic theorizing? An answer may be found in one recent court decision involving a notary's professional liability. The notary had prepared a deed of sale of immovable property where the vendor was paid partly with the transfer of a third-ranking hypothec (similar to "mortgage" in common law) on another property.

The notary performed all relevant verifications as to the legal validity of the hypothec, such as the unpaid balances on the previous-ranking hypothecs, property taxes and assessments, insurance coverage, etc, and found everything to be in order. Accordingly, he certified to the vendor that the claim transferred to him by the purchaser was a valid third-ranking hypothec. When the hypothecary debtor later defaulted, leaving no equity to cover the vendor/creditor's claim, the vendor sued the notary, who was held liable by the court on the ground that he had not fully informed the unfortunate vendor, not as to the legal validity, but as to the economic value (i.e. degree of risk) of the claim. The vendor was awarded full payment of the hypothecary claim plus legal costs.

The notary is expected to give legal advice.

The giving of legal advice to parties has already been discussed to some extent, but it should be added that giving advice is a notary's duty. It is automatically required where a notary has been asked to complete a transaction. A notary who does not fulfil his duty to inform or advise must obtain a waiver in writing from the party concerned to explain why the notary has been relieved of his professional duty. The reason must be sound, such as the personal knowledge and know-how of that party, or the existence of an independent adviser.

A notary may act as adviser to one client, but in that event, he is not allowed, ethically, to complete the transaction unless all parties, being properly informed of his status as a one-party adviser, expressly request that he draw up the official document. Nonetheless, professional guidelines do recommend that a notary not accept such a request lightly.

Notaries Draft Legal Documents

Drafting legal instruments for consenting parties is at the core of notarial services and is still the hallmark of notaries. The services of notaries (graduates of law school) are retained most often for the preparation and drafting of legal documents and instruments for clients. In Quebec, notaries prepare two types of notarial documents:

1. The minute, an original document that obeys strict rules of formalism, is dated and recorded with a serial number, and is retained by the notary, who must keep it in a fire-proof safe or vault. Parties are given certified or true copies of the original, which copies have the same legal evidential force or probative value as the original.

These originals are public documents and must never be destroyed. When a notary ceases to practice, for whatever reason, the originals in his possession, together with the repertory (register), index, and related documents are transferred to another notary in practice or to the clerk of the Superior Court of the notary's judicial district.

2. The brevet is an original like the minute but has no serial number and is remitted to the parties in duplicate, triplicate, or more, as need be. The brevet is normally used to serve short-lived needs were the law does not require the form en minute.

Notaries Authenticate Documents

The function of authenticating is closely linked to the publica fides seen earlier. In short, authenticity means that the document is true, genuine, and must be honoured.

When parties consult a notary, they usually expect authentication, even if not familiar with the concept; the notary must authenticate unless he has valid grounds not to do so.

Authentic instruments, unlike other private writings, have a distinctive and valuable feature, namely, the notary (author) need not testify in a court challenge to one of his documents unless it is set aside for non-compliance with the rules of the formalism. An authentic document is proof in itself and there is normally no point in calling the notary to testify.

Notaries Keep Records Of Transactions

Unless a document serves for a short-term purpose, such as the sale of a motor vehicle, the notary must retain the original en minute as aforesaid and keep a record of it in his register. In so doing, the notary ensures to all interested parties that the transaction instrument will always be available and that authentic copies can always be issued. It also ensures a record of the transaction date.

Interestingly, in Quebec, original notarial documents of all kinds, dating back three hundred years to the early days of the colony, can be referred to and consulted by historians and researchers.

III. DISTINCT CHARACTERISTICS OF THE QUEBEC NOTARIAL PROFESSION

Though of Latin origin, the Quebec notarial profession is evolving in a North American business environment. This explains some divergence between it and the international standard of the profession.

Numerus clausus

Contrary to the practice of most Latin-notary countries, the number of notaries in Quebec is neither limited nor linked to a specific number as a function of population. The Netherlands and Puerto Rico are two other examples of countries without restriction as to the number of members in the notarial profession.

No Territorial Exclusiveness

A notary may exercise his profession anywhere in Quebec, and even abroad if his services involve Quebec residents or if the object of the transaction is situated in the province. Most Latin notarial professions operate on the basis of territorial exclusiveness, although many are now moving away from this restriction.

Bilingualism

A Quebec notary may draft documents in either French or English, at the parties' request. If he also speaks another language, he may record, in an instrument drafted in either French or English, the consent of a person who understands neither official language. This is the typical North American "open-minded" rule.

IV. ORGANIZATION OF THE PROFESSION

General Considerations

Quebec is probably the most advanced society in the Western World in the organization of liberal professions. Through the Professional Code enacted in 1974, it has imposed a uniform set of rules on all bodies governing professional activities in the province.

The Code provides a general framework for the organization of all professional orders: general meetings, board of benchers, executive committee, officers, voting, inspection committee, discipline officer, indemnity fund, framework for the adoption of specific rules for admission into each profession, disciplinary procedure and committee, processing of complaints, professional liability insurance, etc.

A statute has been enacted for each of the 43 recognized professions, with specific sets of by-laws and regulations, the most important being codes of ethics.

The Chambre Des Notaires Du Qubec

The professional order of Quebec notaries is called the Chambre des notaires du Qubec, governed by a board composed of 24 regionally elected benchers, 4 non-members appointed by the Office des professions (the supervising body of all professional orders), and a president elected by all notaries directly.

The Chambre is the oldest (or first) organized professional order in Canada, created July 28, 1847, and has always been considered one of the most professionally managed orders. Its organization was the inspiration for the model in the Professional Code.

Particulars Of The Profession

The notary is a professional under the close supervision of his professional order. To explain that particularity one must bear in mind the unique status of public officer, and further, the importance of his role in handling huge sums of money in trust accounts. Recent gallup polls have shown that notaries, together with doctors (62%), are the most trusted professionals in Quebec society, advocates ranking much lower, at 30% on the public's scale of credibility.

The public's faith in notaries is not surprising, as this profession was the first in Canada to institute periodic compulsory professional inspections (1931), create an indemnity fund (1966), launch semi-annual sessions of continuing legal education (1961) (with attendance at each session averaging 40% of membership), establish liability insurance together with the law society of Manitoba in 1986. I could go on with the list of "firsts." In addition, last March, members were notified that as of January 1998, paper support would no longer be used in communications between the professional order and its members. This indicates how far notaries have gone in computerizing their practice, with their own software-development firm (Notarius) and their own intranet called "Inforoute notariale."

V. AREAS OF NOTARIAL PRACTICE

Notaries may serve the public in all sectors of legal activity except, as mentioned, litigation and advocacy, although their traditional activities are in areas where the law has required notarial deeds and instruments.

Conveyancing Of Immovables

In Quebec, hypothecs must be drafted by notaries, and the conveyancing of immovables and related legal services constitute, on average, 55% of total notarial activities in Quebec. The creation of divided co-ownership (condominiums), for instance, must be effected through notarial deeds en minute.

Wills And Successions

The notarial will is the most popular of the three forms of testamentary documents in Quebec, since it does not require probate for validity. It comes into force immediately upon the death of the testator. It is not surprising, then, to find that notaries are very active in the drafting of wills, planning of estates, and settlement of successions. The renunciation of a succession ("estate" in common law), for whatever reason, must be notarial, as well as the transmission of immovable property to heirs or legatees, and proceedings relating to minors or incapable persons.

Taxation And Estate Planning

Nowadays, many notaries have master's degrees in tax law; a great many have specialized in the field of estate planning and have been instrumental in increasing the popularity of trust wills and testaments.

Commercial Law

The establishment, sale, or purchase of a business, the constitution, amalgamation (merger) or reorganization of a company, commercial financing, and trademarks are the daily bread and butter of all notaries practising commercial law.

Other Areas Of Practice

In Quebec, many notaries have developed expertise in various new legal sectors such as international private law, international adoption, maritime mortgage, intellectual property (copyright), telecommunications law, family and commercial mediation and arbitration, etc.

Clearly, notarial services cover a wide range of needs and can easily be adapted to new trends of activity in our ever-changing world.

VI. THE LATIN NOTARY AND THE NOTARY PUBLIC

I have been asked to explain the difference between the Latin notary, on the one hand, and the notary public of the United States and English Canada, on the other hand.

Legal Education

Notaries in Quebec receive a full legal education and article before being admitted to the profession, while notaries public are not subject to any prerequisite other than being persons of good reputation with basic educations. As such, the notary public is not a professional but strictly a commissioned clerk.

Legal Counselling Or Advice

Legal counselling is an essential part of the Latin notary's function, while the notary public is neither permitted nor competent to give legal advice.

Lifetime vs Short-Term Appointment

The Latin notary is licensed for life and may be suspended for ethical reasons only. The American notary public's commission expires with time.

Certification Authority

The notary public has the power to certify, but his certification has limited probative effect.

The Latin notary is not obliged to testify before a court of justice with respect to notarial instruments unless their authenticity is challenged. Notarial deeds are proof in themselves, prima facie.

In the United States, a notarial seal means that certification is presumed to be authentic and clear, and convincing evidence must be brought to rebut certification. However, this presumption covers only the acknowledgement and genuineness of signature.

The fundamental difference between the two certifications resides in the fact that the notary public's certificate is not deemed to certify or guarantee the facts stated in the document to which it is attached. The notary public's certificate cannot override the hearsay rule; this justifies the exclusion of documents certified by a notary public from in-court testimony.

Fundamental Difference Between Civil Law And Common Law

The last distinction between the powers of certification of the Latin notary and the notary public calls for a few words on the essential philosophical approaches of the civil law and common law systems.

Until recently, the common law was a non-codified set of rules of law issued from the corpus of court decisions. In English tradition, judges pronounce the law and the judiciary adapts the law to cope with evolving society. In such a system, courts are the preeminent agents of law-making and the courtroom is where cases of law must be dealt with; thus the greatest value is given to court testimony.

Another element of this system, an almost complete absence of formalism in contracting, finds its source in the high moralistic values of a puritan society where one's word and a handshake were to be honoured in virtually all instances. Take, for example, the following typically Anglo-Saxon expressions: fair play, gentlemen's agreement, etc.

The civil law approach is found in societies with more secular philosophical values and is predisposed toward the value of writing. For civil law lawyers, testimonial evidence is "seen as temporary and susceptible to many subjective factors that might affect its value. Documentary evidence on the other hand is perceived as more objective and more reliable because it is contemporaneous with the act or accord amongst the parties and because it is prepared prior to the inception of litigation," not to mention the weaknesses of human beings, memory being an example.

In the civil law system, the written word is paramount in judicial proceedings, and the notarial document has been singled out for its particular probative value.

VII. TRENDS IN TODAY'S JUSTICE IN AMERICA

The "judicialization" of American society and the ever-increasing proportion of the GNP of the United States taken each year by the million-plus lawyers south of our border resulted, over a decade ago, in an in-depth examination of the American system of law.

I know of two such initiatives, the first being the creation of the Preventive Law Center of the University of Colorado. A team of professors and lawyers is considering the division of the legal profession and the introduction of a properly educated and trained non-litigious lawyer.

The second initiative is less ambitious but promises to produce quicker results: the creation of the CyberNotary.

In 1993, the Information Security Committee of the American Bar Association, searching for means to certify and secure electronic commerce, found a solution in the Latin notarial profession. The CyberNotary concept was developed and a distinct CyberNotary Committee was created in close collaboration with the United States Council for International Business and the International Union of Latin Notaries.

In short, the ABA committee would like to create another lawyer, distinct from present-day lawyers, with characteristics much like the Latin notary. Their main duty would be to ensure the security of business communications on electronic highways. If the concept materializes, as it may in the near future, the CyberNotary will be the first official specialization in law. Will this model then spread to other jurisdictions?

VIII. CONCLUSION

In 1948, the Quebec notarial profession was one of the founders of the International Union of Latin Notaries, a voluntary association with branches on four of the five continents.

Sixty-two countries are members, i.e. all Western European countries (except Denmark and England), Poland, Hungary, the Czech Republic, all South American countries, Japan, Vietnam, and four African countries. Many others have applied for admission: China, Russia, the Ukraine, Indonesia, and others. In 1985, Quebec was invited by the government of the People's Republic of China to help establish the Chinese notarial profession and is currently sponsoring its admission into the I.U.L.N. Presently, Quebec notaries are helping to establish a Latin notarial profession in the Ukraine. The project is sponsored by the Canadian government, which has participated to the extent of $1 million through a bilateral agreement between the governments of Canada and the Ukraine.

I will end here by adding that the Quebec notarial profession (probably because it has been until very recently a true civil-law island in an Anglo-Saxon sea of common law) is the one notarial organization under the spotlight of the international profession, since with globalization, Latin notaries of other countries are now feeling the pressure of American lawyers' battalions. They urgently need someone to tell them how to survive and develop in a world more and more dominated by American culture in all aspects of life. Now you know who that someone will be!

Footnote

I strongly recommend to those who would like to know more about the Latin notary to read an excellent paper by Notary Pedro A. Malavet in the Hasting International and Comparative Law Review, Spring 1996, entitled: Counsel for the Situation: The Latin Notary, A Historical and Comparative Model.

Reprinted with permission of the author.

Chapter 27

Becoming An Attorney At Law - Bar Admission In The U.S.

In the U.S. lawyers are referred to as Attorneys At Law. Some lawyers call themselves "Counselors At Law." This chapter will explore how to become an Attorney At Law.

The U.S. - Law School And Bar Admission

The process of becoming a lawyer in the U.S. is similar to the process of becoming a lawyer in Canada. There is a pre-law period, followed by three years of law school and then admission to the bar. **The most important difference between the U.S. and Canada is the process of bar admission. Whereas in Canada, one must successfully complete a lengthy bar admission course, in the U.S. one must pass the bar exam of the state in which one wants to practice.** The bar exam may be taken in the summer after completion of law school. This means that one can become a lawyer much faster in the U.S. than in Canada. There is no U.S. state which requires articling! (There are however some states which will allow you to be admitted to the bar based on "law office study." See the chapter on Non-Traditional Ways To Become A Lawyer.")

Each state sets its own bar exam. It is passing that bar exam and subsequently being admitted to the bar that gives one the right to practice law. The bar exam is not like the LSAT. Not everybody can take it. In order to take the bar exam one must have graduated from a law school approved by the American Bar Association (referred to as an ABA approved school) or have permission to take the exam by reason of having an equivalent kind of education. Anybody who graduates from an ABA approved school can take the bar exam. Graduates of other schools may take the bar exam under certain conditions, in certain places and at certain times. It is not automatic. In the past graduates of Canadian law schools (including the author of this book) have been granted permission to take the bar exams of certain states.

Let's backtrack a little and talk about each step of the process in more detail.

Pre-Law - The pre-law process is similar in both Canada and the U.S. In the U.S. students receive a Bachelors degree in four years. Hence, the overwhelming majority of applicants to U.S. law schools have a four year degree. When you research U.S. law schools you should ensure that you are eligible to apply to that particular school on the basis of having a three year Canadian degree. (I am aware of at least one school that questioned whether a Canadian was eligible to apply based on a three year B.A.) The best way to research U.S. law schools is by obtaining a copy of *The Official Guide To U.S. Law Schools* which is published by Law Services (and is now available online at www.LSAC.org). It contains a description of every ABA approved law school along with a discussion of the admission requirements of each school. The book will tell you what combination of grades and

LSAT score one needs to be competitive. This will allow you to determine whether you have a realistic chance of admission at that particular school. There is a greater range in standards for admission at U.S. schools than at Canadian schools. The most competitive are more competitive than the most competitive Canadian schools. The least competitive are much less competitive than the least competitive Canadian schools. It is essential that you apply to a large number of U.S. law schools. Before applying to U.S. law schools you must assess your chances of admission. As is the case in Canada, there is no specific pre-law curriculum.

The LSAT - The LSAT is required for admission to U.S. law schools. It is exactly the same test given at the same time on the same days.

The Law School Experience - Law school in the U.S. is a three year program. Because U.S. states are common-law jurisdictions, law school in the U.S. is very similar to law school in Canada. In fact the first year curriculum is almost identical. At the end of three years at a U.S. law school one graduates with a "J.D." degree. (The letters J.D. stand for Juris Doctor. In the U.S. law degrees are graduate degrees. The Canadian LL.B. stands for Bachelor of Laws.) J.D. and LL.B. degrees play the same role in determining eligibility for bar admission.

Bar Admission - In Canada admission to the bar of a province gives one the right to appear in the Federal Courts of Canada and the Supreme Court of Canada. In the U.S. admission to a state bar gives one the right appear in the courts of only that particular state. There are separate bars (and therefore admission requirements) for admission to the bars of federal courts and the Supreme Court of The United States. It is not difficult to be admitted to the bars of federal courts. For the most part it is conditioned on being a member of a state bar. Some Federal Courts require a separate exam and/or trial experience. Nevertheless, the primary hurdle that must be cleared is the bar exam of the state in which you wish to practice.

State Bar Exams: In most states the bar exam is given twice a year and lasts for two or three full days. In addition most states require that an additional exam in legal ethics be successfully taken. Although each state is free to develop its own bar exam, in practice one of the two days is a multiple choice (similar to the LSAT) test of general law called the "Multistate Bar Examination." The other day could consist of anything the individual state requires. In New York the bar examiners test approximately thirty subjects. The result is a very stressful period of time which culminates in two exhausting days of tests. Many states also require applicants to pass a separate ethics exam. To make matters worse a large number of people do fail the bar exam. For example, John F. Kennedy, Jr. failed the New York bar exam. At the end of this chapter you will find a wonderful "first hand" account of the stress of the bar exam by a law school graduate.

Who Controls Admission To The Bar? - In Canada admission to the bar is under the control of the law society in the province in which you wish to practice. In effect this means that your license to practice law is under the control of your business competitors. In the U.S. admission to the bar is under the control of (for the most part) the court of the state in which you wish to practice.

Is There A Citizenship Requirement? - During the early 1970s the Supreme Court of The United States held that a citizenship requirement to practice law was unconstitutional (In Re Griffiths). Therefore, one can be admitted to the bar in the U.S. without being a citizen.

The Effect Of NAFTA - This has created opportunities for the cross-border mobility of lawyers. See the chapter on "Mobility" for further details.

Immigration Requirements - Being admitted to a state bar will give you the right to practice law in that state, but will not give you the right to live in the U.S. Bar admission is unrelated to immigration considerations. If you are serious about wanting to move to the U.S. then you should consult a U.S. immigration lawyer. (NAFTA will give you the right to work in the U.S. under certain circumstances.)

U.S. Law School And Bar Admission In Canada - If your goal is to become a lawyer in Canada and practice law in Canada then you are better off going to a Canadian law school from the beginning. Although some

Canadian law schools will allow transfers from U.S. law schools you will find that it is very difficult. There are very few transfer spaces available in Canadian law schools. Hence, if you start off at a U.S. law school it is very likely that you will finish there and receive a J.D. degree. If at that point you wish to be admitted to the bar of a Canadian province you will find that your education will be assessed by the National Committee on Accreditation which may require you to take further Canadian legal studies. Once again, you will be faced with having to gain admission to a Canadian law school.

Although it is possible to attend a U.S. law school and do the Bar Admission Course in Canada you will find that it is more difficult. Hence, you should be careful about how you proceed.

You will find that the National Committee On Accreditation will be involved even if you have been admitted to a U.S. bar. (For more information, consult the "Mobility" chapter in this book.)

The Brain Drain - U.S. Law Firms Recruit Canadian Grads!

U.S. law firms have begun to hire graduates from Canadian law schools directly out of law school. Those fortunate to have this opportunity will work in the U.S. at much higher salaries. In addition, they can be admitted to a U.S. state bar faster than they can be admitted to the bar of a province. Hence, the Bar Admission Course can be avoided.

What Are The U.S. Bar Exams Like?

Read the following comments by a U.S. law school graduate.

"As I soon discovered, one day of the two-day bar exam is devoted to the Multistate Bar Examination (also referred to as the Multistate or simply the MBE). It covers six subjects that most states and territories consider basic to the practice of law, namely, contracts, torts, constitutional law, criminal law, real property, and evidence. Most of us hadn't even looked at those subjects since the first year of law school.

On the other day of the exam, you don't take a standardized national test. Instead, you answer questions posed by the state's bar examiners. The questions might require essays, or even a brief in which you tell an imaginary judge why your hypothetical client should win.

The examiners also reserve the right to cover a lot of different topics on the state portion. Here is what they told me about the New York exam that I was going to take:

In addition to the six subjects covered by the MBE, the New York section may also deal with Administrative Law, Agency, Bankruptcy, Carriers, [Ethics], Conflict of Laws, Corporations, Damages, Domestic Relations, Equity, Federal Jurisdiction, Insurance, Labor Law, Municipal Corporations, Negotiable Instruments, New York Constitutional Law, New York Practice and Procedure, Partnership, Personal Property, Sales, Suretyship, Taxation and Trusts and Estates. More than one subject may [appear] in a single question.

This was scary. I had worked in a law firm during my second summer. After that, I had decided to spend my third year of law school studying corporate law rather than preparing for the bar exam, so that I'd be ready for the demands of the job when I started work after graduation.

Besides, as a "national" school, _____ didn't even offer courses in some of the New York bar exam subjects. New York Civil Procedure, for example, was a nightmare of more than 120 legal-sized pages in my bar review book, and I'd never seen any of it before.

Thus, after three years in law school, I hadn't studied even half of the 23 non-Multistate subjects on which New York planned to test me. I had to learn or review them all in the two months between graduation and the July bar exam."

-A U.S. Law School Graduate

Conclusion

This has been an overview of the process of becoming a lawyer in the U.S. To learn about the exact requirements for admission to the bars of state courts and federal courts you should read the requirements for that specific jurisdiction.

APPENDIX

A Canadian At A U.S. Law School

"Life at DCL/MSU.

Growing up in London, Ontario Canada, I would never have imagined myself going to school in the United States. However, after completing four years in pursuing a Bachelor of Arts, Honors Degree at the University of Western Ontario, attending law school "south of the border" seemed the most vibrant and exciting option to me.

I came to the Detroit College of Law at Michigan State University because I wanted to endure the American "college experience". Football games with four downs instead of three, huge marching bands, and professors that required words like "favour" to be spelled with an -"or". DCL/MSU was also attractive to me as a Canadian because it offered many International Law Programs and Exchanges, not to mention a wide variety of Canadian-based courses.

My initial plan was to get my Juris Doctor Degree and head back north to practice. The Canadian course content and International Law background that DCL/MSU could provide was of absolute importance if I was to transfer back to Canada and write the BAR without spending years in "equivalency classes". After a year and a half living in East Lansing, however, my perspectives have changed. Now, I plan to stay in the United States and practice law. While obtaining a NAFTA VISA to remain will be difficult it will be no more difficult than finding a job in the saturated Canadian market.

My time at DCL/MSU has made the "college experience" more than I had ever anticipated. I have met fascinating and inspiring people, ranging from professors, legal speakers, and fellow students. I have sat in the upper deck bleachers of Spartan Stadium with the brisk, November wind pounding on my cheeks as the Green and White took on a mighty Big Ten opponent and I have made many great friends. Most importantly, however, I have learned the law and had a great time in doing so."

Chapter 28

Becoming A Barrister Or Solicitor - Bar Admission In The U.K.

The U. K. maintains the historical distinction between barristers and solicitors.

What Is The Distinction Between Barristers And Solicitors

"The barristers of England have not been replicated here as of this writing."

-F. Lee Bailey - 'To Be A Trial Lawyer'- Chapter 14

At the risk of oversimplification, the difference between barristers and solicitors is that barristers are lawyers who have been specifically trained for and specialize in trial work. North America (with the exception of Quebec) has not retained the distinction between barristers and solicitors.

Solicitors do some kinds of trial work and all other kinds of legal work.

Expanding On The Role Of The Barrister

By definition, a barrister provides advocacy service to the legal profession. A case will begin with a solicitor and that solicitor may refer the case to a barrister. Barristers are independent and objective. Their highly competitive training in litigation and advocacy, together with their specialist knowledge and experience in and out of court, can make a substantial difference to the outcome of a case, whether criminal or civil. Whatever the nature of the legal problem, it is important at an early stage to decide whether to involve a barrister. Solicitors tend to be more general practitioners, albeit now with increased rights of audience in the courts. The practice of a barrister is restricted to trial work. The practice of a solicitor is much broader and may include certain kinds of trial work. In the U.S. and the common law provinces of Canada all lawyers are licensed to do any kind of legal work. Interestingly, Quebec maintains the distinction between the Advocate and the Notary (roughly corresponding to the difference between a barrister and a solicitor). The point is that England and Quebec recognize a legal professional who is a specialist in advocacy!

The Need For Specialized Trial Lawyers

Should any lawyer be licensed to conduct trials? Many people think not. According to noted trial lawyer F. Lee Bailey:

"If there is a trial, it is to be hoped that a trial lawyer will be in command of the controversy. I say "to be hoped" because too many lawyers who do not have the experience or skill to do a professional job at handling a lawsuit will march into court nonetheless and "give it a whirl." There is little to prevent this, because our law has been far too slow to designate and certify specialists.

If you are a doctor who is other than a general practitioner, you choose early on the medical specialty that you wish to pursue and you concentrate on it. The training is long and rigorous, and the standards are high. The status of a "board certified" brain surgeon, psychiatrist, or cardiologist denotes a high level of skill and experience, carefully tested, and a solid protection for the public. Most people know that if you have a special medical problem, your doctor will recommend a specialist. A hospital will not extend staff privileges to a surgeon unless he truly is one.

Alas, courts offer the public no such protection. The unsuspecting client is led to believe that unless a lawyer is actually a specialist in trials, the judge would not allow him to try the case. Maybe things should be that way, but they are not. The fact is, with very few restrictions, any general practitioner of the law can walk in to court and conduct a trial. Judges may cringe at the ineptitude lawyers display at times, but, sadly, they seldom do anything about it. It is little wonder that many clients finish a trial bitterly disappointed not only with the results, but also with the poor service they have received."

-F. Lee Bailey - 'To Be A Trial Lawyer"- Chapter 1

Those who have lost a trial because the other side had a better lawyer would agree with Mr. Bailey.

Expanding On The Role Of A Solicitor

A solicitor's role is to give specialist legal advice and help. As society becomes more complicated the need for the services of the solicitor rises, and the profession's influence expands. Solicitors are the main advisers on all matters of law to the public. A career as a solicitor offers the chance to combine intellectual challenge, interest and variety with the opportunity to work with and for people.

General Practice

Solicitors in general practice usually work in a small or medium-sized firm, and serve the local community, dealing with the legal problems of the public.

They may carry out conveyancing (the buying and selling of houses and land), investigate claims which arise from injury, or advise and represent people in court on their client's behalf in criminal matters. Family law and child care law are important nowadays, and solicitors often represent clients in court in divorce cases. They make wills and administer the estates of people who have died.

Solicitors often advise businesses on such matters as employment laws, contracts and company formations.

Specialist Practices

Many large firms, particularly those in the City of London, or the business areas of other large cities, specialize in the large, corporate client who sometimes has urgent, multi-million pound deals. Such firms often have multi-national clients, and may have offices in major financial and business centres throughout the world. Many solicitors and firms specialize in areas of law in which they are expert, and specializations can include corporate and commercial law, insurance, the registration of patents and copyrights, shipping, banking, entertainment and media law and many others.

Other Opportunities

Not all solicitors work in private practice. It is possible for solicitors to work as in-house legal advisers to a commercial or industrial organization, to a government department or a local authority. The largest employer of lawyers in England and Wales is the Crown Prosecution Service, which advises the police about prosecution and prosecutes cases in the courts. Other opportunities include the Magistrates' Courts Service, law centres, charities, voluntary organizations and even the armed services. Many qualified solicitors, therefore, are in the enviable position of choosing when and how they work and the kind of work they wish to do.

The qualification is also recognized as a route of entry to wider business careers. The skills learned in law school and in the "Legal Practice Course", enable students to be flexible. Most want to go into the solicitor's profession, but some will branch out into other areas which require the range of techniques that you can gain with a legal background.

The Law That Governs Becoming A Barrister Or Solicitor

Under the Courts and Legal Services Act 1990 the Law Society (in the case of solicitors) and Bar Council (in the case of barristers) are responsible for laying down the qualification regulations in respect of those seeking to qualify as solicitors and barristers. The relevant web sites are:

For the Law Society: www.lawsociety.org.uk

For the Bar Council: www.barcouncil.org.uk

The Route To Becoming A Solicitor

The route to becoming a solicitor is more flexible than the route to becoming a lawyer in North America. There are three routes.

Route 1 - Graduating With A Degree In Law

Route 2 - Graduating With A Degree In Something Other Than Law

Route 3 - As A Non Graduate

Each of these will be discussed in turn.

Route 1 - Graduating With A Degree In Law

The steps in Route 1 are:

Step 1: Earn a "qualifying law degree" based on the foundations of legal knowledge.

The Content Of A "Qualifying Law Degree" - The Subjects

A program leading to a "qualifying law degree" includes the foundations of legal knowledge and development of legal research skills.

The Foundations of Legal Knowledge are:

1. Public Law, including Constitutional Law, Administrative Law and Human Rights;

2. Law of the European Union;

3. Criminal Law;

4. Obligations including Contract, Restitution and Tort;

5. Property Law; and

6. Equity and the Law of Trusts.

In addition, students receive training in legal research. This is quite similar to law school in North America.

Qualifying Law Degrees - Length, Format, Etc.

There are many ways of completing Qualifying Law Degrees. They include:

- 3 and 4 year full time law degrees

- 4 to 6 year part time law degrees

- joint and mixed honours degrees

- senior status law degrees both full and part-time

- University of London, External LL.B. Degrees

- exempting law degrees

- the Open University LL.B. degree

These formats offer far more flexibility than anything available in Canada or the U.S.

Step 2: Complete the "Legal Practice Course" which takes one year of full-time study or two years of part-time study.

The Legal Practice Course is analogous to the teaching component of the Bar Admission Course in Canadian provinces. There is, however, one major difference. The Legal Practice Course in England has a number of providers. In Canada the course is run by the Law Society.

The Legal Practice Course Format

The curriculum of the Legal Practice Course comprises:

Core Areas

These are identified as necessary to set certain contexts for the course or to cover an area of practice reserved for solicitors. They comprise:

The Ethical Context - an introduction to the principles of

Professional Conduct and Client Care, including the Solicitors'

The Skills Context - an introduction to the legal skills of advocacy, interviewing and advising, writing and drafting and practical legal research.

The Taxation Context - an introduction to the principles of taxation, trusts and tax planning.

The European Context - an introduction to the principles of EU Law.

Probate & Administration of Estates - the basic principles of testate and intestate succession, and of the practice and procedure of obtaining grants of representation and the winding up of an estate.

Compulsory Areas

- Litigation & Advocacy

- Business Law & Practice

- Conveyancing

All three areas will combine substantive law, procedure and practical skills work.

Elective Areas

Students will be required to study three electives from a range covering subjects of interest in 'Private Client' and 'Corporate Client' work. It is open to practitioners and other groups to suggest to the Legal Practice Course Board areas of law for inclusion as elective areas and these will be communicated to the teaching institutions on a regular basis.

Pervasive Areas

Certain topics have been identified as of such importance that they should be taught and assessed through the relevant compulsory and elective areas of the course. These topics include:

- Accounts

- Professional Conduct and Client Care (including Financial Services)

- European Union Law

- Revenue Law

Skills Areas

The course will seek to develop certain essential skills including:

- Practical Legal Research

- Writing & Drafting

- Interviewing & Advising

- Advocacy

Step 3: Complete a two year training period.

The two year training period is analogous to the Articling component of the Bar Admission Course in a Canadian province.

The basic purpose is to consolidate and develop the skills learned in the Legal Practice Course. During the training period, a Professional Skills Course must also be completed.

As is the case with the articling experience in Canada, training periods can be served with both large and small firms. With a large firm the training period is likely to be more structured.

A number of organizations and individuals are involved in the training process. However, some duties and responsibilities are a matter of good practice. An outline of the roles of those involved in training is given below:

The Law Society - determines the requirements of the Training Contract, Training Code and Professional Skills

Course; provides advice and guidance to trainees and firms; monitors firms and course providers to ensure that the requirements are being met.

The Training Establishment - is the firm or organization authorized to provide the training. It must meet the requirements of the Training Code, appoint a Training Principal and comply with the obligations of the Training Contract. Authorized firms are routinely monitored to ensure that they are providing adequate training in accordance with the Training Code. The Training Principal - is nominated by a training establishment and is a partner or solicitor of equivalent status. The Training Principal undertakes to comply with the Training Code and takes responsibility for the student.

Supervisors - The Training Principal may delegate the day-to-day supervision of work to another solicitor, partner or experienced legal executive. Depending upon the size of the firm the "trainee solicitor" may be supervised by more than one person during his or her training period.

The Trainee Solicitor - Enters into a Training Contract and takes on certain responsibilities and obligations.

The Professional Skills Course

During the training period and before applying for admission to the roll, one must satisfactorily complete the Professional Skills Course (PSC). This course comprises compulsory courses in:

- Financial & Business Skills

- Advocacy & Communication Skills

- Ethics & Client Responsibilities

Step 4: Be admitted to the Roll of Solicitors.

To apply for admission to the roll one must have satisfactorily completed:

- the training and your training principal must confirm this; and

- the Professional Skills Course

Route 2 - Graduating With A Degree In Something Other Than Law

Those with a degree in a subject other than law, must complete a one year full-time (or two year part-time) course leading to the Common Professional Examination (CPE) or the post-graduate Diploma in Law (PgDL). These courses are offered at a number of institutions. Successful completion of either the CPE or PgDL is the equivalent of a Qualifying Law Degree and allows one to enter the Legal Practice Course, followed by the training period, the Professional Skills Course and admission to the Rolls.

Note that (at the time of writing) it is possible to take the course leading to either CPE or the PgDL if you are a graduate of an overseas university. (Those North Americans who always wanted to become English Solicitors should take note.)

Route 3 - The Non Degree Route To Qualification

This route is similar to "law office study" which is available in some U.S. states. No analogy for this exists in Canada.

Legal Executives

For those who do not wish to earn a degree, it is possible to qualify as a solicitor by obtaining employment in a legal office, joining the Institute of Legal Executives and taking the examinations to qualify as a member and subsequently a Fellow of the Institute of Legal Executives. This can be a stepping stone to qualifying as a solicitor.

The process is lengthy, demanding and academically difficult, but enables the non-graduate to qualify as a solicitor. Further information about this, and a career as a legal executive, can be obtained from the Institute of Legal Executives, Kempston Manor, Kempston, Bedford, MK42 7AB.

The Route To Becoming A Barrister

Introduction

By definition, a barrister provides a specialist consulting and advocacy service to the legal profession. Solicitors tend to be more general practitioners, albeit now with increased rights of audience. The majority of barristers work in private practice. About a quarter are employed by a range of organizations including the Government Legal Service, the Crown Prosecution Service, industry, commerce and the armed forces.

Increasingly employers are looking for graduates who possess specific skills fitting them for the changing world of work. Flexibility and the ability to adapt and manage change are essential requirements. The situation is no different for 'would be' barristers. There are discernible skills which students must be able to demonstrate if they are to be successful in qualifying as a barrister and surviving in a competitive professional and business world.

These skills include:

- academic ability

- written and oral communication skills

- numeracy skills

- interpersonal skills

- personal effectiveness

- IT skills

- professional responsibility

- a commitment to continuing professional development

Training as a barrister is divided into **three stages - academic, vocational and practical.**

Stage 1 - Academic

The academic stage is common to both barristers and solicitors and can be completed by taking either a Qualifying Law Degree or a degree in another subject supplemented by the conversion course, which could take the form of the Common Professional Examination (CPE) or an approved Post Graduate Diploma in Law (PgDL). The academic stage is designed to ensure that the student has a basic body of legal knowledge, which can be assumed and built upon at the vocational stage.

Stage 2 - Vocational

The vocational stage of training comprises the Bar Vocational Course (BVC). Before commencing a BVC, a student has to be a member of an Inn of Court. Training in the course builds upon the theoretical knowledge learned during the academic stage and helps ensure that students intending to become a barrister acquire the skills, knowledge of procedure and evidence, attitudes and competence to prepare them for "Stage 3."

The Bar Vocational Course - Further Comments on Stage 2

Course Format and Assessment

The purpose of the course is to ensure that students intending to become a barrister acquire the skills and knowledge to prepare them, in particular, for the more specialized training in the twelve months of pupillage. The full-time Bar Vocational Course (BVC) runs for one academic year and the part-time course for two years. All students are required to be admitted to an Inn of Court before registration on the Bar Vocational Course.

Bar Vocational Course Content

The main skills taught in the Bar Vocational Course are:

Case Work Skills Which Include:

- Fact Management

- Legal Research

Written Skills Which Include:

- General written skills

- Opinion-writing (that is giving written advice)

 - Drafting (of various types of documents)

Interpersonal Skills Which Include:

- Conference Skills (interviewing clients)

- Negotiation

 - Advocacy (court or tribunal appearances)

The main areas of knowledge taught in the Bar Vocational Course are:

- Civil Litigation

- Criminal Litigation

- Evidence

- Sentencing

- Two optional subjects selected by the student

Stage 3 - Practical

 The practical stage of training on the job, namely twelve months of pupillage. (analagous to articling in Canada)

Pupillage -Comments on Stage 3

All those wishing to practice at the Bar of England and Wales are required to do twelve months pupillage. This is divided into two six-months periods, the non-practicing and practicing. Pupillage is the final stage of the route to qualification at the Bar, in which the pupil gains practical training under the supervision of an experienced barrister. It is analogous to the Canadian articling requirement.

Are Pupils Entitled To Be Paid?

Canadian articling students are paid. This may not be true of English "pupils." On March 10, 2000 the English Court Of Appeal ruled that "pupils" in barristers' chambers are not entitled to be paid. Basically, the court held that a "pupil" barrister was not a "worker" under the relevant employment statute. A recent article in Law Times reported that as many as 43 percent of pupils are not paid at all or are paid under 6000 pounds per year! Those Canadian articling students who complain about their plight should take note!

The Bar Council recently approved the extension of continuing professional development to all practicing barristers throughout their careers. This is consistent with the trend in many U.S. states where continuing education is mandatory.

How Can Foreign Lawyers Become Solicitors In England?

It is not overly difficult. The primary requirement is to pass the Qualified Lawyer Transfer Test (QLTT).

Overview Of The Qualified Lawyers Transfer Test

The Qualified Lawyers Transfer Test (QLTT) is a conversion Test which enables lawyers qualified in certain countries outside England and Wales, as well as UK Barristers to qualify as solicitors. In an increasingly competitive business world, lawyers with a dual or more qualifications will be able to offer a more comprehensive service to clients.

The Test covers four Heads:

Property

Litigation

Professional Conduct & Accounts

Principles of Common Law

The Law Society will determine which Head or Heads you must pass dependent upon your primary professional qualification. You will need to apply for a certificate of eligibility from the Law Society before you apply to sit the Test. Contact the Law Society at www.lawsociety.org.uk for further information.

Conclusion

This chapter has explained the distinction between barristers and solicitors. It has explained how to become either. Finally, it has described how "foreign" lawyers can become U.K. solicitors. For real anecdotal experiences, read the following appendixes.

APPENDIX A

A Canadian Lawyer Is Admitted To The U.K. Bar

For what it is worth, anecdotal evidence suggests that it is very easy for North American lawyers to become solicitors in England. Consider the following perspective from a Toronto lawyer who became a U.K. Solicitor.

The new face of practicing law: multiple calls to the bar

Gil Lan

I recently obtained my qualification as a solicitor in the United Kingdom. In addition, I am already a qualified Canadian and American lawyer. Many people (including lawyers) have asked me why and how I became a lawyer qualified in the United Kingdom. This article briefly answers those questions.

1. Why become a U.K. solicitor if you are already a Canadian/American lawyer?

"The world is becoming one big global village" - I practice primarily business law. Since the early 1980's there has been a large increase in international business transactions. These international transactions frequently involve the laws of other countries such as England. Being a qualified U.K. solicitor assists me in advising my clients about transactions involving English law or the laws of any other Commonwealth country.

Competition - As stated above, the ability to practise law in England can be a very useful asset. This allows me to offer my clients expertise that many other lawyers don't have. My increased accessibility to clients is also a two way street. Not only do Canadians who wish to do business in the U.K. contact me, but also, businesses from the U.K. who wish to do business in Canada call me as well.

Prestige - England is originator of the system of law called the "common law". Many other former Commonwealth countries, including Canada, Australia, New Zealand, Singapore, Hong Kong etc., have their legal system based upon English common law. As a result, a U.K. solicitor is a respected and recognized lawyer in many parts of the world.

Options - the world is an ever-changing place and the more options you have, the better. Since I am a U.K. solicitor, I have the option to practise law there if I wish someday. In addition, I would have an easier time qualifying as a lawyer in many common law countries since the U.K. system of law is well recognized.

2. How does one become a U.K. solicitor?

First, qualify as a Canadian or American lawyer - If you are a Canadian or American lawyer, you can apply to become a U.K. solicitor. You must have at least two years working experience as a lawyer.

Second, complete detailed exam application form - there is a detailed exam application form that must be completed and submitted to the Law Society (England and Wales). You will have to send certified academic records and certificates establishing that you are a lawyer in your home country. Based upon your education, experience and country where you practise law, the Law Society will determine how many of their qualification exams you must write. Typically, Canadian lawyers have to write fewer exams than American lawyers. This is due to the close similarities between the Canadian and U.K. legal systems.

Third, write and pass your designated exams - The U.K. bar exams are held 2-3 times a year. You don't have to fly to England to write them. If you are a Canadian, you can write them here in Toronto where they will be supervised by the Law Society of Upper Canada.

Fourth, upon passing exams, apply to be registered as a solicitor - upon passing the exams, you will be given a certificate indicating that you have passed. You need to fill out an application form to be registered as a solicitor and submit it to the appropriate governing body in England.

3. The future - As countries become much more globalized, one can expect to see an increase in the number of international legal issues arising. In such a global economy, it would be a good idea to be qualified as a lawyer in more than one country. While some people view this as more work in addition to getting your standard law degree and qualification, it is certainly worthwhile. Being a lawyer is more than getting a law degree. Going to law school and getting a law degree is just the beginning of the journey and obtaining multiple international qualifications is just one of the roads you may wish to consider.

About the Author: Gil Lan, B.Sc., LL.B., LL.M. (International Trade and Competition Law) is a lawyer practising international and local business / corporate law. He is a qualified lawyer in Canada, U.S.A. and the United Kingdom. In addition to practising law, he is a part-time professor at Ryerson Polytechnic University where he teaches business law courses. He is the instructor for the "Legal Aspects of International Trade" course for the Forum for International Trade Training. He is also a co-author of the book "Counselling Corporations and Advising Businesses" which is a reference and guide for lawyers.

Reprinted with permission of the author.

APPENDIX B

A Canadian Attends Law School In The U.K.

What follows is a very interesting perspective (written in 2000) from a Canadian university graduate who is currently attending law school in England.

"I hope that you will find the information contained in this letter helpful, but this letter provides the information "as is" and makes no representations or warranties of any kind regarding it. I disclaim all liability of any kind whatsoever arising out of your use of this letter and the information contained in it.

'The following is a statement of opinion not fact.'

Part 1 - Prior To Leaving - My Decision To Attend Law School In England

"I studied Philosophy at the University of Western Ontario and graduated in 1999 with Honors. I am currently enrolled in a four-year program where I spend two years at the University of Exeter, in England and another two years at the University of Connecticut in the U.S. At the end of which time I will have my LL.B. and my J.D.

I am enrolled in what is called a Senior Status LL.B. that allows anyone with a previous degree to enter into the second year of the LL.B. program. Most of the Universities in England have similar programs. In the second year of the program you do Tort, Contract Law, Criminal Law and Constitutional Law. After the third year of the program, providing you maintain a high average and you meet the 'regular' requirements of admission, you will be enrolled into the J.D. program at the University of Connecticut. The two programs are independent of each other in two ways. Firstly, there is no automatic entry into the J.D. program at the University of Connecticut, although a good performance at Exeter will secure you a place. You will normally apply to Connecticut at the end of your first year at Exeter. You may enroll in the University of Connecticut for a year as a visiting student or as an LL.M. student or if you are prepared to spend a second year you would be eligible for the J.D. Secondly, the courses you take at Exeter only count towards your LL.B. It is not possible to take courses for credit towards your J.D. while in England. The fee structures are also independent of one another, so, while you will pay International tuition fees in England, of around $6500 -$ 7800, you will also pay, as an International student, around $22,000 - $30,000 per year in the U.S. for tuition, books, etc.

To gain admission into a British University or college, you must apply through UCAS (Universities and Colleges Admission Services). It is similar to OLSAS except, the application is for all the Universities and Colleges in Britain. It operates as the only central applications service for full-time undergraduate courses in the U.K. You can choose up to six courses, but if you are applying for medicine, dentistry, veterinary medicine or veterinary science, you can only choose four. After reading the prospectuses from the Universities that were of interest to me, I sent in my application and was subsequently accepted into all of my six choices. The institutions assess your application on the basis on your qualifications and therefore it would be particularly erroneous to believe that you have a greater chance of entry into law school in the U.K. based on the fact that you only need your 'A' Levels for admission. If your grades are poor, chances are, you will not be offered a place, especially not at one of the top ranking Universities. How do you know which Universities are top ranking? The Times has many articles and rankings of the Universities in the U.K. and you can find that information online to enable you to make a more informed decision.

You must also bear in mind that not all programs are published in the Universities prospectuses. In fact, there was no information regarding this program in the prospectus for the University of Exeter. I enquired about dual degree programs and one of the lecturers at the University of Connecticut wrote to me telling me of this opportunity. You have to do as much research as possible and ask as many questions as you need in order for you to make an informed decision.

You can choose to do a combined LL.B./J.D. such as the one I am enrolled in or you can do the LL.B. with a year in any country in Europe, some programs even allow you to graduate with the relevant degree from the country of study. Most of the Universities in England have the combined LL.B. with European study. For example, if you have advanced French, you can choose to spend a year in France studying the law in that country and you will graduate with your LL.B. with French Law.

The notion that at the end of your four years you should have two degrees and not one degree is particularly apposite in an era where the competition is fierce. I consider any dual degree qualification worthwhile, whether it is your LL.B./J.D., LL.B./M.B.A., LL.B./MA etc. It is important to do your research and figure out where you want to practise law, what general area of the law interests you and then make your decision.

My decision to leave Canada was not an easy one and the choice to pursue my current path filled with trepidation. I originally wanted to enroll in the dual qualification program that was offered by the University of Windsor but its cancellation marked a watershed in my decision making process. For me this decision became increasingly easier the more information I had. U.S. law firms, particularly the larger law firms in states such as N.Y. and Massachusetts, pay graduates a starting salary of $100-$150 K (USD) and during the summer internships you get paid $2400 (USD) per week. That is not including the bonuses, potential for upward mobility and your yearly increase in salary based on your performance. The difference is certainly appreciable between the practice of law in Canada, England and the U.S. With the comparatively low starting salaries for lawyers in Canada, the tax structure, the competition for firms on 'Bay Street', and the lack of dual degree jurisdictional programs, my choice seemed like no choice at all.

I chose to do the J.D. as opposed to the LL.M. even though I wish to practice in New York because I want to be more marketable. The majority of the states require the J.D. along with other requirements for the admission to the Bar. The choices are numerous and whatever decision you make will in all probability, bear consequences both positive and negative. Certainly try to place yourself in the best position for future employability wherever you are, bearing in mind what you would like the eventual outcome to be. Good Luck!"

Part 2 - After Arriving - How I Experience Law School In England

The Good, the Debatable and the Ugly!

The Good:

The potential opportunities while studying in England are endless. I am sure there are equivalent opportunities in any country you choose to study. In England, there are many opportunities to improve your language skills, which have become increasingly important to employers. You are almost expected to be fluent in more than one language.

Universities in England operate Erasmus schemes where students from the U.K. do part of their degree in a European country. There are a variety of choices, for example you can do the European LL.B. and do half of the last year in France and the other half in Germany. Living in England affords you the opportunity to travel to anywhere in Europe for prices well below 100. There are always student specials and you can experience the rich culture and language of Europe while getting a first class education.

Tuition expenses are considerably lower in comparison to that of U.S. schools. The fees for Universities in England can be anywhere from 6,200- 7,800. If you are an International student in Canada, the fees are almost the same, depending on the province in which you choose to live. For example, your fees for the University of New Foundland will be much cheaper than your fees for a school in Ontario. Living in Hall in Exeter cost around 88-97 per week for catered accommodation (this includes three meals a day, seven days a week) and 48- 80 for self catered accommodation. These prices reflect all of England although the popular cities have higher living expenses. I lived in Toronto for a year and I find that the overall expenses for food and accommodation are cheaper in Exeter than in Toronto.

The Debatable:

It is debatable as to whether doing your LL.B. and J.D. is smart decision. One needs only look at the countless articles from lawyers who have pursued this path to see that it may not be as clear cut a path to success as it seems (then again, nothing ever is).

The issues get increasingly complicated as you progress into your course. I am technically in the second year of my LL.B. program and students studying law around the world are at this very moment applying to law firms for internships during the summer 2001. My opportunity for gaining an internship seems to be a bit precarious to say the least. Where do I apply for internships? Do I apply in Canada, England or the United States? If your answer to this question would be Canada, you should at least be aware of the difficulty of obtaining an internship in Canada.

Firstly, law firms in Canada have very little places in relation to the number of students who apply every year.

Secondly, the firms want to know that you are going to practice in Canada when you complete your studies. If you plan on doing this, your best bet would be to attend law school in Canada, rather than face the uphill battle to obtain not only internships for your summers, but, admission to the bar when your studies are completed.

You will also face some difficulties if your answer to this question was the United States. There will undoubtedly be U.S. law firms who will be greatly interested in you because of your potential fluency in both jurisdictions. However, you will still have to deal with the fact that you are in second year, but are only equipped with one year of law school and that year, is one year of English Law with no knowledge as yet of U.S. law. You will most certainly have grave competition for law firm internships in the United States, at least during your second year.

That leaves England! The choices become even more complex with the split in the legal profession between Barristers and Solicitors. Should I do a pupillage (internships for Barristers) or should I enroll on a vacation scheme (internships for Solicitors)? You will still be faced with the difficulty of having only one year of law, however, you may be able to overcome this because you would have a Bachelors degree and perhaps some work experience and not many English students will be able to compete with that.

Suffice it to say, the path to your legal career armed with your J.D./LL.B., although exciting and filled with opportunities, is also filled with an incredible amount of trepidation. With the globalization of legal services, it is hard to see why there are restrictions on foreign attorneys and foreign-trained law graduates, particularly in the United States. It may not be as important to understand this as it is to acknowledge that these restrictions exist and make your decision with all the relevant facts.

The Ugly:

If you study law in England you will undoubtedly be surrounded by teenagers 18-20 years of age. You are sometimes faced with the occasional barbs and comments intended to be facetious but are unpleasant nevertheless.

These comments are in regards to your age and the amazement of these students that you can still be studying after age 24! If you live in hall, you may also face the problem of loud music, students getting wasted and in tears the following morning because they were not able to do their assignment. They also tend to get upset at the most trivial of things, like you not being able to accompany them to the mall. This may be related to immaturity rather than physical age.

You crave the friendship of someone your own age who can relate to your experiences and understand the things you say and rates for international calling in England are very high and therefore you cannot call your friends or family at home too often. The food in England is bland and I eat a lot more salt as a result! The weather is depressing because it rains almost all the time and when it is not raining it is overcast.

How do you deal with these issues? The comments do not bother me for more than a mere second or two until I come to the realization that firstly, any vituperative epithets are frequently insulting to pride rather than disparaging your reputation. Secondly, these issues are mere peccadilloes in the grand scheme of things. Thirdly they are too young too know any better and hence can be exculpated as a result. If the truth were told, it also feels good to know that, not only do you know the meaning of the word 'vituperative', you also know how to handle your work much better than an 18 year old can.

Conclusion

I really believe that in life there will always be negative and positive aspects to whatever decisions you make, whether it be choosing a law school or choosing where to eat for dinner. It is not always certain what choices will yield the greatest benefit but I am a consequentialist and believe that there must be a way to achieve the things you want in life, you must however accept the good with the bad. That being said, I will take my chances on the J.D./LL.B. option. I trust that with the globalization and rapidly increasing cross-border legal services required to help clients achieve their objectives across a wide range of jurisdictions, my fluency in both jurisdictions will appeal to at least some international law firms. Any potential problems along the way are merely challenges that must be overcome. I am doing well in my course and enjoying studying law in England, I do about 5-8 hours of work per day not including class time. The required hours of study are about 3 hours per day. Classes are usually 8 hours per week with 2 hours per week of workshop. I will be enrolling in a three-week intensive course in Strasbourg, France in March to attend lectures on comparative legal systems. I feel confident about my decision to pursue the LL.B./J.D. and I do not have any regrets."

Reprinted with permission of the author.

APPENDIX C

A Senior Barrister's Perspective On Student Barristers

"Stemming the young bar tide

Ronald Thwaites

Ronald Thwaites Q.C. likens the huge number of aspiring barristers to modern-day refugees from central Europe. He says the profession must radically improve its border controls

London is to the legal profession what Hollywood is to the film industry.

Droves of your hopefuls are hypnotized by the bright lights and by the idea that the streets are paved with legal aid certificates and traineeships.

The young do not heed warnings, nor do they read statistics about failure rates. Thousands of surplus young people arrive at the English Bar; like modern day refugees from Eastern Europe, on one-way tickets, carrying their possessions in a bedspread, homeless and in search of a better life.

They are student barristers, known as pupils, who have found no permanent place in the profession. Most complete their compulsory twelve month pupillage and stay on in the legal ghetto for a time, doing further spells as pupils or "squatters" as they have become known.

Some are fortunate and manage to find a tenancy in good, decent or half-decent chambers and from there they can look forward to building a legal career. Others take temporary refuge in minor sets, or sets that are badly run or have no work "clip-joint chambers" who simply want to bleed the young of rent, while providing no backup or prospects.

Those who are desperate cling on in the forlorn hope that somehow work will come in. In the end, after enduring further hardships and privations, without obtaining their legal passports, weighed down by debt and disillusionment, many are deported back to the real world.

There are nearly 10,000 barristers in England and Wales (more than half of them are in London), but there is too little work to keep all barristers fully employed. For a tiny minority there is too much work, but for the general run of barristers there is a struggle to maintain and improve their position. Around half the Bar is less than 10 years call.

Barristers, die or they retire, or become judges and fall out of fashion. But vacancies through natural wastage are not clear cut. If a senior leaves changers, his work may be re-distributed to others there or just disappear. It is not like the civil service where an empty desk represents a job to be done. Life at the Bar is more ephemeral in nature and quite often when a barrister disappears, his work does too.

There are a small number of real vacancies every year - varying between 300 and 500 at most - but at least 1000 new pupils want to start each year. How can they be accommodated when there are no jobs for them?

The educational requirements have risen, so that these days most aspiring barristers must have at least ABC at A level and an upper second degree. But the number of aspirants keeps rising, encouraged in part by the proliferation of course providers.

Universities would provide degree courses in kite-flying, roller-blading and repairing typewriters if they thought that students would pay fees to them in large enough numbers. But, they would not provide job opportunities in any of these fields.

It appears we are unable or unwilling to control entry into our profession because of cries of "restrictive practices or monopoly" that might be heard. This is typical of the cowardly approach we are notorious of adopting in relation to our professional affairs.

It must surely be better to control entry, than to have an open-door policy that slams shut in the face of the would-be barrister after he or she has spent years of their life and thousands of pounds struggling to qualify. Veterinary surgeons have strictly controlled entry to their profession to ensure that they have only sufficient vets to service demand. It is tough to get into, but at least those who make it are sure of being successful in finding a job. Perhaps we could learn something from them.

In addition to being swamped by new recruits, the Bar has suffered upheavals elsewhere.

At least half the Bar's members (and perhaps many more) rely wholly or in part on criminal work. A number of factors have affected that source of work.

Fewer cases are being committed for trial at crown court. Committal proceedings themselves have been simplified, take less time and provide less work for the Bar.

Solicitors are also doing more of the work in-house that was traditionally sent to the Bar. Standard (and significantly lower) fees have been introduced and are spreading to more and more cases. Publicly funded work, has been, or is being capped.

Meanwhile prosecution work will be further reduced when the Crown Prosecution Service (backed by the Government) gets rights of audience in all courts.

And on the civil side, an increasing number of City companies are using their own in-house solicitors to settle pleadings, a job that until recently went to counsel.

The concept of "no win no fee" is the latest unwelcome U.S. import, which inevitably means that in a portion of cases barristers will not be paid for their work (depending on a combination of skill, judgement and luck).

Methinks Mrs Worthington, you would be better to put your daughter on the stage.

But what can be done? One suggestion I would make is that if you want to practice law, do a law degree as your first degree. It is an expensive indulgence to take history or English only to spend an extra year on the conversion course. The other advantage of a law degree is that it teaches you how to use a library (something that does not come naturally to many) and to distinguish between a crime and a tort.

But the most fundamental change I would introduce would be to bring back the correspondence course as a means of qualifying for the Bar. I did the Bar exams myself by correspondence course while I was employed full-time in the City earning my own living.

Many people took the Bar correspondence course to enhance their promotion prospects. In its olde worlde form as "barrister-at-law" it became a standard qualification for those who wanted, for example, to become a company secretary.

Many others, like myself, took the course because they wanted to practice at the Bar, but lacked the funds to do the nine-month full-time course, while their local authority refused to pay for it.

There will be those who claim that the new Bar course - with its emphasis on practical exercises, advocacy training and court visits - could not be completed by correspondence. But in over 20 years of selecting and monitoring pupils and assisting in choosing them as tenants, I have not noticed any improvement in their starting abilities, either on paper or on their feet, since the "practical" content was introduced.

It is only the essential training they get in pupillage that will equip them to be released on a trusting public. They can cut their teeth on small work and start the long training that will eventually turn them into creditable journeyman barristers.

I do not believe that we should be paying money to third year undergraduates, as was proposed by Peter Goldsmith Q.C. in his latest contribution to the future of the Bar.

If graduates went out to work and spent time in business and commerce while studying for the Bar, they would acquire valuable knowledge of the world. They gain business and commercial maturity and, if a career at the Bar did not materialize, they would have useful contacts to help them pursue a different career path.

We will never be able to guarantee a pupillage at the Bar, to all those who want one, but we could improve things by making it cheaper to qualify. The only way of achieving that, unless we pay students, is the correspondence course. I do not know why that method was abolished in the first place."

Reprinted with permission of the author.

APPENDIX D

Joining An Inn

Introduction

There are four Inns of Court (Lincoln's Inn, Inner Temple, Middle Temple and Gray's Inn). Anyone wishing to train for the Bar must join one of the Inns and the Inns alone have the power to call a student to the Bar. Only those called are able to exercise rights of audience in the superior courts of England and Wales as barristers.

The Inns are principally non-academic societies which provide collegiate and educational activities and support for barristers and student barristers. These include a library, lunching and dining facilities, common rooms and gardens. They also provide a limited number of grants and scholarships for the various stages along the way to becoming a barrister.

Admission to an Inn is required before registration in the Bar Vocational Course, although many undergraduates join before this stage in order to participate in the activities, use the library, or start dining. A student's choice of Inn does not affect the area of law in which they wish to practice or their choice of pupillage or tenancy.

Students are required to complete 12 qualifying units in order to be called to the Bar. This can be achieved through a number of different ways:

Attendance at:

- Weekends either in the Inn or at a residential centre such as Cumberland Lodge

- Education Days (primarily for out of London students) - Education Dinners (with lectures or talks) - Domus Dinners (when students and seniors dine together) - Social Dinners (such as Grand Night or student guest nights or dinners at the providers). The weekends will count as 3 units, the days will count as 2 units and dinners and Call Night will count as 1 unit.

Each Inn runs advocacy training courses for their pupils. The programs vary in format and length and combine advocacy training with lecturers on particular areas of law or forensic skills.

Additionally, each Inn has student societies and supports involvement in debating activities which range from internal events to inter-Inn, national and international competitions. The students organize their own social events through their Inns' student association and some Inns also support sporting societies.

Further Information
Lincoln's Inn
Students' Department
Treasury Office
Lincoln's Inn
London WC2A 3TL
Telephone: 0207 405 0138

Inner Temple
Education & Training Department
Treasurer's Office
Inner Temple
London EC4Y 7HL
Telephone: 0207 797 8250

Middle Temple
Students' Department
Treasury Office
Middle Temple
London EC4Y 9AT
Telephone: 0207 427 4800

Gray's Inn
Education Department
8 South Square
Gray's Inn
London WC1R 5EU
Telephone: 0207 458 7900

Book VI - A Report

The World Is Your Oyster
- Lawyers' Mobility In A Global World

Summary And Introduction

My Advice To You Is ....

Think of yourself as a "global professional" right from the beginning. Take all possible steps to enhance your professional mobility. In law school take courses that will give you exposure to the Constitutions of Mexico, Canada and the United States (NAFTA Partners). Learn about the law of the European Community. Joint law degrees are great things. And again, get yourself admitted to the bar of more than one country.

Your career as a lawyer will be completely different from the career your parents may have had as lawyers. There are more opportunities in terms of both the work a lawyer does and where the lawyer may work.

Book VI, will alert you to "mobility issues in a global world." It will also provide suggestions for how you may wish to prepare for a global world right from the first day of law school.

In Book VI, I will play the role of a "international career consultant" introducing you to various locations you may work.

Book VI - Chapter Summaries

29. Canadian Lawyers And Law Graduates - Foreign Bar Admission And Working Abroad

Focus: Take that Canadian law degree and/or Bar Admission and use it to pursue opportunities in other countries, NAFTA, eligibility to take the Bar Exam, Foreign Legal Consultants, etc.

30. Foreign Trained Law Graduates And Lawyers - Canadian Bar Admission

Focus: So, you are a lawyer from outside North America. How do you get your license to practise law in Canadian provinces or U.S. states?

Chapter 29

Canadian Lawyers And Law Graduates - Foreign Bar Admission And Working Abroad

Using Your Law Degree To Work Around The World

The practice of law ceased to be provincial (no pun intended) a long time ago. It is becoming increasingly likely that Canadian and U.S. law graduates will make use of their skills in another country. The purpose of this chapter is to explain how that can be done. What follows is:

"All you need to know about lawyers' mobility, but didn't even know to ask."

Let's begin with two stories of two Canadian lawyers.

A Canadian Immigrant Takes His Legal Education Home

November 21, 1997

"Young lawyers, rule of law both struggling in Vietnam

Brad Daisley

Born in South Vietnam, but raised and educated in Canada, Tim Dang returned to his homeland a year ago to open Burns Solicitors' office in Hanoi.

In association with the Vietnamese Ministry of Finance, he is working on a proposal for developing the country's securities market.

He also works as in-house counsel for an Australian-Canadian mining consortium that is exploring in North Vietnam.

It's home, I can talk the language, but in terms of the values, in terms of the lifestyle, I am almost a stranger, even though I have become more and more assimilated back.

To my surprise, I like it here [in the north part of Vietnam] more than in the south, even though I was born in the south.

There is a marked difference [between the north and the south]. In the south, the economy is more dynamic, the people are less conservative, more easy-going and more commercially oriented.

But it can also be a nastier place if you are not careful. In the north, even though they are more reserved, [they] are easier to get along with. We [Canadians] have some reserve ourselves.

The biggest problem here is that the rule of law is not respected. The bureaucracy is probably the biggest problem [and] can tear you down.

The value systems are almost completely opposite to what we know in Canada. In relations between the state and individuals and between business associates, it is very personal—it depends on who you know, rather than how much you know. So it can be quite a challenge.

I've never met any upfront, open hostility from any government officials [when representing Canadians].

It's due to many factors, one of which is that the [Vietnamese] culture is more subtle. People don't come out and say you're not nice. It's almost like Canada.

As a professional, I think people here look up to us whichever profession we are in.

Most [Vietnamese lawyers] are trained in the Soviet style of legal thinking, [which is] very ideologically driven. In terms of pure technical skills, they have not been well-exposed to international standards. They have not been exposed to legal texts.

The profession is very tightly regulated. Even though [law] has become a favourite among university students, it's [difficult] to enter a law school even though they might have a previous degree.

Many law graduates have to give up their dream of becoming a lawyer because it's almost impossible to meet the requirements of becoming a lawyer here.

You have to spend at least two years articling, for almost nothing. And it's almost next to impossible to find a law firm to hire you. The system is based very much on who you know, and therefore, if you don't know anyone who is willing to hire you, you are finished.

If I had [one] wish for the Canadian embassy here, it would be that they have a more current Globe and Mail available. Every time I have a friend come and visit me, I say bring me a couple of newspapers.

There is no access to Internet here. This is a Big Brother state. They have a law that requires email providers to be responsible for the contents. So that's another aspect of life here that's [different from] life in Canada.

> *Brad Daisley - The Lawyers Weekly*

Second, a Canadian lawyer goes abroad to work for the Hong Kong office of a Toronto firm.

A Canadian Lawyer Works In Hong Kong.

Hong Kong market booms for lawyers

> *Brad Daisley*

VANCOUVER—Hong Kong's lawyers are enjoying a huge increase of business in the days before the change of government on July 1.

"It's clear that things are booming, and it's certainly a seller's market for lawyers right now," Steven Trumper of Osler Hoskin Harcourt's Hong Kong office told The Lawyers Weekly.

"I think for the moment, the Hong Kong economy is doing very well and legal practitioners are very busy. You can see that in the number of job advertisements that are in the weekly lawyers' magazines, and by anecdotal evidence."

And despite those who warn of doom and gloom under a communist regime, the locals see good times ahead.

"We expect business to increase after the handover," said Irene Lau, assistant director of external affairs for the Law Society of Hong Kong, which governs the colony's 4,200 solicitors and 400 foreign lawyers.

"The legal profession, in general, welcomes the change of sovereignty with an open mind, very much like other people of Hong Kong."

However, she added that the law society is concerned that the rule of law and an independent judiciary be maintained, "because these are the cornerstone of Hong Kong's stability."

Mr. Trumper said Hong Kong's foreign lawyers are particularly optimistic that the change of government will give their clients better access to the huge Chinese market.

"We're quite hopeful that...having done away with the political barriers, Hong Kong will remain a very important source of funding for raising capital for China, and that that will provide good business opportunities for us."

He also said more Chinese companies are interested in using Canadian stock markets to raise capital, and that more Canadian companies want to do business in China.

Another Osler Hoskin lawyer, Olivia Lee, says every firm in Hong Kong is expanding.

"As far as the solicitors are concerned, I think they have reacted quite positively to the changeover, and as activities between China and Hong Kong increase, there will be more work for lawyers."

She added that the investment climate in Hong Kong is so good that every law firm is very busy, and that many are having trouble handling the volume of work.

"The demand right now for lawyers is pretty high. The recruitment advertisements are getting thicker."

Ms. Lee also said the legal community is quickly becoming dominated by "law firms who have lawyers who are western-trained but can speak, read and write Chinese and experience in PRC law."

Hong Kong's 600 barristers are, however, concerned about changes to the court system that will come about after the July change of sovereignty.

In particular, they are worried about the requirement that all courts be bilingual, said Audrey Eu, chair of Hong Kong's Bar Association.

She explained that new laws will require that all courts use both English and Chinese. While Hong Kong's lower courts have been bilingual for some years, many lawyers are concerned about the impact bilingualism will have on the superior courts.

"There are people who see the pace [of change] as too fast, and that this is going to jeopardize the common-law system, because English is the language of the common law," Ms. Eu said.

"And there are a lot of questions asked whether Hong Kong is ready for it, and whether it is good for Hong Kong."

Ms. Eu said nobody disputes that there should be Chinese in the courts, "but it is a question of how much and how to have the balance."

The Bar is also concerned about the constitutional legitimacy of the government that will take over July 1.

"The Bar Association actually passed a resolution on Sept. 2 last year saying that they do not support the provisional legislature as consisted by the preparatory committee," Ms. Eu noted.

"In short, it's not in accordance with the provision in the basic law."

She said this could have far-reaching consequences for the rule of law and the appointment of the judiciary, and that the constitutionality of the government may eventually be challenged in court.

Ms. Eu added that barristers are not seeing the boom in business Hong Kong's solicitors are experiencing. "As far as the situation of individual barristers is concerned, I think it varies a great deal. If you are popular and in demand, you are always very busy. We do have some barristers who are struggling and finding it difficult."

How the transfer of power will affect the PRC's lawyers is, however, much more difficult to gage.

Just 15 years ago, there were only a handful of lawyers in China. Today, there are more than 80,000, with the profession expected to expand to 100,000 by the turn of the century.

Brad Daisley - The Lawyers Weekly

Qualifying To Practice Law In Other Jurisdictions

Introduction - The Opportunities

U.S. law firms from New York, San Francisco and Boston (and I am sure that there will be many more to follow) have begun to recruit Canadian law graduates. In many cases the career benefits for those graduates are considerable. Those who stay in the U.S. may choose to not be admitted to the bar in Canada - thus bypassing articling and the rest of the Bar Admission Course.

British firms (London England) have begun to actively recruit Canadian lawyers - creating tremendous opportunities for professional mobility and career satisfaction.

Lawyers are increasingly moving from jurisdiction to jurisdiction. In the 21st century I predict that "lawyer mobility" will continue to become part of a normal career path.

This chapter will explore issues surrounding the professional mobility of lawyers. We will consider practicing law in another jurisdiction both with and without being a member of the bar of that jurisdiction.

Two Ways To Practice In Another Jurisdiction

You may practice law in another jurisdiction in one of two ways:

1. As a foreign legal consultant - for example a Toronto lawyer goes to New York and practices only Canadian law in New York (never being admitted to the New York bar); or

2. By being admitted to the bar of that other jurisdiction and practicing the law of that jurisdiction. For example, a Toronto lawyer decides to move to New York, is admitted to the New York bar and practices New York law.

What follows are some comments on each.

NAFTA And Opportunities For The Foreign Legal Consultant

As the world becomes more and more global, the practice of law has become less and less provincial (no pun intended). The practice of law in the modern world requires both a professional and cultural fluency with other jurisdictions.

As the world gets smaller and smaller the demand for lawyers with knowledge of foreign legal systems will continue to increase. For example, there are U.S. lawyers practising U.S. law in Toronto. There are Canadian lawyers practicing Canadian law in New York. There are Tokyo law firms that have internships for U.S. law students to make use of their expertise on the U.S. legal system.

NAFTA (The North American Free Trade Agreement) has resulted in new opportunities for Canadian lawyers to practice Canadian law in the U.S. and Mexico. Here is how it works.

Article 1210 of NAFTA contains a general provision to facilitate the delivery of cross-border services - including legal services. NAFTA specifically refers to "Foreign Legal Consultants." Basically a foreign legal consultant is a lawyer who is a member of the bar of one country who practices the law of his home country in another country. Example: an Ontario lawyer practicing Canadian law in New York or Mexico City.

On June 19, 1988 relevant representatives of the legal profession in Canada, the U.S. and Mexico agreed on a model rule (binding on all three countries) permitting foreign legal consultants. The leading features of the model rule (in a general way) are as follows:

1. A permit to act as a Foreign Legal Consultant in another country may be issued if:

- the applicant is a member in good standing of the legal profession of his home country;

- the applicant is subject to discipline and regulation by the relevant professional association in his home country;

- the applicant is of the good character and reputation that is required to practice law in his home country;

- the applicant agrees to carry adequate insurance

2. Once issued the permit to act as a Foreign Legal Consultant the applicant may practise and advise on the law of the country where he is admitted to the bar.

3. There is no requirement that a Foreign Legal Consultant be either a citizen or resident of the country where he acts as a Foreign Legal Consultant or to establish or maintain a representative office in the foreign jurisdiction.

4. A Foreign Legal Consultant must describe himself as a Foreign Legal Consultant and not as a member of the bar in the country where he is acting as a foreign legal consultant.

Finally, a permit to act as a Foreign Legal Consultant does not preclude the need for the Foreign Legal Consultant to comply with the applicable immigration and visa requirements set out in Chapter 16 of NAFTA. The issue of what you can do if allowed to go to a foreign country is different from whether you can go there!

Becoming A Member Of The Bar

Scenario 1 - Canadian Law Graduates And U.S. Bar Admissions

To be admitted to U.S. state bars one must sit and pass (what is typically) a two day state bar exam. Graduates of Canadian law schools are allowed by many U.S. state bar examiners to take the bar exam in that state. Bottom line: it is possible!

Professional licensing exists only for the purpose of protecting the public. A license to practice law should be required only to the extent that it is necessary for the protection of one or more public interests. The public interest includes (but is certainly not limited to) the interests of the legal profession. When it comes to Law Societies and Bar Associations there will always be a number of members who use and develop rules for bar admission for the purpose of keeping applicants out.

For the most part U.S. state bars have been very open to Canadians, allowing those with Canadian law degrees to take the Bar exam. The reverse has never been true. For a list of states that will allow Canadian graduates to simply take the state bar exam see www.ncbex.org

Scenario 2 - U.S. LL.M.s (Masters degree in law) and U.S. Bar Admission

There are approximately ten U.S. states that will allow those with a U.S. LL.M. to take the bar exam. For more information see www.ncbex.org

Scenario 3 - Canadian Lawyers And Admission As A Solicitor To The U.K. Bar

Whereas in Canadian provinces lawyers are both barristers (do trial work) and solicitors (non-trial work), in the U.K. lawyers are either barristers or solicitors. This discussion is about how to become a "solicitor" in the U.K.

A Canadian lawyer can be admitted to the bar in England (as a solicitor) by applying to the Law Society (U.K.).

They require:

(1) a recognized LL.B.;

(2) a call to the bar in a Canadian province

(3) at least two years experience working in law

This distinction is important. This is because Canadian and U.S. lawyers may be subject to different exam requirements.

Scenario 4 - Canadian Lawyers And Inter-provincial Mobility

How easy is it for a member of the bar in one Canadian province to transfer and become a member of the bar in another province? What is required? Historically it has been easier and taken less time to become a Solicitor in the U.K. or a member of a U.S. state bar, than to be admitted to the bar of another province! Sounds strange, doesn't it? An agreement signed on December 7, 2002 appears to have changed that.

By way of background: Section 6(2) of the Canadian Charter of Rights speaks to this issue:

6(2) Every citizen of Canada and every person who has the status of a permanent resident of Canada has the right

(a) to move and take up residence in any province; and

(b) to pursue the gaining of a livelihood in any province.

In order to respect the Charter, the Federation Of Law Societies has agreed upon a protocol to facilitate the mobility of lawyers from province to province.

2002 may well be remembered as the year that the barriers to the "inter-provincial mobility Canadian lawyers" came crumbling down.

On December 7, 2002 representatives of eight law societies across Canada signed an agreement which essentially allows Canadian lawyers to provide legal services in any province that is a party to the agreement. The highlights include an understanding that:

- there will be a national registry of practising lawyers;

- members of the bar in one of the provinces will be able to practise the law of another province for up to 100 days per year on a temporary basis (without becoming a member of the bar of the other province) without a permit;

- members of the bar in one province will be able to become a member of the bar of another province without having to pass transfer exams. They will have to satisfy a reading requirement determined by each signatory province.

The bottom line is that, for all intensive purposes membership of the bar of one province will give you the right to both practise and become a member of the bar of another province. Great news!!

The provinces who signed the agreement are: Alberta, British Columbia, Saskatchewan, Manitoba, Newfoundland and Labrador, Nova Scotia and Ontario. Quebec is the eighth province to sign the agreement. Since Quebec is a civil law jurisdiction different criteria will apply. My personal opinion is that the remaining provinces will eventually sign on.

Conclusion

Lawyers are becoming more and more mobile. My advice would be to get yourself admitted in as many jurisdictions as possible. Increasing mobility makes law schools that offer joint law degrees more and more attractive.

Chapter 30

Foreign Trained Law Graduates And Lawyers - Canadian Bar Admission

Canadian Bar Admission - The Starting Position

In general, in order to be admitted to the bar of a Canadian province one must complete the bar admission course in that province. At present a candidate may be admitted to the bar admission course only if one has either a Canadian LL.B. or a "certificate of equivalency" from the National Committee On Accreditation which is based in Ottawa. Therefore, graduates of foreign (including U.S.) law schools who wish to enter the bar admission course must apply to the National Committee for a "certificate of equivalency." The application is necessarily based on the foreign law degree, the fact of bar admission in a foreign jurisdiction and actual lawyering experience.

National Committee On Accreditation

What Is It And What Does It Do?

The National Committee on Foreign Accreditation is appointed by the Federation of Law Societies of Canada and the Committee of Canadian Law Deans. Its purpose is to assess the quality and content of foreign legal studies with a view to determining what Canadian legal studies are necessary to ensure that the applicant has the equivalent of a Canadian law degree.

A "certificate of equivalency" issued by the National Committee is considered to be equivalent to an academic qualification for admission to the Bar Admission Course in Ontario. The certificate is also officially recognized by the Law Societies of some other provinces as a way of qualifying for admission as a student-at-law and enrollment as a barrister and solicitor.

After completing a review of an applicant's file the committee will make one of the following three recommendations.

1. That the applicant be denied further standing. (This means the applicant must earn a complete Canadian law degree.)

2. That the applicant take further education at a Canadian law school. (This will generally be one or two years. The applicant is responsible for applying to law school as a "National Committee applicant." This will not guarantee that the applicant will be admitted. If admitted, the applicant is not eligible to receive an LL.B. degree.)

3. That the applicant write examinations in specified areas of Canadian law. Examples include, constitutional law, civil procedure, etc. The Committee issues a "certificate of equivalency" upon successful completion of

the requirements set out in its recommendation(s).

4. Enter the Bar Admission Course.

Please note these requirements are subject to change.

For additional information about the National Committee you may visit: http://www.flsc.ca

The Societal Benefit To Having Lawyers From Other Countries

Canada is a country composed of many minority and immigrant groups. Many people need the services of a lawyer who speaks their language and understands their concerns. Wherever there is an immigrant community, there is a need for lawyers who are members of that community. This principle is demonstrated in the following article.

March 10, 1992

The Financial Post

A shortage of lawyers?

Ethnic communities seek relaxed bar admission

Michael Crawford

Believe it or not, there's a shortage of lawyers in Canada. At least, that's the belief of some members of ethnic communities who say foreign-trained lawyers face too many hurdles in gaining admission to the provincial bars.

Lawyers who understand the language and culture of many immigrant communities are few. Cornelia Soberano, among the few lawyers of Filipino descent practising in Toronto, says clients often wait months just to see her.

"There's a crying need from these communities for more lawyers," she said.

Although the law societies are sympathetic, they say the barriers are to protect the public. But a lawyer familiar with accreditation procedures around the world suggests they're also about protecting home turf.

Through a joint committee that meets only a few times a year, law societies carefully screen lawyers with foreign credentials. Most are told they must go back to school for at least one to two years, article with a law firm and go into a bar admission program.

The accreditation body gets more than a thousand queries a year. About 200 actually make applications — mostly lawyers with U.S. or British training.

Others may be deterred by a lack of time and money. Soberano said there are more than 100 Filipino-trained lawyers in Toronto alone and only two have been accredited.

But the committee has one mandate. "Our focus is only on whether the person is qualified to go and render services to the public," said Vern Krishna, a University of Ottawa professor and secretary of the joint body.

Looking at the applicant's schooling and experience with the common law system used in much of Canada, the body sets the "credit hours" of retraining needed. If applicants are from a non-common law country, such as Japan, chances are they will get no advance credits. Even lawyers with less than three years in Quebec's civil law regime must be evaluated before working in another province.

Krishna suggests it's wrong to imagine a great wealth of untapped legal talent out there. Most "are fresh young graduates who have just come out of school in their country or Canadians who have gone abroad to study."

However, the committee is trying to help immigrants by giving them three or even five years to meet the requirements. But the hurdles don't end there, Soberano said.

While most schools reserve a few positions for requalifying lawyers, they're not guaranteed a spot.

"What we want is an objective qualifying exam," she said. "They are not asking for any special favors or to lower the standards. They're saying let us have access on our merit."

Reprinted with permission of the author.

Perceptions Of And Experiences With The National Committee

Two Positive Experiences With The National Committee

Here are some accounts of successful applicants.

Perspective 1. From Canada To A U.S. Law School To The Ontario Bar

Students in Canada continue to be interested in the possibility of attending law school in the U.S. and returning to Canada for bar admission. The following perspective is interesting because the writer went to law school in Michigan and then without actually practicing law in the U.S. returned to Canada, spent one year at Osgoode Hall Law School, completed the Bar Admission Course and is currently practicing law in Toronto.

PLEASE NOTE THAT THIS ARTICLE SHOULD NOT BE CONSTRUED TO BE THE BLUEPRINT FOR HOW TO BE ADMITTED TO THE ONTARIO BAR WITHOUT GOING TO LAW SCHOOL IN CANADA. WHAT WORKED FOR ONE PERSON MAY NOT WORK IN THE SAME WAY FOR ANOTHER!

"Studying law in the United States of America:

In considering where to go to law school, most Canadian applicants will think only of opportunities to study and practise law within Canada. The following are my impressions and experiences as one who studied law in the United States and has since returned to practise law in Canada.

Reasons for studying law in the United States:

There are any number of reasons for looking to the U.S. as a place to study. The first one that comes to mind is that there are over 170 accredited law schools in the U.S. (as compared to fewer than 20 in Canada). Put simply, by looking south of the border for your legal education you will instantly gain the benefit of widening your choices by a factor of ten.

One benefit of U.S. studies is that, should you choose to return to Canada to practice, you will have an excellent foundation in American jurisprudence. This can be put to good use when dealing with Canadian clients operating in the U.S. or American clients operating in Canada.

Another reason for looking to the U.S. is, in my opinion, particularly relevant to those students hoping to practise private international law. There are two main reasons for this. First, the two greatest centres in the world for this field are New York City and London, England. If you want to practise a high level of international law, you would do well to aim your efforts at those cities. Of course, this is not to say that by going to law school in Canada you will not be able to move at some later date. However, an American legal education should be considered if this is your goal.

Why I went to the United States:

I graduated from the University of Toronto in 1992. At that time I was looking at law schools both north and south of the border. In the end I accepted an offer from the Detroit College of Law at Michigan State University (DCL-

MSU) because of its proximity to Toronto and because of its Institute for Canadian Legal Studies. Once there I found that I was not alone. Canadians accounted for nearly 5% of the student body. I received a Juris Doctor in 1996 and was subsequently admitted to the State Bar of Michigan. I then opted to return to Canada in order to complete my studies and Canadian licensing requirements as quickly as possible.

Canadian Accreditation:

Accreditation is the process that all foreign trained lawyers who wish to practice in Canada must complete in order to be admitted to a Canadian bar association. The process is more awkward than it needs to be but, in the end, can be dealt with in fairly short order.

The reason that accreditation is not a simple process is that there are several institutions which must be satisfied before one can be licensed here. These institutions are: 1. the National Committee on Accreditation (NCA); 2. the provincial law society; and 3. possibly a Canadian law school. Below is a brief summary of the process.

To be licensed to practice in Ontario one must first pass the Bar Admission Course (BAC) as set by the Law Society of Upper Canada (LSUC). The LSUC will not permit a foreign lawyer to article or to sit for the examinations without a Certificate of Accreditation from the NCA. Upon graduation from a foreign law school the applicant interested in returning to Canada must first apply to the NCA. The NCA will then require that the applicant complete anywhere from 30 to 60 credit hours of Canadian legal studies (1 to 2 years). These studies can be done either at a law school in Canada (to which one applies as a NCA student) or by correspondence courses.

Once the NCA has admitted you to its programme you can then apply to the LSUC for admission to the BAC. If this sounds a bit complicated, that's because it is. However, if you are interested in going to the U.S., don't let the accreditation process worry you too much. Being licensed in multiple jurisdictions is, in my opinion, worth the extra effort.

In my case, after graduating from DCL-MSU and sitting for the Michigan State Bar exam, the NCA required me to complete one year of studies in Canada. To that end I applied, and was admitted, to Osgoode Hall Law School. After completing my year of Canadian legal studies I began articling with a Toronto law firm.

American and Canadian legal studies compared:

I can say, unequivocally, that studying in the U.S. was a great move for me. My time at Osgoode Hall was well spent and it is my opinion that both the Faculty and the student body there are excellent. However, I found my legal education at DCL-MSU to be more rigorous and, finally, more satisfying.

It should be noted that Canadians and Americans share a legal system inherited from the British. Both countries are common law jurisdictions (with the obvious exception of Quebec which retains a civil law system). As such there is substantial common ground between the two systems. For this reason the transition from American to Canadian law, from a lawyer's perspective, is quite straightforward.

The Socratic Method:

Many law schools in the U.S. still employ the Socratic Method as the primary means of education. Briefly, this style of teaching involves a high level of student participation and in-class interaction between the students and the professor. If you would like to get a better feel for the Socratic Method, I recommend that you rent the film "The Paper Chase" or, better yet, read Scott Turow's excellent biographical account of first year law school called "One L" (in the U.S. first year students are referred to as 1L's, second year students as 2L's and, as you may have guessed, third year students are 3L's).

From the first day of first year we were expected to be prepared to brief cases if called upon. We were required to know relevant case law and statutes, to be able to distinguish cases, to have opinions and, most importantly, we had to be able to defend our positions. Attendance for first year classes was mandatory and nobody could avoid being "called on" by the professor. This was often a nerve wracking experience but it was perhaps the most important part of my legal formation. We were obligated, from the first days of law school, to practice our advocacy skills. For me this has proven to be the most useful product of going to law school in the U.S.

Osgoode Hall Law School does not use the Socratic Method. Lectures there resemble undergraduate lectures. They proved less challenging in terms of day-to-day preparation and, consequently, less satisfying. By this I do not mean to say that Osgoode Hall's professors are poor lecturers. Quite the contrary. The lectures, as lectures, were fine. However, the absence of student-teacher interaction meant that advocacy skills were not developed in the class room setting. In my opinion students benefit greatly from the Socratic Method.

Conclusion:

For some of you, a legal education outside of Canada will be the last thing from your mind. That's fine. The overwhelming majority of Canadian lawyers were trained here. However, if you are considering studying law outside of Canada I recommend that you look closely at the possibilities south of the border. Learning the legal system of another country is an invaluable experience. It will make you useful to clients with interests outside of Canada and may also broaden your employment opportunities. In my articling interview, it was represented to me that I was being interviewed because of, and not in spite of, my foreign education.

In the end, going to the U.S. extended my legal education by one year (3 years in Michigan, 1 year in Ontario). For my troubles I will have two licenses to practice law. Would I do it again? Yes. Going to law school in the U.S. has worked out well for me and, for those of you seriously considering this option, I would recommend it."

Perspective 2. An American Lawyer Moves To Canada And Is Admitted To The Ontario Bar

"You may have heard that it is straightforward for a Canadian lawyer to gain admission to a state bar in the United States of America. And, it is. For many states, all the Canadian lawyer need do is sit for a two-day bar examination (and pass it, of course). You may assume that it is equally simple for a US lawyer to gain admission to the Ontario bar. Well, this is not the case.

For a lawyer from a foreign jurisdiction, entry to the Ontario bar is a two step process. First, the lawyer must obtain accreditation of his foreign law degree from the Joint Committee on Accreditation of the Federation of Law Societies of Canada. The lawyer completes a detailed application outlining his education and employment history. Official transcripts from each school attended must accompany the application. Additionally, the applicant must supply references from each prior legal employer. Finally, the required application fee must be paid. The Joint Committee reviews the application, then notifies the applicant what he must do in order to receive accreditation of his foreign degree. The Committee may require the applicant to attend a Canadian law school for a period of years, pass Joint Committee examinations in specified areas of the law, or a combination of the two.

In my case, I had obtained a Juris Doctor cum laude from the Temple University School of Law in Philadelphia in 1984. I have been a member in good standing of the Pennsylvania Bar since 1984, and had actively practiced law for nine years prior to my Joint Committee application. Based on my education and experience, the Committee required me to pass five essay examinations, which I was permitted to study for independently. My examinations were in Civil Procedure, Tax, Evidence, Corporations, and Constitutional Law. Each examination was three hours, and administered at Osgoode Hall. Incidentally, each examination carried a separate fee.

Upon successfully completing my examinations, I received a Certificate of Accreditation from the Joint Committee. This certificate permitted me to apply for admission in the Law Society of Upper Canada's Bar Admission Course. As you may already know, the Course consists of three phases. Phase I entails one month of instruction to prepare the student for Phase II, the Articling Term. In Phase II, the student works as an Articling Student with a lawyer for twelve months. Following successful completion of his articles, the student then enters Phase III. Phase III includes three months of classroom instruction and nine examinations, all of which the student must pass.

An experienced lawyer from a foreign jurisdiction may apply for a waiver of Phase I and an abridgement or waiver of Phase II. Because I had practiced for nine years, I decided to apply for a waiver of both Phase I and II. To do so, I was required to submit an application, accompanied by a Certificate of Good Standing from the Pennsylvania Bar, my law school and undergraduate transcripts, and payment of another fee. I was also required to solicit from every prior employer a detailed letter describing the experience I had obtained in each of twelve legal practice skills. (Yes, again.) The Law Society Articling Director reviewed my submissions and granted a complete waiver of Phases I and II.

Once I received my waiver, I was permitted to enroll in Phase III. And yes, there is a separate tuition fee for Phase III. I successfully completed my examinations, and was admitted to the Ontario Bar February 26, 1998.

So, any student considering crossing the border to attend a US law school should be aware of the process he will face on returning home to ply his trade. It is not a simple matter of enduring a two-day exam." Author's Note: The preceding two perspectives were written when the Ontario Bar Admission Course was different in format from the current format.

Two Negative Experiences With The National Committee

Rightly or wrongly, the National Committee has not been friendly to law graduates of many countries. Lawyers from countries that do not have a "common law based legal system" have experienced problems with the National Committee. The main criticisms seem to be that no credit at all is given for foreign legal experience and that neither the criteria nor the reasons for decisions have been adequately explained (a lack of transparency).

Perspective 3. A Lawyer From Turkey - No Credit Given For Foreign Legal Experience

"When I came to Canada as a foreign-trained lawyer, I was pretty optimistic that becoming a lawyer in Canada wouldn't be too difficult for me since I had already passed an entry exam to a law school, graduated from that school, passed the bar exam, and finally amassed five years experience working as a lawyer in my country. "If I'm already a successful practising lawyer, I can easily become a lawyer in Canada once I gain command of the English language," I told myself. But except for the LSAT preparation with Richardson, my experience trying to become a lawyer in Canada wasn't easy at all.

After going through my full share of frustration and spending one and a half years learning English, I had a pretty good score on the TOEFL. Now I was ready to get my credentials and become a lawyer in Canada. Maybe I was going to have to take a couple of courses in Canadian Law, I thought. I contacted the National Committee on Accreditation and was almost sure that I could get at least some credits for my background. But instead of credits, I got a letter starting with "Unfortunately....." In that letter, I found out that I was not seen as a lawyer but as a university graduate who could first take the LSAT, then apply to law schools, and finally upon graduation take the bar exam, and only then become a lawyer. I went to pieces. My ten years spent on law - four years in law school, one year in training as a lawyer, and five years experience in working as a lawyer - meant and still means nothing - correction: it means only a university degree. Initially, I thought "It is not fair, and I am not going to do it all again." I blamed Canada, its accreditation system, and myself for coming to Canada, but blaming did not wipe out the reality that I had to start from scratch if I wanted to be a lawyer again. Two options crossed my mind: going back to my country, or changing my career."

Perspective 4. A Lawyer From Yugoslavia - A Lack Of Transparency - Is The Process Fair?

"When I learned that, contrary to the information I was initially given by the NCA offices, there are cases in which lawyers with eastern European civil law background were granted advanced standing, I decided to explore the issue further.   On my first request to learn about earlier application cases, I was advised that all this was confidential and comes under the scrutiny of the Information to Privacy Act. I was rather disappointed that this piece of legal advice I received on the letterhead of the Federation of Law Societies of Canada was a misleading one. There is no Act by that neatly italicized name. The committee's attitude did not change when I specified that I had no interest in any previous applicant's personal data, that I was concerned exclusively with anonymous legal backgrounds that had been granted advanced standing for admission to Canadian law schools. The next obstacle was of a technical nature: the files were in storage; it was not feasible to fetch them; the files had never been reviewed by any applicant; and why would I need them at all? Having been denied any advanced standing for law school study upon my second application, I asked to be provided with reasons, especially in view of the similar cases which I then was able to name. The NCA's executive director, Vern Krishna, wrote the reasons. All I was told was that "there are sufficient differences between your case and the other applicants." When I submitted letters of consent for disclosure from former applicants, Mr. Krishna wanted them to file affidavits in that regard. Once the affidavits reached the offices of the executive director, various formal objections were raised. As soon as one had been complied with, and a new affidavit reached Mr. Krishna's attention, a new objection was raised. From three applicants, the committee received a total of six affidavits. However, instead of receiving disclosure, I was advised by Mr. Krishna that I will receive a photocopy of the application forms and that he will prepare for me "an overview of each candidate's profile."   It has been a year and a half since my first request to learn anything about the committee's prior assessment grounds—and I am still waiting. The only way to see whether one's treatment is fair, and to assess the standards as clear and understandable, is having a chance to compare one's case with previously decided similar cases. Besides, isn't the previously decided case the law? And isn't this the most salient principle of the common law whose glorious tradition, oddly enough, this very committee represents in Canada?"

Conclusion

Mobility in the legal profession is increasing. Law students - while in law school - have opportunities to position themselves for a modern and global world! Having said this though, it seems clear that Canada is a country that is not friendly to foreign lawyers and law students. One is left with a strong feeling that Canadian law societies are confusing the "public interest" and the interest of the profession. Those interested in exploring this issue further, will find the following appendices to be of interest.

APPENDIX A

Should It Even Matter Where You Attend Law School?

The issue of where one attends law school and where one is eligible to practice law is interesting. How does it bear on the public interest in ensuring that lawyers are competent? The focus of the National Committee is on how an applicant's foreign legal education compares to a Canadian LL.B. This inquiry assumes that the Canadian LL.B. should be the required educational standard for entry into the Bar Admission Course. It may be worth rethinking this assumption. As long as the Bar Admission Course exists, there may be no policy reason to require a Canadian LL.B.

Canada in general, and Ontario in particular has the most restrictive and time consuming standards for bar admission in the world. By way of comparison, the U.S. has no articling and bar admission course. One must pass a two day bar exam. Now, the bar exam either tests one's ability to be a lawyer or it doesn't. If one can pass the bar exam - why should it matter where one attends law school? There are even some U.S. states that don't require a J.D. from an ABA approved law school. New York is a prime example. New York has confidence in its bar exam. It hasn't erected barriers to keep people out. This has resulted in New York having a particularly diverse legal community. That's why the motto of many a foreign law graduate is "I Love New York."

In Canada bar admission is handled differently. Instead of taking a two day bar exam - law graduates are required to complete a bar admission course that lasts from 12 to 18 months depending on the province. Candidates take a number of exams along the way. At the present time only graduates of Canadian law schools or those with a certificate of equivalency from the National Committee On Accreditation are allowed to participate in the Bar Admission Course. Why should graduates of only certain law schools be allowed in? It is difficult to even invent a reason.

Professional licensing exists only for the protection of the public. Now the Bar Admission Course either teaches and tests lawyering skills that are necessary for the protection of the public or it doesn't. If it does, then where one graduates from law school is irrelevant. If it doesn't, then there is no legitimate reason to have it in the first place. Given the length of the Bar Admission Course, there is less reason to require graduation from a Canadian law school to enter the Ontario Bar Admission Course than there might be for New York to require a U.S. law degree to make one eligible to take the New York bar exam.

I can see only one possible reason to condition entry into the Bar Admission Course on graduation from a specific law school. This reason would materialize only if the Bar Admission Course is failing to do its job. If the Bar Admission Course does not properly teach and adequately test the lawyering skills that are necessary for the protection of the public - well then - it might matter what kind of legal education students bring to the Bar Admission Course! But if the Bar Admission Course does its job, then shouldn't simply passing the Bar Admission Course be sufficient?

Competitive pressure from the rest of the world and common sense suggest that the question of the requirements to become a lawyer in Ontario and the rest of Canada should be revisited! Licensing requirements for admission to the bar must become consistent with common sense and the trend of globalization.

APPENDIX B

Evaluating The National Committee - Setting The Stage For Reform

It is easy to see why the National Committee has been the subject of criticism. Many think that, regardless of its purpose, its effect is to keep foreigners out the of the legal profession. The stage for reform was set in 1997 when Toronto bencher Gavin MacKenzie wrote a report on the National Committee. The report addressed a number of issues. But, most significantly it addressed the issues of:

1. The National Committee's credibility in assessing the experience of foreign lawyers and law graduates (think of the lawyer from Turkey);

2. Transparency of process - what exactly are the guidelines and how are they applied in the case of specific applicants (think of the lawyer from Yugoslavia).

The MacKenzie report is discussed in the following article.

July 18, 1997

LSUC endorses accreditation committee review - July 18, 1997

Questions raised about fees charged foreign students at U. of T.

Paula Kulig

TORONTO—A report that recommends little more than the status quo for the often-criticized body that accredits foreign-trained lawyers in Canada has been endorsed by the Law Society of Upper Canada. But despite the minimal changes proposed in the report, the executive director of the National Committee on Accreditation suggested to Convocation last month that they go too far.

The report on the NCA, written by Toronto bencher Gavin MacKenzie, comes after an extensive study of the 20-year-old organization. In it, he notes the many complaints directed at the NCA by both applicants and law schools-particularly concerning the way the organization assesses qualifications. "As we shall see, questions have been raised by both applicants and legal educators concerning the adequacy of the NCA's assessments. "Indeed, the difficulty in obtaining accurate and consistent prior learning assessments is at the root of most concerns that have been raised about the accreditation process," Mr. MacKenzie wrote. Although applicants and schools agree that there are problems with the assessment process, they often disagree on whether it's too stringent or too lenient, he said, adding that there are "very significant tensions" among the NCA, foreign-trained lawyers and law faculties.

Among the report's 11 recommendations are that:

- The LSUC should continue to support the NCA;

- a person with a background in comparative education and prior learning assessment should review the NCA's guidelines to determine if they need to be amended, to ensure that applicants meet the necessary level of competence, and that they are treated equitably;

- an orientation program for NCA students accepted into Ontario law schools should be offered before classes begin;

- the law society should meet with the University of Toronto law faculty to discuss the higher fees charged by the school to NCA students and the fewer services they receive in return;

- the NCA should include a visible minority representative from among foreign-trained lawyers; and

- applicants with experience working as law clerks in Canada under the supervision of one or more Canadian lawyers should be given appropriate credit.

- Except for the proposal on U. of T.'s law school, the law society is not empowered to act on the recommendations. They'll now be turned over to the Federation of Law Societies-of which the NCA is a standing committee-for further consideration, but the federation is under no obligation to support them. While the report, commissioned by the LSUC's admissions and equity committee, passed almost unanimously, NCA executive director Vern Krishna spoke against the recommendations on law clerks and visible minority representation. Mr. Krishna, a bencher, said the NCA doesn't have the means to evaluate law clerk experience, and recognizing such experience could return the lawyer-accreditation system to pre-1957 days, when there was no formal law degree in Ontario. As for having a member of a visible minority on the committee, Mr. Krishna, a native of India, angrily denounced the idea, saying it "pandered" to political correctness and assumed people from many different countries had the same views because of the colour of their skin.

- But several benchers supported the idea saying, it would bring to the table the views of someone who has been through the process and could provide a different perspective. The NCA evaluates the legal training and experience of people who obtained their credentials in foreign countries and want to practice law in common-law jurisdictions in Canada.

- The body meets three or four times a year to review the material submitted by applicants, and assesses them using a uniform standard. Factors considered include the reputation of the applicant's law school, the quality of the applicant's degree (whether it's a first, second or third-class degree, where applicable), and the length, nature and quality of the applicant's professional legal experience.

Mr. MacKenzie's report noted that in 1995-96, roughly two-thirds of applicants were required by the NCA to attend a Canadian law school either part-time or full-time, and complete a stipulated number of credit hours (usually from one to two years' worth) to bring their qualifications up to par with an LL.B. in this country.

Those with superior qualifications and experience were allowed to write "challenge" exams in certain subjects without enrolling at law school. Still other applicants not found eligible for advanced standing could be required to enroll in a full LL.B. program in Canada. Following successful completion of either law school of the challenge exams, foreign-trained lawyers must then enroll in the Bar admission course and article before becoming accredited to practice law here.

"Applicants object that although they admittedly require education in Canadian laws, as lawyers who are qualified to practise in other jurisdictions (often for many years), being required to return to law school is neither the fairest nor the most effective way to accomplish this objective," Mr. MacKenzie wrote."

Reprinted with permission of the author.

Book VII - A Report

Learning About Lawyers And The Legal Profession

Summary And Introduction

My Advice To You Is ....

Don't approach law school with the idea that you want to be any particular kind of lawyer. Keep your eyes open to the opportunities. There is a legal dimension to every aspect of human activity. Don't ask: what area of law would interest me? Do ask: how can I pursue my personal interests in the capacity of being a lawyer?

What exactly do lawyers do? Is the practice of law a business or a profession or both? Where do they work? How much do they make? Are they happy? How are lawyers regulated? By what are they regulated? Those who wish to explore these issues beyond Book VII will find numerous books about lawyers and the profession. For those of you in Canada, I would particularly recommend Jack Batten's books on Canadian lawyers.

Book VII will provide important perspectives on the legal profession for those of you who wish to be lawyers.

In Book VII I will the play the role of a "fly on the wall" listening, looking and reporting back to you about lawyers and the legal profession.

Book VII - Chapter Summaries

31. What Do Lawyers Do? - Wide Ranging Scenes From The Legal Profession

Focus: The wide range of lawyers' activities

32. Who Are Lawyers And How Much Do They Earn?

Focus: The diverse demographics of the legal profession. The wide range of lawyers' incomes

33. Lawyers, Ethics And The Law - "More Than An Ordinary Citizen"

Focus: The heightened legal and ethical restrictions on lawyers

34. A Career In Law - Both A Business And A Profession

Focus: Lawyers and unpopular causes, business aspects of the practice of law

35. 21st Century Compliance - Globalization, Technology And The Practice Of Law In The 21st Century

Focus: Be Prepared! How globalization and technology are affecting the practice of law

36. Lawyers - A Balance Between Job Satisfaction And Quality Of Life

Focus: The sometimes precarious balance between professional and personal lives

37. Law, Society And The Law Society - How Canadian Lawyers Govern Themselves

Focus: The Canadian legal profession as a self-governing profession, the role of the Law Society

Chapter 31

What Do Lawyers Do? - Wide Ranging Scenes From The Legal Profession

"The knowledge and skills that you acquire at law school will in turn give you an opportunity to pursue a career that is both stimulating and worthwhile. For most of you the career path will be a life in the law - a profession rich in tradition, rich in opportunities for service to people who will entrust their most important and personal problems to you, and ultimately rich in possibilities for service dedicated to the preservation of the great values of law and justice that are the foundation of our nation."

-Chief Justice Brian Dickson

When It Comes To Opportunities - It's The Economy Stupid!

There are many opportunities available to law school graduates and lawyers. Lawyers are very much a part of the economy. They play an important part in the decisions made by many corporations and entrepreneurs. In general, lawyers make good incomes. They are however, a part of the economy. As such, the demand for legal services (along with all other services) will be heavily influenced by the state of the economy.

"Feast To Famine" - Famine

I wrote the first edition of this book in 1992. At that time North America was in the depths of a vicious recession. It was no surprise that there were fewer jobs in those areas most affected by the recession. The 1992 edition of this book included the following comment from The Economist:

"For the past two years the legal business has been battered by a transatlantic tripleblow recession, collapsed property markets and a slump in corporate dealmaking. According to the American Lawyer, a trade magazine, revenues at America's top 100 law firms rose last year by just 3%, to 132.9 billion, after a 9% increase in 1990 - two successively more painful years for an industry in which anything less than double-digit growth had become a dim memory. British lawyers say they have done no better."

-The Economist - July 18, 1992

Opportunities in the legal profession will never be "recession proof." But, as long as there is society, there will be social problems. There is no social problem that does not eventually become a legal problem. Government continues to be a growth industry throughout the world. Consider the following comment from The Economist:

"Lawyers around the world grew busier as lawmakers did the same. In America the number of pages added each year to the Federal Register, which compiles all new laws and regulations, has quadrupled since 1960. In 1970 a similar book of EC rules was three inches thick. Last year the volumes of new rules stretched three feet. East European governments have lawyers, foreign and local, working frantically on their codifications and privatizations. "As rule of law has been extended," says Marc Galanter, a law professor at the University of Wisconsin, "so has the rule of lawyers."

"Feast To Famine" - Feast

What a difference five years can make. As always, the economy moves from bust to boom.

Consider the following:

August 8, 1997

Help wanted —— and fast!

Jobs for lawyers are suddenly opening up right across Canada

Monique Conrod

TORONTO—Dust off your CVs: Bay Street is hiring.

And not only Bay Street, but Calgary, London and New York are in the midst of a hiring frenze for lawyers with the right stuff.

"There's a shortage on the ground of lawyers with relevant skills," says Christopher Sweeney of ZSA, a professional recruitment service operating out of Toronto.

The current economic upturn means more business activity, which in turn means more work for lawyers in a wide range of corporate finance, securities, debt financing, acquisitions and banking.

The problem is, after years of constraint, many firms don't have enough experienced lawyers to handle the workload, and they're starting to hire again in a big way.

The economic resurgence is widespread, but the impact is especially strong in Toronto, perhaps because Toronto was hit more dramatically in the last recession, Mr. Sweeney said.

"I would say the two most vibrant legal centres [in Canada] right now would be Calgary and Toronto."

ZSA set up shop in Toronto about six months ago, an offshoot of the London, England-based recruiting firm ZMB, where Mr. Sweeney worked for the past five years. The agency places ads for law firms or corporations, and pre-screens the responses to help match the right applicant with the right positions.

A successful ad could bring in as many as 100 resumes. Of these, maybe 10 will have the necessary qualifications.

In addition to advertising across the country for major law firms like Tory, Tory, Goodman Phillips & Vineberg and Gowling, Strathy & Henderson, as well as for corporations, ZSA also handles ads for positions in New York, London, Hong Kong and Singapore.

"[U.S. and U.K.] law firms in all of these areas are willing to look at Canadians with the relevant abilities because they're extremely busy, and they're having problems filling positions with existing candidates in the various geographical areas," Mr. Sweeney said.

The international legal brain drain is compounding the local lawyer shortage, according to Gary Ostoich, chair of the associates committee of McMillan Binch in Toronto.

"They're grabbing prospective candidates in Toronto as they never have before."

McMillan Binch has been going through its own hiring boom recently. The large business law firm hired back 100 per cent of its most recent crop of articling students.

Increased hireback rates are a "Bay Street-wide" phenomenon, according to Mr. Ostoich.

It's a sharp contrast to the trend of the past few years, when students were lucky to find an articling position, and getting hired back didn't even enter into the equation for many.

But the real market is for those with two years experience.

"Once you have some experience, you're very marketable," said Mr. Ostoich, "especially in the securities and debt financing areas."

Mr. Sweeney blames the dearth of experienced young lawyers on the short-sightedness of firms who have not hired back enough articling students in the past years.

"As a result, there's now an absolute shortage of lawyers with anywhere from two to five years experience in these areas," he said. "The law firms were just not training up these types of lawyers."

So, for those who are in the right place at the right time, things are looking very good. Not only are there more jobs, but salaries are being adjusted accordingly.

Associates with three years' or more experience at McMillan Binch have seen a salary increase of 10 per cent over last year, as well as bonuses of 15 per cent.

The question, of course, is how long will it last?

"I believe we're just at the start of a wave," said Mr. Sweeney.

"[Current hiring practices] are a strong signal that firms expect this economic activity to continue for the foreseeable future, and that these lawyers will be needed in the coming years."

But Mr. Ostoich is not so sure.

"It's going to continue as long as the economy continues [to do well]. So whenever you think the crash is going to take place, that's when you wonder how much longer it's going to go.

"If I had to predict, I'd say a year or two, max."

Monique Conrod - The Lawyers Weekly

"Feast To Famine" - The Feast May Be Ending

Let's "fast forward" to May of 2001. The inevitable cycle continues. Although the climate for lawyers is far from famine, there is evidence that the feast may be coming to an end. The "dot com" boom has begun its implosion. It stands to reason that the lawyers who "feasted" off it, may need to control their eating. Consider the following comments by Cameron Stracher in the May 14, 2001 Wall Street Journal. These comments come from an article titled:

"Let The Lawyer Layoffs Begin"

"Now that the downturn has finally come, the "L" word is being whispered again in hallways and conference rooms, and associates nervously await pink slips. `We're all looking over our shoulder wondering when the ax will fall,' says one."

Law is a diverse field and is a service profession. In general the economic fortunes of law firms will ride the normal and natural ups and downs of the economy.

Are There Too Many Lawyers? The Answer Is No!

From time to time rumors arise to the effect that there are too many lawyers. The practice of law is saturated! There are no jobs! Or some variation of the above. Before buying into this idea, allow me to make two points:

1. Opportunities in the legal profession follow trends in society. Therefore, there are always some areas of law where opportunities are decreasing and some areas where opportunities are increasing. For example, the advent of "title insurance" will diminish opportunities for real estate lawyers. Our move into the computer age will increase opportunities for lawyers in the IT area.

2. There are always opportunities for good people. Go to law school. Do well. If you do well the opportunities will take care of themselves.

What The "Experts" Are Saying

Professor David Stagar a University of Toronto economist published a book in 1990 called Lawyers In Canada.

Take careful note of the predictions he made writing in 1990.

First, on the question of whether there are too many lawyers?

"Are There Too Many Lawyers?

The assertion that there is a surplus or oversupply of lawyers is usually a reaction to any of the following conditions: decline in lawyer' relative earnings, slower growth in lawyers' real incomes, rising unemployment among lawyers, decline in the rate of return to investment in legal education, lower quality of legal services, or an increase in unnecessary legal work generated by lawyers. While any of these might represent a labour market adjustment, when supply is increasing at a rate greater than demand, none is necessarily evidence of a surplus or of the need to control supply." - page 318

Second, on the question of future demand for lawyers?

"Is There An Impending Shortage Of Lawyers?

In the next decade, the most likely outcome will be that demand increases more quickly than supply. On the assumption that real economic growth will average about 2 percent annually over the next decade, the demand for legal services could increase annually by 3 percent, possibly 4 percent. Compare this conservative estimate of growth in demand with the estimated maximum increase in supply of 3 percent annually. ... Therefore, a surplus of lawyers in the next decade seems most improbable. Rather, a shortage is more likely. To the extent that this occurs, it would be evidenced by an increase in relative earnings for lawyers. But this would be only another stage in the inevitable, continuing fluctuations in the lawyers' labour market." - page 320

> *David Stager - Lawyers In Canada - (1990)*

Career Possibilities - The Incredible World Of Lawyers

Students want to become lawyers for different reasons. Some are attracted to law for money, some are attracted for prestige, some are attracted for intellectual stimulation. Still others see a legal career as a possible vehicle to solve the social problems which are part of our society. The legal profession is sufficiently broad and diverse to accommodate any of these interests. In fact the work of a lawyer is so broad that it is entirely possible for two people to both be lawyers and be completely incompetent to do each other's work. The work of a lawyer is sufficiently broad so that it is possible to change careers throughout one's life and still be a lawyer.

When one considers specific career opportunities for lawyers one must consider both where lawyers work and the kind of work lawyers do. Each of these will be considered in turn.

Where Do Lawyers Work?

The short answer is everywhere. Some lawyers practise law in a traditional sense and practise law with both large and small firms. Some work as in-house counsel in the legal departments of corporations. Many lawyers make their career in the government. Others work in business. Some teach. Some enter politics. As human beings lawyers are an extremely diverse group of people and their influence is felt in every conceivable range of human activity. The range of possibilities is limitless and extends far beyond the traditional practice of law. In order to expand your horizons, you should read the following eight perspectives. Some lawyers are not involved in the practice of law in the traditional sense. Again, these perspectives are not offered as suggestions for areas of law you might consider, but as examples of the diverse range of opportunities available.

Perspective 1:

November 2002

James Lockyer

Jack Batten and Derek Finkle

Standing before a packed auditorium at the Law Society of Upper Canada in Toronto last weekend, James Lockyer is about to tell the story of one of his favourite clients. The audience is there for a conference put on by the Association in Defence of the Wrongly Convicted (AIDWYC), a group of which Lockyer is the director, and they're expecting to hear a woeful tale of an individual crushed by our justice system.

Lockyer, a Toronto criminal lawyer, played a key role in winning exoneration for, among many others, two of Canada's best known wrongly convicted, David Milgaard and Guy Paul Morin. But on this occasion, he elects to put aside Milgaard and Morin in favour of a less recognized victim, a Nova Scotia man named Clayton Johnson who, Lockyer says, "the system had buried for the rest of his life."

Johnson lived in the small town of Shelburne, Nova Scotia, with his wife Janice and two daughters, aged 11 and 8. He worked as a high school industrial arts teacher and was a pillar of the local Pentecostal Church. At 7:40 on the morning of February 20, 1989, Johnson waved his daughters out the front door to the waiting school bus. A minute or two later, as Janice chatted on the telephone to a friend, Johnson left the house himself to drive to work. At 7:51, a neighbour and his little daughter arrived at the house by appointment and found Janice dying in a pool of her own blood at the bottom of the basement stairs.

Everyone believed the poor woman had tumbled down the stairs until Clayton Johnson made what was perceived as an incriminating blunder. Three months after Janice's death, seeking a mother for his two daughters, Johnson wooed and later wed a pretty young woman named Tina from the Pentecostal congregation. Nasty tongues wagged in Shelburne. An RCMP sergeant of Javert-like tenacity got on the case and concluded it wasn't a tumble that had killed Janice, it was a bludgeoning.

On May 4, 1993, a Shelburne jury convicted Johnson of first-degree murder, and the judge put him away for 25 years in the Atlantic Institution in remotest Renous, New Brunswick.

While in Renous, Johnson composed a three-page, hand-written letter that painstakingly made the case for his innocence. The letter found its way to Lockyer, who did his due diligence and got what he calls "the little ping of recognition" that lets him know when the Canadian judicial system has delivered yet another wrong verdict. "It was the phone calls that struck me," he says. Shortly after seven on the morning Janice died, Johnson placed two calls at his wife's request. One was to the neighbour for whose little daughter Janice had promised to babysit that morning. The second was to Janice's brother, who had planned to drop off clothing at the Johnson house. Johnson had the same message for both men: Janice would like you here before eight o'clock.

"An innocent man makes those calls," Lockyer says, "not a man who plans to batter his wife in the next 45 minutes."

The key to establishing Johnson's innocence, Lockyer reasoned, was to account for the position of the killing wounds on Janice's head. Lockyer consulted an independent pathologist, Dr. Linda Norton of Dallas, Texas, who concluded that all the investigators and medical people involved in the case had been operating from a false first premise. All of them assumed that Janice had gone down the stairs face first. She hadn't. She had, Norton said, fallen backwards. That explained the arrangement of wounds on her head. There had been no blows, no murder, just a terrible accident. "I cross-examined Norton in her office for seven hours," Lockyer says. "Her analysis held up."

In November 1997, Lockyer traveled to the Renous prison for his first face-to-face meeting with his client. He told Johnson about Norton's findings. He told him how he planned to apply under section 690 of the Criminal Code for a new hearing before the Nova Scotia Court of Appeal, how he intended in the meantime to request bail for Johnson. Lockyer talked for an hour, and through the hour, Johnson sat silent, his expression flat, without change or nuance.

"Are you still religious after all you've been through?" Lockyer asked at the end, curious about Johnson's demeanor. "I thought you might have renounced your God."

Johnson spoke up. "God has helped me to bear all of this."

"The reason I asked," Lockyer said softly, "is because I've set out for you everything I think will happen and you've shown no emotion whatsoever."

Johnson looked at Lockyer, then his eyes burst in such sudden tears that Lockyer moved back in his chair as if to avoid the flood.

"He'd been holding it in for years," Lockyer says. "The poor abandoned man thought that was the thing to do, to be stoic. It's what can happen to these innocent guys."

Ten months later, Lockyer won bail for Johnson. But it wasn't until February 18, 2002, that the Nova Scotia Court of Appeal finally declared Johnson innocent. When the judge announced his verdict that morning, Lockyer tells his conference audience, there was barely a dry eye in the room.

Lockyer was born on December 21, 1949, in the Kent, England, community of Orpington into a family he says was "conservative and Conservative but conscious." He went to a good public school, St. Edwards Oxford, then into law at the University of Nottingham where he turned both hippie and radical. He let his naturally curley hair grow down his back, LISTENED TO HIS SHARE OF Grateful Dead anthems and went on demonstrations. He marched against South African apartheid, American capital punishment, fascist suspects everywhere. "By the time I left university," Lockyer says, "I was a committed socialist." The commitment remained when he emigrated to Canada in the early 1970s to teach law at the University of Windsor. He became known around town as the guy who organized a tenants' rights protest, helped to run Amnesty International, led demonstrations against the Pinochet regime in Chile. And when he moved to Toronto to practise law a few years later, he ran as the NDP candidate in the federal elections of 1979 and '80. "Lost my deposit both times," he says, "but I doubled the party's vote from six percent to thirteen and a half."

In 1980 he joined forces in a criminal law practice with Jack Pinkofsky, a man so intense in his clients' interest that he is easily the least popular defence counsel in Toronto among judges and crown attorneys. The practice flourished, and, until recently, the firm of Pinkofsky Lockyer, with about 25 lawyers and a branch office in Ottawa, was the largest firm in Canada devoted exclusively to criminal law.

Earlier this month, however, Lockyer announced that he is leaving Pinkofsky Lockyer under amicable terms to start a new firm with fellow defence counsel Phil Campbell as of next January. What is remarkable about the Lockyer-Campbell partnership is that it will specialize in wrongful conviction cases - something that has never before existed in the Canadian legal profession.

Wrongful convictions are something that have been worrying at Lockyer's conscience since 1968, when he first heard the story of Timothy Evans. On January 14, 1950, Britain hanged Evans for the murders at Croydon in Surrey of his wife and baby daughter. But Evans didn't commit the crimes. A backstreet abortionist named John Christie killed the wife and daughter as well as several other women whose bodies he buried in his cellar. Christie was convicted of the murders and hanged on March 10, 1950. Eighteen years later, the British government got around to formally pardoning Evans.

"I thought at the time of the pardon, 'Now what? Do they dig up Evans' body and tell him they're sorry?'" Lockyer says. He shows no hint of sanctimony when he describes the pardon as "a seminal point" in his life. "The Evans case taught me the judical system can make terrible mistakes."

All of which meant that Lockyer felt he was overdue to even the score for Evans when he had the chance to get involved in the appeal of Guy Paul Morin, a man Lockyer considers his "first lost cause." And the same attitude went into the lost causes that followed Morin into Lockyer's office.

It was Lockyer who confirmed beyond question David Milgaard's innocence of the 1969 murder in Saskatoon for which he served 23 years by negotiating DNA tests which pointed to the real killer. Lockyer also helped to exonerate Gregory Parsons after Parsons' wrongful conviction of his mother's 1991 murder in Newfoundland. (In fact, just two days before the AIDWYC conference, Parsons was in court testifying at the sentencing hearing of the man now convicted of the crime.)

Lockyer figures there are ABOUT THIRTY men presently serving sentences in Canadian prisons for murders they didn't commit. "I've got ten clients right now, convicted men, whom I believe to be innocent. I would say even five is a lot TO handle at once. That's the trouble with lost causes - they need so much time."

One of Lockyer's five "lost causes" right now is Robert Baltovich, who was convicted on March 31, 1992, of second degree murder in the death of his girlfriend, Elizabeth Bain. The couple met as students at the University of Toronto campus in Scarborough, the suburb where both had lived all their lives. Bain vanished in the early evening of June 19, 1990, never to be seen again, alive or dead. Hers became a murder case with no body, no direct eyewitnesses, no forensic evidence. But homicide detectives fastened on Baltovich, mostly because he was the boyfriend, and they built a circumstantial case against him. A jury bought the cops' version, and the judge sentenced Baltovich to life without parole for seventeen years. Baltovich appealed, and in February 1999, still in prison, frustrated at the lethargic pace of the appeal process, and dissatisfied with his own lawyer, he phoned James Lockyer from Warkworth Penitentiary.

"I gave Rob the same warning I gave Guy Paul, the same warning I give all my potential clients in his position," Lockyer says. "I told him if he wanted me to take over his case, I had to satisfy myself first that he really was innocent."

Reading Baltovich's trial transcript and other post-conviction documents, Lockyer found plenty of iffy material. The police had keyed their case on Baltovich driving Bain's car to dispose of her body even though Baltovich didn't know how to operate a gear-shift vehicle, which is what Bain's happened to be. But it wasn't the obvious stuff that made Lockyer tingle, it was Baltovich's bizarre episode of spying. From seven p.m. to nine p.m. on the last day Bain was seen, she was supposed to take a mandatory lecture at Scarborough College. Shortly before nine, Baltovich showed up, unplanned and unannounced, outside the lecture room. He noticed someone he later described as "a dark-haired Italian-looking guy" lingering in the hall. Maybe he was Bain's former boyfriend whom Baltovich suspected of insinuating himself back in her life. Baltovich ducked up a flight of stairs and stood concealed on a balcony where he could observe whether Bain greeted the Italian-looking guy. But the guy went off with another woman from the class. Embarrassed, Baltovich waited in his hiding spot for Bain to emerge but the lecture room emptied with no sign of her. Baltovich came down from the balcony and went looking for Bain at her home. Neither he nor anyone else ever found her.

The homicide people said Baltovich had made up the incident. It didn't fit the police theory because it would have had to have happened when the cops posited that Baltovich was elsewhere getting rid of Bain's body. The episode was brushed off at Baltovich's trial, but in a post-conviction police disclosure Lockyer discovered that the detectives had in fact interviewed a woman in Bain's class who met a boyfriend at the end of the lecture. The boyfriend's appearance and clothing matched Baltovich's detailed description of the Italian-looking guy.

Lockyer experienced his ping. He drove out to Warkworth and told Baltovich he was accepting the case.

A year later, on March 31, 2000, Lockyer won bail for his new client. What happens next still remains a matter of negotiation between Lockyer and the crown attorney's office; perhaps the Court of Appeal will hear full argument in the case or perhaps all parties will proceed directly to a new trial.

Whether either of these possibilties or some third course is pursued, Lockyer expects to present new evidence indicating that Bain's real killer might have been another former Scarborough native, Paul Bernardo, the infamous sadist convicted in 1995 of murdering two teenaged girls in Ontario's Niagara region.

After Baltovich's conviction, Bernardo was shown to have been active as "the Scarborough rapist," sexually assaulting more than 20 young women in the area, over a period ending a couple of weeks before Bain's disappearance.

Bain may have been Bernardo's final Scarborough rape victim and his first ever murder victim. Lockyer seems not just sanguine about his future chances for Baltovich but exhilarated at the prospect of arguing on Baltovich's behalf. "I love this work," he says. "Representing people I'm certain are innocent makes me feel, as a lawyer, I'm doing something profoundly worthwhile."

AIDWYC, which now encompasses a floating membership of several dozen lawyers, was created in 1993 out of an ad hoc committee set up to help prove the innocence of Guy Paul Morin. It has set itself two objectives. The first is to act as clearing house and possible saviour for people convicted of crimes who insist on their innocence and have exhausted their appeal remedies. The application of each person who approaches AIDWYC goes through a review process by lawyers who look for new physical evidence in the case, for fresh eyewitness testimony, DNA possibilities, for facts that only emerge with the passage of time, for anything to hang an evidentiary hat on.

(Only once, in the case of Roy Kenshin Lee, convicted of a 1987 murder in Niagara Falls, Ontario, has a DNA test failed to exonerate an AIDWYC client.) The search is not for legal errors in past court proceedings but for a factual case that can be made for the person in the prison cell.

If AIDWYC's review comes up positive, a lawyer will accept the case.

AIDWYC's second objective is, in Lockyer's words, "to put ourselves out of business." The Association's lawyers want the federal government to take over the job they created and have assumed for the last decade, and at the top of their wish list is the establishment in Canada of something almost exactly like Britain's Criminal Cases Review Commission. This body opened operations in 1997, government funded, generously and expertly staffed, but entirely independent. It examines cases for the possibility of wrongful convictions, and when it finds such a possibility, it refers the case to the appropriate court of appeal. In its first fifteen months, the Commission completed 308 cases, sent 12 to courts of appeal, and of the two appeals which have been completed, each was successful. More astonishing, the Commission helped to uncover three more Timothy Evans characters, three men whom the state hanged years ago for murders they are now revealed not to have committed.

Ottawa doesn't like the idea of a Criminal Case Review Commission in Canada, especially the part about being independent. Lockyer and other AIDWYC directors lobbied the then Minister of Justice, Anne McLellan, for such a commission at a meeting on February 23, 1998, and in subsequent written submissions. But in June 2000 when McLellan announced legislation designed to address wrongful convictions, her plan called for insider treatment of the problem. The people who would examine and judge the workers in the judicial system who may have messed up in the first place would themselves be workers in the same system.

"The proposed changes are ridiculous," Lockyer says. "I don't know why the Justice Ministry even bothered. We've somehow got to derail Ottawa on this one."

Over time, AIDWYC has also fought some memorable battles on behalf of Canadians it perceived had been wronged in other countries. In 1998, Lockyer unsuccessfully attempted to halt the execution of Stan Faulder for murder in Texas, not so much because he felt Faulder had been wrongly convicted but because of his staunch opposition to capital punishment and questions about the way Faulder's trial had been conducted.

The following year, Lockyer and Rubin "Hurricane" Carter, AIDWYC's executive director, traveled to Ottawa to meet with the Vietnamese ambassador to discuss the plight of Nguyen Thi Hiep and her mother, Tran Thi Cam.

Both had been convicted of trying to smuggle heroin out of Vietnam to Canada. Despite evidence presented to the Vietnamese that both women had been unwitting drug couriers (known as "pigeons"), Nguyen was, despite the best efforts of Lockyer and others, executed. Soon after, though, the Vietnamese bowed to serious diplomatic pressure and returned her mother to Canada in September of 2000, despite her life sentence.

Lockyer is currently on another mission to save a Canadian facing a death sentence abroad. Bill Sampson, who awaits execution by beheading in Saudi Arabia, was convicted of two car bombings that killed one Briton and injured several others. The fact that Sampson's trial was held in secret, without defence counsel, is, on its own, cause for concern, but what gave Lockyer his "ping" was Sampson's videotaped confession. When Lockyer saw the tape aired on television, it was obvious that Sampson was reading from a script written by someone for whom English was a second language. Moreover, bombings just like the ones that Sampson and his co-accused, a Briton, were convicted of igniting have continued since their imprisonment two years ago.

This time, though, it looks like Lockyer will have some legal heavyweights in his corner. At a press conference the day before the AIDWYC conference in Toronto got under way, Johnnie Cochran and Barry Scheck, two prominent members of the "dream team" that successfully defended O.J. Simpson who are now actively involved in the wrongful-conviction cause, made headlines when they condemned Sampson's treatment and offered to be part of a delegation prepared to travel to Saudi Arabia in an attempt to save his life and secure him a fair hearing.

Robert Baltovich is eating chicken wings at the Bo Peep Family Restaurant in the eastern reaches of Scarborough. The Bo Peep has been in Baltovich's neighbourhood forever. It's where he had his grade eight graduation party more than two decades ago. The sign in front of Jimmy's Smoke Shop, the variety store that Baltovich's father opened right across the street in 1952, is still there despite the fact that his father closed the store down a year ago. The only person who had been missing from the scene lately was Baltovich himself, having served eight years in the prisons at Millhaven and Warkworth.

Baltovich is preppy-looking and proper, and has a habit of speaking with elaborate gentility. When he says "the environment I was in," he means prison. Maybe it's his training. He holds a BA in psychology, earned from Scarborough College earlier in the same month that Elizabeth Bain disappeared, and in May, 2001, a little over a year after Lockyer and co-defence counsel Joanne McLean got him released on bail, he graduated from a course at nearby Seneca College which gave him a diploma in library science. He then went on to work for a year at the library of the Royal Ontario Museum and is now enrolled in a Masters degree program at the University of Toronto.

Baltovich's conversation invariably circles back to Lockyer. He speaks of Lockyer out of an impulse that appears to reflect, in different parts, gratitude, hero worship and amazement that this accomplished lawyer has put himself on the line for Baltovich in such a simpatico way.

He says it was the way Lockyer handled the telephone calls that first indicated to Baltovich that he was dealing with a man who was different from any other lawyer he had ever encountered, in fact different from any other person.

"The first thing you have to realize is that no phone call was frivolous for a person in my position, innocent and locked up," Baltovich says. He was as ecstatic as he allowed himself to get when Lockyer accepted Baltovich's initial call (all phone calls from prison are collect), and he was astonished that Lockyer kept on taking all the calls that followed.

Unbeknownst to Baltovich, Lockyer had instructed his assistant to chat with Baltovich whenever he was out of the office. That way, Lockyer felt he was able to give the guy in prison at least some outside human contact; he also set up a weekly system of calls to provide Baltovich with updates on the case. "I thought it was all extraordinary," Baltovich says, seeming still dazed at the thoughtful treatment.

"When I first went into prison," Baltovich says at the Bo Peep, "whenever I said to the guards or the administrative personnel, 'I'm innocent,' they treated me as if I was from Mars. But by the time I left, the same people were saying, 'Well, maybe you're right.' Public attitudes towards people like me are changing, and the change is mostly thanks to one man."

Baltovich pauses a beat for emphasis.

"James Lockyer."

Reprinted with permission of the authors.

Perspective 2:

In The Field: The Role Of Jag Officers On Operational Deployments

Major Michael Gibson

When I tell other lawyers what I do for a living as a JAG officer, I often find that their initial conception is coloured by the images which they have gleaned from the eponymous American television program. While the reality does not quite accord with the vibrant Hollywood image, it is nevertheless always challenging, sometimes frustrating, frequently rewarding, and unquestionably unique.

Civilian lawyers are often curious in particular as to what it is that JAG officers do when they are deployed to Bosnia, or Kosovo, or East Timor, or Turkey, as I am at the moment with the Canadian Forces Disaster Assistance Response Team which is providing assistance to the victims of a devastating earthquake.

Legal officers on the establishment of the Office of the Judge Advocate General of the Canadian Forces occupy a unique position amongst members of the Bar in that they are both lawyers and serving commissioned officers in the Canadian Forces. One of the most important roles of JAG officers is also one of the most unique: to serve as the in-theatre legal adviser to commanders of Canadian Forces contingents deployed abroad. The Canadian Forces exist as a primary policy instrument for the accomplishment of the defence and foreign affairs policy objectives of the Government of Canada. Operating in this role, contingents of the Canadian Forces may be deployed anywhere in the world, often on very short notice, in a variety of roles, from disaster relief and humanitarian assistance, to peacekeeping, peacemaking, peace support or peace enforcement missions. When required, they can also operate as combat forces as part of United Nations or coalition forces. In whatever role Canadian Forces are deployed in, there will always be a need for the provision of timely and effective legal advice to operational commanders, in order to ensure that they remain in compliance with both Canadian and international law.

What types of advice are legal officers required to provide on deployment? The answer is that the gamut of the fields of law upon which legal officers may be expected to provide advice is extremely broad, and in this sense JAG officers on deployment are expected to be the ultimate generalists. However, they are expected to be experts in some particular areas of law, operational law being foremost on the list.

There are six broad areas of law upon which JAG officers on deployment may be called upon to provide advice: Operational Law, Criminal and Disciplinary matters, Procurement issues, Civil-Military Relations with the governmental authorities of the host nation, Claims, and what might broadly be described as Personnel legal issues.

Operational Law might broadly be described as applied Public International Law. It encompasses such matters as international humanitarian law, embodied in both international conventional law such as the four Geneva Conventions of 1949 and the Additional Protocols thereto of 1977, as well as international customary law. It also deals with the use of force, the very heart of the ultimate raison d'etre for armed forces. In addition to the international Law of Armed Conflict, the use of force will always be regulated by Rules of Engagement ("ROE"), which are orders issued by the competent national authority regulating the circumstances and the purposes for which force is authorized to be used. In Canadian doctrine, ROE are issued by the Chief of the Defence Staff on behalf of the Government of Canada. Legal, diplomatic, policy and operational factors all affect the ROE which will be issued for a particular mission. Given the volatile nature of the operational situations into which the Canadian Forces may find themselves deployed, JAG officers must be fully conversant with Canadian law and doctrine regarding ROE and the use of force. This, in colloquial terms, is where the rubber meets the road, as operational commanders are rarely interested in esoteric dissertations from their legal adviser on the niceties of the law in this regard: in a crisis situation what they want to know is, "can my soldiers use force, and, if so, to what degree", and they want the answer NOW. A premium is placed on getting the answer right, for obvious reasons. The provision of advice on operational law also requires the legal officer to understand and interpret the legal mandate which the force is operating under, which is often embodied in various Resolutions of the United Nations Security Council.

The heart of any armed force is discipline. The unfortunate experience of the Canadian Forces in Somalia, and its aftermath, provide a graphic illustration of the potentially disastrous consequences of breakdowns in discipline. In the Canadian Forces military discipline is enforced by the Code of Service Discipline, which is part of the National Defence Act. The Code of Service Discipline consists of all offences which are offences under other acts of the federal Parliament (including all Criminal Code and Controlled Drugs and Substances Act offences) as well as a number of uniquely military offences. The Code is enforced by service tribunals, which can be one of three types of Summary Trial (summary trial by Commanding Officer, Delegated Officer or Superior Commander) or four types of Court Martial (General Court Martial, Disciplinary Court Martial, Standing Court Martial or Special General Court Martial). Which type of service tribunal has jurisdiction will depend upon a number of factors, including the rank of the accused, whether the accused has elected to be tried by court martial, and the nature and gravity of the alleged offence. The role of the legal adviser in the field on deployed operations is to review unit and military police investigations and to advise on the laying of charges, as well as to provide advice to unit and military police investigators on the conduct of investigations into alleged offences. When charges are laid they may be tried by officers in the operational chain of command by summary trial, or they may be tried by court martial, in which case the prosecutor will be another JAG officer on the staff of the Director of Military Prosecutions.

No operation can be sustained for very long without effective logistical support, and this often involves the legal officer in advising on procurement issues, such as supply contracts for the procurement of goods and services from local sources, leases for the property used by the force, and employment contracts for the use of local civilian labour in the capacity of cooks, cleaners, translators, drivers and general labourers.

The area of civil-military relations with the governmental authorities of the host nation is often one of the most interesting areas in which the legal officer provides advice. The status of the force and its relationship with local host nation authorities is usually governed by a Status of Forces Agreement ("SOFA"), which will govern such issues as criminal jurisdiction of the local authorities and the Canadian Forces, the carrying of arms, local procurement, exemption from taxation by the host nation, drivers licences, customs, how tort claims will be handled, and a host of other issues. If there is no pre-existing SOFA, or if it needs to be amplified, the legal officer will often become involved, together with officials of the Department of Foreign Affairs and International Trade, in drafting and negotiating a SOFA with the host nation. In the event that members of the Canadian Forces come into conflict with the local law, sensitive negotiations will often be required with the host nation legal authorities to determine which nation will take jurisdiction in dealing with the matter.

The fifth area involves claims in tort (often described as Claims against the Crown) which may arise from vehicle or personal injury accidents and damage to property caused by the operations of the force. In many situations (such as Bosnia, for example) the SOFA or other agreement will provide for the resolution of claims by a system of arbitration tribunals. The resolution and payment of claims will usually be the responsibility of the contingent legal officer. This role can often lead to some incongruous situations. For example, I can recall trooping into the offices of a law firm in a small town in Bosnia in order to settle a claim made by one of their clients, clad in my combat uniform with the mud of the field fresh on my combat boots, with my sidearm on my hip, carrying a satchel of money, only to find a set of lushly-appointed offices populated by lawyers in Gucci suits with plush leather armchairs and gleaming oak boardroom tables which would do any Bay Street law firm proud. Amongst lawyers some things, it would seem, are universal.

The final area in which the legal officer might be called upon to provide advice might be broadly described as personnel legal issues. Soldiers are human beings like anybody else, of course, and the complexities of their life do not cease merely because they happen to have been deployed half way around the world from Canada. The "Dear John" letter is still an unfortunate occurrence which sometimes befalls members of the Canadian Forces on deployment, and, to the extent possible without compromising our primary obligation to be legal advisers to the chain of command, legal officers will often find themselves being called upon to assist individual soldiers with advice in the areas of family and estate law.

This brief survey illustrates the enormous variety of legal issues which can face JAG officers on deployment on international operations. One thing which can be said with certainty is that each mission presents its own set of challenges and rewards, and that there indeed is, in the words of the recruiting slogan, no life like it in the practice of law."

Major Gibson is a graduate of the University of Toronto Faculty of Law and a member of the Ontario Bar who, when not deployed on operations, is the Deputy Judge Advocate at Canadian Forces Base Trenton, Ontario. He is currently deployed in Serdivan, Turkey, with the Canadian Forces Disaster Assistance Response Team.

Reprinted with permission of the author.

Perspective 3:

June 24, 2002

The Globe and Mail

Yukon lawyer has a hand in the future of a nation

Terrence Belford

It wouldn't be a stretch to call Yukon lawyer James Harper a modern father of Confederation.

As a specialist in treaty negotiations and a principal adviser to Yukon First Nations for the past 16 years, Mr. Harper's practice in the tiny settlement of Pelly Crossing is proof that the process of hammering out the terms of Confederation did not end in 1867.

This time, 14 First Nations are at the bargaining table with bureaucrats and politicians. When the process is finally finished — it has been under way for almost 30 years now — Yukon will have 14 new essentially self-governing states within its borders; in effect provinces within a territory. Each First Nation will have the power to collect taxes, administer justice, create and administer social, health and educational programs.

Despite the size of the task, only four lawyers specializing in treaty negotiations live in Yukon, with Mr. Harper the only one outside Whitehorse.

Mr. Harper moved to Pelly Crossing — a settlement of about 300 Northern Tuchone, 280 kilometres north of Whitehorse — in the mid-1980s soon after graduating from the University of British Columbia Law School. To date, eight First Nations have signed treaties giving them self-government. All were his clients during that process and many remain so. Four more — including two of his clients — are in the process of ratifying agreements. Two more First Nations are still at the bargaining table.

At stake is ownership of 16,000 square miles of land — with full mineral rights to 10,000 square miles. Through the deals that he helped broker, the First Nations now share in the provincial oil and gas royalties, which previously went to the territorial government. The discreet Mr. Harper won't place dollar values on the natural resource wealth flowing to clients.

"All I can tell you is that it has provided meaningful revenues for my clients," he says.

Mr. Harper readily admits it was not just the legal work involved with forming new mini-states in Yukon that captivated him. He fell in love with the people and the lifestyle.

"It has been extremely challenging work," Mr. Harper says. "It is a situation where you know that what you do can greatly impact the future of entire peoples and, in the end a nation."

His role is not to suggest policy, he stresses. That is up to the elected First Nations's leadership. His role is to be an adviser and negotiator. For example, from the late 1970s to the late 1990s, he was an adviser to the Council of Yukon Indians, which negotiated and formulated the framework for subsequent individual treaties. Once that framework was in place, he became a main negotiator to many of the individual First Nations. Then, when the treaties were ratified and in place, his role shifted again, this time to being an adviser on the legal aspects of specific programs.

"I don't want to give the impression that I worked alone on all of these things," he points out. "I have an entire support structure to call upon both in Yukon and down south. Several First Nations have on staff people who are trained as lawyers, but have never been called to the bar. I do not do litigation, for example, so if litigation is involved the clients will retain outside counsel."

Still, there is more than enough work to keep him on the road for between 25 and 50 per cent of the time. His own estimate is that he travels 35,000 km a year, either in his Buick Riviera or regional air carriers.

"The thing is, what I want is a practice that lets me live life the way I want to," he says. "Working 60 hours a week for a big southern firm is not for me. If I had a separate office and staff instead of working out of my home, I would have to raise my rates and charge my clients more. I don't want to do that either."

While he will not discuss rates, he does say that those in Yukon are a bargain, compared with southern cities. He says corporate work can command $250 an hour in Whitehorse, compared with double that in Toronto.

"What we are doing here is not about money," he says. "I am doing the kind of work I love, living in a community I enjoy. This kind of law is very personal. You get the work because the clients know you and trust you. I could not ask for more."

Reprinted with permission of the author.

Perspective 4:

November 26, 2003

Called to the sports bar

Robert Thompson

Financial Post

Ask Glen Grunwald, general manager of the Toronto Raptors, what NBA stands for and he won't hesitate to give you an answer.

"Nothing but attorneys," says Mr. Grunwald, the 6-foot-8 former co-captain of the Indiana University Hoosiers.

These days two of Toronto's top professional sports franchises — the National Basketball Association's Raptors and the National Hockey League's Maple Leafs — are being run by former jocks who also happen to be lawyers.

Mr. Grunwald, who once practiced law in Chicago, has run theRaptors since being appointed the club's general manager in 1997. In August, he was joined by former player agent and lawyer John Ferguson Jr., who was hired to take over the role of general manager of the Toronto Maple Leafs.

As labour issues have increasingly come to dominate professional sports, it is not surprising to see an increase of lawyers in administrative roles. These days, lawyers like Gary Bettman and David Stern, the commissioners of the NHL and NBA, respectively, have played central roles in defining their sports.

Though Messrs. Ferguson and Grunwald have both landed in sports management roles that utilize some of their legal training, the two took different paths to their current jobs.

Mr. Ferguson, 36, viewed law school as a way of landing a front office job in sports, while entering into management at a professional sports franchise was not a consideration for Mr. Grunwald, 44.

The son of a former Montreal Canadiens standout, Mr. Ferguson pursued a career in professional hockey, playing in the AHL, hockey's top minor league, after a stint in college. But when it became clear that his abilities as a player would not lead him to the NHL, Mr. Ferguson shifted gears and decided to go to law school.

Having taken his law school admissions test while at university,

Mr. Ferguson, then 26, pursued a law degree at Suffolk University in Britain. "The real change for me was the work load," he says. "Sport is so physical, but I ended up doing something that is mentally taxing."

Supported by his wife, a lawyer who was just starting to practice, Mr. Ferguson remained involved in hockey while going to law school, scouting for the Ottawa Senators while interning at the NHL's head office in New York.

Labour issues always interested the former hockey player, and he points to an internship involving the Rhode Island correctional guards as one of his first forays into collective bargaining.

"It really made a lot of labour issues clear to me," he says. He passed the Massachusetts State Bar in 1996, and was soon snapped up by the St. Louis Blues to become the club's assistant general manager, a position he held until joining the Maple Leafs in August.

For Mr. Grunwald, playing basketball was always viewed as a means to an end. Having injured his knee in high school, he hoped university basketball would help finance his education, rather than be a springboard to the NBA.

"Going to Indiana gave me not only a tremendous opportunity to play basketball, but also allowed me to get a great education," he says.

Though he was drafted by the Boston Celtics, Mr. Grunwald says knee injuries forced him to consider options other than playing in the NBA.

He credits Bobby Knight, then the controversial coach of the Hoosiers, for helping get him scholarships that helped to finance law school.

He attended Chicago's Northwestern University, where he earned his degree in 1984. Mr. Grunwald also has a Masters in business administration, which he completed in 1986.

After leaving school, Mr. Grunwald landed a job practising corporate law at the respected Chicago firm Winston and Strawn. Basketball seemed far away.

"I really enjoyed corporate law," he says. "I wasn't sending out any resumes anyway."

But after spending time helping a client search for an NBA franchise to acquire, Mr. Grunwald found himself drawn back to the game. Only this time it was in the office and not on the floor.

After helping a client obtain the Denver Nuggets, he quit his job at Winston and Strawn and took a position with the team, where he was responsible for all legal and human resources issues, while also managing salary cap issues for the team.

"It was just by chance that I got involved in the NBA," he says.

In 1994, Mr. Grunwald joined former Indiana teammate Isiah Thomas at the upstart Toronto Raptors franchise as assistant general manager and legal counsel, being elevated to general manager in1997.

Both GMs say their legal background helps in dealing with Maple Leaf Sports and Entertainment Ltd., the parent company that runs the Leafs and the Raptors.

But Mr. Ferguson clearly attempts to define himself as a hockey executive who happens to have a legal background. Having a law degree doesn't help in evaluating talent, he points out.

"I view myself as a hockey guy with legal training," he says. "Being a lawyer has given me a lot of confidence. It allows me to espouse opinions and positions that may not have been expressed in the past. Being a lawyer certainly helps me do my job, but it isn't a prerequisite."

Like Mr. Ferguson, Mr. Grunwald says that his training in the law is always part of his makeup and factors into many of his personnel decisions.

"Once a lawyer, always a lawyer," says the Raptors' GM. "It gives you perspective and understanding of the business."

Despite the uses he has found for his legal experience, Mr. Grunwald says it is the sports world that keeps him enthralled now.

While some question Mr. Grunwald's success in Toronto (the team has faced significant turmoil over the past few seasons and is sitting on a record this year of 6-7), he now views himself as more of a sports executive than a lawyer.

"Could I go back to practicing law? Sure. But I enjoy this job a lot more."

Reprinted with permission of the National Post

Perspective 5:

The apprenticeship of Eddie Greenspan

Kirk Makin

It was one of those acrid cross-examinations in which witness and interrogator go blow for blow. But Eddie Greenspan had no intention of settling for a draw.

Plopping down on the courtroom floor, he ordered Tanya Sidorova to demonstrate exactly how his client, Toronto businessman Kirby Inwood, had supposedly throttled her just days after she arrived in Canada to become his bride. He was convinced she had seduced Mr. Inwood in hopes of gaining free passage to Canada and then fabricated an assault to be rid of him.

Ms. Sidorova did her best to re-enact the attack but clearly was rattled by the startling break in courtroom decorum. Word of the stunt travelled quickly on the legal grape-vine, and the grumbling grew. Had Fast Eddie lost perspective?

Fifteen years later, Mr. Greenspan winces. "It was an error. I should never have projected myself as an exhibit. You can cross-examine a witness vigorously, but you should never embarrass a witness. I embarrassed her and, in doing so, I embarrassed the administration of justice, which is my God."

It is a rare anecdote because it reflects badly on Mr. Greenspan; most stories about him revolve around impeccably timed bon mots that cracked up a judge or spell-binding addresses that left juries limp with doubt. But the Sidorova incident speaks volumes because afterward Mr. Greenspan resolved never again to trot out an unconventional tactic or question without first running it by trusted colleagues.

Now he is in the news again because of his controversial accusation in a secret court hearing that investigative journalist Stevie Cameron was a secret RCMP informant.

The accusation has aroused some familiar questions. Is the old Eddie Greenspan back? Was he just throwing up a smokescreen to divert attention from his own client, Karlheinz Schreiber, the high-flying Toronto businessman fighting extradition to his native Germany?

Mr. Greenspan insists that he was making a sincere attempt to uncloak a scandal that may reach into the upper echelons of government. Unlike the Sidorova incident, he betrays no regret or uncertainty.

Indeed, just weeks from his 60th birthday, he seems to be someone whose convictions have gelled and who is consummately confident of his approach to the law.

The apprenticeship of Eddie Greenspan, the small-town outsider who quickly became the toast of Toronto's criminal bar, is long over. The remarkable string of clients he has amassed includes former Nova Scotia premier Gerald Regan; Mr. Schreiber; theatre impresario Garth Drabinsky; and three men convicted of notorious murders — Robert Latimer, Peter Demeter and Helmuth Buxbaum.

The epitome of a hotshot, big-city criminal lawyer, Mr. Greenspan has a secure place in legal history. However, his daring tactics and larger-than-life personality seem destined to provoke debate until the day he hangs up his gown.

Turning 60 may be a time of reflection and refocusing for many, but for him, it is just a way station. Eighteen years ago, he came to grips with his mortality, long before his peers began to have similar thoughts because he believed that, like his father, a scrap dealer, he would be gone at 42.

Joseph H. Greenspan had died of a heart attack. Obsessed, his son planned his entire life around his premature departure. Assuming he had little time to make his mark on the law, he worked long hours, smoked three packs a day and compulsively consumed junk food. After all, what did it matter?

But then "I woke up when I turned 43," he recalls, "and I had no plans. Everything since then has been bonus time."

His superstitious nature also has its amusing side. For instance, his office contains a sizable freshwater aquarium, and he named one of its first occupants Morris Fish after a good friend. The very next morning, he arrived to find Morris floating upside down. Mr. Justice Morris J. Fish of the Supreme Court of Canada never learned what had happened, and Mr. Greenspan vowed never to name another fish.

In the courtroom, he is careful to neither clean nor switch his gown during a trial. Beyond that, however, the secret to his success is just hard work. Determined not to coast, he still camps in his office, in a beautiful, restored bank building downtown, six days a week and logs well over 60 hours of work. His case preparation is unflagging, as is his commitment to spreading the gospel of defence advocacy.

Much sought after as a speaker, he devotes long hours to speeches on the noble role of the defence lawyer and the need to force the state to live up to its ideals. (He also often lionizes his wife, Suzy, for giving him the freedom to pursue his work. Daughters Julianna and Samantha have made similar sacrifices, with Julianna so bitten by the legal bug that last year she joined her father's firm as a lawyer.)

Ask what drives him and he will say a pure love of the law. But others suggest it's a fear of falling from his perch and a desire to silence those who dismiss him as more showman than tactician. Which leads back to the Stevie Cameron episode, in which Mr. Greenspan regaled the court with his theories.

"Other lawyers told me afterward that it was a mesmerizing performance, but I wasn't trying to do that." He was outraged, he claims, that federal authorities embarked on a case that smeared former prime minister Brian Mulroney on the apparent say-so of a journalist.

But a Crown prosecutor scoffs at this: "It was a stunt. I guarantee you Eddie did it thinking about what the headlines would be."

According to the prosecutor, well-timed manoeuvres draw many clients to Mr. Greenspan. "This is all about the man and the myth," he says, "but the man has to at least come close to the myth for it to be sustained over any period of time, and Eddie is absolutely deserving."

In fact, prosecutors tend to think twice before locking horns with him, which gives him an edge. This willingness to drop the gloves is rare among senior, A-list lawyers, says James Lockyer, himself a leading defence counsel. "A lot of good lawyers, as they get older, tend to do cross-examinations without getting their knees dirty."

Mr. Greenspan approaches a jury trial as a performance. The basic script is provided, but the rest is a blend of choreography and improvisation. His first move is to establish a rapport that will rub off on his client. Throughout, his "antennae" constantly assess the mood. "I watch juries very closely," he says. "I watch for their approval or disapproval. If one of them shakes his head, I make a note of it."

This attention to detail spills over into other aspects of his life. Friends and colleagues point to such rituals as carefully stacking papers or cigarette butts in an ashtray. "He will come in your office and move your stapler to make it parallel to your desk," says Todd

Ducharme, a former member of his firm. "I don't know if that is an indication of a serious obsessive-compulsive disorder, but I certainly found it striking."

Out-of-town trials pose a special challenge. Mr. Greenspan must do battle with his own reputation as the heavy hitter from big, bad Toronto. So he eats in local beaneries, chats up strangers and, in court, is careful to treat jurors as his peers.

It may look like part of the performance, but he says he's a small-town boy at heart even if he has a North Toronto mansion and hobnobs with society figures. "I love ordinary people. . . . I would rather eat a hamburger than Beef Wellington. . . . I want a jury to feel that I am real; that I am flesh and blood. It's not an act."

Born Edward Leonard Greenspan and raised in Niagara Falls, Ont., he went to school with kids from every social stratum, which allows him, he says, to relate to anyone from Conrad Black to a street sweeper. "I'm not Toronto. I am Niagara Falls. And I've never forgotten that."

A graduate of York University's Osgoode Hall Law School, he made $3,200 in his first year as a lawyer. In despair, he considered returning to Niagara Falls, but then acted as a junior defence counsel to lawyer Joseph Pomerant in the high-profile Demeter murder trial. His colourful quotes and energetic cross-examinations thrust him into the public eye.

He remained there, becoming a favourite of reporters and television interviewers in search of a penetrating quote or a clever quip. His love of the media and their ability to influence public opinion inspired him to write the best-selling Greenspan: The Case for the Defence, and to produce with writer George Jonas the popular television series called The Scales of Justice.

Now, he cuts a dramatic figure in court. He sweeps in, drapes himself over a chair at the defence table, and fixes his opponent with a stony glare. He switches from self-deprecation to biting antagonism in a flash, and his instincts for the moment are second to none.

"Very few cases are won or lost because of an advocate's reputation, but some get a better hearing based on who the advocate is," the Ontario prosecutor says. "It's very hard for a judge in Orangeville to bounce Eddie out of court 10 minutes into submission, whereas the same judge might do it for a less well-known lawyer."

Mr. Greenspan's impact is even more paradoxical given his frequent accusations that authorities are biased or hide evidence or conspire against his clients. A lesser lawyer's credibility would melt away. How does he get away with it?

"Greenspan doesn't make the common mistake of personally vouching for his client's good character and innocence . . . which always sounds contrived," says David Schermbrucker, a federal prosecutor in Nova Scotia and former defence lawyer in Toronto. "Far better to attack your attackers."

"His main weapon is his mouth. He knows how to state an issue in simple, direct fashion that immediately points out why the Crown, or other foe, is seriously offside in going after his client."

Another key is his firm belief that the state is a grasping, authoritarian monster. "As criminal lawyers, we see it all the time," he says. "I don't trust the state. I think the state should interfere with our lives as little as possible."

Mr. Greenspan does not come cheap. His office alone suggests that his clients have deep pockets, and Helmuth Buxbaum paid more than $1-million to fight, unsuccessfully, the charge that he murdered his wife. In fact, the Greenspan image as a defender of the wealthy and powerful annoys many lawyers who defend the downtrodden.

"Most of his naysayers speak from envy and resentment," Mr. Schermbrucker says. They see Mr. Greenspan as having limited "depth" when it comes to intricate legal issues and appellate argument, he explains. "To them, it's frustrating that he gets so much attention. But that's the market. I do think he is one of the great defence lawyers of all time."

Mr. Lockyer has made a crusade of representing the wrongfully convicted (and been mocked in a Greenspan speech for wanting only clients who are innocent), but says he doesn't resent upscale defendants. "To be perfectly honest, I'd love to have one or two of them."

But he says Mr. Greenspan's big legal fees propel him into a different realm. He espouses the ideal that defence lawyers must represent even the most hated or indigent clients, Mr. Lockyer says, but "he says it in the context of a $500,000 retainer. He is not a lawyer who takes them on legal-aid certificates. This means he is not really involved in the day-to-day machinations of the criminal law."

Stung by such accusations, Mr. Greenspan points out that he began as a no-name lawyer with empty pockets and a legal-aid clientele. The fact that he now leaves most of his firm's legal-aid cases to lawyers who share his office does not make him a dilettante. "Ninety-five per cent of my cases are done alone in the shadows. I go from court to court like anybody else. You don't know that I was in Cornwall yesterday. Or that I was in Chatham a week ago. I'm as excited by a common assault as a murder case."

The other knock on Mr. Greenspan is the publicity that seems to follow him around. But he feels the crime or the accused really generates the publicity. If the police and press begin to crucify a client, he is compelled to go public to blunt their angle. "I don't believe I've ever done something to somehow advance myself. Everything I do is for the client."

Mr. Ducharme says critics are wrong to assume Mr. Greenspan's showmanship lacks substance. "Cross-examination can be a real dance, but Eddie is so quick on his feet that he can do things we lesser mortals can only dream of. . . .. Eddie can change gears and go with the flow so quickly. And, yes, he'll use theatrics when he needs to."

And yet the great showman is frustrated at times that he is so rarely ranked with lawyers considered civil libertarians even though he is a long-time director of the Canadian Civil Liberties Association, and constitutional principles are at stake in many of his cases.

In 1987, he even abandoned his practice for six months to fight the return of the death penalty. His finest day in law came 14 years later when, in one of his cases, the Supreme Court squashed any prospect that capital punishment would ever be restored.

Still, his 35-year career has surpassed his wildest dreams. "I love what I do. I haven't lost a bit of interest, enthusiasm or energy. I love fighting for people. I love fighting the state. I wake up every morning and I can't believe I'm a lawyer."

Reprinted with permission from The Globe and Mail

Perspective 6:

Canada's first pet lawyer is just purring along

donalee Moulton

On a typical day the sounds that emanate from Kristin Graver's Vancouver law office might include the jangling of a phone, the whirring of a fax machine, and the quiet voices of a lawyer and her client in conversation. Oh yes, there might also be the yelp of a Chihuahua, the purr of a tabby and the chirp of a budgie.

You see Kristin Graver is the only lawyer practicing exclusively in pet and animal law in all of British Columbia and most likely in all of Canada. It's a fitting vocation for a woman who helped pay for her university education by working part time in a veterinarian's office.

"I definitely love animals and I have a real connection with animals," Ms. Graver told The Lawyers' Weekly in an interview.

"It's fun," she added, "but sometimes it's distracting having an animal running around your ankles."

Ms. Graver, who graduated with her law degree from the University of British Columbia two years ago, spent a year articling for a downtown Vancouver law firm. She quickly discovered that she did not enjoy civil litigation.

"I wasn't engaged with my clients' causes," she said.

It was her sister who suggested the idea of pet and animal law, a suggestion Ms. Graver at first pooh poohed. However, after doing her research Ms. Graver discovered there was merit in the idea. Indeed, the field is gaining momentum in the United States where the number of pets, and therefore issues regarding their welfare and the rights and responsibilities of pet owners, continue to grow.

Basically pet and animal law covers any type of law that has as its subject matter a pet or an animal, explained Ms. Graver, who has her own firm, Graver & Company, in North Vancouver. Indeed, the specialty requires knowledge of federal law, provincial statutes and municipal by-laws, running the gamut from leash regulations to livestock acts.

Dog bites and related injuries are usually the first thing people think of when they think of legal issues related to animals and Ms. Graver has certainly been called upon to represent clients in disputes where an animal, usually a dog, has harmed a person, another animal or caused property damage. However, there's much more to the field than this, she noted.

One emerging area is that of wills. Many people put their pets in their will as beneficiaries, which is not legal. Pets are considered property in Canada (and the United States) and cannot therefore inherit. Ms. Graver recommends that a clause be put in a will giving the pet to someone as a gift, obviously with that person's consent. A sum of money can then be set aside for that person, or another person, that is to be used for the continued care of the pet. If desired, pet owners can also set up a trust, although that is not very common, said Ms. Graver.

Another area of interest, she added, is landlord/tenant law. One common problem revolves around the right to keep an animal in an apartment. Sometimes tenants are even threatened with eviction if they continue to keep their pet, an action that is not, however, usually allowed by law. In Ontario, for example, it has been shown that the pet by-laws cannot be enforced, which provides somewhat of a precedent for other jurisdictions. There are also sticky issues, such as keeping a guide animal in an apartment, that were frequently not considered when the by-law or the lease was originally prepared.

Often municipal by-laws are too broad or too detailed, either way they are invalid, said Ms. Graver.

As well, she added, if landlords do not act quickly enough they will have been said to have waived the no-pets clause in their lease.

Ownership disputes also arise over pets and other animals, particularly among breeders. Ms. Graver, who was called to the bar in British Columbia last fall, recommends against co-ownership agreements unless it is absolutely necessary or unless the period of time in question is relatively short. For example, such agreements may be put in place as security while an animal is being bred.

At present, it is rare to have the issue of pets arise as part of a separation or divorce agreement, however, family lawyers may be handling these types of problems as part of the broader divorce settlement. But that may change with the emergence of pet and animal law in Canada. Ms. Graver, for example, is currently working with another lawyer on a divorce settlement. She is handling only those issues related to the couple's pet.

Indeed, many lawyers are relieved to know there's someone out there who is familiar with pet and animal law. Otherwise they have to spend valuable time digging through statutes that are often conflicting. And pet and animal law is all that Ms. Graver practices.

Although she doesn't think it will become a growth area like Asian law or tax law, there is clearly sufficient work to keep her busy. The rates are standard for the marketplace. Drawing up a contract for a breeder, for example, would cost approximately $200, the going rate for other types of contracts.

Best of all, said Ms. Graver, the work is not dull or routine.

"I wasn't sure at first but the law is very challenging and mentally stimulating. You have to construct some pretty complex arguments and construct new arguments," she noted.

Indeed, at present Ms. Graver is writing an article on the issue of pets as property, which means they are of very little importance under the law. She'd like to see a different way of classifying pets and animals, which are often a very beloved member of the family and of far more consequence than the dining room table.

Ms. Graver also volunteers for animal welfare organizations such as the Society for the Prevention of Cruelty to Animals (SPCA) and the Domestic Animal Committee, a local group that addresses practical issues of concern to pet owners.

Of course, the 27-year-old Vancouver lawyer also understands pet issues first hand. She and her partner are the proud owners of Zola, a kitten they brought home recently from the SPCA, and Terra, a five-month-old Samoyed."

Reprinted with permission of the author.

Perspective 7:

Sunday December 21, 2003

The great marijuana debate

Outspoken law professor at forefront of crusade to reform Canada's pot laws

Made career out of challenging state's power

Tracey Tyler

The word "liberty" is scrawled on the blackboard as Alan Young launches into one of his asides.

Did you know, he asks his students at the University of Toronto, that commercials for a well-known sexual performance-boosting drug could be illegal?

A section of the Criminal Code bans advertising drugs intended to promote sexual virility, he explains.

"Don't try telling me they're not promoting virility — the guy's dancing," says Young, the outspoken law professor at the forefront of the crusade to reform Canada's drug laws.

A decisive moment in the battle is expected Tuesday when the Supreme Court of Canada rules on whether banning recreational pot smoking is unconstitutional. Young is a long-time lawyer for one of three men at the centre of the fight.

Under the circumstances, it seems entirely appropriate that Young is getting ready to show a movie called Grass. But first he takes the class through a discussion of other hot-button topics, including assisted suicide, abortion and a nasty case involving a group of amorous blood relatives in Nova Scotia who went to court to challenge the country's incest laws.

Young wonders aloud if they didn't have a point about the government butting out of their lives, even though he finds their pastime creepy and "repulsive."

"There are enough sexual partners out there, I think, that you can leave the family members alone," he says. "But does the state have the right to ban it?"

Young's provocative manner is a hit with students.

"He's my favourite professor," says Elizabeth Pluss. "He makes it interesting."

For Young, 46, pushing boundaries is standard fare.

From defending a dominatrix who ran a "bondage bungalow" to a shopkeeper charged with selling "obscene" records, the Harvard-educated, self-described "neurotic" has made a career out of challenging the state's power to use the criminal law to intrude into people's lives — and a name for himself as a controversial scholar and showman. Quite an accomplishment for someone who never wanted a career in law.

Young's most recent case was a mixed success. Earlier this fall, the Ontario Court of Appeal ruled that the federal government was unconstitutionally restricting the rights of medical marijuana users and paved the way for large cannabis growing collectives.

But the court also recriminalized simple possession.

Young hasn't been above some high-profile shenanigans to focus attention on the cause, including leading a "million marijuana march" through downtown Toronto. While he enjoys the entertainment factor, the merry-making usually has a purpose, according to those who know him best.

Young is a "natural advocate" and "very bright" academic who thrives on teaching himself and others about the law, says criminal lawyer Marie Henein, a friend and former student.

And he is a great educator because he "can connect with any audience"—— young people especially, since he has a vast knowledge of pop culture and loves showing it off, says defence lawyer Paul Burstein, one of Young's closest friends.

Those teaching skills, in turn, make him a good courtroom lawyer because, in essence, "he is educating the judiciary."

But is Young too talented for his own good? "There are those in the profession who have very high regard for Alan" — for the quality of his work, his courtroom results and the countless hours he's devoted to cases free of charge, Burstein says. But some "have very little respect."

"With some of them, it's just politics," he says. "They don't like his approach to the whole institution of law. They don't like him rocking the boat."

"And this book is not going to help."

The book he is referring to is Young's newly published Justice Defiled. In it, Young rips apart the entire "criminal justice industrial complex." His most vicious criticism is reserved for law schools, which he calls breeding grounds for "politically correct little bastards."

He realizes that exposes him to charges of hypocrisy, since the profession is how he's made his living, but says he wrote the book while he was coming out of a difficult period personally and professionally and considering leaving the law altogether.

Within the space of a couple of years, Young's marriage broke up, his sister died of cancer, he was defrauded by a colleague and became the target of a student harassment complaint, which ultimately wasn't pursued. To cope, he took a leave of absence, moved into an apartment with his Belgian Shepherd, Salem, and spent a year studying Japanese flute and Shiatsu massage.

For a while he eased the pain by plunging into dozens of minor criminal trials. When he was asked to write a book, it served "as a bit of a purge."

In it, he urges ordinary people to "reclaim lost turf" through an alternative justice system, one that would allow them to represent themselves in many cases. They'd "get killed" doing that today because the system is monopolized by a rude and abrasive "knowledge elite" called lawyers, he says.

Where has it got us? The state is squandering resources prosecuting cases involving little more than controversial "lifestyle choices" — such as recreational drug use — and not devoting enough attention to serious crimes like home invasions or serial murders, he says. The needs of victims often get overlooked, he adds.

Being a lawyer was never Young's ambition.He had always wanted to be a writer, but eventually went to law school, in part, to please his parents.

He worked as a law clerk for Chief Justice Bora Laskin at the Supreme Court of Canada and later landed a job with leading criminal lawyer Alan Gold, who advised him that practising law "is a series of lows punctuated by the occasional high."

Young says he considered the advice so important he's passed it along to other young lawyers. But it's something he could never accept.

"Some lawyers will ride a jury acquittal for the rest of the year, but it never worked for me," says Young, who reached a turning point in 1985, while representing one of several men charged in a huge marijuana and hashish smuggling conspiracy. The ringleader was sentenced to 18 years in prison. Young's client got 14 years.

Considering people "were going down for two years less a day" for attempted murder, the outcome left Young feeling disillusioned and angry.

He escaped into academia. As a professor at Osgoode Hall law school at York University, Young made a speciality out of challenging laws he saw as nothing more than "exercises in moral hygiene."

He says he's "seriously independent" by nature and the cases he's taken on have "suited my personality," even though some might consider them on the fringe. "Doing conventional murder and robbery cases largely doesn't change the world."

He began to grow dispirited with teaching law in the mid-1990s. Part of the problem, he says, was an atmosphere of political correctness sweeping the school. He also came to believe the faculty valued only academic research and didn't respect his work as a lawyer.

For the past four years, he has been on leave from Osgoode and teaching first and third-year criminology students at U of T.

Last summer, he was quietly remarried, to a woman named Laura, who contacted him after seeing him on TV. Surprising, he says, since he vowed he would "never remarry." Sort of like how he has vowed to leave the law? "The fact of the matter," says Henein, "is he loves the law."

Reprinted courtesy Torstar syndication services.

Perspective 8:

Camp Julien, Afghanistan

Cristin Schmitz

Three years ago, David Sinclair was eking out a living in a small-town general practice and hating it. Today, the 32-year old native of Truro, N.S., is advising army generals and colonels on the rules of engagement in Afghanistan and loving it - notwithstanding the carnivorous camel spiders, sweltering heat and numbing cold, land mines, drafty outhouses and sundry other hazards in and around Camp Julien, the main Canadian army base southwest of Kabul.

"If you had told me when I was in law school that I would be here, I would have told you you were crazy, but now I wouldn't be anywhere else," says the University of New Brunswick law graduate who was called to the Nova Scotia Bar in 1999.

Back home, Captain Sinclair is the resident legal adviser at Canadian Forces Base Petawawa, near Pembroke, Ont. Now half-way through his first six-month tour of duty overseas, Sinclair finds his responsibilities have been ramped up in Kabul, where he advises the chain of command on discipline issues for 1,700 Canadian soldiers, and gives legal opinions on often-risky peacekeeping missions.

"We are dealing with rules, orders that could mean the life and death of Canadian soldiers or the life and death of people in Afghanistan," Sinclair explained.

At times, he still marvels at how far he has come. "It's a big responsibility to be the adviser on suicide bombers or the use of force when a patrol is out," he said in an interview outside the modular tent he shares with other officers of the national command element of Operation Athena, Canada's military mission in Afghanistan.

"We've had situations where you have to think about contingency plans, that if things go pear-shaped, we are going to have to kill people, and to think about how the rules of engagement apply, whether it be protecting the president [of Afghanistan, Hamid Karzai,] down to criminal activity. We are dealing with real-time life-and-death stuff."

Operational lawyers are essential players in the modern-day military, but fast-paced problems on the ground demand a "common-sense approach," Sinclair says. "I don't really consider myself an academic. I am more 'How are we going to do this? What are the pros and what are the cons? What's the risk analysis? Can we do it or not?' That's what I think you need in the field. We need to do it tomorrow - we don't have six months to do research."

The threat of terrorists, or Afghan warlords, deploying suicide bombers against peacekeepers in the NATO-led International Security Assistance Force (ISAF) is ever-present in Kabul. Last June, four German soldiers were killed and 29 injured when an explosives-rigged taxi rammed into their bus. As the recent attempted rocket attack on Camp Julien illustrates, the risk remains live in the days leading up to the Dec. 10, 2003 Loya Jurga, when Afghan leaders meet in the capital to ratify a new constitution that is supposed to pave the way for general elections next year.

Among the legal questions suspected suicide bombers pose for ISAF commanders are: what is the threat level? And can soldiers use deadly force to intercept them?

"Maybe it's cold, and they have got a bulky jacket on," Sinclair points out. Certainly Canadian Forces commanders on the ground have access to considerable legal resources. In addition to the ISAF rules of engagement in Afghanistan, which are classified, there is a manual which covers the legal foundations for the use of force; key concepts such as self-defence and proportional use of force; principles on the use of force; levels of force; definitions of "hostile act" and "hostile intent"; and controlling the use of force.

But it is still not easy to abide by, and apply, rules developed in countries governed by the rule of law in a land that is still controlled, in large part, by warlords with private armies financed by the opium trade.

Another not-infrequent problem confronting peacekeepers is children who carry toy 9mm pistols that look so authentic, they even cock like the real thing.

When Prime Minister Jean Chrétien was to fly into Kabul for a brief visit with Canadian troops, a Canadian soldier patrolling his route in advance spotted an eight-year-old boy pointing a pistol. The soldier drove back, spoke to the child, and then relieved him of the gun, which turned out to be a replica.

"Could the child have had a real weapon and shot him? Maybe," Sinclair acknowledges. "One of the cases we had, the mother grabbed hold of the kid and gave him a beating because she knew that if the soldiers thought he had a real weapon, they could use up to and including deadly force and shoot the child."

When soldiers perceive a threat of physical harm, they are trained to employ escalating measures, starting with a shouted warning, progressing through several other phases, up to deadly force.

"Sometimes a soldier on the ground only has a few seconds to decide what kind of force, and they learn drills to know," Sinclair explains. "If you have a kid that's throwing rocks at you, you can use force but you can't shoot him. You can go over and grab hold of him, or something proportional."

Sinclair stresses that his role is not to command, but to advise those who do command. "They can come to me and say: 'What does this mean? What does that mean? Here's the situation we have - how does it fit in? Are we right or wrong?'

As the adviser on domestic Canadian legal issues to ISAF deputy commander Maj.-Gen. Andrew Leslie, Canada's top soldier in Afghanistan, Sinclair spends about half his time dealing with discipline issues. "Discipline is the foundation of the military, really. If we don't have attention to detail then it could mean lives. Discipline is a command issue ... but the legal world gives [commanders] tools," he says.

In the first four months of Operation Athena, there have been about 40 summary trials and, as yet, no courts martial.

At a summary trial, presided over by a senior officer trained by the office of the Judge Advocate General, the accused is helped by an "assisting officer" rather than a lawyer. The process is designed to be used quickly as a corrective tool within the unit, so the soldier can be returned to service as quickly as possible.

The presiding officer combines the roles of prosecutor, defender and judge, with a mandate to look out for the soldier's best interests. "The presiding officer comes to me for pretrial advice - what are the elements of the offence? Are there any evidentiary issues that we have to be concerned about? Advice on punishments," Sinclair says.

Summary offences committed in Kabul have run the gamut from negligent discharge of weapons to being absent without leave and failing to shave before donning a uniform. Fines for negligent discharge have ranged from $400 to $1,500, with the most severe punishment, a $2,000 fine, being meted out for an alcohol-related offence.

General Leslie has himself presided over several summary trials, including a major convicted of negligent discharge and a warrant officer convicted of insubordination. Quarrels and disturbances, drunkenness, absent without leave and insubordination usually are handled at summary trials, as is "conduct to the prejudice of good order and discipline" if it involves infractions of rules related to "dress, deportment, kit and quarters".

"We are not going to give you an election for court martial because you have dirty boots or because you didn't call the Sgt.-Major 'Sgt. -Major', you called him 'hey buddy,' " says Sinclair. When not working on discipline or operational issues, Sinclair settles traffic accident tort claims against the military and points soldiers with private legal problems in the right direction.

Sinclair says the hardest part of being deployed abroad is missing his wife and year-old daughter. "That being said, I think I'll be home more when I'm home than when I was practising in private."

He has no regrets about forsaking general practice. In the military, "you are not worried about the money, you are just worried about practising law," he smiles. "The phone rings and you can say, 'How can I help you?' as opposed to, 'How can I get a retainer out of you?' That's what I wanted to do - practise law."

He says the military offered a sense of adventure, a solid pay cheque, a pension, four weeks vacation, fitness and language training "and the chance to come somewhere like this." Having started in the military at $54,000 per year, he currently earns $60,000, soon to be boosted by his annual performance bonus. In 2004, after four years in, Sinclair will be promoted to major, earning $80,000.

Senior majors can make $120,000 per year. After five years in he will get five weeks' vacation. And when he retires at age 55, Sinclair will have amassed a considerable pension.

"I know lawyers back home who can't retire because they lost so much money when the stocks went belly-up a couple of years ago," says Sinclair. "You don't have to worry about your pension" in the military.

More importantly, Sinclair says his career gives him deep satisfaction. "I wouldn't do anything else now," he observes. "It's a cool job, and you feel like you are part of a bigger thing. When I retire I am going to be a veteran. I don't go out and do patrols, but I am still part of it and Remembrance Day means something different now than it did four years ago.

"Wearing a uniform has become an important part of my life, not just my career. What you do is you serve your country and you do it with the skills you have. I don't know if I'm making a difference, but we are making a difference, and I'm part of the machine that does that."

Cristin Schmitz - The Lawyers Weekly

Persective 9

Calming Troubled Waters

By Moira Tobin, Law '83

Running the legal aid clinic in the remote northern B.C. community of Hazelton can be tiring, lonely, and at times thankless work, but even after 13 years on the job Linda Locke, Law'84, remains committed.

Linda Locke, Law'84, recalls how sad she was when the Inlander Hotel in Hazelton, B.C., burned down last September. "It wasn't just another local news story about the loss of a landmark," she says. "Some residents lost their livelihoods, others their homes. The hotel was a place for people who had no other place to be."

The fire ripped yet another hole in the heart of this remote village on the Skeena River, 290 kms northeast of Prince Rupert, B.C. Hazelton and the nearby Gitsxan and Wetsu'wet'en communities are home to about 10,000 people.

There is a large aboriginal population here, and because most residents work in resource-based industries, times are tough. The local economy has been hit hard in recent years by downturns in forestry, mining, and fishing, and by provincial government cutbacks. Unemployment has soared, and with it poverty and social problems.

Linda Locke knew all this, just as she knew many two dozen people whose lives and livelihoods were affected by the Inlander Hotel fire. Determined to help these people, Linda worked with members of the local business community to set up a bank account and organize a fundraiser featuring local musicians, games, gourmet food, and an auction. The event raised more than $1,200. While that wasn't enough to rebuild the hotel or solve everybody's problems, every dollar helped. And the gesture itself was important.

It was this kind of community spirit and involvement that earned Linda Locke the prestigious Canadian Bar Association's Community Service Award in 2003. Known for her work with aboriginal people and for building bridges to all members of the community, Linda has been the driving force behind the Hazelton Legal Aid Services clinic. In fact, if it wasn't for her, the office might well be closed. In 2002, B.C.'s newly elected Liberal government axed the funding for the Hazelton clinic and for 60 others across the province.

Linda continued to work *pro bono* while she marshaled support to keep the doors of the Hazelton clinic open. Working in partnership with the Upper Skeena Counseling and Legal Assistance Society's Board of Directors (with support from the community and with some funding from the B.C. Legal Services Society, the Law Foundation of British Columbia, Aboriginal Justice Canada, the Skeena Native Development Society, and the Royal Bank of Canada), Linda worked a small miracle.

Miraculously, the Hazelton legal aid clinic is one of the very few in B.C. that survived the cuts.

"We're still standing!" says Linda. "We're still operating in the red, and we survive from year-to-year on the strength of contracts that we have to provide legal services to various agencies, but we're trying to be innovative and creative in how we operate. We've got to be. This office has to survive. Most of our clients are aboriginal people who've been especially hard hit by the economic troubles and government cutbacks."

Linda is intimately familiar with the problems aboriginal people face. She herself is a member of the Sto:lo nation from the Fraser Valley.

"Legal processes are incredibly important in a town like Hazelton, and the legal aid clinic offers a neutral place to go, a place to be heard, a place where people can express themselves and move toward resolving conflicts," says Linda.

Working in a small-town legal aid clinic isn't easy, nor is it as lucrative as working in a private practice or in a government ministry might be. But Linda Locke is committed to what she does, and she does it well.

Linda attributes her legal skills to her education and to her varied work experience. Before studying law at Queen's, she earned a degree in Social Work from the U of Calgary in 1974, spent time as a probation officer, and became familiar with courts, the justice system, and the roles that lawyers play. Says Linda, "After a while I began to think, 'I can do that, too.'"

She enrolled in the Native Law Program at the U of Saskatoon as a trial venture. The intent of the rigorous eight-week course was to determine whether students had the aptitude for law. It turned out that she did. Although Linda had her pick of three law schools, she chose Queen's. She now says it was the right choice for her for many reasons. "The people I met were great, so welcoming," she says.

Linda's first year of studies, 1980-81, proved to be a huge challenge. She encountered a different culture; many of her classmates were younger; and many had parents who were lawyers or business people. Linda also struggled to learn to "think like a lawyer."

With time, a lot of perseverance, and some welcome support from professors and friends, she grasped the reasoning processes behind law and lawyering. So well so that after graduating from Queen's, Linda furthered her legal studies in Ottawa, and then taught Native Studies at the U of Saskatoon.

During this period, she realized she's an activist at heart, not an academic. Linda returned to B.C., where she articled with the Vancouver firm Mandell Pinder, and specialized in aboriginal law. As part of her articles, she enrolled in a Human Rights Internship Program at the U.N. Centre in Geneva before being called to the provincial bar in the fall of 1989. Soon afterward, she joined a Native Community Law Office (Legal Aid Clinic) in the town of Terrace, in northern B.C. Two years later, Linda moved to Hazelton.

From Day One, she knew her job there would be "a challenge." On her first day, Linda sat in one of the rickety office chairs, and it collapsed. But office furnishings were the least of a Linda's concerns.

Setting up a filing system, training support staff, and finding the money to keep the clinic open proved to be far bigger challenges.

In the end, everything somehow came together. Linda, a paralegal, and two support staff now provide a vital service for some of the area's neediest residents.

Linda is still struggling to ensure that the clinic's doors remain open and even to expand its outreach and educational initiatives. In the meantime, she's trying to find the time and energy to further her own training. Linda has been honing her mediation skills in hopes of being able to share the techniques and help people find new ways to resolve conflicts without going to court.

"I have no idea how long I'll be in Hazelton. The workload can be overwhelming at times; there's just so much to do, and it wears you down," says Linda. "But I want to stay as long as it takes to make sure things are running smoothly and the office can carry on. It's like a pool of water. When the waves have settled and the water is calm, I'll know then it's my time to go."

"Being the only lawyer in a legal aid clinic in a remote northern B.C. town isn't easy, nor is it as lucrative as working elsewhere might be, but even after 13 years, Linda Locke remains committed."

This article originally appeared in The Spring 2004 issue of the Queen's Alumni review magazine. It is reprinted with the kind permission of the Review and of the author.

What Are Some Specific Areas Of Law?

Most large law firms provide legal services in many areas of practice. Let's take a tour of a major Toronto firm. This particular firm has over 230 lawyers practicing out of its Toronto office. In the reception area you will find brochures describing the firm's areas of expertise. The firm describes itself as organized to provide integrated legal services in the following practice areas:

Aboriginal; Admiralty & Shipping; Aviation; Banking & Finance; Biotechnology; Capital Markets; Casualty; Commercial Transactions; Communications & Broadcasting; Competition Marketing And Advertising; Computer & Information Technology; Construction Surety & Fidelity; Corporate; Criminal; Defamation; Education; Entertainment & Sports; Environmental; Estates; Expropriation; Family; Franchising & Licensing; Golf Industry; Health; Hospital; Immigration; Insolvency & Bankruptcy; Insurance; Intellectual Property; International Business; Investment Funds; Labour & Employment; Mergers & Acquisitions; Mining & Natural Resources; Municipal Planning & Public Environmental; Mutual Funds; NAFTA; Pensions; Personal Injury; Personal Services; Products Liability; Real Estate; Regulatory & Criminal Defence; Securities; Structured Financing & Leasing; Taxation & Trusts.

The Trend Toward Specialization

It is unlikely that as future law students you recognize all of these areas of practice. You are not alone. Many of the lawyers at this particular firm (although they recognize the areas of practice) know little about most of them. The practice of law is becoming increasingly specialized. There is a consensus that it is becoming harder and harder to be a "generalist." John Hennessey writing in the April 1999 issue of the Canadian Bar Association Digest commented that:

"Never has the lawyer - particularly the hewer of wood and drawer of water who specializes as a generalist - been more challenged: technology, paralegals, globalization and competition, not to mention public image."

As a lawyer it is possible to completely change careers many times in your life and continue to practise law.

Here are three points you should remember as future law students:

1. Your formal legal education will not include direct exposure to the majority (or even many) of these areas of practice. There are too many areas. Hence, the purpose of a legal education is to teach you how to continue to learn about various areas of law. In other words - law school is about learning how to learn the law!

2. Start law school with the attitude that you seek exposure to as many different areas of law as possible. This will help you identify those areas that interest you most.

3. It is completely unnecessary to choose an area of law. There is no area of human activity that does not have a legal aspect to it. I recommend that you just continue in your area of interest and work in the legal aspects related to it! If you don't believe this is possible, read the Appendix to this chapter about a woman who did just that!

Possible Growth Areas - The Trend Is Your Friend

The law follows trends in society. There will be "lawyering opportunities" available to you down the road that don't exist today. As society changes, new areas of practice will develop. Here are three examples of societal trends that have created new areas (and enhanced existing areas) of legal practice.

Trend 1 - The Baby Boomers Are Getting Older!

Most readers of this book are not part of the baby boom generation. Nevertheless, you will be in a position to build a successful legal career around them. As the boomers move into retirement age whole new areas of law will mature, evolve and be created because of them. Consider that one of this decades most popular books is "Boom Bust Echo - How To Profit From The Coming Demographic Shift" by David Foot (a U. of T. economist.) Headlines from recent newspaper articles include:

"Lawyers find more work among seniors"

"Aging boomers mean future boon to estates lawyers"

In one of the bestsellers of the late 1990s, "The Millionaire Next Door", the authors suggest that lawyers who specialize in the areas of estates, taxation and immigration will find their services to be in high demand.

Think of the business and legal and business opportunities which will exist in the area of retirement planning.

Trend 2 - ADR: A Huge Growth Area In Law!

ADR stands for Alternative Dispute Resolution. ADR includes mediation, negotiation, arbitration, and any other of facilitation that is for purpose of managing conflicts. In the past (with the exception of informal efforts on the part of lawyers to settle cases) the courts and certain administrative tribunals have been the primary forums for dispute resolution. There are may disadvantages to using the courts to resolve conflicts. These disadvantages include:

1. The astounding cost which has the potential to bankrupt the average person.

2. The incredible delay. It is not unusual for cases to take years to work their way through the courts.

3. The likelihood that the dispute will be resolved strictly according to the law. This is not always a good thing. Laws can be unfair and their application will result in a winner and loser.

4. The destruction of relationships. After having been to court - no further relationship between the parties is possible. Often complete destruction of business or family relationships is the result of the adversarial nature of the litigation process.

Disputants who opt for ADR construct their own method for resolving disputes. These methods range from private courts (a number of retired judges are now in the business of providing private courts), arbitration (getting a third party to make a decision either in accordance with the law or not) and mediation (a mediator, rather than rendering a decision, helps the parties resolve the dispute themselves). In many cases ADR will facilitate a result that each party is happier with, that is less costly and that is faster. ADR can be so effective that I predict that within 10 years ADR will be the normal method of resolving disputes and the courts will be the alternative mode.

Lawyers are scrambling to get into ADR. No license (at least at present) is required to be an arbitrator, mediator or negotiator. Although a law degree is an asset, there is no requirement of a law degree or membership in the bar to enter this field. You will be hearing a lot more about ADR as the years go on.

ADR has moved into cyberspace. "E-Justice", online arbitration, web based mediation and electronic courts are proof of the trend toward using the internet to resolve disputes.

Trend 3 - Growing Up Digital

"The law of the internet is expanding at light-speed, and even traditional practice lawyers can't afford to ignore it any longer."

-A Legal Commentator

The explosion in telecommunications has created new industries overnight. A whole body of law will continue to develop around it. The demand for IT lawyers is booming. In fact, one Canadian law firm donated money to a law school for the purpose of funding a chair in IT law.

Conclusion

As a lawyer you can have a career that involves any area of human activity. Don't ask - what are the career opportunities for lawyers? Rather, ask - How can I do what I like to do in the capacity of being a lawyer?

Chapter 32

Who Are Lawyers And How Much Do They Earn?

Introductory Note:

The actual amount that lawyers make (like all incomes) is subject to change. The purpose of this chapter is to show you how lawyers make money and how lawyers' incomes differ depending on the kind of lawyer. For this purpose, data is used from the late 1990s and early 2001.

Part A - The Demographics Of The Legal Profession

"A Snapshot In Time" - The Canadian Legal Profession

In order to see a complete breakdown of the demographics of the profession, please visit the website of the Federation Of Law Societies at: www.flsc.ca

These statistics are updated annually.

Small provinces have smaller numbers of lawyers. The largest province - Ontario - has the largest number of lawyers (approximately 28,000 which is approximately 1/3 of the total of number of lawyers in Canada).

Demographic Trends And Admission To The Bar Of Ontario

The bottom line is that the percentage of women and minority groups admitted to the Ontario Bar is increasing each year. In fact, 1999 was the last year in which more men than women were admitted to the bar. In 2000 equal numbers were admitted and in 2001 and 2002 more women than men were admitted. According to the Law Society of Upper Canada:

Ontario - 2001 Bar Admission Course Enrollment

	% of Ontario Legal Profession	% of General	% BAC 2000	% BAC
Women	30.1%	50.8%	51.6%	53.4%
Vis. Min.	7.3%	17.5%	16.1%	20%
Franco	2.8%	3.3%	N/A	5%
Abor.	0.6%	1.4%	1.8%	1%

Women, Men And Admission To The Bar Of Ontario

Year	Total	Female	% Total	Male	%Total
1999	1039	489	47%	550	53%
2000	1074	537	50%	537	50%
2001	1047	539	51%	508	49%
2002	1055	558	53%	497	47%

Part B - Lawyer's Incomes - So How Much Do Lawyers Earn?

A Voice From The Past - Have Times Changed?

"No lawyer can make rich out of the practice of law. Some there are who have - like men in other pursuits - who have been fortunate in speculation, or who have in other ways or by other means outside of the practice of their profession acquired considerable wealth - but the truth stands out and may not be gain said that no lawyer can grow rich from the practice of his profession alone."

> - From An Address To The Ontario Bar Association By The Hon.
> Justice W.R. Riddell - December 1907

So, How Much Do Lawyer's Earn?

It is impossible to generalize. Lawyers work in many different places and do different kinds of work. Furthermore, the state of the economy is in a constant state of flux. Therefore, what is accurate statistical data today, will be inaccurate tomorrow.

It is impossible to say what kind of income you will have as a lawyer. So, why include a chapter on this subject at all?

The purpose of this chapter is to show you:

1. How lawyers generate income;

2. How incomes may be influenced by various factors including: the type of law practised, the length of time one has been a lawyer and how you practice (big firm, small firm, in-house counsel, partner, associate, government lawyer, etc.);

3. How lawyers incomes are influenced by the general state of the economy - including competition.

But, leaving these factors aside, for those of you who just want to know how incomes in law compare to the average income, consider the following findings by Statistics Canada in 2000:

"Lawyers earn 146% more than average Canadians."

There are as many different income levels as there are kinds of lawyers. What follows is an attempt to provide a snapshot of what lawyers have earned in the recent past. We will consider levels of remuneration for lawyers in private practice, lawyers employed by the government and lawyers who work as "in-house counsel." I would emphasize that these are average amounts. There are some lawyers who make considerably more - and some who make less.

Part 1 - How Lawyers Generate Income

Lawyers In Private Practice

Lawyers in private practice are either employees of the firm called "associates" who are paid a fixed salary by the firm or "partners" who are entitled to a share of the firm's profits.

The practice of law is a business. Lawyers sell time (commonly referred to as billable hours). In return for their time, lawyers expect to be paid. Lawyer's typically charge their time out in one of four ways:

1. By the hour - In this case the gross revenue of a law firm may be calculated by multiplying the number of hours billed "billable hours" by the hourly rate of the lawyer doing the work.

2. By the job - In some cases a lawyer will charge a flat fee for a service rendered. This type of billing arrangement is most common when the lawyer is able to assess in advance the time required to perform a job.

3. Contingency fees - In most North American jurisdictions, lawyers will charge the client a percentage of the dollar amount recovered.

4. By acquiring a share in a startup - This is a new trend and is associated with work done for "new economy" businesses.

In addition to paying for the lawyer's time, clients must pay for "disbursements" of money that the lawyers are required to pay to third parties while servicing the client. Examples include (but are not limited to) fees for government filings. The profits of the firm are calculated by subtracting expenses from gross billings. The overhead to run a law firm is high. Overhead typically includes payments for: rent, office equipment, telephones, staff, liability insurance, law society membership fees, etc. Canadian Lawyer magazine recently estimated that these expenses consume an average of approximately fifty-five percent of billings. This implies that the average level of profit to the firm is forty-five percent of billings. There is a strong incentive for lawyers to control their expenses.

The Concept Of The "Billable Hour"

Historically the "billable hour" has been the most common way of charging clients and the most common way of measuring the productivity of a lawyer. Many in the profession are growing increasingly uncomfortable measuring their life and incomes in this way.

"Removing the shackle of billable hours

by donalee Moulton

Billable hours do not only hurt the practice of law, they actually hurt the profession of law, says the past president of the Nova Scotia Barristers' Society (NSBS).

"A lot of lawyers recognize that billable hours have a lot of problems. Most (however), don't recognize the effect it has on us psychologically and on how we work," John Merrick told The Lawyers Weekly in an interview.

Mr. Merrick, a partner with the Halifax law firm Flinn Merrick notes that not only do billable hours result in very high legal fees, they also play a critical role in the changed perception of what lawyers see themselves as doing.

"It's harder to get satisfaction out of the work you do when you have to account for every minute of your time. (But) your income depends on this. You begin to see the task in terms of units of time as opposed to 'What can I do for this client?'" says Mr. Merrick.

In a recent column that appeared in the Barristers' Society newsletter, he told lawyers that, "We have been suckered. The billable hour wasn't just a record-keeping concept. Rather, it has fundamentally affected how we practise and, most importantly, how we think about what we do and how much we enjoy what we do."

"Think about it. The vast majority of us are now governed by the practice, in most cases the requirement, that we track and account for all of our working day. Managing partners tell us we must bill a certain minimum amount of our time. Our success and our futures in the practice are held out to depend on how well we log our hours."

Indeed, one of the first questions recent law grads want answered is how many hours will they have to bill. In Canada, the answer to that question is 1500 hours a year, on average. In order to bill 6.5 hours, however, a lawyer usually has to put in 10 hours in the office.

"Even low quotas of six hours a day are hard to achieve," says Mr. Merrick. "You fixate on this and go home dissatisfied. (But) you may actually have accomplished something even if you didn't get your hours. What this fixation on billable hours creates is a mind set that transforms the lawyer from a counsellor into a technician. The result, Mr. Merrick, noted in his NSBS' article is that "we have shackled ourselves to an assembly line."

So how does the profession free itself from the albatross of billable hours? There are no easy answers to that question, says John Merrick. Alternatives to billable hours usually mean one of two things for a firm and their lawyers — less money or more money. If the solution is to move away from billable hours and into enhanced service for the client, firms will likely have to hire more lawyers, or prepare to earn less money.

On the other hand, many alternatives put forward to replace an hourly billing system, are really just ways to drive fees even higher, says Mr. Merrick. "They are driven by financial concerns not professional ones and therefore the solutions are not satisfactory." For example, he says, "value billing is a euphemism by lawyers for getting a bigger piece of the pie. (It) may have given the lawyer more money but the lawyer doesn't go home at the end of the day feeling any better about themselves."

What happens is that feelings of dissatisfaction chip away at members of the profession and many start to leave. Others sour. "When I say these things to lawyers they all nod their heads but one of the repercussions of billable hours is that we don't have time to reflect and discuss and therefore there is not a lot of feedback from colleagues," says Mr. Merrick.

Still the message may be getting across. Annual targets for billable hours seem to be declining across the country and some law firms are emphasizing lifestyle and client service as much as money. A firm in New Glasgow, Nova Scotia, for example recently placed an ad seeking a lawyer to join the eight lawyers already on its staff. The title of the ad was, "Want a Life?" and it stressed the need for a balance between work and leisure.

Thirty years ago, notes Mr. Merrick, graduates emerged from law school and did a little bit of everything. In the process they found out what areas of law they liked and what ones didn't appeal to them. Billable hours has essentially eliminated that self-selection process.

"(It) has really made a smaller profession," says Mr. Merrick.

There is also concern that the profession's use of billable hours actually discriminates against women and excludes some people altogether. Bertha Wilson, a former member of the Supreme Court of Canada, raised this issue four years ago when she said that law firms have a legal responsibility to allow women with children to work up to 20 per cent fewer billable hours – but not suffer a comparable cut in pay or loss of opportunity for advancement.

It is a new, and perhaps, much-needed way of thinking. Or rethinking.

"The problems we're facing aren't just a question of money," says Mr. Merrick. "There's the problem of self identity. It's self fulfilling. Eventually we will become nothing more than technicians...(We) have to take the shackle of the billable hour off (our) leg."

John Merrick is optimistic this will happen. "The more we see written about this and the more we talk about this the more we will start to resolve the problem."

Reprinted with permission of the author.

Part 2 - How Incomes Are Influenced By Various Factors ...

So, What Do Lawyers Actually Make?

Every June Canadian Lawyer Magazine publishes its annual compensation survey. In June of 2001 Kirsten McMahon reached the following conclusions.

2001 National Average Salaries For Associates

Year of Admission To Bar	Middle Range
2000	$33,800-$57,440
1999	$38,520-$64,440
1998	$40,980-$78,000
1997	$51,220-$93,360
1996	$48,790-$103,420
1995	$52,920-$100,530
1994	$51,940-$103,890
1993 and on	$56,080-$123,990

Partners - 2001 Law Firm National Averages

Percent Of Partners in Income Category	Income Category
38.0%	$50,000-$100,000
28.0%	$101,000-$150,000
12.0%	$151,000-$200,000
8.0%	$201,000-$250,000
4.0%	$251,000-$300,000
3.0%	$301,000-$350,000
1.0%	$351,000-$400,000
0.0%	$401,000-$450,000
4.0%	$450,000 +

Although this is the most current "bottom line" information, it doesn't provide a great deal of information. To provide a better picture, I will introduce you to the information in the June 1998 compensation survey which was done by Michael Crawford. Although the figures are a bit older, you will see how different lawyers earn different incomes.

How Much Do Lawyers Typically Charge Clients?

In his 1998 Legal Fees Survey Mr. Crawford analyzed both what lawyers charge on an hourly basis and what lawyers typically charged for performing certain kinds of legal services. His conclusions were interesting:

Lawyers Hourly Rates: Mr. Crawford concluded that the hourly rate depended on the number of years of practice and what part of the country you are in. This is not surprising. His results are as follows:

Years Of Lawyering Experience	Geographic Based Range
Ten	$170-$250 per hour
Five	$120-$165 per hour
New	$90-$125 per hour

Once again, these are simply averages. The hourly fee of many lawyers is far higher.

Average Fees Billed For Certain Types Of Work Across Canada:

Category	National Average	Large Firm
Uncontested Divorce	$734	$723
Contested Divorce	$7578	$9641
One Day Criminal Trial	$1804	$1992
Probate	$2582	$2914
Two Day Civil Trial	$14445	$21245
Shareholders Agreement	$1123	$1285

Note that the fees of large Toronto firms will be considerably higher.

So, What Do The Lawyers In Private Practice Actually Take Home?

A 1997 Snapshot

The following information is very general and is based on Michael Crawford's National Compensation Survey published in Canadian Lawyer.

Partners - 1997 Law Firm National Averages

Percent Of Partners in Income Category	Income Category
16.7%	$50,000-$100,000
25.5%	$101,000-$150,000
14.0%	$151,000-$200,000
8.6%	$201,000-$250,000
5.5%	$251,000-$300,000
2.4%	$301,000-$350,000
2.3%	$351,000-$400,000
3.3%	$450,000 +

These figures are very general and account for neither geographical differences nor differences based on the kind of legal practise. They are also based on 1997 data. In any case, it should be clear that lawyers take home very decent incomes.

What Do Government Lawyers Earn?

Lawyers employed by the government are "employees." In general they are paid less than their private sector counterparts with equal amounts of experience. The pay of government lawyers will depend on their years of experience and the kind of work they are doing. Many government lawyers work as prosecutors. A 1998 article in the Toronto Star suggested that prosecutors earn a yearly salary in the range of $50,000 to $130,000. A prosecutor in Ontario with eleven years of experience could expect to make approximately $85,000. Top criminal defense lawyers in private practice routinely earn far more.

In-House Counsel - Some Very Attractive Opportunities

An "In-House Counsel" is a lawyer who works in the legal department of a corporation that is not a private law firm. Almost all large companies have "in-house" legal departments and hire lawyers to work in those departments. A small number of examples include: General Motors, Sun Life, Toronto Hydro, etc.

Why Do Companies Hire In-House Counsel?

I suggest there are two main reasons.

First, cost efficiency. In many cases it simply costs less to have a lawyer on staff who is paid a salary. This is particularly true of large companies with lots of legal work. The cost savings to the company can be enormous!

Second, business efficiency. One in-house counsel commented that: "An in-house lawyer is a business person with legal expertise, as opposed to looking after business needs." All companies need to solve their legal problems in ways that are most consistent with the business objectives of the company. The best "legal solution" to a problem may not be the best "business solution."

The Trend Is Your Friend - The Future Of The In House Counsel

These two reasons for hiring in-house counsel suggest that more and more companies will hire in-house counsel. In fact one in-house counsel commented that:

"Being in-house is where it's at. As we move into 2000, if you are a bright young person who wants to accomplish something, use your mind, be part of a team and help people build a business, the only one place you will use all of that is as a corporate counsel."

Show Me The Money! - The Salary Of An In House Counsel

The base salary of an in-house counsel may be less than a lawyer who is with a private law firm. But this difference may be offset through bonuses and perks which can include stock options. In addition, since in-house counsel are paid a base salary, they don't have to worry about "billable hours."

In-House Counsel - 1997 National Averages

Type Of Lawyer	Middle Range
General Counsel	$93,625-$205,875
Associate General Counsel	$90,250-$146,750
Senior Lawyer (more than five years)	$66,250-$118,750
Junior Lawyer (less than five years)	$37,500-$72,500

Please note that the remuneration of in-house counsel varies greatly by geographic region and by industry. The possibility of "stock options" can make the life of an "in-house counsel" very lucrative. In general, the life of an "in-house counsel" does not include worries about billable hours!

An interesting perspective on the life as an in-house counsel follows.

February 20, 1998

So you want to become a corporate counsel?

Norman MacInnes

"TORONTO-Getting a job as corporate counsel seems, at first glance, pretty straightforward, says Jonathan Marsden, managing consultant at QD Legal Recruitment in Toronto.

"You reply to ads in the paper, you register with a couple of recruitment consultants, and you put the word out," he said.

But in-house counsel work may not be all that it's made out to be, Mr. Marsden warned. Young lawyers should investigate what being a corporate counsel is really like, he said.

Some corporate counsel jobs are "fantastic jobs" that give a broad experience and a variety of challenging work; others may be more limiting.

Many young lawyers approach Mr. Marsden saying they want to leave major law firms and join the business world as an in-house counsel.

Their reasons are varied, he said. They may want to get more involved in business, or to learn about a particular business or product rather than juggling a lot of different clients.

As well, a lot of lawyers don't really want to be lawyers. They see law as a stepping stone to being a businessperson.

Other lawyers say they want to switch for quality of life reasons-they don't want to work the long hours that they do in private practice.

But on this point, they may be deceiving themselves, Mr. Marsden said: in-house lawyers work hard.

They have a very demanding client to serve, so the pressure is still there.

In fact, Mr. Marsden encounters many lawyers who, having spent several years in-house, want to return to private practice.

Sometimes they miss the cutting-edge work and the team atmosphere in a law firm, or the excitement of consistently working on big transactions.

Sometimes they can't get used to doing a major joint venture one day, and then the next day having to litigate some small product liability claim.

And sometimes they miss the money, because-when times are good-law firms make more than corporate in-house departments.

The bottom line, said Mr. Marsden, is that you should identify your medium- and long-term career objectives, and then try to structure your career around that.

Georgia Sievwright, general counsel, secretary and director of corporate relations at Hewlett-Packard (Canada) Ltd. in Mississauga, Ont., believes potential in-house counsel should be good communicators who are able to market their services internally to the corporation, and should have some knowledge of technology.

In a law firm, the clients traditionally come to junior lawyers through senior partners. But corporate counsel need to have a personality that will attract business from their internal clients.

They must be able to network, and should be politically astute enough to know what's going on in the business.

Corporations look far and beyond law school marks when hiring in-house counsel, she told The Lawyers Weekly. They look for a particular fit to the firm's unique culture.

Consequently, it's difficult to generalize about their requirements, but since most businesses have "channels of distribution," previous experience with retailing, pricing and marketing strategy is extremely helpful.

She added that a big part of the work of in-house counsel is managing relationships. Counsel must understand their internal "customers" and what their needs are.

A corporation looks for more than just cost savings from in-house counsel, Ms. Sievwright said.

The value that in-house lawyers can add is a thorough understanding of the company's business.

Consequently, she said, young lawyers who wish to become corporate counsel must be prepared to learn as much as possible about how the business operates.

Ms. Sievwright stressed the importance of networking.

"I believe than an awful lot of corporate counsel jobs are found through networking-they're not advertised," she said.

"I often get calls from people looking for people, and from people who are looking for a job."

It's also a good idea, she said, to try to find a mentor who is a corporate counsel-someone who can be asked questions in confidence.

How does one find a mentor? It's unlikely that there are any lawyers in private practice who wouldn't know a least one in-house counsel, she observed.

As well, she suggests attending Canadian Bar Association section meetings and continuing legal education conferences."

Norman MacInnes - The Lawyers Weekly

Part 3 - How Incomes Are Influenced By The State Of The Economy

A 1998 - Hot Economy - Recent Graduates At New York Firms

In 1998, The Wall Street Journal reported the following information about salaries and year end bonuses at some major New York law firms.

First, salaries: new recruits now get at least $100,000 as annual compensation. (This is roughly three times what articling students are paid at top Toronto firms.)

Second, year end bonuses: $10,000 to $15,000 to lawyers with at least one year of experience.

2000 - Getting Hotter - The Effects Of The Dot Com Frenzy

"Rookie lawyers cash in on Silicon Valley frenzy" was the title of a recent article in the Globe. Apparently the dot com companies have been providing lucrative job offers to newly minted lawyers. This "internet brain drain" has had the effect of luring lawyers away from traditional firms. In order to keep prime legal talent the firms have been forced to pay even higher salaries. For example, one New York firm recently raised its base salary for rookie lawyers to $125,000 U.S. dollars. With bonuses their pay could go to $160,000 U.S. Not bad to start!

Not to be outdone, a leading Boston law firm which represents emerging technology and internet companies, has increased pay for young lawyers in order to stem defections to high tech companies. It recently notified its associates that it was increasing total compensation to associates to a maximum of $155,000 per year.

U.S. Firms Look North - U.S. Opportunities For Canadians

U.S. law firms are now recruiting Canadian law graduates. The benefits to Canadian law graduates are two- fold.

First, Canadian law graduates can avoid articling and the Bar Admission Course.

Second, there may be considerable financial benefits.

After comparing a New York lawyer's starting salary in Canadian dollars with what the lawyer would make at a Toronto firm, Julius Melnitzer, writing for Law Times concluded that:

"Measured in Canadian dollars, then, the base salary of Toronto first-year lawyers is roughly 40 percent of the amount earned by their New York counterparts. Even factoring out currency considerations, the Toronto base salary is less than 60 percent of U.S. earnings."

Canada's Response To U.S. Competition - Increasing Salaries!

The days that Canadian law graduates must article with a Toronto firm are over. Toronto firms must now compete for the legal talent they want. The following perspective demonstrates the beginning of a "wake up" call in the Toronto legal community.

May 09, 2000

Law firms raising the bar on novices' salaries

Jonathon Gatehouse

National Post

Battling a greed drain that has seen hundreds of young lawyers head to the financially greener pastures of New York and San Francisco, Canada's biggest law firms have hiked their associates' pay for the second time this year.

The latest round of salary escalations kicked off a week ago when Bay Street titan Torys (last in the news as Tory Haythe when Thomas Haythe, its senior New York partner, resigned amidst allegations that he had drunkenly groped female colleagues) raised its compensation for first-year associates to $88,000, plus bonuses. By week's end at least two more blue-chip Toronto-based firms, Goodman Phillips & Vineberg and Osler, Hoskin & Harcourt LLP, had followed suit. Most other large firms are expected to announce similar increases in the coming days.

The raises, retroactive to Jan. 1, come a little more than four months after Torys raised the bar all over Bay Street by giving its first-year lawyers an unheard-of $80,000 a year. Salaries generally increase $10,000 to $15,000 per annum over the first five years in practice.

With the economy booming, associates at Canada's largest firms are also earning hefty annual bonuses, typically in the range of 20% to 30% of their gross pay.

But it's not just the good times that are fueling the rapid expansion in compensation for sharks in suits. It's the lure of American lucre boosted by the publication of confidential salary information on the Internet.

"The market for talent knows no borders," Les Viner, Torys' managing partner, said yesterday.

"Every firm, including ours, has lost some people to the States. It's not a flood, but it's an unnerving trend."

Big U.S. firms have been aggressively recruiting at Canadian law schools for the past three or four years, hyping the advantages of larger salaries and lower taxes south of the border.

But a raging pay war between America's East and West coasts is now drawing the attention of young lawyers who have already started to practise in Canada.

In early January, San Francisco law firm Gunderson Dettmer Stough Villeneuve Franklin & Hachigian raised its starting salaries to US $125,000 from US $95,000 to stop associates from defecting to Silicon Valley. Within hours the massive raise was the talk of lawyers coast to coast thanks to a popular Internet salary billboard (www.greedyassociates.com). Firms in other big cities, including Toronto and Vancouver, have been forced to pony up in order to keep their stable of young talent.

"We believe our associates are as good as anyone else and deserving to be compensated that way," said Dale Lastman, managing partner of Goodman Phillips & Vineberg, and son of Mel Lastman, the Toronto mayor. "We have no choice if we're going to remain competitive in this marketplace."

As an added incentive, Goodmans has offered its lawyers an all-expenses-paid long weekend for two in the Bahamas. Associates have also been given the choice of a Palm Pilot, DVD player, 19" colour TV or fax machine. Mr. Lastman said the electronic goodies did not come from his family's chain of Bad Boy furniture stores.

"I'm certain my brother will kill me if you print that," he said.

In Vancouver, Farris, Vaughan, Wills & Murphy is raising its first-year rate to a reported $73,000.

Yesterday, an Internet site that gives Canadian lawyers a chance to gossip and compare salaries (www.infirmation.com) was starting to register the latest round of Toronto increases, and associates were taking notice.

"Everybody's been talking about it," said one young lawyer. Though his firm has yet to announce another big raise, he said associates are confident one is in the works.

"It's monkey see, monkey do," he said. "It just takes some time."

Reprinted with permission of the National Post.

Conclusion

This chapter has been designed to demonstrate that:

1. Lawyers are relatively high income earning people.

2. Different kinds of lawyers make different amounts of money.

3. There are different ways that lawyers can bill their time.

4. The state of the economy will influence incomes.

5. Competition drives salaries higher.

This chapter is based on data from 1997 - 2001. Obviously, it is subject to change.

APPENDIX

"Living History - Boom To Bust To ...."

I was called to the Ontario Bar in 2000 and was a practising lawyer in Toronto.

Prologue - Mid-2000 - The "Dot Com" Boom

In Mid-2000, I was driving down Highway 101, the main artery in Silicon Valley, to an all expense paid interview with a very large California law firm. At first glance, it was difficult to get a sense of the extent of wealth which had been created in the region during the technology boom. During the drive, I saw many globally famous names, Intel, Oracle, Sun, Cisco, to name a few. Obviously, these companies needed many services, attorneys were at the top of the list.

This demand was the catalyst for the skyrocketing growth of law firms in Silicon Valley. There was a dire shortage of attorneys to service the "dot com" generated work. California law firms began poaching lawyers from New York firms and firms in other large US cities. The recruiting efforts went beyond the U.S. border. Toronto became a recruiting ground.

Recruiting was only the beginning of the story. Law firms were having trouble retaining the lawyers they had recruited. The reason was simple - money. Many young lawyers left law firms for the greener pastures (more greenbacks) of Internet companies. Consequently, law firms were forced to bring their compensation structure in line with what the local market was offering. The effect was that first year salaries (including my own) started at $125,000 plus bonuses.

In summary, in 2000 at the height of the "dot com" boom, California law firms didn't have enough lawyers and couldn't keep the ones they had. Therefore, incomes for lawyers were high and getting higher. I was very excited to be invited for an interview in such a good market for lawyers!

The interview at my law firm was comprehensive. Seven attorneys, at various levels, interviewed me. For the most part, they were friendly and welcoming. Although curious about the Canadian legal training, they agreed that practising corporate transactional law is really not jurisdictionally confining. Thus it was that I became a Canadian transplant to Silicon Valley. I entered the U.S. pursuant to the NAFTA Agreement. All I needed to immigrate was my law degree and job offer. (I was allowed to stay in the U.S. only as long as I had the job.) The California bar exam was challenging but achievable. With a focused approach, I passed and became a member of the California bar.

At the beginning , the law firm reeked of wealth, promise, opportunity and excitement. The parking lots of law firms had the hallmarks: many BMWs, Mercedes, high-end SUVs, etc. The attorneys, especially young ones indulged themselves with expensive cars. Since suits were unnecessary, lawyers also indulged themselves with designer shoes - Salvatore Farragamo and Minolo Blahnik. Socializing at fancy places after work was the norm. However, the outings happened late at night because people were really busy at work until then. Times were good!

The law firm culture was remarkably different from the large Toronto law firm culture. The firms were managed by a much younger set of partners and were remarkably open and transparent in their dealings with associates. It was truly a joy to work with such a fine group of very talented attorneys. Clients were approachable, interested and interesting. The pace of life was fast with opportunities to participate in many interesting transactions. Attorneys were given a far greater access to clients, independence and encouragement to be proactive.

Late 2000 - The Beginning Of The "Dot Com" Bust

Until late 2000, law firms had lots and lots of work. Many law firms would turn down work because they were operating at maximum capacity. Small companies would make futile efforts to retain some of the big law firms and would consider themselves lucky if a small law firm agreed to do their work. Law firms could afford to pay their attorneys generously because they had, what looked like, an unstoppable tide of deal flow.

2001 - The "Dot Com" Bust Gains Momentum

In early 2001, the signs of a slowdown started appearing. Golf courses were busy during the day. Lunches were longer, shopping trips were made, and happy hours were earlier and notably longer. Initially, most people attributed the slowdown to just an economic adjustment. This was wishful thinking. It became a very protracted slowdown. The deal flows at law firms were reduced to a mere trickle. Law firms were still optimistic that the economy would "turn around" and the state of affairs would be restored to its glory days. Based on this belief, they reassured their associates and continued to pay them. Although it was easy to see the rationale, given their earlier experience of finding and retaining talent, it did not make economic sense.

By mid to late 2001, some firms started laying attorneys off and some offered generous buy-out packages. The writing was on the wall.

2002 - The End

The cut backs continued well into 2002. Some nimble law firms recalibrated their focus from corporate to litigation. Some law firms were too large to quickly refocus and hence suffered economic losses. To add to their woes, many law firms were locked into long term expensive real estate leases negotiated at the height of the boom 1999-2000.

Late 2002 - My Return To Toronto

Like many I accepted a termination package. Without a job I was forced to leave the U.S. I am now back in Toronto, practising law again but through my friends keep informed about the developments in the legal field. Most of my friends have found alternative employment with law firms or companies.

2003 - Epilogue - A Final Symbol Of The "Dot Com" Bust

In January 2003, the most notable example of the spectacular fall out from the "dot com bust" is the blue-chip law firm of Brobeck. After 77 years in business, it fell victim to the adverse economic conditions, it shut its doors and filed for bankruptcy, collapsing under the weight of its debt and expenses.

The "dot com bust" was responsible for the San Francisco area, in 2003, having the most rapid population decline of any part of the U.S.

The Moral Of The Story Is That ......

The job market for lawyers is just as subject to local economic conditions as anything else.

But, the experience was great!"

Reprinted with permission of the author.

Chapter 33

Lawyers, Ethics And The Law -
"More Than An Ordinary Citizen"

"You are a member of a learned profession. Keep abreast of the law. Take advantage of the great opportunities now available for continuing legal education. At all costs, be honourable. And, that means more than simply being ethical in the sense required by the detail of your professional code. It also involves at all times treating your fellow lawyers, adjudicators, government officials, and particularly your clients with civility and, in the case of clients, with sensitivity to their needs and problems. Recognize also the call that the requirement to "assist [your] fellow subjects" places on you. In particular, it requires not just competence in the representation of those who can pay but being alert to the plight of those who cannot and for whom legal aid is not available or insufficient. Put aside time for pro bono work whether you are practising alone, for a major national or international law firm, or somewhere in between. Have the courage, even as a new associate in one of those large firms, to find out about and, if necessary, work for change in the firm's pro bono work policies. Become a member of a community group which can draw usefully on your expertise. Don't see every out of office involvement in terms of its potential for additional remunerative work for your practice.

Beyond this, I also want to emphasise particularly the public service component of the Law Society's foundational objectives. Lawyers have played a major role in the public life of this country. Indeed, it is to be lamented, not celebrated that the number of lawyers in Parliament and the legislatures is apparently diminishing. Your training and skills fit you particularly well for effective and informed participation in the political and broader public life of Canada. The Charter notwithstanding, Canadians still depend mightily on Parliament and the legislatures for the framing of laws which are respectful of fundamental constitutional and legal principles. Whether as elected members, advisors to parliamentarians, or lobbyists in the cause of appropriate respect for the rule of law and the fundamentals of our legal system, lawyers have a vital role in our democratic processes."

Excerpt from the speech of Queen's Law Professor David Mullan on February 14, 2002 at the call to the Bar ceremony in Ottawa. Professor Mullan was awarded an Honourary Doctorate by the Law Society Of Upper Canada.

"More Than An Ordinary Citizen"

Lawyers hold a unique position of trust in our society. We tell them the most intimate details about our business affairs and personal lives. We entrust them with our money. They are "officers of our courts." As a result, it is reasonable and appropriate to expect lawyers to subscribe to the highest standards of ethics and honesty!

Law Societies in every province have elaborate rules of professional conduct which regulate the conduct of lawyers. Good character is required to be admitted to the bar. Honest behavior and adherence to the rules of professional conduct are required to remain a member of the bar. It is regrettable that the pressures of the practice of law cause some lawyers to violate these canons of professional conduct and in some cases the criminal law. In some cases conduct violates the rules of professional conduct. In some cases it violates the Criminal Code. In some cases it violates both.

Conduct Resulting In Criminal Code Violations

In general, lawyers hold themselves (and are held) to high standards of ethical conduct. Nevertheless, there are many examples of lawyers having been convicted of violations of the criminal code. Think back to the chapter on the character requirement for admission to the bar. Those of you who want to explore this topic more deeply will find numerous examples of lawyers in trouble with the law.

I would recommend the book, "A Matrix Of Evidence" by Bruce Olson. It tells the story of a lawyer accused of murdering his business partner.

The consequences for lawyers who are convicted of offenses under the Criminal Code include:

1. Punishment for the crime itself; and

2. Very often being disbarred.

Conduct Violating Rules Of Professional Conduct

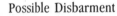

Possible Disbarment

July 1, 2000

The National Post

Clinton faces historic humiliation

Arkansas court seeks disbarment over 'dishonesty, fraud'

Jan Cienski

WASHINGTON - Bill Clinton, the U.S. President, was sued yesterday by a committee of the Arkansas Supreme Court for misconduct involving "dishonesty, deceit, fraud and misrepresentation" in covering up his affair with Monica Lewinsky, the former White House intern.

If the suit is successful, Mr. Clinton would become the first sitting president in U.S. history to have his lawyer's licence removed. But in addition to this unprecedented humiliation, it would mean an official body was satisfied that he committed the perjury for which the House of Representatives judiciary committee recommended his impeachment in 1998.

The five-page lawsuit accuses Mr. Clinton of "serious misconduct" and asks John Ward, Pulaski County Circuit Judge, to disbar him for conducting "himself in a manner that violates the model rules of professional conduct as adopted by the Arkansas Supreme Court."

Mr. Clinton's lawyer, David Kendall, said the President would fight the suit, adding: "We fundamentally disagree with the complaint filed today and will defend vigorously against it."

Shortly after the news, the President arranged an evening round of golf to begin the Fourth of July holiday weekend. He has said his lawyers told him that if he were to be treated like other lawyers, there would be "no way in the world" that he could lose his licence.

The court's Committee on Professional Conduct voted May 19 to sue Mr. Clinton over his January, 1998, testimony in the Paula Jones sexual harassment case, in which he denied under oath having sexual relations with Ms.

Lewinsky.

In a later deposition, Mr. Clinton insisted that oral sex — which is as far as his relationship with Ms. Lewinsky went — did not mean sexual relations, as he understood the term. Ms. Jones, who accused Mr. Clinton of making a crude pass at her while he was still governor of Arkansas, eventually settled the case out of court for US $850,000. Mr. Clinton was later fined US $90,000 by the judge in the case for contempt of court.

Mr. Clinton's deposition set off an investigation by Kenneth Starr, the independent counsel, and eventually led to the President's impeachment by the U.S. House of Representatives.

The U.S. Senate acquitted Mr. Clinton, even though one of the two charges under consideration accused the President of obstructing justice in the Jones case. A related charge that he provided false and misleading testimony in the Jones case — the current grounds for the Arkansas Supreme Court action — was dropped by the House.

While Mr. Clinton dodged the bullet in the Senate and got to keep his job, the special counsel who replaced Mr. Starr, Robert Ray, still hasn't rejected the idea of prosecuting Mr. Clinton once he leaves office next year.

The professional conduct committee was unsparing in its criticism of Mr. Clinton in yesterday's filing.

"The conduct of Mr. Clinton ... was motivated by a desire to protect himself from the embarrassment of his own conduct," the committee wrote. It went on to accuse Mr. Clinton of misconduct involving "dishonesty, deceit, fraud and misrepresentation."

The committee said that it was basing its action on complaints filed by the federal judge in charge of the Jones case and by a conservative Atlanta group, the Southeastern Legal Foundation.

Judge Ward, the judge selected in a random computer draw to handle the case, is a former Democratic state representative who was in office while Mr. Clinton was Arkansas governor.

If he were to disqualify himself from the case, the computer would select another judge at random. Regardless of the outcome in local court, it is expected the case will ultimately end up before the State Supreme Court.

This is the first time an effort has been made to strip a sitting president of his law licence. New York pulled Richard Nixon's law licence, but that came after he resigned the presidency Aug. 9, 1974, during the Watergate scandal.

Mr. Clinton, a licenced lawyer since Sept. 7, 1973, was attorney-general of Arkansas from 1977-79 and once taught at the University of Arkansas law school. He has not practiced law since the early 1980s, between his first and second terms as Arkansas governor."

Reprinted with permission of the National Post.

Conclusion

As citizens, lawyers are subject to the law of the land. As lawyers they are subject to a higher standard of conduct than the average person.

Chapter 34

A Career In Law -
Both A Business And A Profession

"It is...disquieting to realize how things have changed in the fifty years since I graduated from law school...I am talking about the changes in our profession, in the practice of law...When I graduated from law school, the law was an esteemed and honored calling...Lawyers regarded themselves as charged with a public trust...Over the years, however, something seriously disturbing has been happening to the legal profession. We have become a business, dominated by "bottom line" perspectives. In too many of our firms, the computer has become the Managing Partner as we are ruled by hourly rates, time sheets and electronic devices...We are making more and achieving less, and in the process, I am afraid, we have lost a great deal of what we were meant to be."

- Sol Linowitz (Senior Counsel of Coudert Brothers) addressing the Cornell Law School Centennial in April 1988 as reported in 'The Lure Of The Law' by Richard Moll

A Business And A Profession

The practice of law is both a business and a profession. Although a profession may include a business, a profession implies more than a business. A business is for the sole purpose of gaining a livelihood. The practice of a profession involves more than pursuing the gaining of a livelihood. Admission to the bar implies an adherence to a code of professional conduct. Adherence to this code of conduct (among other things):

- places a lawyer in a fiduciary relationship with the client;

- places a lawyer in special relationship with other lawyers;

- imposes on the lawyer obligations vis-a-vis society as a whole;

- places a lawyer in a special relationship with the courts. In the words of one commentator, a member of the bar is:

"More Than An Ordinary Citizen"

Many of these principles are expressed in rules of professional conduct. A lawyer is simply not free to practice law in any way that he or she sees fit.

Law - The Profession Aspect

What does it mean for one to be a member of a profession? How does it differ from being in a business? A profession cannot be defined with precision. But, the following excerpts from the address to the February 2000

Call to the Bar in Ottawa by the Right Hon. Beverley McLachlin, Chief Justice of Canada, do provide us with some insight.

"The message I wish to leave with you can be summed up in one word: professionalism.

Professionalism in the legal world is about commitment to three things: to the learning and discipline of the law; to the service of society and to yourself.

The first ingredient is commitment to the learning and discipline of the law. The law is, above all, a way of thinking, a way of ordering society and a way of solving, or even better, preventing, the conflicts and tensions that can arise in our society. It is also a repository of learning that has been passed on to us, and which we in turn, with some adjustments, will pass on to others.

To be a good lawyer - a true professional - you must immerse yourself in your chosen area of the law. You must seek the best solution [which is] revealed only to those who possess a profound and enduring understanding of their particular area of the law. This thorough understanding separates the mediocre practitioner from the true professional. Lawyers who make a mark in their profession and a mark on the world all possess a passionate and profound interest in the law in general, and in their chosen field of practice in particular.

The second requirement of true professionalism is commitment to the service of society. The notion of service is embedded in our legal language. The lawyer serves the client. The lawyer renders - bills for - services.

The professional lawyer sees service not as a duty, but as part of the privilege of practising law.

The law has great power to improve society and improve people's lives. It was the law that won the right for women to be considered "persons" so they could take up professions and participate in the governing of society. But it was also the law, through various human rights cases, that continues to tackle the evil of discrimination based on false and stereotypical notions of people's abilities and worth. It is the law that has identified and addressed sexual abuse and sexual harassment.

The professional lawyer also owes the client not just a duty of competency but a duty of fidelity and loyalty. True service is uncompromisingly doing the right thing whether anyone knows or not.

True professionalism involves yet a third commitment - commitment to oneself. The poet [Rudyard] Kipling captured the essence of this commitment in his memorable line of advice,

"Above all, to thine own self be true." Your years at law school have transformed you, your "self" from layperson to lawyer. The law is now a part of you. You are forever changed. If you are true to this new self, the other commitments of which I have spoken - commitment to the learning and discipline of the profession and commitment to the service of society - will follow naturally.

There is no set path to finding one's place in the law and thus oneself. But I offer this piece of advice: Avoid getting prematurely boxed in to an aspect of the law that you do not truly enjoy.

Keep your options open. Keep trying until you find something that suits you and gives you deep and lasting satisfaction. Do not be put off by a bad day, three bad days, or even five.

But if all the days - or even most of them - are bad, perhaps the reason is that you have wandered into an aspect of the legal profession that does not suit you, that does not maximize your potential, that does not, to return to Kipling's phrase, allow you to be true to yourself."

Professionalism And Unpopular Causes

One of the characteristics of a lawyer as a professional is that a lawyer must not be swayed by the tide of public opinion. A lawyer may often be obliged to advance positions that are unpopular. A lawyer will often act for clients and advance causes that are disagreeable to the lawyer on a personal level. Consider the comments of this defence lawyer who is a true professional in every sense of the word.

June 14, 1999

Toronto Star

Defending a 'monster'

Steven Skurka

If I ever needed an education in defending an unpopular client, I received my degree with my defence of John Paul Roby.

Working with a wonderful team of lawyers, I have spent much of the past year defending the man described as the monster of Maple Leaf Gardens. I must say that, to the end, I always saw the human side of my client and preferred to leave matters of judgement of my client to a jury of his peers. A lawyer takes on a case not a cause.

For a lawyer undertaking an unpopular case, there must be a steely resolve not to be diverted from the task by the outpouring of anger and bitterness that constantly surround them. Whether it be the campaign of stares that greeted me regularly on my way into court or even the threats directed at me in the midst of my jury address, nothing moved me from my spot on the courtroom floor.

The Roby trial brought to mind the description by Irving Stone in his biography of Clarence Darrow of a notorious case Darrow participated in the early part of the century in Idaho:

"The reception Darrow received in Boise would have poisoned a less hardy man, one less inured to the kind of universal condemnation, this all-pounding hatred; he would have shrivelled under it, become ill, been forced to flee. When he walked the streets, when he went into public buildings, when he entered restaurants, he found icy faces of loathing turned upon him or passionately burning eyes of aversion and contempt.

"He is defending the killer," said Boise, "so he must be in league with killers"'.

It is precisely the unpopularity of the case, the tremendous stirring of public emotion and anger, that sets the stage for a potential injustice. It is tempting to discard principle for vengeance when the allegations are particularly stark and brutal. A democratic society cares about injustice in every case. In how many countries would Roby have received a fair trial?

Yet there will always be some, even political leaders, who will decry the "sympathy" defence counsel demonstrate toward their "criminal" clients and the great disservice they occasion on victims. Our critics do not command the plain of moral virtue. It is only the verdict of the jury that dictates who the true victims and who the true criminals are.

As a society, we understandably condemn the imprisonment of the innocent. However, a system of justice devoid of rigid safeguards and checks and balances invites miscarriages of justice. The presumption of innocence becomes a hollow legal sham, unless we sustain the right of vigorous cross-examination to pierce the shield of deception worn by false complainants.

Most cases are decided on issues of credibility of witnesses, and miscarriages of justice will not always be rescued by magical potions of DNA. As I told the jury in Roby in my closing address, injustice is the drink that stirs the soul of the defence.

And what of the Roby case, this most unpopular client? For me as his lead counsel, it marked the adversarial system at its very best. A thorough prosecution, a strong and relentless defence, all supervised by a trial judge who cared deeply that justice would be served.

While for many the memory of this trial will be the tumultuous 10 days of jury deliberations, I will always recall that great shining moment when the jury arrived on Mother's Day with their verdict. Confronted with the daunting task of assessing the credibility of 60 complainants and similar act witnesses, this jury met the incredible challenge of treating each allegation as a separate trial.

In the end the jury would not find Roby guilty on any of the six cases of recovered memory, the scourge of our justice system. Equally, they found him not guilty on all but a few of the most serious and evasive allegations of sexual conduct challenged by the defence.

If there is one lesson I take from the Roby case, it is that the measure of a fair system of justice is the manner in which we deal with the most unpopular of cases, where the emotional climate is most intense. And yes, I do sleep well every night; yes, I can hold my head up high. I am very proud to call myself a criminal defence lawyer.

Steven Skurka is a Toronto criminal defence lawyer. He is no longer lead counsel in the Roby case.

Reprinted with permission of the author.

Law - The Business Aspect

As future lawyers you will be interested in how lawyers make their livings. This part of the book is to provide insights into this issue. What follows are 6 short articles which have been included to provide "glimpses" into the "business aspects" of the legal profession.

Glimpse 1:

The Lawyers Weekly

Treat law as business, not a practice, grads told

Resources are available for new calls, but they have to work to find them

Neil Seeman

TORONTO—Three lawyers speaking to new calls at a recent Canadian Bar Association-Ontario (CBAO) conference on career search strategies all agreed on one key strategy: get out there and be aggressive.

Sole practitioner Jennifer Keenan of Toronto, and founder of a support group for sole practitioners with less than five years' experience, gave the CBAO forum the inside scoop on starting up one's own practice.

After one year of practice at a firm following her call to the Bar in 1992, Ms. Keenan found that she was "fundamentally unhappy."

"I felt that I needed to get more control over my life, and I wanted to do something more entrepreneurial," she said.

Ms. Keenan withstood some criticism at the outset for starting out on her own at such an early period. "Many of my colleagues at large firms couldn't even imagine not getting inter-office mail delivered to them, let alone practising on their own at such a young stage of their career," she said. "I looked at it and thought, 'There really isn't a better time of life to start up on my own.'" Some useful pieces of advice offered by Ms. Keenan to those considering opening up their own practices included: Buy yourself a good computer. "Your computer will be as valuable to you as your law degree." Look into renting board-room space downtown. This is a good way to meet clients in a professional environment at a relatively low expense. Acquire a good accounting package. "I wish I had invested in my computer accounting package from the start as opposed to a year down the road." Become active in professional associations. These are a great source of contacts, role models, information and potential referrals. For start-up capital, approach the banks and use their business proposal kits. "The banks will be tripping over you trying to get you in the door. Believe it or not, as a lawyer, you're seen as a relatively good client." Above all else, however, Ms Keenan counselled new graduates to take initiative. "There are a lot of resources out there, but you have to find them," she said. She also encouraged young lawyers to actively seek out mentors who could offer them assistance. "You'll be amazed at how willing people are to lend you a hand," Ms. Keenan said.

Another panelist, sole practioner Lauren Bernardi of Mississauga, Ont., gave new calls who were just starting out a reason to be confident. "I'm here to tell you how losing my job was the best thing that ever happened to me," announced Ms. Bernardi. At first she was emotionally devastated, since she knew she wanted to be a lawyer. She felt she had not been exposed to a sufficiently wide variety of practice areas, and was thus worried about starting up on her own. Undeterred, she decided that she was to become an employment lawyer "come hell or high water." After doing some market research, Ms. Bernardi found that there was considerable demand for employment law counselling as it related to human resource management. She therefore decided to become an expert. "I just read about it. It's not rocket science. I learned at the library," Ms. Bernardi told the CBAO conference. As she began her practice, she also took college-level courses in marketing and business strategy. "It made me realize that I'm not starting a practice, I'm not hanging a shingle: I'm starting a business, and I damn well better start thinking of it as one," Ms. Bernardi recalled. Ms. Bernardi learned that it was critical for sole practitioners to become aware of their competitive advantage. "For me it was being a hybrid, being two things at once, both a lawyer and a human resource advisor," she said. Once she had carved out her niche, her confidence began to build quickly. "People like sole practitioners. They are tired of the big law firms with the big marble floors, and knowing that they're paying for all these things. "I now have no problem stealing away clients from big law firms. They don't feel that we're a threat, but we are," said Ms. Bernardi. As for her advice, Ms. Bernardi said that everything centres around effective marketing. "One of the first things I did was to get business cards. It helps to make you look more professional,"she advised. Other tips included writing legal articles for free, and doing market research. "There are a lot of things you can do, but you've got to get out of that box of thinking of yourself as a practitioner, and hanging your shingle and hoping people will come knocking on your door, because they won't. You have make it happen."

Toronto lawyer Bernard Morrow offered the CBAO seminar several other tips on the subject of marketing one's legal wares. "As lawyers, we should see ourselves as human resources. We're not hired guns," said Mr. Morrow. "People are interested in having lawyers who aren't only interested in lining their pocket books," he said. As a lawyer with a large firm, Mr. Morrow felt he was not portraying an image which he found attractive in a lawyer. "I realized that I spent too much time playing the hired gun, winning battles, but seemingly losing the war in the end. I was going home at night not feeling very fulfilled, and I thought, 'There must be another way of helping people,'" Mr. Morrow said.

Neil Seeman - The Lawyers Weekly

Glimpse 2:

Contract work part of the profession's future

Carefully prepared resumes, interview preparation key to getting positions

Neil Seeman

TORONTO—The professional world has changed dramatically, and lawyers need to adapt just like other professionals, according to two speakers at a recent Canadian Bar Association-Ontario careers seminar for recent call to the Bar. Elaine Franklin, a legal recruiter and lawyer from Thorek Scott in Toronto, gave new graduates the "recruiter's point of view." "There's definitely a demand out there," she said but advised new lawyers to be mindful of important strategies when looking for work, especially when using the services of a recruiter. "Recruiters are match-makers," Ms. Franklin said, but the matches they inspire are not like arranged marriages. "It's entirely consensual, it's entirely by way of looking for the best fit...It's for the benefit of the employer as well as the employee." Ms. Franklin's firm ensures complete confidentiality of all its clients. When a resume comes in, she said, it goes nowhere until a candidate gives her the authority to send it out.

Representatives of the firm then describe the candidate's skill-set on an anonymous basis to prospective clients, and if a client expresses interest, only then are candidates approached.

If you want to make the most of recruiting service, advised Ms. Franklin, there are certain tips to bear in mind.

First, the resume has one purpose, which is to get an interview. So when you are made aware of an opening, it is critical to review the resume's accuracy at that time.

As for the interview itself, there are some fundamentals: always be positive, enthusiastic, and interested. "Let them know you're a real person," she suggested. If you encounter a question about why you were terminated from your earlier job (or not asked back), your answer "should be short and sweet, and then get on to what really matters." At all costs, cautions Ms. Franklin, do not make disparaging remarks about your former employer. "Don't try to make yourself look better by putting your former employer down. You won't succeed, but you will raise a lot of question marks in the eyes of your potential employer. Always speak with respect about your former employer." Other do's and don'ts for interviews include:

- Don't ask prematurely about salary. "It should be one of the last things you talk about. On the other hand, don't be afraid to talk about it."

-"Everywhere you go, be enthusiastic about what you do, about what you offer...Enthusiasm goes a long way. There's a certain exuberance which comes out of people who really care about what they're doing, and it's contagious."

Another recruiter on hand was Ronald Krueger of Toronto's Catalyst Career Strategies Inc., who gave a talk on the "new rules of work" and how graduates could apply these rules to their advantage. Given the increased complexity of legal services, it is essential to first find out "what it is that you are good at and what you can offer to the world. "This is the only route to success," said Mr. Krueger.   "You need to know who you are, what problem-solving abilities you have, and this will then often answer where it is you want to go." Mr. Krueger advised that a law degree still carried an enormous amount of weight these days, but that it was necessary to think strategically in order to translate one's education into a job. "What is happening out there is happening to the whole of society. "We're in the middle of a vast change in the way workforce operates," said Mr. Krueger. Now that jobs are not seen as being permanent—the audience was told that the average job today lasts four years—Mr. Krueger advised that a new ethos in hiring was emerging among employers: "hire the talent to do the job." This means that a lot of work in the future will be contractual in nature, and that people should expect to work in short-term spurts. In addition to keeping apprised of new trends, job-seekers should rid themselves of common misconceptions about the job-market, Mr. Krueger said. One such misconception is that all companies are amidst a period of "downsizing," the buzz-word of the late nineties. "They're not. They're hiring and firing at the same time. So just because a company's firing people, that doesn't mean it's not looking for people," Mr. Krueger advised. Some   other misconceptions highlighted by Mr. Krueger included:

-Your resume is your most important marketing tool. "You are your most important marketing tool," said Mr. Krueger.

-Most, or even a significant portion, of available jobs are advertised. In fact, only a very small percentage of jobs are advertised.-It is better to look for jobs when you're already employed. In actuality, if you are looking for work seriously, said Mr. Krueger it is a full-time job."

Neil Seeman - The Lawyers Weekly

Glimpse 3:

Small firms survive and flourish in the late '90s

 Elizabeth Raymer

TORONTO—Small is beautiful, small is big and smaller may be better.

Speakers at a recent meeting of the Canadian Bar Association-Ontario's Law Practice Management Section extolled the virtues of the smaller law practice, and told the audience why smaller firms are often better positioned to serve the client market.

"There is a growing concern among the sole practitioners that it's getting too tough out there," said the meeting's co-chair, Michael Crawford of Crawford Reid Consulting.

"We have accountants...[and] lots of other people infringing on the territory that lawyers traditionally felt that they had."

But there's lots the small practitioner can do to overcome these challenges, he said. And smaller firms often have an inherent advantage.

Changes in the marketplace and technology are among the reasons why smaller firms can outperform their larger competitors, said speaker Ward Bower.

His management consultant firm, Altman Weil Pensa, in Newtown Square, Pennsylvania, publishes the annual Small Law Firm Economic Survey.

"Of our clients who came through the recession [of the early 1900s] best, in the U.S...it was some of our small- and medium-firm clients that did so. The clients that got hurt the worst were some of our large-firm clients."

Small-and medium-sized firms were very lean and focused, and so were able to withstand the leaner times.

Practitioners prefer small firms for numerous reasons, Mr. Bower said, among them flexibility, self-determination, a feeling of contribution to the business and the ability to manage the organization better.

But "there's one inherent competitive advantage in small law firms that most...don't take advantage of," Mr. Bower pointed out, "and that is their ability to act quicker, to implement quicker, to react quicker, than larger firms."

Overhead is much lower for smaller firms of less than nine lawyers, which allows them to charge less.

On a cost-per-lawyer basis, "there's a $20,000-per-year difference, in the 1996 survey of law firm economics, between under-five-lawyer firms and over-75-lawyer firms," Mr. Bower said, a result which is consistent with the previous 25 years of surveys.

"That is what we see as one of the competitive advantages that a small firm has, and it's part of the reason why small is beautiful," Mr. Bower said.

He stressed that firms need a plan, and that success depends on prioritizing and doing the most important things first.

Mr. Bower's keys to successful small-firm practice are:

Cost Containment—Average per-lawyer overhead in American firms has increased at a greater rate than per-lawyer revenue over the past ten years, Mr. Bower said. Average overhead has increased about 60 per cent, compared to about 50 per cent for revenue.

"We see increasing cost pressure in U.S. and Canadian law firms...being driven by four factors that need to be managed very carefully."

Supply and demand will likely push support staff labour costs up "dramatically in the foreseeable future," Mr. Bower said, as there are increasingly less trained and qualified people working as support staff (e.g. secretaries).

Occupancy costs are usually the second biggest overhead costs after labour. Mr. Bower suggested restricting lawyer offices to work space rather than meeting space, the latter being more expensive to decorate and usually larger.

Expenditures are also increasing in the area of marketing and promotion in business development, but this is important for increasing firm profile and attracting clients, Mr. Bower said.

In the area of technology, Mr. Bower said that the promised benefits are beginning to be seen in decreasing support staff costs. Per-lawyer expenditures on information technology have doubled every three years since his firm started surveying in this category in 1980 in U.S. law firms, Mr. Bower said, and for a long time with no appreciable reduction in support staff employment costs.

However, in the 1992 survey of law-firm economics, there was a very small decrease in the lawyer-support staff ratio, and this has continued. Mr. Bower attributed this to lawyers using computers more, and thus decreasing reliance on secretaries.

Fee Realization—The biggest problem in small firms is either the inability to get bills out or the inability to follow up on bills, "and as a result you only get paid for a portion of what you do," Mr. Bower advised.

This is partly due to a lack of discipline in things like time-recording, and a refusal to say "no" to cases even where clients are known to be delinquent in paying accounts.

Specialization—It's better to specialize, Mr. Bower noted. With the "convergence" movement among corporate lawyers of the 1900s, small-and-mid-sized firms get outsourced business because they are seen to offer better value.

Alternative Pricing— Small law firms can charge less, which is obviously attractive to clients. It is also easier for them to know their costs, and it's easier for them to offer a variety of pricing options.

Economic Globalization—There are international legal opportunities for small-and-mid-sized firms to be domestic importers of international legal work, or to take in-bound domestic work on behalf of foreign-based businesses investors.

"That is a huge growth area, and there is no reason a smaller firm can't make itself the firm of choice" in this type of work, Mr. Bower said. These firms can become "international boutiques."

Technology Utilization—With new technology such as voice recognition, in which one can speak into a microphone and see one's words appear on a word processor, "there's a huge opportunity to substitute capital for labour and begin to get control over that fastest-rising and largest element of the overhead of law firms of all sizes, which is support-staff/occupancy costs," Mr. Bower told his audience."

Elizabeth Raymer - The Lawyers Weekly

Glimpse 4:

New practitioners fly solo

Need commitment, good business plan

Neil Seeman

TORONTO-For some recent calls, being proactive has meant opening up their own shops.

John Kingdon articled with a small criminal firm in Toronto, and knew all along that he would have to start his own practice if he wished to continue as a defense lawyer.

He started to investigate the viability of his idea after the summer of his second year of law school at the University of Toronto.

"It's the only way to do criminal work, and this is what I love to do," said Mr. Kingdon.

When he approached banks for start-up loans, "they were not overtly hostile to the idea," joked Mr. Kingdon.

Speaking by phone to the Lawyers Weekly from his newly minted home office, Mr. Kingdon shared some of his initial learning experiences.

His advice to those thinking about starting their own practice: "Be sure this is something you're committed to, and make sure you have a good business plan."

Mr. Kingdon received guidance from a number of sources.

He attended a conference presented by the Law Society of Upper Canada advising new calls on the basics of start-up businesses.

"It was very impressive," said Mr. Kingdon.

At the same time, he has discovered that the criminal defence Bar has been very supportive. "[It] is extremely collegial," he noted.

Assistance from senior members of the criminal Bar is suspicious, given that Mr. Kingdon hopes to draw his initial clients chiefly from referrals. He has also signed up for the law society's Lawyers' Referral Service, and hopes to attract some legal aid certificate work.

Preparing for his future clients has thus far been a full-time job. Mr. Kingdon has been searching out downtown office space to rent for client meetings. He has also designed his own accounting software package with a spreadsheet.

"I'm lucky in that I'm very computer literate," said Mr. Kingdon. He therefore did not require any secretarial assistance, a savings which has been essential to his new practice.

For the time being, Mr. Kingdon is holding off on any added expenses, such as advertising. "I've talked to a lot of people about advertising....Some say it's a complete waste of time, others say go for it, so I'm still investigating."

Mr. Kingdon does admit that starting off on one's own can be an intimidating experience.

He not only has to concern himself with administrative chores but also with keeping professionally competent, he said.

And so he heads the latest books and attends continuing legal education programs to keep up to speed with the newest developments in criminal law.

Another recent call, Gavin Naimer, has adopted a similar proactive approach to starting up his legal career.

Instead of opening his own practice, Mr. Naimer has chosen to do a form of freelancing for large Quebec firms which need litigation work done in Toronto. "I didn't want to sit around and wait for the jobs to come to me," Mr. Naimer said.

As he makes more contacts, his referral base has increased considerably. "I've made some excellent contacts during this period. And you never know how it's going to benefit me down the road," Mr. Naimer noted.

What's his advice for other unemployed grads? "Opportunities will present themselves, but you've got to maintain an open and dynamic approach to seize upon the opportunities as they come up."

Neil Seeman - The Lawyers Weekly

Glimpse 5:

Opportunities and obstacles face young family law practitioners in wake of legal aid funding cuts

Janice Zima

TORONTO—The legal aid crunch's heavy-handed swipe at Ontario's family Bar, with its unrealistically low tariff restrictions and low returns on docketed time, has fed both disillusionment as well as unexpected opportunities for a new generation of family law practitioners.

Tanya Road, a 1997 graduate who set up her Toronto practice with associate Simon Jellinek last spring, contends that since she began taking on legal aid clients, she has had a "horrendous time" with Ontario Legal Aid Plan (OLAP).

According to Ms. Road, the biggest problem with OLAP is that the complexity of many legal aid clients' issues means the tariffs are often hopelessly inadequate.

"They're fairly complicated issues, and they require a lot of work, and I find that OLAP doesn't allow for the complication of the matter," Ms. Road said.

She finds legal aid client problems are often "extremely complex," because many other bureaucratic agencies are frequently involved in OLAP client affairs.

Consequently, OLAP matters often require more time than the files of many paying clients, "who often have their lives together better," she said.

Logging endless hours of unpaid work, Ms. Road said she has sometimes spent up to 90 hours on files with 20-hour budgets because, from her ethical perspective, the additional effort is necessary to "put the case forward properly."

Still, according to 1993 call Cori Kalinowski, while legal aid tariffs are clearly too low in some areas, it is possible to structure an effective OLAP practice.

"You have to learn to run a case really efficiently," said Ms. Kalinowski, who set up her own practice last April.

"It's a little tricky, and you have to sort of work at it for awhile and talk to people to figure out the ins and outs of the system."

Ms. Kalinowski, who practises a mix of family and employment law, reported that 20 per cent of her practice is currently comprised of legal aid clients.

She said that OLAP has diversified her practice, both providing interesting work and bolstering her client base.

Although Ms. Kalinowski had law firm and court experience before taking on her first legal aid clients, she believes there is a definite "learning curve" for OLAP practitioners.

She acknowledged, however, that even with an efficient practice, the tariffs can be too low to provide sufficient time to ensure good client service.

"Everyone I've spoken to ends up putting in more hours than [they] get paid for, "Ms. Kalinowski said.

"But you have to do it so that you meet your obligations as a lawyer and you provide the service."

Other lawyers have found that the frustrations of legal aid in the '90s have influenced their decision to simply not develop any legal aid practice.

James Edney, a 1993 call who practises with Harris & Harris in Toronto, found that OLAP cuts actually had a positive impact upon his practice, by encouraging him to provide competitively priced legal services.

"What happened," he told The Lawyers Weekly, "was that people who wanted the legal work found ways to afford it, and young lawyers could provide very good services at cost efficient rates.

"So I think it was a real help for my practice in the first few years." He believes the market for affordable family legal services has actually been bolstered by restrictions on legal aid funding.

"I think [the cuts] help them, because it makes [young counsel], generally being the most affordable counsel, the most attractive to a lot of these people," said Mr. Edney, whose $200/hour fee nearly doubles what he charged when he began his practice five years ago.

He adds that the dearth of legal aid funding has allowed him to develop a practice of paying clients.

"That is very key in these cash-conscious times, and when you have large payments due to the law society and for insurance, you make sure you stay on top of it, rather than waiting for legal aid receivables," he said.

Ms. Road, who articled at a full-service Bay Street firm, has found the accepted standards of practice within the legal aid system somewhat disillusioning.

"What I see from some more senior legal aid lawyers is that they just don't care about their clients," she said.

"I don't find that the legal aid system allows you to care about people and to do a good job because it doesn't support you economically in doing so."

Ms. Road added that while there is plenty of legal aid work available, the pro bono work she ends up doing means she cannot afford to take on more than one or two cases per month.

Ms. Road is convinced that legal aid standards are lower than they should be, because "there's no way you could do the work that's required and put together materials the way they're supposed to be put together on a legal aid budget."

Concurs Ms. Kalinowski: "[Legal aid lawyers] end up feeling that they're almost funding the system, because they're providing their time pro bono....The low tariffs can make it quite difficult to manage these files."

According to Ms. Road, among the main difficulties as a newly called lawyer out on her own is the administrative aspects of legal aid practice, which are not taught in Bar Ads or in law school.

"You're acting as a lawyer, a secretary, and a law clerk, and you're doing all the administrative stuff, all your filing, all your document prep...everything," she said.

"I wouldn't consider representing somebody unless I was going to do the whole nine yards, regardless of whether I'm going to get paid for it. These are people's lives." Ms. Kalinowski said that administrative work related to legal aid work "adds substantially" to her unpaid hours, although she says that she has managed to develop methods of keeping this time to a minimum.

"There's sort of a unique way to practising the legal aid files," she said. "But it helps with your other practice, too; the more efficient you are, the better."

"Even when you're not practising legal aid files, you still have to watch your hours all the time. And you want to make sure that what you're billing as work is representative of the work you did," she said.

Ms. Kalinowski added that at $67/hour, legal aid work can be lucrative if files are managed efficiently, since OLAP fees can provide a fairly steady income with "no collection issues."

Ms. Road and Ms. Kalinowski support the recommendations of the recent McCamus Report on Legal Aid to allocate a greater proportion of OLAP resources to family cases.

"There has to be more funding going to family," said Ms. Kalinowski. "If there's any way that there can be more funding for the family law program, it would really help young lawyers to run a business."

"With [legal aid] cuts, I'm afraid there are a lot of people going to court unrepresented who shouldn't be," she said.

"It's really frustrating as a lawyer, because you really don't want to turn people down because they simply can't afford to retain you.

"But you can't do it for free."

Janice Zima - The Lawyers Weekly

Glimpse 6:

Dawn of the brand-name firm

American law firm franchise setting its sights on the Canadian legal marketplace

Brad Daisley

A marketing expert who helped establish a real estate company, a car rental chain and a Chinese food franchise is bringing brand-name marketing to Canadian lawyers.

The practice of law "lacks a market leader," said 41-year-old Gary Swernik, who was instrumental in developing the Century 21 real estate chain, HOJ car rentals and the Yuchu's fast food outlets. "If you look at real estate or the stock brokerage business, they all have a few key strong companies that really dominate the business, and law doesn't have that."

His solution is First American Law, an international association of independent law firms based on a central marketing strategy.

In the United States, it's already started with several firms in Tampa, Florida, and hundreds more across the country waiting for their applications to be screened.

And First Canadian Law is not far behind.

"We will launch it in Canada. Realistically, I can say [within] six months to a year," Mr. Swernik told The Lawyers Weekly.

He also said much of First American's and First Canadian's start-up capital came from Canadian investors.

The company already has a Toronto office, and much of the American firm's operation is handled from there. First American Law is not affiliated with First American Title Insurance.

"We looked at it and we realized that there was an opportunity to do something in the area of consolidating law firms on some basis, and we decided to do it from a marketing point of view," said Mr. Swernik, a McMaster University marketing and economics grad.

"We provide member law firms with a high-frequency, high-profile professional marketing program that includes TV, radio, print, public relations, direct mail campaigns and a Web site."

First American's goal is to create brand-name recognition for its member firms, much the same as Century 21's marketing provides brand-name recognition for its member real estate companies.

"What we offer is...the power and credibility of brand name, the customer loyalty that brings and the ability in some respects to dominate the field," Mr. Swernik explained.

Much of First American's advertising is directed to public relations programs and event sponsorship designed to create an image of professionalism and integrity, such as a recent program to purchase infra-red helmets for a Florida fire department.

"This is all marketing," he said, "designed to elevate the name 'First American Law' and to cause the consumer, whether it be a business or non-business consumer, to think First American Law when they need an attorney for something."

"We're not out there with these aggressive, American-style ambulance-chasing ads," he stressed.

"These are...corporate, [with] high production values. They're definitely not the typical U.S. lawyer ad."

"We are positioning [First American] as the Merrill Lynch of law," he noted. "We are definitely not going to be perceived as the K-Mart of law."

Mr. Swernik and his partners—Derek Tennant, founder and former chairman of Holiday Rent-a-Car, and investment banker John Penny—began researching the legal market in 1995.

They quickly discovered a market that was competitive and mature, but fragmented and without a really dominant firm.

They also hired three of the best ethics attorneys in the United States to make sure their plans didn't run afoul of state Bar regulations.

First American is targeting small to mid-size firms with fewer than 50 lawyers. In larger communities, First American also targets firms according to the area of law they practise, in order to reduce competition between members.

Applicants must pass a screening program that includes a review of any complaints to the state Bar association and any insurance claims.

Member firms remain independent and First American, which is owned and operated by non-lawyers, does not control individual law firm operations and does not share in individual firm profits.

Instead, it charges affiliates a flat fee, based on the number of lawyers in the firm and the cost of advertising in the firm's region.

Plans for future members services include professional development programs, discount purchasing for office supplies and group insurance. Member firms are expected to refer work outside their field of expertise to other firms, and there is a toll-free phone referral service as well.

First American also conducts satisfaction surveys with every client, and reports back to the firm that served them.

State Bar ethical rules prohibit First American from disciplining member lawyers unless the lawyer is disbarred or convicted of a felony.

Mr. Swernik said his screening process should keep problem firms out. He also expects member firms will monitor each other's performance to ensure no one devalues the brand name. To date, only a few firms have joined the fold, but it's still early in First Americans' life and Mr. Swernik hopes soon to have 2,000 affiliates across the United States.

One of the first firms to join was Tampa's Wetherington, LeFloch and Hamilton, a five-member firm that specializes in business law.

"So far we've had little success in getting a lot of referrals, but it's in its infancy and therefore we sort of expected that," said partner Eugene LeFloch.

"We've had of couple of referrals that have been very good."

His firm signed on in January after seeing First American's TV ads.

"That's what sold me on them. They were very, very professionally done and they were very tasteful. They weren't these traditional ambulance-chasing ads."

Mr. LeFloch added that his firm doesn't really expect to see the benefits of its association with First American for at least a year. "It's just getting going," he said.

Brad Daisley - The Lawyers Weekly

Conclusion

The practice of law is both a business and a profession. The "business" side of it pays the bills (and for many lawyers does far more). The "profession" side is what makes it interesting and unique.

Chapter 35

21st Century Compliance - Globalization, Technology And The Practice Of Law In The 21st Century

"As some of you may know, I will be retiring on January 7, 2000. I will be leaving it to this Court, including its newest member, to deal with the legal problems of the next millennium. Of course, none of us can know precisely what those legal issues will be. But having been a judge for almost a third of this century, I think I can at least predict what some of the broad areas of legal controversy may be. It will fall to you, Justice Arbour, and your colleagues on the Supreme Court of the 21st Century to address these matters.

No doubt, for example, there will be a great deal of legal uncertainty surrounding a range of biomedical matters such as new reproductive technologies, genetic engineering and cloning. In addition to the obvious moral and ethical concerns, one can only imagine the vexing legal issues that may arise from scientific developments in these areas. But they will surely include difficult matters of intellectual property, family law and regulatory law.

To take an example that is not even the slightest bit far-fetched, even at present, what law will apply to the growing world of telemedicine, in which, for example, in which a Canadian citizen may receive at base camp on Mount Everest from a para-medic who is sending computer generated data by satellite to a cardiologist at Yale Medical Centre in the United States for analysis and diagnosis. Against whom, in what jurisdiction, in which court, applying which country's laws and what forms of evidence could a medical malpractice suit be brought in such circumstances?

And it is not just in areas of scientific and medical advancement that legal challenges will arise. The evolution of our own thoughts and attitudes about some areas of the law is almost as rapid as the rate of scientific innovation.

I am thinking about areas such as discrimination on the basis of gender, sexual orientation and disability; aboriginal and treaty rights of first peoples; the definition of and legal responsibilities among family members; the place of the victim in criminal law; globalization of the law through mutual legal assistance, extradition and, of course, international criminal tribunals."

—From the Remarks of the Right Honourable Antonio Lamer, P.C. Chief Justice Of Canada and of the Supreme Court Of Canada on the Occasion of the Swearing-in of the Honourable Louise Arbour October 4, 1999

International Criminal Tribunals - Now That You Mention It!

Law and the practice of law follow changes in society. For every change in society there will be a change affecting the practice of law. Some areas of law will become extinct. Other areas of law will spring into being. The recently created Hague tribunal has created an opportunity to practise a new kind of criminal law. Canadian lawyers have been quick to involve themselves in it.

Tuesday July 17, 2001

The Globe and Mail

Canadians key players at Hague tribunal

Lawyers from Victoria and Toronto among many taking major roles in Milosevic's trial

Paul Knox

"Eight years ago, secure in his post as president of Serbia, Slobodan Milosevic could hardly have believed that one day he would sit in a prisoner's dock and hear himself accused of crimes against humanity.

Nor could he foresee that the long legal process bringing him to court in The Hague would be studded with Canadians in key roles.

Call it a peculiar vocation for international criminal law. Call it mere coincidence. For whatever reason, a remarkable number of Canadians have been closely involved with Mr. Milosevic's case.

Most prominent in the days since the former president's July 3 court appearance have been Dirk Ryneveld, the Victoria prosecutor leading the legal assault against him, and Christopher Black, the Toronto lawyer helping him counterattack.

But they're just the tip of the iceberg.

A Canadian — Madam Justice Louise Arbour — supervised the preparation of the 1999 indictment against Mr. Milosevic. She was then chief prosecutor for the International Criminal Tribunal for the former Yugoslavia (ICTY).

James Stewart, a Toronto lawyer on leave from the Ontario Attorney-General's office, helped assemble the prosecution's legal team. Stephane Bourgon, a former Canadian Forces military lawyer, is chief of staff for ICTY president Claude Jorda of France.

And if Mr. Milosevic's case reaches the appeal stage, he could well find yet another Canadian arguing the case for the prosecution. In all, 60 Canadians are serving among the ICTY's 1,120 staff members, including lawyers, police investigators and support staff. "They're all fine people," said William Schabas, a Canadian expert on international criminal law who teaches at the National University of Ireland in Galway. "They do us proud being there."

Canadians have also been prominent in a parallel criminal tribunal for Rwanda, and in efforts to set up an International Criminal Court. Philippe Kirsch, former chief legal adviser to Canada's Foreign Affairs Department, chaired negotiations that led to the ICC's approval in 1998.

"Canadians have a particularly well-developed sense of justice . . . ," Mr. Ryneveld said. "For a country with a very small population, we're at the cutting edge of developments in this area."

The Canadian thread in the pursuit of Mr. Milosevic began in 1992, when the United Nations set up a commission to investigate atrocities in the former Yugoslav republics.

A key member was Bill Fenrick, then a Canadian Forces expert in the law of war and now senior legal adviser at the ICTY.

At the time, there was talk of punishing the perpetrators of so-called ethnic cleansing and the leaders who ordered it. But the commission on which Mr. Fenrick served was starved for funds, and posed a slim threat to major players.

The rebellion in the Serbian province of Kosovo that led Mr. Milosevic to send in troops in 1998 and the North Atlantic Treaty Organization's bombardment of Serbia the following year were far in the future.

Mr. Fenrick was skeptical in those early days about the chances of linking powerful figures to atrocities and bringing them to trial.

"I wouldn't have been surprised at the idea of there being an indictment of Milosevic, but I would have been surprised at seeing a trial, yes," he said from The Hague.

Mr. Fenrick joined the ICTY staff after the UN Security Council established it in 1993 as the first war-crimes court since Nuremberg.

One of its 11 judges was Jules Deschend, formerly of the Quebec Superior Court, who headed a royal commission on war criminals during the 1980s. He resigned from the ICTY in 1997 because of poor health and died last year.

Judge Arbour left the Ontario Court of Appeal in 1996 and took over as the ICTY's chief prosecutor. By the end of her three-year term, there were more than 60 public indictments and an unknown number of secret ones.

The most famous was the May, 1999, indictment of Mr. Milosevic, who was then president of Yugoslavia. He was accused of committing crimes against humanity and breaking the laws of war in connection with mass deportations and killings of ethnic Albanians in Kosovo, and was handed over to the tribunal last month.

The senior trial attorney on the case is Mr. Ryneveld, a long-time B.C. prosecutor who handled an inquest into a 1978 air disaster in Cranbrook that killed 42 people.

His team works under Mr. Stewart, the ICTY's chief of prosecutions, who as an Ontario Crown attorney worked on the early stages of the Paul Bernardo sex-slaying trial.

Also at the ICTY is Norman Farrell, a former Ontario prosecutor and lawyer for the International Committee of the Red Cross. As the longest-serving member of the tribunal's appeals section, he's a logical choice to handle arguments if the Milosevic case gets that far.

And the ranks of Canadians could swell even further.

Sharon Williams, a professor at Osgoode Hall Law School in Toronto, was named last month as one of 27 judges on call to clear up a backlog of cases at the ICTY and handle an expected increase. And Marlys Edwardh, a Toronto trial lawyer, was interviewed this month for a prosecutor's job.

Canadians say that taking part in the ground-breaking ICTY was too good an opportunity to pass up.

Mr. Stewart, 54, had appeared before Judge Arbour in Ontario and said it was her appointment as chief prosecutor for both the ICTY and the Rwanda tribunals that triggered his interest.

"She had a gap that needed to be filled, and I was able to supply that need," he said.

Dutch-born Mr. Ryneveld, 55, said the mixture of elements from British, continental European and military law practised at the tribunal can be confusing.

"Whatever you learned back home you park at the door," he said. "You have to re-educate yourself."

The largest leap may be from domestic criminal law to the law of war, which bars the deliberate targeting of civilians but allows "collateral damage" if the tactics used are appropriate for the military objective in sight.

"In normal criminal-law situations, killing is absolutely wrong," Mr. Farrell said. "In wartime situations, killing is not [necessarily] wrong. . . . It's difficult to get your head around this concept of proportionality."

Reprinted with permission from The Globe and Mail.

Additional Trends - The Trend Is Your Friend!

The Hague tribunal is of course only one example of how a change in society has created a whole new area of law. Our society is in constant change. Information technology and computers are the backbone of the new economy - changing the way that we work and communicate. Anyone can now communicate with almost anyone else via email or a telephone call in seconds. Do you miss seeing the person? Not a problem. People can communicate in real time while viewing one another on the internet. Do you need to reach out and physically touch the person?

There is no part of the world that you can't get to within 24 hours. Are these options for communication expensive? Not a bit. All forms of communication are far less expensive than they used to be. Costs are still falling. To put it simply - nobody is "out of touch" regardless of his or her location. What are the implications for society as a whole? Like all adjustments there will be winners and there will be losers. Here are "some suggestions":

- the presumption that buyers and sellers may be found in the same geographical vicinity has ceased. How many of you have bought a book from Amazon.com instead of from your local bookstore? The line between national and international markets has been greatly diminished.

Winners: businesses that want to enter markets that used to be local

Losers: local businesses that used to have captive markets

Real World Winner: Amazon.com (assuming it becomes profitable) - buyers will have access to a larger number of sellers. This means that competition among sellers will become even more fierce.

Winners: most businesses and all consumers

Losers: businesses with inflated prices or cost structures

Real World Winner: Ebay.com (buying and selling everything on the internet)

- more and more people will work from somewhere other than fixed company premises. This will result in new opportunities for "part-time" and "self-employment".

Winners: everybody who wishes to take advantage of these additional opportunities

Losers: The owners of office buildings in downtown areas. For many businesses expensive space in downtown locations may not be necessary.

Real World Winner: For an innovative lawyer see: www.electriclawyer.com- capital in the 21st century is more likely to be a function of your knowledge, skills and ability to continue learning. The value of education and intellect is likely to increase.

Winners: those who acquire the skills needed for a lifetime of learning

Losers: those who target very industry specific jobs that could become obsolete.

Real World Winners: Those who acquire "learning skills" as opposed to "technical skills"

- the trend toward free trade and globalization is likely to continue. NAFTA and other treaties promoting free trade will become stronger. The borders between countries will blur (evidence of this is clearly available in Europe). The legal profession is beginning to understand that their clients are becoming more international and have interests in a number of different domains.

Lawyers And Proximity To Serve Clients

Law firms need to have a presence in the same places as their clients. In the modern world, that presence can be either virtual or physical.

Creating A Virtual Presence

It is now possible to run certain kinds of law practices from the internet. For example a lawyer specializing in domain disputes might never even have to meet his client. Immigration lawyers can service clients from outside North America without ever having to meet them. The advantage is that the law firm can be open 24 hours a day, 7 days a week.

By way of example, read the following letter from a young lawyer:

The Law Offices Of

Former Big Firm Associate

123 Main Street

Vaughn, Ontario

L6A 1R8

mail@formerbigfirmassociate.com

(416) 666-6666

John Richardson

www.prep.com

Box 19602, Manulife P.O1

55 Bloor St. W.

Toronto, Ontario

M4W 3T9

December 15, 2003

Dear John:

I am very pleased to advise you that I will be opening my own law office effective January 2, 2004. As of this date I will be operating offices in North York and Vaughn Ontario. My mailing information is indicated above.

All matters handled by me on your behalf at (Previous Big Firm) remain at (Previous Big Firm). If you have any questions about this, please do not hesitate to contact me.

My practice will be limited to national and international intellectual property related matters, namely patents, copyrights, trademarks, trade secrets, industrial designs, non-disclosure agreements, plant breeders rights, inventions and development, entertainment and e-commerce law.

My office will be almost entirely electronic in nature, thus reducing unnecessary overhead, with the resultant savings passed on to all clients. This will result in an unprecedented speed of service to all clients in all matters. It is my intention to provide quality service that is dollar-for-dollar superior to that provided by Bay Street in Toronto for the same of less-inclusive services.

On my launch date of January 2, 2004, I will hope that you will take the opportunity to visit any of my web sites on-line at: www.formerbigfirmassociate.com

Apart from the wealth of information on the sites above, I will also be participating in a number of public speaking engagements, and the details of these engagements will also appear on the site on an on-going basis.

If I may be of assistance to you; please do not hesitate to contact me.

I wish you the very best of the holiday season and hope to hear from you in the very near future.

Yours very truly,

Former Big Firm Associate

Creating A Physical Presence

In order to enhance proximity to their clients law firms have (1) merged, (2) created associations and (3) created Multidisciplinary Partnerships (MDPs).

---

1. A Larger Physical Presence Through Law Firm Mergers

In August of 1999 the British law firm Clifford Chance and U.S. counterpart Rogers & Wells agreed to merge and set the stage for Germany's Puender, Bolhard, Weber & Axster to join them to create the world's largest law firm. The new firm would have revenues of more than one billion U.S. dollars, thirty offices and more than 2700 lawyers. Why? "There are more international deals being carried out, and clients don't want the time delays and the expense that comes from working with many firms around the world. They want one top-tier firm," Keith Clark, senior partner at Clifford Chance said in an interview.

The proposed merger is an example of the trend toward globalization and "one-stop shopping." In the long run, the creation of international law firms is sure to create competitive difficulties for Canadian firms that have relied on legislative monopolies to maintain their client base.

Consider the following perspective on "World Wide Law Firms"

October 2, 1998

Get ready for worldwide law firms—and soon

Door may have closed on firms still seeking to go global, lawyers told

Brad Daisley

"VANCOUVER—Global law firms that offer a complete range of services worldwide will soon be a reality, delegates to the International Bar Association's conference in Vancouver were told.

"We've got a handful of United States firms that appear to be almost ready for the implementation of this strategy," Philadelphia-based consultant Ward Bower told an overflow crowd of several hundred lawyers attending a workshop on the globalization of law firms.

Four London firms are looking to expand globally and a few firms in other parts of the world are considering globalization but face restrictive regulatory markets and schemes, he added.

Other firms thinking about expanding to the global market-place may be too late, Bower warned.

"It may well be that we are in a position where the aggressive amalgamators who capture market share in an economy like we've got right now are going to be the winners in the long term, and the faster they can get there, the better off they may be."

According to a 1997 survey by The Economist magazine, U.K. lawyers predict there will be 10 to 20 global law firms within a decade: three to six from England, five to ten from the United States and another two or three associated with the major accounting firms that have already set up global offices.

Bower defines a global law firm as something much bigger than an international law firm.

"Global means full service, with localized services in virtually every location in which the firm is serving...tied together in a one-firm concept," he said.

"In that sense, global networks of law firms are something less than global law firms. International law firms are not on the ground in all the places they need to be."

Driving the demand for globalized legal services is the international economy and global corporations that demand one-stop shopping for multinational advice.

Typical global legal markets include project financing, mergers and acquisitions, privatizations, customs and cross-border trade issues.

Bower said global clients like "the idea of instructing lawyers in a particular location and having those instructions executed in 10 or 12 different jurisdictions, and being able to hold the firm accountable through the lawyer in the office in which the instruction was made."

Sophisticated clients also want "cross-border consistency" from their professional advisors.

Studies of other professions that have already globalized—what Bower calls "precursor markets"—suggests lawyers should expect rapid consolidation among the large firms similar to the recent mergers that saw the so-called "Big Eight" accounting firms shrink to the "Big Five."

"We've got four independent law firms in the world currently claiming over 1,000 lawyers, and in the U.S. alone, we have another 100 [firms with] 300-plus [lawyers] and almost 400 firms of 100 or more lawyers."

Bower said global firms benefit from brand-name recognition—which a 1994 U.K. study suggested is worth the extra 10 to 15 per cent in premium billing for a professional services firm.

And they spend more on marketing and advertising than local firms. Currently, law firms spend only 1.6 per cent of revenue on marketing, compared to almost seven per cent for other professions.

Bower predicts a new structure will emerge for the legal profession. At the top of the ladder will be a very few global firms that specialize in international financial transactions and are based in the major capital markets of New York, London and Asia.

On the next rung will be global firms handling corporate/commercial matters that fall short of the major capital market transactions.

Following those firms, he sees the international firms that have offices in several countries but not worldwide.

Bower said there are also opportunities for international boutiques—such as intellectual property firms—and for domestic firms that provide "on-the-ground services" for foreign investors.

But other speakers cautioned lawyers to avoid being mesmerized by the prospect of global firms.

"Ninety-five per cent of the profession worldwide do not belong to mega-firms and are not likely to do so," said London based law firm consultant David Andrews.

He told the largely American and European audience they should examine what the"non-mega firms" can and should be doing in the increasingly complex and international market-place.

He also noted that virtually all of the so-called mega-firms took decades to build their practices to their current stature.

"It's not an easy field to break into, and those who aspire in newer, younger firms to compete head-on as full service firms with the mega-firms may be being somewhat unrealistic," he said.

"It may be possible to nibble on the heels of some of the mega-firms in certain areas of practice, but to try to emulate them across the board is, I think, perhaps an unrealistic strategy."Andrews said mid-sized firms must gear their infrastructure to their client base and avoid diluting their profitability through over-expansion.

He also urged the smaller firms to develop strategies to attract the best lawyers and to keep them at the firm.

Recent studies conducted by Andrew's own consulting firm revealed the most common reason for lawyers leaving firms was an inconsistent work ethic among the partnership.

Other factors were divergent levels of competence, poor management and simple boredom. "You don't see any mention of money," he noted.

"I'm not saying partners never move for money reasons. But what I am saying is that the majority are not motivated by money."

Andrews also noted compensation is rarely a factor when top-level law school graduates are looking for work. The firm's sense of direction, management and working conditions are much more important.

Other factors include the quality of work and the opportunities for career development."

Brad Daisley - The Lawyers Weekly

---

2. A Larger Physical Presence Through Law Firm Associations

Law firm's mergers are not always necessary in order for firms to serve their clients in other jurisdictions. The same result can be accomplished through informal associations. For example, some firms are part of a global network of firms. The advantage is that the firm stays independent, but has the benefit of being part of a global network. Daniel McHardie writing in the Globe in 2000 tells the story of how:

"...12 years ago, New York lawyer Lowell Lifshultz had an inspiration. He dreamed of a partnership of medium-sized law firms worldwide designed to share knowledge, expertise and clients.

Mr. Lifshultz, a partner in the New York firm Epstein Becker & Green, went out and formed the International Lawyers Network, which now has 4,000 lawyers from 72 firms in more than 50 countries."

The benefits of this are easy to see. With a shrinking world I predict an expanding number of global networks.

---

3. A Larger Physical Presence Through Multidisciplinary Partnerships (MDPs)

MDP's have resulted from the changing nature of business, globalization and the need to be competitive. They are attractive because they give the client the option of "one-stop shopping."

A MDP has been defined as a business arrangement where individuals with different professional qualifications practice together in a partnership or other business arrangement. MDPs can vary in size and scope. Examples include a law firm practicing within a worldwide accounting or consulting firm and a law firm that forms a partnership with a paralegal.

Clients require accounting and other professional services as well as legal services. Hence, associations between law firms and accounting firms can make good sense and are the earliest examples of MDPs.

Notable associations creating Multidisciplinary Practices between law firms and accounting/consulting firms include:

Donahue & Partners - Canada's first multidisciplinary law firm

This arrangement results in a business services entity that allows the business to provide both:

1. A larger range of services by category (legal and accounting); and

2. A larger range of services geographically.

Such arrangements are common in other countries. For example, in France five of the six biggest law firms are affiliated with accounting and/or consulting firms and more than ten percent of the countries lawyers work for them. I predict that we will see much more of this kind of arrangement. The trend is your friend!

Conclusion

There are hundreds of additional examples. However, life in the 21st century will be characterized by:

- rapid change;

- international as opposed to local markets;

- heightened competition;

- increased personal flexibility and mobility;

- the birth of new industries and the death of old industries;

- globalization

21st century compliance will require lawyers to be more flexible and better educated than ever. Remember, it's not that people plan to fail, it's just that they fail to plan. The time to start thinking about these issues is now!

APPENDIX A

There will be many opportunities. In order to take advantage of those opportunities (both within and outside the legal profession) you must make yourself "21st Century Compliant." Consider the following advice about "preparing your legal career for the 21st century", by Gil Lan, a young Toronto lawyer. In his article he shares his perspectives on what will be helpful to the lawyer of the 21st century. The three topics discussed are (1) language skills (2) qualifying to practise in multiple jurisdictions and (3) graduate education.

Preparing your legal career for the 21st century

Gil Lan

Language skills

"The nature of the legal profession has changed drastically over the last two decades. Despite the glamorous depictions of wealthy and affluent lawyers on television, the reality is that the legal industry has become extremely competitive. Gone are the days where a license to practice law guaranteed one of a stable income. Much more is required of today's lawyer than ever before. To that end, I shall endeavor to provide my opinion regarding how one may prepare a successful legal career in the 21st century.

One of the most significant events in the last decade has been the rapid globalization of the world economy. Such globalization refers to (1) the extensive trade between various countries and (2) the influx of immigrants to North America and other parts of the world. The practical impact of globalization is that language skills have suddenly acquired a vast new significance.

The ability to speak a second language is invaluable in today's legal market. A second language opens the local markets at home (the local population speaking the second language). Often a client must share very sensitive and intimate information with his/her lawyer. The client feels much more comfortable communicating such information in his/her native language. Furthermore, by communicating in the client's native language, you reduce the chances of a misunderstanding or not receiving clear instructions from your client. Frequently, prospective clients will specifically seek out lawyers that can speak their native language.

Alternatively, even if your client speaks fluent English, in today's global economy, there is a significant likelihood that your client may be doing business or be otherwise involved with a person who does not speak English. For example, your client may be involved in a dispute with a foreign business overseas. If you can speak the relevant foreign language, you can provide value-added service to your client by speaking directly to the foreign entities involved.

The value of language skills has been recognized by many prominent law firms. I frequently see recruitment ads where a prestigious law firm requires a particular set of language skills. In fact, sometimes the law firm will disregard your lack of experience in the particular legal area and offer to train you provided that you have the language skills! Quite clearly, language skills are a valuable asset for you as a lawyer.

If you don't already speak a second language, the time to learn is now. Once you start practicing law, it will be very difficult to learn a new language in addition to your responsibilities as a lawyer. You can take the language courses as part of your undergraduate studies or learn outside of university. In fact, the ability to speak a second language might even assist you in being accepted to law school since the admission committees frequently look for "well-rounded" candidates.

With the ability to speak a second language, you will have one more qualification that will set you aside from the legion of other lawyers out there. In many instances, all other things being equal, it may be the deciding factor in whether a client retains you or a law firm hires you as opposed to another lawyer.

Qualifying as a lawyer in multiple jurisdictions

There are two good reasons for qualifying in multiple legal jurisdictions. The first reason is that, in the global economy, your client's legal issues may often involve more than one jurisdiction of law. For example, your client's factory may be in New York but perhaps he/she has a branch office in Toronto and sell the goods in Canada as well as the United States. If you are qualified as both an American and Canadian lawyer, you would be able to advise your client on how both American and Canadian law impacts on his/her business. Alternatively, if you are an American lawyer and your client already has a Canadian lawyer, you will at least be able to communicate more effectively with the Canadian lawyer since you understand both legal systems.

Such a dual qualification is a valuable asset to you as a future lawyer. As the world increasingly becomes more inter-connected, the value of the ability to practice law in more than one jurisdiction increases as well.

The second good reason for qualifying in multiple jurisdictions is job mobility. You may find that your legal practice is not as fulfilling in your home jurisdiction as you once thought it may be. If you qualified as a lawyer in more than one jurisdiction, you have the option of moving to the other jurisdiction and practicing there. Very recently in Toronto, the major prominent law firms were very concerned that many prospective young lawyers were moving to New York for higher salaries. The response of many Toronto law firms has been to increase the benefits and compensation offered to young lawyers now.

You should obtain your multiple qualifications very soon after law school. It will be very difficult to go back and write another bar exam if you are in the middle of a full-time law practice later on. In addition, when you are fresh out of law school, your "test taking" skills are still fresh in your mind and you are more likely to pass the various bar exams that you are writing.

You can inquire about the various requirements of foreign legal jurisdictions by writing to the relevant local bar association. If you are already qualified in a recognized jurisdiction, there is the possibility that you may be allowed to waive certain examinations. While there is some time and effort involved in this process, the benefit of being able to practice law in several jurisdictions is well worth the effort.

Graduate education

The legal profession has changed dramatically in the last two decades. There is much more competition among lawyers for business. In addition, many lawyers find that they do not enjoy practicing law and eventually leave the practice of law. One method of preparing your legal career for either of the two possibilities mentioned above is to pursue graduate legal education.

The typical "law school" law degree (a J.D. in the U.S.A. or an LL.B. in Canada or the United Kingdom) is an undergraduate degree. A graduate legal degree would be a Master of Laws degree or a doctorate in law.

There are three good reasons to pursue graduate legal education. The first reason is that an undergraduate law degree is no longer a guarantee of a successful legal career. There is stiff competition amongst lawyers for business and they all have an undergraduate law degree. By pursuing a graduate legal degree, you can increase your specialization in a chosen area of law and become more competitive in that particular legal field.

The second reason is that graduate legal education raises your credibility and profile in both the academic and professional legal community. Graduate legal education, unlike undergraduate legal education, is very specialized. Typically, you will write a thesis on a very narrow topic as part of your graduate legal education. As a result, you may become somewhat of an expert in that particular area. As you write more about that area, your profile as an expert increases. This leads to more clients coming to you for your expertise in a particular area of law.

The third reason for graduate legal education is that it provides you with more career options. As I mentioned, many lawyers find they do not like the practice of law and choose to pursue careers in different fields. If you still like law but do not wish to practice law, you can always teach law. However, a graduate law degree is highly recommended if not an absolute necessity, for being considered for a teaching position.

In addition, many other fields value a graduate degree. For example, business management consulting firms will often consider lawyers for a position. If you have only an undergraduate law degree, the business consulting firm will consider you with all other undergraduate applicants. However, if you have a graduate law degree, you will be considered with the graduate applicants. The positions for applicants with a graduate degree generally have higher salaries, greater responsibility and more prestige.

You should apply for graduate legal education very soon after you obtain your undergraduate law degree. It will be much more difficult to "go back" and obtain a graduate degree after you run a full-time law practice. Most graduate law degree programs are much shorter than graduate degree programs in other disciplines. For example, in North America a typical Master of Laws degree program is only one year full-time. Hence, the opportunity cost of attending graduate school in law is not at all onerous compared to other graduate programs.

Graduate legal education can greatly enhance your future legal practice by assisting you in establishing your expertise in a particular area of law. In addition, a graduate legal education provides you with greater career options should you choose not to practice law or should you find that there are better career opportunities for you outside of law. You can inquire about various graduate legal education programs and their requirements by contacting the relevant university's faculty of law admissions director. Given that graduate legal education improves your career possibilities both within the legal profession and outside of it, it is an option you should seriously consider."

Reprinted with permission of the author.

APPENDIX B

The Wave Of The Future?

Multidisciplinary "People" - The Global Business Professional

A multidisciplinary partnership involves different kinds of professionals working together. Instead of those how about becoming a "jack of all trades" - a global business professional with skills in many areas. The "global business professional" may be arriving soon!

Monday, May 8, 2000

The Globe and Mail

New professional designation sounds familiar

Royston Greenwood and Roy Suddaby

"Last month, eight leading professional institutes announced their intention to create a new international designation. The "global business professional" designation is intended to span several disciplines, including law, accounting, finance and management consulting. A task force has been formed, led by former Bell Canada chief financial officer Robin Hamilton Harding, whose goal "is to create a globally recognized designation that would enable professionals to seize opportunities presented by an increasingly globalized economy."

The arguments for a new professional designation seem compelling. Business is increasingly global and requires professionals who can move easily across geographic boundaries. A primary objective of creating the designation is to negotiate international acceptance that will enable professions to go from one jurisdiction to another. A second justification for the new profession is that business transactions are increasingly complicated and tend to span disciplinary boundaries. So it is important for clients to have access to individuals trained in a number of disciplines.

The areas identified by the task force for the new global business professional include accountancy, business law, change management, information technology, knowledge management, performance measurement and project and risk management.

A closer examination, however, suggests we have seen this phenomenon once before. In its earlier form, it was called the multidisciplinary practice or MDP and was proposed as an elixir to many of the same business problems. MDPs — or firms comprising accountants, lawyers, management consultants and others — have been touted as the future for professional service firms. But the concept has met with resistance from professional regulators. Legal associations have erected significant barriers; in Ontario, for example, they require that MDPs be limited to firms controlled by lawyers. The American Bar Association, similarly voted overwhelmingly against allowing lawyers to practice with accountants "unless and until additional study demonstrates that such changes will further the public interest without sacrificing or compromising lawyer independence."

The concept has also come under fire from the powerful U.S. Securities and Exchange Commission. Its chairman, Arthur Levitt, has publicly decried the potential for conflicts of interest and client confidentiality concerns that arise when auditors, management consultants and lawyers are housed in the same organization. An independent investigation performed on behalf of the SEC revealed "thousands" of conflict-of-interest violations at Price Waterhouse Coopers. Mr. Levitt is rumoured to have a more ambitious goal, to force the Big Five accounting firms to split audit work from their more profitable management consulting practices. Shortly after the

PricewaterhouseCoopers investigation, the accounting giant announced a dramatic restructuring plan to split into a number of separate business units. KPMG, similarly, announced that its consulting practice would be moved to a new corporation.

The new professional designation appears to be an attempt to revisit the MDP issue from a different level of analysis. The reasoning appears to be that although firms composed of multiple professionals may violate norms and ethical standards, some of these difficulties may be avoided where individuals have a multiple professional designation. Dual designation professionals have existed for some time, particularly in the legal profession where tax lawyers may also be chartered accountants and business lawyers may also hold MBAs. These professionals, however, elect to present themselves under a primary designation (usually as lawyers) in order to avoid the regulatory and ethical problems identified with MDPs. It isn't clear how creating a new designation will resolve that difficulty.

The new designation raises additional concerns. Although the intention is to create a superprofession that embraces other professions, the "eight leading professional institutes" behind the new designation are composed, almost entirely, of accountants. The founding members of the task force include professional accounting associations in Canada, the United States, Australia, Britain, Scotland, Ireland, New Zealand and South Africa. No professional associations in law are represented. Their absence is significant, as it is the lawyers that have produced the strongest resistance to MDPs.

Ultimately, the success or failure of the new designation will depend upon the underlying intention of its founders. If the task force makes a serious effort to address the issues of ethics and conflicts of interest raised in the debate about MDPs, then the new designation is a step forward. But if it represents an effort to divert attention from these serious issues by placing old wine in new bottles, the global business designation will never achieve the legitimacy of a true profession."

Professor Royston Greenwood and doctoral student Roy Suddaby are members of the Centre for Professional Service Firm Management in the Faculty of Business of University of Alberta.

Reprinted with permission of the authors.

Chapter 36

Lawyers - A Balance Between Job Satisfaction And Quality Of Life

"Never confuse having a career with having a life!"

   - Unknown

"Let's get out the word that our profession can be very satisfying and socially helpful and financially rewarding."

   - Toronto Lawyer Morris A. Gross

"Achieve a balanced life. Preserve and enhance your greatest asset, yourself, by continually renewing your physical, spiritual, mental, social and emotional dimensions. Most successful people I know are able to do it."

   - Michigan Lawyer Eugene Gargaro addressing the first year students - University of Detroit School Of Law (1999)

The Need To Strike A Balance

For any person, there are career conditions that will make you happy and conditions that will make you unhappy. The trick is to gravitate toward the conditions that make you happy. For most people these conditions will include a balance between work, family, personal interests, etc.

Balance And Time Management

In my own life I have found that I am most productive when the amount of time that I have available to work is limited. You may have heard the expression that the amount of work expands to fill the available time. It is important that you control your time and not that your time control you.

On the issue of working hours consider the following thoughts in relation to U.K. lawyers suggesting that long hours are a sign of poor practice:

"But consistently working long hours is usually a sign of poor time management. Some of the best workers are those who leave the office at 5:30 pm, after putting in an intense seven-hour day. If you have really worked hard for this period, you feel as if you have just sat two university exams - and there is very little point in staying on for another three hours. You should go off to see a film or relax in some other way..."

But, There Are Lawyers Who Leave The Profession

There are some who do not find fulfillment in the role of a practising lawyer. Why not? The reasons vary. In order to find an answer, read the following perspectives.

Perspective 1:

October 16, 2000

The Globe and Mail

Lawyers courting new careers

Natalie Southworth

Ask career-switching lawyers what they'd like to be next, and you may expect to hear "consultant," or "head of business development for a dot-com."

But Oprah Winfrey?

Randi Bean, a recruiter and consultant for disillusioned lawyers, says it's an answer she hears surprisingly often from would-be law refugees.

"The big response is 'I'd like to be Oprah.' The answer starts off as a joke, but ends up being informative. We discover what about being Oprah is so appealing."

Swiping Ms. Winfrey's job is a long shot, but Ms. Bean has managed to place lawyers in e-commerce startups, publishing companies and management consulting firms.

The 31-year-old former criminal lawyer runs Life After Law Inc., a seven-month-old Toronto agency that helps lawyers who have grown tired of their career get off to a fresh start.

She sits down with them, discusses their career goals and tries to match them with new employers. "Some people are miserable. They hate their work environments. Other people feel they aren't using all of their skills."

This disenchantment reflects the fact there are more reasons than ever to get out of law. Job pressures are weighing heavily on young associates, it takes more time to make the coveted partner, and a string of new career options are emerging outside the profession.

"The perception is lawyers are more unhappy now and are looking elsewhere," says Gillian Hadfield, a professor of law at the University of Toronto.

"The number of hours lawyers are working is increasing, the job is more stressful and in the New Economy, the rewards are greater for people with good analytical skills and education," adds Prof. Hadfield, who studies alternatives to the legal profession. Consider one province's experience. In 1990, 2,175 lawyers practicing in Ontario left the profession to start careers in other areas, according to the Law Society of Upper Canada. In 1998, that number almost doubled to 4,143.

Ed Borkowski, communications adviser for the law society, says the organization has anecdotal evidence that suggests three major reasons why lawyers have left:

They were never really interested in private practice to begin with.

The long hours became taxing on family life.

A large number were moving into the technology industry. "That lure is one reason we keep hearing," Mr. Borkowski says.

But it's not as easy as it sounds, argues Christopher Sweeney, director of ZSA Legal Recruitment, an agency with offices across Canada.

Although the skill set of lawyers is touted as desirable, they can find it hard to make the shift to business.

"There are not as many opportunities for lawyers outside of law as you would think or as I would like to see. To say a law degree opens up all doors is misleading."

Between 10 and 20 per cent of ZSA's candidates are lawyers looking to leave the profession, but only 1 to 2 per cent of them are successful in their job search, adds Mr. Sweeney, a former property lawyer.

"Lawyers are not as much in demand as we would like to believe."

He says lawyers involved in high-end corporate finance have a much easier time moving into business; criminal lawyers are better prepared for careers in politics. But making the shift means breaking down widespread views that people trained to be lawyers are capable of only practising law, he says.

Ms. Bean has matched several young candidates with e-commerce startups as business development managers; some of her more experienced candidates have moved into management consulting.

"I have candidates from some of the big firms and from really small boutiques. Many people are looking to take advantage of their true skills."

Ms. Bean, who herself left a job as a criminal defence lawyer after one year, says people often enroll in law school because they don't know what else to do. Once there, they don't have time to question their decision. "It is very easy to see six years of your life go by without realizing what you're doing."

Martin Perelmuter, 31, was one of those students. He studied at York University's Osgoode Hall Law School in Toronto, focusing on corporate work. Before he knew it, he was a first-year associate at Goodman Phillips & Vineberg making $60,000 a year.

"I didn't feel I was making much of a difference. I dealt with paper much more than I dealt with people."

Leaving his job behind, Mr. Perelmuter started Speakers Spotlight, an agency that places speakers at engagements all over the world.

He has no regrets, but is thankful for his education. "Law ingrained me with discipline. I don't procrastinate and I always return phone calls really quickly."

Mr. Perelmuter doesn't plan on returning to law — he went so far as to severe his association with the Law Society of Upper Canada.

And Ms. Bean isn't going back either.

"In the past, I was giving advice to people charged with criminal offences. It was isolating and draining. Now I talk to people in a friendly way."

Reprinted with permission of the author.

Perspective 2:

A Former Lawyer And Law Professor and Law Dean Weighs In

Why Do They Do It?

Philip Slayton

About fifty thousand people practise law in Canada. Forty thousand of them complain about it.

So, why do they do it? What got all these lawyers into legal practice in the first place? What do they think about their career decision now?

I am a lapsed lawyer. I have personal answers to these questions. But I won't rely on such dross for an article in a respected professional publication. I have done research. I have gone into the field, as they say in the universities. I have done a "survey."

From my retirement house by the sea in Rugged Cove, Nova Scotia, I sent an e-mail to a handful of Canadian lawyers of my acquaintance, all of them actively practising their profession one way or another.

Hardly a scientific survey, this, certainly worthless by any rigorous standards (law school standards, for example), and politically incorrect in the extreme (no women or visible minorities). I began my e-mail with a suitably whimsical preamble, and then got down to business. I asked the simple questions I mention above and added another: "Why do you keep at it?" It went to one or two former students (I was a law professor once), erstwhile colleagues, and friends.

A few replies to my e-mail weren't very polite. A common thread in these impatient replies was that whereas I, sitting by the sea in Nova Scotia, apparently had unlimited leisure and, so it appeared, was free to pursue any will-o'-the-wisp that occurred to me, the recipient of my communication, being an actively practising lawyer, didn't have time to fool around. He, the recipient, was very busy. Maybe, it was suggested, I just don't remember what it's like to be a working lawyer. Oh yes I do. That's why I am a retired lawyer sitting by the sea in Nova Scotia.

I've never known a lawyer who wasn't very busy. When I practised on Bay Street, there was a standard elevator conversation, overheard and, indeed, engaged in, by me many times a day.

Lawyer A: Hi. How are you?

Lawyer B: Very busy. Very, very busy.

Lawyer A: Me too. I'm very busy.

Heads of government, I suspect, have down days, days when they're not that busy, when matters of state aren't very pressing, but not lawyers. But then heads of government do not measure out and record their days in one-tenths of an hour, hoping for a respectable total by six p.m. or later.

One of the polite replies I got to my e-mail was from Randy Hahn, a Toronto lawyer and a cultured gent with a doctorate from Oxford University.

A lawyer to his toes, Randy wrote, no doubt with one eye on his day timer: " I'm not at this time answering the questions posed, but providing you with insights already on file." He then presented a collection of quotations concerning the practice of law taken from the writings of Tolstoy, Dickens, Hugo, George Eliot, Swift and Boswell (I told you he was a cultured gent). At the end of the collection, continuing to be lawyerly, Randy put forward a disclaimer: "Having attended both law school and graduate school, I think there is a reasonably good chance that the above has been taken out of context or misrepresented."

The Hahn Collection, in or out of context, misrepresented or not, hardly encourages those contemplating a career in the law. For example, Tolstoy in The Death of Ivan Ilych wrote the following about the main character: "And the further he departed from childhood and the nearer he came to the present the more worthless and doubtful were the joys. This began with the School of Law."

I e-mailed Randy back: "Enough with the fancy quotations, answer the questions." He replied: "I decided to pursue law as a career in the hope that it would allow me to make a living that would be intellectually challenging, financially rewarding and socially useful. I keep on practising law in the hope that it will yet prove to be intellectually challenging, financially rewarding and socially useful."

One young lawyer in a big firm (he's not a partner yet - I won't mention his name) made a similar point (although he didn't say anything about being socially useful): "I went into the practice of law for the intellectual challenge and financial security. I stay in it for the financial security."

Nathan Cheifetz is a corporate solicitor and a partner in a big Bay Street firm. As to why he went into the practice of law in the first place, Nathan wrote: "I came from a hippie background without much objectively verifiable principles and I wanted to sink my teeth into something real. I was also attracted to the idea of fighting for people's rights and freedoms." What does he think about legal practice now? "I can't say that I've been fighting for too many rights and freedoms. The last time I checked I was fighting for the inclusion of a comma in the middle of a paragraph."

And why does Nathan keep at it? "Clean work, indoors. What law doesn't offer, I try to find in other areas of my life."

Jim Hodgson, former president of The Advocates Society, left a big Bay Street firm two or three years ago with some of his partners to start up what has turned out to be a successful litigation boutique.

Why did Jim go into legal practice? "It seemed (at least according to the TV shows of the time) like it might be an interesting job, the money would be pretty good and for the most part you would function independently."

"I keep at it," wrote Jim, "because I really don't know anything else that I could do - at least that people would pay me for - and it's an interesting job, the money's pretty good and for the most part (especially now) I have a fair degree of independence." Mark Halpern, a Canadian lawyer who practises in Japan, took a pragmatic approach similar to Jim Hodgson's

"I enjoy being my own boss. People treat me with respect. I try to keep occupied with work I'm confident I can do well, and I take some pride in giving good service to my clients at a fair price, as a lawyer and as a cross-cultural communicator."

Mark's message finished on what, I thought, was a wistful note: "What drove me to law was an intellectual interest in substantive law - and that has not disappeared. But in my day-to-day solicitor's practice, I'm not really dealing with many issues of substantive law." Like Nathan Cheifetz, Mark concluded: "Yet I find other pleasures to keep me feeling fulfilled."

Henry Kloppenburg, a Saskatchewan Rhodes Scholar, has practised law successfully in Saskatoon for thirty years. Henry's reply to my e-mail was the longest and most detailed, and in some ways the most troubling, that I received. He characterized his reply, at the end of it, as a "mixed and spotty and unenthusiastic picture of the law."

A lot bothers Henry about the practice of law in Saskatchewan. Accountants are encroaching on the territory of lawyers; a no-fault regime for automobile accident insurance has removed lawyers from automobile injury compensation; and salaried legal aid lawyers have largely replaced the private bar in delivery of services in criminal courts.

Moreover, writes Henry, the incoming system of computerized land titles is an invitation to title insurers, banks and others to assume roles lawyers have played in real estate practice without enhancing the quality of services to the public or doing so at a true lower cost. Added to all of this is a loss of civility among lawyers.

To me Henry's most interesting general comment was this: "I believe I am seeing the decline of fact based and principle regulated conflict resolution. It's all how one feels or what is your interest in getting this solved."

With compelling honesty, he wrote: "I stay at lawyering because I have, in the Saskatchewan environment, no other place to go. I have a successful practice by local standards. I generally speaking like living in Saskatoon."

Henry, claims Henry, has no place to go. Someone else, whose name I can't mention, came to the same conclusion: "Having done whatever it is I do for so long I am concerned that I have forgotten how to do anything else." As if to prove the point, my unnamed correspondent wrote earlier in his e-mail: "I'm not sure what the `it' stands for in your question on what I think of 'it' now. If it refers to my practice, see my earlier comment on what I do. If it refers to the practice of law as carried on by the vast majority of practitioners, not very much."

David Jones is an Edmonton practitioner, twenty-seven years at the Bar. For fourteen years he was a full-time law professor, first at McGill and then at the University of Alberta. "I went into law," he wrote, "because I saw it as a way to shape society (on a macro basis) and a way for individuals to cope with society (on a micro basis). I had always been interested in rules," continued David, "making them better or more accurate, using them." And now? "Now I am not so sure that there is a direct linkage between law and behaviour. There is a linkage, to be sure, but the whole relationship is much more complicated and indirect. I am not sure any longer (if I ever was) that objective justice exists."

David Matas, a distinguished Winnipeg human rights lawyer, is an erudite man, author of books, and a recipient of an honourary doctorate from Concordia University. David wrote, simply: "I keep at the practise of law because I believe in the ideal of justice and the worthiness of the effort to pursue that ideal." I know David well enough (I've known him for over forty years) to know that he means what he says. It takes your breath away, a comment like that from someone who's been practising law for thirty-five years.

Money, intellectual stimulation, independence, the pursuit of justice. These reasons, or some combination of these reasons, are why someone decides to become a lawyer.

Maybe there's a few practising lawyers out there who think it's all worked out for them, who think they are getting what at the beginning they had hoped to get, but I don't think there are many such people.

Money? There are, of course, lawyers who routinely earn hundreds of thousands of dollars a year. For the most part, these lawyers are the partners of Canada's major firms. How many of these people are there? I don't know (there's probably some serious survey out there which gives us the answer), but, as an educated guess, I'd say two thousand big earners - that's four per cent of the practising profession - at the most.

And the other ninety-six per cent? These are the lawyers who don't have offices in the downtown cores of Canada's three or four largest cities. These are the lawyers who practice in the suburbs of those cities, or on the prairies, or in the Maritimes, or in the North. These are the lawyers of the hinterland. These are just about everybody in the profession of law in Canada. And in my experience over many years these lawyers aren't doing that well at all. They likely would have been better off financially as managers of village bank branches, or as minor government bureaucrats.

(A footnote on the plutocratic four per cent. Many of them, although cash flow wealthy, are also envious. Envious of whom? Envious of their entrepreneurial clients who amass capital wealth even although, as the envious lawyers will tell you, the clients are not all that smart, certainly not as smart as the lawyers!)

Intellectual stimulation? Almost all lawyers learn, and they learn it fast, that most of the time the practice of law is boring. Not all of the time - but most of the time. And this is true no matter what kind of practice you are talking about. Does anyone really think that high-flying corporate solicitors, working on those "big deals" that are so breathlessly reported in the trade magazines, are enjoying themselves for more than an odd moment or two now and again? Most of the time they are making endless trivial amendments ("fighting for the inclusion of a comma") to mountains of documents that no one will ever read. And high-profile litigators, constantly reveling in courtroom cut-and-thrust? The trouble is that most litigators spend less and less time - in many cases almost no time at all - at the courthouse. And if Messrs. High Flyer and High Profile are not enjoying themselves, who is?

Independence? Yes, to some degree, next to some occupations, but not to any impressive degree. Remember, lawyers have as many bosses as they have clients.

Socially useful? Let's be honest. In some abstract sense we lawyers believe that we are an essential part of the legal system, from which everyone benefits. But is our behaviour in any discernible way influenced by this belief? Do we feel the need for justice? Do we ever act on our abstract belief?

"I find other pleasures to keep me feeling fulfilled," said one of my correspondents. "What law doesn't offer, I try to find in other areas of my life," wrote another. These are the judgments of experience."

Reprinted with permission of the author.

Conclusion

Living a balanced and happy life is the key. One of the best discussion of these issues is in the following article by Mr. Justice Frank Iacobucci, former dean of the University Of Toronto law school and Judge of the Supreme Court Of Canada.

APPENDIX

Striking A Balance: Trying to Find the Happy and Good Life Within and Beyond the Legal Profession

Frank Iacobucci*

I. Introduction

As probably most of you have, I have noted an alarming trend of late. Articles in the popular press and professional journals report that talented, committed people are leaving the law. *Harvard Magazine* describes a partner who abandons his firm to edit a local newspaper, while an associate in corporate practice puts aside her dictaphone to take up the jazz saxophone.[1] In an article entitled "The Best and Brightest, Bored and Burned Out", the *American Bar Association Journal* reports that a survey of second-year associates found that more than half were dissatisfied with their work. [2] I have just come back from the United Kingdom and have heard disquieting reports there about the increased commercialization of law. Most sobering, perhaps, in *Canadian Lawyer*, a lawyer who withdrew from a successful practice in a large urban firm confesses:

If I practised law any longer, I felt my entire soul would be swallowed up; that the practice being what it is, I'd never be able to do the things in life that had personal meaning for me or even remain capable of appreciating those things.[3]

I set out to confirm whether these lawyers' reactions were mere aberrations, but I have found that these feelings are, in fact, not uncommon within the Canadian legal profession. *In Transitions in the Ontario Legal Profession: a Survey of Lawyers called to the Bar between 1975 and 1990*, the Law Society of Upper Canada reports that, while the majority of lawyers are satisfied with the nature of their work, their relationships with colleagues and the possibilities for job security, a significant number are distinctly dissatisfied with their working conditions. They emphasize particularly the hours required, stress imposed, and difficulty of balancing professional duties with personal and family life.[4] The Law Society also discovered that, although more and more men are expressing dissatisfaction with the toll their commitment to career takes on their lives outside the law, women are the ones expressing the deepest dissatisfaction and the ones most inclined to act upon this dissatisfaction by withdrawing temporarily or permanently from the profession.

In my remarks today, I would like to examine the disconcerting trend of both men and women leaving the legal profession. They are leaving because they despair of the possibility of ever being able to integrate their personal lives with their professional lives. They are also leaving because they are disillusioned with the law profession itself. I wish to suggest that both these complaints arise, in large part, out of a failure of the profession to respond to its members' need for meaning in their lives and in their work. I will also point to what I view as the salutary effect these lawyers' demands for accommodation of family and personal responsibilities are having upon the flexibility and responsiveness of the profession.

II. Distinguishing features of "professions"

A profession, and certainly the profession of law, is something more than a commercial enterprise. On other occasions,[5] I have spoken about the tension between practising law as a profession or as a business. The profession of law involves service as the main aim, and profit as the incidental purpose, to paraphrase the late Roscoe Pound.[6] Of course, the challenge is to strike the proper balance between earning a livelihood and rendering service to one's clients and one's community. In other words, the emphasis should be on the right line, not on the bottom line.

Professor Eliot Freidson has defined the features which distinguish a profession such as law from callings. A profession is an occupation whose members have special privileges, such as exclusive licensing, that are justified by the following assumptions:

(1) That its practice requires substantial intellectual training and the use of complex judgements.

(2) That since clients cannot adequately evaluate the quality of the service, they must trust those they consult.

(3) That the client's trust presupposes that the practitioner's self-interest is overbalanced by devotion to serving both the client's interest and the public good.

(4) That the occupation is self-regulating — that is, organized in such a way as to assure the public and the courts that its members are competent, do not violate their client's trust, and transcend their own interest.[7]

It will surely be clear to you that the development of exclusive forms of expertise over periods of intensive study is a feature law shares with many other professions and occupations. The cabinetmaker who learns to turn a chair which is both elegant and strong carries expertise developed over centuries and passed on through a period of apprenticeship. Similarly, the cabinetmaker's work cannot properly be assessed by those who not have the same expertise. While we might appreciate the beauty of a piece, most laypeople would be unable to assess whether it would stand up to repeated use or to the vicissitudes of our more corpulent houseguests. We trust therefore that cabinetmakers love their art more than they value the profits it brings and that their integrity will not allow them to rest their reputations on shoddy goods.

If cabinetmakers fail in fulfilling these obligations, they are disciplined by the adjudicative apparatus of the community at large, while lawyers are judged and disciplined by a community of our peers. What sets the profession of law apart from other callings is not the fact that we bear exclusive knowledge. The distinguishing feature of the practice of law is the fact that this knowledge carries with it both great power to influence private lives and public affairs and, correspondingly, great responsibility to our clients and community.

In giving effect to this unique sense of responsibility, our forebears in the profession of law developed a canon of ethics designed to ensure that our effort and attention serve the interests of our clients and our communities rather than those of ourselves or of our colleagues.

III. Changing identity of practitioners

Let me emphasize that I am honoured to have been a member of the legal profession and to have made what I hope is a contribution to it; but I am — and I hope I have some witnesses who will back me up — equally committed to the roles I have played outside the law as husband, father, son, citizen and member of my community. I believe the development of a movement within the profession towards recognizing that lawyers must be well-rounded people who participate meaningfully in the varied areas of their lives is owed in part to the growing presence of women in the profession. By insisting that they cannot and will not be made to choose between their obligations to their families, women are expanding the horizons of all lawyers, male and female, in considering what the limits of the "good life" in law might be.

Clara Brett Martin, the first woman in the British Commonwealth admitted to the practice of law, became a member of the Ontario bar in 1897. However, the representation of women in the legal profession, both here and in the United States, remained quite small for decades after that landmark event.[8] In fact, my wife was one of the brave souls who sought to make a career in law before it was truly open to women, as she graduated from the Harvard Law School in 1962, one of 25 women in a class of 550. Although she finished with an A average, graduating *magna cum laude*, and although she had been an editor of the Harvard Law Review, when she was interviewed at a top law firm in Boston (where incidentally her father and older brother had worked after law school), she was offered a job at a salary considerably less than the going rate offered to male graduates. When she asked for an explanation of the differential, she was told that she would not be expected to work as long hours as the men. She refused the job. It is interesting to note, however, that as a result, the firm subsequently changed its policy, and years later a senior partner told her how much the firm regretted the approach they had taken with her and other female candidates.

In her book *Women in Law*, Cynthia Fuchs Epstein explains that this earlier wave of female lawyers was channelled into areas of practice, such as trusts and estates, in which crises giving rise to lengthy time demands were minimal. The expectation that women would not work as long hours was based on two assumptions. The first was that any compromises that needed to be made in order to provide family care would be made by the woman. The second was that regardless of how hard a female associate worked, she knew she would never make partner and would thus govern her working life accordingly.[9]

It has only been in the last 20 years or so that women have entered the profession in significant numbers. Women are now represented in every sector of legal practice, in the legal academy and, increasingly, on the bench.

I was a professor of law at the University of Toronto when the proportion of female students began to approximate that of their male counterparts. I recall that my colleagues and I felt that the inclusion of women held great promise for the profession. By bringing with them different attitudes and different life experiences, we felt that our female colleagues would redefine the nature of both the law and legal practice. Indeed, I believe feminist analyses of several substantive areas of law, such as family, constitutional, tort, and criminal law have had a profound influence on the development of Canadian jurisprudence.

This is not to suggest that there is some essential genetic or moral difference between men and women that grows out of their biology — that women qua women bring a different perspective to law — but that different patterns of socialization, different expectations and different occupations prior to entry into the profession may lead women to have different approaches to the law. I have certainly felt that my experiences in different occupations and my family history as the son of working class immigrants to Canada have provided me with a special perspective which I have drawn on in my roles as practising lawyer, legal educator and judge.

In her controversial book[10] that nevertheless has become quite influential in legal scholarship, Harvard psychology professor Carol Gilligan has argued that there is more than one way of conceptualizing ethical dilemmas. The "ethic of justice" which pervades our adversarial system of justice frames moral problems as a conflict of rights and describes the process for resolving such conflicts as a matter of identifying the nature of the rights at stake and determining which should take priority in a given case.

In conducting comparative studies of male and female subjects of various ages, Professor Gilligan detected another mode of moral theorizing which analyzed moral dilemmas as a conflict of competing obligations of the parties to each other and to others not immediately involved in the dilemma. Subjects were asked how they would resolve the following problem:[11]

Heinz's wife is gravely ill with cancer. There is a medication which will heal her, but Heinz has no money with which to purchase it. He knows that the medication is available at a local pharmacy. Should Heinz steal the drug?

While an "ethic of justice" analysis might tell us to weigh the competing property claim of the pharmacist against the right to life of Heinz's wife and ultimately to conclude that Heinz may steal the drug because the value of human life must take precedence over that of property, an analysis based on what Professor Gilligan describes as the "ethic of care" would seek a solution that satisfied all the parties and preserved their relationships with each other. For example, one might suggest that Heinz simply approach the pharmacist, explain his position, and offer to work out a payment schedule or work off the value of the drug through helping out in the store.

Professor Gilligan does not purport to explain the etiology of these differences, nor does she suggest that those who employ the different modes of analysis are invariably of one sex. She does note, however, that women predominate among those resorting to an ethic of care while men predominate among those employing an ethic of justice. Other theorists, such as professors Nancy Chodorow[12] and Dorothy Dinnerstein[13], suggest that this different orientation towards resolving moral dilemmas may grow out of fundamental psychological processes involved in the development of gender identity. Others, like Professor Sarah Ruddick[14], suggest that this orientation grows out of being socialized towards, and being involved in, the practice of mothering. Where the conflicts one must routinely resolve involve one's children, an adequate response will not be one in which somebody is the loser. Rather, one must develop approaches and strategies which permit the attainment of often contradictory goals while preserving the integrity of individual interests and relationships. An adequate resolution will only be one that respects and preserves the interests and needs of all parties.

It may be that this orientation towards characterizing an adequate resolution as one which satisfies competing claims rather than chooses among them is one which leads women to seek creative solutions to the challenge of integrating career and family, rather than choosing between the two. It may also be, given women's historic and continuing role as primary providers of child care, that women have no choice but to find a way of integrating these demands. For whatever reason, many women in law are suggesting that the profession must recognize and make a place for involved mothers and fathers who also wish to contribute to the cause of justice through the practice of law.

When my peers and myself consider our early careers, many express regret at not having spent more time with their children while they were growing up. Very few express regret at not having spent more hours in the office. Looking back at my own experience, I have often said that my wife is due by far the major credit to the extent that our three children are making their way positively in their lives. That she was the primary care-giver in our family is an understatement. I do not mean to suggest that I am ashamed of my role — but I always felt a great tension between my professional involvement and my family responsibilities.

While many male lawyers have relied and continue to rely on their spouses to provide childcare, such options do not yet appear to be available to women. Women's progress towards equality of opportunity in the profession of law and elsewhere in the marketplace has not been matched by a changing distribution of labour within the home. Studies of the general population have found that when women work outside the home, their share of the domestic and childcare responsibilities does not diminish accordingly.[15] Even in instances of two-professional-career couples, women generally retain major responsibility for home and child care. It is disproportionately women who deal with childcare crises, who rush home to relieve the babysitter, who look after sick children, and who care for elderly parents. It is also most often women who surrender their employment in order to permit their husbands to pursue lucrative career opportunities through relocation.[16]

The Law Society of Upper Canada study mentioned earlier suggests that these findings apply to women in the legal profession as well. Female lawyers reported that they were responsible for 49% of childcare while male lawyers felt they were responsible for 26% of such work in their families. Men reported that the slack was taken up by their spouses in 61% of cases, while women reported that they were more likely to share childcare responsibilities with a paid domestic worker (26%) than with their spouses (21%). Female lawyers are far more likely to take on the lion's share of housework responsibilities (39% vs. 4%) and to leave work to look after sick children or attend children's activities (52% vs. 8%)[17]. These findings are replicated in studies of the profession carried out in Saskatchewan,[18] Alberta,[19] British Columbia[20] and the United States.[21]

This is not to suggest that men necessarily feel that this is an appropriate division of labour. Numerous studies of male lawyers report that they too resent being absent from the everyday lives of their children. Male respondents to the Law Society of Upper Canada study stated:

I wish there were more time to pursue non-professional activities and to spend with my children and wife. There is too much to do in our one life, and the law takes up too great a proportion of it, leaving me less rounded and involved than I would choose to be. I am finding it very difficult to be a competent, conscientious lawyer, a good father and husband and to do volunteer community work. My wife and I are expecting a child in the coming months and I am very concerned about increasing pressure in our firm and others to increase the number of hours docketed. Time with my family will be a priority for me and if my career interferes too greatly, I shall seek alternative employment (perhaps [as] in house counsel).[22]

IV. Departures from active practice for professional reasons

The Law Society of Upper Canada report notes that while women compose only 30% of the profession in Ontario, most of whom graduated quite recently, women represent 66% of those taking temporary absences from practice but expressing in intention to return, and 37% of those who leave practice altogether.[23]

Why are good lawyers abandoning the law? Lawyers of both genders report that they leave the practice of law because they are dissatisfied with long hours, a practice focused on the production of billable hours rather than of quality of work, and a sense that they are hired guns in the service of client demands rather than in the service of the greater cause of justice. They feel that there is insufficient meaning in the work that they do and insufficient time outside of work to attend to other areas of life from which they might derive meaning.

Pride in one's professional role is an essential aspect of fulfilling working life. In the Barrister's Oath taken by all Ontarians upon admission to the bar, you pledged to serve your individual clients and to preserve and promote the administration of justice. The Oath reads in part:

You are called to the Degree of Barrister-at-law to protect and defend the rights and interests of such of your fellow citizens as may employ you. You shall conduct all cases faithfully and to the best of your ability. You shall neglect no one's interest nor seek to destroy anyone's property. You shall not pervert the law to favour or prejudice any one, but in all things shall conduct yourself truly and with integrity. In fine, the Queen's interest and your fellow-citizens you shall uphold and maintain according to the constitution and the law of this Province.[24]

I share the concern of many young lawyers that the profession has become excessively skewed towards fulfilling only the first goal of client service, often through single-minded pursuit of wealth maximization. In performing their work, the attention of some lawyers has been directed away from quality towards quantum. In the process, some have lost sight of the broader function to be played by the profession and its members in the life of the community and the country.

Lawyers have historically seen themselves as playing the role of confidante and counsellor to individual and corporate clients. On this model, clients seek out the expertise of lawyers to assist them in articulating and resolving complex legal problems or in structuring involvement in corporate transactions and regulated activities in a manner which will adequately protect the clients' interests and avoid bringing them into conflict with the law.

In their study of large law firm practice in the United States, Professors Robert Kagan and Robert Rosen suggest that this model no longer describes the working lives of many involved in large corporate practices.[25] Rather than playing the role of independent and influential counsellor, many lawyers perceive themselves to be technicians giving effect to the dictates of sophisticated consumers of legal services who require counsel to determine how a project may be done rather than whether it ought to be done. They play the important roles of giving effect to client demands and insuring against client exposure, but have seen their role diminish with regard to structuring those demands in accordance with the legitimate dictates of justifiable regulations or the interests of third parties and the community at large. Quite properly, these lawyers feel that an important element of what distinguishes the profession of law from a trade in legal services has been undermined. The authors note:

Although lawyers sometimes justify the type of service they provide in terms of what clients demand, professions traditionally have justified their privileged positions by the claim that professional standards, not merely client demands, govern their work. The professional does not simply take the task as given to him. "The client, unlike the customer, is not always right". This statement would seem especially true of the practice of law, where third party and collective interests are significantly affected by the client's law-related decisions and directives. Hence corporate lawyers who pass up opportunities to act as influential and independent counsellors, because corporate managers have not asked them to do so, would   seem to be forsaking an important aspect of professionalism.[26]

Professor Karl Llewellyn has described law as "a profession in theory, and a monopoly in fact; a monopoly not merely by force of skill and brain but established and maintained by law. Only through lawyers can the layman win in fact the rights the law purports to give him."[27]

While it is indeed a key aspect of the lawyer's role to vindicate the interests of his or her client, we must not forget that our obligations as officers of the court, and as human beings, compel us to look beyond the immediate interests of particular clients. Without scrupulous effort on our part, the rights won through historical development and political struggle are rendered meaningless for our clients, ourselves and our community. We must ensure that our actions do not merely satisfy the letter of the law, but go further to enhance the spirit which underlies it. The society we create through our work is the society that we and our loved ones must live in. A commitment to justice must permeate all elements of the work we do as lawyers. This is the task we have sworn ourselves to undertake. In pursuing our profession with these goals in mind, we may also find that we recapture the vision of a just and equal society which led us to the law in the first place.

V. Making a place for meaningful activities outside work

Lawyers are also leaving the profession because they find there is no time for, or value placed upon, their obligations outside the workplace. Many women who are leaving the profession, temporarily or permanently, report that they find that the tensions between maintaining the hours expected of them by major firms and their obligations and desires to be with their children put them in an untenable position. Some women leave because they cannot find the quality of childcare for the lengthy hours they require for the limited remuneration they are able to offer. A 1988 survey of female graduates of the University of Saskatchewan College of Law found that one quarter of those responding employed live-in domestic workers or nannies, another quarter relied on babysitters who took children into their own homes, and the rest relied on some combination of daycare and care by relatives or spouses. It was noted by the authors that few male spouses of female lawyers had chosen to withdraw from the workforce in order to provide care for the couple's children.[28] As noted earlier, men also express concern over failing to discharge adequately their obligations as fathers; but they have traditionally been able to juggle their dual obligations by relying upon wives who may be full-time homemakers or who may take part-time work which allows them to work around their husbands' schedules.

Indeed, flexibility within the workplace is often identified by female lawyers as the key factor which enabled them to remain in the profession during their child-bearing years. The level of support available from their firm or employer may be gauged by the availability of maternity leaves, extended leaves, part-time work, and the absence of a "mommy-track" which penalizes those who view their families as a priority by rendering them permanent associates. These options are becoming more available, but they must be expanded and made accessible to parents of both sexes before lawyers can truly begin to make real decisions regarding the balance in their lives between career and home obligations.

Many firms now have maternity leave policies but there are still significant deficiencies. The length of leave is often linked to years of service, a policy that is not of much use to young women who begin their legal careers as they enter their childbearing years. This difficulty is exacerbated in some firms where eligibility for maternity leave is limited to partners, people who have typically put in at least six or more years. One respondent to the Law Society of Upper Canada study commented:

Leaves based on number of years of service discriminates against the very people who are most likely to require leave—women of child-bearing years. When a woman is in the early years of practice, she is also in her prime child-bearing years. She should not be forced to postpone child-bearing in order to qualify for a reasonable length of maternity leave (6 months). If law firms would begin to support their employees in this area, they would find that they had grateful and loyal employees in the years after child-bearing. After all, a woman's productive years of lawyering number far more than her productive years of child-bearing.[29]

A small number of workplaces now make paternity leaves available to new fathers. An even smaller number provide adoption leaves to new parents of both sexes. These are salutary developments which are to be encouraged.

Some firms have also begun to negotiate part-time work for parents, so they may work, for example, four days a week at a pro-rated salary, or work some hours at home. While it might initially appear costly to provide office space and support services for lawyers who do not work a full week, this expense is compensated for by the fact that experienced counsel are able to bill at a higher rate than would a full-time, more junior associate hired to replace them. The hours which these experienced parents put in might well be more efficient and productive.[30]

Professor Carrie Menkel-Meadow has noted, however, that the presence of these options for women will not bring about meaningful change in the practice of law until it also becomes acceptable to use them:

Some law firms proudly proclaim their commitment to maternity leaves and "flexible" working arrangements for women lawyers with children, but many women who have availed themselves of such plans have quietly acknowledged that they are never again accepted as serious members of their firms.[31]

Similarly, the availability of paternity and adoption leave may prove to be an illusory advance in light of the fact that few men take advantage of them for fear that they will be viewed by the firm as not being "serious" about their careers. A study by the Stanford Law Project found that of workplaces where paternity leave policies were enacted, only half of them had ever seen their policies used. When they were used, however, they were used consistently.[32] One author suggests that this may mean that paternity leave policies are used where the firm makes it clear that they support such decisions.[33]

While demands for change are only now being brought forth by members of the legal profession, the precept that moderation is an essential feature of a fulfilling life is by no means new. In the *Ethics*, Aristotle counselled that the happy life is one which integrates satisfaction of the fundamental need for gainful employment, physical and sensual needs, honour and contemplation of the good.[34]

VI. Conclusion

Good lawyers should not be leaving the law. The profession of law must reclaim its traditions of meaningful engagement with issues of justice while developing a new tradition of providing for a lawyer's involvement in the equally meaningful work of raising a family and fulfilling broader civic obligations in the community.

At the moment, our profession is undergoing dramatic changes and I am optimistic about our future. I say this because of the dialogue which is already going on. I commend those responsible for the studies undertaken in Alberta, British Columbia, Ontario, Quebec and Saskatchewan, and elsewhere.[35] I am greatly encouraged by the work of the Hon. Bertha Wilson and her colleagues on the C.B.A. Task Force on Gender Equality in looking at the role of women in profession. I am also encouraged by the vast majority of lawyers I know who recognize the problems I have mentioned and are willing to face realistically and sensibly the challenges they raise. I remain upbeat, but we must all do our part to bring about these necessary changes. I encourage you to work towards making the legal profession a place in which the practical, intellectual and emotional needs of clients and practitioners are responded to with sensitivity, respect and humanity.

I end on a challenge and a hope. We in Canada have taken pride—usually modestly and quietly - in the fashioning of a society that strives to ensure equality of opportunity and fairness for all. Canadians are willing to assert individual claims while recognizing community interests and we have many examples of Canadian institutions, traditions and values that distinguish us in these respects. Those of us associated with the legal profession must resolve to show similar leadership in effectively taking on the issues that I have briefly identified in these remarks. If we succeed—when we succeed—we will have created a proud legacy for the future members of our profession, and an impressive model for other professions and occupations; equally importantly, we will have performed an important service for our fellow citizens.

ENDNOTES

*The Honourable Mr. Justice Frank Iacobucci, of the Supreme Court of Canada. This address was delivered by him at a meeting of the Young Lawyers Division of the Canadian Bar Association - Ontario on May 21, 1992.

1. Glenn Kay, "Free of the Law", *Harvard Magazine* (January-February 1992) 60 at 62 and 65.
2. *ABA Journal* (May 15, 1987) 28 at 28.
3. Mary Otovos, "Why I'm Leaving Law" *Canadian Lawyer* (February, 1992) 12 at 13.
4. *Transitions* (May 1991) at 101.
5. See "The Practice of Law: Business or Profession", remarks given by the Hon. Frank Iacobucci to B.C. Fellows of the American College of Trial Lawyers, 49:6 *The Advocate* (November 1991) 859.
6. Historically there are three ideas involved in a profession: organization, learning, i.e., pursuit of a

learned art, and a spirit of public service. These are essential. A further idea, that of gaining a livelihood is involved in all callings. It is the main if not the only purpose in the purely money-making callings. In a profession it is incidental. Roscoe Pound, *The Lawyer From Antiquity to Modern Times*, cited in Geoffrey C. Hazard, Jr. and Deborah L. Rhode, eds., *The Legal Profession: Responsibility and Regulation* (Mineola, New York: The Foundation Press, 1985) at 89.

7. Eliot Freidson, "In the Spirit of Public Service" (1986) *ABA Report on Professionalism* at 10, cited in Rudolph Gerber, *Lawyers, Courts and Professionalism: The Agenda for Reform* (New York: Greenwood Press, 1989) at 12.

8. Mary Jane Mossman, "Portia's Progress: Women as lawyers, Reflection on the Past and the Future", prepared for the Law Society of Upper Canada Continuing Legal Education Program. *Women in the Legal Profession,* May 13, 1986.

9. Cynthia Fuchs Epstein, *Women in Law* (New York: Basic Books, 1981) at 318.

10. Carol Gilligan, *In a Different Voice: Psychological Theory and Women's Development* (Cambridge: Harvard University Press, 1982).

11. Gilligan, *supra* note 10, at 25-26.

12. Nancy Chodorow, *The Reproduction of Mothering: Psychoanalysis and the Sociology of Gender* (Berkely: University of California Press, 1978).

13. Dorothy Dinnerstein, *The Mermaid and the Minotaur Sexual Arrangements and Human Malaise* (New York: Harper and Row, 1976).

14. Sara Ruddick, "Maternal Thinking", in Joyce Trebilcot, ed., *Mothering: Essays in Feminist Theory* (Totowa, New Jersey: Rowman and Allenheld, 1983).

15. Statistics Canada, *General Social Survey Analysis Series: Where Does Time Go?* (Ottawa: Ministry of Industry, Trade and Technology, 1991) at 50-60.

16. William Michelson, *From Sun to Sun: Daily Obligations and Community Structure in the Lives of Employed Women and Their Families* (Totowa, New Jersey: Rowman and Allenheld, 1985) at 69; F. Diane Pask and M. L. McCall, eds., *How Much and Why?* Economic Implications of Marriage Breakdown: *Spousal and Child Support* (Calgary: Canadian Research Institute of Law and the Family, 1989) at 65.

17. *Transitions, supra* note 4, at 46-50.

18. J. Savarese, M. Keet and K. Sutherland, *Survey of Women Graduates From the College of Law* (Saskatoon: *Women and the Law,* College of Law, University of Saskatchewan, 1988).

19. D. Fromm and M. Webb, "The Work Experience of University of Alberta Law Graduates". (1985) 23 *Alberta Law Review* 366.

20. J. Brockman, *Identifying the Barriers: A Survey of Members of the Law Society of British Columbia* (April 1991), prepared for the Law Society of British Columbia's Subcommittee on Women in the Legal Profession.

21. D. L. Chambers, "Accommodation and Satisfaction: Women and Men Lawyers and the Balance of Work and Family", (1989) 14 *Law and Social Inquiry* 251.

22. *Transitions, supra* note 4, at 78-79.

23. *Transitions, supra* note 4, at 65.

24. Rule 51 (1) made under the *Law Society Act,* R.S.O. 1980, c. 233.

25. Robert Kagan and Robert Rosen, "On the Significance of Large Law Firm Practice", (1985) volume no. 37, *Stanford Law Review* 399.

26. *Ibid* at 440.

27. Karl N. Llewellyn, cited in Ralph Nader and Mark Green eds., *Verdicts on Lawyers* (New York: Thomas Y. Crowell Co., 1976) at ix.

28. J. Savarese, M. Keet and K. Sutherland, *supra* note 18.

29. *Transitions, supra* note 4, at 90.

30. Nancy Blodgett, "Whatever Happened to the Class of 81?" (June 1, 1988) *ABA Journal* 56 at 58.

31. Carrie Menkel-Meadow "Women in Law? A Review of Cynthia Fuchs Epstein's *Women in Law*", (1983) *American Bar Foundation Research Journal* 189 at 197.

32. Stanford Law Project, "Gender, Legal Education and the Legal Profession: An Empirical Study of Stanford Law Students and Graduates", (1988) 40 *Stanford Law Review* 1209 at 1272 .

33. Chris Tennant, "Discrimination in the Legal Profession, Codes of Professional Conduct and the Duty of Non-discrimination", (1992) [forthcoming] at 15.

34. Aristotle, *The Nicomachean Ethics*, translated by David Ross (Oxford: Oxford University Press, 1925).

35. The body of research expands daily. While editing this speed for publication, I read of similar studies in Alberta and Quebec. See "The Old Boy's Club Lives: Alberta Law Society Survey Finds Bias Against Women", 19:5. *National* (Summer 1992) 1; "Practique Professionnelle: La Cohabitation Avec le Sexe Oppose au Bureau", *LeJournal Du Barreau* (juillet 1992) 28.

Reprinted with permission of the author.

Chapter 37

Law, Society And The Law Society -
How Canadian Lawyers Govern Themselves

"Over the last three years the operations of the Law Society have seen tremendous change. We have changed our structure, the way we operate, the types of programs and services we provide, methods of service delivery, communication to members of the public, the legal profession and our workforce and the way we manage our resources.

...

We are on the right path to creating the kind of organization necessary to effectively serve the legal profession and the public. It is a process of continuous improvement as we strive to be 'best in class'. We are not there yet. While there is much to be proud of, there continues to be much to do."

-M. Heins - Law Society CEO

How Canadian Lawyers Govern Themselves

A Self-governing Profession

In Canada, the legal profession is a "self-governing" profession. What is the rationale for giving lawyers this special privilege? The theory is that only lawyers have the knowledge and expertise that is required to ensure that the profession is regulated in the interests of the public.

The Law Society

Canadian lawyers are regulated very differently from their U.S. counterparts. They are governed by the Law Society of their province. Although U.S. states do have committees that oversee the profession ("Board Of Bar Overseers"), ultimately U.S. lawyers are governed by the court that admitted them to the bar.

No discussion of the Canadian legal profession would be complete (or could even be fully understood) without a discussion of the Law Society (the organization that governs lawyers) and the Law Society Act (the legislation that governs the behavior of individual lawyers and the Law Society).

How The Legal Profession In Canada Governs Itself

Every Canadian province has a Law Society. They are very similar to each other. I will use Ontario as the model for this chapter. For further information about the Law Society, visit their web site at: http://www.lsuc.on.ca.

1. What Is The Law Society And What Is It For?

The Law Society is the organization that governs lawyers and other aspects of the legal profession. It is also the body that administers the Law Society Act. Law is a self-governing profession. This means that (at least in theory) the Law Society is to govern lawyers in the public interest.

The Law Society states that:

"The Law Society of Upper Canada exists to govern the legal profession in the public interest by:

-   ensuring that the people of Ontario are served by lawyers who meet high standards of learning, competence and professional conduct;

-   upholding the independence, integrity and honour of the legal profession;

-   advancing the cause of justice and the rule of law."

These noble ideals suggest that (at least in theory) The Law Society exists only to protect the public. Many think that there is a huge gap between that theory and reality.

2. Is It In The Public Interest For The Legal Profession To Be Self-Governing?

Many think not. The legal profession must be and must be seen to be independent of the government. That does not necessarily imply that the government cannot set the basic parameters for how the profession should be run. For the moment, the legal profession in Canada remains self-governing. But, it will remain "self-governing" only as long as the Law Society governs and is seen to govern the legal profession in the public interest.

On this point, consider the following summary of an article that graced the front page of the U.K. Telegraph on March 23, 2000.

"Lawyers and accountants face competition inquiry

In the U.K., the government is beginning to seriously question whether it is in the public interest for the legal profession to remain "self-governing." A Competition Act was recently enacted in the U.K. Interestingly, both the legal and accounting professions were exempted from its terms. In March of 2000, the U.K. Daily Telegraph reported that lawyers and accountants would be the subject of a "competition inquiry" - in part to review whether the legal profession should remain self-governing and whether it should be exempt from the provisions of the Competition Act. The commission was to focus on three aspects of the profession.

First: restrictions on entry, including disproportionately high standards for obtaining and retaining the right to practise;

Second: restrictions on advertising - including regulations preventing the advertising of fees; and

Third: requirements forcing people to use lawyers when others could also do the work."

The three factors considered by the U.K. competition commission are also issues in Canada. It may well be time for provincial governments to reconsider whether the legal profession should remain self-governing. It is important to note that jurisdiction and powers of The Law Society are defined by the terms of The Law Society Act.

3. Which Lawyers Actually Govern The Legal Profession?

All lawyers are "members" of the Law Society. At specified intervals, every "member" is entitled to vote on which lawyers will govern the profession. Those lawyers who are elected to govern the profession are called "Benchers." The "Benchers" elect a single bencher to become the head of the Law Society. That elected "Bencher" is called the "Treasurer." The Law Society conducts its business at a meeting which is called a "Convocation."

4. What Is The Origin Of Terms Like Bencher, Treasurer And Convocation?

An ad for a well known mutual fund reads: "Proud of our past, confident of our future!"

The Law Society - Proud Of Its Past

The Law Society is clearly proud of its past. Hundreds of years ago in England, senior lawyers ate at special benches. Hence, they became known as "Benchers." The rent had to be paid and one of the "Benchers" was designated as the person responsible for collecting the rent. Hence, the origin of the designation "Treasurer."

The present day offices of the Law Society are at the corner of Queen and University - on one of the most valuable pieces of real estate in the city of Toronto. A beautifully landscaped lawn is surrounded by black wrought iron fence. The fence was originally designed to keep the horses out. The building also includes a library for members of the bar, lecture rooms to run continuing education programs, administrative offices and a dining room for members of the bar. The basement is rumoured to include a cellar of the finest wines money can buy. The Law Society's building and land is similar to Darlington Hall in the movie "The Remains Of The Day." Lord Darlington, Stevens the Butler and all the other support staff of Darlington Hall have their direct parallels and analogies in the Law Society which is housed in Osgoode Hall.

The Law Society is both proud and protective of this property. A new opera house and a 44 story office and residential complex were proposed for the corner of Queen and University - across the street from the Law Society's offices. In 1999, the Globe and Mail reported that the Law Society objected to the new construction, on the grounds that the office tower would cast a shadow on its building and land. The complaint has put the Law Society in direct conflict with the interests of the public and will probably generate a whole new set of lawyers' jokes!

In 1997, Canada Post honoured the Law Society by issuing a special stamp that commemorated the 200th anniversary of its founding.

The Law Society - Confident Of Its Future??

"What I want to say can essentially be boiled down to a sentence or two. Like all other institutions, the legal profession and the Law Society are having great difficulty in adjusting to the pervasive and rapid changes of the late twentieth century. Those changes represent a brute reality. We cannot ignore them; we cannot reverse them; and very likely we cannot offset their effect on the profession, even if we wanted to, by moralizing, threats of punishment or even strategic planning conferences."

-Former Osgoode Hall Dean Professor H.W. Arthurs - 'Law, Society and The Law Society"

A second legal academic weighed in by saying:

"A traditional knock on the legal profession is that it normally lags behind the rest of society by 10 or 15 years. Despite the fervid efforts of a coterie of super-trendy benchers, this remains true of the legal profession in Ontario."

- University Of Western Ontario Law Professor Rob Martin For Law Times - January 31, 2000

As the above commentators suggest, the Law Society is out of touch with the modern world. It is big, bureaucratic and ill suited to exist in a world of globalization, efficiency, competition and openness. For two hundred years the Law Society has operated as a centralized power. As Paul Hoffert (of Lighthouse fame) pointed out in his insightful book ("The Bagel Effect") power is moving from the center to the periphery. The Law Society, as a centralized power in the legal profession may be in its final days. In order to survive it must evolve into an organization that:

- allows foreign lawyers to be admitted to the Ontario bar without regard to the effect on the competitive interests of the local bar;

- treats its members (Ontario lawyers) as clients to which it provides services and NOT as cows to be milked for membership dues;

- ensures that membership dues is no higher than is necessary to provide services desired and no higher than in comparable jurisdictions;

- uses the dues of its members to provide only the services its members want and NOT those that are perceived as irrelevant;

- recognizes that paralegals are here to stay and governs the legal profession in a manner that allows lawyers to compete with paralegals;

- recognizes that there are certain areas where paralegals can provide legal services more efficiently.

5. What Are The Most Important Sections Of The Law Society Act?

The Law Society Act defines:

1. What the Law Society is allowed to do;

2. What the Law Society is required to do; and

3. How it must go about doing what it does.

The most visible sections of the Law Society Act provide that:

A. A license is required to practise law and the practise of law is restricted to lawyers.

Rationale: A license to practise law is necessary to protect the public from unethical and/or incompetent practitioners.

Practical Effect: The requirement of a license gives lawyers a monopoly on the delivery of legal services.

B. Lawyers are required to be of good character and successfully complete the bar admission course of the province in question.

Rationale: The protection of the public by ensuring that those who are granted a license to practise law are educationally and morally qualified to practise law.

Practical Effect: It provides some assurance of a minimal level of competence.

(More information on the Bar Admission Course may be found in the chapter on Bar Admission.)

C. Law is a "self-governing profession." Within the parameters set by the Law Society Act, the legal profession governs itself. The Law Society has the authority to enact numerous bylaws and regulations governing the profession. These bylaws and regulations govern the conduct of lawyers, the annual fees lawyers must pay to practise law and standards for completing the bar admission course.

Rationale: Only lawyers have the knowledge to judge the competence of lawyers. Hence, it is logical that lawyers should govern themselves. (This assumption is increasingly coming under attack. Many are of the view that Law Societies use the principle of self-governance to govern the profession in the interests of lawyers and not in the interests of the public.)

Practical Effect: The supervision of the Law Society is difficult, expensive and time consuming. At present, Law Society conduct can be reviewed only in the courts. A self-governing profession is not free to do anything it wants.

Rather, a self-governing profession governs its day-to-day activities within the framework of the existing statute.

In summary: The Law Society Act is a statute of the legislature. This Act allows for the Law Society to enact bylaws and regulations. Furthermore, since the Law Society is "self governing", the Law Society (and not the government or an outside agency) administers the Act.

6. What Is The Relationship Between The Law Society And The Public?

Public Benefit And The Law Society

Through its licensing standards, the Law Society ensures that lawyers have attained a minimal standard of competence before being "called to the bar." After lawyers are called to the bar, the Law Society is the organization that receives and processes complaints about lawyers. 1999 Law Society Act amendments give the Law Society the power to monitor the competence of lawyers.

On another level, the Law Society has undertaken initiatives simply to help the public. The "Feed The Homeless" program is one example.

Public Detriment And The Law Society

Not all legal problems require the services of a lawyer. In recent years a profession has emerged which is called (for lack of a better term) "Paralegals." "Paralegals are restricted in what they can do. They are, however, perceived to offer better service at lower cost in certain areas. Examples include: traffic offenses, landlord and tenant disputes and certain aspects of immigration matters. The Law Society has been relentless in its prosecution and persecution of Paralegals. It argues that this is for the protection of the public - but a number of setbacks in the courts calls their credibility and motives into serious question.

Fortunately, the report of an Ontario government inquiry led by Justice Cory, recognizes the permanence and value of paralegals to the legal system.

7. What Is The Relationship Between The Law Society And Members Of The Bar?

There is tension. On the most basic level, the Law Society sets the rules that one must follow in order to become a lawyer and make a living as a lawyer.

To its credit, in 1999 the Law Society hired Earnscliffe Communications to research and prepare a report on a number of issues including "prevailing attitudes and opinions toward the Society among its members." Part of the summary stated that:

"On balance participants did not believe that the Law Society provided value for money. The Law Society would have received a failing grade from a majority of participants and a bare pass from the rest. We found no single audience that is clearly in the corner of the society, while there were several that exhibited high levels of negativity."

On balance, the report suggests that the profession views the Law Society as somewhere between irrelevant and obstructive. The report suggests that the Law Society is most visible to its members when it announces a new restrictive and/or expensive measure. In the words of one commentator the Law Society's ratings range from "never watch" through "hardly watch" through "hate to watch." "In other words, somewhere between irrelevant and obstructive."

The basic relationship between the Law Society and its members revolves around the "ubiquitous presence" of the Law Society which is financed from annual fees (dues) paid by the members.

The Ubiquitous Presence

The Law Society is involved in every aspect of law school, bar admission and the practice of law. An ad for a well known insurance company reads:

"Like a good neighbour _____ is always there."

The same can be said about the Law Society. It plays a role in every stage of the "legal life" of a lawyer. It is present at the conception, birth, life and death of every Ontario lawyer.

Your Conception And The Law Society

- prior to your graduation from law school (the Law Society regulates your contact with law firms in your search for an articling position);

- at the moment of graduation from law school (the Law Society welcomes you to the Bar Admission Course);

- during the Bar Admission Course (the Law Society regulates articling, your bar exams and the rest of the course);

Your Birth And The Law Society

- at the moment of officially becoming a lawyer (Your "call to the bar" is run by the Law Society);

Your Life And The Law Society

- your first expenditure as a lawyer (mandatory annual fees payable to the Law Society);

- your conduct as a lawyer (all aspects of your professional life are regulated by the Law Society);

- your annual filing (keeping them abreast of your activities during the year);

- at the moment of the first complaint against you (the Law Society will receive the complaint and possibly invite you to a hearing).

Your Death And The Law Society

- your legal career can end in any of the following ways: disbarment, resignation or death (unless you die off their premises, the Law Society will be directly involved)

Your Personal Life And The Law Society

Is it reasonable for the Law Society to involve itself in the personal life of its members? Should the Law Society be able to investigate every aspect of your life? The late Pierre Trudeau once commented that the state has no business in the bedrooms of the nation. What about the Law Society?

July 13, 2000 - National Post

Lawyer with messy apartment may lose right to practise

James Cudmore

"EDMONTON - An Alberta lawyer who was ordered yesterday to vacate his unkept and putrid-smelling apartment may lose the right to practise law in Alberta if the law society decides he has harmed the reputation of the legal profession.

James McLeod, deputy secretary of the Law Society of Alberta, said yesterday he has begun an examination into the conduct of John M. Grindley, a Stettler lawyer who was convicted of drunk driving in June and who yesterday had an eviction order that had been brought against him by a public health authority upheld.

Under Section 47 of Alberta's Legal Profession Act, any lawyer who brings disrepute to the legal profession is subject to investigation and possible sanction by the society.

Yesterday, Mr. McLeod said he will "look into it and make a decision in due course."

Mr. McLeod was referring to a decision in an Edmonton courtroom in which Mr. Justice William Giggulis agreed with an assessment by Melvyn Cherlenko, a public health inspector, that Mr. Grindley kept an untidy abode so strewn with garbage that it had become a hazard to public health.

"I considered it pretty bad," Mr. Cherlenko said. "If you walked through the hallway you could detect the odor quite strongly. There was a lot of garbage in the place and comestible food items. "I didn't feel there was anybody who could live there."

"I got a messy apartment," Mr. Grindley said yesterday. "they want me out, they took a back-handed stab at me. And this health thing? It's just absolute nonsense."

Mr. Grindley said he would appeal the health inspector's decision.

The law society will examine allegations that Mr. Grindley failed to report an upcoming appearance in Camrose on July 19 to answer to a second set of drunk driving charges."

Reprinted with permission from the National Post.

Annual Fees And Insurance - "A Tax By Any Other Name"

The two areas where the Law Society is most visible to the average lawyer are in the areas of annual fees and insurance. Once admitted to the bar, lawyers must pay an annual fee to the Law Society. Insurance is mandatory for those in private practice.

Why Must Lawyers Pay Annual Fees?

It is the obligation of the profession to finance the affairs of the Law Society. Once a year, every lawyer receives a bill for an annual fee. For the 2000 year a lawyer's annual fee of $1390* was broken down as follows:

General membership fee	$895
Capital and Techonology Fund	$75
County Library Levy	$210
Lawyer's Fund For Client Compensation Levy	$210
Total Annual Fee	**$1390**

According to the Earnscliffe Report lawyers express frustration over:

- the amount of the annual fees they pay;

- the fact that they receive no services in return; and

- the fact that there is little accounting of where the money goes.

*Law Society fees have fallen since 2000

The Power To Tax Is The Power To Destroy!

Annual fees are really a tax on a lawyers right to practise his or her profession. A failure to pay the fee will result in a suspension of the lawyer's right to practise. Even Canada's newest Law Society, the Law Society of Nunavut, which has only twenty members charges an annual of fee of seven hundred dollars per lawyer. One would expect that Ontario, with approximately 28,000 lawyers would have a much lower annual fee. Not so. In fact Ontario has the highest annual fees in Canada (and in North America.) This is surprising since Ontario has the largest number of lawyers in Canada. By way of comparison, New York state has far more lawyers than Ontario. The annual fees in New York are approximately 15% of the fees in Ontario. There is no evidence that Ontario lawyers are the recipients of more or better (or any) services. As borders become less important, Ontario fees will (and deserve) to come under intense scrutiny. Sooner or later (and the Earnscliffe Report suggests sooner), Ontario lawyers will ask: where does all our money go?

Insurance Fees

Insurance is mandatory. Once again, it is interesting to note that Ontario (with the largest number of lawyers) has insurance premiums that are among the highest in the country. The Law Society has granted one insurance company a monopoly on providing insurance to Ontario lawyers. It is hardly surprising that many lawyers feel that there should be competition in the market for professional liability insurance. It seems fairly obvious that the cost of insurance should be driven by market forces.

8. What About The Law Society And The Rule Of Law?

The Law Society proclaims its role to include: "advancing the cause of justice and rule of law." In all of its activities, the Law Society has a particularly strong obligation to respect the rule of law in both substance and procedure. As the most visible part of the legal profession, the Law Society should work hard to set an example for all lawyers.

The Law Society And The Charter Of Rights

The Constitution is the supreme law of Canada and the Charter Of Rights is part of the Constitution. A failure to support the Constitution is a failure to support the "law of the land." Enacted in 1982, the Canadian Charter Of Rights is to ensure that individual rights are respected by governments and by extension the self-governing professions. Rather than support the "law of the land", Law Society objectives and policies have been among the biggest victims of the Charter. Since 1982, Law Society restrictions concerning requirements for admission to the bar (Equality rights), advertising (Freedom of expression) and lawyers' mobility have been held to violate the Charter. Recent amendments to the Law Society Act have given the Society increased powers of "search and seizure." I predict that these provisions will eventually face Charter scrutiny.

The Law Society And The Discipline Of Lawyers

The Law Society is responsible for the regulation and (if warranted) discipline of lawyers. This responsibility must be exercised in a manner that is fair to the individual lawyer and fair to the public.

Fairness To The Individual Lawyer

The following perspective is both interesting and disturbing. It is indicative of both good news and bad news.

First, the good news. The Benchers mentioned in this article had the wisdom and courage to quash the conduct of the Law Society's administrators.

Second, the bad news. The article suggests that, at the administrative level, the Law Society is not paying attention to its obligation to advance the rule of law. George W. Bush reminded Al Gore that one should not have a White House without a controlling legal authority. Nor should there be a Law Society without a controlling legal authority that recognizes the Law Society's obligation to advance the cause of justice.

June 8, 2000

The Globe and Mail

Ontario law society hammers internal investigation process

Lawyers probing misconduct complaints became like a law unto themselves, panel says

Kirk Makin

"The body that governs Ontario lawyers blasted its own investigative branch yesterday for carrying out a "ridiculously protracted" 10-year investigation that systematically abused the rights of a high-profile lawyer.

The Law Society of Upper Canada said its investigators dithered, improperly suppressed information and generally acted like a law unto themselves while investigating complaints of misconduct against Thomas Baker.

The unprecedented attack was written by a panel of three of the law society's elected governors - Roger Yachetti, Seymour Epstein and Gregory Mulligan.

"In the opinion of this committee, the sword of Damocles has been hanging over Mr. Baker's head for far too long," they said, throwing out each of three charges of professional misconduct and five counts of conduct unbecoming a solicitor.

"This case was screaming for attention," it said. "Yet, the law society ignored this case."

Mr. Baker, former president of Seven-Up Canada Inc., faced allegations of conflict of interest after acting as executor and trustee of, and solicitor for, the estate of Frederick Rosbrooke, which held shares of Seven-Up Canada before Mr. Baker became president. He also faced charges relating to assertions that he conspired with a former Toronto police inspector to obstruct justice.

The panel was hearing an application to have the complaints thrown out because of abusive treatment by the investigators.

Chris Paliare, a lawyer who represented Mr. Baker, described the case in an interview yesterday as a "horrendous struggle. The law society's behavior from the very beginning can only be described as scandalous. We had to fight tooth and nail for every scrap of disclosure."

The panel gave short shrift to an argument by the law society's special prosecutor, lawyer Edward Greenspan, that the societal importance of the case helped excuse the long delays.

"Our system of jurisprudence at every level does not condone the sacrifice of individual rights at the altar of societal interest," it said.

It said the delays in the case were both astonishing and arbitrary and noted that Mr. Baker had a right to have his discipline hearing held within four months. "Five years later, the hearing of the merits of the complaint has yet to begin," it said.

Mr. Baker became a lawyer in 1976. He entered the world of business full-time in 1988, quickly becoming president and chief executive officer of Seven-Up Canada Ltd. and amassing millions of dollars.

His name has appeared frequently in the news media in relation to outstanding criminal charges of tax evasion, his professional troubles, and his marital litigation with his ex-wife, Monica Francis. (Last year, the Supreme Court of Canada awarded substantial support payments to Ms. Francis in a major ruling.)

Mr. Paliare said yesterday that law society officials obviously pre-judged Mr. Baker in 1989 when they embarked on their crusade to bring him down and they never altered their viewpoint.

He noted that the first panel struck to review the case was dismantled by a Superior Court judge because of numerous incidents that gave rise to an apprehension of bias against Mr. Baker.

"Virtually no other lawyer would have had the [financial] resources to do what Tom Baker did here," Mr. Paliare said. "That is, to not buckle under. Put simply, the law society were bullies in this case."

The law society launched its investigation in 1989 based on tips from someone who, according to yesterday's decision, bore "deep personal animosity" toward Mr. Baker.

The investigation was initially done internally by the law society, but in September of 1990, the society contracted the job out to the firm of Lockwood & Associates.

"Over the next two years, there is no evidence that the Lockwood firm did a single thing to further the investigation of the Rosbrooke complaint," the panel said yesterday.

After the Lockwood investigators produced their report on April 19, 1994, the law society took "the unprecedented step" of appointing Mr. Greenspan's firm to reinvestigate the allegations, the panel said.

Mr. Baker never received a copy of the report.

Mr. Greenspan submitted his own report on Jan. 25, 1995. A month later, the official complaints were finally laid.

Meanwhile, the law society waged a running battle to withhold much of its investigative data and findings. The panel said Mr. Baker had a legal right to most of the material, yet investigators were "extremely aggressive" in attempting to block it, including going to court to overturn internal rulings ordering it to disclose the information."

Reprinted with permission from The Globe and Mail.

Fairness To The Public

Is it possible that fairness to the individual lawyer could be unfair to the public? Consider the following perspective.

December 2, 2000

The Globe And Mail

The Law Society failed the public

"The Law Society of Upper Canada faced a telling choice in the case of lawyer Kenneth Murray. It could probe whether he breached his ethical duties by concealing Paul Bernardo's wretched torture videotapes. Or, it could sidestep the whole debacle and fervently hope few would notice.

Those familiar with the sorry history of how lawyers police their own will know instinctively the route it chose.

The law society deflected attention by striking an impressive and badly needed panel of experts to develop disclosure guidelines. It went on to justify its decision by claiming the pertinent issues in the Murray case had been adequately aired at his criminal trial last spring. It said no public interest could be served by rehashing what Superior Court Judge Patrick Gravely delved into when he acquitted Mr. Murray of obstructing justice.

For the record, here is what Judge Gravely actually said in his ruling: "I want to make clear that my function in this case is limited to deciding if Murray has committed the crime of obstructing justice, not to judge his ethics."

Could a judge have issued a clearer invitation to a professional body to do its duty?

In ignoring his hint and sweeping the Murray case under the carpet, the law society has insulted the same country that recoiled in horror upon learning that Mr. Murray secretly warehoused the torture videotapes for 16 months.

Consider some of the ethical issues the law society could have examined, had it not opted to shirk its duty.

Clutching a crude diagram drawn by his client, Mr. Murray rushed up to the Bernardo home on May, 6, 1993. Police had just spent 71 days tearing the premises apart in a fruitless search for them. Within minutes, an excited Mr. Murray was burying them in his briefcase.

Was this an ethical breach?

In mid-1994, Mr. Murray was granted several days to question Ms. Homolka in prison. He passed up the opportunity to trap her using his knowledge of the tapes, undermining his whole rationale for concealing them. And he continued to hide them. Was this an ethical breach?

In August, 1994, Mr. Murray begged lawyer John Rosen to take over the case, but kept him in the dark about the inutterably damning videotapes.

After handing over the murder file to Mr. Rosen, Mr. Murray hung onto the file on Paul Bernardo's Scarborough rapes. He proceeded to obtain odd, written instructions from Mr. Bernardo allowing him to transfer material — potentially including the videotapes — to the rape file.

Shortly afterward, a lawyer Mr. Murray had hurriedly retained advised him to hand over the videotapes. Mr. Murray did so, but failed to reveal he had made duplicates until he was confronted.

Were these ethical breaches?

Judge Gravely concluded that Mr. Murray's conduct misled Mr. Rosen, nearly deprived a jury of critical evidence and "had the potential to infect all aspects of the criminal justice system."

And, lest anyone forget a particularly lamentable byproduct of the affair, Karla Homolka engineered a notoriously lenient plea bargain while the videotapes were in hiding. She will soon rejoin us in the outside world.

Judge Gravely said he couldn't convict Mr. Murray. The burden of proving beyond a reasonable doubt that he intended to pervert justice was simply too high a threshold. Thus, the Murray matter reverted to its rightful place — before a jury of his peers.

We pass no judgment on whether Mr. Murray ought to have been suspended, disbarred or merely admonished. What the Canadian public was deprived of was the chance to see lawyers police themselves and define critical ethical duties.

His worries behind him, Mr. Murray now talks placidly about his need for closure. What about ours?

As for the law society, its members are fond of pointing out that the public cannot have confidence in the system unless it perceives justice to be done. Justice is blind, they say.

Except, apparently, when it comes to lawyers.

Reprinted with permission from The Globe and Mail.

9. What Is The Future Of The Law Society?

The pace of globalization will increase pressure on the Canadian legal profession to be run more like the legal professions in other countries. Over time, like all taxes, lawyers' annual fees must decrease to levels consistent with those of other jurisdictions. In all probability licensing requirements will become more like the requirements in other countries. This implies the abolition or the changing of articling and the rest of the Bar Admission Course. Once the Law Society has less money and less to do, it will become like the Governor General. That is, nice to have around for historical reasons, but basically irrelevant.

Conclusion

As the legal profession evolves, the Law Society is sure to evolve. The election of University of Ottawa law professor Vern Krishna as Treasurer may have started a process that will make the Law Society more functional and modern.

APPENDIX

A Possible New Beginning?

July 27, 2001

National Post

Passion for justice

Sandra Rubin

The steel behind Vern Krishna's passion for justice may well have been tempered one desolate day in the acid fires of racism. Alone in Canada, far from his family in India, he was 20 and working as an apprentice accountant in a large Toronto firm. A senior partner approached him and told him he was a "bright young man" and should consider specializing in tax, one of the most challenging fields.

Mr. Krishna was feeling very proud that the older man, a respected senior partner, should single him out for praise and encouragement when the man added, "and that way the clients won't have to see you." Today, he says, aside from "the psychological bruising of a young boy's emotions," he owes the man a debt.

Mr. Krishna took his advice, went into tax, then tax law, where he has been more than moderately successful. He was just named treasurer, or head, of the Law Society of Upper Canada, the venerable body that governs the largest group of lawyers in the country.

He has power, prestige and a platform to push for wider access to justice for ordinary Canadians, an issue that has become something of a passion.

"I have had an enormously different life from the other treasurers," Mr. Krishna acknowledged in an interview. "I wasn't well off, I started at the absolute bottom and studied and worked. I had no inherited wealth. I had no silver spoon in my mouth."

"The law society was at one time an enormously wealthy and privileged group, but to its great credit it has been adaptive and changed with the times."

He says his appointment sparked an outpouring of "enormously touching and very personal letters."

Many came from strangers, especially immigrants, who spoke of how much it meant to them that he had pierced the veil of colour and class that shrouded the law society's top position for more than 10 generations.

One of Mr. Krishna's priorities is a pilot project designed to make access to the justice system more affordable for the middle class. It is believed to be the first program of its kind in Canada.

He says the cost of hiring a lawyer has put justice out of reach for most people unless they are extremely wealthy or qualify for legal aid.

"What I am concerned about is that huge group of people who earn between $40,000 and $85,000, and I ask you this: How many people can throw even 10,000 after-tax dollars at a lawsuit to obtain a remedy to what they consider a wrong?"

"Even in something as common as divorce, people are squeezed and have to take out a second mortgage, or use their RRSPs, or risk not having their interests protected. It's an access-to-justice issue that is often overlooked in our society, and we are very conscious of this problem. It's a huge issue."

Crusading for more affordable justice may seem a remarkable endeavour for any body of lawyers, particularly for the august 204-year-old Law Society of Upper Canada. However, Mr. Krishna is clearly a remarkable choice to lead the organization.

He is the consummate outsider: an academic who forged his career far from the corridors of power and influence, and the first member of a visible-minority group to sit in the symbolic, high-backed red leather treasurer's chair and govern 30,000 lawyers in Ontario.

The son of a doctor, Mr. Krishna was born in the Punjab and sent to study in England at 16. At 20, he came to Toronto where he worked at the accounting firm "for the princely sum of $350 a month." He knew no one and lived in the downtown YMCA for $3 a night.

He submerged his loneliness in his insatiable hunger for education: an MBA and law degree at the University of Alberta, a Master's in law from Harvard University and diploma in comparative law from Cambridge University. He is still a professor of business and taxation law at the University of Ottawa and teaches an annual course in international tax at Harvard.

But Mr. Krishna's crusade to widen access to justice may be where he makes his most visible mark. The program, if successful, could be adopted by law societies across the country.

"Each of the provinces is very conscious of what the other provinces are doing," said Richard Marggets, president of the Law Society of British Columbia, which oversees approximately 10,000 lawyers. "So, yes, we will be watching."

"We would definitely be interested in monitoring what they are doing," said Don Thompson, executive director of the Law Society of Alberta, which governs 6,400 lawyers.

Mr. Krishna says a co-ordinator has already been hired to run the pilot project, and free, or discounted, services will become available in stages. "It will be in limited areas and, up to a certain amount, will be free of charge," he said. "It's in the embryonic stage; the parameters have not been settled. It won't be free — there will be certain costs — however, it will not be income tested."

He says the law society and its partners, the Law Foundation of Ontario and Legal Aid Ontario, are still determining how the program will work.

Contingency fees and class-action lawsuits are other methods of broadening access to the justice system, he says.

Contingency fees, in which lawyers are paid a percentage of the award if they are successful but receive no compensation if the case fails, allow people to retain a lawyer without making a large financial commitment. Ontario is the only province that does not permit them. Mr. Krishna says he intends to approach the Ontario government this fall about changing the law. Previous treasurers have approached the attorney-general of the day and been told it was not politically expedient.

"The great problem the public has with contingency fees is the perception that lawyers will gouge you. That's why we want a structure. We are concerned there should be some protection," he said. "The contingency fees could be capped, they could be subject to judicial approval, there would be a system for pre-registering the fees before the matter is actively undertaken.

"That said, I think a fee of 30% on a big, complex case is not an exorbitant amount. Remember, you have to take into account the risk the lawyer is taking, and they may have to carry that risk for eight years. It's like a junk bond — it is a classic example of a high rate of return against a higher risk."

Class-action lawsuits are another avenue, he says, because they allow people to pursue a case in situations, as in Bre-X Minerals Ltd., where the legal fees could outweigh the money a person lost.

Harvey Strosberg, a former treasurer of the law society, says he has no doubt Mr. Krishna's passion for access derives from his own background.

"He was born into a caste society and it has affected him in many strata," he said. "But there is no doubt he was moulded by overt and covert racism."

Mr. Krishna returns to that day in Toronto, when the senior partner at the accounting firm briefly punctured his dreams.

"The beauty of it is it put me into a subject matter that I find absolutely delightful, challenging, intellectually stimulating, that I thrive upon and I get up every day and I'm happy to work with."

"So everything from that incident turned out well. The story has a remarkably happy ending. That is the ultimate justice."

Reprinted with permission from the National Post.

Book VIII - A Report

Recognizing Historical Barriers To Access

Summary And Introduction

My Advice To You Is ....

Lawyers are uniquely positioned to take a "leadership role" when it comes to combating discrimination. Unfortunately most don't. The concepts of making a living and making the world a better place are not mutually exclusive.

Minority groups have been discriminated against for many years and in many ways.

They say that lawyers are a conservative profession. The truth is that lawyers and the legal profession have not taken an enlightened approach when it has come to eradicating discrimination. Minorities have fought hard for the privilege of becoming lawyers. Even after becoming lawyers, they have experienced discrimination at the hands of the profession. The legal profession has been no better or worse, than the rest of society in its treatment of minority groups. Book VIII will not be of interest to all readers. But, those who are interested in human rights, will see that lawyers are uniquely positioned to play a special role in combating discrimination.

The great Toronto lawyer, the late J.J. Robinette, once remarked that a lawyer is nothing more than a practical historian. In Book VIII, I will play the role of a historian. Those who understand the past have a better chance of influencing the present!

Book VIII - Chapter Summaries

38. Minorities And Discrimination - Law School, Bar Admission And The Practice Of Law

Focus: Discrimination based on race, sex, religion, political orientation, citizenship, disability ...

39. Women - As Law Students, Lawyers And Judges

Focus: From the common law prohibition from practicing law to their majority status in law schools

Chapter 38

Minorities And Discrimination - Law School, Bar Admission And The Practice Of Law

Discrimination And Access To The Legal Profession

"For a long time, law, like other professions, was a male profession... Now, it seems to me, we must devote our energies to ensuring that there is a high degree of sensitivity in our admissions programs to those from different ethnic and economic backgrounds. Canada is a country that prides itself on adherence to the ideal of equality of opportunity. If that ideal is to be realized in our profession then law schools, and ultimately the legal profession, must be alert to the need to encourage people from minority groups and people from difficult economic circumstances to join our profession."

-Chief Justice Brian Dickson

"In making admission decisions, law schools should give special consideration to applicants who are members of cultural, ethnic or racial groups that have not had adequate opportunities to develop and demonstrate potential for academic achievement and would not otherwise be meaningfully represented in the entering class. Schools should make reasonable accommodations to the special needs of disabled applicants."

-The Law School Admission Council's Statement of Good Admission Practices

"Making legal education equally accessible to all sectors of our society - to women, to all races, religious and ethnic groups has been a vital step in the development not just of the legal profession but of Canadian democracy. For lawyers are the dominant profession in our system of government. Lawyers outnumber any other professional group in our elected legislatures and at the highest level of our bureaucracies. In the judicial branch of government, since the last century, ordinary citizens, except for occasional jury duty, have been squeezed out and the legal profession has a virtual monopoly on decision-making power. If the media are the fourth estate, the legal profession is surely the fifth estate in our system of government (and, I am not referring to a television program!). How essential it was for the growth of our democracy to remove barriers that prevented over half our population to even qualify for membership in this fifth estate."

-Professor Peter Russell - Changes In Our Legal Culture And Professional Inheritance

Foreward - Chapter Guide

Discrimination is a complex topic. It is far easier to recognize than to define. All laws and practices make distinctions among different groups of people.

Who Discriminates?

Public Discrimination Laws vs. Private Discrimination Practices

People suffer discrimimation from governments through laws that discriminate. People also suffer discrimination from people who discriminate through practices.

Two Kinds Of Discrimination - Intent And Effect

In one of the Supreme Court of Canada's first decision on the Charter Of Rights the court ruled that when considering whether laws violate the Charter, attention must be paid to both the intention and the effect of the law. Hence, the question of discrimination must be considered from both perspectives.

Not All Differing Treatments Are Discriminatory

Laws and practices often make distinctions among groups. Distinctions in treatment may or may not be discriminatory. For example few would think the following would be examples of discrimination:

1. A law requiring somebody must be 16 to drive.

2. A parental rule requiring an 8 year old to be home by 6:00 p.m.

To constitute discrimination, one must (at the very least) be treated differently in a manner that cannot be justified.

Different Treatment May Be Required To Avoid Discrimination

Consider this example. A parent wants to buy each of two daughters a new dress. The goal is to buy each of them a dress the daughter likes. Imagine a sitution where daughter A likes blue dresses and daughter B dislikes blue dresses and likes red dresses. The parent buys each of them a blue dress. Even though the daughters are being treated in an indentical manner, daughter A will be happy and daughter B will not. In this case different dresses need to be purchased for each daughter to ensure they are treated equally with respect to the purpose of making them happy.

Chief Justice Dickson (writing in the context of laws) once made the point that:

"The true interests of equality may require differentiation in treatment."

Laws by definition make distinctions among groups of people. For example, the law requires that one must be over 19 to drink alcohol. Although this law distinguishes people based on age - few would argue that it is discriminatory. Therefore, not all distinctions made by laws result in discrimination.

There are some laws that distinguish people in ways that are discriminatory. For example, laws taxing people based on their national origin would constitute discrimination.

When governments enact laws that make distinctions among groups, they often bear the burden of demonstrating the distinction in the law is not discriminatory.

Private Sector - Practices Or Customs That Discriminate

What about a law firm that won't hire religious minorities? What about a landlord that won't rent to people of colour? What about a restaurant that won't serve certain groups? History has been replete with examples of this type. In most instances this type of discrimination is prohibited by law. In these cases, the government enacts laws prohibiting private sector discrimination.

How Does This Apply To The Legal Profession?

When considering discrimination, one must consider both intentional and systemic (effect based) discrimination in the context of both public sector laws and private sector practices. The legal profession presents an unusually rich context for discrimination of all types. A "road map" for this chapter is as follows:

Introduction - Unflattering Truths

Part A - Intentional Discrimination

- Religion

- National Origin

- Sex

- Citizenship

Part B - Discrimination In Effect

Admission To Law School

- Blacks - Dalhousie's IBM Program

- Native Canadians - Saskatchewan Native Law Institute

- The disabled and the LSAT

Bar Admission

- Native Canadians

The Practise Of Law - The reality of finding a job

Conclusion

- Treasurer Vern Krishna

Appendix

- Michael Baxter

Introduction - Unflattering Truths

In December of 1998 the National Post reported that the Law Society of British Columbia apologized for preventing a Communist from becoming a lawyer during the Cold War. Gordon Martin, who graduated in 1948 from the first class of the U.B.C. law school died in 1974. His widow welcomed the apology. Today the B.C. Law Society bars only incompetents and criminals.

In the summer of 1999 The Natal Law Society (South Africa) apologized posthumously to Mahatma Ghandi for opposing his 1894 application to become a lawyer. His application was rejected because he was not white - he was Indian. The apology was extended to all aspirant lawyers whose applications to practise law were rejected on racial grounds.

Would the result have been different if Ghandi had applied to be a member of a bar in Canada? The answer is not clear. In Canada's brief history, during different times and in different places, a number of minority groups have been prohibited by law from becoming a lawyer. These groups have included: women, Roman Catholics, Aboriginal

Peoples, Asiatics, those who were not British Subjects and some people who were not Canadian citizens. Some of these rules were part of the common law (women and non-citizens) and some had their genesis in local conditions. Even if not legally prohibited from becoming members of the bar, lawyers with certain ethnic and religious orientations have been subjected to terrible discrimination.

Discrimination is a complex topic. Some forms of discrimination are intentional. Examples include: discrimination based on race, national origin, religion and citizenship. Other forms of discrimination may not be intentional, but may have the effect of discriminating against certain groups. For example, many policies have had the effect of discriminating against the disabled. Some laws or policies may discriminate both in intention and effect.

Part A - Examples Of Intentional Discrimination

In cases of "intentional discrimination" certain groups were prohibited by law or custom from becoming lawyers. Part A will canvas examples of discrimination based on religion, national origin, sex and citizenship.

Intentional Discrimination Based On Religion

In Canada's early years Roman Catholics were barred from the legal profession. In later years, religion may not have been a legal bar, but it was a practical bar.

The late Bora Laskin was the Chief Justice of Canada and a law professor at the University of Toronto. He is regarded as one of the finest jurists Canada has ever produced. He was also Jewish. He earned a Masters degree in law at the Harvard Law School and returned to Canada in 1937. The following passage from The Making of a Chief Justice: Bora Laskin, The Early Years by Irving Abella tells the story of a past that many would like to pretend never happened.

"On his return from Harvard in 1937 this brilliant legal scholar with two Masters degrees could not get a job in a Toronto law firm. His friend, Maxwell Cohen, who was still at Harvard, had warned him about Toronto. As Cohen wrote their mutual friend, Caeser Wright, then a teacher at Osgoode Hall, for Bora " ... the Jewish problem in Toronto presents a serious obstacle, but personal interviews might do a little to offset the initial disadvantage of name." Apparently they did not. Laskin's brother Saul recalls the bitterness of the first rejections, the shattering disillusionment with the profession he loved and in which hoped to make his career. In later years, Laskin would occasionally remind his family how "waspy" a city Toronto once was and how he was shunned by the large law firms. Eventually he did get a job; writing headnotes for the Canadian Abridgment at 50 cents a note, hardly the job he expected or was trained for."

> *- The Making of a Chief Justice: Bora Laskin, The Early Years - page 190, Volume XXIV, Number 3 of the September 1990 Law Society of Upper Canada Gazette*

Intentional Discrimination Based On National Origin

The following excerpt from page 36 of a History of The Law Society of British Columbia by Alfred Watts reveals the spirit of discrimination that once characterized the legal profession.

"In another matter, the Vancouver law students "persuaded" all too well. On January 19th 1918 they petitioned the Benchers that Asiatics be prohibited from becoming members of the Law Society. At that time the provincial Electors Act (R.S.B.C 1911, chapter 72 as amended by Chapter 20, 1913) prohibited Asiatics the right of being on the voters' list. Acting on the law students' petition the Benchers amended Rule 39 to require applicants to be among other requirements:

'a British subject and who would, if of the age of twenty-one years, be entitled to be placed on the Voters' List under the Provincial Elections Act.'

This situation continued until the Provincial Election Act was amended in 1949 and until that date had the effect of barring among others the native Indians of British Columbia, who obviously should have been entitled. Alfred Scow, now a Provincial Court Judge in Courtenay, was the first Indian of the Province to be called in 1962. Discrimination of this sort, which was general and not by any means the property of the Law Society, has now happily, passed."

Intentional Discrimination Based On Sex - Women

"A large number of women have been admitted to Canadian law schools, have performed superbly there, and are now embarking upon successful legal careers which will, inevitably, lead them to the pinnacles of the practicing and judicial branches of the profession."

> *- Chief Justice Brian Dickson*

At common law women (along with non-citizens) were barred from the legal profession. Women currently constitute approximately fifty percent of the students in North American law schools. The integration of women into the legal profession will be treated in a separate chapter.

Intentional Discrimination Based On Citizenship - Non-citizens

The Bible

"You are to have the same law for the alien and the native-born."

Leviticus 24:22 (NIV Translation)

"Do not mistreat an alien or oppress him, for you were aliens in Egypt."

Exodus 22:30 (NIV Translation)

"Viewing the profession of the law as the source from which the superior judicial magistrates must be derived, and from which a large proportion of enlightened and efficient public officers is usually selected, every one must naturally feel solicitious that it should not fall into such hands as would lower it in the national opinion. It would be difficult to avoid this consequence if aliens were entitled to admission; for legal acquirements and private worth may subsist with inveterate prejudices against the principles of our government. In such an arrangement society would cease to derive that benefit from the profession which it now affords, by supplying a continual succession of men qualified and worthy to preside in the Courts of justice. No longer a nursery in which merit is trained under the directing hand of experience, and qualified to render manly and essential services to the community, the legal profession, "in its nature the noblest and most beneficial to mankind; in its abuse and debasement the most sorid and pernicious," would sink into a mere mercenary instrument, without sympathy in the public prosperity, and without hold on the public confidence".

> *-Justice Taylor of the Supreme Court of North Carolina delivering judgment in the 1824 case of Ex Parte Thompson*

"I find citizenship to be a personal characteristic which is relevant to the practice of law on account of the special commitment to the community which citizenship involves and not merely because the practical familiarity with the country necessary for that occupation can necessarily be expected of citizens."

> *-Justice Taylor of the Supreme Court of British Columbia delivering judgment in the 1985 case of Andrews v. Law Society of British Columbia*

At common law aliens were prohibited from becoming attorneys. This prohibition was, along with the common law, imported to North America. Of the many minorities who have been barred from the practice of law in Canada, the prohibition against non-citizens practicing law remained the longest.

Until 1989 non-citizens were precluded from bar admission even if they completed law school in Canada, suffered through the articling process and passed the bar exams - simply because they were not Canadian citizens (in some provinces) or British Subjects (in other provinces). The citizenship barrier fell, not because of Law Society or government initiatives, but rather because the Supreme Court Of Canada held that the requirement violated the "equality rights" section of the Charter Of Rights. The Federation Of Law Societies (on behalf of the Law Societies of each province) argued that the citizenship requirement should be retained. David Lepofsky commenting on this issue wrote:

"In its first pronouncement on the Charter's equality guarantee, the Supreme Court Of Canada struck down as discriminatory and unjustifiable legislation in British Columbia restricting membership in the legal profession to Canadian citizens. ... The fact that the Federation of provincial Law Societies across Canada intervened before the Supreme Court Of Canada in an effort to defend such legislation as justifiable in a free and democratic society is something about which we should question critically."

-David Lepofsky - A Time Of Transitions

A citizenship requirement to be a Solicitor was changed in England in 1974. A U.S. citizenship requirement was struck down by the Supreme Court of the United States in 1974. Like the Supreme Court of Canada, the U.S. Supreme court ruled that a citizenship requirement to practice law violated the "equal protection" rights in the U.S. constitution. Surprisingly, there is still mention of a citizenship requirement in some Law Society Acts.

Enlightened Judges

On the relationship between citizenship and bar admission modern judges have commented:

"It is the lingering vestige of a xenophobic attitude which as we shall see, also restricted membership in our bar to persons who were both male and white."

-Justice Mosk of the Supreme Court of California

"The common law generality enshrined in Coke ... no more than a predisposition designed to preserve the integrity of the legal profession."

-Justice Street of the New South Wales Court of Appeal (Australia)

Now that non-citizens are eligible to practice law there is no class of persons who is barred by law from the becoming a lawyer.

Part B - Discrimination In Effect - Groups Under represented in Law

In cases of discrimination by "effect", certain groups while not prohibited by law from becoming lawyers, have been historically very under represented in the profession. I will canvas this issue from the perspective of law admission, bar admission and career opportunities.

It All Begins With Admission To Law School

Anyone is now eligible to become a lawyer. Access to the legal profession begins with access to law school. There is now a heightened sensitivity to:

1. The need for minorities to be represented in law school; and

2. The need for minorities to become lawyers.

Minority Representation In Law School - One Example

"Although blacks number between 30,000 and 40,000 in the province, there are fewer than a dozen local blacks in the provincial bar and "less than a handful" of black Nova Scotians studying law at Dalhousie. There are no indigenous native (i.e. Mic Mac) lawyers in the province, and only one native has ever graduated from the law school, even though there are 12,000 natives in Nova Scotia."

- Anne Emery 'Dalhousie goes after black, native students"- The National - June 1989

In 1989 Dalhousie Law School established the Law Programme for Indigenous Blacks and Mi'kmaq (Indigenous Blacks and Mi'kmaq Programme). The goal of the Programme is to increase the representation of Indigenous Nova Scotian Blacks and Mi'kmaq in the legal profession by making Dalhousie Law School more accessible to applicants from these two communities. Dalhousie Law School, after wide consultation with the public, recognized the problem of under representation of Indigenous Blacks and Mi'kmaq in the legal profession in the Province of Nova Scotia.

Since 1989 the I.B.M. (Indigenous Black and Mi'Kmaq) program has experienced some growing pains. Consider the following two articles by donalee Moulton.

Report on Dal's I.B.M. Programme under attack

donalee Moulton

A review of the Indigenous Black and Mi'Kmaq (I.B.M.) Programme at Dalhousie University's School of Law has concluded that although the Programme is beneficial work now needs to be done to enhance and improve it. However, the factors on which those conclusions are based have proven to be unacceptable to many members of the Black and Mi'Kmaq communities inside and outside the university.

"Reviews of programs are a regular management tool to ensure quality. The whole law school was reviewed in 1991-1992 but the I.B.M. Programme was too new then," Dawn Russell, dean of the Dalhousie Law School, said in an interview with The Lawyers Weekly.

"Overall," she added, "(the review) is very positive. This is a unique program and it should continue."

Carol Aylward, director of the I.B.M. Programme, points out that this initiative, established in 1989 to enhance participation of Blacks and Mi'Kmaqs at Dal, is an affirmative action program. It is not an academic program. In this context, she says, reviews are not a regular management tool.

"We have never reviewed the admissions criteria known as 'mature students' or 'students with disabilities,' all of whom would be predominantly white. We have to conclude that this review is a review of affirmative action based solely on race and this is unacceptable."

Concerns have also been expressed over the review committee's use of marks and other academic measures as indicators of the Programme's success. In their report the committee noted that, "It appears that a significant number of I.B.M. students enter law school without a university degree. Students with university courses had academic averages in the range of 68 per cent to 70 per cent. LSAT scores were often below the 50th percentile, and usually below the 30th percentile. This contrasts with non-I.B.M. student academic averages in the low 80s and LSAT scores in the 80th percentile or greater."

"The report doesn't say those statistics are bad," says Ms. Russell. "It doesn't say I.B.M. graduates are less bright. It docs say there is systemic discrimination. (But) if they've graduated they have shown they can do (the law school program)." But the report raises concerns because the majority of I.B.M. students are graduating in the C to B range and this leads to questions about poor performance, notes Ms. Aylward. "Obviously what they have to be saying is that C's and B's are poor performance. Then they need to say that for the whole school."

She adds that the Dal Law School grades on a bell curve so the maximum number of A's that can be given out in any year is 10 per cent, and often that number is not reached. Last year, for example, only seven per cent of Dal law graduates had an overall grade of A.

"Marks are really no indication of success. The graduation rate is extremely high (in the I.B.M. Programme) compared to similar programs across Canada and the United States. The failure rate is extremely low. The white failure rate is much higher," says Ms. Aylward.

"This review process should not have included grades or employment as a measure of success for students who have successfully completed the (bachelor of law) degree, since no such review has been or will be undertaken with respect to white law graduates," notes Heidi Marshall, the executive director of the Mi'Kmaq Justice Institute.

In a memo to Dean Russell and Dr. Deborah Hobson, the university's vice president, academic and research, Ms. Aylward notes that, "If hiring was done exclusively on the basis of grades, and grades accurately measured competence, then all law graduates in the C+ to D range (not just the I.B.M. students as the report suggests) would be incompetent, unemployable and unemployed. If this were true the Law School should treat all grades falling below a B as a failing grade for all students and revise its pass/fail criteria accordingly.

"Moreover, the Law School should revoke the degrees of students of all races and from all years who graduated with an average in the C+ to D range. This would invalidate the degrees of 201 alumni who graduated in this range during the period from 1992 to 1996 alone."

Another concern has been raised over comments in the report about the number of I.B.M. students that come into the Programme without a university degree. "Ignoring the fact that 76 per cent of I.B.M. students do come in with a university degree, this tries to put in place a new admissions standard for Black and Native students," says Ms. Aylward, "The normal requirements are zero to 10 credits. It sets up an exclusionary barrier."

"I defy anybody to look at the degree that hangs on my wall and say that my degree is any different from the degrees of my fellow students who graduated with me," says Burnley "Rocky" Jones, an I.B.M. student who was valedictorian of his graduating class.

However, he adds, "if you were a client looking for a lawyer, after reading what's been out there in the press, would you go to a person that you felt was inferior academically?"

Dean Russell also has serious misgivings about the coverage of the issue in the local press. The comments in the report that have come under scrutiny, she says, "play a minor role in the report. This is almost an attempt to subvert the discussion that will take place with faculty council. We don't decide things through a town hall mechanism. This seems like an attempt to pre-empt this process."

The report, she adds, will not be retracted as has been requested by members of the I.B.M. Programme and the Black and Mi'Kmaq communities.

"The report is advice. We don't have to take it although given the background and experience of those involved we'd be foolish not to give it careful consideration."

The four members of the I.B.M. review committee are Dal law faculty members Michael Deturbide and Bruce Wildsmith, who teaches aboriginal law and represents the Union of Nova Scotia Indians, and I.B.M. Advisory Board members Judge Corrine Sparks, the first Black woman judge in Canada, and Patrick Johnson, director of Mi'Kmaq Student Services at the University College of Cape Breton. In addition there were two external peer reviewers: Professor Joanne St. Lewis of the Faculty of Law at the University of Ottawa, and Professor John Burrows, director of the First Nations Program at the Faculty of Law at the University of British Columbia.

But the argument that the report on the I.B.M. Programme cannot be discriminatory because racial minorities were represented on the review committee is a discriminatory remark in and of itself, says Ms. Aylward.

The review of the Dal Law School in 1991 was conducted by an all white review committee, she points out, and yet faculty disagreed with some of the recommendations in that report, and in some cases recommendations were unanimously rejected. However, no one argued that the law faculty couldn't make those comments because the reviewers were white.

"There is," she adds, "a divide and conquer mentality when issues of discrimination and racism arise. Do all whites agree?"

There is also concern from both sides that not everyone touched by this controversy is going to feel free to speak up. "There is a fear of speaking out. This is especially true of students in the institution," says Ms. Aylward. "(But) you do not ignore people who have been aggrieved because all 48 (I.B.M. graduates) don't speak up and say so. That's ridiculous."

If the report had not been leaked, she adds, the discussion could have been conducted differently. "But those more obnoxious and exclusive recommendations will not pass. I don't think that those people who are anti-affirmative action are going to win on this one."

Reprinted with permission of the author.

Report and recommendations spark controversy

donalee Moulton

In their 25-page report the four members of the committee established to review the Indigenous Black and Mi'Kmaq at Dalhousie University's Law School have come forward with 22 recommendations. Those recommendations, they believe, will contribute to the long-term survival of the I.B.M. Programme.

Indeed, the importance they have placed on these recommendations — and the Programme itself - -are captured in a quote from one of the two external peer reviewers who assisted the committee.

"The I.B.M. Programme is useful, has enjoyed some great successes, and will continue to be demanded by people from these communities. Despite the Programme's challenges and problems, not one person we interviewed questioned the need for its continuation at Dalhousie Law School beyond 1999 (after which time funding has not been guaranteed)," said Joanne St. Lewis, a member of the law faculty at the University of Ottawa.

"Through this review," she added, "the law school has a great opportunity to work on processes and mechanisms that will ensure that the vision of a more representative law school and legal profession can be realized."

Needless to say, not everyone endorses the report and its recommendations. In an editorial in The Chronicle Herald newspaper, Evangeline Cain-Grant, an African Canadian lawyer practicing in Halifax, noted that, "The I.B.M. review report completely forgets the goals that the I.B.M. Programme was designed to achieve namely to address the long history of discrimination against the Black and Mi'Kmaq people of Atlantic Canada with respect to both the educational system and the legal system."

"Those communities," she added, "need lawyers who will recognize the expertise of the Black and Mi'Kmaq people of Nova Scotia in identifying adverse effects of discrimination, and who will listen to and take seriously the voices of the members of these communities when they cry out against injustice, instead of denying the truth of everything they see."

Among the 22 recommendations put forward by the review committee are that:

* The I.B.M. Committee, with input from the I.B.M. Program Advisory Council, should evaluate how the needs of both Black and Aboriginal students can best be addressed through the position currently designated as the Director. The Committee should report its recommendation to the Dean within the next year.

* Dalhousie Law School should make the Indigenous Black and Mi'Kmaq Programme accessible to Black and Aboriginal candidates from communities across Canada, with the stated policy that some preference will be given to Indigenous Black and Mi'Kmaq candidates from Nova Scotia.

* In assessing applicants for admission to Dalhousie Law School through the I.B.M. Programme, the Admissions Committee should generally require at least 10 full university credits and a minimum LSAT score at the 20th percentile.

* The number of Mature persons accepted to the Programme (i.e. candidates with fewer than 10 university credits) should be limited to a maximum of two per year. The Admissions Committee should require all mature students to complete some university level courses before being considered for admission.

* Demonstrated community activity and commitment should be weighed as important factors in assessing applicants to the I.B.M. Programme, especially with respect to Mature students.

* The I.B.M. Committee should have the responsibility of ensuring that statistical information is regularly received from the Law School administration, and should oversee external communications about the Programme.

* Faculty members should be given the opportunity of receiving instruction on how to teach a culturally and racially diverse class, and in particular on the different learning methods of students from diverse cultural backgrounds.

* The Director should report to the I.B.M. Committee at the end of each term, and at any other time that may be prudent, on the academic progress of the I.B.M. students. Students in academic difficulty should be identified and offered enhanced assistance.

* The I.B.M. Committee, in consultation with the Advisory Council, should consider renaming the I.B.M. Programme to more accurately reflect an equity education initiative.

* The Law School, through its Dean, Faculty members and I.B.M. Programme Director, should vigorously promote the career achievements of Black and Mi'Kmaq graduates.

* More communication and interaction between the Nova Scotia Barristers' Society and Dalhousie Law School is required to educate the Bar about the I.B.M. Programme. The I.B.M. Committee should investigate and implement education and placement initiatives with the Nova Scotia Barristers' Society and governmental departments.

* Assistance in substantive law issues should be provided by upper-year student tutors. The current tutoring program provided by the I.B.M. Programme should be expanded and I.B.M. Programme students should be advised to make use of this resource."

Reprinted with permission of the author.

Minority Representation In Law School - Native Canadians

"I know that in recent years several law schools, and the profession as a whole, have made sincere efforts to encourage more Canadian native people to embark upon a legal career. The pre-law course for native people at the University of Saskatchewan and the special admissions programs at most Canadian law schools come to mind. I applaud them. But there are still problems, in law schools and in the profession. I know that many native people have real problems once they get to law school and, if they succeed there, once they begin the early years of their practice. Quite simply, there is a need to translate the good intentions that we all have and the good start that many of you have made into better results. I call, therefore, on the university, the bar and the judiciary, to be diligent and imaginative in seeking out ways to involve more actively Canadian native people in the important work of our profession."

- Chief Justice Brian Dickson

There is no group in Canadian society who has a better claim to minority status than native Indians. There have been very few natives who have become lawyers. Hence, it is not surprising that many Canadian law schools have a special application category for "Natives." For those applying in the "Native Canadian" category, an offer of admission may be made conditional upon the applicant's completing an eight week pre-law summer course at the University of Saskatchewan's Native Law Centre. The Native Law Centre is described by the Law School as follows:

"The Program of Legal Studies for Native People has been offered at the University of Saskatchewan since 1973. It began as a pilot project to facilitate access to legal education for Aboriginal people. After studying a similar program established at Albuquerque, New Mexico, the University offered the inaugural session.

When the Program was established there were only 4 lawyers and 5 law students of Aboriginal ancestry in Canada. The Program has been very successful in increasing that number. Program alumni have become lawyers, judges, government officials and professors. Many pursue graduate studies in law. However, the Aboriginal community is still under represented in all areas of the legal profession. In 1998 there were about 500 Aboriginal law graduates in Canada. If the Aboriginal population were proportionately represented in the profession there would be approximately 1500 Aboriginal lawyers.

Course Description

Approximately 40 students from across Canada attend the Program every year. Women and men are represented equally and the students' ages vary from 20s to 60s.

The course is 8 weeks long and is taught by lawyers and law professors from across Canada. The subject taught is property law, which is broken down into three components: personal property, real property and Aboriginal property. The course is representative of a first year property course offered at Canadian law schools. Each week students spend 15 hours in class in addition to attending tutorials, writing seminars and plenary sessions. Optional seminars on current legal issues are also offered. Reading and writing requirements are heavy and students are expected to be prepared for classroom participation. Students are required to write mid-term practice exams as well as final exams.

The Program focuses on teaching students the skills necessary to succeed in law school. To facilitate the focus on study skills the Program offers a support structure staffed by both writing consultants and teaching assistants. Skills are emphasized in law classes, as well as in tutorials and plenary sessions which focus on writing and study skills which are essential to success in law school. The sessions evolve as the students develop their legal analysis skills.

The Program's teaching group includes Elders who provide guidance, counseling, instruction and a cultural component in the Program. Student volunteers and Teaching Assistants work with the Elders to arrange cultural events. Among Aboriginal traditions incorporated into the Program are talking circles, sweet grass ceremonies, sweat lodges, feasts or round dances.

Participants comments about the program include:

"I found the program to be very rewarding. [It] gave me a valuable advantage when I entered into law school; as well I was brought closer to the traditional values of my people. I feel it is important to bring such values into the profession of being a lawyer."

"It served as a timely cultural focus for myself and others. . . . I can easily reflect back upon the summer and be comforted in knowing that I will get through this experience intact. By this I do not mean physically or academically. I am strictly addressing the cultural and spiritual aspect."

Evaluation

At the end of the Program the teaching group assesses each student's performance. This evaluation is based on two components. First, marks received in each writing assignment and exam are assessed. Second, the student's legal analysis skills, writing skills and work habits are considered. The final grade and an overall assessment and recommendation is sent to each student and to each law school the student designates.

Several Canadian law schools recognize the property course offered by the Program for credit as a first year law class, providing the student has completed the Program at a satisfactory level. Satisfactory performance means receiving a grade of at least 60% in two of three course components. A list of schools which give credit is available from the Program.

Admission

The Program is open to all Canadian students of Aboriginal ancestry whether they are status or non-status Indian, Metis or Inuit, providing they have been admitted, conditionally or unconditionally, to a law school. Law schools may admit students through a general admissions category on the basis of grade point average and Law School Admission Test (LSAT) score; or, because inequities result from strict application of these criteria, law schools also admit students through a discretionary admissions category. The discretionary category considers various additional factors such as work experience, age and background. Aboriginal students may be accepted on the condition that they successfully complete the Program of Legal Studies for Native People.

A Saskatchewan Human Rights Commission Order permits restriction of enrollment to Aboriginal students.

Information about the Native Law Centre may be obtained by writing:

Native Law Centre

101 Diefenbaker Place

University of Saskatchewan

Saskatoon, Saskatchewan

S7N 5B8

(306) 966-6189

Fax: (306) 966-6207 www.usask.ca/nativelaw"

Minority Representation In Law School - The Disabled

For many "Law School Bound" students the first step in applying to law school is taking the LSAT. The LSAT is administered under severe time constraints. Time constraints do pose a problem for people experiencing various kinds of physical disabilities. In fact, Law Services has been sued, for failing to provide sufficient time to do the test.

On December 7, 1999 the Associated Press reported that the Civil Rights Division of the U.S. Department of Justice filed a lawsuit against LSAC. The suit alleged that LSAC violated the Americans with Disabilities Act when it denied four people with physical disabilities, including cerebral palsy and juvenile rheumatoid arthritis, extra time on the test. The grounds for the lawsuit are described by the AP as follows:

"The disabilities law requires private firms and organizations that give admissions test for postsecondary schooling to offer those exams in a place and manner that will accurately reflect the applicant's ability and aptitude for the training or career they seek rather than reflecting the person's disability. Adjusting the time for the test is a common modification for the disabled, the government said."

The Department of Justice lawsuit appears to be very similar to the lawsuit launched by Christina Helden, a Hamilton, Ontario woman with Lupus, who has also sued LSAC. Ms. Helden's statement of claim alleged that:

"The medical opinion stated that the Plaintiff needed three things to be fairly tested, namely:

a) More time to write each LSAT module;

b) Short breaks in between each module;

c) An acknowledgement her illness qualified her for special accommodation.

The defendants refused the most important of the three, namely, more time to write the LSAT modules. They did so without reason."

LSAC's procedure for dealing with requests for special accommodation may be found on their web site at www.LSAC.org. These lawsuits (particularly the one from the Department of Justice) are sure to be a public relations nightmare for LSAC. I expect they will force LSAC to rethink their procedures.

Minorities And Bar Admission

It is not enough for minorities to graduate from law school. They must also be admitted to the bar. There has been discrimination with respect to both who can practice law and the treatment of minorities who can practice law within the profession itself.

Native Canadians And Bar Admission

Discrimination can exist in both purpose and effect. The legal profession no longer has a purpose of discriminating against minority groups. However, laws and procedures can have the effect of discriminating against certain groups. The Bar Admission ceremony used to require applicants take an oath of allegiance to the Queen. The following two articles illustrate how this requirement has discriminated against Native Canadians in its effect.

Mohawk law student plans court challenge of oath of allegiance

"A member of the Mohawk Nation studying law in Ontario is going to court to avoid having to pledge allegiance to the Queen before being called to the bar.

In a statement of claim to be filed in the Ontario Supreme Court today, Patricia Monture says that, as a member of a sovereign people, the Mohawk Nation, she should not have to swear an oath to a foreign monarch.

The oath of allegiance reads: "You do swear that you will be faithful and bear true allegiance to her Majesty Queen Elizabeth the Second, her heirs and successors according to law. So help you God."

Anyone who refuses the pledge is not admitted to the bar and cannot practice law in Ontario.

Ms Monture's claim says the demand for such a pledge violates her rights under the Constitution Act of 1982, which recognizes aboriginal rights, and that it also violates the Charter of Rights and Freedoms.

"The whole concept of an oath is offensive to me," Ms Monture said in a telephone interview from Kingston, Ont. "In my culture, we do not distrust people and make them swear to tell the truth. My people carry an eagle's feather to symbolize that they will tell the truth."

Ms Monture graduated from Queen's University law School in May and plans to pursue a master's degree at Osgoode Hall in the fall. She expects to be called to the bar in about two years.

"I'm taking legal action because I want to know now if it's worth articling. If I lose this case, I will not practice law," she said.

She said that while her fight may appear trivial, it could have important ramifications if the court upholds her claim.

"This case has the potential to be very important because the courts can finally recognize that aboriginal people should be judged by different standards because we are different cultures and nations... Our sovereignty has been recognized through treaties and customs and we have never given it up," Ms Monture said.

She said the Canadian legal system is inherently racist and oppresses natives. Her case is a way of "taking on the system in a positive way," something she hopes to do in her legal career by working for change from within.

"The concepts of crime and punishment are alien to aboriginal people but, because law is the major hurdle we must jump to succeed, I have chosen to practice law in your culture," Ms Monture said.

Her lawyer, Ronald Price of Queen's University, said the lawsuit is "not a run-of-the-mill civil liberties case. The sovereignty issue is at the heart of this case."

The defendants, the Attorney-General of Ontario and the Law Society of Upper Canada, have 20 days to respond to the claim."

Reprinted courtesy Torstar syndication services.

To it's credit the Law Society abolished the oath to the Queen requirement. But, as the following account demonstrates, the decision was far from unanimous.

November 14, 1991

The Toronto Star

Lawyers scrapping oath to Queen

Lisa Priest

The Law Society of Upper Canada has voted to stop swearing the oath of allegiance to the Queen.

Last night's vote follows an impassioned speech by Darrell Doxtdator, a lawyer of Iroquois heritage, who spoke of the struggle of his ancestors and his allegiance to Mother Earth.

"It's one small step towards attaining equity in the legal profession," said Doxtdator, 29, adding that he refused to swear the oath when he was called to the bar in the spring.

Doxtdator told about 100 people at the law society's annual meeting that he isn't anti-British or disrespectful of the Queen; he just sees himself as her ally, not her subject.

The society is the governing body of Ontario's lawyers and is responsible for their education, licensing, supervision and discipline.

In a voice frequently broken with emotion, Doxtdator said his great uncle, Tom Longboat, fought in World War I and was declared missing in action three times before finally being declared dead.

"His wife remarried and he came back to find his life had been disrupted greatly," he said. Another uncle lost his eye in a mortar attack in Holland during World War II.

Despite the losses of Indian lives, "we were not given war veterans' allowance or (government-funded) funerals," he said, adding that it was only this Remembrance Day that the heroic war efforts of First Nations members were recognized.

The stirring speech touched off an hour-long debate.

Ken Harris of Mississauga said that, as a member of the Royal Canadian Air Force, he swore the oath of allegiance to Her Majesty with "great pride."

He said dropping the oath would be "tearing down what I consider to be my culture, and my heritage."

But Graeme Mew, who described himself as a British citizen, said: "It's not necessary to swear this oath to discharge one's abilities as a solicitor and barrister."

Last year, the New Democrats removed the Queen from the oath taken by police, causing a public-relations headache for Premier Bob Rae.

"(The law society's vote) just boggles my mind," said John Aimers, dominion chairperson of the Monarchist League of Canada.

"I'm disgusted," he said.

Reprinted courtesy Torstar syndication services.

Post Bar Admission - The Actual Practice of Law

Minorities, Equality In Employment And Career Opportunities

Although bar admission is a tremendous achievement and a worthy goal, it merely signals the beginning of one's legal career. For most newly admitted lawyers, admission to the bar, marks the beginning of a search for employment as a lawyer or (in the case of those who create their firms) a search for clients. Tribunals like the Ontario Human Rights Commission exist (in part) to combat discrimination in the employment market. The following comments by Mr. Michael Baxter, demonstrate that minorities continue to be excluded from desirable opportunities in the legal profession.

"The year is 1998. We approach the next millennium. Do black lawyers still have a problem gaining access to Bay Street firms? Many Bay Street lawyers would deny that a problem ever existed. But they would go on to say that, even if one did exist in the past, today's black lawyers have as good an opportunity as their white counterparts to practise on Bay Street.

Here is the reality. Based on the 1997 Canadian Law List, there are about 23 Bay Street firms in Toronto. These 23 firms represent a total of about 3,117 lawyers. Of these 3,117 Bay Street lawyers, about 20 are black. This represents six-tenths of one percent! Only one of those 3,117 Bay Street lawyers is a black partner. One black partner among 23 firms and over 3,000 lawyers. Is there an access problem? You need not be a rocket scientist to figure it out."

-Michael Baxter - 'Black Bay Street Lawyers And Other Oxymora"
The complete text of Mr. Baxter's insightful article is reproduced in its entirety at the end of this chapter.

Discrimination Based On Disability

David Lepofsky is a lawyer with the Constitutional Law And Policy Division of the Ontario Ministry of the Attorney General. He is one of the finest Constitutional Law lawyers in the country. He is also blind. As a part of an address in the Call To The Bar Ceremony he made the following point:

"Let me tell you just a bit about Canada's disabled population. This group is a large and substantial minority, numbering between 10 and 15 percent of the total population. It suffers from intense systematic exclusion from the mainstream of Canadian life, reflected for example in unemployment rates among employable-aged disabled persons of up to 50 to 80 percent - a figure usually seen in the populations of third world countries."

As Mr. Lepofsky makes clear, the disabled constitute a significant percentage of our society. There are many forms of disabilities. Each form will pose a special challenge for the disabled individual. These challenges have manifested themselves in the law admissions process, bar admission and the practise of law.

Disabilities And Practice Of Law - It Is Possible!

The following two perspectives are proof positive that the disabled can achieve extraordinary things in the legal profession! It is possible!!

Technology boon — and bother — for deaf lawyer

donalee Moulton

Henry Vlug is a lawyer. He's also deaf.

In many ways modern technology is helping him serve his clients better, work with colleagues more efficiently and conduct research quickly and conveniently. However, the full promise of technology has not yet been attained.

For me, technology is both a blessing and a curse, Mr. Vlug told The Lawyers' Weekly in an e-mail interview.

One of the first major technological advances to help deaf people communicate was the TDD/TTY, or telecommunications device for the deaf. Little more than a decade ago the Canadian Radio and Telecommunications Commission ruled that telephone companies in this country had to offer TDD services for the deaf community.

This involved establishing relay centres where an operator could act as intermediary between a speaking person and a deaf person. The operator types into a TDD/TTY machine what the speaking person says and then relays the deaf person's response, which they have typed into their home or office TDD machine. It can be a time consuming process but it has provided — for the first time — deaf people with the opportunity to speak with friends, family and colleagues around the world.

"The phone relay services allow me to make and receive phone calls just like anyone else," said Mr. Vlug, who practices deaf law part time in Vancouver.

"But," he added, "there is quite a bit of extra effort involved and I have found that most hearing lawyers avoid using it if they can — they will fax and even e-mail me instead."

In addition, the relay service is not that effective in handling the voice mail systems that many lawyers now have. This newer technology came after the development of the TTD/TTY and relay system.

"It's a pain using it so I find myself avoiding using the relay service more and more too," said Mr. Vlug.

Surprisingly, he noted, very little communication with other lawyers is currently done through the Internet. However, he does conduct some business with non-lawyers this way. Mr. Vlug, for example, uses the Internet to undertake research for advocacy groups.

But e-mail, in particular, does hold out great promise for deaf individuals.

"E-mail has absolutely revolutionized the world for deaf people," Jamie MacDougall, an associate professor of psychology at McGill University and president of the Canadian Deafness Research and Training Institute in Montreal, said in an interview.

"There's a tremendous social experience going on," he added. "It really is an exciting time for the deaf."

It is also business as usual. For Mr. Vlug that means using a state-of-the-art TTY setup, which includes a computer modem that can handle TTY calls, as well as modem calls.

"Theoretically," he pointed out, "anyone with a modem would be able to call me direct without using the relay service but no one has done so yet."

As well, he noted, "my modem should also be able to handle all my faxes. I tried to have it do so for a while but it simply could not handle it so I added a smart ring feature to my phone services and a Brother multi function machine to do my printing, faxing, copying etc."

Mr. Vlug, who does not have any secretarial or clerical help, does all his own typing and bookkeeping. It's not that difficult, he said, thanks to computer software programs such as Word Perfect and Quickbooks.

Deafness is becoming more common in North America, especially as the population ages. One in 1000 people have profound sensory neural deafness but approximately one in 10 people have a hearing problem, in particular, the elderly.

"A lot of people are getting older; a lot of people are going to lose their hearing," said Mr. MacDougall.

But there are more modern advances on the way. Closed captioning, for example, has allowed individuals, especially older people with a hearing problem, to continue enjoying television. But closed captioning may also be an option for continuing legal education programs, especially distance education.

Likewise real-time video enables business to be conducted by individuals in two different — and often distant — locations. If an interpreter was on hand in one location it would enhance efficiency while reducing costs. It would also open doors that, at present, are just slightly ajar.

But then opening doors is what technology is all about. Just ask Henry Vlug.

Reprinted with permission of the author.

Computer revolution key for blind lawyers

Norman MacInnes

TORONTO-It was not unusual for blind people to practise law before the advent of computers, "but the technology has facilitated an absolute explosion in doing it," says David Lepofsky.

"The point is, we could do it back then," he told The Lawyers Weekly. "What this has done is not make it go from impossible to possible, but from possible to even more possible."

Mr. Leposfsky, who had partial sight in one eye as a child but was completely blind by the time he went to law school, is counsel with the criminal appeals section of the Office of Crown Law at Ontario's Ministry of the Attorney General in Toronto. He has practised civil litigation, constitutional and administrative law, and has also served as co-head of the Public Law Section of the Ontario Bar Admission Course.

Rapid advances in technology-most within the last ten years-have enabled him to practise more effectively, efficiently and independently, said Mr. Lepofsky.

He cited developments such as personal computers (PCs), speech synthesizers, on-line legal information databases, document scanning, the vastly expanded storage capacity of hard drives, laptop computers, and the growth in the number of other lawyers who use PCs.

The key technology for Mr. Lepofsky is a PC equipped with a screen-reading program and a speech synthesizer. The computer reads aloud the words that appear on the screen.

"You buy two different things," he explained. "You buy the screen-reading program and the speech synthesizer separately and then you run them together."

The speech synthesizer is the hardware-"a little box, about the size of a paperback book, that you plug into the serial port." The screen-reading program is the software.

"Think of the [speech synthesizer] as the vocal chords, and the screen-reading program is the brain," he suggested.

Mr. Lepofsky was one of the first lawyers to use a PC and to do much of his own word processing.

"For me, word processing is important not just for the convenience of correcting, but it's an accessible way to read and write and produce something in printed form," he said. "Now I can type a factum, and edit and proofread it.

"Also, because we are all now using the same software, I can now give it to my secretary, and other lawyers can give me stuff they want me to read on disk and the computer will read it back to me."

The increasing availability of legal documents in electronic form has helped to put him on a more nearly equal footing with sighted lawyers.

No longer does he have to wait for someone to read the documents aloud and make a tape recording.

"When I do an appeal, my secretary will contact the court reporter and try to get the transcript on disk, if possible," he said.

"If that doesn't work, we use a document scanner and optical character reader [OCR] software."

The OCR can also be used to convert all kinds of printed information-textbooks, cases, journal articles-into digital form, thus making it accessible to him. Mr. Lepofsky pointed to the rapid growth in online legal databases as another development that has helped blind lawyers.

"For sighted people, QL [Quick-Law] is an enhanced research tool. For me, it's an online legal library."

"I'll dial in there and if there's a decision that I want to read, I'll download it and the computer reads it [aloud] to me," he said.

"It used to be," Mr. Lepofsky recalled, "when nobody was using QL much, and the few who were weren't very adept at it, if the Supreme Court of Canada released a major Charter decision, the headnote would be faxed in, and then you'd have to wait a day for the decision to arrive in the office, and if it was 100 pages you'd have to wait another day for it to be photocopied and circulated-and then I would have to wait until somebody allocated the resources to having it read aloud and recorded on a tape recorder."

"Now," he continued, "a decision comes out at 10:30 in the morning, I have it downloaded by 2:30 in the afternoon, and I can have read the headnote as quickly as anybody, and have blasted through the decision and be giving responses and feedback on it very quickly."

The exponential growth in the storage capacity of hard drives and the advent of laptop computers have enabled Mr. Lepofsky to work portably-and therefore more productively.

He is able to go to court with all the necessary transcripts, factums, statutes and caselaw stored on his computer.

This helps to level the playing field, he said. "A sighted person can bring all the materials he or she needs, can open a book, or go upstairs and look it up in the library. For me, it's all on my computer."

A laptop with earphones also enables him to make better use of his time. "If you were flying to Ottawa to argue an appeal, you'd bring cases on the plane to read-well, so can I.

"If I'm in court and we're on the list the whole day, and we're not reached until three in the afternoon-what do sighted lawyers do? They'll bring some of their work and they'll sit and read it while they're waiting to be heard."

"Until I had a portable computer," said Mr. Lepofsky, "that was dead time for me. I can now sit in the court with my laptop and, if another case is being argued, I'm 'reading' and writing and preparing. With earphones, I'm not bothering anybody."

"So really, it's enabled me to do what sighted people do to make effective use of their time."

The technology available to blind lawyers has changed dramatically in the last 15 years.

When Mr. Lepofsky attended law school from 1976 to 1979, he used a tape recorder and a typewriter. He relied on others to read aloud and tape-record casebooks and other written materials.

He dictated his lecture notes with a microphone into a tape recorder.

"There were two types of people at law school," Mr. Lepofsky recalled. "There were those who hated me because it was distracting, and those who loved me because it gave them what the prof said on the rebound."

At graduate school (Harvard, 1981-1982, where he obtained an LL.M.), he used a court reporter's steno mask, so that he could tape lecture notes without distracting others.

He acquired his first PC in June 1983. "It was a 64K machine with a walloping five-megabyte hard drive-that was huge." Mr. Lepofsky remarked wryly.

Computers were of limited utility to a lawyer at that time. There were incompatibility problems (it seemed "every computer used a different language"), and because few other lawyers used computers, Mr. Lepofsky couldn't give them documents on disk.

As well, few legal materials were available in electronic form.

But "for me, it was a huge breakthrough," said Mr. Lepofsky. "That was the first time I could compose and read back what I had written on my own."

The next breakthrough occurred in 1987, "when I got my first IBM PC. It was an XT, using WordPerfect 4.2."

"For the first time, I could give a document to my secretary [on disk], she could change it, and I could read it again," said Mr. Lepofsky.

By the time Bob Fenton, who practises civil litigation at McCarthy Tetrault in Toronto, entered law school in 1989, technology was considerably more advanced.

Mr. Fenton, who has always been blind, used an XT-level computer equipped with a speech synthesizer during first-year law school.

In second year, he graduated to a 386-level PC. He also started to use a scanner to scan textbooks and casebooks, although he was still listening to books recorded on tape.

But "by third year, I was not using tapes at all," Mr. Fenton recalled. "I was scanning everything."

Not only had the accuracy of scanners with OCR software evolved sufficiently to make this practical, but the electronic storage capacity of computer hard drives was by this time large enough to store the prodigious quantity of reading material generated by law school courses.

It helped, of course, that he did not need to store graphic images, which take up a lot of spaces on a hard drive.

For a blind person, a key advantage of the legal profession is that most law is expressed in the form of words-and words can be written or spoken.

Mr. Lepofsky agreed that the "huge strides forward" in the speed and accuracy of scanners in recent years have helped him to practise as effectively as sighted lawyers.

"I used to say categorically that I would not do a heavy paper litigation matter when I was doing civil work," said Mr. Lepofsky, "although I could work on it with a team. Because of this technology, that has become less of a concern than it used to be.

"I'm talking about a perception I had in 1982 versus 1997," he noted.

"Because in 1982, if somebody produced two boxes of documents, you would have to have a sighted person sit and read them all to you or read them onto a tape. And then you wouldn't be able to search through them-you'd have no search capability."

Now he can scan documents into the computer and use the computer's searching tools to find critical information.

A comparatively minor but useful development is the ability to send a fax directly from his computer, which has enabled him to perform "a very sighted activity," said Mr. Lepofsky.

"A sighted person can print a document then walk over to a fax machine and slap it down. I can print a document, but I can't readily walk over and put it on a fax machine. However, I can fax from my laptop or my desktop."

But e-mail has become a preferred method of communication, one that has become more useful as more lawyers acquire e-mail addresses and learn how to use it.

Where a sighted person might say, "Please fax it to me," Mr. Lepofsky instead asks, "Please e-mail it to me."

Mr. Fenton finds the Internet an increasingly important resource, giving blind lawyers access to information that was previously difficult or expensive to obtain.

"I can log into the Internet and get newspaper stories, Supreme Court of Canada decisions [from the Supreme Court of Canada Web site], the Rules of Professional Conduct from the Law Society [of Upper Canada] Web site, American cases, House of Lords cases-I can get all that stuff for free," he said.

As well, he noted, real audio and video legal resources from the United States and the United Kingdom are available on the Internet.

Norman MacInnes - The Lawyers Weekly

The Future Of Discrimination

Times are changing. Perhaps not as fast as many would like, but discrimination is diminishing. The diminishment is not, however, because the legal profession (or society as a whole) is more enlightened or tolerant. The reason is that many law firms are realizing that it costs them money to discriminate. The fact is that so called "minority groups" have substantial buying power and they need legal services. Furthermore, many of these groups are demanding legal services from lawyers who speak their language and understand their culture. Therefore, it is in the interests of law firms for their lawyers to include representatives from as many different groups as possible. By including minority lawyers, law firms will attain the language skills and cultural fluency that are necessary to do business in the 21st century. A fascinating example of this principle at work appeared in the July 2000 issue of Canadian Lawyer magazine. In an article called "Soaring Like An Eagle Through A Glass Ceiling", Bill Rogers describes how the Toronto firm of Aird & Berlis created a practice group composed exclusively of aboriginal lawyers. It is a fascinating article and I recommend it to anyone interested in this issue. The theme of the article is that:

"With a growing entrepreneurial demographic and billions of dollars of land claims flowing into aboriginal communities, law firms are starting to see an unfolding market for legal services - but one with cultural sensitivities. In some cases, these client concerns can only be satisfied when the lawyers themselves are Aboriginal Peoples - and that has led some forward-looking firms to create practice groups composed exclusively of such lawyers."

The article profiles the practice of the four young aboriginal lawyers who compose the "Aboriginal" law practice group at Aird & Berlis in Toronto.

Conclusion

Minority access to and representation in the legal profession has come a long way. We will close with the comments of Professor Vern Krishna writing in his role as Treasurer of the Law Society.

"As the body which regulates Ontario's almost 34,000 lawyers, our mandate is to govern the profession in the public interest. As the Governor General pointed out, to do this properly, we must do all we can to help create a profession as diverse, as reflective of the society it serves as possible. Only then can we achieve a legal system truly accessible to all. I am proud of the Law Society's efforts and of the strides made by our profession in recent years. I am equally proud that few of us intend to rest on our laurels. Despite perceptions to the contrary, the face of the legal profession is changing.

Over the past decade, we have seen greater diversity within our ranks, a diversity expanded each year as new lawyers are called to the Bar. For each of the past three years alone, women called to the Bar have progressively outnumbered men. In October 2002, 54 per cent of those called to the Bar were women.

As a law professor and as head of the Law Society, I have seen these changes first-hand. For example, law year nearly 17 per cent of those students enrolled in our Bar Admission Course were visible minorities and roughly 53 per cent of those in the program were women."

- Professor and Treasurer of the Law Society Vern Krishna, Q.C., FCGA - writing in the Ontario Lawyers Gazette - Spring 2003

APPENDIX

We will conclude the chapter with the fascinating and motivational keynote lecture given by Michael St. Patrick Baxter at the University Of Western Ontario. Enjoy it!

BLACK BAY STREET LAWYERS AND OTHER OXYMORA

MICHAEL ST. PATRICK BAXTER*

I am honoured to have been invited to address the students and faculty at Western. It has been almost 19 years since I graduated from these halls. But the memories are vivid. I remember, as if it were yesterday, my first-year moot for Professor Rayner. I remember Professor Hunter's inspiring address on the last day of our Torts class. I remember Dean Johnston's 8:30 a.m. Company Law classes. I even remember Professor McLaren's assignment in first-year Contracts to write an essay on "consideration." The truth be told, I also remember being a bit of a procrastinator. By the way, Professor McLaren, about that consideration essay, I will have it done by this Friday!

I also remember being the only black person in my class. Oddly enough, I do not recall being consciously aware of that fact until the day I graduated. After the commencement exercises, a classmate, a professor and I were looking at the class portrait hanging on the second floor of the Law School. My classmate, who, by the way, is now a good friend, laughingly remarked: "you certainly add colour to the class." That was the first time I actually remember myself focusing on my race in law school.

A. BAY STREET CIRCA 1979

The year was 1979. After graduation, I articled for a Bay Street firm. I use the terms "Bay Street firm" and "Bay Street lawyer" to refer to large corporate law firms and the lawyers in such firms, wherever in Canada they may be located. Although there are exceptions, law firms of at least 50 lawyers are generally regarded as Bay Street firms. Bay Street firms, then and now, are recognized to be the elite of corporate law firms.

I was one of the firm's six articling students. I was the only black articling student at the firm. In fact, with the exception of a black woman in accounting, I was the only black person in the entire firm. Moreover, during my articling year, I did not encounter another black lawyer or articling student on Bay Street.

Of the six articling students at my firm, three were asked to return to the firm as associates. I was not among them. I sought employment opportunities at over 50 Toronto law firms. Surely, my academic credentials and my Bay Street experience (and the photograph of my smiling face, which appeared on my resume) would yield many opportunities. They yielded one interview at a small firm, but no job offer.

Obviously, my credentials were not good enough. Or so I believed. Determined to overcome this, I worked hard to finish in the top one percent of the Ontario Bar Admission Course. I served as a law clerk to the Chief Justice of Ontario. I published a law review article. I received an LL.M. from Harvard Law School. And I took a one-year position at a prestigious American law firm to get some cutting-edge legal experience.

The year was 1984. I was halfway through my year at Covington & Burling. I was confident that now I was ready for Bay Street. I sent my resume (this time sans photograph) to the best of the Toronto Bay Street firms. The response was immediate. I was invited to fly up for interviews, all expenses paid. I was surprised when my interviews yielded only one job offer. Still, I was not too disappointed because the offer came from a firm that was at the top of my list and which I regarded as the best corporate firm in Toronto.

Shortly after I received the offer, I learned that one of my Harvard professors had recommended me for a teaching appointment to the Dean at Harvard Law School. I was flattered by the recommendation and was asked by the professor not to make any commitments until I had heard from the Dean. I informed the Toronto firm of this and was told that they were impressed by the development and that it would not be a problem.

A few weeks later, I was sitting in my office at Covington & Burling when I received a telephone call from one of the senior partners at the firm from which I had received the offer. He advised me that the partnership was reviewing its needs and had decided that they could not make me an offer. I was speechless! Somehow, I managed to find the words to reply that the firm had already made me an offer. I inquired if what he meant was that the offer was being revoked. He confirmed this. I was shocked beyond belief! When I asked, "Why?" he simply repeated that it was the result of the firm's reviewing its needs. I inquired as to whether the offer had been made without authority or whether the firm could no longer support an additional lawyer. He said that neither was the case.

I was so confused by the entire situation that I actually called the senior partner several days later to see if he could better explain the decision to me. I never received a better explanation.

B. THE LESSON

That experience was a pivotal one for me. At the time, I believed that ability transcended race. I felt that race simply was not a factor in my career. I believed that I could achieve whatever I wanted if I were prepared to work hard enough. And I was. I was convinced that whatever failures I encountered were simply personal failures that reflected the limits of my ability.

The experience was the beginning of my own Epiphany. It started a long, difficult process of self-doubt, reappraisal, reflection and insight. The process ended almost a decade later, when, in 1993, I was invited to participate in a panel discussion at the Delos Davis Law Guild conference in Toronto. The subject was "Breaking Through the Glass Door - The Firm Hurdles." I was preparing to give my usual talk - colour is irrelevant on Bay Street; all that matters on Bay Street is ability; if you work hard and do good work, you will succeed. But an odd thing happened. The preparation forced me to relive my Bay Street rejection. For the first time, I came to grips with it. More importantly, for the first time I spoke about this experience to others. For me, it was a defining moment. I learned that colour is relevant on Bay Street. I learned that hard work and good work do not ensure success. I learned that my colour could be a more powerful limitation on my success than my own ability.

Many black lawyers and students have already learned these lessons. Some have heard of these lessons, but reject them. I, too, had rejected them. These were lessons that I had heard for a long time but never really believed could happen to me. I usually had been successful in my endeavors. When I had met with rejection, I refused to acknowledge that it could possibly have anything to with my colour. I had always rationalized that another candidate had even better grades or better references or better experience or better whatever. In fact, I had used rejection to redouble my efforts to make me an even stronger candidate the next time.

For the first time, I did not find my rationalizations persuasive. I was forced to come to grips with the reality that, in 1984, a "black Bay Street lawyer" was an oxymoron.

C. DO BLACK LAWYERS HAVE A PROBLEM GAINING ACCESS TO BAY STREET FIRMS?

The year is 1998. We approach the next millennium. Do black lawyers still have a problem gaining access to Bay Street firms? Many Bay Street lawyers would deny that a problem ever existed. But they would go on to say that, even if one did exist in the past, today's black lawyers have as good an opportunity as their white counterparts to practice on Bay Street.

Here is the reality. Based on the 1997 Canadian Law List, there are about 23 Bay Street firms in Toronto. These 23 firms represent a total of about 3,117 lawyers. Of these 3,117 Bay Street lawyers, about 20 are black. This represents six-tenths of one percent of the Toronto Bay Street lawyers. Six-tenths of one percent! Only one of those 3,117 Bay Street lawyers is a black partner. One black partner among 23 firms and over 3,000 lawyers. Is there an access problem? You do not need to be a rocket scientist to figure it out.

Still, some say that those numbers simply indicate that black lawyers are not interested in Bay Street. Indeed, you will hear that explanation from some of the few black lawyers on Bay Street. Others will say that the numbers simply reflect the scarcity of qualified black law graduates.

I reject both of these explanations. They are the same tired excuses that were offered by Bay Street in the '60s when Jews were excluded and, more recently, when women were excluded. These explanations let us feel more comfortable with the status quo and do not threaten our idealistic view of an egalitarian profession.

The uncomfortable reality, however, is that, despite a substantial increase in the number of black students attending law school over the last 20 years, blacks still constitute only an insignificant percentage of Bay Street lawyers. We continue to be overwhelmingly and disproportionately concentrated in small practices and government jobs. A 1992 survey of black law students, articling students and recently called lawyers found that a majority of the respondents believed that Bay Street is effectively closed to them.

I am reminded of a remark by billionaire investor Warren Buffett last year at the annual meeting of his company, Berkshire Hathaway. Buffett is widely regarded as the most successful investor in modern times. In commenting on his success, Buffett remarked that he had won the "ovarian lottery." By that, Buffett explained, he meant he was born white and male in a society where women and minorities are put at a disadvantage.

That blacks face a barrier to access on Bay Street is clearly reflected in the relative absence of black lawyers in Bay Street firms. That there is a problem with access has been almost universally denied by Bay Street. And, until recently, it has been largely ignored by the rest of the profession.

Just last year someone stated that there was "systemic discrimination and inequality within the legal profession." Who do you think made that charge? A civil-rights activist? A civil-liberties organization? A feminist? If you guessed any of those, you would be wrong. It was the venerable Law Society of Upper Canada. In its Bicentennial Report, the Law Society of Upper Canada acknowledged the existence of systemic discrimination and inequality within the legal profession. Moreover, the Law Society accepted the responsibility to take the lead in eliminating discrimination and racism in the profession.

When an institution as traditional, as conservative and as Bay Street as the Law Society makes a ground-breaking statement like that, we have to sit up and take notice. Those of us in denial have to open our eyes to reality. I commend the Law Society. But I regret that it took 200 years to reach this milestone.

D. WHY SHOULD YOU CARE?

Why should anyone care if black lawyers face barriers to entry on Bay Street? As a black person, it is obvious that I should care. However, if I were white, I may be wondering "What does that have to do with me?" I may be asking myself, "Why should I care?" The best I can do is to suggest some reasons everyone should care.

First, Bay Street firms represent the elite of our profession; therefore, we ought to care not only whether, but why, any group is systematically less likely to gain admission to this select Bar.

Second, corporate clients are increasingly aware of the value of diversity. They have long recognized that their leadership ranks can no longer consist exclusively of white males. Corporate clients increasingly are expecting their law firms to reflect diversity. By the year 2006, visible minorities are expected to make up one-sixth of Canada's population. By the year 2005, it is projected that women and minority men will make up 62 percent of the work force of the United States. In this age of globalization, maintaining a glass barrier that impedes the progress of blacks or other minorities simply will not be good for business.

Third, many Canadians value diversity. Our cultural mosaic has long been celebrated as one of the hallmarks of Canada. Bay Street firms that continue to be homogeneous may find themselves at a competitive disadvantage with their more diverse peers in law school recruiting.

Fourth, all Canadians would benefit from the easing of social and professional tension that would accompany a leveling of the playing field in the legal profession.

Finally, as lawyers, we are members of a profession that has been a staunch advocate of the principles of nondiscrimination and equal opportunity. We have always viewed the practice of law as more than just a business. If we, as a profession, continue to be apologists for discrimination, then our profession's claim to the high moral and ethical ground of society will be seriously undermined.

E. SHOULD BLACK LAWYERS BE INTERESTED IN BAY STREET?

Why should black lawyers be interested in Bay Street? For some, Bay Street holds no allure. Still, I think it would be a mistake for black lawyers to foreclose Bay Street practice. There are many reasons for this.

First, Bay Street firms by virtue of their client base are centers of power and influence. More black lawyers need to gain access to these centers or forever we will be on the outside looking in.

Second, membership in these firms automatically imbues one with credibility. Right or wrong, that is the reality. This is not to say that one cannot achieve similar credibility as a small-firm practitioner. But if a Bay Street firm can offer us an advantage in this area, why not take it?

Third, Bay Street firms perpetuate themselves. The tenure of a small firm usually is tied to the longevity of its principals; however, a Bay Street firm is an institution with a life of its own. If black lawyers continue to be rarities in such firms, the future will hold more of the same.

Fourth, Bay Street practice generally will expose a lawyer to more professionals than will practice in a small firm. Because of the size and nature of Bay Street practice, the Bay Street lawyer has a greater opportunity to work with more lawyers, bankers, accountants and corporate executives than a lawyer in a small-firm practice. The importance of this should not be underestimated. One reason blacks have difficulty gaining access to Bay Street firms is that the Bay Streeters who make the hiring decisions have not had much professional or personal experience with blacks. As a result, their actions and decisions are influenced by black stereotypes. Greater interaction of black lawyers with other professionals will assist in dispelling these stereotypes.

Finally, even if one later chooses small-firm or government practice, the Bay Street credential will assist mobility. It is far easier to move from Bay Street to a small firm or to government, than the reverse.

F. WHY DO BLACK LAWYERS HAVE A PROBLEM GAINING ACCESS TO BAY STREET FIRMS?

Why blacks have a problem entering Bay Street firms is subject to debate. My own view is that the problem is attributable, in large part, to the fact that the people who, historically, have controlled the portals of the Bay Street firms generally have suffered from a lack of personal experience with blacks. These "gatekeepers" generally have had little interaction with blacks. Indeed, their firms may never have had a black lawyer. Their interaction with blacks is usually limited to blacks in subordinate positions. Without the benefit of substantial personal interaction with blacks, the gatekeepers tend to rely on the stereotypes so readily available through the media and have a tendency to make conscious or unconscious assumptions about black lawyers based on these stereotypes. To understand the effect of this, one needs to examine the recruiting process.

The recruiting process of Bay Street firms can be divided into two stages: the "credential" stage and the "interview" stage. In the credential stage, the firm evaluates an applicant's objective credentials, such as grades and law school status. In the interview stage, the firm makes a subjective determination about the applicant's personality and fit.

In the credential stage, it is difficult for Bay Street firms, today, to discriminate. A firm is unlikely, for example, to refuse interviews to black applicants whose credentials are superior to those of the white applicants selected for interviews. Still, even well-credentialed black applicants often are at a disadvantage compared to their white colleagues in the credential stage of the recruiting process. Why?

We all are products of our environment. From an early age, we are bombarded through the media with stereotypical images of blacks and myths of black intellectual inferiority. As a result, we tend to see each other through assumptions and predispositions that are connected to race. These "race-coloured glasses" are so subtle that most of us seldom are conscious we wear them. Bay Street interviewers are no exception. They tend to have certain conscious or unconscious stereotypes about blacks. These stereotypes are reinforced by the relative scarcity of blacks in positions of power and prestige, and the virtual absence of black lawyers on Bay Street. As a result, Bay Street interviewers tend to question the credentials of black applicants more than those of white applicants.

For example, a black applicant at the top of his or her class has a greater likelihood than his or her white counterpart that an interviewer will probe the difficulty of the black applicant's courses or even question his or her professors to determine whether the black applicant deserved the high standing.

I recall a job interview I had years ago at the Ontario Securities Commission. The interviewer, a graduate of Harvard Law School, seemed genuinely surprised that I was attending Harvard. We had an exchange that went something like this:

Interviewer: So, you're attending Harvard?

Baxter: Yes, I am.

Interviewer: You must have done well at Western to go to Harvard?

Baxter: I wasn't the gold medalist, but I did well.

Interviewer: I suppose that you must have gotten a lot of A's?

Now, the interviewer had my resume, which disclosed that I had made the Dean's Honour List at Western, articled on Bay Street, finished in the top one percent of the Bar Admission

Course, clerked for the Chief Justice of Ontario, won a Canada Council doctoral fellowship and published an article on derivative actions in the McGill Law Journal. Still, he probed to satisfy himself that I had earned the grades to go to Harvard. It became clear to me that the interviewer was having difficulty accepting the fact that I could have performed well enough to gain admission to Harvard. Consequently, he felt the need to probe behind my credentials to see if I had earned them. The fact that I was at Harvard was running smack into his assumption, conscious or unconscious, that blacks are unable to perform well enough to get into Harvard on the basis of merit.

Passing the credential stage of the recruiting process does not land you on Bay Street. Once an applicant advances past the credential stage, the law firm's hiring decision will be driven largely by its assessment of the applicant's "personality and fit." This occurs during the interview stage of the recruiting process.

At the interview stage, Bay Street firms are less inclined to base their decisions on objective criteria. Moreover, because this stage of the recruiting process is not observable, firms can act more or less with impunity. Indeed, firms generally will not review writing samples or ask substantive questions during the interview to test legal knowledge and analytical ability. Instead, the focus at the interview stage is primarily on whether the applicant will "fit" at the firm. Although firm-fit is important in any hiring decision, Bay Street firms tend to emphasize personality and fit in the interview stage to the virtual exclusion of assessments of analytical ability and writing skill.

The emphasis on personality and fit at the interview stage disproportionately disadvantages well-credentialed black applicants who have passed the credential stage. Why? First, the interviewer's conscious or unconscious stereotypes about blacks will affect the interviewer's subjective determination of personality and fit. Second, because of the white interviewer's general lack of significant interaction with blacks, the interviewer may not feel as comfortable or connected with the black applicant as with the white applicant. As a result, in a competition between a white applicant and a black applicant, the interviewer's subjective determination, not surprisingly, may often be that the white applicant "connected" better during the interview and, consequently, would "fit" better at the firm.

Let me be clear. I do not mean to suggest that the barriers that blacks face on Bay Street are the result of intentionally racist views held by Bay Street firms. To the contrary. I have met very few people whose discriminatory actions I believe to have been the result of malice or ill will toward blacks. In my experience, discriminatory treatment usually is at the hands of basically good people who have had little experience with blacks and who let assumptions and negative stereotypes affect their conduct.

Ironically, this type of discrimination is more insidious than discrimination born from malice or ill will because it is more difficult to deal with. It does not occur in the open, where all can recognize and deal with it. It occurs behind closed doors and in private discussions, and it manifests itself in discriminatory actions that catch you when you least expect it. Indeed, in many instances, the actor is not even aware of the discriminatory basis of his or her actions.

G. ADVICE FOR BLACK LAW STUDENTS

What advice would I offer black students who seek to practice on Bay Street?

First and foremost, take advantage of your law school years to get your professors to know you. Please notice that I did not say "get to know your professors." I said "get your professors to know you." Take an active role in class discussions. Try to get research positions with your professors. Most professors are happy to act as a reference for a student. The best references, however, are from those professors who have had a substantial opportunity to know both your work and you.

Second, develop your credentials. This begins with performing to the best of your ability in law school. It may surprise some of you to learn that your academic performance in law school will follow you for the rest of your life. You cannot afford to do other than your best. If possible, try to obtain an advanced law degree, such as an LL.M., from a well-regarded school. American law schools, such as Harvard and Yale, are particularly favoured by Bay Street firms. Try to secure a judicial clerkship. An advanced law degree and a clerkship not only will burnish your credentials, but also will expose you to other professors and judges, who, if favourably impressed, will readily provide you with a strong reference.

Third, article with the best law firm available to you. Law firms are very hierarchical. It is much easier to go from a Bay Street firm to a small firm or to government than to go from a small firm or from government to Bay Street.

Fourth, find a mentor. Success on Bay Street is virtually impossible if you do not have a mentor. A good mentor will look out for you, guide you and counsel you. Most importantly, your mentor will ensure that you receive the essential training required to succeed on Bay Street. This is key. You cannot succeed on Bay Street if you have not received the necessary training. By the time an associate comes up for partnership, the associate must have acquired the necessary skills to function as a partner. The associate must have been exposed to a variety of challenging assignments that allow him or her the opportunity to develop an area of expertise, sound legal judgment and the ability to take charge of matters. Most importantly, the associate must have been exposed to clients to develop the necessary client-relations skills. Is this unique to black associates? No. It is true for all associates, regardless of colour.

The structure of Bay Street firms is somewhat like a pyramid. The firms hire a large number of law school graduates. Generally, after six to eight years, firms will admit to partnership those associates who have demonstrated the greatest potential. This process produces a pyramid-type structure because not all of the associates will make partner. A typical Bay Street firm will have a large number of associates and a much smaller number of partners. Since not all of the associates will make partner, it does not make economic sense for firms to train all of their associates. Through an informal selection process, certain associates will receive the best training. Black associates are less likely to receive the training necessary for their success - just as the barriers on Bay Street make it less likely that they will be hired in the first place.

For one thing, black associates are less likely than their white peers to find mentors who will give them demanding work and client contact, and counsel them about how to succeed at the firm. A primary reason for this is the natural affinity that we all have for people who remind us of ourselves. In other words, we all like to mentor people who remind us of ourselves. Mentors will gravitate towards associates with whom they feel most comfortable and with whom they most identify. These associates are not likely to be the black associates. Consequently, it is more difficult for black associates to form the mentoring relationships that are critical to their success on Bay Street. In addition, even in the exceedingly rare instance in which the firm has a black partner, such partner may not be quick to mentor a black associate. The black partner may believe mentoring to be unnecessary because he or she may have succeeded without such mentoring. Moreover, the black partner may fear that mentoring a black associate will be seen as race-based.

Despite the difficulties, you must find a mentor. Your success will depend on it.

Fifth, view discrimination as just another obstacle to overcome. It is out there, so you have to deal with it. Inevitably, it may lead to some rejection. Nevertheless, it is absolutely essential that you not internalize this rejection. There is a tendency to treat such rejection as representing far more than it does. For many years I took my Bay Street rejection as a shameful indication that, after all my efforts, I still lacked the "right stuff" to become a Bay Street lawyer. Only much later did I understand that the rejection was not a reflection on my ability or character. Remember, discriminatory actions are merely a reflection of the ignorance of the discriminator. Never let it lead you to question your own ability.

However, recognize that black associates face higher costs from making mistakes than their white peers. Black lawyers do not come into a firm with a presumption of competence. Instead, they come in having to prove themselves. When partners expect black associates to be mediocre or less than competent, any mistake will be seen as confirmation of this. By contrast, white associates are presumed competent in the absence of conclusive evidence to the contrary. As a result, their mistakes are more likely to be dismissed as aberrational or inexperience.

Sixth, have a passion for your work. Bay Street is a demanding and intense place to work. If you have a passion for your work, you will thrive in that environment.

Seventh, seek opportunities to grow. While some opportunities may come your way, most opportunities have to be pursued and seized. Do not wait for opportunities to land in your lap. Seek out the work, the experiences and the relationships that will best prepare you for partnership. Periodically, take stock of your experiences and evaluate your skills. Only by doing this can you ensure that you are developing as you should.

Eighth, demand the best of yourself. You are your own best rival. Measure your achievements against your potential.

Ninth, get to know your black colleagues. Some of us have a tendency to feel self-conscious when we get together with a group of our black colleagues. I think we fear that it will make us stand out even more as outsiders on Bay Street. We prefer to keep our heads down to avoid drawing race-based attention. I think we fear that Bay Street may use our cohesiveness as a group to define us by race - which, in turn, may lead to our lack of acceptance by Bay Street as "lawyers."

This is not an irrational fear. There is a tendency in society to define us as "black" first, and "lawyer" second. We simply want to be accepted as "lawyers," and not to be defined by our race. I do not want to be known as a "black lawyer." I want to be known as a "lawyer," period. I am a lawyer, who just happens to be black. My race affords me a different perspective on many things. But it does not define who I am. It is not the sum total of my existence.

Despite the risks, we should make an effort to connect with our black colleagues. There is strength in numbers. It is a good place to network. It is an even better place to share your experiences and to learn from the experience of others.

Finally, build bridges - don't burn them. While we are part of the black community, we are also part of a larger community that is not connected by race. Become an active part of that larger community rather than retreating into the relative comfort of the black community. Only by taking our place in the larger community can we eliminate the barriers that now impede our access.

Building a bridge may mean that you have to work on a relationship with a person or a firm that has discriminated against you in the past. These are the most difficult bridges to build because there is a natural tendency for us to become embittered by the experience of discrimination. It will not be easy, but I encourage you to work past any feelings of bitterness because that bridge is an important one to build. You, yourself, may never be given the opportunity to cross that bridge. But your efforts will allow others who follow an opportunity to go where you were denied. When the first person crosses your bridge, you will take as much pride in the knowledge that you have built well, as that person will take in his or her ability to make it across.

Success is not a solo endeavor. Many of us cross bridges today that were built by our predecessors. Each of you, whether knowingly or unknowingly, has taken advantage of the efforts of your predecessors. While it may be personally gratifying to believe that your success is solely the result of your own efforts, recognize that many who have gone before you have laboured to make your journey an easier one than they had.

All that being said, I would be remiss if I failed to caution you. Even if you follow my advice to the letter, it still may be virtually impossible for us to succeed on Bay Street, today, if we lack one critical quality. To succeed on Bay Street, today, a black lawyer must transcend race. What do I mean by that? You must be able to function as if oblivious to race. Moreover, it is not enough simply to act as such. You must believe it with every fibre of your being. To succeed on Bay Street, you must be able to walk into a roomful of people in which you are the only black person, yet never have the thought occur to you that you are the only black person in the room. I guarantee that that thought will occur to everyone else in the room - but it probably would not occur to the successful black Bay Street lawyer. To succeed on Bay Street, you must believe in your heart that your colour has had and will continue to have no effect on your career.

Why is this quality essential? Because if you do not possess it, you are unlikely to pass the critical personality-and-fit assessment which occurs in the interview stage of the recruiting process. If you do not possess this quality, you will be unable to signal to the Bay Street recruiters that you will "fit" at the firm. And even if you were to successfully fake this signal, your thoughts eventually will betray you during your tenure on Bay Street and will work to undermine your support at the firm.

Make no mistake, I do not counsel you to deny your race. I seek only to direct your attention to the reality that both the current structure of Bay Street recruiting and the nature of the training of Bay Street associates penalize black law graduates and lawyers who do not believe that Bay Street is colour-blind. Does this colour-blind mindset accord with reality? I wish it did. The sad truth is that virtually all people view each other through "race-coloured glasses." It is a natural result of the pervasive myths and stereotypes of blacks that exist in this society. Fortunately, the extent to which these myths and stereotypes influence one's actions will vary from person to person and is inversely related to the quality of the person's experiences with diverse people.

Is this colour-blind mindset a good thing? Ignorance is seldom a virtue. But sometimes it is easier to meet the challenges in one's life with less than complete information.

Last year, I had a conversation with a white high school friend. We were also both college and law school classmates at Western. He had read a news report of an address that I delivered in 1994 at the annual symposium of the Black Law Students Association of Canada. He said that the address made him proud of me and that he was proud to have been my classmate. I was moved.

What he said then floored me. He said that he wanted to apologize for all of the "stupid things" that went on behind my back in high school. Up until that conversation, I believed that I had had a completely race-neutral high school experience. After all, I had been on student council, played football and graduated in the top of my class. It never occurred to me that race-based things - in respect of me, of all people - could have been going on in high school.

My friend was truly remorseful and apologized - not only for himself - but said that he was apologizing for all of the others. Imagine being told something like that after 23 years.

The point of the story is simply this: one's perception may not always accord with reality. Sometimes that may be a good thing. I would not like to have known then what I know now.

H. AFTER BAY STREET

What should black lawyers do after they get to Bay Street? There is a temptation once we have gained access to Bay Street to sit back and enjoy the fruits of our labours. Having beaten the odds and arrived, we often become elitist. As a consequence of this mindset, the black Bay Street lawyer, consciously or unconsciously, may refuse or neglect to assist other black lawyers or students seeking access. He or she may deny to those who follow the benefit of his or her experience. Since today's black Bay Street lawyers may have made it without similar assistance, they may believe it to be unnecessary to those who follow. Moreover, they may fear that assisting other blacks will be seen by their white colleagues as race-based.

Having gained access to Bay Street, we must resist becoming elitist. Share your knowledge and experience with those who follow. The fact that more black lawyers, with your assistance, will become Bay Street lawyers will not diminish your achievement. Indeed, it will serve to memorialize it. Being the first black lawyer at a Bay Street firm is a substantial accomplishment. But that accomplishment will be temporary and easily forgotten if not built upon. Whatever your professional accomplishments may have been, if you leave your Bay Street firm with no more black lawyers than when you arrived, you should question whether you really have been successful.

All of us remember Jackie Robinson, the first black baseball player to play in the Major Leagues. Generations of baseball players who did not even have the opportunity to see Robinson play have benefitted from his remarkable achievement. By opening the door to other blacks, Robinson created an unforgettable legacy.

Too often we are afraid to advance another black candidate for fear of being criticized that we are doing so only because he or she is black. Learn that there is nothing wrong with supporting a black candidate in whom you believe. Everyday there are examples of groups assisting their own. For the last 200 years, the "old boys' network" has helped its own. Does anyone seriously question whether that will continue? Lift as you climb. Do not be too absorbed by your own career to extend a helping hand.

Recognize that each black lawyer is a model by which the others will be judged. In a world full of stereotypes, there are those who will be quick to judge the worst in each of us as typical of all of us, but slow to attribute the best in each of us to the betterment of the rest of us.

We also are role models for the black lawyers who follow us. Our success gives added confidence to our successors. Do not underestimate the power that you have as a role model.

In my first year in Washington, I had the opportunity to observe oral argument at the U.S. Supreme Court. I remember seeing the late Justice Thurgood Marshall on the Bench. I cannot describe the sense of pride that I felt to see him seated among the other Justices on the United States Supreme Court. Intellectually, we all know that blacks can hold positions of power and prestige. But I tell you, actually witnessing it through one's own eyes can be an inspiring event.

I. CONCLUSION

So what does the future hold? I am and have always been optimistic. Clearly, there is greater opportunity for black lawyers today than there was for me 14 years ago. Twenty black lawyers of the more than 3,000 lawyers on Bay Street may seem insignificant, but it represents an infinite increase over the number just 14 years ago. We are no longer an oxymoron.

Still, any celebration would be premature. Bay Street is nearly as segregated today as the entire legal profession was almost 50 years ago.

Today's black law graduates hold the best promise for taking our place on Bay Street. The Law Society of Upper Canada, at last, has recognized the problems with access faced by black graduates. Take advantage of this changing climate to gain access to areas where we were denied in the past.

In closing, I am reminded of one of the most inspiring speeches in American history. In his "I have a Dream" speech delivered more than 30 years ago, Martin Luther King, Jr. spoke of his dream that his children one day would live in a nation where they would not be judged by the colour of their skin but by the content of their character. This is not just a dream of black America. It represents an ideal that speaks to the very best in each of us. It is not limited by national boundaries, race, creed or colour. I believe every one of us shares this dream. Let us each do our part to make it a reality.

* LL.B. (Western), LL.M. (Harvard); partner, Covington & Burling, Washington, D.C. This paper was delivered as a keynote lecture at the Faculty of Law, The University of Western Ontario on February 9, 1998. The paper is based on Michael St. P. Baxter, Black Bay Street Lawyers: Looking Back, Looking Ahead, 28 GAZETTE 32 (1994). I have benefited immensely from discussions with my friends and colleagues, and from the seminal work of David B. Wilkins & G. Mitu Gulati, Why Are There So Few Black Lawyers in Corporate Law Firms? An Institutional Analysis, 84 CALIF. L. REV. 493 (1996).

Reprinted with permission of the author.

Chapter 39

Women -
As Law Students, Lawyers And Judges

"A large number of women have been admitted to Canadian law schools, have performed superbly there, and are now embarking upon successful legal careers which will, inevitably, lead them to the pinnacles of the practicing and judicial branches of the profession."

-Chief Justice Brian Dickson

From The Common Law Prohibition To A Common Majority

The Common Law Prohibited Women From Becoming Lawyers

Present Day Reality - Facts Are Stubborn Things!

Intentional discrimination against women has long since disappeared. By the fall of 2004, four of the nine judges of the Supreme Court of Canada were women. As of 2002, every Canadian law school with the exception of the University of Western Ontario had a higher percentage of women students than men students. In every year since 2000 more woman than men have been admitted to the bar in Ontario.

Furthermore, this state of affairs is not restricted to law schools. Lysiane Gagon writing for La Presse notes:

"This fall, the Universite de Montreal has twice as many female students as male. Women make up 80 percent of the medical school's student body. The same inbalance can be found in most departments, including dental, veternarian and law school. Most criminals are male, but when they are brought into court, they'll be surrounded by female lawyers and judges and observed by female criminologists and psychologists. ... This is not the kind of world that '60s feminists dreamed of. The idea was to develop a balanced society, where men and women would equally share power and responsibilities, both at home and at work. Instead, what's developing looks like a complete reversal of the old order, with women gaining full power over men - something that only radical, man-hating feminists used to wish for."

-Lysiane Gagaon - Here's A Shock For Women - October 12, 2002

A Bit Of History

Of course, it hasn't always been this way. The integration of women into the legal community has been a gradual process. The purpose of this chapter is to describe some of the historical milestones.

In 1990 University of Toronto economist David Stager and Professor Harry Arthurs of York University published "Lawyers In Canada." It was a fascinating study of the legal profession. In 1990, Michael Crawford, commenting on the book noted that:

"Perhaps the biggest change to hit the legal profession, Stager says, is the growing number of women. In 1970, women represented 13% of law students and 5% of practising lawyers. Today, they make up half of the law school graduates and a quarter of the lawyers and the numbers are rising by about 1% to 2% each year.

More telling, by 1988 women represented 42% of lawyers under 30 - the next wave of lawyers.

I have made the forecast to a few of my lawyer friends that within the decade there will be a woman who is managing partner of one of the top 10 or 15 firms," says Stager. "And in fact they're going to dominate the profession in a decade or so."

- From Michael Crawford 'Women Making Gains"- the Financial Post, December 27, 1990

Were Professors Stager and Arthurs right in their prediction? They are clearly on the right track. Two points are worthy of note.

1. The year 2000 was the first year in which more women than men were called to the bar in Ontario.

2. Christine Legarde, a fourty-four year old French lawyer became the first woman to head Baker & MacKenzie which is one of the world's largest law firms.

The History Of Women In The Legal Community

Historical Beginnings

The common-law prohibited women from becoming lawyers. This was probably one of many restrictions which burdened women prior to the twentieth century. At the beginning of the twentieth century women began their attempts to become members of the legal profession. In both Canada and the United States, the conflict moved to the courts. The climate of the early part of the twentieth century can be understood from the following comments of Mr. Justice Saint-Pierre who was a Quebec judge.

"...I hold that to admit a woman and more particularly a married woman to the profession as a barrister, that is to say, as a person who pleads cases before judges or juries in open court and in the presence of the public, would be nothing short of a direct infringement upon public order and a manifest violation of the law of good morals and public decency."

- from Dame Langstaff v. The Bar of the Province of Quebec

Historical Discrimination

The records of law societies across Canada outline the initial efforts of women to become lawyers. In 1897, Clara Brett Martin of Ontario, became the first female lawyer in the British Commonwealth. The following article from the *Law Society Gazette* traces the history of women in the legal profession.

The Law Society Gazette

Admission of Women to the Bar: An Historical Note

John de P. Wright

"Nature has given women so much power that the law has wisely given them little," so wrote Dr. Johnson in a letter to the Reverend Dr. Taylor in 1763.

Certainly the legal profession was loath to share its power and prestige with women.

The first woman to become a lawyer in the British Empire was an Ontario lady by the name of Clara Brett Martin.

Miss Martin attempted to gain admission to Osgoode Hall Law School in 1891. The Law Society concluded that it had no authority to admit women and refused her.

The Ontario Legislature solved this problem by passing an Act authorizing the Law Society to admit women.

The Law Society then resolved that it was inexpedient to frame rules for the admission of women and this was communicated to the applicant.

The benchers of the day thought that this had put an end to the vexatious question. They were wrong. Sir Oliver Mowat, Attorney General and ex-officio, a bencher moved that Convocation "do proceed to frame rules for the admission of women as solicitors." This motion was carried twelve to eleven.

The Minutes of Convocation record what happened next.

"Mr. Riddell entered after the question had been put and carried, and claimed the right to vote, having been in the building and in court, and having entered the Convocation room while the vote was being taken and before being concluded. The chairman ruled against Mr. Riddell's right to vote. Mr. Riddell then asked to leave to record his vote.

"Mr. Kerr moved, seconded by Mr. Martin, that Mr. Riddell be allowed to vote. Ruled out of order.

"It was then ordered by unanimous consent that Mr. Riddell be at liberty to say how he would have voted, and record the same. Mr. Riddell stated that he would have voted "nay."

"Moved by Mr. Osler, seconded by Mr. Moss, that it be referred to the Legal Education Committee to frame Rules respecting the admission of women to practice, and to report on the same at the next meeting of Convocation.

"Mr. Martin moved in amendment that the motion stand adjourned until the 27th day of December instant for further consideration.

"The vote was taken on Mr. Martin's amendments which was lost...

"The vote was then taken on Mr. Osler's motion and stood as follows: [Yeas-12, Nays-12]

"The Chairman voted with the yeas and the motion was declared carried."

Miss Martin was finally admitted as a student-at-law in June 1893, just two years after the date of her petition for admission and was called to the bar three years later.

The editor of the *Canadian Law Times* (and presumably the majority of the profession) was upset.

"By a vote of twelve to eleven the Benchers resolved to admit women to practice as solicitors. The vote we believe does not represent the opinion of the profession, nor that matter the real opinion of the Benchers, some of whom voted either out of compliment to the Attorney General, or because they thus got rid of what was likely to prove a troublesome question.

"The fact is that the majority in the Legislature was very small. The question was shelved there by giving the Law Society power to admit, and the Attorney General used his persuasive powers to induce the Benchers to take the responsibility on themselves of a radical change in the law.

"The question is not one of the mere domestic affairs of the Law Society. It is an extensive and radical question of politics, and ought to be so treated. If the responsibility is cast upon the Benchers, who themselves are but a representative body, it is certainly taking a great responsibility upon themselves for the twelve out of the thirty elective Benchers to make such a radical change in the government of the Law Society without taking the sense of the Profession upon it. We feel confident that the good sense of the Profession is against the measure. To argue that many women practice law in the United States is of no avail. Monkeys are mimetic. Men should act upon reason and judgement."

A year later the same editor had the occasion to comment upon the failure of the Legislature to allow women to vote.

"It is curious to observe the action of the Legislature with regard to the adjustment of the "rights" of women. It has solemnly declared that they may practice medicine and law, and that no restriction shall be imposed on them in that respect by reason of marriage. The Attorney General took enough interest in female solicitors to give them his personal attention at a Convocation of Benchers. But when a radical member of the house arose to extend the franchise to them all without restriction, the same authorities denied them that privilege as vehemently as they had asserted their right to enter the Professions. A Legislature composed of women could not have acted more impulsively or illogically. Women may be entrusted with our lives and our property, but must not express an opinion on political questions. It cannot be that our homes would be more broken up and desecrated by the voting of women than by their going out daily to bleed and blister and issue writs. [The reference to "bleed and blister" refers not to the legal profession, of course, but to the medical profession which had been forced to admit women a decade before.] So it must be that our legislature have such a mean opinion of politic that they do not desire their wives and daughters to soil their hands with them - and perhaps they are right."

The battle to admit women to the bar in the United States was not won by default.

In **The Matter of the Motion to Admit Miss Livinia Goodel to the Bar**, Ryan, C.J. said: "This is the first application for admission of a female to the Bar of this Court. And it is just matter for congratulation that it is made in favour of a lady whose character raises no personal objection: something perhaps not always to be looked for in women who forsake the ways of their sex of the ways of ours....

"There are many employments in life not unfit for the female character. The profession of the law is surely not one of these. The peculiar qualities of womanhood, its gentle graces, its quick sensibility, its tender susceptibility, its purity, it delicacy, its emotional impulses, its subordination of hard reason to sympathetic feeling, are surely not qualifications for forensic strife. Nature had tempered women as little for the juridical conflicts of the courtroom, as for the physical conflicts of the battlefield. Womanhood is molded for gentler and better things. And is not the saints of the world who chiefly give employment to our profession. It has essentially and habitually to do with all that is selfish and malicious, knavish and criminal, coarse and brutal, repulsive and obscene, in human life. It would be revolting to all female sense of the innocence and sanctity of their sex, shocking to man's reverence for womanhood and faith in woman, on which hinge all better affections and humanities of life, that woman should be permitted to mix professionally in all the nastiness of the world which finds its ways into courts of justice; all the unclean issues, all the collateral questions of sodomy, incest, rape, seduction, fornication, adultery, pregnancy, bastardy, legitimacy, prostitution, lascivious co-habitation, abortion, infanticide, obscene publications, libel and slander of sex, impotence, divorce; all the nameless catalogue of indecencies, la chronique scandaleuse of all the vices and all the infirmities of all society, with which the profession has to deal, and which go toward filling judicial reports which must be read for accurate knowledge of the law. This is bad enough for men. We hold in too high reverence the sex without which, as in truly and beautifully written, le commencement de la vie est sans secours le milieu sans plaisir, et la fin sans consolation, voluntarily to commit it to such studies and such occupations... Reverence for all womanhood would suffer in the public spectacle of women so instructed and so engaged. This motion gives appropriate evidence of this truth. No modest woman could read without pain and self abasement, no woman could so overcome the instincts of sex as publicly to discuss, the case which we had occasion to cite supra King v. Wiseman. And when counsel was arguing for this lady that the word, "persons," in Section 32, Chapter 119, necessarily includes females, her presence made it impossible to suggest to him as reductio ad absurdum of his position, that the same construction of the same word in Section 1, Chapter 37, would subject woman to prosecution for the paternity of a bastard, and in Sections 39, 40, Chapter 164, to prosecution for rape. Discussions are habitually necessary in courts of justice, which are unfit for female ears. The habitual presence of women at these would tend to relax public sense of decency and propriety. If, as counsel threatened, these things are to come, we will take no voluntary part in bringing them about. The motion is denied."

Reprinted with permission of the author.

Intentional Discrimination Ends - The Profession Evolves

Since the early 1900s there has been no legislative intention to discriminate against women in the profession. That does NOT mean that women have not been discriminated against. It means only that discrimination has been systemic.

Systemic (Unintentional) Discrimination Against Women

Prologue - 1990

There are two kinds of systemic discrimination in the legal profession. The first is the treatment that women lawyers receive from other lawyers in what has been until recently still predominately a male profession. In other words, do women have to work harder than men to become partners in law firms? The second kind of systemic discrimination is faced by all women in dealing with the legal system. Some commentators have taken the position that laws themselves and the legal system reflect strong gender bias. The highest profile proponent of this view has been Madame Justice Bertha Wilson, formerly of the Supreme Court of Canada. According to the "Toronto Star", Madame Justice Wilson, in commenting on gender bias in the legal system, stated that:

"A distinctly male perspective is clearly discernible and has resulted in legal principles that are not fundamentally sound."

Grappling With Systemic Discrimination Through the 1990s

The 1990s was the decade that the legal community addressed issues that impacted primarily on women. Each of the profession, the law schools and the judiciary were impacted by this.

The Profession in the 1990s

The following article from the *Toronto Star* in 1991, summarizes more of Madame Justice Wilson's views on this subject. The issues identified in it guided much of the debate on this issue through the 1990s. Justice Wilson was responsible for "Touchstones For Change," the 1993 Canadian Bar Association report describing the status of women in the legal profession.

August 20, 1991

The Toronto Star

Wilson knows first-hand gender bias lawyers face

David Vienneau

Bertha Wilson recalls how as a young lawyer in a male-dominated profession, an outraged man stung her by saying, "I don't want any bloody women drafting my will."

On other occasions, the former Supreme Court of Canada judge would march into all-male corporate boardrooms only to see "their faces fall" because she was a lawyer and not a secretary.   While that type of blatant, overt discrimination is no longer as evident today, many women lawyers still face systemic stumbling blocks their male counterparts don't experience, Wilson says.

It's for this reason she has agreed to head an unprecedented Canadian Bar Association task force on gender bias in the legal system.

"There is no doubt about the fact that women face obstacles in attempting to practice their profession," Wilson told a news conference at the association's annual meeting.

A recent investigation by the Law Society of Upper Canada found most of Ontario's female lawyers have experienced sexual discrimination during their careers and earn less than their male colleagues.

It also revealed that many women quit the profession early in their careers.

Wilson's six-member task force will look at parental leave policies for both women and men lawyers, ways for women to have successful legal careers while fulfilling their roles as mothers, part-time work and on-site child-care centres.

It will also examine remuneration, equality in hiring, how to promote the upward mobility of women in the profession, and the problems resulting from sexual harassment.

"Trying to reverse decades, indeed centuries of injustice to women in law places a heavy burden on the task force," association president Wayne Chapman told about 1000 people yesterday.

"I am confident in its ability to find solutions. The final duty, however, rests with our association and every one of its members."

Convincing the normally shy Wilson, who retired from the court in December, to head the task force is considered a coup by many legal observers and feminists.

She has been an outspoken critic of the gender bias that exists in the law.

A year ago she gave a milestone speech in which she said, "A distinctly male perspective is clearly discernible and has resulted in legal principles that are not fundamentally sound."

Wilson, 67, has been a role model for many women lawyers. After practising in Toronto, the native of Scotland became the first women appointed to the Ontario Supreme Court and the Ontario Court of Appeal.

She capped her career in 1982 by becoming the first women appointed to the Supreme Court.

Interestingly, the first time she walked into the judges' conference room, seven of the eight men then on the court politely stood. The exception was Chief Justice Antonio Lamer, who saw Wilson as a judge and colleague, not a women.

Wilson said while the discrimination is probably more subtle now, the reality is that women who want to advance their careers face a much tougher challenge than men.

"When a women is promoted or moves up she constantly has to prove herself," she said. "Whereas when a man moves up it is assumed he is thoroughly competent or he wouldn't have got there.

"Women still face the problem every time they move into a new group. Assuming we're talking promotion, people wonder if they are really competent. Why was she moved up? Can she really do the job?"

"Any women who is hoping to aspire to reach the higher echelons must assume that at every fresh level she must start from scratch and prove herself all over again to a new group of people."

The other members of the task force are lawyers Sophie Bourque of Montreal, Daphne Dumont of Charlottetown, Patricia Blocksom of Calgary, Alex Robertson of Vancouver and John Hagen, a University of Toronto law professor.

Originally, the bar had planned to have only one man on the task force. But Wilson, true to her conviction, insisted there must be two to avoid the appearance of tokenism.

The task force is to present its report at the association's 1993 annual meeting in Quebec City.

Reprinted courtesy Torstar syndication services.

Canada 1993 - Touchstones For Change

In 1993 The Canadian Bar Association under the leadership of Justice Wilson released its task force report: Touchstones For Change: Equality, Diversity and Accountability. The report is comprehensive and is well worth reading. The authors conclude by saying:

"This Report sets a momentous challenge for the legal profession. Study after study has shown that women lawyers are discriminated against within the profession. The results of our research and consultations serve as further proof that gender bias exists in all sectors of the profession and on a national basis. Evidence of gender inequality abounds in the restricted nature of employment opportunities available to women, in the limits placed on their career advancement, in the lack of accommodation of family responsibilities and in sexual harassment."

A Choice Between Work And Family?

Touchstones For Change spoke of "the lack of accommodation of family responsibilities. The following perspective on this issue certainly provides "food for thought."

December 11, 2000

The Boston Globe

Female lawyers seen fed up with major firms

Diane E. Lewis

BOSTON — Donnalyn Kahn was a lawyer at a big Boston law firm three years ago when she took a 50-per-cent cut in pay to work for the city of Newton, Mass.

Ms. Kahn quit after watching what she described as the subtle harassment of female lawyers at the firm who had chosen to work less than 60 hours a week.

"People were expected to put the firm first. If you put anything else first at any given time, you were not committed," said Ms. Kahn, 38, who left the firm after the birth of her second child. "When I was at the law firm, I considered working part-time after the birth of my first child five years ago, but I never asked because I saw what was happening to other women."

Of U.S. women who leave law firms, 40 per cent reported in a recent survey that their firm's reaction to reduced-hour working arrangements led to their resignations.

Female lawyers, burned out and fed up with what they perceive as the gruelling hours and lack of flexibility at Massachusetts' major law firms, are forgoing six-figure salaries and the prestige of a partnership for jobs in government, business or at smaller firms where hours are shorter and personal satisfaction is higher.

The survey by Massachusetts' Women's Bar Association, which looked at 45 large law firms, found that the growth rate of female representation at the biggest firms is down from 12 per cent in 1995 to just 0.8 per cent in 1997, the last year data were available.

"We wanted to figure out why, with so many women in the pipeline at law schools, we were not seeing an increase at the partnership or senior lawyer level at the big firms," said Nancer Ballard, co-author of More Than Part-Time: The Effect of Reduced Hours on Retention, Recruitment and the Success of Women Attorneys.

"What we found is that part-time policies are not nearly as important as the messages the firms send," Ms. Ballard said. "If a firm begrudgingly says, 'Yes, take tomorrow off,' and then turns around and indicates that the person is now a marginal attorney, that lawyer is not going to feel valued."

Asked about the study, Joel Reck, chairman of the real estate section at Brown Rudnick, said women have had difficulty balancing work and family at major law firms.

"Many women lawyers who work part-time feel they are not valued as highly as full-time lawyers," he said. "They need interesting work to be valued, but law firms must also make the situation work if we want to keep and attract young women. . . ."

"At the same time, when a woman takes part-time employment, she needs to understand exactly what's involved," he said.

The study tracked women who left Massachusetts law firms between 1996 and 1998, as well as female lawyers who began working part-time last year.

Women constitute 28 per cent of lawyers employed by the 100 biggest firms in the state, but represent 40 per cent of the lawyers who leave each year, the study said.

The study also found that female lawyers with reduced hours left big firms at a higher rate than full-time women and at a rate that was 70 per cent higher than their full-time male peers.

Sarah Orlov, 35, left a law firm two years ago to work for a title insurance company in Boston. Ms. Orlov, with three children, said her old employer offered her a part-time arrangement when she submitted her resignation, but she declined. Today, she earns more and has far more flexibility.

"The whole mindset of the firm just wasn't conducive to it," she said."

Reprinted courtesy of The Boston Globe.

The U.S. 1998 - Presumed Equal

In 1998, CareerPress published a book called: "Presumed Equal - What America's Top Women Lawyers Really Think About Their Firms." (ISBN: 1-56414-313-9) The authors, Harvard Law School graduates Elizabeth Westfell and Suzanne Nessel, describe the impetus for the book as follows:

"The impetus for Presumed Equal arose more than two years ago when, as second-year law students at Harvard contemplating jobs at large firms, we were alerted to the complex set of issues and conflicts facing women in private legal practice. ..."

The authors' findings include a statement that:

"Among the most striking findings of our study is the fact there is no single "woman's" experience at any firm. The attorneys at each of the firms surveyed varied considerably in terms of their impressions of their workplaces. That women diverge in their accounts of what individual firms are like is not surprising. Women attorneys come from diverse backgrounds and have varying priorities and expectations. Attitudes and tones that make some women feel right at home can make others very uncomfortable. Assignments systems that give some women tremendous opportunities can leave others feeling underutilized and frustrated. Differences in perceptions may be attributable to distinct personalities, different hopes in terms of professional satisfaction, or varying levels of talent drive and stamina."

- Presumed Equal - page xii

This finding is hardly surprising.

The Law Schools In The 1990s

The General Climate

Approximately half of all law students are now women. Hence, it is reasonable to assume that women will be admitted to the bar in the same numbers as men. Some believe that women experience law school differently from men. In her 1999 book: "A Woman's Guide To Law School", Professor Linda Hirshman begins by writing:

"Three years of private law school costs upwards of $75,000 in tuition and living expenses. A very nice suit no more than $750. It turns out that men and women don't fit into law school in exactly the same way any more than they fit into the suit in the same way. You'd try on a suit before you bought it, especially one that was originally designed for a man! This book was written to enable you to do the same thing with the much more important decision about law school."

You may visit the author at www.lawwomen.com.

Professor Hirshman, a U.S. law professor, argues that some U.S. law schools are more "women friendly" than others. This idea is consistent with the theme of an article in the October 95 issue of the National Jurist (a U.S. magazine for law students). The article identified and ranked the best law schools for women. The rankings were based on the percentage of students and faculty members that were women, the percentage of women who occupy leadership positions in the law school, and how women perceive they are treated on campus.

Institutionalizing Equality

Queen's University, was one of the first schools to institutionalize a formal policy of equality. On page 3 of *The Law School Calendar 1991-92*, it stated:

"The Faculty of Law recognizes the right of all persons to equality and the fact that the fundamental principles of equality are not well enough served by the legal community which remains disproportionately male and white. The Faculty has demonstrated a commitment to ameliorating the historic and current inequalities between women and men. ... so that female and male pronouns appear alternatively or conjointly...When the materials are perceived by the instructor to omit significant legal issues relevant to the historic or current unequal treatment according to women and members of minority groups, or to inadequately represent them or their interests, the instructor should endeavor to compensate for such omissions or inadequacies in his or her discussion of the published materials ..."

Law Schools In The 1990s - Feminist Course Content

Professor Linda Hirshman suggests that law school was originally designed for men. Justice Bertha Wilson has commented that in the law "... a distinctly male perspective is clearly discernible and has resulted in legal principles that are not fundamentally sound."

During the 1990s, a number of schools (and some professors) adopted measures to include feminist legal theory in the curriculum. One well known example is the Feminist Perspective Bridge week at the University of Toronto law school. The "Bridge Week" is devoted to a week long study of feminist legal theory. It has been reported that these measures were controversial. At a minimum law students were introduced to a feminist perspective on the law. At its maximum impact, the introduction of feminist legal theory divided faculty and students and resulted in some unpleasantness. For example, The Globe And Mail in an article titled "Feminist Content In Course Creating Rift At Law Schools" by Kirk Makin (December 26, 1989) report the following problems in the law schools:

- members of Queen's University law faculty have been accused of sexual harassment and insensitivity;

- a professor at the University of Ottawa was attacked for supporting the position stated on a poster he put up. The poster promoted a controversial court decision and implied that sexual assault does not constitute serious bodily harm;

- the University of Western Ontario was split by accusations of sexual harassment by unnamed law professors. Adding fuel to the fire was a published study by a feminist law professor that claimed widespread sexual discrimination against female faculty members.

It is hardly surprising that this discussion found its way into campus newspapers. Consider the following:

"I think feminist perspectives are great but I don't want to see it in other classes. I want to learn the damn law and that's all I care about."

> *- A 3rd year Osgoode law student.*

The Judiciary In The 21st Century

Canadian women have made unprecedented progress in the judicial branch of the legal profession. The Supreme Court of Canada is the highest branch in the land. It's decision have a profound impact on every aspect of Canadian society. Since the Charter of Rights and Freedoms, judges have the power to strike down laws which they decide are contrary to the Constitution. In 1989, three of the nine judges on the Supreme Court were women. There are few countries, (if any), where women have such representation in the judicial branch of the legal profession. By 2004 - at the time of writing - four of the nine judges are women. In addition, Madame Justice Beverly McLachlin is the Chief Justice Of Canada.

September 28, 2000

The National Post

Judges share unique judicial friendship

Luiza Chwialkowska

OTTAWA - A frosty wind blew across the escarpment beneath the Supreme Court building last night as Madam Justice Claire L'Heureux-Dube, of the Supreme Court of Canada, stood by a side entrance, shivering in a black evening dress, watching her hands turn blue from the cold.

Suddenly a black car pulled up, and Judge L'Heureux-Dube rushed headlong into the gale and into a warm embrace as Madam Justice Ruth Bader Ginsburg, of the United States Supreme Court, began her first visit to Ottawa.

The two women rushed into a secret, wood-panelled judges-only elevator. Judge Ginsburg is in Ottawa for a conference to mark the 125th anniversary of the Supreme Court, but she and Judge L'Heureux-Dube had decided to skip the opening reception for a private chat in the judge's book-lined chambers.

While Judge Ginsburg hung her coat, the Canadian judge described the long personal relationship that links the continent's two top courts.

"The first time that I contacted Judge Ginsburg was after she was appointed to the Supreme Court and I wrote her a letter," she recounted.

"I read her life story in The New York Times. I thought there was so much similarity between her life and mine that I wrote her to say that. I told her, you don't have to respond. But she did."

The commonality between the women is as personal as it is professional.

Both are the second female judges appointed to their respective courts. From Quebec City and Brooklyn, the two jurists have followed similar paths to the highest courts — paths marked by personal tragedy, uncommon determination and a shared vision of the law as a tool for achieving equality.

"I'm older than Ruth — not by much," said Judge L'Heureux-Dube. "But we are of the same era, when women had no place in the law. They had no place in law firms, and a reluctant place in the courts."

Judge Ginsburg added: "When I graduated from law school in 1959, there was no woman on an appellate bench in the United States.

"People ask me, 'did you aspire to be a judge?' I tell them, 'I just aspired to get a job!' "

At this Judge L'Heureux-Dube smiled and nodded in recognition.

The parallels between their lives are deep and sometimes tragic.

Judge L'Heureux-Dube once worked as a secretary in a cod-liver oil plant before leaving for law school when she realized she was smarter than her boss.

After graduating from Cornell University, Judge Ginsburg worked in an Oklahoma welfare office where she was demoted, given a pay cut and denied training after becoming pregnant.

Judge Ginsburg's sister and mother died before she graduated from high school. Judge L'Heureux-Dube's husband committed suicide more than 20 years ago; her son, who suffered from depression, died in 1994.

While Judge L'Heureux-Dube was a rare female lawyer fighting for women in Quebec family law courts, Judge Ginsburg's struggles with the American legal system are legendary.

One of nine women at Harvard Law School in the 1950s, she was asked by the law dean to justify why women should be allowed to occupy seats that could otherwise go to men.

She earned top marks at Harvard and became editor of the law review — while at the same time getting married, giving birth to a daughter and helping her husband, Martin Ginsburg, finish his law degree when he was stricken with cancer.

After graduation from Columbia Law School she was rejected by every law firm to which she applied. And despite glowing recommendations, she was also passed over for a Supreme Court clerkship by Mr. Justice Felix Frankfurter, who declared "he just wasn't ready to hire a woman."

But, like Judge L'Heureux-Dube, Judge Ginsburg's experiences strengthened her resolve to use the law to fight for equality.

"People sometimes say that women of my generation were elite white women who were trying to get a place only for elite white women," she said. "That is so far from the truth."

When she finally found employment as a law professor (though at a lower salary than her male colleagues because her "husband had a good job"), Judge Ginsburg began working as an advocate for the American Civil Liberties Union, specializing in sex discrimination cases. She challenged laws that treated men and women differently, even if the differences had been intended to help women, and won in five of the six discrimination cases she took to the top court.

In contrast, Judge L'Heureux-Dube is known for championing the view that difference in treatment is sometimes necessary for "equality of outcome." "In order to be equal, you have to take differences into account," she said.

Judge Ginsburg agrees, but only to a point, it seems.

"That is most easily seen in the case of disability," she said. "The difference, when it comes to women and race, is that there is nothing readily identifiable that makes them different."

Stopping herself, she said — "Except pregnancy" — and explained that maternity leave is necessary for women to enjoy equality.

Judge Ginsburg will speak to the gathering of judges and scholars today about the growing "globalization" of the law.

"I think we all learned from World War II that even popularly elected legislatures need the check of the higher law," she said of the proliferation of human-rights laws around the world.

"The U.S. court used to have an isolated mentality," she said. "But more and more I think my court is going to be looking outward."

Will it look to Canada?

"I read about 99% of all your decisions," said Judge L'Heureux-Dube to her guest.

"I make sure that I read her decisions," Judge Ginsburg replied, adding with a smile: "Because she sends them to me."

Reprinted with permission from The National Post.

Conclusion

This chapter has canvassed the history of women in the legal community. At the beginning of this century, women are well represented in the law schools, the profession and the judiciary. The voices of women have been helpful in identifying a number of "lifestyle issues" in the legal profession. Perhaps it is time to realize that many of these issues also apply to men.

APPENDIX

May 15, 2000

The Globe and Mail

Christine Legarde Heads International Law Firm

Margot Gibb-Clark

Toronto-On law firm Baker & McKenzie's Web site, Christine Lagarde describes her office location simply as "global."

At 44, the French lawyer is the first woman to head what is one of the world's biggest legal practices. Her job as chairwoman keeps her away from her Paris home 85 per cent of the time.

Instead of practising antitrust and employment law, she now builds strategy and consensus among 2,700 lawyers in 35 countries-a task anybody who knows the profession would recognize as difficult.

Last week she was in Chicago and Toronto; the week before, in Paris; and the one before that, in Jakarta and Tokyo.

"It's a challenge every day," she says, noting that lawyers cherish their autonomy and can argue better than anybody. "But it's also very gratifying and a very exciting period of my life."

On the professional side, "it is a challenge because the competition has now recognized that what we started to do 50 years ago is exactly the right thing to do."

By that, she means the thrust for global presence. In January, London-based Clifford Chance merged with firms in New York and Germany, and overtook Baker as the world's biggest. The Big Five accounting firms have been increasingly offering legal services, although so far they are truly competitive only in tax law, Ms. Lagarde says.

From the time it was founded in Chicago in 1949, Baker & McKenzie has sought international business and tried to be on the ground in most of the world's financial centres.

Its global revenue last year was $818-million (U.S.), and it has 60 offices from Azerbaijan to Vietnam. Last year it was named the world's best global firm by British magazine The Lawyer.

Not surprisingly, Baker is known for cross-border transactions and international dispute resolution as well as tax-its first major international practice area.

It does what its lawyers characterize as "major projects" that require input from several legal specialties and countries. One example is a Hungarian highway, built with funding from London and New York. It involved contract, construction and financing expertise, Ms. Lagarde says.

Some of that international flavour is reflected in the firm's Web site (http://www.bakerinfo.com). In the lawyer directory, right under a person's name, is a list of the languages they speak, with the adjectives "native," "fluent" or "good."

With the exception of U.S. offices, individual lawyers often list several languages. In the case of Ms. Lagarde, they are French (native) and English (fluent). Her English is close to perfect, tinged by a slight British accent. She also speaks some Spanish.

Asked to name the major challenge of her three-year term as chairwoman, she identifies the effort to maintain a culture which is in some ways familial while adapting to provide increasingly sophisticated services to clients.

For example, a few years ago clients might have been billed for hours of work on a draft contract for amalgamating a foreign acquisition. Now, with advanced technology, Baker could send them a standard contract within an hour.

Other international law firms should not underestimate the work it takes to resolve the cultural issues from having offices in so many countries, Ms. Lagarde cautions. Practising law in Taipei is pretty different from Tijuana.

To deal with that, Baker gets lawyers from around the world together in small training classes where they can learn about one another, as well as about cases.

The firm sends its lawyers to Northwestern University's Kellogg School of Management for a specially tailored course to help them understand management issues and appreciate how they affect clients. "We need to understand what they face and what their thinking is," Ms. Lagarde says.

One of those issues, which Baker faces increasingly in the world of e-commerce, is the request by startup clients for law firms to take equity rather than charge hourly fees.

Although the firm is considering the idea, Ms. Lagarde is skeptical. "To the extent that you have a strong vested interest in a venture, are you still going to be able to render the independent opinions that are essential?"

Several of Baker's practice groups are global, including one specializing in World Trade Organization law that Ms. Lagarde helped create. She describes it as a virtual group with no real home, drawing lawyers from Brussels, Geneva and Washington.

A spinoff of the WTO group is an unusual pro bono project. Baker lawyers are offering free legal advice to each of the world's 48 least-developed countries.

Among the firm's other policies are three months paid maternity leave for women lawyers, a policy Ms. Lagarde shepherded through the executive committee, although she says it was suggested by a pregnant American lawyer.

"It would have been impossible and so politically incorrect for the other seven members [of the committee] at the time to argue that it was uneconomical," she says.

Other Baker lawyers may also have been sensitive after getting stung with a huge lawsuit in 1994 after a U.S. partner sexually harassed a secretary. The woman won $3-million and legal costs doubled that amount. Partners around the world had to pony up several thousand dollars each. The firm has since offered sensitivity training courses.

Ms. Lagarde has spent her whole legal career with Baker & McKenzie, joining as a trainee in Paris in 1981 after completing a post-graduate law degree. She chose the firm partly because the Paris office had a woman managing partner, then a rarity. "I thought that was a very encouraging sign."

She was also influenced by a stint as a scholarship student at a U.S. prep school which made her interested in diversity. "I felt Baker & McKenzie could offer the same collegiality, diversity, tolerance."

Her female mentor has since died, but Ms. Lagarde still tries to meet with women lawyers and clients at each of the offices she visits. They ask her how she juggles personal and professional duties, she says, as well as discussing issues affecting women in business.

Her answer: When she travels she usually gets up at 5 a.m. and often spends evenings until 11 at events representing the firm. Her only time to herself seems to be swimming in hotel pools. She was once a member of France's synchronized swim team, though today she limits herself to swimming lengths.

She also sets her alarm for 7 a.m., French time, no matter where she is, to be able to speak to her sons, 14 and 12, before they leave for school. "Lately they've told me 'don't bother, we'll be able to get up', which is good news," she says with a grin."

Reprinted with permission from The Globe and Mail.

APPENDIX

Part A - A Report

Introductory LSAT PREP - Get Off On The Right Foot!
Part A - Introducing The LSAT - A PREP Primer

Summary And Introduction

My Advice To You Is ....

On the one hand, you should recognize the important role that the LSAT plays in the admissions process. On the other hand, don't blow it out of proportion. Your goal should be to score high enough so that you won't be rejected from law school because of your LSAT score. Prepare responsibly. In an ideal world, you should take the LSAT the first June that you are free.

Like it or not the Law School Admission Test ("LSAT") has a well established and important role in the law admissions process. I have taught LSAT courses for more than twenty years. Those years of experience have allowed me to give you some excellent introductory advice. This Appendix is not intended to be a complete LSAT book. But, it will get you moving in the right direction. Furthermore, it will show you how to PREP for the LSAT in the most effective way.

You should also be aware that I am the author of a complete book on the LSAT: Mastering The LSAT - How To Prepare Effectively And Successfully (ISBN: 0-9696290-3-6) and teach live LSAT programs in Toronto. www.richardson-prep.com - 416-410-PREP.

In Part A, of this Appendix I will play the role of the "LSAT PREP Trainer."

In Part B, I will discuss the LSAT from the vantage point of "past, present and future" - playing the role of an "LSAT Historian."

Appendix - Part A - Introducing The LSAT - A PREP Primer

Appendix Part A - Chapter Summaries

40. Prologue - Focused Beginnings - The Nuts And Bolts Of The LSAT

Focus: What does the test look like? How do you register? How is the LSAT used?

41. Inside The LSAT - Twenty-Six Effective Principles For Percentile Performance

Focus: Twenty-six effective principles of approach

42. Understanding Your LSAT Score - What Your Score Means

Focus: Although a higher number is better than a lower number, students often have questions about how to interpret LSAT scores

43. You've Finished The LSAT - Post Mortem Considerations

Focus: When should you cancel your score? When should you repeat the LSAT?

Chapter 40

Prologue - Focused Beginnings - The Nuts And Bolts Of The LSAT

Part I - Prologue

How do people experience the LSAT? What follows is the perspective of a National Post reporter who took the June 11, 2001 LSAT.

July 28, 2001

The National Post

Trial by multiple-choice

If you want to be a lawyer, you have to take the LSATs.

A National Post reporter goes through the ordeal

Rebecca Eckler

It's early in my working life but I now know one thing for certain: I will never be a lawyer.

Like thousands of other would-be lawyers, I got the results of my LSAT test from the Law School Admissions Council last week. And how did I do, I hear you ask? I got lower than the 60th percentile, lower than the 50th percentile, lower than, well, why go on? It's humiliating. Suffice to say I will never be Ally McEckler.

Between 5,000 and 7,000 applicants compete for about 2,340 first-year places in Canadian law schools each year — and each and every one of those aspiring lawyers must take the LSAT, which is administered four times a year, in June, October, December and February.

It is designed to measure skills considered essential for success in law school: reading comprehension, analytic reasoning and logic. There is also a one-page essay designed to see how well the candidate can form an argument. Because so many apply, academic achievement simply isn't enough.

I decided to take the test to find out what it was all about. I know a lot of people who have considered going into law, and I wanted to find out why friends who have taken the LSAT find it a painful subject to discuss. So I signed up over the Internet in early May, charging the $133 fee to my credit card.

Most people who take the LSAT study at least three months for it. I have heard of people studying for six. Many don't do well enough. They can take it again — up to nine times — but only three times in a single year. One friend, a single mother, took it twice but didn't do well enough to get into law school either time. This is a woman who had aced university.

"It's great if you have the support and live at home and can take three months off to dedicate yourself to studying," she says. "I didn't have that option."

The Law School Admission Council says repeat test-takers improve their scores only "slightly," though some law schools average the results.

Two days before the test, I decided I better at least look at some practice LSAT questions, so I went to Chapters to buy an LSAT study book.

There weren't many left. A young woman I encountered there suggested I buy two volumes of LSAT: The Official TriplePrep Plus with Explanations — for $90! (I saw Legally Blond this week. Those are the books Reese Witherspoon's character uses.)

"I'm on the waiting list to get into law schools," the nice young woman told me. When I asked her how she'd done on her LSAT, she shook her head violently. "I can't talk about it," she said, then held her stomach. "Really, I can't."

For the next two days I studied maybe a total of eight hours. I was soon to discover that simply isn't sufficient.

My boyfriend, a corporate lawyer, tried to do some of the practice tests with me and had just as much trouble figuring out the right answers. When he did his LSAT, he studied hard and ended up in the 90th percentile. Maybe that just means he's a good test taker.

- - -

On Monday, June 11, at 11:30 a.m., I made my way to the downtown campus of the University of Toronto to sit for the test.

People arrive at least an hour before the required time of 12:30. The process takes a total of six hours, though only three hours are spent actually writing the test. There is one 10-minute break.

Most of the students taking the test with me were university aged, though there were a few in their 40s.

One of my fellow test-takers, armed with a handful of sharp orange HB pencils (necessary for the test), shared a theory with a few of us.

"What if," he ventured, "someone is playing a joke on us and sent out falsified letters telling us the test was taking place here, but the test really is taking place somewhere else, just so they'd get a competitive edge over us?"

The dozen or so of us, sitting on the floor near him, laughed nervously. Fierce competition coupled with stress breeds paranoia.

"There's no way," he continued, scoping the hundreds who have gathered, "that all of us here can become lawyers. No way."

He's right. I realize there's no way I'm going to do well. Reading I get. But I'm not very logical. And I've never done well at math.

I discovered that timing is everything. You have only 35 minutes to finish a section. There are five sections with up to 26 questions in each. You have about a minute to answer each question. Many people bring stop watches to keep themselves on track.

Before we went into the room, I talked to some of my testmates. The consensus was that taking the LSAT is like playing blackjack in Vegas: a gamble.

"I don't agree with the LSAT at all, not at all," said Heather McConnell, 24, who was taking it for the first time. "I have lots of friends who are lawyers who I have been talking to throughout this process for insight for the best way to do well, and most of them took the test four or five times. Others said, yeah, they got 65% or 75% on their LSAT and managed to get in, but it doesn't appear to have anything to do with their careers or law schools. And others, who became lawyers before the LSAT was so important said there would be no way they'd be lawyers now if they had to do the LSAT again."

Ms. McConnell, like most of the test-takers, had paid for an $850 five-week preparation course, taken on weekends. There are also on-line study options at about $500. Still others take LSAT study courses — Kaplan or Richardson's are the most famous — which can cost thousands.

"Sure you can take the test a number of times, if you can afford it. And you will eventually do well. You're basically buying your way in," says Ms. McConnell. "I couldn't imagine doing it without the course. It was helpful and they gave you step-by-step analysis of right and wrong answers, and helped examine the language of the questions. The problem is you can't possibly use all the tools you learn in the time you are given in the test."

"Nowadays, it becomes a question of how much money you can afford to spend so you can get to the point where you may get a good mark on the LSAT. It excludes a lot of people who may not have that money."

- - - Finally, it was time to start.

The close to 200 of us taking the test that day were divided into three classrooms.

We were acquainted with the rules: No food or drink in the test area. No cellphones or pagers. For security reasons, we were fingerprinted and required to show photo identification.

No one is allowed to leave early.

And cheating is nigh impossible: There are a number of versions of the test, with the questions listed in a different order, so there's no question of looking over at someone else's test.

At the end of the test, we were a pretty disgruntled bunch.

"Please don't use my name," begged one test-taker, worried lest anything he says is used against him. "But they have a bunch of idiots running the test. We show up on time, they don't. It takes them forever to get you organized, when we've studied forever. And the so-called supervisors and assistants helping them kept whispering during the whole thing. How is that possibly fair?"

On the floor where my test was administered, there was one women's washroom with one stall, which meant nearly 20 of us spent our 10-minute break not eating a snack or drinking juice but waiting in line to pee.

"I don't know about your room, but there was no clock on our wall," said another. "You just assume there would be one. I should have brought a stop watch. I mean, it's the year 2001 and they're counting down by writing on the board we have five minutes left for each section."

- - -

I was exhausted for three days after the test. It seemed to me that the main purpose of the LSAT must be to test how badly one wants to become a lawyer.

Lots want it very badly.

The Faculty of Law at the University of Toronto gets 1,600 applicants a year vying for 170 first-year places. To get in, your median grade-point average on your university transcript had better be at least 3.8 out of 4.0.

"Very few candidates," it says in the law school's admission book, "are admitted with an LSAT score below the 85th percentile and cumulative academic averages below 78%."

Even with a B-plus grade average, and a 75% to 84% LSAT score, acceptance is unlikely. At Osgoode Hall Law School at York University, about 2,000 applicants apply and 287 are admitted.

"To stand a realistic chance of acceptance at Osgoode," they write, "a regular applicant should have at least an A-minus average on their university work and a percentile rank of 80 or higher on the LSAT."

The Faculty of Law at the University of Calgary suggests at least a B average and at least 50% on the LSAT.

I recently talked about the LSAT to Ron Daniels, the dean of law at the University of Toronto, the toughest Canadian law school in Canada to get into.

"The LSAT is first and foremost an aptitude test. There is a debate as to whether or not courses do or do not help," he says. "We have a number of students who take the LSAT on a whim with no preparation and score in the 99th percentile. We've seen it regularly."

That didn't cheer me up.

"The LSAT," he concluded, "is part of the right of passage to becoming a lawyer."

Reprinted with permission from the National Post.

Author's note: (By the way, the reference in the article to LSAT Preparation courses costing in the thousands is incorrect. I know of no LSAT course that costs in the thousands.)

The above article, which is a great read and contains some fact and some fiction. The rest of this chapter will separate the fact from the fiction.

The LSAT And The Law Admissions Process?

The letters "L S A T" stand for Law School Admission Test. The LSAT is required as part of the admissions process for most of North America's "common law" schools. (At present Moncton, McGill and the French common section of the University of Ottawa do not require the LSAT.) The LSAT is developed and administered by Law Services in Newtown, Pennsylvania.

Why Was The LSAT Conceived?

The LSAT is the great equalizer. It is the one thing that all law school applicants have in common.

" ... (admissions committees) are confronted with a situation where all law school applicants have high marks. Since there is no designated pre-law curriculum, and law schools tend not to discriminate on the basis of where a student did his undergraduate work, it is clear that another mechanism was needed to evaluate the large numbers of applicants in a fair way. Enter the infamous LSAT."

- 'The LSAT In Perspective"

When Can You Take The LSAT?

The LSAT is available to be taken four times a year. In general it is administered in early October, early December, early February and mid June. Every administration except for the June administration is on Saturday mornings. The June administration is on a Monday afternoon. Alternative dates are available for those who observe the Saturday Sabbath. Special arrangements can also be made for those suffering disabilities. (See the LSAT Registration Book for full details. The appendix to this chapter also includes a perspective of interest to those with disabilities.) There are many who think that the "special arrangements for those with disabilities" may not be sufficient. In December of 1999 the U.S. Department of Justice launched a civil suit against Law Services alleging that the "special arrangements" did not go far enough.

A Good Source Of Free LSAT Information

The <u>LSAT Registration Book</u>, which is available free of charge, contains a wealth of information about the LSAT (including sample questions). (The same questions are also available at www.LSAC.org) The Canadian edition also includes "entry level" information about each of Canada's common law schools. Needless to say, I encourage you to obtain a copy of this book. You will find it in the admissions office of law schools and your university career centre.

How Can You Contact Law Services?

The address and phone number for Law Services are:

Law School Admission Services

Box 2006

Newtown, PA 18940-0963

U.S.A.

(215) 968-1001 - They do not have a toll-free telephone line.

The easiest way to find information about the LSAT is at www.LSAC.org.

How Do You Register For The LSAT?

You may register for the LSAT online at www.LSAC.org, by telephone or by mail using a registration form. Information about these options may be found in the LSAT Registration Book which is available free of charge.

There is a fee to take the LSAT and pre-registration is required. To learn how to register refer to the LSAT Registration Book. At the present time there are three ways to register for the LSAT.

1. Regular registration by mail, telephone or online - approximately five weeks before the test.

2. Late registration by mail - a window period that extends after the deadline for regular registration expires.

3. Late registration by telephone or online - A window period that extends after the deadline for regular registration expires. The vast majority of applicants apply online.

The most inexpensive way to take the LSAT is by registering through "regular registration."

You will find that the LSAT is administered at most universities in Canada and the U.S. It is up you to select the test centre which is most convenient for you.

Warning!! It is common for certain test centres to fill up. Hence, it is to your benefit to register as early as possible!

What Is The Present Format Of The LSAT?

The LSAT has had many different formats over the years. At present, the LSAT is a multiple choice test, consisting of five thirty-five minute sections and a separate writing sample section. Four of the five sections count towards your LSAT score. The remaining section is experimental. Its purpose is to allow the test designer (LSAC/LSAS) to try out questions for future use. The four sections that count are as follows:

1. Reading Comprehension - four passages - approximately 28 questions

2. Analytical Reasoning - four sets of conditions - approximately 24 questions

3. Logical Reasoning - approximately 16 arguments and approximately 25 questions

4.   Logical Reasoning - same as number 3 above

The experimental section will be a repeat of one of these four sections.

(In Part II of this chapter I will introduce you to the format of some sample questions.)

The writing sample is administered separately either before or after the main LSAT is over. It is a thirty minute exercise. A copy of the writing sample is available along with your LSAT score to every school that receives a copy of your LSAT score. The writing sample is not graded and is placed in your file for possible consideration.

Warning!! Warning!! It is likely that in the near future that the LSAT will adopt a new format. In order to verify the current format of the LSAT, I encourage you to visit www.LSAC.org.

How Is The LSAT Used?

Your LSAT score which is based on the number of questions you answer correctly is reported on a scale of 120 - 180. There is no penalty for selecting the wrong answer. Hence, it is important to always ensure that your best guess is on record. The LSAT is not a pass or fail exam. Your score is a reflection of how you perform relative to everybody else taking the test. Each school is free to decide how to use the LSAT and to decide what score will satisfy its admissions requirements.

Under the present rules, there is a limit to the number of times you may attempt the LSAT in a fixed time period. You should also be aware that some schools will take the average of your LSAT scores and some will take the highest. Therefore, the LSAT should never be taken for practice!

What Does Your LSAT Score Mean And What Is A Good Score?

Your scaled score from 120 - 180 is a reflection of how you performed relative to all test takers. You need not get all the questions right to get a score of 180. It is possible to get some questions wrong and still get a score of 180. In other words, a perfect LSAT score does not necessarily mean a perfect performance.

Your score report will also describe the percentile ranking that your scaled score (120 - 180) is equivalent to. For example a score of 180 would mean that you scored better than approximately 99.9% of all test takers. For those interested in a more complete discussion of what your LSAT scores means, see the chapter on "Understanding Your LSAT Score", which is later in this book.

Who Receives Your LSAT Score?

If you have not yet applied to law school, then only you will receive your LSAT score. At the point that you apply to law school, the school will request your score from Law Services. Law Services will report multiple test scores. The policy on the number of scores and how old of a score Law Services will report, changes from year to year. Current information may be found in the LSAT Registration Book.

May I Take The LSAT And Cancel The Score?

Yes. At the present time, it is possible to take the LSAT and decide after the test is over that you do not want to have the test scored. (You will never know what your score was.) The information for when and how to cancel your score may be found in the LSAT Registration Book. (For a more detailed discussion of this issue, see the "Post-LSAT Considerations" chapter, which is later in this book.)

When To Take The LSAT

You should take the LSAT as early in the year as possible. By taking the LSAT earlier you will be giving yourself an opportunity to take the test again (should that option be desirable). By taking the test in June or October you will be taking the test:

A. At a time when you will have the least pressure from other academic commitments; and

B. At a time that will leave you the opportunity to take it again (should that be necessary).

You should also know that many law schools have a "rolling admissions" process. This means that your application will be considered at the time it is complete. If you don't have an LSAT score, your application will not be complete and cannot be considered.

The Case For The June LSAT - The Most Ideal Situation

For those who want very specific advice: Take the LSAT the first June that you have the time. There is no reason to delay taking the test until the June immediately before your application is due. An extra year of university will not improve your LSAT taking skills.

How Far In Advance Of The LSAT Should You Begin Training?

In my experience students worry about the LSAT far longer than they actually train for it. Students often presume a much longer training period than is required. Proceed on the assumption that a minimal but reasonable period is required to train. I suggest that you:

1. Take the LSAT at a time of the year that gives you an opportunity for a retake; and

2. Begin by assuming a period of approximately four to six weeks. This period should be a time of serious dedication to LSAT training.

3. During your training period you must work consistently and in the early part of the day. When it comes to the LSAT one hour of practice in the morning is equivalent to three hours of practice in the evening.

4. Extend your training beyond the four to six week period only if you find that in your specific circumstances a longer training period is required. (This can be determined practicing with real LSAT exams. More on that later!)

Bottom line: Presume a minimum training period and don't extend beyond that time period Unless there is clear evidence that you need it.

The best way to become acquainted with the directions to the LSAT and the question types is by studying the descriptive material in the LSAT Registration Book. (You might even wish to have this book with you as you read the following discussion.) What follows is a very brief discussion which is designed to acquaint you with the format of the LSAT question types, the directions to each type and what skills each question type is designed to measure.

Warning!! Please note the following questions are representative of the format of LSAT questions. They do NOT AND ARE NOT INTENDED to represent either the level of complexity in design or objective difficulty of real LSAT questions.

Analytical Reasoning

The directions to the Analytical Reasoning section of the test read as follows:

"Each group of questions in this section is based on a set of conditions. In answering some of the questions, it may be useful to draw a rough diagram. Choose the response that most accurately and completely answers each question and blacken the corresponding space on the answer sheet."

Format: Each thirty-five minute section will consist of four sets of conditions. Each set of conditions will be followed by approximately six questions.

Tip: In Analytical Reasoning the response that "most accurately answers the question" is objectively correct. As a result, you do not have to read every choice before you choose an answer choice. This is different from most of the Reading Comprehension and Logical Reasoning questions.

Law Services describes the purpose of the Analytical Reasoning section in the following way.

"Analytical reasoning items are designed to measure the ability to understand a structure of relationships and to draw conclusions about the structure."

What follows is a sample set of Analytical Reasoning questions. The purpose of these questions is to illustrate the general nature of this section. Remember that you will receive four of these sets to do in thirty-five minutes on the actual LSAT!

"On Saturday, Sunday, and Monday of every Victoria Day weekend, a small charter plane company uses each of its three planes, plane 1, plane 2, and plane 3, for separate all-day trips. Their flying assignments for Victoria Day weekends are distributed among four pilots, K, L, M, and N, in accordance with the following restrictions:

K does not fly plane 2.

M flies plane 3 only.

N must not be given more flying assignments than L on any Victoria Day weekend.

Each of the pilots must be given at least one flying assignment on a Victoria Day weekend.

1. If on a particular Victoria Day weekend N's only assignment is to fly plane 3 on Saturday, all of the following must be true EXCEPT

(A) K is assigned to fly plane 1 on Sunday.

(B) L is assigned to fly plane 2 on Monday.

(C) plane 1 has the same pilot throughout the weekend.

(D) plane 2 has two different pilots in the course of the weekend.

(E) The flying assignments for Sunday and for Monday are identical.

2. Which of the following must be true of L's flying assignment for any Victoria Day weekend?

(A) L flies plane 1 only once, if at all.

(B) L does not fly plane 3.

(C) L is given at least two flying assignments.

(D) L flies on all the days that M flies.

(E) L flies on all of the days that N flies.

3. If on a particular Victoria Day weekend N's entire flying assignment is to fly plane 1 on Saturday and again on Monday, which of the following must be among the flying assignments for that weekend?

(A) M flies plane 3 on Saturday.

(B) M flies plane 3 on Sunday.

(C) K flies plane 3 on Monday.

(D) L flies plane 1 on Sunday.

(E) L flies plane 3 on Monday.

4. If K and M are given an equal number of flying assignments for a particular Victoria Day weekend, which of the following could also be true of that weekend's flying assignments?

(A) K and L have an equal number of flying assignments.

(B) L and N have an equal number of flying assignments.

(C) M and N have an equal number of flying assignments.

(D) K's assignments are all for different days than M's assignments.

(E) L's assignments are all for the same days as N's assignments.

5. If N is assigned to fly a different plane on each of the three days of a particular Victoria Day weekend, which of the following could be true of that weekend?

(A) On one of the three days, K flies plane 3.

(B) On one of the three days, K and M both fly a plane.

(C) On one of the three days, L flies none of the planes.

(D) K and M have an equal number of flying assignments.

(E) M and N have an equal number of flying assignments."

Reading Comprehension

The directions to the Reading Comprehension section of the test read as follows:

"Each passage in this section is followed by a group of questions to be answered on the basis of what is stated or implied in the passage. For some of the questions, more than one of the choices could conceivably answer the question. However, you are to choose the best answer; that is, the response that most accurately and completely answers the question, and blacken the corresponding space on your answer sheet."

Format: Each thirty-five minute reading comprehension section will consist of four passages. Each passage will be followed by from six to eight questions.

Tip: The "best answer" in reading comprehension is usually not the kind of answer you would create by yourself. Since you are asked to select the "best answer", it is essential that you read every word of every choice before selecting an answer! If you look for an answer that is objectively correct you will become very frustrated very fast!

Law Services describes the purpose of the reading comprehension section in the following way.

"The purpose of reading comprehension questions is to measure your ability to read, with understanding and insight, examples of lengthy and complex materials similar to those commonly encountered in law school work."

What follows is a sample set of reading comprehension questions. The purpose of these questions is to illustrate the general nature of this question type. Remember that you will receive four of these sets to do in thirty-five minutes on the actual LSAT!

"In an economic community, there is a separation between those who prefer a secure though modest return — that is to say, a mere livelihood — and those who play for big stakes and are willing to assume risk in proportion. The first compose the great bulk of manual workers of every description ... while the latter are, of course, the entrepreneurs and the big business men. The limited or unlimited purpose is, in either case, the product of a simple survey of accessible economic opportunity and of a psychic self-appraisal. The manual worker is convinced by experience that he is living in a world of limited opportunity. He sees, to be sure, how others - for instance - businessmen are finding the same world a store-house of apparently unlimited opportunity. Yet he decisively discounts that, so far as he is himself concerned. The businessman, on the contrary, is an eternal optimist. To him the world is brimful of opportunities that are only waiting to be made his own.

The economic pessimism of the manual group is at the bottom of its characteristic manner of adjusting the relation of the individual to the whole group. It prompts also the attitude of exclusion which manual groups assume towards those regarded as "outsiders." Again the manualist's psychology can best be brought out by contrast with that of the fully developed businessman. Basically the businessman is an economic individualist, a competitor par excellence. If opportunity is plentiful, if the enterprising person can create his own opportunity, what sane object can there be in collectively controlling the extent of the individual's appropriation of opportunity, or in drastically excluding those from other localities? Nor will this type of individual submit to group control, for he is confident of his ability to make good bargains for himself. If, on the contrary, opportunity is believed to be limited, as in the experience of the manual worker, it then becomes the duty of the group to prevent the individual from appropriating more than his rightful share, while at the same time protecting him against oppressive bargains. The group then asserts its collective ownership over the whole amount of opportunity, and, having determined who are entitled to claim a share in that opportunity, undertakes to parcel it out fairly, directly or indirectly, among its recognized members, permitting them to avail themselves of such opportunities, job or market, only on the basis of a "common rule." Free competition becomes a sin against one's fellows, anti-social, like a self-indulgent consumption of the stores of a beleaguered city, and obviously detrimental to the individual as well. A collective disposal of opportunity, including the power to keep out undesirables, and a "common rule" in making bargains are as natural to the manual group as laissez-faire is to the business man.

6. The passage indicates that those who prefer a secure and modest return hold the view that:

(A) entrepreneurs are hoarding money that "belongs to the people"

(B) opportunity is limited for all people

(C) opportunity does not exist for them

(D) they are entitled to a fixed minimum wage

(E) their interests will best be served by joining a union

7. The passage indicated that the beliefs of manual workers concerning the amount of available opportunity are responsible for:

(A) entrepreneurs creating their own opportunities

(B) the entrepreneurs adjusting their relations to the group of manual workers

(C) the manual workers not appropriating the entrepreneurs' opportunities

(D) manual workers consenting to having part of the existing available opportunity rationed to them

(E) manual workers "sinning" against each other

8. It can be inferred from the passage that:

(A) the manual worker will increase his standard of living by becoming part of a group

(B) the collective ownership of the available opportunity increases the amount of opportunity available to the group members

(C) membership in a group will protect the individual from oppressive bargains

(D) the entrepreneurs will get richer

(E) entrepreneurs and manual workers are enemies

9. The passage suggests that a manual worker will feel most comfortable living in which of the following kinds of living accommodations?

(A) a co-operative housing development

(B) a condominium apartment building

(C) a middle class suburban neighborhood

(D) a government subsidized housing project

(E) a Manhattan penthouse

10. The author of the passage supplies information that would answer which of the following questions?

I. Why would a person want to join a labor union?

II. Do labor unions protect workers from oppressive employers?

III. Are manual workers oppressed by entrepreneurs?

(A) I only

(B) II only

(C) I and II only

(D) II and III only

(E) I, II, III

11. The most appropriate title for this passage is:

(A) Are Unions Effective for Their Members?

(B) Is Opportunity Limited for the Entrepreneur?

(C) A Theory of the Labor Movement

(D) The Eternal Conflict Between Manual Workers and Entrepreneurs

(E) How Manual Workers Can Reap the Rewards Earned by Entrepreneurs

12. The author of the passage would most agree with which of the following statements?

(A) Manual workers have less ability than entrepreneurs.

(B) The major determinant of whether one is an entrepreneur is mental attitude

(C) Entrepreneurs always make good business deals.

(D) Laissez-faire is natural to the manual worker.

(E) Manual workers who are excluded from unions suffer from this exclusion.

Logical Reasoning - Argument Analysis

The directions to the Logical Reasoning section of the test read as follows:

"The questions in this section are based on the reasoning contained in brief statements or passages. For some questions, more than one of the choices could conceivably answer the question. However, you are to choose the best answer; that is, the response that most accurately and completely answers the question. You should not make assumptions that are by common sense standards implausible, superfluous, or incompatible with the passage. After you have chosen the best answer, blacken the corresponding space on your answer sheet."

Format: Each logical reasoning section will consist of approximately twenty-five questions.

Tip: The "best answer" is rarely objectively correct. Since more than one choice could conceivably answer the question it is imperative that you don't select an answer until you have read every word of every choice! If you look for an answer that is objectively correct you will become very frustrated very fast!

Law Services describes the purpose of Logical Reasoning in the following way.

"Logical Reasoning questions are designed to evaluate a test taker's aptitude for understanding, analyzing, criticizing, and completing a variety of arguments."

What follows are some sample Logical Reasoning questions. The purpose of these questions is to illustrate the general nature of this question type. Remember that you will get twenty-five of these questions to do in thirty-five minutes on the actual LSAT!

13. Below is an excerpt from a letter that was sent by a company recruiting new employees to an applicant seeking an interview:

Unfortunately we are unable to grant you an interview. Our hiring committee has been forced to refuse interviews to many well-qualified applicants because we must select the applicants we interview in accordance with the "affirmative action" guidelines laid down by the government.

Which of the following can be deduced from the excerpt?

(A) Only those applicants who were well qualified were granted interviews

(B) This particular applicant was considered to be one of the most well qualified applicants.

(C) This particular applicant was not well qualified enough to be granted an interview.

(D) Few of those who applied for interviews were well qualified.

(E) The qualifications of the applicants were not the only considerations in deciding which ones to interview.

Questions 14 and 15

What do I say about Tom McMillan running for the U.S. Senate? In order for a U.S. Senator to be effective he must be smart. McMillan plays professional basketball for the Atlanta Hawks. The result of the ETS Professional Basketball Potential Examination (PBPE) indicates that the average I.Q. of pro basketball players is well below that of the national average. A follow-up study has indicated that the Hawks are no exception to this: i.e. there is no significant difference between the average I.Q. of an Atlanta Hawk and the average I.Q. of a player on any other team. Clearly the Hawks are as stupid as all the rest of the players, and since McMillan is a Hawk, he is just as stupid as all of the other players, just plain stupid.

14. Which of the following most closely parallels the reasoning used by the author to show that McMillan is stupid?

(A) Russian threats are no news. Therefore, Russian threats are good news since no news is good news.

(B) To press forward with a properly ordered wage structure in each industry is the first condition for curbing competitive bargaining; but there is no reason why the process should stop there.

(C) Since every third child born in New York is a Catholic, Protestant families living there should have no more than two children.

(D) It is necessary to confine animals and lock up dangerous lunatics. Therefore, there is nothing wrong with depriving people of their liberties.

(E) Narcotics are habit forming. Therefore if you allow your physician to ease your pain with an opiate you will become a hopeless drug addict.

15. Which of the following, if true would most weaken the author's claim?

(A) Many members of the House of Representatives have had low I.Q.'s and have been effective members of the house.

(B) Pro basketball players have low I.Q.'s as a result of years of playing basketball which has the effect of lowering I.Q.'s.

(C) Without McMillan on their team the I.Q. of the Hawks would be lower than that of the rest of the league.

(D) McMillan was a Rhodes Scholar and all Senators who have been Rhodes Scholars have been effective.

(E) The average I.Q. of a U.S. Senator is lower than the average I.Q. of a pro basketball player.

Questions 16 and 17

The blanks in the following passage indicate deletions from the text. For each question select the completion that is most appropriate in context.

Ask yourself what products are currently (16) . Postal service, elementary and secondary schooling, and railroad passenger transport would surely be high on the list. Ask yourself which products are most satisfactory and have improved the most. Household appliances, television and radio sets, hi-fi equipment, computers and, we would add, supermarkets and shopping centers would surely come high on that list.

The shoddy products are all produced by government or government-regulated industries. The outstanding products are all produced by private enterprise with little or no government involvement. Yet the public — or a large part of it — has been persuaded that private enterprise (17) , that we need ever vigilant government employees to keep business from foisting off unsafe, meretricious products at outrageous prices on ignorant, unsuspecting, vulnerable customers.

16.

(A) most available and reasonably priced

(B) most necessary to day-to-day living

(C) most satisfactory in terms of quality

(D) in greatest demand and least available

(E) least satisfactory and have shown the least improvement over time

17.

(A) don't produce what products are demanded

(B) produces high quality products

(C) produce products that are too high cost to the consumer

(D) produce low quality products

(E) produce unsafe products

Answers: 1. D 2. C 3. B 4. C 5. A 6. C 7. D 8. D 9. A 10. A 11. C 12. B 13. E 14. E 15. D 16. E 17. D

The Writing Sample

The writing sample is a thirty minute exercise which is administered separately from the LSAT. It is handed out separately and collected separately. The writing sample is administered either before or after the five thirty-five minute sections. The amount of space that is provided is equal to the amount of space on one 8 1/2 by 11 piece of lined paper.

All writing sample topics have the same format. The topics require you to argue for one of two alternatives. You will be provided with specific information to use when you argue for one alternative instead of the other. Remember that the writing sample does not count towards your LSAT score. It is included along with your LSAT score whenever a school receives your LSAT score.

Law Services has provided the following comments about the role that the writing sample is intended to play.

"There is no `right' or `wrong' position on this topic. Law schools are interested in how skillfully you support the position you take and how clearly you express that position. How well you write is much more important than how much you write. No special knowledge is required or expected. Law schools are interested in organization, vocabulary, and writing mechanics."

What follows is a sample writing sample topic which is similar to what you will encounter on the LSAT.

"Read the following description of the choice open to Don Davidson, who has successfully worked for an eminent New York City Publishing company for six years. Then, in the space provided, write an argument for the career choice you would advise Don Davidson to make. Use the information in this description and assume that Don Davidson highly values the following:

1. The well-being of his family;

2. Eventually owning his own business.

Don Davidson has drawn on extensive editorial and marketing experience (with his father's weekly newspaper) and two years of post-graduate religious studies to revive the slumping performance of his publishing houses's Religious Books Division, most of whose publications are directed to the general reader. He has received a sizable raise and has been promoted to manager of that division. He has been told that his chances of further advancement are very good. His wife, employed by a fast-growing advertising firm, has been promoted to creative director. Although, their apartment is cramped and overpriced, both Don and his wife enjoy New York's cultural and intellectual life. Their two children, aged six and eight, attend excellent schools. The younger child's dyslexia was diagnosed early and the disability is being given state-of-the-art treatment.

One of the oldest and closest friends of Don Davidson's father recently contacted Don. This man owns a small publishing company specializing in academic books in the fields of religion, history, and anthropology. The profit margin has been chronically slim but the business has survived for a long time. Don has been invited to manage this business and then buy the business when the older man retires in several years. The company is located at a small town in the Midwest, a twenty minute drive from the state university which is a cultural center and major employer in the region. Spacious, inexpensive housing and good schools are available. Both children would enjoy playing more freely outdoors. The older child could finally have the dog she's longed for. Lower living expenses might compensate somewhat for an initially sharp drop in family income were Don to take the new job. In the long run he might make more money than he could in New York. The older man's offer has made Don realize how much he would like to eventually own his own business and be his own boss, but he doesn't want to harm his wife's career or in any way jeopardize the well-being of his family."

This is an excellent example of the format that the writing sample will have.

Conclusion

The preceding discussion was to provide basic factual information about what the LSAT is about and a taste of what the questions look like. The next chapter has been designed to give you some insight into the hurdles that you must clear in order to perform well on the LSAT. The chapter contains twenty-six very important principles of approach. You will see that the LSAT is not like any other test that you have encountered.

APPENDIX

Disabilities - Special Accommodation

Law Services has developed a special process so test takers with disabilities receive special consideration. The principles are described in the LSAT Registration Book. What follows is the experience of a student who successfully navigated this process.

"Many individuals with learning disabilities avoid and are afraid of standardized tests because these disabilities can impede the outcome of such tests. I have discovered that LSAC accommodates individuals with `documented' disabilities. This means if you can prove to LSAC that you have a disability that will potentially affect the outcome of your LSAT score then they will consider accommodating you in order to place you on an even level or playing field with the other students writing the test. Learning disabilities are most often diagnosed in grade school and are likely documented in your school records.

The process of applying for accommodations is time-consuming and somewhat painful but if you believe that you qualify then I highly recommend going through the process. In the LSAT Registration and Information Book (pg 6 of the 2000-2002 edition) it is recommended that candidates submit all of their information and all of their supporting documentation well in advance of the deadlines. I cannot stress enough how time consuming this process is and how important it is to allocate ample time to the task. I began this process in September and was not organized enough for the December LSAT.

I began by phoning the Accommodations Department of LSAC (215-968-1001). I knew that I could download all of the required documents from: www.LSAC.org but I wanted to be sure that I was a likely candidate and that I received all of the relevant information. I ordered all of the documents through the mail. Once I received the documents I had to find a psychologist who could perform the required testing and complete the forms that I was sent.

The easiest and cheapest place to begin the search for a good psychologist is at your university's disability/accessibility/accommodations office. When I began my search private doctors were quoting prices more than twice what was offered at my university and often their appointment schedules were less flexible. The university's testing was priced at approximately $700. If you begin this process early enough there may be time to apply for a grant for this type of testing either through the disabilities office or through OSAP.

The actual testing was not totally painless. For those of you who have experienced this type of testing before it is tiring and often alienating and perhaps even humiliating. Some of the tests I preformed included but were not limited to: reading lists of words and numbers; reading both silently and aloud and answering corresponding questions; hearing and repeating and or reading aloud non-sense words, memorizing and repeating lists of words; repeating lists of words in reversed order; ordering stores using picture blocks; space and ordering tests with multi-coloured blocks; spelling tests; math tests; and examples of short essays. The testing took about eight hours and was preformed over two days.

After the testing is completed the process is out of your hands. The psychologist will examine the results of your test, make a diagnosis and file a report with recommendations to LSAC. LSAC then decides which, if any, of the recommendations they will accept. In my case I was not granted accommodations for all of the recommendations that the psychologist made but I was granted a test that I believe will more accurately reflect my abilities.

My final piece of advice is that you apply for the LSAT prior to the deadline for the accommodations because although you may be granted accommodations there is no guarantee that there will still be a seat available at the LSAT testing centre of your choice. It all seems to take appropriate timing."

Chapter 41

Inside The LSAT - Twenty-Six Effective Principles For Percentile Performance

Multiple Choice Is Your Friend!

"The 23th Rule Of Life"

"Multiple choice is my friend; I shall not worry.

It maketh me love taking tests and teacheth me what a number 2 pencil is for. It gives my life new meaning (Life is nothing more than a long multiple choice test).

It leadeth me down the right road to the answer in spite of my ignorance.

Yea though I live with the terror of logical games, I will fear no failure.

Thy susceptibility to the power of answer elimination comforts me.

Thy format inspires me because I know the right answer lies before my very eyes.

It giveth me the ability to identify the answer even though I understand nothing.

Confidence and right answers shall follow me through the "test preparation stage of my life" and I will be healthy, wealthy and wise for the rest of my days."

> *- The Wise Words Of A Test Prep Coach*

An LSAT PREP Primer - Multiple Choice Is Your Friend!

"When I took the weekend prep-course (LSAT), the first thing the guy said was, `Stop thinking this is an exam. It's not an exam, it's a game, and you just have to learn how to play the game,' ... `They (the course) teach you tricks on how to get the answers which obviously shows it's not a test of knowledge. ...'he said."

> *-A student's perception of the LSAT*

The purpose of this chapter is:

To Give You An Understanding Of "LSAT Reality",

Which Will Shape Your Attitude,

Resulting In A Workable Goal For Your Preparation,

With Information About How To Train For That Goal.

How To Use This Chapter - Twenty-Six Important Principles

Note: You should read this chapter after you have read or seen (and perhaps tried) a real LSAT. Real LSATs are available from Law Services and from many bookstores. You may download one for free at http://www.lsac.org.

This chapter has been designed to prepare you for the LSAT on an emotional level. It contains an extensive, but by no means complete discussion of the LSAT. It is not a substitute for practicing actual LSAT questions or a more complete LSAT PREP manual or an LSAT Preparation Course.

Understanding The Layout Of The Chapter

Each component of this discussion is summarized by a principle. This chapter will introduce you to twenty-six important principles of the LSAT. Knowing these principles is only a beginning. You must practice their implementation. Remember: It is not sufficient to "know what to do." You must also be able to "do what you know!"

Many students approach the LSAT and LSAT preparation the same way they approach other tests. This is a great mistake. Success on most tests in your academic career depends on a knowledge and understanding of the subject being tested. In addition, it is usually possible to get "part marks." For most tests it is possible to predict some of the exact questions with certainty.

The LSAT is the exact opposite. It tests neither knowledge nor understanding nor is it possible to get "part marks." The exact questions cannot be predicted. Your LSAT score is a reflection of nothing more than a measure of your ability to do the LSAT - on that particular day! Hence, your LSAT preparation must focus on learning how to take the test. Learning how to take the LSAT consists of:

1. Learning specific principles of approach; and

2. Practicing those principles on test questions.

But first, let's get one student's perception of LSAT preparation.

How to prepare and how not to prepare for the LSATs

Bonnie Redekop

In this bureaucratized and stratified society in which we live, it sometimes becomes imperative that we submit to the rigours of stringent testing which aims to classify us as worthy of further education. Thus, we have the LSAT as a test one must undergo in order to enter Law School.

You may well ask, why would a relatively intelligent university-educated person such as myself desire to seek such a profession? Let's just say that I am mildly twisted and misguided, actually feel I can have a worthy and rewarding career as a lawyer, or both.

Anyway, my purpose here is to enlighten other LSAT-bound students, and those students who are even remotely considering such a venture.

The LSAT is a half-day, standardized test, and consists of five thirty-five minute sections. The sections comprise the topics of analytical reasoning, reading comprehension, two logical reasoning sections, and one section for experimental purposes. It is intended to assess the skills that are judged to be necessary for success in law school.

Your first step should be to pick up a copy of the LSAT Registration and Information Book. This book will be your bible for the coming months. In it you will find information on each law school in Canada.

It also contains information on how to plan and pace yourself in order to maximize your LSAT performance.

Finally, the book provides addresses where you can send away for preparation materials, and the LSAT registration form itself.

Having obtained a copy of the Registration and Information Book (also known as the pinkie-purplish book), I sent away for a preparation kit, which I found to be helpful, because I could work through the questions at my own pace.

I found the test stressful, but was able to get through it without imploding and sinking into an unidentifiable puddle under the desk. The time constraint was apparent, and I found myself randomly answering questions that I had not thought through, in the hope of winning at the game of chance.

Six weeks later, the results came, and while not totally disappointing, I felt that a Supreme Court appointment was just slightly out of reach. Another try at the LSAT was definitely in order. To prepare myself for the second test, I attended an LSAT preparation course at the University of Toronto. Given by John Richardson, a lawyer with both American and Canadian law degrees, the course was both informative and entertaining. I discovered that the answers to the LSAT questions were not lodged deeply in the recesses of my brain after all, but were right there in front of me on the page. Imagine my elation at this news!

The course gave me a new way of looking at the structure of the LSAT and solving the questions.

I have compiled a list of LSAT do's and don'ts, derived from my own experiences as an average but under-prepared test-taker.

DO's

1. Get the pinkie-purplish (LSAT Registration) book and READ it.

2. Register for the LSAT in plenty of time so as to avoid the late-registration penalties, and fill out the registration form carefully.

3. Do as much preparation as you can. Bookstores and libraries are also good sources of information.

4. Get a lot of sleep and good food before the test, and bring along a snack for the break. I firmly believe in the mind-body link, and if your body shuts down, those neurons will soon follow.

DON'Ts

1. Don't make the mistake of likening the LSAT to an IQ test, or anything which requires no preparation. Studying can help, believe me.

2. Don't go into the test with a negative attitude. Believe you can do it, or you're wasting your money.

3. Don't dwell endlessly on questions you can't answer. Do your best, and move on.

4. Don't see one LSAT grade as the end-all or be-all of your existence. You can take the test a number of times, so it's not as if your professional fate is decided in the course of one day.

A good LSAT mark is only one part of the process for entering the field of law. Law schools also assess GPA, and many schools use letters of reference, work experience, community involvement, and extra-curricular activities (why do you think I'm writing this article!). In other words, don't lose your perspective.

So good luck and happy writing, and remember, if you totally bomb, so what? This war-ridden and ozone-eroding world is bound for destruction anyway. Your positive attitude is all you really have, so don't lose it!"

Reprinted with permission of the author.

LSAT PREP - The Big Picture

The "Big Picture" is the sum of:

I. LSAT reality

II. Attitude

III. Defining a "Workable Goal."

Each of these components will be discussed in turn.

I. LSAT Reality

Your LSAT score is determined by and only by the number of questions you get right. There is no penalty for guessing. Two important principles follow from this.

Principle 1: Ensure you have an answer filled in for every question whether you have looked at the question or not. Guess if necessary!

Principle 2: Every question on the LSAT has the same weight. Easy ones count as much as the hard ones. Therefore, do the easy questions first!

The LSAT is a <u>multiple choice</u> test which is administered under strict time constraints. This ensures that you will always be behind schedule. Your score reflects <u>your performance relative to others</u> taking the test. Each of these factors is important to our process.

The LSAT Is Multiple Choice

The fact of multiple choice is both good news and bad news. The bad news is that you either will or will not find the "credited response." The good news is that the "credited response" is right there on the page. You can see it. All you need do is identify that response. You are not required to understand the response.

This is a critically important point. The directions to every section of the LSAT instruct test takers to choose the "best answer." This may be (with the exception of "Analytical Reasoning") different from the "objectively correct answer." Many test takers search for an "objectively correct" answer. This misses the point. The issue is not what is the objectively correct answer to the question asked, but rather which of the five choices comes closest to fitting the requirements of the "best answer." Hence, success depends on keeping one's eyes on the answer choices.

Principle 3: The issue is not what is the answer to the question, but rather which answer choice comes closest to fitting the requirements of the question! Don't ask what is the answer to the question. Ask, which of the actual choices comes closest to fulfilling the requirements of the question. Keep your eyes on the answers! Nurture a habit of aggressively seeking and eliminating answer choices that are clearly wrong. In life and on the LSAT, it is always easier to know what is wrong than to know what is right. It is usually easy to eliminate two or more of the answers. The quick elimination of some answer choices focuses you on the remaining choices - making the focus on these remaining choices easier.

Principle 4: Be aggressive about eliminating the answer choices that are clearly wrong. This will require conscious effort and a great deal of practice. In order to accomplish this you must spend at least as much time looking at the answer choices as looking at the questions!

Deciding What Is Wrong - A Helpful Beginning

What will allow you to quickly eliminate an answer choice? Identify the "operative words" of the question. The "operative words" are the words that define the relationship between the right and wrong answers. For example if the question asks you:

1. What **must** be true you would eliminate choices that could be false.

2. What **could** be true you would eliminate choices that must be false.

3. What **must be false** you would eliminate what **could be true**.

4. What **could be false** you would eliminate what **must be true**.

Begin by determining the relationship between the right and the wrong answers.

Then, eliminate the answer choices that are clearly wrong.

Principle 5: The key to eliminating wrong answers is to identify the "operative words". This will help determine the relationship between the right and wrong answers - allowing for faster elimination of what is wrong.

The Problems Of Strict Time Constraints

Reality!! Reality!! You will run out of time. It is important to train yourself to run out of time when you encounter the questions that are hardest for you.

Time is the currency of the LSAT! If test takers had unlimited amounts of time most would be able to correctly answer the majority of the questions. **Since your score reflects how you performed relative to all others:**

You will score better than some and worse than some.

The test maker ensures that the LSAT is difficult for all by forcing test takers to work at an uncomfortable rate of speed. Test takers are always behind schedule. Most test takers will be unable to finish the test in any meaningful way. There is no penalty for selecting the wrong answer, so guess if you haven't finished a question!)

Principle 6: You will run out of time and you will be behind schedule.

Lack of time raises three considerations. These are:

1. The number of questions to do; and

2. The appropriate order to do the questions that you do; and

3. The amount of time to spend on the questions that you do.

The Number Of Questions To Do

The "trade-off" is speed versus accuracy. The faster you work the less accurate you will be. You must learn how to pace yourself. Thirty-five minutes is a relatively long time. It is easier to pace yourself through a shorter section. As a result, you could think of each thirty-five minute section as being four nine minute sections. Each section of the exam is really structured as follows:

1. Reading Comprehension - 4 passages each with 6 - 8 questions.

 (Each passage and question set is a nine minute test.)

2. Analytical Reasoning - 4 games each with 5 - 7 questions.

 (Each game and question set is a nine minute test.)

3. Logical Reasoning - 24-26 questions

4. Logical Reasoning - same as 3 above

(Each group of 6 questions set is a nine minute test.)

Each thirty-five minute section consists of four tests. Your only concern is how to maximize your number of correct answers within that thirty-five minute period. Some test takers achieve a larger number of correct answers by working more slowly on a smaller number of questions. I.e. spending their time doing three of the four tests and simply guessing on the final one. This approach would necessitate a "blind guess" on 1/4 of the questions in any thirty-five minute section. (For "blind guesses", put the same letter for each question. This will increase the chances of getting more than one correct.)

You must recognize the speed versus accuracy "trade off". Your optimal rate of speed will be determined by practice.

Principle 7: Each thirty-five minute section consists of four nine minute tests. For each section you must, through practice, determine whether to answer three or four of those tests.

The Order To Do The Questions That You Do

This question must be answered from the perspectives of:

1. The order to do the four tests; and

2. The order to do the questions in each test.

The Order To Do The Tests

In Reading Comprehension the four passages will be about different topics. In Analytical Reasoning the four sets of conditions will be of different types. In Logical Reasoning there is a tremendous range in the types of questions. If you have determined that you are going to do three of the four tests, spending twelve minutes on each test you should follow the following procedure for each question type.

Principle 8: Reading Comprehension - Omit the passage that you are the least comfortable with. Then do the remaining passages in the order that you are most comfortable. Your goal is to run out of time when you hit the passage where you believe you would score worst. If you do all four passages spending nine minutes on each passage, do the passages in the order you feel most comfortable.

Principle 9: Analytical Reasoning - Omit the game that you are the least comfortable with. Then do the remaining games in the order that you are most comfortable. Your goal is to run out of time when you hit the game where you believe you would score worst. If you intend to do all four games spending nine minutes on each game you should do the games in the order you feel most comfortable.

Principle 10: Logical Reasoning - Omit the six questions that you are the least comfortable with. (You may want to omit them as you go along.) Do the remaining questions in the order that you are most comfortable. Your goal is to run out of time when you hit the questions where you believe you would score worst. If you intend to do all four question sets spending nine minutes on each question set you should do the questions in the order that you feel most comfortable.

Principle 11: LSAT questions do not appear in each section in ascending order of difficulty. Hence, it would be wrong to assume that difficulty with earlier questions will prevent you from answering later questions.

The Order To Do The Questions In Each Passage Or Game

A reading passage or individual logic game will have a number of questions based on it. The order that you do these questions will have a major impact on:

1. The number of questions you complete; and

2. The accuracy with which you complete those questions.

LSAT questions consist of two parts. The first part is the statement or condition. This is the information to which the questions and multiple choice answer choices relate. For a large number of LSAT questions there will be a number of questions which relate to one statement. For example in Reading Comprehension you will have six to eight questions based on each passage. In Analytical Reasoning you will have approximately six questions based on each set of conditions. It is impossible for the test designer to create a large number of questions from one passage or set of conditions and not have a considerable degree of overlap. If understood and used properly, test takers can turn this overlap to their advantage.

Principle 12: The information in LSAT questions and the answer choices overlap. By learning to recognize and take advantage of the overlap you will improve your score.

In order to take advantage of overlap of information, you must be deliberate about the order you do the questions. For some sets of conditions in Analytical Reasoning it is possible do only three of the six questions and use your work from those three questions to answer the remaining three. This results in a more efficient use of your time and a higher score!

Principle 13: Test takers can take advantage of the principle of overlap of information by learning to do certain questions in a certain order. If you answer the questions in the order LSAT lays them out you will underperform!

The Amount Of Time To Spend On The Questions You Do

Learn to cut your losses. Learn how long to invest in a question before guessing. In general for each question you should:

1. Eliminate all choices that are clearly wrong.

2. Focus on the remaining choices. Be willing to guess if necessary.

Understand the concept of "opportunity cost." You may be uncomfortable with the idea of eliminating two or three choices and guessing one of the remaining choices. Make every effort to choose an answer before guessing. There are, however, times when you simply must guess. Ensure that your best guess is on record. Time spent agonizing over which of two remaining choices is correct can often be better spent doing another question. Learn when to cut your losses and guess!

Principle 14: Become comfortable with the idea of eliminating what is clearly wrong and then ensuring that your best guess is on record.

Ensure you select an answer at the time that you have read the question. A single reading of the answer choices will allow you to eliminate some wrong answers. Decide on an answer then and there! At the very least, you should ensure that your best guess is on record. This will protect you from running out of time and then "blindly guessing" an answer choice that you had eliminated earlier!

Principle 15: When you start a question, finish the question. This will ensure that (at the very least) your best guess is on record.

Your Score Is Relative To Others - The Good News And The Bad News

The Good News - You will score better than some people.

The Bad News - You will score worse than some people.

And Some More Bad News - you will not experience the feeling of total control that many of you have felt when you were performing well on a test! There will be many times when you will feel that your future dreams are slipping away from you!

This is the feel of the test. It may not bear much relation to your actual performance.

Principle 16: Don't become disillusioned if you feel that the test is difficult. This is the "feeling" of most test takers.

II. The Right Attitude

I have taught LSAT preparation courses for many years. At the beginning of my teaching experience I thought of myself as a teacher who was there to impart valuable information and principles of approach to the students in my classes. I was totally oblivious to the fact that the biggest problem that people have with the test is emotional. The emotional problem is rooted in the fact that most students think of the LSAT as a test. Since most tests are for the purpose of testing understanding, many students' emotional orientation toward the LSAT is that it tests an understanding of the questions. This is dangerous. Don't concentrate on the questions to the point that you ignore the answer choices. The identification of answer choices is the only thing that you receive credit for. It is difficult to eliminate the wrong answers choices if you are not paying attention to those choices.

LSAT scores would improve if people stopped thinking of the LSAT as a test. It should be thought of as a game! The object of the game is simply to find the best answer! This places the focus on the answer choices.

Principle 17: The LSAT should be thought of as a game where the object is to identify better answer choices by eliminating worse answer choices.

Why The Difficulty In Focusing On Answer Choices?

The emotional need for understanding prevents test takers from looking at the answer choices as completely and aggressively as they should. Many test takers refuse to look at the answer choices until they have tried to understand the question and determine the correct answer. Believe me, many answer choices can be eliminated as a result of a cursory reading of the question and answer choices! The emotional need to understand first and answer second results in inattention to the answer choices.

Multiple Choice Is Your Friend - Achieving The Mindset

What matters is **answer identification!** "Understanding" is necessary only to the extent that it is needed to eliminate wrong answers. Focus on the answer choices and understand only as much of the question as is required.

Principle 18: The appropriate focus is on the identification of answer choices. Understanding is a tool that should be used only when necessary to identify answer choices.

III. Defining The Goal

So far we have talked about LSAT reality and about making the identification of answers the priority. Let's tie these ideas together into a workable goal. Our goal is to:

Identify the best answer to as many questions as we can.

This is a goal that each and every test taker can achieve. Let's consider the components.

Identify - We are concerned with the identification of answers and not with the understanding of questions. Learn to aggressively eliminate wrong answers.

Best Answer - The significance of this is two-fold

First the directions to each section of the test require that you select the "best answer." In Reading Comprehension and Logical Reasoning the "best answer" is often not objectively correct but is simply better than the other choices. In Analytical Reasoning the "best answer" is objectively correct.

Second, there will be many times on the test when you will eliminate three choices and guess one of the remaining two. In instances like this you are doing the best that you can under the time constraints.

As Many Questions As You Can - On the one hand, you will select an answer to every question (remember there is no penalty for guessing). On the other hand, you won't have time to "think" about every question. There will be questions that will simply be too difficult or that you will not reach.

All of this is to easy to understand, but hard to implement. Fortunately:

"Perfect Practice Will Help You Make Perfect!"

Principle 19: You must practice identifying answers, by eliminating wrong answers, until this process has been internalized into your psyche.

IV. Realizing The Goal - Effective Preparation

The Requirement Of Preparation For The LSAT

Even Law Services has taken the position that preparation for the LSAT is an important part of the LSAT experience. Law Services has commented that:

" ... it is clear that in order to be mentally prepared to take a difficult, timed, objective examination designed to test skills more than knowledge you can take certain steps. Make sure you know what the LSAT is about, practice under test conditions and understand the directions. It is impossible to know when an individual has prepared enough, but very few can achieve their full potential by not preparing at all."

Why Is It Possible To Prepare For The LSAT?

Law school applicants take the LSAT at different times of the year. The integrity of the test depends on specific scores meaning the same thing no matter which LSAT. For example, a score of 165 on the June LSAT must mean the same as a score of 165 on the October LSAT. This requirement can be accomplished if and only if each LSAT tests exactly the same things. In order to serve its purpose the LSAT must "measure" consistently. This consistency can be ensured only when every edition of the LSAT requires that the same things be done in the same way! The consequence of this design requirement is that both the questions and the answer choices on the LSAT must be designed in a consistent way for each LSAT!

Principle 20: Every edition of the LSAT must test the same things in exactly the same way.

The test designer is faced with a problem. On the one hand every edition of the LSAT must be the same. On the other hand, it must have questions and answer choices that look different from test to test. The only way that the test designer can resolve this dilemma is by ensuring that **all of the answer choices and the actual questions are developed by using a specific design formula.**

Principle 21: LSAT questions consist of questions and multiple-choice answer choices. Every edition of the LSAT must consist of questions and answer choices which follow the same design requirement.

The test designer is designing a test where the scores are normally distributed. This means that the test can function as intended only if, for any given question, a certain percentage of test takers are selecting the "credited response." Answer choices must be designed so that:

A. Test takers will be attracted to answer choices that are wrong; and

B. Test takers will be repelled from the answer choice that is right.

Principle 22: An important task of the test designer is to obscure the "best answer." The job of obscuring the "best answer" must be done the same way for each LSAT and will therefore be done in predictable ways.

LSAT questions are not inherently difficult. They become difficult because of severe time constraints. The test designer understands this and uses this reality to his advantage. The more complex the answer choices, the more difficult the LSAT question. LSAT answer choices are often long and comprehensive. They are designed to attract you to them when they are wrong and repel you from them when they are right. An understanding of the requirements for how the wrong answers are designed will allow you to discriminate among the answer choices quickly, eliminating the answers that are wrong and selecting the answer that is right!

Principle 23: It is essential that you learn the principles of design that allow the test designer to obscure the wrong answer!

Ways To Prepare For The LSAT

Every person should begin by obtaining a copy of the <u>LSAT Registration Book</u>. Study the descriptive material and the sample test which has been included. This will give you a good look at the questions, but little insight into how to approach them. After having done this, you have two additional options. First, everybody purchases books. Second, large numbers of test takers also enroll in formal LSAT preparation programs.

Your time spent preparing for the LSAT will be spent doing two things. These are:

1. Learning: This involves learning background skills and principles of approach that will allow you to identify answers quickly.

Background Skills: These include specific topics like conditional statements, categories of questions, different reading styles for different parts of the test, different ways to diagram conditions, etc.

Principles of Approach: These include question order, answer elimination, the right number of questions to do, the design requirement for questions and answer choices, and how the test is designed to obscure the right answer and attract you to the wrong answers.

2. Practice: This involves practicing the background skills and principles of approach that you have learned on thirty-five minute test exercises. Practice should be done using only actual LSAT questions or questions that follow exactly the same design requirement!

Principle 24: LSAT Preparation must include learning and practice. It is essential that the process be focused and efficient.

How Should You Go About The Preparation Process?

Everybody buys books (with or without software). Some people take courses. What books should you buy and what courses should you take?

Books Containing Real LSAT Questions

First, the good news. Law Services publishes books of actual questions. Since, the use of actual questions is essential in the preparation process, it is imperative that these books be acquired.

Now, the bad news. The sample LSAT questions (with small exceptions) come with answers but no commentary. As a result, most people need additional books or courses to learn systematic approaches for answering the questions.

"After Market" Books Containing Commentary

Definition - "After market" books are books about the tests that are not written by the test designers.

First, the good news. Some "after market" books contain excellent commentary that will teach you approaches that may be applied to actual test questions.

Now, the bad news. In most cases "after market" books don't use actual test questions. If the acquisition of sample questions, is your SOLE reason for purchasing a book, you are better off simply purchasing the actual test questions from the test designer.

"After market" books should be used for commentary and not for practice questions.

Principle 25: For the purposes of duplicating LSAT questions, you should purchase the actual LSAT exams. For the purposes of finding essential commentary, you should purchase one or more "after market" books.

Courses - Should You Take One?

A long time test prep instructor once made the point that:

"A good course will help some people a lot and a lot of people some."

There are many courses all claiming to do the same thing. Some are excellent. Some are terrible. It pays to do research when selecting a course.

How Should You Research And Select A Course?

Recently I received the following email from a student:

"I find that these days there's so many LSAT prep courses that are being offered to students. As a student I find it hard to know which course will prove beneficial to me. I would appreciate any form of guidance you could offer."

Here is the text of my reply:

"I know that there are a lot of courses. They all promise the same things and market in the same ways. So I agree, if I were a student, I would have difficulty deciding what to choose as well.

The first point that I would make is that anybody has access to actual past exams. It is essential that you have lots of exposure to actual exams. So, make sure that the course you choose uses actual exams.

The second point that I would make is that you don't take a course from a test prep company (although you do give your money to them), you take a course from a specific instructor. So, you want to go "instructor shopping."

The third point is that your good instructor must be teaching systematic approaches rooted in the design and concepts of the actual test. A systematic approach will teach you how to proceed when you don't know the answer to the question.

Now let's look at your options.

First, there are the companies that try to run courses everywhere (national companies) They tend to be at the more expensive end of the market. These companies are in the position of having to hire a lot of instructors. Although, I am sure that many of these instructors are good, some companies have so many instructors that you want to inquire about the experience level and ability of the specific individual teaching the exact section in which you wish to enroll.

Second, you have local private companies. They tend to be smaller operations, with fewer instructors. The quality of instruction can be very high (especially if the company owner/operator is doing the teaching). It takes a long time to teach LSAT effectively.

Third, the continuing education divisions of local colleges and universities often run courses. But, they rarely have their own course. They simply put their name on somebody else's course and contract with that other person to deliver the course. I am not saying that a university course is good or bad. I am just saying that it probably was not developed by the university and has no connection with it. (On occasion, I have taught LSAT courses for universities.)

Fourth, short courses or long courses? In the test prep industry courses range in length from the convenient weekend format to courses that last months. I have authored test preparation books. I also have taught all variations of courses over the years. Every person has his/her own learning style. In other words, the question is not: Is a long course better than a short course? The question is: Given the kind of person that I am, will a weekend format be better (which guarantees immersion) or is a longer course better (which puts a strong onus on you to do the work between the classes)? I hope this helps you think about how to select an LSAT course. I wish you well."

Principle 26: All that is worth paying for in an LSAT Preparation Course is a good approach and an experienced, quality instructor. Investigate these thoroughly before enrolling in a course.

Conclusion

"Success Favors The Prepared Mind." Make sure that you prepare for the LSAT effectively and efficiently. The LSAT Should Be A Once In A Lifetime Experience!

If you are finding this "LSAT PREP Primer" to be helpful, you might want to consider

my complete book on LSAT Preparation:

Mastering The LSAT - How To Prepare Effectively And Successfully

ISBN: 0-9696290-3-6. Visit our web site at www.richardson-prep.com - 416-410-PREP

Chapter 42

Understanding Your LSAT Score - What Your Score Means

It is not necessary to understand how LSAT scores are calculated to understand that the more questions you answer correctly, the higher your score. Nothing will change that basic fact. Understanding LSAT scores is primarily a matter of personal interest. For those who are interested, here goes.

First Comes The Raw ...

Every LSAT is intended to have 101 questions. (On rare occasions a test will have fewer than 101 questions. For example, one question on the October 1997 LSAT was withdrawn reducing the number of questions to 100.) All questions count the same and there is no penalty for guessing. Hence, it is essential that you answer every question. Guess if necessary. Your "raw score" is the number of questions that you answer correctly out of 101. Does this mean that a test taker who gets 75 questions right on the October test would receive the same score as a test taker who got 75 questions right on the February test? Not necessarily. In the words of Law Services:

" ... one test form may be slightly easier or more difficult than another." Hence, a method is needed to compensate for these differences in difficulty. The method used to achieve this is "scaling."

Then Comes The Scaling ...

Compensating For Levels Of Difficulty

So, what is a scaled score? Your scaled score is your raw score converted to the familiar 120 - 180 scale. In the words of Law Services:

"The scores from different test forms are made comparable through a statistical procedure known as equating. As a result of equating, a given scaled score earned on different test forms at different administrations reflects the same level of difficulty."

Let's compare the June 1999 and December 1998 LSATs. How many correct answers were needed to achieve the same scaled scores on the 120 - 180 scale on each test?

# of right answers to achieve score

Scale	June 99	Dec 98
180	99	97
175	94	91
170	88	85
165	80	78
160	71	70
159	70	69
158	68	67
157	66	65
156	64	64
155	63	63
154	61	60
153	59	59
152	57	57
151	56	55
150	54	54
149	52	52
148	50	50
147	49	49
146	47	47
145	45	45
144	44	44
143	42	42
142	41	41
141	39	39
140	38	37
135	30	30
130	24	24
125	18	19
120	0	0

It appears that it is only in the higher score ranges that different raw scores result in significantly different scaled scores. Note that to achieve a 170 three more correct answers were needed in June 99 than in December 98. Note also that in the average score range of 152, 57 correct answers were needed on both tests. The implication is that the two tests differed in the upper level of difficulty.

How Many Additional Answers Are Needed For A 5 Point Increase?

How many additional right answers would a test taker need (increase in the raw score) to raise his or her score by five points on the 120 - 180 scale? The answer is: it depends from where you start. For example, looking at the June 99 LSAT we find that to go from:

120 - 125 would require 18 additional right answers

125 - 130 would require 6 additional right answers

130 - 135 would require 6 additional right answers

135 - 140 would require 8 additional right answers

140 - 145 would require 7 additional right answers

145 - 150 would require 9 additional right answers

155 - 160 would require 8 additional right answers

160 - 165 would require 9 additional right answers

165 - 170 would require 8 additional right answers

170 - 175 would require 6 additional right answers

175 - 180 would require 5 additional right answers

How Many Additional Right Answers Are Needed For A 1 Point Increase?

In general, the higher you move in the score scale the fewer the number of additional right answers needed to increase your score by one point. For example, to more from 171 - 172 typically requires only one additional right answer. But to move from 150 - 151 typically requires two or more additional right answers.

Finally Comes ...

The Scaled Score Implies A Percentile Ranking

Your scaled score (120 - 180) reflects your performance relative to other test takers. Hence, the scaled score must tell an admissions officer how you performed relative to other test takers. Each score on the 120 - 180 scale also corresponds to a percentile ranking. In the words of Law Services:

"A percentile rank is also reported for each LSAT score, reflecting the percentage of candidates scoring below your reported test score. The percentile for a score is based on the distribution of scores for the three-year period prior to the year in which your score was reported."

This implies that your score represents how you performed relative to test takers in the preceding three years. Don't forget that Law Services incorporates an experimental section on the LSAT to try out questions for further use.

What follows is the percentile chart for the 1994-95 LSAT year. (Changes in the percentile chart from year to year are so small that they are insignificant.)

1994-1995 LSAT Percentile Table

(June 1991 - February 1994)

180	99.9 %	149	40.9 %
179	99.9 %	148	37.3 %
178	99.9 %	147	33.1 %
177	99.8 %	146	29.6 %
176	99.7 %	145	26.4 %
175	99.6 %	144	23.4 %
174	99.5 %	143	20.3 %
173	99.3 %	142	17.6 %
172	99.0 %	141	15.4 %
171	98.7 %	140	13.2 %
170	98.2 %	139	11.0 %
169	97.6 %	138	9.7 %
168	96.9 %	137	8.1 %
167	95.9 %	136	6.9 %
166	94.8 %	135	5.7 %
165	93.4 %	134	4.8 %
164	92.1 %	133	4.0 %
163	90.1 %	132	3.3 %
162	88.0 %	131	2.8 %
161	85.4 %	130	2.3 %
160	83.1 %	129	1.9 %
159	80.0 %	128	1.5 %
158	76.8 %	127	1.2 %
157	73.5 %	126	1.0 %
156	69.5 %	125	0.9 %
155	65.9 %	124	0.7 %
154	61.9 %	123	0.6 %
153	67.5 %	122	0.5 %
152	53.7 %	121	0.5 %
151	49.2 %	120	0.0 %
150	45.3 %		

And Finally, The New Kid On The Block - Score Banding

In an effort to discourage the overly precise use of LSAT scores, LSAT has introduced a concept called "score banding." Score bands are expressed as ranges of scores that reflect a high probability of containing your actual LSAT proficiency level. The intent is to allow admissions officers to focus on the range that an LSAT score falls into. Since the June 1997 LSAT, each LSAT score report includes a "score band" of plus-three and minus-three points with each LSAT score. By way of example, a test taker with the score of 161 would receive a score band of 158 to 164. According to Law Services, the score band will contain an applicant's "true score" approximately 68% of the time.

Conclusion

When a school requests your LSAT score, Law Services will report all scores over a fixed period of time. (In other words, there is no way to ensure that the school sees only your highest score.) In addition to the scaled score, percentile ranking and score band, Law Services will report the average of multiple scores. By the way, in evaluating LSAT scores, some schools average, some take the highest, some take the scaled score and some take the percentile ranking! As far as repeating the LSAT - there is a limit to the number of times you can take the test over a fixed period of time. See the LSAT Registration Book for details.

But, as interesting as all this is (or isn't), your job is to:

"Ensure that your best guess is on record for every question."

Possible LSAT Changes!

The information in this book is accurate on the date of publication. We believe that there will be no format changes to the LSAT during the life of this edition. Should there be any changes we will post them online. Any changes to the format of the LSAT that take effect between the publication of this book and the publication of the next edition of this book may be found at:

www.masteringthelsat.com

If there is no mention of a format change - that means that there are no changes.

Any format change(s) will also be published in our "Law School Bound" email newsletter. To receive a FREE subscription simply email us: **lawnews@prep.com**

Finally, the LSAT is produced by Law Services. Information on the test may be found on their site at:

www.lsac.org

Information about our live LSAT Programs may be found at:

www.prep.com

For information about our "Law School Bound" book and program visit:

www.lawschoolbound.com

Chapter 43

You've Finished The LSAT - Post-Mortem Considerations

Should You Cancel Your Score - Repeat The Test?

The purpose of this short chapter is to discuss issues that arise after you have taken the LSAT. Some issues arise both before you have received your score and some after you have received your score.

Part I - Issues That Arise Before You Have Received Your Score

The Option Of Canceling Your Score

If you leave the LSAT feeling certain that you did not perform up to your potential, you have an opportunity to cancel your score. This is another reason to take the LSAT earlier rather than later. It would be tragic to delay taking the LSAT until the last possible moment, feel that you should cancel your score, but be unable to cancel, because this was the latest LSAT you could take for fall admissions! The procedure for canceling an LSAT score may be found in the *LSAT Registration Book*. If you cancel your score, Law Services will report that you took the test but that the score was canceled. There is nothing that the admissions committees can infer from this.

When Should You Exercise The Option Of Canceling Your Score?

You should cancel your score only if you honestly believe that you did not perform up to your potential. You may not have performed up to your potential for a variety of reasons. These reasons include having been forced to take the LSAT under adverse testing conditions and/or being underprepared. Let's first focus on the problem of adverse conditions.

Adverse LSAT Testing Conditions - Poor LSAT Scores

For the most part Law Services does a good job of ensuring that testing conditions are adequate. There have, however, been some (in the extreme minority) instances of conditions being sufficiently bad to impact adversely on candidate's scores. Examples of adverse conditions can include:

- inadequate lighting (wish I had some advice);

- background or other noise (complain immediately);

- incorrect timing of sections by the proctors (bring your own watch and time yourself!);

- extreme room temperatures (dress in layers).

If you find that the conditions at your test centre were bad and that they hurt your performance, you must complain immediately! At the same time you must consider whether to cancel your score. You may or may not find Law Services to be sympathetic. There have been some instances of Law Services offering to let students retake the LSAT at no additional charge.

In the event that you complain, keep copies of all correspondence between you and Law Services.

If you allow your LSAT to be scored (which I would not recommend unless you have no choice) you must have documented evidence of the nature of the test conditions and the fact that you complained! The correspondence between you and Law Services should suffice.

There are two groups of people who have LSAT scores which were adversely affected by the test conditions. Members of the first group are applying with only that (adversely affected) LSAT score. The second group have a subsequent LSAT score which is higher. What follows are some suggestions for "damage control" for each of the two groups.

Applicants With One (Adversely Affected) LSAT Score

You will have to argue forcefully that your LSAT score should not be given the weight that it normally would. Since all schools require an LSAT score it is unlikely that you will be able to get the committee to discount the score. Your goal is to get the committee to place less emphasis on it!

Applicants With A Subsequent Higher LSAT Score

It is easier to argue that your LSAT score was affected negatively by the conditions if you have a subsequent LSAT score that is significantly higher. If you have a subsequent score that is higher - ask the school to disregard the first score. (This will be of benefit to you if you are applying to a school that averages LSAT scores.) **In this instance your goal should be to persuade the committee to discount your first score!**

Adverse Testing Conditions Resulting In No LSAT Score

Some students taking the LSAT at York University in Toronto Canada on September 26, 1998 experienced adverse testing conditions resulting in no LSAT score. The power went off in the building where the LSAT was being written. There were three groups of people affected.

The first group had finished the complete test and therefore were eligible for an LSAT score and did complete the "writing sample" for inclusion in the law school application file.

The second group had finished the multiple choice portion but had not completed the writing sample. In other words, this group was eligible for an LSAT score but was not able to provide the "writing sample" for inclusion in the application file. Law Services responded by: offering this group the opportunity to complete the writing sample on Saturday October 17. Participation in this exercise was optional and if candidates did not attend, Law Services would forward a letter to law schools indicating that "through no fault of their own" the applicant was not able to complete the writing sample.

The third group had not finished the multiple choice portion or the "writing sample" and was therefore not able to receive an LSAT score and was not able to provide a "writing sample" for inclusion in the file. Law Services responded by: offering this group the opportunity to take a "make up" LSAT on Saturday October 17, 1998. This "make up" test was a non-disclosed LSAT (meaning that a copy of the test questions would not be provided to the test takers). I assume that it was the same as one of the LSATs administered at another non-disclosed LSAT administration. Candidates unable or unwilling to take the October 17 "make up" LSAT had to wait until the December LSAT. (Candidates received notification of this option on October 14. The late notice angered many students affected by this problem.)

Part II - Issues That Arise After You Have Received Your Score

Should You Take The LSAT Again? Under What Circumstances?

Law Services would like you to believe that it is unlikely that you can increase your LSAT score. Over the years I have observed many students increase their scores by retaking the test. It is possible to increase one's LSAT score - but it will require work! In fact it is common for students to perform better on the second attempt than on the first attempt. It is also possible to score lower on a subsequent attempt. How should this issue be decided? For what it is worth, here is what I suggest.

There are four principles:

First, your goal is to score high enough so that you will not be rejected because of your LSAT score. Most law school applicants do not need as high of a score as they believe.

Second, as a general principle, schools claim to average multiple LSAT scores. However, if you underperformed the first time, all may not be lost. If you are able to significantly improve your score you may have grounds for an admissions committee either disregarding your first score or giving it lesser weight. (It is your responsibility to check with individual schools on this point.)

Third, under the current rules you can take the LSAT only a fixed number of times in any two year period. (But, remember that the rules can change each year. Please keep up to date!) Therefore, if you do plan to take the test again - don't do so until you have grounds to believe that your score will improve. You can gauge your progress by practicing with actual LSAT exams.

Fourth, if you take the test again and achieve the same score, you will have (from the perspective of the admissions committee) reinforced that first score. That could be good or bad depending ...

In my experience people are dissatisfied with their LSAT scores regardless of the score. I receive calls from high scorers, average scorers and low scorers wondering whether they should take the test again.

I suggest that you should take the test again if you have more to gain than to lose. How can this be determined?

Warning!! Warning!! You must discuss this issue with your academic advisor. What follows are NOT suggested guidelines, but rather an example of how one hypothetical individual might (with solid grades) decide whether he has more to gain than to lose.

60th percentile or less ...

The chances are that he has more to gain than to lose. Hence, he ought to consider taking the test again. But, he must make certain that he has prepared sufficiently so that he does not reinforce that first score. Score improvements may be monitored by practicing with actual LSAT exams under timed conditions.

60th percentile to high 60s ...

Probably more to gain than to lose. But remember that without effective preparation he runs a risk of reinforcing the first score.

70th percentile to high 70s ...

This is a very hard call. He already has a credible LSAT score. With high grades that score may be enough. Since he is starting from a credible score he will have to work harder to improve than someone who is starting from a lower score. But, improvement is still very possible. He must be careful:

- the LSAT should be repeated only when he has clear evidence of score improvements on actual LSAT exams.

80th percentile to high 80s ...

Leave well enough alone. There is a chance of scoring worse the second time around - more to lose than to gain. Also, if he fails to improve, he will leave the admissions committee with the impression that he could not have scored better.

90th percentile ...

Stop thinking about the LSAT. He must move on to a new stage of life that will include worrying about new things.

Finally, he must not take the LSAT again until he has taken all necessary steps to improve!

Conclusion

Although the "LSAT Should Be A Once In A Lifetime Experience", the experience may not end when you leave the room. Remember this chapter. If you need guidance after the test is over - read this chapter again!

APPENDIX

Part B - A Report

Introductory LSAT PREP - Get Off On The Right Foot!
Part B - Studying The LSAT - Past, Present And Future

Summary And Introduction

My Advice To You Is ....

The LSAT does evolve. Make sure that you use information about the current format when you prepare for the LSAT!

This part of the appendix will not be of interest to everyone. But, there are always some people who wonder where the LSAT came from, what formats it has had over the years and where it may be going.

This section will describe the past and present formats of the LSAT. Furthermore, it will discuss the probable evolution of the LSAT into a Computer Based Test.

In Part B of the Appendix I will play the role of the "LSAT Historian."

Appendix - Part B - Chapter Summaries

44. Past And Present - The "Paper And Pencil" LSAT Through The Years

Focus: A short history of the LSAT - for LSAT historians

45. The Future - The Possible Evolution Of The LSAT

Focus: The possible future of the LSAT - possible new question types

Chapter 44

Past And Present - The "Paper And Pencil"
LSAT Through The Years

A Short History - For LSAT Historians

Introduction

The LSAT is similar to the SAT which is taken by virtually all American high school students as part of the admissions process to university. David Owen, commenting on emotional fallout caused by the SAT said that:

"But of course most people's feelings about the SAT and other standardized tests are not entirely rational. The tests have a power out of all proportion to their actual content, and they awaken smoldering insecurities in the people who take them. The intensity of their anxiety doesn't have much to do with the size of their scores. Low scorers worry that the tests are definitive and binding; high scorers worry that they are not.

For people who do poorly on standardized tests, low scores are a heavy burden. A psychoanalyst I know told me that low SAT scores are one of the most common and powerful sources of unhappiness in his young patients. A low grade in a course is just one teacher's judgment, but a low SAT score is a brand for the ages. Even when reality seems to contradict them, the numbers cast a spell of their own. ... Even in adult life one occasionally encounters people who, in anxious moments, find ways of inserting their scores into casual conversation. People who can't remember their shoe size don't forget what they got on the SAT!"

> *-David Owen - None Of The Above*

I suggest that these comments are just as applicable to the LSAT experience.

As you read this chapter you will find two themes. The first is the positive effect that New York's "Truth In Testing" law has had on access to information about the test. Publications that contain actual LSAT questions would never have existed without this legislative initiative. The second theme is the fear that LSAC/LSAS has about the possibility of and effects of preparation for the LSAT. As long as the LSAT is a multiple choice test LSAC/LSAS will not be able to design an LSAT that students will be unable to prepare for! The LSAT always has and always will be the result of a very predictable design requirement. Your job is to learn what that requirement is and how to take advantage of it!

The LSAT In Perspective

Genesis

In the beginning the world of law admissions was without order and void, and uncertainty was upon its face. The spirit of a group of original wise old law professors was rising to come to grips with the problem.

Then, in 1947 a group of legal educators (acting under the authority of the group of wise old law professors) set out to create a uniform national examination for admission to law school. And this group of educators said, "Let us be called the Law School Admission Council"; and they were called the "Law School Admission Council" (LSAC) and they saw that they were good. And there was evening and there was morning, one day.

And LSAC said, "Let there be an operating corporation through which we can conduct our activities." And LSAC created Law School Admission Services (LSAS) which became the operating corporation through which all their activities were conducted. And LSAC/LSAS said that the purpose of our operating corporation is to generate revenue and for that we need a product and customers for that product. And LSAC/LSAS saw that it was good. And there was evening and there was morning, a second day.

And LSAC/LSAS said, "Give us a product for our new corporation to sell!" And LSAC/LSAS created the Law School Admission Test (LSAT). And LSAC/LSAS thought that the areas that were likely to be useful on the LSAT included: paragraph reading, analogies, syllogistic reasoning, inconsistencies, practical judgment, "productivity of ideas," and quantitative reasoning. And LSAC/LSAS saw that it was good and that it was to be. And LSAC/LSAS said we need buyers for our product. The law schools emerged and provided the market for the product by forcing applicants to law school to pay for the LSAT. By the 1970's the LSAT had established a well defined role as a very important part of the admissions process in nearly every ABA approved law school in the United States and most law schools in Canada. And there was evening and there was morning, a third day.

And LSAC/LSAS said let there be consultants for the purpose of designing the LSAT format and questions. And it was so. By contracting with representatives of the College Board, and later the Educational Testing Service, and later still the American College Testing Program, LSAC/LSAS was able to generate the LSAT. And so the LSAT moved from being a theoretical concept to the reality that characterizes the life of young lawyers-to-be. And LSAC/LSAS saw that it was good. And there was evening and there was morning, a fourth day.

And LSAC/LSAS said, "Let the LSAT be designed as a test to be used in determining basic competency for legal education." And so it was so. The first LSAT was a multiple choice exam designed to measure certain abilities important to the study of law and, thus, to aid law schools in assessing the academic promise of their applicants. The test was intended to cover a broad range of academic disciplines. It was designed to give no advantage to candidates from a particular academic background. The multiple choice questions yielding the LSAT score were designed to measure the ability to read, understand, and solve problems in matters and contexts thought to be relevant to legal study. And LSAC/LSAS saw that it was good. And there was evening and there was morning, a fifth day.

And LSAC/LSAS said, "Let all activities surrounding the development and questions and answers to questions on the LSAT be shrouded in secrecy." And it was so. All information concerning test development, the actual test questions, and the answers to these questions was secret. LSAC/LSAS simply reported an LSAT score to test takers without giving any opportunity for test takers to know what sections they had performed well on and what sections they had performed badly on. In addition, there was no opportunity to know what answers were credited as correct or any opportunity to challenge the wisdom of LSAC/LSAS. Many promising careers were ruined. And LSAC/LSAS saw that this was good. And there was evening and there was morning, a sixth day.

And on the seventh day, ...

Evolution Of The LSAT

The LSAT has always been multiple choice. From 1947 to 1982 candidate's scores were reported on a scale of 200 - 800. During this time period there were many differences in the nature of the actual tests which produced these scaled scores. These differences were differences in the length of the LSAT, the types of questions that were used, and the number of actual scores that the test yielded. These differences may be summarized by the following chart.

Year	Length	Scores
The LSAT Before Test Disclosure Laws		
First three years	full day	200-800 (LSAT)
1950's to 1961	half day	200-800 (LSAT)
1961-1971	full day	200-800 (LSAT)
		20-80 (Writing)
		20-80 (General)
1971-1982	half day	200-800 (LSAT)
		20-80 (Writing)
The LSAT After Test Disclosure Laws		
1982-1983	half day	10-50 (LSAT)
1982-1991	half day	10-48 (LSAT)
1991-present	half day	120-180 (LSAT)

As you can see from 1947 to 1982 the LSAT score itself was reported on a scale of 200 to 800. Candidates were required to sit either a half day or full day test and during some years candidates were given separate scores based on a "General Background" test and a "Writing Ability" test. These scores were reported on a scale of 20 to 80. The "Writing Ability" test was basically a test of English grammar and usage. Although there was always an LSAT score reported on a 200 to 800 scale, the nature of the questions which were used to make up the LSAT portion of the test changed drastically from 1947 to 1982.

LSAT Question Types From 1947 - 1982

Pre-Test Disclosure Era

From 1947 until 1951 the LSAT had eight to eleven sections and emphasized reasoning, reading, arguments, classification, and data and figure interpretive questions. In 1951 when the LSAT changed to a half-day test the strongest of the existing question types were retained. Some of the major components of the test used through the 1950's were reading, reasoning, data and figure interpretation, and questions concerning principles applied to cases. In some editions directed memory and error recognition exercises were used. During the 1960's the LSAT component of the full-day test was similar in content to the LSAT of the 1950's. During the 1960's candidates also took a "Writing Ability" test and a "General Background" test. Each of these scores was reported on a scale of 20 to 80.

The "general background" test was discontinued at the start of the 1970's. The "writing ability" test was retained. Beginning in 1971 both the LSAT and "writing ability" test were administered in a morning only. (The actual testing time was approximately three and one half hours.) The content of this test evolved in stages from 1971 to 1982. According to LSAC/LSAS in Law School Admission Test: Sources Contents And Uses:

"All LSAT's of the 1970's shared cases and principles as well as sentence correction question types. The early seventies' tests had reading comprehension and recall questions, data interpretation items, and error recognition exercises. In a notable shift, the test introduced in 1975 replaced the reading questions with logical reasoning and practical judgment exercises. By the winter of 1978, a usage section had replaced error recognition on the LSAT. Forms of that late 1978 type remained in use through February 1982."

In June 1989 Reading Comprehension emerged as the most important section on the LSAT. This continued to June of 1991. At that point "Logical Reasoning" became the most important section on the LSAT. It is interesting to see that from 1975 to 1982 the LSAT had no sections that tested "Reading Comprehension" directly!

LSAT Question Types From 1982 On

The Post Test Disclosure Era

What Was Test Disclosure And Why Was It Important?

Testing is a big business. It is impossible to move through school and a career without being subjected to a variety of standardized multiple choice tests. All of you know about the LSAT. But each of you has also have friends who must take MCAT's, GMAT's, DAT's, TOEFL's, SAT's, GRE's, etc. This list goes on and on. After you finish law school those of you who want to be admitted to state bars will have to take the Multistate Bar Exam. This is a standardized test of general law which is given twice a year across the United States. Testing is pervasive. The consequences of scoring badly on the LSAT may be severe. To put it simply, your dream of a career in the law may be shattered. The reality of the role of testing in today's society is two-fold:

1. Everybody must take tests; and

2. The consequences of low scores are enormous.

Daniel J. Burns in an article entitled "Truth In Testing: Arguments Examined" noted that:

"What began thirty-three years ago as a fledgling research group devoted to designing aptitude test questions for college bound high school seniors, has today become a one-hundred-million-dollar-a-year organization that administers aptitude test to nearly seven million persons annually. Examinees range from pre-schoolers and high-schoolers to stockbrokers, lawyers and doctors, automobile mechanics and police officers. It is the contention of E.T.S. that, by means of these tests, it can predict the performance of test-takers in their academic, professional, or occupational endeavors. Whether, and to what extent, the instruments which determine these predictions should be disclosed to the consumer who pays a fee to take such a test, is the center of a major controversy over the purpose of E.T.S. and its influence upon the lives of those persons who buy its services."

Given the important individual interests at stake in testing it is vitally important that:

1. There be a mechanism to review the quality of the questions, the answers, and the candidate's answers; and

2. That the results of the test be used only for the purpose the test was intended for.

Prior to January 1, 1980 the testing industry operated under a veil of secrecy. Little information was published about the test itself. There was no way to see any of the questions after the test. As a result there was no way to challenge the accuracy of the "credited responses". The testing industry was not accountable to anyone and would not disclose any information to anyone. One was simply given one's LSAT score and that was that. This was an intolerable state of affairs which could no longer be permitted to exist. At a minimum, the rules had to change so that the answers were subject to independent verification.

By the late 1970's there was a great deal of dissatisfaction with the testing industry. The climate was favorable to legislative intervention. One of the leading detractors of the use of standardized testing results was Senator LaValle of New York state who drafted and introduced SB 5200A which has become known as "the Truth-in-Testing" law. LaValle's motivation for pushing for "truth in testing" may be gleaned from the following excerpt from one of his speeches:

"Despite the immense impact of these tests, however, those who take them and those who use them, have little access to information that would help them understand their value and significance. The testing industry has surrounded itself in a mantle of secrecy that leaves it unaccountable to the public, who should be able to independently assess the accuracy and validity of its products."

The practical effect of the proposed "truth in testing" law was that upon payment of a fee a test taker was entitled to a copy of his or her answer sheet, a copy of the questions that were used to determine the test score, and the correct answers to those questions. As you might expect this law was strongly opposed by the testing industry. It is understandable that the industry would be upset by any attempt to pierce its mantle of secrecy and make it accountable. It was reported that representatives of the testing industry attempted to prevent the enactment of the "truth-in-testing" law through the use of paid lobbyists to influence the New York Legislature. Their principal objection to disclosure of test questions was that the questions could not be used again, making the process of equating and test development more expensive. Other objections were less clear but the following quotation from The War On Testing: Detroit Edison In Perspective, a pamphlet published by ETS in 1979, shows how far the testing industry was prepared to go to retain its place in the sun.

"Tests are under attack today, as they have been throughout most of this decade. The battle over test security is only the latest battle in what is turning out to be a long war, increasingly fought on two main fronts. Struggles in courtrooms continue; struggles in legislative halls are just beginning; and the question we must ask ourselves, the basic, underlying and overriding question is why.

I believe that the answer is this: Tests are under attack today because they tell us truths about ourselves and our society; partial truths, to be sure, but truths nonetheless and, in recent years, many of these truths have been unpleasant and unflattering. Seen in this perspective, the attack on tests, is to a very considerable and very frightening degree, an attack on truth itself by those who deal with unpleasant and unflattering truths by denying them and by attacking and trying to destroy the evidence for them."

As you can see the "truth-in-testing" debate took place in an extremely volatile emotional climate.

In the end the forces of good prevailed over the forces of evil, Senator LaValle was successful and effective January 1, 1980 "truth-in-testing" became part of the law of the State of New York. On July 13, 1979 upon signing "truth-in-testing" into law Governor Carey (the then Governor of New York) stated:

"The standardized tests are a very important element in one of the most crucial determinations in a young person's life. Tests of this type are imprecise, open to potential misinterpretation. It must be a candidate's right to have access to his results."

The war was over!

How Did The Testing Industry Respond To The Actual Law?

On December 30, 1979 the front page of the New York Times ran an article titled "5 Exam Groups Drop Opposition To Law on Tests - They Now Back Principles of `Truth In Testing.'" The first paragraph of the article read as follows.

"In a sharp departure from their earlier position, the leaders of the Educational Testing Service and four of the major college and graduate school admissions testing programs have endorsed the fundamental principles of New York State's new "truth in testing" law, which goes into effect Jan.1."

The article went on to say that one of the "graduate school admissions testing programs which endorsed "truth in testing" was none other than the Law School Admission Council. To its credit LSAC/LSAS had agreed to comply with the law.

After having lost the battle in the legislature, some testing organizations, rather than complying with the law, took the battle to the courts. The Association of American Medical Colleges went to court to request an injunction to prevent the application of the "truth-in-testing" law to the MCAT. The plaintiffs raised constitutional issues of due process, equal protection and unlawful infringement of existing federal copyright laws.

Test Disclosure And The Fallibility Of Testing?

It didn't take long for people to challenge the answers to test questions. The first important challenge to ETS came in 1981, when a high school student by the name of Daniel Lowen successfully challenged ETS's answer to a math question on the SAT exam. Of greater interest is the fact that LSAC/LSAS was forced to rescore the February 1981 LSAT when it became apparent that they had credited the wrong answer to one of their math questions. (Yes, there used to be a math section on the LSAT.) This is extremely significant because it was the very first LSAT administered after the "truth in testing" law came into effect! The testing industry does make mistakes but you will have difficulty getting them to acknowledge them when anything except a math question is involved.

Truth In Testing And The Availability Of Practice Questions

Since 1980 all of the major testing organizations have published books which consist of actual past exams. Until February of 1989 LSAC/LSAS sold all of the LSAT's administered from June of 1982 to October of 1988. In addition they sold two books called The Official LSAT Sample Test Books (Volumes I and II). These publications have been a great assistance to students preparing for the LSAT. At the present time LSAC/LSAS sells the vast majority of released LSAT exams. See the LSAT Registration Book for current information.

How Did Truth In Testing Change The Format Of The LSAT?

LSAC/LSAS has indicated that the "truth in testing" law was directly responsible for the massive format change the LSAT underwent in 1982. To understand why this was so, consider the way in which the LSAT is used. The LSAT score is sent to a law school where it is seen by a member of an admissions committee. It is important that a score of say 150 on one version of the LSAT represent the same ability as a score of 150 on another version of the LSAT. Different versions of the LSAT must be "equated." Prior to 1980, when it was not necessary to retire a test after using it once, "equating" was done by new LSAT's being administered along with previously administered versions of the LSAT. By comparing how applicants performed on various editions of the test, it was possible to assess the difficulty of the new LSAT's relative to the old LSAT's. Test disclosure meant that an LSAT had to be retired after it was used. Without any undisclosed editions of the LSAT to be administered along with the new LSAT a different method for equating various editions of the LSAT had to be developed.

After an appropriate amount of research LSAC/LSAS developed a section called "section pre-equating." In this process, equating is achieved by studying results on individual sections of the test used in trial form. The "trial sections" are administered experimentally for the purpose of obtaining data for future test use. LSAC/LSAS has also indicated that a "critical requirement of the new process is that each section of the LSAT be equally timed." As a result, all sections on the LSAT are of equal length.

Format Of The LSAT Beginning In June Of 1982

Effective June of 1982 the LSAT consisted of exactly six thirty-five minute sections. Four of the six counted toward the LSAT score. The remaining two were "experimental" and were for the purpose of pre-equating the various editions of the LSAT. There was no way to know exactly which of the two sections were experimental. In addition, an unscored thirty minute "writing sample" replaced the multiple choice grammar sections which previously yielded the "Writing Ability" score. The four sections that contributed to the LSAT score were:

1. Issues and Facts   36 - 40 questions

2. Logical Reasoning   24 - 26 questions

3. Reading Comprehension   27 - 29 questions

4. Logic Games   23 - 26 questions

The only section retained from the February 1982 version of the LSAT was the "Logical Reasoning." Although "Issues and Facts" and "Logic Games" were new, it is interesting that they returned to "Reading Comprehension" which had been on the test until 1975. Why the change in the kinds of questions? LSAC/LSAS provided the following two clues:

1.   The need to produce new tests rapidly created a need to produce question types that could be written and edited with greater facility than some of the question types in use in 1980; and

2.   Concerns such as test security and short term coachability could also be addressed by the construction of a new test.

On the issue of short term coachability LSAC/LSAS stated:

"LSAC and LSAS strive to offer a test which is as free from potential effects of short term preparation courses as possible."

How Was The LSAT Score Calculated From June 1982 To February 1989?

Effective June 1982 LSAT scores were reported on a new scale. The 200 - 800 scale was abolished and replaced with a 10 - 50 scale. The 10 - 50 scale was replaced by a 10 - 48 scale after the first full year of the new test format. LSAC/LSAS gave the following explanation for abolishing the 200 - 800 score scale.

"The 200-800 score scale of the LSAT was established in 1948. It was based on a performance of candidates who took a test far different from the one now being administered. Over time, new versions of the LSAT, containing different types of questions, have been introduced gradually and equated to previous versions. Despite these changes, the 200-800 score scale was preserved.

Because of the major change in questions employed on the new LSAT this version will not test the same qualities that were tested in exactly the same ways. Consequently, even if the 200-800 scale were to be retained, scores on the old and new versions would not likely mean the same thing. While there is no change in the measurement objectives for the test, or the intended use of the test, groups of applicants might be ordered slightly differently by the new test than they would have been on the current LSAT.

In addition, the particular 200-800 score scale employed in the LSAT program has been a subject of concern to LSAC/LSAS for some time. The three-digit score scale can create an impression of precision that is not warranted.

It has been determined that an entirely different score scale will deal most effectively with these and the many other considerations which must be taken into account when making a decision about the scale to be used on a test such as the LSAT. The scale decided upon will yield scores across the range 10-50."

The actual LSAT score was calculated by totaling up the number of correct answers and multiplying by a number that was approximately 0.5. From this a constant factor (between 6 and 13) was subtracted to calculate the actual LSAT score. The constant factor was for the purpose of equating the difficulty of various editions of the LSAT. For example let's assume a student got 100 correct answers and the constant factor was 10. That student's LSAT score would have been:

$(100 * 0.5) - 10 = 40$

Format Of The LSAT From June Of 1989 To February Of 1991

In June 1989 the following changes to the LSAT took place:

1. "Issues and Facts" was dropped.

2. The remaining three sections were expanded.

3. The format of the LSAT became four forty-five minute sections with one experimental section and the three remaining sections that counted.

4. The "reading comprehension" sections began to use passages extracted from "law review and like articles."

In other words the format of the LSAT was:

Section	Content
Writing Sample	30 minutes (not part of LSAT)
Logical Reasoning	45 minutes (33 - 35 questions)
Logic Games	45 minutes (29 - 31 questions)
Reading Comprehension	45 minutes (33 - 35 questions)
Experimental Section	45 minutes (29 - 35 questions)

The LSAT score was still reported on a scale of 10 - 48.

It is interesting to note the reasons for retiring "Issues and Facts." In its Report On The Revised LSAT, LSAC/LSAS offered the following reasons:

"1. Easiest item type, consequently low discrimination among most able examinees.

2. No substantial addition to the predictive validity of the test.

3. Very difficult to produce quality items that do not pose possible defensibility problems.

4. Most format-driven and therefore potentially the most affected by practice."

It is interesting to note that reason "4" reflects their continuing concern with short term coachability. It was so easy to prepare for this section that I could teach any student to get over thirty-five of these questions correct!

Was The June 1989 LSAT Harder Or Easier Than Its Predecessor?

LSAC/LSAS had indicated that even though the easiest section of the LSAT had been eliminated, the overall level of difficulty of the LSAT had not been changed. Presumably this implies that Reading Comprehension, Logical Reasoning, and Logic Games on the June 1989 LSAT were easier than those sections were before June of 1989.

How Was The LSAT Score Calculated From June Of 1989 To February of 1991?

The LSAT score was still reported on a scale of 10 to 48. LSAC/LSAS had taken steps to ensure that scores on the revised LSAT (June 1989) would have the same meaning as scores on the pre-June 1989 LSAT. This was the result of the statistical process of "equating." The method of "equating" has changed since June of 1982. From

June of 1982 to February of 1989 LSAC/LSAS used a method of "equating" by section. Since June of 1989 LSAC/LSAS has been equating using an "Item Response Theory" equating model. I.e. equating is done question by question. June 1989 was the first time that the "Item Response Theory" of equating was used with the LSAT. LSAC/LSAS has indicated that this is significant because:

1. It provides the best available technology to allow continuity and score meaning. I.e. it results in scaled scores that neither advantage nor disadvantage those who took the revised (June 1989) LSAT.

2. The Item Response Theory Conversion process does not use a multiplier and constant to convert the number of correct answers to a reported score on the LSAT scale as the past procedure did. The LSAT score is no longer determined by multiplying the number of correct answers by a number that is approximately 0.5 and subtracting a constant factor. Instead a conversion table is provided. The conversion table shows the LSAT score that corresponds to each possible number of questions answered correctly.

What Were The June 1991 LSAT Changes?

The LSAT now consists of five thirty-five minute sections. Four of the five sections will count. One is experimental. The four that count are:

1. Logical Reasoning   23 - 26 questions

2. Logical Reasoning   23 - 26 questions

3. Reading Comprehension   26 - 28 questions

4. Logic Games   23 - 25 questions

Since June of 1991 it has become clear that reading passages are no longer restricted to social sciences! I.e. the October 1991 LSAT had one passage that was a science passage. In addition, the "Multiple Option" question format has been discontinued.

What Is The New Scoring Scale?

The current LSAT score is reported on a scale of 120 - 180. Notice how similar this is to the old 200 - 800 scale. I.e. if you take away the first number of the 120 and 180 and add the number "0" to each at the end you will be back to the 200 - 800 scale. Remember what LSAC/LSAS said in 1982 about having a three digit LSAT score? The reasons given by LSAC/LSAS for changing the score scale were:

1. It was too difficult to make meaningful distinctions among test takers; and

2. The 10 - 48 scale did not result in the kind of score distribution the test required. To put it simply: too many people were getting high scores.

Concern About The Effects Of Short Term Preparation

When LSAC/LSAS announced the 1991 changes to the LSAT it continued to voice its concern about the effects of preparation. In other words they do their best to create a test which is as free from the effects of preparation as possible. LSAC/LSAS continues to discourage people from taking preparation courses or buying books that are commercially available. They do, however, try very hard to sell their own books on LSAT Preparation. I recommend that your preparation include exposure to actual LSAT questions.

Conclusion

Why Will You Always Be Able To Prepare For The LSAT?

The answer is simple. The LSAT is a multiple choice test. Multiple choice tests are unique in that the answer to the question is right there before your very eyes! Your job is to identify the answer. This will often involve eliminating those answers that are wrong. There is no requirement that you understand the answer. In fact, for many students, the attempt to understand (which takes a great deal of time) actually results in their obtaining lower scores than they would if they simply concentrated on eliminating answers that were obviously wrong!

* This article was originally written by the author in 1991 right after the 1991 changes went into effect.

Chapter 45

The Future -
The Possible Evolution Of The LSAT

In 1995 Law Services began to research the viability of new LSAT question types. Some of these question types were administered by a computer. It is possible that the LSAT may become a computer based test - which happens to have a "Computer Adaptive Format" - better known as a CAT. In all likelihood this will become a reality. When? Only Law Services would know for sure. But, it would not be surprising, if by the end, of the first decade, of the 21st century, the LSAT became computer adaptive. By implementing a "Computer Adaptive LSAT", Law Services will continue the trend toward computer based testing. In recent years many multiple choice tests, including the GMAT and GRE have become Computer Adaptive.

What Is A Computer Adaptive Test (CAT)?

A CAT is administered on the computer. But, the test is adaptive. This means that the questions adapt to the computer's assessment of the test taker's ability. The basic principle is that the computer will begin with a question of average difficulty. If the test taker answers it correctly, the computer will assume that the test taker's ability level is higher and generate a harder question. If the test taker answers incorrectly the computer will assume that the test taker's ability is lower and generate an easier question. The purpose of generating questions is to determine the ability level of a given test taker. This will occur after a certain number of questions have been answered. In fact the earlier the question the more it is likely to tell the computer about the test taker's ability level. Once this ability level has been determined the computer will generate a score based on that ability level.

Features Of A Typical CAT

There are a number of features that are worthy of note.

First, CAT tests are not standardized tests. All test takers taking the LSAT currently are invited to answer the same questions. On a CAT, the computer generates custom questions for each test taker.

Second, the computer must know your response to each question asked. Hence, every question must be answered and the questions must be answered in the order given.

Third, not all questions count the same. Earlier questions count more than later questions.

The Possible Advantages Of A Computer Adaptive Test

The possible advantages are:

First, the test can be administered on demand at any time. Hence, the LSAT would no longer be restricted to four dates a year.

Second, fewer questions need be answered in order to determine a test taker's ability level.

Third, more question types can be asked on a CAT than can be asked on a "paper and pencil" LSAT.

Conclusion

So, What Are The Chances?

I have neither a crystal ball nor inside information. It seems clear that changes to the LSAT will occur during the first decade of this century. The LSAT evolves slowly. It is possible that changes will be made to the current (paper based) format before the test moves to a computer based format. To stay tuned visit our website at www.richardson-prep.com and www.lawschoolbound.com

APPENDIX

Possible CAT Related Changes In LSAT Questions Types

Question Types Unveiled Informally Between 1995 and 2002

The following possible changes are based on my experience with the prototype of the experimental LSAT questions since 1995. New question types have been unveiled at the "Law Forums". Early indications are, that there will be substantial changes if and when the new LSAT is adopted. Some changes that LSAT has experimented with are:

- some of the question types will cease to be multiple choice. LSAT has experimented with non-multiple choice question types in the areas of logical reasoning, analytical reasoning and reading comprehension.

- LSAT has explored a "listening comprehension" section to be part of a new LSAT.

The 2002 LSAT Field Testing

On October 19, 2002 Law Services ran the first of their LSAT Field tests throughout North America. The purpose of the field test was to allow Law Services to try out new question types for future use. The format of the LSAT has not changed since June of 1991 and there have been no new question types introduced (in terms of the sections) introduced since 1982. After 20 years, the test is due for some changes and the field test provided strong indications of where the test is going. Reports from the October 19 test suggested that the test had something new, something old and something borrowed. Most importantly, the "Field Test" was used to experiment with the new question types discussed in the previous paragraph. The content of the "Field Test" suggests major changes are coming.

The most significant (possible) change is the inclusion of question types that go beyond the traditional multiple choice format.

The first of these is (are you ready for this) a test of listening comprehension. (How often have you heard the suggestion that lawyers don't listen?) Apparently candidates were asked to listen to a tape and then answer questions based on what they thought they had heard.

The second is a question type that tested whether test takers could recognize the effect that certain word changes would have on a passage.

The familiar logic games and logical reasoning question format continued to appear as part of the "Field Test".

What follows is a description of the morning from one test taker:

"Section 1 was 30 marks and was an audio CD that was played with conversations. Some were three minutes long and you had to answer 4-6 questions after the conversation. Some were 9 seconds and there was only one question. The questions were all comprehension type questions and applying what the format of an argument was when given a different situation. You were given a scrap piece of paper and were allowed to write notes during the questions.

Section 2 was a logic section and there were 24 questions and 35 minutes to answer. The questions were all things like, you have 5 places in a hat store and three types of hats. Given conditions (about 5) what are the order of the different hats. Or what could not be the order. Or if place 1 is _____ then place 2 and 4 can not be _____. There really wasn't enough time for this section and I thought it was the easiest.

Section 3 was 27 questions in 35 minutes and was comprehension. Given a passage about an argument or a specific topic you were asked to do analysis on the types of arguments presented. There were questions like... if you substituted _____ word in for _____ word in line 24 which word would mean the same. Other things were what is the argument about?

Then we had a break..about 20 minutes.

Section 4 was the same as section 1 - 30 marks and was audio tape conversations.

Section 5 was like section 3 but the passages were longer and there were about 5-8 questions on every passage. It was out of 27 and was 35 minutes long."

Law Services continues to run "Field Tests" and "LSAT Pilots." What question types will they try out? A clue comes from the following Law Services comment in conjunction with the "LSAT Pilot."

"The purpose of the pilot test is to try out various new kinds of questions to see whether they provide useful information for making law school admission decisions. Law schools are particularly interested in getting information about applicants' writing ability, and the trial questions will be assessed for their usefulness in providing such information."

- An LSAT test taker

Book And DVD Ordering Information

If you would like to order John Richardson's:

1. Law School Bound - ISBN: 0-9696290-2-8 - $49.95; or

2. Mastering The LSAT - ISBN: 0-9696290-3-6 - $31.95

3. "Getting Into Law School" DVD (see below)

Please contact us at: info@lawschoolbound.com or 416-410-PREP

Richardson Press
Box 19602, Manulife P.O.
55 Bloor St. W.
Toronto, Canada
M4W 3T9

Interested In the Law School Bound DVD?

A DVD is available of John Richardson delivering a live "Getting Into Law School" course in Toronto, Canada. This is a great product for reinforcing specific points or for those of you who prefer video to books. The approximate length is three hours.

For information email:

Info@lawschoolbound.com

Put Over 25 Years Of Test Prep Experience To Work For You!

► **LSAT**

► **GMAT**

► **GRE**

► **MCAT**

www.richardson-prep.com

Improving Scores Since 1979!

416-410-PREP